PURSUED BY FURIES

A LIFE OF MALCOLM LOWRY

Gordon Bowker

St. Martin's Press
New York

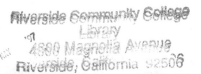

PURSUED BY FURIES: A LIFE OF MALCOLM LOWRY

ISBN 0–312–12748–0 (cloth)   ISBN 0–312–16356–8 (paperback)

Library of Congress Cataloging-in-Publication Data

Bowker, Gordon
Pursued by furies : a life of Malcolm Lowry / Gordon Bowker.
p. cm.
Originally published: London : HarperCollins, 1993.
Includes bibliographical references and index.
ISBN 0–312–12748–0 (cloth)   ISBN 0–312–16356–8 (pbk.)
1. Lowry, Malcolm, 1909–1957—Bibliography. 2. Authors, English—20th century—Biography. I. Title.
PR6023.096Z569 1995
813'.54—dc20
[B]   95–17775
CIP

First published in hardcover in Great Britain by HarperCollins Publishers 1993

First St. Martin's Griffin Edition, March 1997
10 9 8 7 6 5 4 3 2 1

Gordon Bowker

was born in Birmingham where he attended King Edward's Grammar School, Camp Hill. He spent two years in Australia sheep-farming, and three years in the RAF. After training as a teacher, he went to Nottingham University to read philosophy, English and sociology, and later did an MA at London University. He taught sociology at Goldsmiths' College London from 1966 to 1991. He is now a full-time author and journalist.

from the reviews:

'This biography makes an engrossing read. What a four-letter man Lowry was!' JOHN BAYLEY, *Evening Standard*

'The immense problem that a Lowry biographer faces – and it should be said at once that Gordon Bowker has overcome it quite magnificently – is that while the life was chaotic, the work is more chaotic still... *Pursued by Furies* is the product of meticulous but intelligent research that entirely avoids both the anal retentiveness and the wild psychological inference of American-style biography. Nobody has got closer to Lowry than Bowker and I doubt that anyone ever will.' BRIAN MORTON, *TES*

'We may never know exactly how Lowry died but thanks to Bowker's meticulously detailed biography, we know exactly how Lowry lived by retreating into "his own alcoholically inspired world of familiars and daemons". This is no aesthetic appreciation of a gifted author but a bout-by-bout account of a desperate man for whom writing was the one positive way of confronting the Demon Drink. Judged as an alcoholic odyssey it could hardly be bettered.' ALAN BOLD, *Glasgow Herald*

'*Pursued by Furies* is complete enough to make another such book unnecessary for a long time. Bowker successfully inhabits Lowry without being overcome by him.' GEORGE WOODCOCK, *Quill & Quire*

'Gordon Bowker's biography, a full and painstaking route through difficult terrain, is a major achievement in its own right.' *Economist*

'The story of Lowry's self-destruction is terrible and terrifying: every page of this history is soaked in alcohol and, by association, in misery.'
J.D.F. JONES, *Financial Times*

Further reviews overleaf

'Don't read this book if you've got a hangover. No writer can have drunk more than Malcolm Lowry, and Gordon Bowker's glass-by-glass account could put you off the stuff for a lifetime. Arriving in Mexico in 1936, Lowry not only downed tequila and the hallucinogenic mescal by the pint, but on one occasion consumed a whole bottle of olive oil under the impression that it was a hair tonic which contained a high percentage of alcohol... During this Mexican sojourn, he got the shakes so badly that he needed a pulley to lift a glass to his lips. And in this state, somehow, he conceived and wrote his masterpiece about an alcoholic, *Under the Volcano.*' HUMPHREY CARPENTER, *Sunday Times*

'A very absorbing book... that should stand for some time as the consummate Malcolm Lowry biography.' MICHAEL TURNER, *Globe and Mail*

'It is a wretched story, and Mr Bowker tells it compellingly.'
ALLAN MASSIE, *Daily Telegraph*

'The long-awaited new biography of Malcolm Lowry by Gordon Bowker is an awesome achievement... Lowry was an unique phenomeon in English literature and here is an book worthy of the man... a book to savour and enjoy. To call it a must read for all Lowry aficionados is the understatement of the century.' ALAN FORREST, *Malcolm Lowry Bulletin*

'Throughout his life, drink and a quasi-autistic self-centredness combined to make Lowry the house guest from hell... Bowker assembles his portrait of a guilt-ridden paranoid fugitive with intelligence and sustained energy.'
JOHN DUGDALE, *Literary Review*

'A carefully researched yet compulsively readable account of Lowry that, instead of trying to explain him away, recreates the incredibly involved verbal and textual universe Lowry constructed around himself and makes us see that that carefully created universe is what made his writing possible. Bowker's new biography gives Lowry's life a complexity and fullness worthy of Lowry's writing.' MATT COHEN, *Toronto Star*

'Detailed, lovingly researched' ANDRO LINKLATER, *The Times*

'*Pursued by Furies* never loses sight of the man who was a poet with something new to tell us about hellfire. That is its merit.'
ROBERT NYE, *Scotsman*

'I am not much unlike to some sick man
That long desirèd hurtful drink; at last
Swills in and drinks his last, ending at once
Both life and thirst. O, would I ne'er had known
My own dishonour! Good God, that men should
Desire to search out that which, being found, kills all
Their joy of life! to taste the tree of knowledge,
And then be driven from out Paradise!
Canst give me some comfort?'

JOHN MARSTON, *The Malcontent*, Act III Sc I

'. . . if you love a writer, if you depend upon the drip-feed of his intelligence, if you want to pursue him and find him – despite edicts to the contrary – then it's impossible to know too much.'

JULIAN BARNES, *Flaubert's Parrot*

'He was glad that the man was interested in his life, since this was indeed interest in his work at one remove.'

MALCOLM LOWRY,
Dark As The Grave Wherein My Friend is Laid

CONTENTS

ACKNOWLEDGEMENTS

In the preparation of this book I am most grateful to Jan Gabrial Singer, Priscilla Woolfan and Russell Lowry, the latter of whom made available to me his copious writings on his family and his comments on previous biographies. I am also indebted to the following people who knew Lowry: John Aiken, Joan Aiken, The Reverend Betty Attwater, Alan Baddeley, Earle & Esther Birney, Maurice Brown, Colin Brown, Ronald Burghes, Harvey & Dorothy Burt, Arthur & Ara Calder-Marshall, John Carter, Dr Ralph & Adrienne Case, Raymond Fletcher Cook, Alistair Cooke, Dr Victor Drache, Albert Erskine, Eric Estorick, Stanley H. Fox, Robert Giroux, Thomas Boden Hardy, Allanah Harper, Mrs Edward Henriques, James Hepburn, George Hepburn, Fr Maurice Hickin, Ronnie Hill, Jane Aiken Hodge, Carol Hyde, Ralph Izzard, Marjorie Kirk, Robert Lazarus, Gene Lawrence, Dorothy Livesay, Joe London, Clarissa Lorenz, Kenneth Lumsden, William McConnell, David Markson, Evelyn Morrison, Maurice Nadeau, Norman Newton, George Northcroft, Gerald Noxon, James Osborne, Dr Kathleen Raine, Dr Michael Raymond, George Robertson, Dr Sydney Smith, John & Molly Sommerfield, James & Tania Stern, Kitty Sprague, Julian & Mary Trevelyan, E. Kenneth Wright.

I must also acknowledge the kind assistance of the following: Professor Muriel Bradbrook, J. R. Ablett (St Catharine's College, Cambridge), Dr Chris Ackerley, John Best, Mason Bibby, Dr John Baker (St Catharine's College), Dr Carl Baron (Senior Tutor, St Catharine's College), Dr Ronald Binns, Neville Braybrooke, Professor Edward Butscher, the Headmaster of Caldicott School, Carmen Callil, Virginia Capel, Anne Chisholm, Dr Richard Hauer Costa, Dr Halvard Dahlie, Hugo Davenport, Natalie Davenport, Roger Davenport, Elizabeth Douglas, Richard Eberhardt, Dr Dale Edmonds, Dr Adam Egede-Nissen, Rosemary Goyden, Professor Sherrill Grace, Julian Green, Dr John Haffenden, Lisa Hatle, Edvard Hoem, the Headmaster and Mr Geoffrey Houghton of The Leys School, Dr A. D. Kellett-Carding, Dr Suzanne Kim, Francis X. King, Harvey Lloyd, Colin Lowry, Professor Patrick MacCarthy J. K. Mayberry (Secretary, Caldy Golf Club), Dr C. A. Meier, George Melly, Joanne M. Morgan, Dr Betty Moss, the Principal of Newnham College (Cambridge), Jeremy Nichols (Headmaster, Stowe School), Sybella O'Callaghan, Giles Playfair,

H. C. Porter, Marguerite Rea, Catherine Rylance, Dr Kathleen Scherf, Anthony Slide, Cynthia Sugars, Dr Barry Supple (The Master, St Catharine's College), Paul Tiessen, Lord Tweedsmuir, Dr Carmen Virgili, Helge Vold, Hugh Walford, Dr Ronald Walker.

It would have been impossible to write this book without the generous help of the staff of certain libraries and other institutions. My greatest debt is to Anne Yandle, George Brandak and Chuck Forbes of the Special Collections Division of the University of British Columbia Library, Sara Hodson, Deputy Archivist and Carolyn Powell of the Huntington Library, Lori N. Curtis, Curator, Special Collections (University of Tulsa); Rodney Dennis and staff at The Houghton Library (Harvard); Beth Alvarez, Assistant Curator, Archives & manuscripts, University of Maryland, and staff at the Harry Ransom Humanities Research Center (University of Texas at Austin), Princeton University Library (Rare Books and Special Collections), and the University of Reading Library. Great and often miraculous help has also come from the following: W. E. Wilkes (Methodist archivist for Liverpool District); Cheshire Records Office (Chester); City of Manchester Central Library; University of London Library; University of Durham Library; John Rylands University Library, Manchester; Liverpool Library; Liverpool Records Office; Royal Air Force Library; St Catherine's House (London); Public Record Office (London); National Archives of Canada; Robert Duncan & Lynne Williams of the National Film Board of Canada; Queen's University Archives (Kingston, Ontario); Research Collections of Mills Memorial Library (McMaster University, Toronto); Maritime History Archive (Memorial University, Newfoundland); Los Angeles County Record Office; Los Angeles Public Library; Cambridge University Library; Alderman Library (University of Virginia), Columbia University Library, Bellevue Hospital Center (New York); New York City Public Library; Universitet bibliotehet (Oslo); Maritime Museum (Bygdøy); Theatremuseum der Universität Zu Köln, Germany; Norman Holme, archivist, Regimental Museum of the Royal Welch Fusiliers.

In reading and trying to understand Lowry I have benefited greatly from the work of three Lowry scholars in particular: Dr Ronald Binns, Dr Brian O'Kill and Dr Victor Doyen. And my indebtedness to Professor Muriel Bradbrook, whose inspired enthusiasm for Lowry was second to none, is unrepayable.

I am grateful to (Sterling Lord Literistic and the Malcolm Lowry Estate and to Random House (UK) Ltd for permission to quote from Lowry's published and unpublished works. Also to the Estate of Conrad Aiken for permission to quote from his published and unpublished works, and to the University of Georgia Press for permission to quote from Clarissa Lorenz, *Lorelei Two*. The following have also given me permission to reprint materials from their collections: the Huntington Library, Princeton University

Libraries, Houghton Library (Harvard), the University of Tulsa, Harry Ransom Humanities Research Center at the University of Texas at Austin, the University of Pennsylvania Libraries, the University of West Virginia Library, the University of Maryland, the BBC. Extracts from the *New York Times*, copyright © 1947/57 by the *New York Times* Company, are reprinted by permission.

I have been fortunate enough to receive grants for research into this biography from the London University Central Research Fund, the British Academy, and the Society of Authors (The K. Blundell Trust). The British Council also made it possible for me to make a lecture visit to the University of British Columbia where I saw for the first time their remarkable collection of Lowry material.

ILLUSTRATIONS

PREFACE

Trying to follow Malcolm Lowry's life is like venturing without a map into a maze inside a labyrinth lost in a wilderness. The maze itself is a shadow-filled hall of distorting mirrors, some of them cracked. In what little light there is we catch sight, from time to time, of a figure in various disguises, luring us on like a will-o'-the-wisp first down one trail and then along another. The pursuit is made even more confusing by others, travelling in the opposite direction, offering conflicting advice on which way to travel. It is a merry, often exhausting, but always exhilarating dance. No wonder that one of his earliest critics predicted that Lowry would be the despair of his biographer.

Lowry was, of course, the contriver of some of the most complex and compelling fiction of modern times, and his life, it sometimes seems, was his most complex and compelling fictional contrivance of all. This is almost certainly attributable to his sense as a young man that he was somehow different from his contemporaries, a man with a calling, set apart, and fated by virtue of the special creative gifts he possessed to suffer for the sake of producing great literature. To this end, he centred all his imaginative effort around himself and exposed himself to the most appalling dangers, both physical and psychological, in order to have something original to say about the human condition. The central characters in his novels and short stories, therefore, are all Malcolm Lowry in one guise or another.

It is not surprising, then, that the fiction tended to take over the man and transform him into a myth. The real Lowry and the mythical Lowry are often difficult to separate, and he himself worked hard to blur the difference. He romanticized his past life and, like the Ancient Mariner, seemed able to persuade all those on whom he fixed his glittering blue eyes that the legends he wove around his experiences were in fact the truth. Certainly there is always the note of conviction about even his most exaggerated claims. When, for instance, in *Ultramarine*, he refers to his autobiographical hero, Dana Hilliot, as 'a small boy chased by the Furies', one recognizes the feeling he had of being picked out for punishment by cruel gods of his own invention, a theme which recurs throughout his poetry and fiction and which was borne out by many painful experiences.

Perhaps he never grew up, and the remarkable thing is that the small boy, so relentlessly pursued by the avenging agents of fate, survived to the age of almost forty-eight. Certainly he was on the run from an early age, seeking refuge from his private terrors in the imaginative world of romantic literature and the unreal state of alcoholic oblivion. He began drinking at fifteen and at seventeen he escaped to sea, but found it impossible to break free from what he called 'the tyranny of self'. At twenty-four he took off into exile, beginning a journey which led him through innumerable seedy bars, into two unstable marriages and in and out of gaols and mental institutions on three continents. He recorded everything. The reckless flight was also a reckless pursuit of pain and pleasure and the words and images to transform them through language into art.

The pain and terror encompassed many gripping fears – a fear of women and of being rejected by them, of sex and the danger of contracting syphilis, the fear of authority and especially of the police and being spied on, and the fear of being exposed as a plagiarist. Some of the most telling images through which he expressed these painful fears arose out of other, more intellectual obsessions. He was obsessed by the legend of Faust, by German Expressionist cinema, by mirrors and magic, by metaphysical ideas about time and the inventive nature of human life. But perhaps his most abiding obsession took the form of an identity crisis of such agonizing proportions that, according to Conrad Aiken, his mentor, he could only have a sense of existing by taking on the identities of other writers and living, as he put it, 'in introverted comas'.

This sense of having no identity of his own certainly led him to 'take over' other writers – Melville, Conrad, Eugene O'Neill, Nordahl Grieg and especially Aiken himself. But he also came to identify closely with his own characters, with Dana Hilliot in *Ultramarine*, Bill Plantagenet in *Lunar Caustic* and notably Geoffrey Firmin in *Under the Volcano*. In creating these characters, Lowry invented for himself a series of alter egos apparently doomed, like the Wandering Jew, to drift aimlessly through uncharted and hostile territories – the lunatic interior of the psychiatric ward, the hellish landscape of Mexico, the Paradise Garden from which expulsion is imminent. And this chosen underworld of the self in turn became a prison and a purgatory from which he was unable to escape and inside which he was destined to die. It was as if he had become his own torturer and the confessions he extracted from himself provided us with the poetry and fiction which now stand as his epitaph. This image of himself comes to us, as if from beyond the grave, in *Under the Volcano*, in a letter from the Consul, Geoffrey Firmin, to his wife, discovered a year after his death.

> And this is how I sometimes think of myself, as a great explorer who has discovered some extraordinary land from which he can never return to give his knowledge to the world: but the name of this land is hell.

This is at once the underworld of the poet Orpheus, the nightmare Expressionist world of Dr Caligari, the apocalyptic vision of the doomed Dr Faustus. There are echoes here, too, of the shadowy and threatening fictional worlds of Kafka – the disorienting interiors of bureaucratic empires where the lone individual is subjected to the terrifying uncertainty of arbitrary powers.

That is the most powerful metaphor for a life embodied in Lowry's fiction – the journey into a labyrinthine world of menacing shadows, threatening illusions and unpredictable disasters to which the reckless voyager is condemned once he abandons the set and certain path of rectitude and orthodoxy. This vision is given an added significance by Lowry's obsession with the sea, and the title he chose for the grand design which was to include all his novels, *The Voyage that Never Ends*. The destiny of modern man, he seems to be saying to us, is to travel dangerously but never to arrive.

In life, of course, Lowry, like many others of the generation which grew to adulthood in the early thirties, was attempting to break free from the enclosed world of middle-class propriety and guilt-ridden Victorian morality into which he had been born. But whereas writers like Orwell, Spender and Auden set out to find the alternative society through organized political action, Lowry embarked on a lonely and seemingly undirected search for an alternative identity in and through literature. While the mainstream rebels, fuelled and inspired by ideology, sought the mirror-image society, Lowry, the lone wolf, fuelled and inspired by poetry and alcohol, sought the mirror-image self.

The obsession with self was reflected in his life as well as in his art. Lowry's old friend, the short-story writer James Stern, recalled how fascinated he was with mirrors, and others have told of catching him staring at his own reflection. In *Ultramarine*, Dana Hilliot sometimes seems to be more interested in his own performance than in the behaviour of his fellow sailors.

> I put down the glass noisily then picked it up again, and gazed mournfully at my own reflection. Narcissus. Bollocky Bill the Sailor . . . aspiring writer, drawn magically from the groves of the Muses by Poseidon.

But Bollocky Bill was only one of the many images he created for himself. John Davenport, Lowry's friend from his Cambridge days, has noted how he presented different masks to different groups of his friends, and his French translator, Clarisse Francillon, remembered his habit of slyly watching for audience reaction whenever he was behaving outrageously.

In the numerous photographs of him, some of these performances have been captured and frozen – the ukulele-playing poet, the drunken genius clutching his book and his gin bottle, the tough guy with the enormous chest expansion, the Chaplinesque clown with the baggy trousers, the lost and helpless victim of a cruel world, the pioneer hippy and visionary sage at one with nature at his shoreline shack in British Columbia. One picture even shows him holding a mirror reflecting himself being photographed.

His prose also has a mirror-like quality, reflecting not just a life, but a life reflecting upon itself and the world around it. By the time he wrote *Under the Volcano*, the personality had become truly kaleidoscopic, as had the prose. 'You look down,' wrote one of his first reviewers, 'the bottom is never reached, but the reflections are fascinating.' It is this ever-changing, insubstantial, dissembling and elusive quality which he shared with his narrative texts which gave his self-obsession its wider significance. The image purveyed is so blurred and so ambiguous that it could be Everyman.

> I see myself as all mankind in prison,
> With hands outstretched to lanterns by the ocean;
> I see myself as all mankind in mirrors,
> Babbling of love while at his back rise horrors.

This extraordinary ability to project himself on to the world and to reflect the world back upon himself is seen by some of his keener critics as Lowry's most profound achievement. The strong note of irony he brings to his unremitting self-scrutiny enables him to comment shrewdly on the condition of modern man. Stephen Spender, in his analysis of *Under The Volcano*, commented on the way Lowry takes the symbolism evident in the social and political upheavals of the 1930s and 1940s and uses it to create the interior world of his hero, Geoffrey Firmin. Anthony Burgess goes even further, and, drawing a parallel with Goethe's *Faust*, argues that Lowry's genius lies in his ability to transform the suffering of an alcoholic in the 1930s into a parable of universal significance.

However, this life in art, reflected back to him through the reactions of his contemporaries, with all its tragic and apocalyptic reference, was by no means a story of persistent gloom and suffering. Although he deliberately created the conditions for his own destruction, he was always acutely aware of what he was doing, and throughout his fiction, his poetry and his letters there sounds the recurring note of self-mockery, the low chuckle which prevents his work collapsing into sentimentality and self-pity. This is Lowry the narrator, the critical commentator, who, like Nabokov's Hugh Person, in the novel *Transparent Things*, always seems to be at his own shoulder, watching and judging.

We have, then, two versions of Lowry's life, two aspects which are both different and complementary. There is Malcolm in Doom-laden and Spook-ridden Wonderland, and Malcolm Through the Dark and Twisted Looking Glass. And like Alice he always had some magic potion at hand, whisky, tequila or mescal, through which he could transform himself and the world around him, to turn the squalor and misery of the madhouse into a vision of the lunatic city, to make the infernal paradise of Mexico the setting of the greatest modern novel about the struggle of mankind against the forces of evil.

The horrors and terrors which inspired Lowry and enabled him to take on the role of modern Everyman engaged in his own internal struggle for sobriety and sanity, he recognized to be largely of his own making. Although while still at Cambridge he blithely informed his tutor, Hugh Sykes Davies, that he was doomed, he later took the view from Ortega y Gasset that we are all novelists creating the fictions of our own lives. And in very few writers is the work so central to the life, and the life woven so deeply and deliberately into the work. His two tyrannies, he said, were the pen and the bottle, yet no one embraced his tormentors with more enthusiasm. He worked relentlessly and compulsively at both. The mountain of bottles he left in his wake and the mountain of manuscripts he produced are evidence of the ferocious industry he brought to his chief vice and greatest virtue. He drank and wrote recklessly; manuscripts were abandoned, lost, recovered and rewritten. He had the greatest reluctance about finishing anything. Once put on to paper the words were no longer his, and in rewriting them he could again take possession of them. In the same way he was constantly rewriting his past life, reinterpreting it, through Freud, or Jung, through the cabbala or the philosophy of Ortega y Gasset.

As well as the fictional Lowry, the mythical writer who he himself created, there was, of course, the bony reality born on 28 July 1909, who died on 27 June 1957, the twice-married, eternally constipated, accident-prone, self-exiled, syphilophobe who sustained a marginal existence as an alcoholic in London, Paris, New York and Mexico, and who lived in the remote obscurity of British Columbia for fourteen years at his father's expense. There were, however, significant portions of that physical life that went unrecorded. He hated polite society, and a deep sense of alienation took him well away from the mainstream of literary life where friends, devotees and critical voyeurs would have observed and chronicled his movements. Even while married, he might disappear for days on drunken sprees which he was thereafter unable to recall. And his death is probably more obscured in mystery than that of any other English writer of his stature. The physical life, however, provides us with a symphonic structure in many movements, and the inconsistent myth supplies the variations on the many themes that can be discerned – exile, alienation, the search for identity, the Faustian flirtation with damnation, the compulsion to change the self through alcohol and the world through literature.

It is in the constant shifting of our narrative from man to myth, from record to legend and back again, that the story and its meaning will emerge. The labyrinth may not yield up its final secrets, the discordant symphony may continue to bemuse us, but the journey and the struggle for comprehension can be nothing short of fascinating.

PURSUED BY FURIES

CHAPTER I

ROOTS

> The family, with its narrow privacy and tawdry secrets, is the source of all our discontents.
>
> EDMUND LEACH

In the 1940s, Malcolm Lowry wrote a story about a childhood incident which throws light on his relationship with his father and his emergence as a young rebel. The schoolboy narrator sometimes rides with his father in his chauffeur-driven Minerva from their home at Caldy, on the Wirral, to Birkenhead, where the father takes the ferry en route to his office across the Mersey in Liverpool. On the way they invariably overtake a neighbour, a lawyer, who chooses to walk the seven miles from the village to the ferry. The lawyer always smiles and raises his stick in salute as the limousine sweeps past, but the boy's father studiously ignores him. When the lad enquires why, he is told sternly that the man is a drunkard, without self-discipline. But, the boy protests, isn't getting up at five in the morning to walk seven miles to the ferry self-discipline? *They* didn't do that. The father does not answer; to him anyone who drinks is beyond the pale. The boy's heart goes out to the man as it turns against his hard-hearted father. 'He did not know', he says, 'that secretly I had decided that I would be a drunkard when I grew up.'[1]

Whether something like this event took place is not clear, but, since his fiction is so deeply rooted in autobiography, it would seem the seeds of discontent were planted early in Lowry's life. He was the youngest of four sons born to Arthur Osborne Lowry, cotton broker, and Evelyn Boden Lowry, with fourteen years between him and his oldest brother, and was treated as the baby of the family from the outset, which both set him apart and provoked his naturally bad temper.

Lowry is an old Scottish name for fox; it also means a crafty person. The sixteenth-century Scottish poet John Dunbar's reference to a fox as 'an lusty reid haird lowry' is an apt description of Clarence Malcolm of that ilk. The coppery brown hair together with the narrow, intensely blue eyes, and mischievous, slightly buck-toothed smile, gave him a foxy look he was keen to cultivate. 'A fox', he wrote in his school magazine, 'is an animal who in his spare time foxes'.[2] The Lowry family makes no claim to noble ancestry, cultivates no family tree, sports no escutcheons.[3] Like many families on the rise, Arthur Lowry's family regarded its history as a tabula rasa. It had no past, just a future. But in search of a writerly identity, Malcolm created a fictional past to give meaning to his present, inventing a family history, part British, part Scandinavian, which, through his rather shadowy maternal grandparents, was just conceivably plausible. His own parents, however, were substantial enough. Arthur Osborne Lowry was born in 1870, the son of a jobbing builder, at 14 Admiral Street, a three-bedroom terrace house in the respectable lower middle-class district of Toxteth Park in Liverpool – 'that terrible city whose main street is the ocean,' Lowry wrote.[4] Evelyn Boden Lowry was born nearby, at 113 Handel Street, the daughter of a master mariner. 'That terrible city' and the sea which provided its *raison d'être*, were to supply Lowry with two enduring and related visions – that of the lunatic city inside which he was to feel trapped and was to suffer, and that of the pathway to the sea and the ocean voyage, the risk-laden escape route from lunacy into uncertainty.

Arthur was one of the survivors of a family of thirteen, a dark-haired, slightly built boy with a serious demeanour. His parents were from Carlisle, where parish records attest to the presence of Lowrys as far back as the 1690s. There is no recorded memory of his father Edward, nor of his mother Georgina, whose family name was Bradburn. They were, however, strict Methodists, both pious and censorious. Edward brought the fervour of a convert to his Wesleyanism, a powerful commitment shared by his elder brother Richard William, whose son, Richard junior, became a minister on the Liverpool circuit. Richard William and Edward joined together in 1875 to form the firm of E. & R. W. Lowry, joiners, builders and estate agents, at 32 Admiral Street. The Lowry brothers each fathered large families, and for each of them family life revolved around home, the nearby St John's Methodist Chapel in Belvidere Road where the Reverend Richard was the resident minister, and the Admiral Hall Mission for Sailors established at 32 Admiral Street in 1894.

When Edward died that year, Arthur's family moved in with Richard who became paterfamilias of the new joint family. The heavy atmosphere of moral rectitude must have been suffocating for an intelligent boy like Arthur. It certainly left its mark on him, despite his later efforts to break away. The mould into which he was compressed left him incapable of expressing overt emotions. He grew up to believe that open displays of feeling were signs of weakness, and weakness in turn was a sin. That, at least, is the impression he gave his children. The ghosts of these gloomy, puritanical Lowrys cast a long dark shadow over Malcolm's life, and he made early efforts to exorcize them with a lethal pen. In *Ultramarine*, his first novel, he buries them all, 'knocked for a row of milk bottles in the cemetery at Oslo,' the victims of congenital syphilis. They never reappear in any of his subsequent writing. 'The gods', he wrote, 'hugged my forebears to death.' Later in the novel he admits that he had killed them off that way only in his imagination and for pleasure. However, a sense of religious foreboding lived on in his life, and a deep sense of guilt about the damage a sinful life could do to the genius with which he was entrusted.

His mother's family, however, were spared his homicidal malice. Although they were more penurious than the Lowrys, they were seemingly more colourful and venial. Evelyn's father, John Boden, was born at Northwich in Cheshire in 1839, son of a lighterman. Her mother, Betsy Potter, was born four years later in Liverpool. John was lost at sea in 1884, leaving Betsy with four young children to bring up in penny-pinching poverty. Evelyn, it seems, set out early to 'improve' herself and to distance herself from her family as much as possible. She transformed her father into a legendary figure, a romantic sea captain who came to play an important role in the fictional ancestry of her mythogenic son, Malcolm. Evelyn told her children that 'Captain Lyon' Boden was given his first command in his early twenties and disappeared at sea, along with his ship, the four-masted schooner, the *Scottish Isles*, returning from India. In *Ultramarine* we get our first glimpse of the legendary 'Captain' Boden when Lowry's autobiographical hero Dana Hilliot recalls being bathed one evening by his mother.

> Gazing at the picture of my grandfather in the old nursery, I noticed for the first time how infinitely blue his eyes were, and slightly obscene; watery, as though he had never wiped the salt spray from them. 'Why are you so dirty, Dana? My father was always so clean, so spruce. He had a master's certificate before he was twenty-three. When he came ashore he always came in a cab, and wore a top hat. He always wore a deerskin cap . . . He was an angel from heaven. He was bringing me a cockatoo.'[5]

That 'slightly obscene' look Lowry placed in the old Captain's watery blue eyes was clearly a mark of affection bestowed on a much-loved creation. In his story 'Through the Panama' he is a swashbuckling memory 'recalled by Old Hands in Liverpool' for his pugnacity and seamanship, and in the posthumously published *Dark as the Grave Wherein My Friend is Laid* he is spun into a dramatic yarn worthy of a Conrad novel.

> My grandfather was a skipper in sail, he was wrecked, and drowned in the Bay of Bengal. Actually, his ship was blown up. He had a rather heroic death . . . It became quite a legend. They were in the doldrums. The crew had cholera.[6]

He told his second wife that it was at the valiant Captain's request that a British gunboat blew the stricken vessel and all on board, himself included, out of the water. The tale, as told, must have resonated with conviction, and no doubt its gradual elaboration owed something to having been told and retold over innumerable bar-room tables.

Sadly for Lowry's story, the prosaic record blows Captain Boden and the *Scottish Isles* out of the water more effectively than any gunboat. The ship on which John Boden disappeared on 26 April 1884, somewhere in the Indian Ocean, was the Quebec-owned *Vice Reine*, and the 45-year-old master mariner was serving not as its captain but as first mate.[7] The facts, however, were less important to Lowry than a myth he could build upon, and here he had a far more romantic ancestor than any supplied by the gloomy and pedestrian Lowrys, who were so unimaginative and sanctimonious.

After three years at the Liverpool Institute, Arthur left school at fifteen to become an office boy with a shipping company, and must have found the spirit of enterprise which infused Victorian commercial life highly congenial. Liverpool in the mid-1880s was Britain's busiest seaport, a city of opportunities for bright industrious young men like Arthur. Steamship companies such as the White Star, Blue Star and Blue Funnel lines, trading to the Americas, west Africa and the Far East, were extending their fleets. The Mersey was the gateway into which poured the raw material of the old and new British Empires and out through which streamed the products of the factories of the North and Midlands. Arthur was well equipped to succeed in a dog-eat-dog world of wheeling and dealing. He had a natural talent for mathematics, a shrewd commercial brain and a deep-rooted work ethic. By nineteen he had advanced to the position of accountant with the cotton broking firm of A. J. Buston & Co., and by twenty-one he was the company's cashier with a junior partnership.

By the time he was twenty-two he was in a position to consider marriage. At the Belvidere Road Chapel he had met Evelyn Boden whose sister Mary had become engaged to his older brother William. Evelyn was four years younger than Arthur, a small, blue-eyed, extremely pretty blonde, though so proud and aloof that the other members of her family nicknamed her the Duchess. Her mother had settled somewhat stoically into widowhood and her two brothers, Jack and Charlie, had followed their father to sea. Evelyn, however, considered them altogether too uncouth for her liking – her mother kept a corner shop and Charlie came to run a coalyard. Her sights were set on higher things. She had taken up elocution lessons and had cultivated a preposterous upper-class accent. Now she was about to be rescued by Arthur, a young man with prospects.

They were married on 5 June 1894, by the Reverend Richard Lowry at Belvidere Road and moved into a small rented terrace house in nearby Cairns Street. Within six months, Arthur had carried his young wife away from the overcrowded streets of Toxteth Park and the sordid thoroughfares of workaday Liverpool across the Mersey to the more sedate residential district of Wallasey on the north-west tip of the Wirral Peninsula in neighbouring Cheshire. Not only was this a distinct move up the social scale, but it put the wide river estuary between them and their families. The impecunious Bodens and the censorious Lowrys could be gradually ignored and eventually all but forgotten. Now Arthur travelled daily to the Liverpool Cotton Exchange aboard the Birkenhead Ferry in the company of other commuting businessmen. At 5 Churchill Grove, in the old village of Liscard, on 9 May 1895, the Lowrys' first child, Stuart Osborne, was born.

Over the next fifteen years this flight from origins continued. Every four or five years the Lowrys moved house, and after each move there was another addition to the family. The moves charted the steady rise in Arthur's position and fortunes. Their second child, Wilfrid Malbon, was born at a three-storey semi-detached house in tree-lined Sandrock Road in July 1900, and Arthur Russell arrived in September 1905, at the more elegant 'Warren Crest', on the distinctly superior North Drive, overlooking the Municipal Golf Course and the sea. The only set-back to Arthur's advancement was an attack of pneumonia at the end of 1901, so severe that he barely survived. This experience changed him both as a man and as a father. While he was ill, to ease pressure on Evelyn, Stuart was farmed out to the Bodens in Toxteth Park, where, much to her displeasure, he became quite attached to his sailor uncles, Jack and Charlie. Evelyn must in any case have been annoyed to have to depend on a family she now felt was beneath her, and from then on a procession of nursemaids was engaged to take Wilfrid and the other children off her hands until they were sent away to school.

Arthur's illness and its debilitating after-effects threatened to terminate his career with Bustons, where he was still employed in an essentially clerical role. But characteristically he took this reversal as a challenge; the sedentary cashier became a physical fitness enthusiast. He became a keen member of the Liverpool Swimming Club and was awarded a silver medal by the Liverpool Shipwreck and Humane Society for saving a woman from drowning in the Mersey on 15 June 1902. Determined to build up his physique, he enrolled on a mail-order course in muscular development offered by the American strongman Eugene Sandow. Evidently he was a star pupil. He swam and exercised daily and within three years had won the Sandow Medal as England's Best Developed Man of 1904.[8] He proudly wore the gilt medallion on his watch-chain for the rest of his life. His passion for physical culture was passed on to his sons, and with Malcolm it persisted into middle age. But, still in his early thirties, Arthur was not only reincarnated as an athlete but transformed as a parent. He had set out to play the liberal, easy-going father, but by degrees was converted into an autocrat. Evelyn was proving to be an unwilling and ineffectual mother, and Stuart was becoming a rebel. There were complaints from his school and when, barely ten years old, he got into a scrape with the police, Arthur began to take a tough line with all of his sons. He was, by this time, third in seniority at Bustons, with only A.J., its founder, and one other, his cousin Fred, above him. That year he travelled abroad on company business for the first time, on this occasion to Germany, and in the following years he was to handle most of Buston's overseas interests.

Evelyn found his absences stressful. Not only was she finding motherhood distasteful but her new social status made her increasingly uncomfortable. 'Self-improvement' through elocution and marriage had not equipped her with the appropriate social graces, and she was ill at ease in company and unable to entertain. In these circumstances, Malcolm was not exactly a welcome baby. He told John Davenport that he was a mistake – unplanned and unwanted. 'Thrown together by a cotton broker in less than 5 minutes. 5 seconds perhaps,' says his alter ego in

'Through the Panama'.[9] Arthur told him later that during her pregnancy his mother had 'concentrated her thoughts on beautiful things so that her dear boy might have beautiful thoughts.'[10] But at thirty-four, and with an evident dislike of small children, the news that she was again pregnant could hardly have been a cause of much joy to Evelyn.

The summer of 1909, the summer of Malcolm's birth, was hot and sultry. His birthplace, New Brighton, swarmed with holidaymakers. On the day of his birth, 28 July, the newspapers were filled with images of Empire. The Asquith Government was to lay down four new dreadnoughts for the Royal Navy; the newly created Union of South Africa had been toasted by a gathering of Imperial Premiers at London's Guildhall; and cheering crowds were greeting the German Kaiser and the Russian Tsar at Cowes for the yachting. But it was in the air rather than at sea that history was being made. On 25 July, an unknown Frenchman, Louis Blériot, had become the first to fly the English Channel, giving rise to invasion scares in the jingo press.

On Thursday 29 July, the births column in the *Liverpool Echo* announced: '*LOWRY* – July 28th, at Warren Crest, North-drive, New Brighton, to Mr and Mrs Arthur Lowry, a son.' Much the same notice appeared in the *Post and Mercury* the following day. Clarence Malcolm Lowry, as he was soon baptized, was a Wednesday child with much woe to come. He was born, his mother told him years later, at midnight,[11] and Arthur, was no doubt proud and delighted to be a father, even if perhaps an unintended one at thirty-nine. Had he been at all superstitious, he might have noted something portentous in the fact that on that day, according to the *Echo*, the Liverpool cotton market fluctuated nervously.

Lowry liked to recall that he was born close to Rock Ferry where Nathaniel Hawthorne lived as US Consul in Liverpool, the city where Herman Melville had announced to Hawthorne his determination to be annihilated.

Lowry claimed one literary link for himself – that he was named Clarence after Shakespeare's duke who died head-down in a malmsey butt. In fact the name came from a friend of Stuart's. Mercifully it was soon dropped. Evelyn Lowry hinted frequently that Malcolm's entrance into the world had been an awkward one. Six years after it she had a hysterectomy, and thereafter would often sigh dramatically and say, 'I've never been the same since Mawlcolm was born,' a remark which became a catchphrase with the younger boys, to be uttered with a suitably histrionic sigh whenever anything went wrong, like a bad shot at golf, or a failed kick-start on the motorbike. Both Malcolm and Russell recalled their mother as cold, uncaring and self-centred, and Arthur had to blackmail them into showing her affection. In return for some minor favour he would say, 'Give your mother a nice warm kiss, then.' This, too, became a joke with the two younger boys who, as they grew older, became apt mimics of their humourless parents.

Malcolm and Russell, like Stuart and Wilfrid before them, were quickly handed over to nursemaids, and their contact with their mother was minimal. Whether or not Evelyn did, as Arthur maintained, breast-feed Malcolm, Russell remembered them being fed on a milk-substitute called Mellin's Food. And, he recalled, she never ever bathed them at bedtime. As a result, like many little boys of their class, the two youngest became deeply attached to their nanny, Miss Bell, known affectionately as 'Bey'.

In the summer of 1910 the family spent a holiday on the Isle of Man, for which Malcolm came to hold a special affection, and Manx figures crop up occasionally in his novels and stories. On their return, Wilfrid was sent to Caldicott School in Hitchin, the prep school for The Leys, the Methodist public school in Cambridge to which Stuart had been sent the year before.

Meantime, Arthur had met, probably on his daily trips across the Mersey to his office at the Liverpool Cotton Exchange, a German property developer, David Benno Rappart. Rappart was the architect of an ambitious scheme to build an estate for affluent gentry and the nouveau riche at Caldy on the north east coast of the Wirral peninsula, just south of Hoylake. Caldy was a tiny, isolated hamlet – little more than a church, a village green and a manor house. Rappart's Caldy Manor Estate planned a series of detached houses in the grand style, each to be built on at least an acre of land, with a cluster of small separate houses for servants, and use of a nine-hole golf course designed by golf champion James Braid. The seaward prospect from Caldy was magnificent – the broad sweep of the Dee Estuary with the Welsh mountains beyond. From the golf clubhouse on a clear day the snow-capped peak of Mount Snowdon was visible. To the north lay Liverpool Bay, Hilbre Island, and the strange coastline around Hoylake and Leasowe, with its ancient sunken forest and lonely lighthouse. It was an idyllic spot, the perfect place to which to escape from the sordid industrial seaport where Arthur spent his working days. He bought a parcel of land, hired a builder, and on 6 September 1911, Russell's sixth birthday, the family moved into the new house, Inglewood, an eight-roomed mock-Tudor mansion set in two acres of land. It cost Arthur £3,500. He was now a man of substance and most certainly on the way up.

The move was not exactly to Evelyn's taste. The house needed servants, and having to manage them only heightened her sense of social anxiety. Arthur bought her a copy of Mrs Beeton's cookbook, departed immediately on business for Russia, and left her to get on with it. But it was not only Inglewood that worried her; she also found the local social scene intimidating. The new neighbours included two bankers, an insurance chief, and a shipowner who travelled to work in a horse-drawn carriage driven by a coachman in white-topped boots. Evelyn, seemingly overawed by this show of style, retired to her bedroom for most of the day and forbade entertainment at Inglewood. If Arthur needed to entertain business friends he was to do so at the Cotton Exchange. In fact, Evelyn was to live almost entirely isolated from Caldy society for almost forty years, even preferring to shop by phone. She was unwell for a long time following Malcolm's birth and this reticence may have been caused by medical problems and the early onset of menopause. But if she found the role of hostess too painful, Arthur was ready to indulge her in order to maintain the fiction of a happy marriage. Protected from reality by his stern devotion, she was both spoiled and caged. Her family life was largely a performance, and from her children's point of view it was a performance without truth or affection.

Three servants were hired in addition to Miss Bell: Mary, the cook, and Minnie, the housemaid, lived in; George Cooke, the gardener, an old Caldy inhabitant, lived out. Cooke was an old-fashioned countryman (memorable for having had all his teeth extracted by the village blacksmith) who taught the Lowry boys a great deal about rural life. However, the servants and the running of the house soon caused loud quarrels between Evelyn and Arthur. Writing from London en route to Russia shortly after moving into Inglewood, Arthur complained sadly, 'You do sometimes knock down all my castles.'[12]

By 1912, he had acquired a car and hired a chauffeur by the hour to drive him to and from the Birkenhead ferry. His career was at its apogee. He was a prominent and respected member of his profession, with a fine new house, a pretty if rather awkward wife, a young family of healthy good-looking sons of whom he was enormously proud, a car, servants, and excellent prospects. Perhaps to mollify her, he bought Evelyn a full concert-sized Bechstein for the lounge, and around this the family would congregate to sing, mostly hymns from the Methodist

Hymnal. Although he had escaped the excessive piety of his own family, Arthur still insisted on regular church-going, and each Sunday marched his family five miles to the nearest Methodist chapel in West Kirby. As a baby, Malcolm went with Miss Bell to the Caldy parish church, and by the time he was old enough to walk, to an Anglican church Arthur had switched to because it was nearer than the Methodist one.

Trauma struck when the nanny, thinking to better herself, took a job as a stewardess on a cruise liner, and departed suddenly in April 1912, when Malcolm was three months short of his third birthday. When she left, the two youngest wept inconsolably. However, she did not enjoy the experience on the liner (possibly disturbed by the Titanic disaster that month) and on the occasion of his third birthday, 28 July, she wrote Malcolm a sweet letter from Wallasey on SS *Teutonic* notepaper, saying how the sea had not suited her and how sad she grew thinking of her 'dear little baby with a brown face and blue eyes' who sang 'Twinkle, Twinkle Little Star' to her.[13] The letter was opportune because her replacement had been a disaster.

The stand-in nursemaid was the youthful but short-tempered Miss Long, whom Malcolm and Russell disliked on sight, probably for no other reason than that she was not Miss Bell. One day, while the two boys were being walked by Miss Long over Caldy Hill – a stretch of wild grass, gorse and bramble bushes overlooking the Dee Estuary – Russell wandered off, leaving the nanny wheeling Malcolm along in his pushchair. Suddenly he heard loud screams and went running back to find Miss Long and Malcolm emerging from behind bushes, Malcolm in floods of tears and Miss Long in a furious temper. What occurred in the undergrowth will never be known, but Malcolm was later to milk the incident for all it was worth, claiming at various times that he had been beaten on the genitals with a bramble branch, sexually abused, and held upside down over the cliff's edge.[14] The same nanny was also said to have suspended him head-down over a rain barrel. What probably happened was that he had a temper tantrum, and Miss Long, unable to cope with a fractious three-year-old, lost control and belaboured him with whatever lay to hand, perhaps a dead branch lying along the path. In the event, the hapless girl was quickly dismissed, and Miss Bell returned to much rejoicing from the two young Lowrys. But Miss Long had provided Malcolm with a memory trace from which he came to build a sad tale of cruelty and suffering. Not only was she a sadist, but his parents, by allowing this to happen, had neglected him disgracefully.

The return of the much-loved 'Bey' brought happier times. Then, at five, Russell was sent to a local prep school, leaving Malcolm with 'Bey' to himself during the day. He was generally spoiled both by her and the other servants. Mary, German and fierce, was thought to have come to England for love, only to have been jilted. Sarah soon replaced Minnie, but both women had a soft spot for young Malcolm. He claimed later that they gave him wine to make him sleep as a child, but what happened was that once, aged four, he strayed into the larder and helped himself to some of Minnie's home-brewed wine, making himself so ill he was put to bed, where he passed out. The children saw Evelyn only during meals, except dinner, when she and Arthur ate alone. When they were reluctant to eat, she would reproach them with her poverty-stricken childhood. 'Ooh, lovely porridge! I never had anything like this when I was a girl!' Her early deprivation was real enough and no doubt played a large part in the making of her character. Russell remembered her as snobbish, small-minded and mean, with few redeeming qualities.[15] It was she, he believed, who was the main cause of the trouble which slowly began to brew inside the family.

CHAPTER II

UNWILLINGLY TO SCHOOL
1914–1923

> Since my earliest childhood a barb of sorrow has lodged in my heart. As long as it stays I am ironic – if it is pulled out I shall die.
>
> KIERKEGAARD

When Malcolm was five, Miss Bell was dismissed and he was sent to a local day school, Braeside, in West Kirby. After being the centre of such loving female attention, to be thrown back into the unloving arms of Evelyn and simultaneously projected into the aggressive company of other young boys was devastating for him. In stark contrast to 'Bey', Evelyn was a dedicated authoritarian who spelt out her demands in no uncertain terms. Any impudent refusal would be met by instant outrage. 'How dare you speak to me like that! I am the Queen of Inglewood!' – another remark the boys recited gleefully to mimic her. And the 'Queen' and the 'King' were so often engaged in small-minded bickering, about such matters as who should use the chauffeur at what time, that any illusion of happy families was dispelled early on so far as the boys were concerned.

Evelyn became so remote that they not only ridiculed her in secret but defied her openly. She responded with a mixture of pious injunctions and coarse ill-temper which only served to increase their contempt for her. The contrast between her professed religiosity and her cold hostility towards them is doubtless one source of Malcolm's portrait of the witch, Mother Drumgold, in his story 'Elephant and Colosseum', 'a Methodist most wonderfully Methodistic,' who leads her son to speculate on 'the operation of the dark powers among the converts of John Wesley.'[1] Arthur, on the other hand, was someone to be respected: the strict, controlled disciplinarian. Malcolm grew to fear yet admire this small, abrupt, humourless man who 'had plans' for his boys, but never told them what they were. In his own way he was a kind father who went to considerable lengths to help his sons, but the kindness was well concealed behind a tyrannical exterior.

Despite the hard face Arthur presented to his children, his letters to Evelyn show him to have been a sensitive, considerate and even romantic husband. But although he was less 'wonderfully Methodistic' than his wife, he, like her, did not escape his youngest son's retribution.

> My excellent father . . . is now in a home eating the buttons off the chair at clairaudient intervals, and composing a sonnet sequence, *Songs of Second Childhood* . . . While my mother, who occasionally writes me, is going blind. A queer family . . . a queer family. As for myself, I am the only sane member of it, the only one who has escaped the taint.[2]

As with his murdered forebears in Oslo Cemetery, none of this was true, he wrote, but to imagine that it was gave him pleasure. As a child, however, he was more often displeased and ill-tempered, on one occasion hurling Evelyn's prize silver sugarbowl across the table at Russell, narrowly missing his right ear. And he was very sensitive and easily infuriated by remarks about his chubby, ungainly appearance. Stuart was forever provoking him, laughing at his awkwardness and referring to him as 'Baby'. Russell believed that the effect of these jibes led Malcolm to want to become an adult before his time, and he was often withdrawn and preoccupied with his own thoughts.

At Braeside, among strange boys for the first time, his sense of physical inadequacy was sharpened. He suffered chronic constipation, the cause of which went undiscovered for over forty years, and it must have been with hours of childhood misery in mind that he later wrote so pointedly of his 'racked, trembling, malodorous body.'[3] He also suffered every winter from appalling chilblains, his fingers swelling up and bursting open like so many fried sausages.[4] On his first day at the school, taunting bullies reduced him to tears when he could not tie his own tie because of his chilblains, and he was rescued by the school captain, whose words remained with him. ' "Let the bloody boy alone," always I would remember to my dying day. That act of compassion when I was new . . . For that I loved him & his whole family forever.'[5] That boy, James Furniss, and his family, were to be immortalized as the generous and hearty Taskersons in *Under the Volcano*. He often used his writing to sanctify or demonize those he saw as friends or enemies, as he did when he smote his own parents with congenital syphilis in *Ultramarine*.

But awkward and temperamental as Malcolm was, it was Stuart who was giving Arthur his greatest headache. In 1911, he had been removed from The Leys, where, in one splendid gesture, he had been caught breaking several school rules simultaneously in a farcical encounter with his headmaster on the Cam – caught smoking in a punt while playing truant. Arthur promptly packed him off to a school in Switzerland. But by 1913, at the age of eighteen, Stuart was an apparently reformed character, and had been taken on at Bustons as an apprentice.

As war began to threaten in Europe, Arthur's certainties looked vulnerable. During the last years of peace he had travelled widely through Europe and America, journeys about which he wrote home in loving letters to Evelyn. On a second visit to Russia via Berlin in February 1914, he described how, while sailing from Gothenburg to Trelleborg, past the site of the Battle of Copenhagen, he had raised his hat in memory of Nelson. There was no doubting the patriotism of this 'Tory of Tory capitalists on a grand scale,' as Malcolm later called him. One can only imagine how passionately he would have been caught up in the jingoism which swept the country later that year, as old Europe prepared to destroy itself on the battlefield.

According to family legend, in August 1914 Stuart rushed off to volunteer with the words, 'Let's all go off and get killed!' Jokingly, he told Arthur that if he returned, he would climb Liverpool's recently built Liver Building and retrieve one of the two great metal birds (the famous Liver Birds) perched on top of it. He was soon commissioned in the Cheshire Regiment, and stationed for the first two years of the war in Bournemouth. Before going to France in June 1916 he was promoted to First Lieutenant in the 4th Battalion of the Royal Welch Fusiliers. Before leaving he sent a postcard home with the simple message, 'Here we go!'

After a year as school captain, Wilfrid left Caldicott in September and was sent in Stuart's footsteps to The Leys. The following January, Malcolm became even more isolated when Russell in his turn went off to Caldicott. The two elder brothers would travel together to Cambridge where Wilfrid then saw Russell on to his train to Hitchin. When they arrived, a telegram was sent home reading: '*Atwowah*', meaning, 'All travelling went off without a hitch'. From time to time, Arthur would visit his boys at school, proudly taking them out for tea. Perhaps it was his greater isolation which drove the already somewhat introspective Malcolm into books. After the usual childhood favourites of the period, like *Peter Rabbit*, he graduated to school stories – Talbot Baines Reed's *Fifth Form at St Dominic's* and Kipling's *Stalky & Co.* were particular favourites, followed, before the war's end, by *Tarzan of the Apes*. But another great passion had already been ignited. Arthur disapproved of cinema-going, regarding it as time wasting, but in 1916 the boys were taken in a family group to see the D. W. Griffith's silent movie, *Intolerance*, a vivid experience which Malcolm still recalled thirty-three years later.

One grim effect of the war was strong anti-German sentiment. Rappart, the German developer, was interned as an Enemy Alien and shortly afterwards died heartbroken. Even Mary, the Lowry's Hanoverian cook, came under suspicion and presumably escaped detention only because Arthur vouched for her. She did, however, have to report to the police once a week, and Lowry later reflected upon this whole episode as a great injustice.

But the immense amount of wartime naval activity in the Mersey must have been a considerable attraction. The ocean on his doorstep and the teeming port of Liverpool gradually turned the young boy's mind outwards towards the sea. There was in that city, he wrote later, an 'enormous sense of sea and ships,'[6] and there grew in him 'an inborn craving for the unrest of the sea.'[7] Once, home on leave, Stuart observed Malcolm pacing back and forth in front of the great bay windows at Inglewood overlooking the Dee and muttering, 'I wish I had a hook instead of a hand.' Presumably he had been reading *Peter Pan*.

In 1916 Arthur braved the U-boat blockade himself by making the dangerous Atlantic crossing on business to the American South, and Evelyn and Malcolm saw him off on the USMS *St Louis*. Malcolm, meanwhile, was not doing so well at school; Braeside was proving irksome to him. As a day boy he felt excluded from the world of the boarders, the mysteries of mathematics eluded him, and he displayed no talent for languages. He had no idea how to write Greek letters, he told a friend some thirty years later. 'I began Greek when I was acht and forgot it when I was novum.'[8]

After the war, Stuart returned home a Captain. He had survived the trenches unscathed by battle, though shattered by the deaths of so many friends. In France he had contracted arthritis in one foot, making him unfit for active service and destroying his hopes of an army career. Surgeons rebuilt the damaged foot, but it remained a handicap, and he would never scale the Liver Building in pursuit of that mythical bird, despite Arthur, in a weak and tasteless attempt at humour, suggesting that the time had come to redeem his promise. Stuart, however, soon escaped the claustrophobia of Inglewood. While stationed in Bournemouth, he had met the girl he intended to marry, Marguerite (Margot) Peirce, daughter of a veterinary surgeon. But she was Catholic, and both Evelyn and Arthur were vehemently opposed to the match. When they married at St Clement's Church Bournemouth in January 1919 according to the rites of the Church of England, it was therefore without the presence or blessing of the Lowry parents. While Stuart was shunned by his family, Margot was shunned by her church, and was duly excommunicated for marrying a Protestant. By the time Stuart left the army shortly afterwards, Arthur's displeasure had abated sufficiently for him to buy the newlyweds second-class tickets to America. They went to Texas, where Stuart settled down to learn the cotton trade at source. According to Malcolm, the second-class ticket was Arthur's subtle punishment for the son who had knocked down one of his castles by marrying a Catholic.

Armistice celebrations saw successions of warships coming to the Mersey for the jubilant public to visit. On one occasion a Q-ship appeared, a mysterious man-of-war which masqueraded as a freighter to lure surfaced U-boats within range of its concealed guns. Wilfrid, now a part-time officer in the RNVR, took Russell and Malcolm to see it, and the experience stayed submerged in Malcolm's memory only to resurface again in *Under the Volcano*, in which his hero, Geoffrey Firmin, became the youthful commander of the Q-ship *Samaritan*. Such experiences were retained in detail, because Malcolm, it transpired, was gifted with a prodigious memory. He acquired a passion for noting down and memorizing details of anything that caught his eccentric fancy – odd words, names of hymn tunes, street signs, advertisements. On the rare occasions he met them, he amazed his Lowry aunts by knowing the title of any hymn they cared to name by number in the Methodist Hymn Book, and they would ask him again and again to repeat this remarkable party-piece. It was good family fun, but a photographic memory, while in some ways a blessing, could, as he was to discover, also be a curse.

The post-war period brought new interests for the young Lowrys. They were taken to the cinema again, this time to see Griffith's *Broken Blossoms*, which Malcolm always considered one of the great movies of all time, and there was a rare family visit to the theatre to see *Richard II* at the Birkenhead Hippodrome. Arthur loved Shakespeare and always took the text along to read between acts. The theatre became as great a passion as the cinema for Malcolm, but there were simply more films than plays to see in his part of the world, and he would sneak off to the cinema with Russell and Wilfrid at every opportunity. Now aged nine, he was a flourishing young golfer, often turning out at the Caldy club with his brothers, or with friends from Braeside, like Bruce Thompson, or one of the Furniss boys. He was also a keen and natural swimmer, and, encouraged by Arthur, swam at the Liverpool Swimming Baths as well as in the sea each summer.

At the same time he found another new friend. Arthur, who had done well out of the war, as had Buston's, bought an additional piece of land adjoining Inglewood, and built a splendid garage which cost him more to build than Inglewood itself. In an act of uncharacteristic generosity he set George Cooke up in business at the local post office, then took on a full-time chauffeur, an ex-soldier called Coltman who had fought, so he liked to say, on the 'Gall-eye-Pole-eye Peninsul-eye'. Russell disliked him intensely; Malcolm considered him a hero. He had a favourite oath with a whiff of the trenches about it – 'Chew glass and spit blood!' which became their secret greeting, a password, a sign of intimacy with a man from the other side of the tracks.

> It was an extraordinary thing he should have said that, I now think, But with the incredibly grim humour of the English, this absurd catchphrase (was) his way of cheering me up – . . . It was like his favourite song, 'Ain't it grand to be bloomin' well dead'.[9]

The contrast between the grimly humorous Coltman and the humourless and sanctimonious Arthur could hardly have been greater, and Malcolm 'adopted' him as his 'guardian'.[10] There was evidently something in the post-war atmosphere which was already beginning to set boys of Malcolm's and Russell's generation apart from their Victorian parents.

What umbilical attachments remained for Malcolm were severed in January 1919 when he left home for his first term at Caldicott. He had two hard acts to follow. Wilfrid had developed into a first-class athlete, taken most of the school trophies and ended up school captain. Russell, still in the top form, was an academic high-flyer. If anyone seemed like the runt of the litter it was Malcolm. Ever more chubby and ungainly, he had none of Wilfrid's physical prowess, or Russell's ability in the classroom. In sport he had a robust energy which was to make him a usefully aggressive, if uncoordinated, rugby player and he acquired a thrusting sort of style at hockey, and in a small school like Caldicott there was always a place for him in the school team for his age group. As for his studies, only two subjects engaged him fully: Nature Study and English.

Caldicott was established in a large house on the edge of Hitchin as a prep school for The Leys in 1904 by a Leys old boy and previous master, J. Heald Jenkins, and when Lowry arrived there, had some thirty-five boys and five or six staff. The ethos was Wesleyan Methodist. In Wilfrid and Russell's day, Jenkins was still headmaster. He was a fierce moralist with a ferocious reputation with the cane, whose watchword was, 'On no account attempt to be fair. If a wrong has been done somebody must be punished. At once. Wipe the slate clean.'[11] Once, when Russell and a friend were accused of cheating, he did not look into the matter but simply gave them 'six bleeding weals apiece,' then said, 'Well you won't do that again. Here, have a piece of cake.'[12] He was nicknamed 'Pony' because of his whinnying laugh, and, despite his sadistic streak, won the respect of many boys for his cutting wit and brilliant wordplay. Russell, and Malcolm after him, learned to enjoy the cut and thrust of verbal duels with Jenkins and relished his stirring, sometimes humorous readings from Thomas Hood.

By the time Malcolm arrived at the school, 'Pony' had been replaced as Head by the more liberal, and secretly alcoholic, J. Vereker Bindon. A brilliant scholar, Bindon managed to conceal his drinking from parents and governors, if not from the boys – some of whom recalled the smell of alcohol on his breath, even in chapel. It was Bindon who Lowry later claimed sent him to walk his dog and bring in his liquor – an unlikely tale considering his youth at the time – but notes he made on his schooldays suggest a strong sympathy for a man ultimately ostracized and removed from the school because of drink. Jenkins, however, remained a master at the school, where his acts of punitive savagery became legendary. The prevailing atmosphere of heavy sermonizing coupled with threats of dire physical punishment did not greatly distress either Wilfrid or Russell; to Malcolm it was hateful.

For a time, the three brothers took the train journey to school and back together. Wilfrid was in his last term at The Leys, and Russell in his penultimate term at Caldicott. They would all travel to London, where Wilfrid would see the two youngsters on to the train for Hitchin before going on alone to Cambridge. Between trains there was usually time to visit a cinema or theatre; the chief problem for Wilfrid was extracting the other two in time to catch their connections. London, like Liverpool, both excited and horrified Malcolm. 'When I first saw London,' he wrote, 'I thought I was in hell.'[13] But it was a hell he enjoyed visiting, where he could feast himself on plays, revues and musicals, and visit all the cinemas he had time and money to take in. Even though there was a simpler way to travel to Cambridge from Liverpool, when he finally moved to The Leys himself he always travelled via the tempting 'hell' of the metropolis.

For his first two terms at boarding school Malcolm came under the watchful eye of Russell, who was able to steer him through the thicket of school rules and regulations. Among the new friends he made, Eric Firmin may well have surfaced from his prodigious memory twenty years later when he gave his name to his drunken Consul in *Under the Volcano*; Ralph Izzard, whom he knew also at The Leys and at university, crops up in an unfinished Lowry novel, *The Ordeal*, as a ghostly bully. At school, however, Lowry and Izzard struck up a friendship mainly because each suffered from chronic chilblains, and during their first winter at school together, went three times a week for electrical treatment for their swollen fingers.[14] If there was any conflict or rivalry between them, it arose from a joint passion; they both enjoyed writing and soon found themselves competing for school essay prizes.

In the close community of a boarding school a physical oddity can readily attract unwanted attention and cruel comment, and before long Malcolm found himself picked on for two things. His unfortunate habit of going red in the face when angry soon earned him the nickname 'Lobs', short for 'Lobster', and the tiny size of his penis was quickly noticed at bathtime. To his intense mortification he became the object of mocking curiosity. He was not unhappy about the nickname, but the physical deficiency became a psychological obsession with the onset of adolescence.

Not surprisingly perhaps, his closest friendship was with a boy who, on arrival, found himself a complete outsider at the school. William Hywel Jones, from Anglesey in North Wales, was a nervous boy, who spoke only Welsh when he arrived at Caldicott, and spent his first term separated from the other boys while he learned English. Later, he and Lowry shared the same four-bed dormitory and started their own 'Sporting Magazine' together. It was just a handwritten affair, but each wrote to his sporting heroes, soliciting contributions, and Jones actually received a letter from Max Woosnam, a leading Manchester City soccer player. Lowry had no success, so wrote a piece himself on the Caldy

Golf Club,[15] probably his first published work. The golf course was to be one of the most enduring images to emerge on the symbolic landscape of *Under the Volcano*, with the Consul's obscure mental references to the Donga (an old sunken pathway to the seashore at Caldy), and to the names of the golf balls he used (like the Zodiac Zone). Lowry seems to have adopted a protective stance towards his nervous Welsh schoolmate, much as Jimmy Furniss had protected him at Braeside. He already found himself drawn to vulnerable 'outsiders', and the stuttering new boy his doppelgänger befriends in his school story 'Enter One in Sumptuous Armour'[16] is probably based on Jones, the tongue-tied Welshman.

Unlike his older brothers, he was an unenthusiastic Wolf Cub and Boy Scout, though he fell under the spell of the cub-mistress, Miss Ingram, who took the boys on nature walks. She heightened further the love of nature he had learned from George Cooke, a love which was to infuse his later work, and the stark contrast between the 'heavenly' beauty of the world of nature and the 'hellish' landscape of the industrial city became a powerful focus in his poetry and fiction. Possibly of more direct importance to him as a writer was another teacher of whom he grew extremely fond. Gordon Wood was, according to Wilfrid, 'a ripping sport' who 'reads ghosts stories out of Dickens to us before "lights out".'[17] The story before 'lights out' became a school tradition, and once a week one of the boys was allowed to read or tell a story. Malcolm quickly revealed a flair for storytelling, especially ghost stories, and acquired a reputation for surprise endings, so that boys came to look forward to hearing 'a Lowry story' at bedtime.[18] He had discovered the power and prestige which comes from being able to command an audience. He was a natural actor, and finding an exciting use for the words he had collected and memorized, came completely out of his shell once on stage. This power over an audience was a strong drug which he found impossible to resist for the rest of his life.

School holidays meant golf at Caldy and seaside holidays with the family. In the summer of 1919, Arthur took Evelyn to India on a business trip, and Wilfrid took Malcolm and Russell on holiday to the Isle of Man. They stayed at Fort Anne, where they were known as 'the boys'. They played golf and danced and had great fun. Wilfrid was in charge for the first ten days, then Arthur joined them. There was much messing about in boats and finally Arthur chartered a fishing boat in which they sailed around the island. Young Malcolm had trouble getting off boats and up ladders. When he was around, things tended to go wrong, often to the irritation of his brothers who never hesitated to make fun of him, only to spark off his easily combustible temper. When they referred to him as 'Fat-bottom', he coloured up in fury, in his peculiarly lobster-like fashion, and was particularly annoyed that they hoisted him up a ladder to get him on board.[19] It was on this holiday that he first began to have eye trouble, and it was Wilfrid's and Russell's duty to see that he was treated regularly with his prescribed eye-drops. But, discomforting though this must have been, it did not prevent him sneaking off at opportune moments with the others to the cinema.

Arthur was extraordinarily mean and kept the boys very short of money, so they had to scrape the price of a cinema ticket from any source they could, usually by saving the money from what they got for travelling to and from school. Malcolm remembered how once he and Russell were punished for the sin of visiting a cinema in Hoylake, but how Wilfrid, apparently, had pointed out that the cinema in question had been designed by one of their Lowry uncles, an architect. Was it also sinful for Arthur's brother to have drawn the plans? With tactics such as that, wrote Lowry, they had gradually worn the 'Old Man' down so that he became more tolerant, though consequently less true to himself – 'for I think he was a natural tyrant & being decent didn't suit him.'[20] The skill learned as a child of scraping together cinema money must have stood him in good stead later on when trying to scrounge money for another passion and taste which awaited him – alcohol.

Wilfrid, by now a mature young rugby player, was about to bring distinction to himself and the family. He had graduated from the school first team to the local team, Birkenhead Park, and now turned out regularly for his county side, Cheshire. Finally he was picked to play for England at right wing three-quarter against France at Twickenham on 21 January 1920. It was his only game for England, but he became both a family and local hero. Evelyn was especially thrilled by such things and took great pride in the cluster of Wilfrid's trophies which were kept well polished and prominently displayed on the sideboard in the lounge at Inglewood.

Despite the glamour which his sporting success had brought him, Wilfrid was a modest, conventional and utterly reliable young man. In 1920 he was again entrusted to take his younger brothers on summer holiday, this time to Rothesay on the Isle of Bute in Western Scotland. It was the perfect place for the boys. There was not only swimming but an eighteen-hole golf course, as well as a local flea-pit cinema where they could catch up on film-going. There were plenty of social events, and for the first time Malcolm had the opportunity to meet girls. Staying at the Hydro Hotel, they met a Scotsman called Lindsay who owned a thirty-foot yacht and had two daughters more or less Russell and Malcolm's ages. Boys and girls paired off, and spent a great deal of time on the boat. It must have been more painful than ever for Malcolm, anxious to impress twelve-year-old Helen Lindsay, still to be teased about his awkwardness. She was probably the first girl to whom he wrote, in a schoolboyish way, and for whom he developed an attachment – although he did elsewhere claim that his first love was Hilda Cooke, the gardener's daughter.[21]

Russell had moved to The Leys at the end of summer, 1919, and by this time, for some reason, Arthur rarely visited his boys at school. However, Wilfrid now made it his duty to visit them occasionally and to take them both to London for the day whenever he could, once in 1922 to see Douglas Fairbanks in *Robin Hood*. But Malcolm must have felt miserable that neither of his parents ever came to see him at school.

After a year at Caldicott, he was given a new bicycle for Christmas, which was to bring near disaster and a family of new friends. He was freewheeling at high speed down King's Drive, a high winding hill which bisects Caldy village, when he skidded. Edward Brown, who lived at Hillthorpe, a large house at the top of the hill, was driving his family home at the time and they were horrified to see this small boy swerve off the road and fly headlong into the ditch. They stopped, gathered the howling child into their car, and rushed him home, where Mrs Brown cleaned and bandaged a severely gashed knee. The patient was so pleased to be fussed over that he was reluctant to leave, and stayed on to play. There were two Brown boys of about his own age, Maurice and Colin, and a slightly older girl, Carol. Finally he was taken home and his father promptly took him to a specialist to have the gash in his knee sewn up. However, he had found a new family and from then onwards he was frequently at Hillthorpe, playing ping-pong or tennis on the Browns' private court. He had also acquired a spectacular diagonal scar on his right knee, which he later claimed was a bullet wound sustained in crossfire during the Chinese Civil War.

Later in the following year, he had another experience which was to take on as great an importance in his personal mythology as his beating by Miss Long. The eye inflammation which had first afflicted him on holiday two years earlier suddenly became worse; the eye-drops ceased to be effective and ulcers developed. The ulceration, had it spread, could have endangered his sight, so Arthur took him to a Harley Street specialist called Hudson, who scraped his eyes, an extremely painful but effective form of treatment. For a while he was confined to bed at Inglewood, where Maurice Brown remembered being allowed to visit him, a rare privilege, given Evelyn's dislike of visitors. Even children wishing to call on her sons were usually unwelcome, as Lowry noted later:

> Our family was one of those not uncommon in England, that, while tolerant on occasion for business reasons, lives in almost complete isolation from their sons' friends, at the same time being highly critical of them . . . Nor had any other of my friends (been allowed into the house) whose fathers kept liquor in the house or went to a different church . . .[22]

Malcolm returned to school sporting a black eye-patch, and was again, apparently, the object of some derision. However, with his new-found sense of drama, he probably enjoyed playing the pirate-king and imaginatively sporting that longed-for hook. Later he expanded this experience into a sad tale: his eye condition had languished untreated by an uncaring family for so long that he had become blind and unable to read for several years. Being forced to go to school though blind, he wrote, gave him some sympathy with the sufferings of the drunkard Bindon. And he discovered this story of blindness aroused great sympathy, especially among females.[23] However, in a letter home from Caldicott early in 1922, he said very specifically that he was having 'no trouble at all with the conjunctivitis,' and he was 'allowed to do work and do absolutely everything.'[24] But from such misfortunes do great tragic legends rise. One possible source of this blindness legend emerged thirty-three years later when he told his psychiatrist that he had read in books that masturbation made you blind and sex gave you syphilis. That he claimed to have masturbated from the age of nine probably explains his youthful fear of blindness. Certainly the association of sex with syphilis became a powerful obsession for him.[25]

After his great rugby triumphs, Wilfrid could do no wrong in the eyes of his proud parents. He was given a Sunbeam motorcycle as a reward, and on this the three brothers would set off during school holidays to visit the cinema in West Kirby or Hoylake – Russell on the pillion and Malcolm wedged on the petrol tank. He also persuaded Arthur to buy a gramophone, an imposing cabinet affair placed next to the Bechstein in the lounge at Inglewood. Jazzy foxtrots were much in vogue, and Malcolm became a dedicated fan – the Virginians playing 'Aunt Hagar's Blues' and its flipside 'Aggravatin' Poppa' being particular favourites. Jazz became such a passion that later he contemplated a career as a songwriter-musician, and in his novellas, *Lunar Caustic* and 'The Forest Path to the Spring', a jazz musician replaces the more customary writer as his fictional alter ego.

To give consistency to the story of childhood deprivation he complained in later life about the lack of books at Inglewood, but this was almost certainly a false accusation. Russell recalled there being plenty, including Poe's *Tales of Mystery and Imagination*, Melville's *Moby Dick*, Rabelais, and Arthur's volumes of Shakespeare. However, with the exception of the Bible, all books were locked away on Sunday, and the key remained in Arthur's pocket till Monday morning.

Malcolm acquired a taste for P. G. Wodehouse and for romantic novels of travel and high adventure – Kipling, W. H. Hudson and Rider Haggard. Like Geoffrey Firmin as a boy, his 'nose was always in a book.'[26] W. H. Hudson appealed both as a naturalist and as a novelist who wrote romantic stories set in distant lands. *Green Mansions* was a favourite, as was *Far Away and Long Ago*, the celebration of Hudson's unrestrained childhood on his family's ranch in Argentina. Hudson's story of trying in vain to pull an armadillo out of a hole by its tail found its way into *Under the Volcano*, where Hugh recalls the story on his horse-ride round Quauhnahuac with Yvonne.

A writer whose hero came to cast a particular spell over Lowry at Caldicott was Robert Holmes, a prison missionary, whose semi-fictionalized stories of *Walter Greenaway, Spy* were first published in *Blackwood's Magazine* during the war and later as a book. When Lowry was asked early in 1922 to write about his 'favourite character in fiction or in fact', he wrote nine and a half pages on Walter Greenaway.

Greenaway was a quintessential Lowry hero. He was a 29-year-old clerk turned cat burglar who 'got into mischief out of pure fun of it', and took to crime after being wrongly accused of robbery and discovering a facility for climbing over roofs and through windows. After a stretch in prison, Holmes arranged for him to be sent to sea on a windjammer, a career into which he fitted so naturally as to astound his fellow sailors. 'Nobody can learn him anything about a schooner,' the ship's mate wrote to Holmes, 'He knew it all afore he come on board.'[27] In fact, he had learned to sail in Scotland, along the very coast where the Lowry brothers had 'messed about in boats' in 1920. Greenaway was the educated son of a rich businessman, and the sailors were dying to see him fail when ordered aloft, but 'He climbed up in a flash and sat like a monkey thoroughly enjoying himself.'[28] He wrote to Holmes an almost illegible letter scrawled with a blunt pencil on scraps of faded yellow paper; he had gone, posing as a deaf mute, to live among the Bedouin and to spy for the Allies behind Turkish lines in Mesopotamia. Strangely, he wrote of himself as a spy as if he were writing about someone completely other than himself, and had further cast himself away from his roots by marrying an Arab woman. Despite his criminal past he risked his life for his country. His parents, ashamed of their erring boy, had locked themselves away and received no visitors, and sadly they died before news came that their son was, after all, a genuine patriot and hero. Lowry's close identification with a falsely accused and generally misunderstood anti-hero developed into an obsession which seems strangely to foreshadow his own life, as though Lowry, having chosen a role in fiction, was now fated to live it out. Noble but flawed, misunderstood figures subject to public contempt were forever to excite his sympathy – Eugene Aram, the doomed schoolmaster in the poem by Hood; Oscar Wilde kept waiting at Clapham Junction station for hours on his way to Brixton prison;[29] Geoffrey Firmin set upon by fascists and done to death in a sleazy Mexican bar.

Nevertheless, if, like many boys of his age, Lowry thought of himself in heroic terms, he may have already begun to incorporate the deviant hero into his role-model. Walter Greenaway had unintentionally been turned into a crook; Eugene Aram was a betrayed romantic. A sensitive child like Lowry, wretchedly homesick but disguising the fact in cheerful letters home, was also exposed to insensitive and unjust cruelties and arbitrary punishment. Hywel Jones recalled a junior falsely accusing him and Lowry of bullying. In characteristic style, without listening to their story, 'Pony' Jenkins dealt them one of his famous thrashings and sent them to Coventry for a week. Jones went on hunger strike, and was let off. Lowry endured his punishment to the bitter end.[30] He was also, according to Izzard, once brutally thrashed by Bindon ('flayed at seven, crucified at eleven' he wrote in his poem 'Autopsy'), and that may have cut deeper because of his liking for Bindon, who was less inclined than Jenkins to reach for the cane.[31] Walter Greenaway would have understood and been staunchly on his side. Lowry suffered in silence, but secretly he, too, knew he was innocent and a hero.

Lobs Lowry was remembered at Caldicott as a rather fat and clumsy boy of unpredictable temper, 'a non-conformist with no close friends' who, although not deliberately anti-authoritarian at school was something of a rebel.[32] The scouts were too conformist for Lowry and some boys were surprised that Wilfrid's playing rugby for England left him apparently unmoved. But in letters, and in references in stories to miraculously converted tries and the loneliness of the right wing three-quarter, he showed that he *was* proud of Wilfrid's success; though, irked at being constantly compared to his famous brother, no doubt he affected lack of interest. And at Caldicott, although initially sensitive at being teased about his awkward physique, his eye-patch, and about his colourful bad temper, he seems to have adapted cheerfully enough to being regarded as an oddity. He might never hope to match Wilfrid's graceful skill on the rugby pitch, but he could enjoy the hurly-burly of a rugger or a hockey match. In his final year, 1922, he even managed to scrape a place in the school First Hockey XI. The rough-and-tumble of the game he enjoyed, the communal bath afterwards he hated – the joshing and laughing curiosity of boys comparing muscles and penis size was too mortifying, and probably accounts for his loss of enthusiasm for games. Izzard remembered Lowry being judged on the petite side, but not being unduly teased about it. But who can tell when silent wounds are struck? Certainly, as he grew up he became intensely aware of this deficiency – just another reason, added to his ungainly body, his clumsiness, his chilblains and his constipation, for loathing himself. When finally he left Caldicott in the summer of 1923, many of the key strands of his character had been woven. The strange mixture of cheerful mischievousness and intemperance was to remain throughout his life, the passion for storytelling combined with self-dramatization came to characterize his future writing, and his growing identification with the outsider, the weak, the scorned, the put upon – the Bindons, the Hywel Joneses, and the Walter Greenaways of this world – came to dominate his thinking and his personality. There were those who said that because he carried these early characteristics through into adulthood, he never grew up. But he believed strongly that naïveté was a necessary quality for the creative artist. The air of tough sophistication he later developed was no more than a defensive façade.

Like Russell, he made up for being unable to play golf as a school sport by pitching himself into it during the holidays. The only other games at which he was very good were tennis and ping-pong, and he played incessantly at Hillthorpe and Inglewood, acquiring a skill which he could still produce over twenty years later. His main golfing companions, apart from his brothers, were still Bruce Thompson and the

Furniss boys. The Furnisses were a family of 'characters'. Their father, John, a respected local lawyer, lived with his wife Mary and eight children, six of them boys, at Clevelands, a spacious house on Moels Drive, Hoylake, right beside the Royal Liverpool Golf Club.

Lowry haunted Clevelands, and was always there after a day on the course with Jimmy, the boy who had saved him from being bullied at Braeside. John Furniss was unusually liberal and brought up his children in a free and progressive fashion. Arthur disapproved of him partly because, though a lawyer, he was too independent and outspoken, but mainly because he committed the unforgivable sin of keeping drink in the house. The Furniss boys were allowed to drink beer quite freely at home, and had a reputation for unpredictability and boisterousness. The family, said Lowry later, had a veneer of British respectability but were really 'incredibly dissipated'. The Furnisses became a local legend, and the doings of the Furniss boys were long remembered in the neighbourhood. They were amazing walkers, and Maurice Brown remembered Jimmy Furniss once calling at Hillthorpe and saying, 'I've just come from London.' He had walked the whole two hundred miles in three days flat. They became Lowry's Taskerson family in *Under the Volcano*, and from them he acquired a life-long enthusiasm for prodigious walks, and a predilection for excessive beer-drinking and extravagant behaviour.

At Hoylake that September of 1923, Lowry entered a competition for sons of members of the Royal Liverpool Golf Club. To his and his parents' delight he won the Boys Medal for under-fifteens with a score of ninety-five, a creditable performance for a fourteen-year-old player, and by no means the lowest on record, despite his later claim. Nevertheless, here was another small trophy to place beside Wilfrid's many on the sideboard at Inglewood.

Wilfrid's Sunbeam had now passed to Russell, which meant not only more trips to the cinema, but an easy means of escape into the countryside with their books, to laze around and read, and on occasions, to smoke a surreptitious pipe. Years later in Mexico, Malcolm remembered the bliss of those days and the good reading habits he learned from such expeditions with Russell. It was also a way of escaping the atmosphere of parental disapproval and bickering at Inglewood. Although Evelyn loved to hear 'thrilling stories' of her boys' achievements, they had gradually come to despise her and to write her off as a figure too ludicrous to take seriously. But at Inglewood she was a power to be reckoned with. Arthur pandered to her every whim and expected his boys to do the same. However, as time went on they grew more estranged from Arthur, too, which Russell ascribed to his father's growing awareness of his own limited education compared to that of his children, and to a fatal lack of humour. They, on the other hand, had developed an acute, sometimes savage comic wit, begun as a defence against Evelyn's emotional blackmail, but later refined into an intellectual rapier in the battlefield of an English public school.

CHAPTER III

AT THE LEYS
1923–1926

When I was a kid I used to get fun out of my horrors.
EUGENE O'NEILL, *The First Man*

'The first term at an English public school', wrote Lowry, 'was an appalling proposition.'[1] Yet for him, following his brothers to The Leys, things were probably a little easier than for many other boys. At least for his first two terms Russell was there in the same house (West) to be turned to when necessary. On the other hand, as at Caldicott, he had high standards to live up to, and going away to school, with its rules, restrictions and punishments, always held particular terrors for him. Despite becoming ever more alienated from Inglewood, as he journeyed back to school each term he still felt homesickness strike, 'with a yet more alien cold sense of dreadful loneliness and impending disaster.'[2] Caught between these two alien forces, home and school, he recalled his mother's familiar remonstration: 'There are many little boys in the gutter who would be glad of what you have.' 'God,' he wrote, 'how I envied them.'[3]

At The Leys, 'new bombs' faced an intimidating initiation ceremony, known in West House as 'lamb-singing', where new boys were expected to perform a party-piece for the general entertainment. Those getting the critical 'thumbs down' had to run the gauntlet of critics intent on blacking their faces with burnt cork. Stuart escaped blacking in his time with a well-received song, picked up from the music hall or a seaside minstrel show – the 'Wibberlee Wobberlee Song', turned into literature later when Malcolm had Jacques Laruelle recall it in *Under the Volcano*.[4] It was performed, one imagines, with appropriate winks and gestures.

Oh we allll WALK ze wibberlee wobberlee WALK
And we alll TALK ze wibberlee wobberlee TALK
And we alll WEAR wibberlee wobberlee TIES

And-look-at-all-ze-pretty-girls-with-wibberlee-
wobberlee eyes. Oh
We allll SING ze wibberlee wobberlee SONG
Until ze day is dawn-ing,
And-we-all-have-zat-wibberlee-wobberlee-wobberlee-
wibberlee-wibberlee-wobberlee feeling
In ze morning.

Stuart had taught this rakish little ditty to Wilfrid, who in turn taught it to Russell. It was good enough to get them all through 'lamb-singing' free of blacking, and now it was Malcolm's turn. Like the others, he sailed through unscathed. It was, no doubt, a performance of great panache, and passing his initiation in style must have eased considerably the misery of being a 'new bomb'. In retrospect he saw such rituals as another form of beastliness in which a mindless herd, 'They', picked on and terrorized some poor misfit or newcomer. 'They', he wrote, was 'an unusually sadistic and despairing creation.'[5]

The School Deputy Head and resident master in charge of West House was a small, scholarly, reticent, good-humoured Scot, W. H. Balgarnie, classics master at the school for almost a quarter of a century. Some old boys recalled him as a desiccated bore; for others he had a special charm. An earlier pupil, James Hilton, based his famous schoolmaster-hero, 'Mr Chips', on Balgarnie. But in Lowry, 'Chips' (also known as 'the Balfe' or 'the Hooley') was to find a far more eccentric yarn-spinner than the prolific Hilton. And in his turn, Lowry was delighted to discover that Balgarnie enjoyed reading stories to the West House juniors before 'lights out', just as had Gordon Wood at Caldicott.

Being the younger brother of Wilfrid, Balgarnie might well have expected Malcolm to be a promising games player, which he was not – at least at the recognized school games. He did once manage to reach the finals of the junior tennis doubles championship, but his best game, golf, was not played there (except for an annual tournament dominated by the masters), so there were no school golf trophies with which to dazzle the folks back at Inglewood. Nevertheless, he had other talents which the shrewd Balgarnie quickly spotted and began to encourage. In fact, as a potential writer of his kind, Lowry had probably come to as good a school in as good a place as he could have hoped for. The Leys, standing at the corner of Trumpington Road and the Fen Causeway, was a mere five minutes walk along Trumpington Street from many of the great university colleges, Peterhouse, Pembroke, Corpus Christi,

St Catharine's, St John's and Trinity.[6] It was set up in 1875 as the first Free Church public school aimed at sending the sons of Nonconformists to Oxford and Cambridge following the repeal of the Test Acts. It was a Methodist foundation and, like Caldicott, was therefore marked by a strong air of Wesleyan morality, typified by thundering sermons from the Chapel pulpit. The school duly produced its quota of ministers and missionaries, along with a respectable crop of industrialists, scientists and doctors. Three writers of note have emerged from The Leys: the prolific James Hilton, the Booker Prize-winning J. G. Ballard, and Malcolm Lowry.

Although there was no 'fagging' at the school, there *was* thrashing which could be administered as injudiciously as at Caldicott. Ralph Izzard was once beaten for saying 'Dash!', and Lowry was not to escape his share of whipping. A more favoured punishment, however, had boys writing on green paper, purchased a penny a sheet from the school shop, a set of lines composed by an old classics master, E. E. 'Jerry' Kellett: 'Few things are more distressing to a well regulated mind than to see a boy who ought to know better disporting himself at improper moments.'

He hated school routine, being marched here and summoned there, and recalled 'the horror of "crocodiles" '[7] and the school bells which always 'seemed like sombre church bells tolling for a funeral.'[8] The emphasis on games bored him; one of his favourite subjects, Nature Study, was not taught, although there were occasional visiting lecturers on such pastimes as bird-watching. But Lowry claimed that anyone showing an interest in nature was thought a cissy.[9] Immediately after the war, under the headship of the Reverend H. Bisseker, The Leys, like many other schools at the time, was going through a bad patch. The older generation of teachers had largely expired or left the scene, and most of the new generation had died in the trenches. Some older masters, brought back to fill the vacuum, continued to teach a Victorian morality no longer relevant in the post-war world. Keeping order became a problem, and academic standards suffered.

But the cheery, mischievous, untidy, endearingly eccentric Lowry did find good masters who were interested in him, especially two young English masters, R. M. Morris and F. W. Ives, who spotted something distinctive in his oddly written essays. Morris recalled Lowry's reputation for writing 'pour épater le bourgeois', and remembered Ives 'hooting with laughter at his profanities.' Ives, a charismatic figure who went on to teach at Charterhouse, was keen on drama, and made a lasting impression on at least one old boy with a memorable reading in class of Coleridge's 'Rime of the Ancient Mariner'.[10] If Ives and Morris encouraged Lowry's writing, another master, S. C. Gillard, encouraged his dramatic flair. Gillard put him into school plays, remembering him as 'a small boy, tousle-headed, splay-footed, ruddy-faced – all teeth and perpetually grinning – frightfully jaunty and argumentative, rather untidy, terribly fond of talking, and especially fond of listening to sea yarns which I was rather too prone to tell in class, and he would often trap me into telling.'[11]

In spite of his comparative indifference to games, he became rather attached to the sports master, Jesse Mellor, an Old Leysian, and head of South House, who later gave Malcolm extra coaching in classics. Mellor was a Bisley sharpshooter and Cambridge rugger blue and knew all the Lowry boys. He took great pride in Wilfrid's rugby achievements, and for years a photograph of Malcolm taken by him stood on the Bechstein in the lounge at Inglewood. He was a keen photographer and their friendship would have been reinforced by a common passion for golf – Mellor seemed to win the annual school tournament every year. He was an intense rival of Balgarnie's, and, from what Malcolm told Russell three years later, his influence was ultimately a baleful one. By contrast, Balgarnie had the most benevolent influence, guiding him in his first serious steps toward becoming a writer.

Russell left the school at the end of the spring term 1924, the summer which saw the last Lowry family holiday. Arthur and Evelyn and the two youngest boys packed into Arthur's new Minerva and, with Coltman at the wheel, left Caldy for a tour of the West Country, staying for the most part at Budleigh Salterton on the Devon coast. There were trips to Stonehenge and to the theatre in Exeter for a performance of *Outward Bound*, a play which left a lasting impression on Malcolm. A golf course by the sea, a play combining a voyage and a symbolic journey of the dead to purgatory, and a growing interest in the occult, foreshadowed important 'design-governing postures' (a favourite expression) in his later fiction.

After the holiday, Russell stayed on with friends in Cornwall, where he picked up the latest craze, the banjolele, before setting off to study commercial French for a year in Lille. With Russell gone, Malcolm was more than ever on his own. Wilfrid, very much against his mother's wishes, had become engaged, and planned to get married the following year, so was rarely at home. Malcolm, like Russell, had already become cynical about life at Inglewood and was growing increasingly alienated from both his parents. This new sense of isolation may not have worried him that much, for he was in the grip of a new obsession. He had decided to become a writer.

The pressures at home were certainly mounting. A story which Lowry later sketched about a Christmas at home may capture his spirit of rebellion against the unimaginative authoritarianism at Inglewood.

> Father . . . said:
>
> 'I think now we all might take a few minutes to reflect what this great festival of Christmas really means . . . You try and tell us.'
>
> I thought & thought & for some reason I couldn't think. Finally I said, 'The death of Christ, father.'
>
> There was a frightful commotion. For this 'almost blasphemous remark', as my father called it, I was sent to the lumber-room . . . But it had been a genuine lapse. And in the lumber room I was troubled in my heart. I could not understand religion: sermons bored me: the bible was totally obscure to me. But it hurt my heart when anyone said anything contemptuous about Christ to whom I prayed in my way, & now it seemed I had done just that.[12]

The impulsive sin followed by remorse was to become a feature of his life. And it may also have been during Russell's absence that in one of his brothers' rooms he came across the book that introduced him to the dreaded subject of sex, a book full of Methodistic hell-fire and obviously painful revelations (and perhaps an explanation of his earlier eye trouble). 'The . . . books on top of my brother's wardrobe . . . already assured me, if they were true, that I had acquired certain habits and should have gone mad. So I had long got used to having no normal prospects. I looked for death at any moment.'[13] Having learned the innocent pleasures of masturbation, he now discovered the hellish punishment in store for such innocence, and experienced the sense of living as if it was his last day on earth long before Geoffrey Firmin's final Day of the Dead.

By now he had lost some of his earlier puppy fat and photographs showing him stylishly posed on the beach at Budleigh Salterton, or looking wind-blown in front of Stonehenge, suggest that he had developed into a quite attractive youngster. The unruly mop of copper-coloured hair, the florid complexion, the clear blue eyes and slightly projecting front teeth, giving his smile a hint of mischievousness, were still there, but to that was added now an air of theatricality. This rather jaunty style and sense of drama, coupled with that wicked verbal wit acquired from 'Pony' Jenkins at Caldicott, sharpened in subversive coded exchanges with Russell at Inglewood, and further honed with Balgarnie and Ives at The Leys, had begun to produce the eccentric charm which his later friends found so enchanting.

Back at The Leys at the beginning of 1925, Lowry at fifteen was a cheerful, awkward, obsessive bookworm, average both academically and at games, rather slovenly in appearance, and trying in every possible way to circumvent school rules about dress.[14] But Balgarnie had taken a shine to him and, when he sent in some precocious, unsolicited stories to the school magazine, the *Leys Fortnightly*, encouraged him with his writing.[15] The school had suffered three electric light failures at the beginning of the year, and Lowry converted this experience into fiction. In the 13 March issue of the *Fortnightly*, his first short story, 'The Light That Failed Not', appeared. It was signed 'Camel', a simple play on his initials C.M.L. The title, in turn, was a play on that of Kipling's novel, *The Light that Failed*, the story of a Bohemian artist who suffers progressive blindness and the pangs of unrequited love.

Lowry's story was pitched in a comic vein more reminiscent of Wodehouse than Kipling, and shows him already master of such humorous devices as hyperbole, ironic ornamentation, affected pedantry and self-deflating pomposity. The schoolboy hero is one of a class kept in for prep who is surreptitiously reading a novel while pretending to work. In dropping a pin to wake a sleeping neighbour he draws attention to himself, so affects innocence: 'Wormwood Scrubs was written over every face, except mine, in that assembly.' But his novel drops to the floor and how is he to explain? 'I am not like you people sparkling in epigram and epithet, who hand out the honeyed word and the diplomatic smile . . .' Disaster is averted by an electrical failure. 'The Electric Lighting Co. . . . rose to the occasion, and the luminosity, as it were, conked . . .' 'Fortune never favours the horribly guilty, except in grand guignol,' he concludes, 'But as Shakespeare or somebody said – "All fact is fiction and all fiction fact".'[16] The confusing of fantasy and reality, art and life, he admitted just before he died, was to be serious and damaging for him. As a writer and as a man, Lowry had started in the way he was destined to finish.

In May, Wilfrid was married, and at about the same time Stuart returned after six years in America to become a partner at Buston's. He introduced Malcolm to some of his favourite American literature, notably the plays of Eugene O'Neill, and later, having taken up weightlifting in Dallas, to the joys of physical culture. Malcolm took up O'Neill with an enthusiasm bordering on self-identification. He had become fascinated by the lives of his writer-heroes, and searched out information about them wherever he could – books, newspapers, magazines. Once, in *Life* magazine, he found a review of O'Neill carrying his picture, 'with handsome moustaches' and noted approvingly that he had not bothered going to school.[17] The idea that a writer had no need of schooling by uncreative schoolmasters recurred in later stories, especially in his meditation on an author's creative consciousness in 'Through the Panama'.

The boy with his nose always in a book was now reading well beyond the normal schoolboy range of reading, and he became singularly attached to authors of smart, literate novels like Jeffery Farnol, W. J. Locke and Michael Arlen. His enthusiasm for Locke became a West House joke, but it was a noteworthy fascination. In a book like the bestselling *The Morals of Marcus Ordeyne* can be found so many of the ingredients which Lowry later made his own. It is a somewhat racy intellectual romance strewn with references to Burton, Machiavelli, Rabelais, Marcus Aurelius, Dante and Goethe. Faust is quoted, 'Then may the devil take me and do what he likes with me,' anticipating the doomed Consul; and a line anticipating Lowry's own career, 'We will have to go to some new land where attaining fame is easier for a beginner than in London.'[18] He also became attached to John Masefield, and could quote whole chunks from *Sard Harker* and *Odtaa*.[19] And when Balgarnie read W. W. Jacobs's spine-chilling 'The Monkey's Paw' to the House juniors at 'lights out', Lowry decided it was 'the best short story ever written, except for Conrad's "Typhoon".'[20] Conrad was a lasting influence. More than twenty years later, in a storm in the Atlantic, he recalled reading Conrad by torchlight under the blankets in bed at The Leys.[21]

By now too he must have put his nose into the Melville and the Poe in the glass-fronted bookcase at Inglewood. Their doom-laden sentiments appealed to his eccentric taste. He recalled with particular relish in notes for his school story 'Enter One in Sumptuous Armour', opening Poe at random and reading something like, 'Man does not desire happiness, but to be held captive in chains by barbarian hordes, in a land unpeopled and alone,' and adding, 'These were my exact sentiments, I felt, in a sort of amusing way.'[22]

He attached himself to an older boy in his House, Raymond Fletcher Cook, son of the then Australian High Commissioner, quizzing him about life in the Australian outback. Cook, yearning for the wide-open spaces himself, found this young enthusiast an appealing and receptive listener. He discovered that like him Lowry had an agreeable reluctance to getting up on wintry English mornings, and they first met at detention where each was writing the well-known lines on green notepaper for being late for breakfast. Russell, who knew Cook, disapproved of his enthusing Malcolm with the idea of 'roughing it' in the outback. But his interest was not confined to Australia; there were Japanese and Indian pupils at the school (The Leys had a strong missionary tradition) with whom he also spent time, enquiring eagerly about life in their countries, too.

Another older friend was Thomas Boden Hardy. The initial attraction could have been a name combining that of the great novelist with that of Lowry's seafaring maternal grandfather, a striking enough coincidence for Lowry to see in it some important hidden significance. In any event, thinking he seemed lonely, Hardy befriended the boy and he clung on, following him everywhere, rather pathetically, 'like a lost dog'. He said his father had gone suddenly bankrupt and he felt very insecure at home. He spoke of his mother in glowing terms but gave the distinct impression that she was dead. Hardy was taken in and felt duly sympathetic. As a sharpshooter, he cycled twice a week to the Grange Road rifle range in Cambridge, and Malcolm joined him. Once there, however, he would disappear, and turn up again as Hardy was returning to school:

> He'd be waiting for me at this peculiar rather rustic old pub, where he'd found this old couple sitting in front and he raved about them, was going to write a story about them. But on one occasion I was coming back from the shooting range to find Malcolm's bicycle lying in the middle of the road and Malcolm sitting on the curb laughing like a hyaena, drunk as a lord.[23]

The young writer had discovered alcohol.

What caused him to want to write is a matter of speculation. James Hilton, though long an Old Boy, still contributed to the *Fortnightly*. He had been a contemporary of Wilfrid's at the school during the war, had edited the magazine, and been a protégé of Balgarnie's. After The Leys, he went to Christ's College, got a First in English, then became a journalist. By 1925 he had published three novels, the first one written while still at school. Balgarnie doubtless encouraged the unconventional young essayist with the example of Hilton, the successful author, and he first saw himself as a journalist or story writer rather than as a serious novelist.

Hardy recalled that the writer who possessed him most completely, however, was Rabelais. 'He loved Rabelais; he quoted Rabelais all over the place.'[24] He had discovered that physical self-disgust could be rendered more acceptable and express itself to some effect through a gutsy humour. It was as a Rabelaisian character expounding the Rabelaisian philosophy of the inspired drunkard that Hardy remembered Lowry at The Leys. If this was a side of his character he enjoyed parading before his school friends, it was one he carefully concealed from the folks at Inglewood. Concealment, scrounging, duplicity and elaborate self-justification, the arts and practices of the great fraternity of drunkards, were tricks Lowry already seemed to have acquired.

His next story for the *Fortnightly*, 'Travelling Light', also arose from direct experience. It cast an ironic eye over the School Corps, though what sort of soldier this born member of 'the awkward squad' would have made is not difficult to imagine. In this story his protagonist is returning to school late from his brother's wedding (Wilfrid's presumably). He has not only 'to return to general drudgery' but to a Wednesday night full-dress parade of the Corps, at which the school's more martial types display their military fervour. But, he adds in mock-Wordsworthian vein:

> A curse it is these nights to be alive;
> To be arrayed in panoply of war
> Doth aggravate the evil.

There follows a suitably Wodehousean portrait of the good soldier Lowry, on whose back 'the black dog of this parade' sat and whispered that, as well as many other military irregularities, his uniform was dirty, his cap-badge missing, his puttees still muddied from some bygone field exercise. Moreover, 'I imagined myself sloping arms with the rifle upside down and ramming it into the back of my trousers when I unfixed bayonets.'

He is in grave danger of making himself conspicuous. On the train from Liverpool, he falls asleep and dreams that the school has been burned down. The odd charred fragment of uniform and a pair of Oxford bags too wide to be completely incinerated were all that remained. 'It was a cruel sight, and I remember wanting to kick myself as I buried my face in a handkerchief to conceal my lack of emotion.'

But then he tripped over something – 'a human foot in a Corps boot.' He wakes with a jolt to find himself in Edinburgh when he should be in Ely. He has been saved, it seems, from the humiliation of the bayonet in the trouser seat. But has he? he asks, hovering before delivering his last-minute twist, because this has not really happened, and even as he writes he is under punishment for an extra parade. Yet he has 'set down an account of the tragedy in words that may perhaps soothe my troubled feelings. And ruffle yours? One never knows.'[25] The idea of fictionalizing away his misery was to become an important *raison d'être* for his writing. But to do so one first had to be miserable.

Camel was now established both as an oddity who ruffled a few feelings and something of a true eccentric, who, against School rules, wore Oxford bags and got away with it. Nevertheless, he was awarded a minor honour, a prize from the *Fortnightly,* and allowed to select his own books. He chose O'Neill's *Anna Christie,* Michael Arlen's *May Fair* and Stevenson's *The Wrecker.*[26] In the summer of 1925, with Arthur and Evelyn again abroad, Malcolm was packed off for a while to a holiday camp run by the Children's Special Service Mission, a Methodist organization of gospel-promoting Cambridge undergraduates. With him went his friend, Hardy. The camp was under canvas in the grounds of St Andrew's School at Eastbourne, and he soon made it clear to Hardy that he had no intention of following the rules or routines of the camp or hanging around to have his soul saved. 'He immediately dived off and found the cinemas in Eastbourne, and the pubs. And we were there for ten days and I spent ten days literally dragging him out and finding which pubs he was in and keeping him away from people because he was so pickled. But this was Malcolm . . .'[27]

Russell was back home from Lille, in love with Meg Gillies, a Scots girl he had met there, and toting his banjolele. Malcolm immediately acquired one, too, and shortly afterwards they switched to ukuleles which they thought better for picking out jazz tunes. Gradually, over the dining table at Inglewood, or at Stuart's home, they began composing and singing their own songs, becoming, in Russell's opinion, 'reasonably accomplished if noisy performers.'

Russell noticed that Malcolm seemed to have turned sour about school and after a time he confided to him what had happened. Jesse Mellor, with whom he had had such a close relationship, had caught him 'cribbing' and instead of giving him lines, had flown into a rage and thrashed him severely. Lowry's pride was deeply wounded and he felt badly betrayed by the teacher who until then had been so very friendly. In a poem, 'Der Tag', for the *Fortnightly*, he seems to send up the experience. For handing in his imposition late he gets 'three raps upon the pate', his work is consigned to the bin, and he goes 'quite dippy in the dome'.[28] The self-image of the quirky, loopy, batty, but clever chap was beginning to take shape. The impish, brilliant child was becoming ever more alienated, increasingly delighting in teasing the uncomprehending sobersides around him.

The four Lowry brothers, together again in and around Caldy, made an interesting contrast. Wilfrid was moderately tall, slim and fair-haired, Stuart dark, short and muscular, Russell, slight, fair-haired, around five foot eight, and Malcolm, chunky, copper-haired and around five-nine. All were extremely good-looking with bright blue eyes, and each brilliant and witty in his own way. Stuart, Wilfrid and Russell had inherited Arthur's keen business acumen, though Stuart had a rakish Bohemian tendency, and was both widely read and a talented cartoonist. He and Margot settled at Upton, five miles from Caldy, and their house, Corvally, became a second home for Russell and Malcolm. Although he kept a fairly low profile at first, Stuart gradually became leader of an unofficial resistance movement against their parents, and at Corvally the younger boys could vent their feelings freely. Stuart had never quite forgiven their opposition to his marriage, and now Russell was suffering similarly. He wanted to get engaged to Meg, but Evelyn was implacably opposed and Arthur forbade him to see or communicate with her. Being kept under his father's thumb as a poorly paid cotton apprentice and denied his opportunity to marry was a cause of a deep resentment in Russell. The liberal and sophisticated Stuart, though unable to soften his parents' hard hearts, encouraged him to keep in touch with Meg through Corvally. The conspiracy against Inglewood was thus confirmed.

Malcolm was carried along by this anti-parent sentiment. He and Russell composed hymns of hate against Evelyn, whom both blamed for their mutual suffering. He also became fascinated by an interest of Margot's – the occult. Her mother was a sort of Irish mystic, and Margot was both a medium and an adept of the ouija board. In trying to get in touch with the 'other side', she would invoke the spirit of 'the Old Captain', her grandfather, a retired sea captain who had died in Naples. With so many youthful casualties in the recent war, there was, at that time, a great interest in spiritualism. Lowry became hooked and was ever afterwards deeply fascinated by matters mystical.

It was possible for him to confide in Stuart things he could mention to few others – his fears about sex, his growing desire to go to sea. Stuart decided it was time to give young Malcolm a sex education. As an adolescent, he and a friend had discovered the Anatomy Museum on Liverpool's Paradise Street, which had a section designed to warn unwary seamen against the dire consequences of venereal disease. The exhibition was so gruesome it had almost put Stuart off sex for life. Nevertheless, in turn he took Russell and then Malcolm to view these dreadful exhibits, telling them cheerfully, 'You must see it before you see the Isle of Man.'[29] Malcolm, like Russell, was transfixed with horror, but the place took on a strange fascination for him, and he went back to it time and time again. He even copied down the words of warning which accompanied the disfigured foetuses, waxen effigies of ulcerated penises and 'the famous pickled testicles'. 'Man, Know Thyself' read the stern warning sign above the door. It was a vision of hell-fire no preacher could ever rival and it haunted him.

> I thought of . . . the faces of the poor people in Paradise Street, the wax works, one little bit of light would have illuminated even the worst mass of corruption. This seemed . . . an exact picture of people's souls. Physically it didn't frighten me at all . . . It amused me; or it struck home to me, a child, as some frightful drama, some good drama I hadn't seen, better than the Ten Horses of the Apocalypse. I was fascinated by it & was going to go there again & again, I thought, I wouldn't be able to keep away from it 'a slave of the Museum of Anatomy' – as B. had been a slave of the picture palace.[30]

Although Malcolm and Russell were still close, Russell was apprenticed now to Bustons and intent on getting married, despite the unfeeling opposition of his parents. Nonetheless, the boys would whizz off to the cinema on the Sunbeam or get out into the countryside with their books, pipes and tobacco. Malcolm also went on many solitary walks exploring the Wirral countryside. Once he stumbled across a literary landmark – Hilbre Island, where Milton's Lycidas had drowned. He felt it was his own discovery, though it did not help him understand or even like Milton's poem, he wrote. 'But he had drowned . . . that was something . . .'[31] The coast around Hoylake and Leasowe so imprinted itself on his mind that it provided a natural background for the childhood of his Consul, Geoffrey Firmin.

Reading O'Neill, Conrad, Masefield, and Melville and wandering around Deeside and the Mersey, the pull of the sea began more and more to assert itself; a deep chord had been struck, and the romantic

Lowry found himself entranced. He recalled how 'filthy, sinister, clap-stricken old Liverpool was dear to my heart . . . It was the sea that made it dear, the unwinding Mersey, those ships there, the things that told you you could get out of this fearful country altogether.' England, it seemed to him, was 'blighted . . . & damned like some poor famous old tree in a park . . . a tree preserved, and destroyed by civilization.'[32]

Even while playing golf, the sea was not far away – Caldy Golf Course had magnificent views of the Welsh Mountains across the Dee and Hoylake had the open sea to the north across the sand dunes. In September 1925 Lowry again competed in a boys' championship at Hoylake, repeating his success of two years earlier by winning this time the competition for fifteen- to eighteen-year-olds with a respectable score of eighty-eight. Twenty-six years later, for the benefit of an editor he wished to impress, he exaggerated this boyhood success into a score never previously beaten.

His next two stories for the *Fortnightly* were based on his reading of his prizes from the previous term. Both were pastiches, one admitted, the other concealed. 'The Blue Bonnet' appeared 'With apologies to the Author of "Mayfair", "The Green Hat", etc.', a reference to the smart, cynical Michael Arlen, and 'A Rainy Night', owing much to O'Neill's *Anna Christie*, appeared two weeks later with no acknowledgement. 'The Blue Bonnet' is not a very successful piece of writing, defeated by striving too hard for witty effect, the sort of thing Lowry probably produced without effort. It is a compressed tale of the murder, more a brief scenario than a complete short story, and has a number of now recognizable Lowry devices, literary allusions (to Samuel Butler as well as Arlen), hesitant asides – 'as one might say' – and epithetical comments: 'He was a man, one might say, considerably on the seamy side of mediocre', 'He died just before the close of the inverted commas.' It ends with an ellipsis – 'Moreover . . .'[33]

In 'A Rainy Night', Lowry is back in a railway carriage, a narrative setting he found useful; being 'on the move', after all, gives a narrative the impression of movement even when it is standing still. Travelling from Yeovil to Liverpool via Manchester, his narrator enjoys and notes the cinematic view from the window, like a tracking camera. He has sandwiches for the trip, and again the train is empty, 'except for a little wizened, cross-eyed old man, who shivered in the corner of the corridor.' The sympathetic narrator invites him to his compartment and finds he is a Swedish seaman, a fireman going to rejoin his ship at Liverpool. His odd, Scandinavian speech echoes Chris Christopherson, the father in O'Neill's *Anna Christie*. 'Py Jo, Aye forgat' says Lowry's Swede, Christofersen Olivsen, frequently and for no reason. 'Py yimminy, Ay forgat' says O'Neill's Swede, just as often. The narrator thinks the old man is drunk (there is drinking throughout *Anna Christie*), and considers preaching him a sermon. But he is ill and in distress because (as with O'Neill's sailor) while he was at sea his wife and child have died. He refuses money and the offer of a job. The narrator leaves saying 'Good-bye, old Swede.' 'Old Svede,' mutters the man, 'And Aye am only thirty-two!' He is later found in the carriage, dead of starvation. The twist in the tail is that on arriving home the narrator finds he had left his parcel of uneaten food in the same compartment as the starving man.[34]

O'Neill's Swedish captain had a father who died in the Indian Ocean and was buried at sea. The ghost of 'Captain' Boden had obviously made contact from 'the other side' through the medium of O'Neill's play. *Anna Christie* also has an ill fireman, and Lowry's identification with O'Neill and the adaption of Christopherson shows how close he got to the writers he admired. The shadow of the old Swede cropped up again in another guise years later in *Ultramarine*:

> – reminds me of a chap who fell down in New York on Forty-seventh Street . . . Everybody thought he was proper stupefied drunk. Policeman picks him up! This man's not drunk, he says. What's your name? My name is Christopher Christ, the chap says. And I'm starving –[35]

Apart from his lone drinking while Hardy was at the shooting range, Lowry also managed occasional clandestine pub crawls in other company. Ralph Izzard and a group including Lowry often dodged games and hooked it into the town for a surreptitious pint. But some time in 1926 Lowry started slipping off alone to theatres, the Festival Theatre and the New Theatre. In January he was able to feast himself at a Shakespearean Festival at the New (*Merchant of Venice*, *Macbeth*, *The Tempest*, *King Lear*, *Hamlet* and *Romeo & Juliet*), and early in 1927 he took Izzard to see Congreve's *Love for Love*, considered very daring at that time.[36]

In taking his inspiration directly from others, Lowry was quite conscious that he was walking the tightrope between originality and plagiarism, but his attitude was distinctly cavalier, and in May he told a girlfriend that 'plagiarism is the least socially harmful form of theft'.[37] But in his next published story, 'Satan in a Barrel', which has Judge

Jeffreys, judge of the Bloody Assizes, in hell, he starts with an admission 'Pirated history, this story.' At least, he argues, that is what the reader will say. All that needs to be known about Jeffreys is known; it leaves no scope for the imagination. But why not? 'Untruths, especially when they might be true, are most satisfying,' – his own philosophy in telling his friend Hardy about his bankrupt father and dead mother. The reader is being offered a piece of invented history, but also an underlying 'truth'.

Jeffreys is presented as an alcoholic imprisoned in the Tower of London awaiting his fate. Offered salvation by 'the Voice of Grace', Jeffreys chooses Satan. His soul is in hell, he says, and in time his body will be lodged there, too. Although the story takes the form of a disguised religious homily (evil is punished and good is triumphant), some of Jeffreys' arguments must have raised a few pious eyebrows at the Methodistic Leys. 'It is ridiculous to pray,' he says. 'Praying is naught. Praying is canting, hypocritical. One goes down on one's knees and prays honeyed words to a Being you don't understand and believe in less.'[38] He likens the power of prayer to the power of delirium tremens, and curses life, Fate, Christ and Christianity. Lowry had discovered a device for making blasphemy intellectually respectable – it all happened in a dream. 'The psychology of dreams,' he announces, 'is an interesting study.'

'Satan in a Barrel' was a big step forward in Lowry's fiction-writing. We are in strangely familiar territory. The soul of an alcoholic sinner is at risk of eternal damnation. As distant clocks chime out the last hours of his life, he debates ways in which he might have saved himself, hears voices and predicts his own death from drinking too much brandy before choosing hell-fire. There is a sense of Lowry himself speaking, through this fictional dream, with a voice of his own, echoing perhaps the incipient inner conflicts of the young Rabelaisian toper. In this he prefigures an older Lowry, and the doomed Consul who sprang fully grown from his own tormented alcoholic experiences.

If he was regarded by his schoolfellows as an eccentric, this opinion was strongly reinforced at the end of January when he turned his hand to sports reporting. Earlier, the *Fortnightly*'s editors had been criticized by sports master Mellor for the tone of some of their reports. Shrewd readers interpreted this as a ploy to embarrass Balgarnie, his rival. But if he had been upset by what went before, Lowry's reports must have enraged him. Alan Baddeley, then the editor, thought that using Lowry was Balgarnie's way of getting back at Mellor, and in the budding satirist he found a willing ally after his thrashing at Jesse's hands.

Typically, Lowry used a model for his hockey reports – the flowery soccer column by Thomas Moult in the *Sunday Dispatch*, read eagerly every week by the boys in West House.[39] After all, why write pedestrian reports for boring sports addicts when you could write a piece of satirical prose, ruffle a few feathers and amuse the pathologically slothful? Why call a rugby ball a ball when you could call it an oval, or write about a huge kick when you can bring in a Rabelaisian reference? And why pretend that the home team put up a good effort when they plainly stumbled about the pitch like an uncoordinated corps of drunken ballet dancers? Although these hockey reports (signed 'CML') began soberly, the first report concluded that 'Lumsden was torpid' and 'Haller, our goalkeeper, who was compelled to fox for the majority of the game, made one save for us, just before half time, with a Pantagruel kick.'[40] Of one failure after a run of successes he commented, 'Still, Shakespeare had his "Pericles": comfort in that.'[41] And of a drawn match with Peterhouse he noted that the only interesting incident was a nonchalant one-handed catch brought off by a somewhat bored referee. The feat brought one of the few outbursts of applause heard during the match, he wrote.[42]

These modestly amusing reports were clearly excuses for Lowry to indulge his sense of irony, his love of wordplay and teasing obscurity. Three anonymous letters of protest to the *Fortnightly* were aimed as much at Camel the storywriter as at CML the hockey reporter. 'I am in the habit of reading the reports of the hockey matches to refresh my memory with regard to the game,' wrote one. 'Imagine my surprise, therefore, when, on opening my copy of the current issue of the *Fortnightly*, I found, instead of a report, a novelette by W. J. Locke, writing under another name.' No one was more unsuited to writing hockey reports than CML. The majority of readers did not read W. J. Locke or J. Farnol: 'in fact one has to be educated to digest W.J. Therefore may we suggest that the reporter take his "Pantagruel" phraseology elsewhere and put it to better use.' The implication that readers of the *Fortnightly* were too uneducated to understand W. J. Locke suggests Lowry's own hand behind this one. Another letter urged 'let your contributor continue with his undoubted talent . . . in another vein,' while a third demanded explanations of the use of typographical devices such as ellipses and 'absurd words' like 'fox', 'torpid', 'Pantagruelian' and 'Pericles'.[43]

Balgarnie may well have initiated and orchestrated this correspondence for fun and to further 'get one over' Mellor, but in the following issue, Lowry replied to his critics in style. He had not, he wrote, the slightest intention of apologizing. He could not say that he read his critics' 'childish slating' with any interest. From their style he could only assume they were new to the school and not old enough to contribute to the magazine. He wondered whether they *were* actually at the school. Not to understand 'Pantagruel' meant they had not read (perhaps were not old enough to read) their Rabelais. A fox, he condescended, was 'an animal which, in its spare time, foxes. Hence, the verb, to fox.' Finally, the *coup de grâce*: 'One of you remarks that I have undoubted talent: this is an error of etiquette – you should never tell people that they have undoubted talent: you will find me making no such mistake with you.'[44]

Despite this spirited riposte, his next few reports were more restrained, probably because the First Hockey XI were due to visit Paris, and Lowry was set on going along. He therefore held himself back until the last *Fortnightly* of the Spring Term, then filed reports which were more Tom Moultish than ever. One game 'was remarkable chiefly for its inability to "begin" ', some players spent much of the game 'wandering round like mislaid ewes and hitting at this and that,' and the game finally 'sank . . . into delirium.'[45]

His funniest report, of a match with Guy's Hospital, was a model of displaced hyperbole. The editor prefaced the piece with the curt message, 'Our so-called reporter, who has gone away for his holidays, leaving us to grapple with this, is hereby sacked.' There followed a hockey report masquerading as a play review. Unlike rugby, soccer or cricket, he began, hockey was not susceptible to 'romance', but he was called upon to report on a match which was frankly not worth reporting. Hesitating to write a straightforward report he could perhaps compare it to a poor play and write a suitable notice thereof. The first act was 'about as diverting as a musical comedy without any music; the second as a farce without a single laugh (or) epigram.' Having established this device he let his imagination rip. One player not only forgot his lines but sulkily refused to heed the voice of the prompter; another 'suffered from stage-fright and missed several cues.' The backstage crew performed as well as ever, though the goalkeeper, 'so promising, made the unforgivable mistake of shuffling his feet while delivering his lines.' He ended with a flourish: 'It was slightly before the final curtain that I crept (complete with hump) towards a door which, had it been there, would have been surmounted tactfully with the legend EXIT.'[46]

The dramatic slant of this report sprang no doubt from the fact that he was at the same time rehearsing for a part in the school play, Ian Hay's *Tilly of Bloomsbury*. Rehearsals coincided with the games and as he wrote he was also 'waiting to go on'. Reviewing the play in the *Fortnightly*, Balgarnie wrote that 'Lowry acted the character of *Percy* with a delightful breezy abandon which made one regret the unsatisfactory way in which the part peters out in the second act; if he had fault, it was that he was a little too emphatically resolute.' In other words, Lowry overacted.

On 1 April, The Leys' hockey team set off for Paris. Before Malcolm left for France, Russell had tried to teach him a few basic French phrases. It proved difficult, so finally he settled for one all-purpose phrase he could repeat when stuck – '*Ça va*'. He said this so often that by the end of the trip he had acquired a new nickname, 'Monsieur *Ça va*'.[47]

Monsieur *Ça va*, it seems, shared the stereotypical view of foreigners then prevalent among public schoolboys, and on his return he wrote a humorous account of his time amongst the comic French. It is reported that he spent most of his time in the City of Light drunk, having discovered Pernod.[48] Certainly he did not spend all of his time watching hockey, and undoubtedly visited as many cinemas and theatres as he could. He also discovered the Grand Guignol theatre near the Moulin Rouge. This became an obsession to compete with the Paradise Street Anatomy Museum, and later, whenever in Paris, this was one place he insisted on visiting. 'Abroad' was a revelation, and this is probably where he truly got the 'travel bug', something he took a long time to shake out of his system. The excitement of freeing himself from English middle-class restraints would gradually take hold of him – yet another powerful drug to cope with beside acting, writing and alcohol. As usual he memorized the films and plays at various cinemas and theatres, especially the Grand Guignol, and also saw the famous circus troupe, the Ten Fratellinis, storing the memory for future use.[49] But he did watch some hockey, and he did write some reports, mostly full of Wodehousean jokes at the expense of the French players, and once noted a 'sign which read, "*Sportifs! Respectez les décisions de l'arbitre: soyez calmes et silencieux.*" '[50] It foreshadowed another notice enjoining orderly conduct which he later found so fateful and sinister in Mexico. The following term, he gave a talk about the trip to the school Literary and Debating Society. The *Fortnightly* reported that, 'C. M. Lowry . . . gave an amusing account of the Frenchman's characteristics illustrated with excerpts from his vocabulary.'[51]

Following the hockey team, he had found two new friends – Philip Nichol from West House, and Tom McMorran from B House. All were keen on golf as well as hockey and went once a fortnight to play at the Gog Magog course just outside Cambridge. Not long after his return, Lowry and a friend (McMorran perhaps or Jimmy Furniss) went to hear Paul Whiteman and his orchestra, over in Liverpool from America. He made a day of it by taking in the Anatomy Museum first.

> Could the end of the endless hunger that tore us to pieces [bc] that the hunger started to eat the man himself, bit by bit, this I couldn't understand or believe. We went outside past the pickled testicles laughing quietly and spent quite a long time trying to pick up a couple of women, though what we were going to do with them exactly we didn't know. Then we had tea and cakes at my mother's favourite restaurant & then . . . we went to the first house of the Liverpool Empire & heard Paul Whiteman's violinist play Pop goes the Weasel.[52]

The story of following women in the streets with the vague aim of picking them up occurs both in story notes and in his 'lost' novel *In Ballast to the White Sea*, where it became more purposeful and less of a 'lark'. In going to the museum in Liverpool's Red Light district he must have been very conscious of the women touting for business, as well as the dangers of patronizing them. He told his analyst thirty years later that his first sexual experiences were with prostitutes while still at school.[53] But he also claimed that he was still a virgin when he went to sea, so probably, out of fear, these contacts stopped short of intercourse. For someone with Lowry's Wesleyan upbringing and its attendant sense of sin and guilt, combined with the knowledge gained at the Museum of the most pathological cases of advanced syphilis, the whole business of casual sex in the dangerous purlieus of the Liverpool dock area must have been fraught with excitement and terror.

If his childhood was finally in the process of slipping away from him, he parted from it with mixed feelings. Retrospectively, in his poem 'Autopsy', he saw his whole childhood as one of utter wretchedness.

> An autopsy on his childhood then reveals:
> That he was flayed at seven, crucified at eleven.
> And he was blind as well, and jeered at
> For his blindness. Small wonder that the man
> Is embittered and full of hate, but wait.
> At this time, and always lost, he struggled.

In pain he prayed that none other
In the world should suffer so. Christ's
Life, compared with his, was full of tumult,
Praise, excitement, final triumph.
For him were no hosannas. He writes them now.
Matriculated into life by this, remembering how
This laggard self was last, last in everything,
Devoid of all save wandering attention –
Wandering is the word defines our man –
But turned, to discover Clare in the poor snail,
And weave a fearful vision of his own.[54]

CHAPTER IV

LOVE AND THE OCEAN WAVE
1926–1927

Love is like the measles; we all have to go through it.

JEROME K. JEROME

Shortly after returning from Paris, Lowry was smitten by love. Carol Brown, one of the family who had rescued him after the great fall from his bicycle, suddenly became the centre of his passionate attention. She was now eighteen, a fun-loving young woman, a talented tennis player, and about to become a student at the Liverpool City School of Art. Lowry had taken her for a walk in mid-April, serenaded her with his ukulele, and when she gave him some innocent encouragement, he became a man possessed.

He wrote her a nine-page letter from Inglewood after a sleepless night in which he climbed out of the window and walked to Heswall (Walter Greenaway, cat burglar, would have been proud), where he smoked three pipes, walked home in time for breakfast and a bath, and then went otter hunting.

In the throes of desperate love he waxed hyperbolic.

> I'd die for you, Carol. I'd sell my soul for you. If you were bitten – I'd sail round the world to make the fellow who bit you apologise to you for it again . . . I'll love you still when you haven't a tooth or a hair on your head . . . if I'm in your way, I'll . . . run away from home, school, toil, kindred, and become an assistant bartender in Honduras or somewhere without ½ a sou if necessary

He knew he was not much of a catch, but, 'there's always one chance in 1 million twenty thousand, five hundred that I might win the amateur . . . Championship.'[1]

At the end of April she came to see him off on the train back to school then wrote him first an encouraging letter, then one telling how one of her admirers had told her their love was 'predestined'. In a flood of pleading letters he opened his heart to her. He slept with two photographs of her under his pillow, he said, but vowed that his passion for her would not interfere with his work. He and his friends, 'Mac' (McMorran) and 'Nick' (Nichol) formed a sort of Stalky and Co., and Mac was also in love. They sought solace in the verdant Cambridge countryside with their pipes and plenty of navy-cut – or Empire-grown shag in his case – and swore to marry no other but their present loves. He tried to impress her with his commitment to art rather than money, and deplored its sacrifice to public taste. When he sent a good, even clever, story to magazines like *Short Stories* or *Lots o' Fun*, it was often turned down simply because it *was* a good story.

> Dear Sir, (they say) . . . If you are clever enough to lower your art to the writing of a bad enough story for our pages, we should be obliged. If not, not. In the meantime thank you very much for the temporary divertion [sic] you have afforded the Editorial staff of Short Stories, (or Lots o' Fun).[2]

And as for her own work, he warned her that, 'Filthy lucre ruins the romance of the thing.'[3] He described a dream house for them to share which she would decorate with her pictures. They would have their own bathing pool 'with really decent deep salt water, and a high dive – and a tennis court.' He swore that never before had he told anyone he loved them.

This letter, posted on 2 May, should have arrived at her college address on the third. But that day the General Strike began, and when there was no reply he wrote a stream of ever more frantic letters. Extraordinarily enough, he seems to have been oblivious to the cataclysm which was about to shake the nation to its foundations. The national and local press and radio had been full of the impending strike. Apart from the mobilization of troops and special constables nationwide, four thousand Cambridge undergraduates had volunteered as strike-breakers and hundreds were out around the country working both for and against the strikers. With the country at a standstill, Britain was faced with the real prospect of revolution. But all this seems to have passed Lowry by; his passions were directed elsewhere. Although he said thirty years later that as a boy he had thought the strike had been great fun,[4] there is no evidence from his letters that he was anything more than a deaf bystander blinded by love. Throughout that week of social upheaval, he continued writing heartbreaking letters to Carol, pleading with her, 'Why don't you write?' and urging her to set him 'some Herculean labours' to prove his love. Equally distracted by art and passion, Lowry sent his beloved a short story about a man who invents a self-playing piano, and that week, too, the *Fortnightly* published his Paris hockey reports.

Not only did the General Strike pass him by, but lessons became just occasions for composing ever more complex love-letters. In Geometry he wrote:

> I'm so blindly in love with you (the hypotenuse IO is common. Quite so, DP=OQ, being radii, absolutely yes) that I can't see my way properly, and don't know what I'm wishing or what I want, just all I know is that if a quadrilateral is described about a circle, the angle subtended at the center [sic] by any two opposite sides are supplementary, which is stated and proved in the converse theorem, and very neatly avoids sentiment, which you must hate from me.[5]

When a reply finally arrived he sprang for his pen. He had completely forgotten 'this 'ere strike' and been 'smitten, struck, and otherwise afflicted' by the idea that she had so many friends she had forgotten about him. 'Consequently I have been tottering to every post like a swerving snipe to see if there was a letter for me, from you.'

Wanting to impress her with his singularity he gave a deliciously ironic account of how The Leys' authorities regarded him. He had a reputation for being cynical, he wrote, and composed cynical letters to the *Fortnightly* lambasting the school for hypocrisy, though it was no more so than any other public school; it just amused him to say that it was.

> Bisseker actually phoned Balgarnie for half an hour the other night while I was supping with the latter . . . telling him the following home truths.
>
> 1 that I was a danger to the school.
> 2 that the Fortnightly would be blasted everlastingly if they published my latest excrescence on the snobbishness of prefects singing out of one corner of their mouth in chapel, and giving punishments with the other.
> 3 that the Fortnightly would be blasted everlastingly in the after

life, for entertaining such an immoral character as myself on their staff.

4 that my works, fairly smart no doubt, were viper's productions, cheeseparings and hogwash.
5 that he doubted of late whether they were even smart: that they were mere braggartly cynicism.
6 that I had been reading Alec Waugh (which was quite true, rather a hit, that), that not only had I been reading Alec Waugh, but I had been reading Noel Coward, Michael Arlen, Eugene O'Neill, and Samuel Butler.
7 that I was not original, although I thought I was.
8 that it was rot.
9 that I was a disgrace to the school.
10 that I would continue to be a disgrace to the school.
11 that my works were boa-constricterine and adderesque.
12 that they were cheeseparings and hogwash.

Here I went out. When I came back, the great W. H. Barrelorgani was shaking with laughter. 'I don't advise you,' he said, 'to agitate about the insertion of that particular letter. I gather from the Head's remarks that you are (cough) not much thought of by him. That is the horrible effect of being CYNICAL. Have a meringue?' I had.[6]

Carol was intending to come to The Leys' Prize Day, ostensibly to see her brother Colin, who had been there for just a year, and Lowry eagerly offered to find her a room. Although top for Essay, he told her, he did not expect to receive a prize because he refused to answer the set questions or read the set books. However, the *Fortnightly*, which had given him a prize the previous year, might give him hush-money this time.

In reply he received a long, illustrated letter driving him almost delirious, and wrote back telling her of a certain mysterious acquaintance, Richard Connell. Connell was an American writer, whose short stories Lowry had been sending to Carol, passing them off as his own – his first major excursion into plagiarism, the form of theft least dangerous to society, as he later styled it. Connell was, he told her, 'the biggest liar, the biggest coward, the bravest man, the most immoral and the most puritanical man, the most insipid drunkard, and the worst and the best friend alternately that one might hope to have'. He sought for inspiration in drink and went to church to dream up 'a story about dopes'. 'He is, of course, quite mad – having in that respect a very similar temperament to myself.'[7] Then he pretended that Richard Connell was a pseudonym he used in trying to sell stories. However, he had given her a remarkable self-portrait. But if confession was good for the soul it also left him feeling bad about himself. 'I have almost given up hope that you could ever love a misfit like me . . . Every moment I live I love you more and more and realise what a hopelessly inadequate sort of person I am.' He tried to draw her into his work, suggesting they collaborate and publish stories jointly, a tendency he never lost – to involve the objects of his affection in his work.[8]

While wrestling, somewhat vainly, with his passion for Carol, in between examinations and Prize Day, he got away with his friend Hardy for a week in Nottingham. There was a Test Match between Australia and England at Trent Bridge starting on 12 June, and Hardy had invited his Rabelaisian friend home to see it with him. But the first thing Lowry asked for was a map of Nottingham with all the cinemas marked, intending to visit every flea-pit in town. On the first day of cricket, he made an excuse and slipped away, turning up again, apparently drunk, only as the day's play ended, 'weaving about a bit but having written screeds.' His friend decided that it was sometimes difficult to tell whether he was truly inebriated or whether he was acting. Hardy's sister Doris, then twenty-six and the woman of the house, took to the cheerfully delinquent schoolboy and 'spoiled him to death'. He had brought his uke along and, according to Hardy, 'drove the whole bloody house mad' with his perpetual strumming.[9]

Carol duly came to The Leys' Prize Day on 18 June and Lowry persuaded her to slip away for a walk along the Cam behind King's College. Though once again she tried gently to distance herself from him, clearly he basked in her company. Before she left, he gave her a copy of Conrad's *Lord Jim*, telling her that it was the greatest novel ever written. What he did not know was that she was really there to visit the man who *did* interest her, a student at St John's, whom she later married. But he was still hopeful, and on the day she left, wrote to her in the form of a story. Cambridge for three days had been like 'the very devil of a time in Paris' for a poor clerk who normally rotted away in a London office. One day she might come round to his way of thinking, and she was, after all, the 'Only One'. Then came the routine self-abasement. He was, he implied 'a low type of human being' – 'Parallel, a dog: qualities, faithfulness, devotion; only you don't like me nearly as much as that.' And a touch of self-pity: there would be drawbacks to their marriage because 'my eyes aren't exactly the world's best manufactured articles' and so he might have to settle for friendship.

He seems to have realized, too, that drink, with its effect of releasing the drinker from a painful reality, was a useful weapon against those who frustrated him. In a sudden change of mood, he threatened to get drunk if she did not love him. When she wrote back chiding him for intemperance, he quickly repented. He was sorry to have worried her, he said, but he was capable of saying anything in his 'half niblicked frog moods' and if he had not abandoned hope of winning her he would 'just cry hoot' and drown his sorrows in 'seven pints of bitter a day for a week, which would make me tight for a fortnight . . . and this would not be a sign of courage at all, but of superlative weakness.' Meeting her had made him realize that he must pull himself together and look as though he meant something. Apart from a certain ability to write, he was, or tried to be, one of the world's greatest 'don't care two hoots'. And he was not at all stuffy about principles, as she had suggested. 'Religion . . . is like a school tie tied round a pair of white flannels – if it is tight, it is uncomfortable, and if it is loose, you might as well have none at all.'[10]

When she replied that she 'liked 'em bad', he boasted that there was no school rule that he and Mac had not broken. Nor must she think him too literary; he liked reading good books but it was only a whim, like her drawing. Balgarnie had told him, '(cough) Lowry, we mustn't be so irregular, we must (cough) obey school rules more. I was thinking of recommending – er – you for a sub-prefect next term, but I perceive we're going to be irregular . . . (cough) – we mustn't be so irregular – don't be such an *irresponsible fool*!'[11]

There was no reply to this, so on impulse he sent her a telegram, then quickly wrote asking forgiveness. It was, he said, a poor attempt at humour for which the telegram was a poor medium. She replied hoping she had not made him unhappy, but he responded that his unhappiness was 'only a pose'. Nevertheless, to cope with his sense of solitude he went swimming alone in Byron's Pool, which was 'the world's worst place to swim and smelt of people's feet.' Yet it was a nice place afterwards to lie in the sun being lazy and smoke Woodbines, he said. Frustrated love, he hinted, had sent him to the Romantic poets, especially to Shelley. Twenty years later, alone and miserable and reading Shelley again in Mexico, he recalled nostalgically his solitary schoolboy forays into the countryside to read.[12]

In June Nick and Mac went for a weekend to Inglewood. Arthur and

Evelyn were away in Buenos Aires, and in their absence it was easier to have friends to stay. They spent most of their time playing tennis at Hillthorpe, where Malcolm was eager to show off his 'love' to the rest of Stalky and Co. Shortly afterwards, Mac wrote secretly to Carol about Lobs, asking if she realized how smitten he was, and whether the passion was mutual. He got 'the most awful fits of down-heartidness and self loathing' because he could not think how anyone could like him. 'It must be admitted that he doesn't get an awfully good time at home and has had bad luck so far in life . . . I have one or two things I would *like* to tell you about him which would melt your heart but I can't unless you say that you really do love him.' When she replied that she did not reciprocate Lobs's passion, Mac wrote asking her to let his chum down lightly.

> You are quite right when you say that he is a little headstrong and impulsive, but I am doing my best to keep him steady. He's got this journalism on the brain of course and doesn't do a stroke of serious work. I am trying to reform him in that way too, for, if he doesn't do something he'll never be able to get up to the Varsity next year . . . I am about the only friend he has got in the school, although I've introduced him to all my set in my house here, which has been some help to him.[13]

As a result of Mac's plea, Carol decided to end the correspondence and wrote one last letter gently breaking the news. 'Certain happenings', she told him, made it better that they stop writing. In his reply, addressed from 'Deep Elm', he accepted the end of the affair gloomily but with equanimity. He supposed she had fallen in love with 'some priceless old bean'. He always was 'a complete mug', and could never hope that she would love him in spite of his 'hideous rantings, and arrogance.' Carol married her beau from St John's in 1932 and shortly afterwards went off to India, the wife of a District Officer. Thereafter Lowry appeared less inclined to go for girls from his own class. He wanted admiration, but he had decided, like Walter Greenaway, to desert his background and spy on the world and himself from a distance. To prove himself a hero he needed to be more than just a smart and cynical story writer; he needed to get out into the world and prove himself a man.

These extraordinary letters to Carol reveal many of Lowry's characteristics as a writer and as a man which were to became further exaggerated as he grew older. They show that at sixteen he was already a prolific and compulsive letter writer. To each of these intensely composed missives he brought a wild originality, using techniques which were both artful and reflective of the unbounded complexity of his young mind. The reality of a geometry lesson or a conversation with his housemaster interrupt his fantasizing, or fictional characters appear masquerading as real people. And the literary techniques he was able to command as a sixteen-year-old he would later develop into a peculiarly modernist style of his own.

The sortie into hockey reporting and his passion for Carol Brown may have diverted him from serious storywriting briefly, but in the *Fortnightly* of 4 June he produced yet another which reflected his recent experiences and foreshadowed work to come. 'The Repulsive Tragedy of the Incredulous Englishman' owes something to his sea-crossing to France, his friendship with Raymond Cook, and his new-found interest in psychic phenomena. It tells of an English novelist on a boat bound for Australia meeting an Armenian hypnotist who complains of being disdained in his own land and so is planning to try his luck in the Antipodes. The Englishman is sceptical of hypnosis, but his wife is ill and, since the Armenian is a doctor, asks his help. The author is tricked into shooting the Armenian, and then finds his wife dead.[14] It was as if Lowry was already seeing himself as two people – a journeying writer and a despised exile, the one straight and decent, the other malevolent. But as yet the shifting voices within himself, there in his letters to Carol Brown, had not yet found their way so clearly into his fiction.

In August, with Bruce Thompson, he entered for the national Boys' Golf Championship at Coombe Hill in Surrey. At Arthur's insistence they stayed at a temperance hotel, and on 23 August they set out, each hoping to become British Boys' Amateur Golf Champion. Thompson managed to scrape through the first round before being eliminated; Lowry was beaten in the first round. Good natural player though he was, he was not in the same class as the finalists. Possibly he was hungover that morning at Coombe Hill; he told the folks at home that he had been ill with a bad stomach.

Whatever the Head might have thought of Lowry's subversive influence, Balgarnie thought well enough of him to appoint him a sub-prefect at the start of the autumn term, and also to put him on the *Fortnightly* editorial board, though he never, it seems, turned up to meetings.[15] Doubtless Balgarnie felt that giving his 'irregular' pupil a bit of authority might settle him and that as something of an outsider he might exercise some control over other wayward members of the House. He was fortunate to have a man like 'Chips' prepared to look beyond the scruffy, awkward schoolboy exterior to the unusual talent lying within him. In his last year at school, Lowry was given the elbow room he needed to expand as a writer. But he was still thought backward enough to be placed in the Sixth Form Remove.

Being House sub-prefect entitled him to a small study, shared with Michael Rennie, later a film star. Evelyn sent him a few things to make the room comfortable, and in October he wrote to thank her for sending cushions and a tablecloth. 'The study now resembles the bibliothèque of an Armenian professor of down.' Wherever one flung oneself there were cushions. 'It is all very pleasant.' He was disappointed that his father had not taken her to see *Juno and the Paycock* in Liverpool as promised, but added knowingly, 'Perhaps you were the stubborn one.' In any event they had both lost out by missing it, he said.[16]

As well as fiction, he thought he might have a talent for songwriting, and had composed a few things with Russell. One day that same autumn, he wandered into a music room below the school hall and found Ronnie Hill, like him dodging games, improvising jazz at the piano. He had met a boy with 'the piano at his finger tips,' he wrote home.[17] Hill found Lowry rather intimidating – a tough, muscular boy sophisticated beyond his years, who had recently taken to parading around arm-in-arm with Michael Rennie, wearing pointed sideburns and flannel bags minus turn-ups. However, he was persuaded to collaborate on a series of songs, and surprisingly it worked, Lowry concentrating on the lyrics, Hill on the music. They were prolific from the start. There was 'Dismal Swamp', according to Hill, 'full of extraordinary imagery, but very beautiful,' and 'Hindu Babe', which gave Lowry the chance to add to his ukulele accompaniment with rhythmic farts.[18] The enlarged lower bowel identified by doctors some thirty years later could be used as a useful wind instrument, much to the delight of those privileged to hear the maestro in action. There were also 'Goodbye to Shanghai' and what Hill remembered as 'that dreadful "Three Little Doggone Mice" ' with endless verses, often versions of corny schoolboy jokes. 'How do you make a Venetian blind?/ . . . Poke his eyes out, we won't mind.' Playing with the talented Hill, subsequently a BBC dance-band leader, Lowry's ukulele playing improved, and he was later considered by some to be quite professional, (not, however, by Hill, who thought his performances depended mostly on enthusiasm and bravado).[19] As a musician he had one major drawback – his hands were too small to stretch an octave on the piano, though he had learnt to hammer out a lively tune on the Bechstein at Inglewood. He became obsessed with the shape and size of his hands, as he was with the rest of his 'misshapen malodorous body', but his anxieties doubtless began with the appalling chilblains from which he suffered as a child.

By the end of the year the two young composers were confident enough to send some of their songs to sheet-music publishers. Lowry may have gone in person, like his youthful doppelgänger Hugh, in *Under the Volcano*. 'His method was each whole holiday to make the rounds of the music publishers with his guitar – and in this respect his early life vaguely recalled that of another frustrated artist, Adolf Hitler – his manuscripts transcribed for the piano alone in the guitar case, or another old Gladstone bag of Geoff's.'[20]

Reading Shelley to absorb his frustrated passion for Carol Brown had failed to improve his own verse. 'The Old Woman Who Buried Cats' in the 15 October *Fortnightly* was a piece of whimsical doggerel about a woman carrying a dead cat in a case, looking for a place to bury it, oddly anticipating an episode in his own life six years later. In November he published a more serious poem, 'The Rain Fell Heavily' (which leaned heavily on a Kipling poem in *The Light that Failed*).

When I am dead
Bring me not roses white,
Nor austere lillies grimly bright;
But bring me from the garden roses red,
Roses red, wind-blown, sun-kissed;
The roses that my life hath missed –
When I am dead.[21]

His taste in poetry was less well-defined than his taste in fiction. At Caldicott he had learned to enjoy Hood, Flecker, and Francis Thompson. He had already acquired a love for Shakespeare, but Byron, Keats, and Shelley burst into his life only with his first 'pangs of dispriz'd love', and there was a wilful attraction to 'mad' poets like Clare and Blake. Of his alter ego he wrote that what drew him to Blake as a child was reading in his father's *Times* that the poet was 'cuckoo'.[22]

As a drama critic he was more self-assured. Ben Greet, an itinerant player-manager in the Wolfit style, brought a play to The Leys once a year. That October it was *Macbeth*, and Camel was sent to review it. '*Macbeth*,' he wrote, with the confidence of an experienced hand, 'is quite a good play, but it must be supremely well acted to make it "go" at all,' and he could not say for sure that Ben Greet's performance exactly 'went'. The final applause he thought was sincere, and 'although there were some ironical cries of "Author!" I am glad that he was unable to be present.' The witches' cauldron was obviously no cauldron, the thunder no more than 'indifferent work on the bass drum', and the chairs at the banquet clearly out of classroom number six. The witches were 'more like respectable spinsters of West Kensington than witches,' and he could produce a better duel with a knife and fork than the one between Macbeth and Macduff. And how had a piano managed to find its way on to a blasted heath? But the afternoon was not entirely wasted. After all, 'Shakespeare's words are Shakespeare's words.' His conclusion had that firm ring of hesitancy which by now had become his stylistic trademark. 'I should say on the whole that it had its dramatic moments, and some moments which were – er – not dramatic.'[23]

In a sudden burst of energy, he plunged into debating, opposing the motion 'That this Society deplores the literary tastes of the modern schoolboy', and in an issue of the *Fortnightly* (also carrying advice on novel-writing by James Hilton), attacked the idea that 'Public school men are better than self-made men'. This was neither patriotism nor snobbery, but childish. He was not exactly a socialist nor any special kind of fanatic, 'but I do say that the epigram . . . caused one of your most sober and law-abiding readers to feel as though he were being slowly beaten to death by a short-sighted spinster with Freudian leanings with a sack full of wet dough on a rainy February night in Wigan.'[24] Arthur Lowry, the self-made man who sent his sons to Public School, might have disagreed, but he had no reason to believe that his youngest son's claim to be both sober and law-abiding was anything but true. Three or four more years would change that forever.

Maybe in anticipation of soon being out in the world 'roughing it' in the way of sailor-heroes in countless sea novels, Lowry all at once threw himself into physical activity. He quickly won himself a regular place at inside three-quarter in the school Second Rugby XV beside his friend Rennie, and began to gain a slight reputation as a sportsman. 'Lowry – er – wormed his way through the opposing pack several times before being tackled,' wrote a knowing *Fortnightly* reporter, catching something of his bull-in-the-China-shop style of play.[25] 'Lowry had plenty of energy,' wrote another, 'but he was usually tackled with the ball, a fatal thing for an inside man.'[26] In other words he was too much an individualist to be a good team-player. His end of term assessment was 'plucky'.[27]

Arthur, too, needed pluck in 1926, a difficult year for Bustons. The firm had had trouble with an unscrupulous South American agent, and the Buenos Aires trip with Evelyn had been undertaken in an attempt to sort out this muddle. Following a complicated lawsuit, both Buston and Arthur's cousin, F. E. Lowry, retired, leaving Arthur in charge. He immediately took Stuart and Wilfrid in as partners, leaving Russell, however, still in a fairly junior position. He must have been wondering what on earth could be done with Malcolm, and one idea may have been the diplomatic service. Farcical as this may seem, Arthur was a poor judge of character, and Malcolm had become quite adept at concealing his inadequacy behind a jaunty façade. Such a career, however, required a university education, so that Malcolm was expected, unlike his brothers, to try for Cambridge Entrance. But in the meantime he was making his own plans to escape.

The passion to travel and to write was accompanied now by a passion to be loved. Having accepted that his feelings for Carol were unrequited, he was desperate for a girlfriend with whom to indulge romantic dreams of rose-covered cottages and children, and to whom he could write letters of tender and extravagant passion. 'You cannot live without loving' became a key motif in *Under the Volcano*, but now he was the only Lowry without a partner, something he must have felt keenly. The years of emotional starvation following Miss Bell's departure were beginning to tell. The replacement he finally found for Carol not only satisfied his need for love but was to become enshrined as Janet, the adored but absent virgin in *Ultramarine*. Her name was Tessa Evans, and if the basis of the novel is barely disguised reportage, as it seems, she was a shorthand-typist he met at a dance hall in New Brighton. Since he was no dancer and very inhibited, the courage to approach her probably required the fortifying power of a few drinks. Tessa was young and naïve and sentimental, as her letters to him reveal.

She was sixteen and lived with her parents at 26 Thirlmere Street, Wallasey. In *Ultramarine*, she becomes Janet Travena, the surname a part-anagram of Teresa Evans. She was flattered enough by his attention to fall head over heels for the handsome public schoolboy with a well-educated voice, mysterious far-seeing blue eyes and a mop of copper-coloured hair, who spoke poetry and shared with her his dreams of travel and literary success. She called him Lobs, and they spent a great deal of time together wandering the Wirral countryside, playing golf and visiting cinemas and theatres in Liverpool and Birkenhead. Failing to win the socially poised Carol and then sweeping this young typist off her feet must have made him aware of how readily he could charm girls from a lower class. His friend McMorran, now up at Christ's, had a similar experience when he fell for a shop-girl. When his family heard of it they persuaded him to drop her as socially unsuitable. But Lowry did not make McMorran's mistake, and Tessa remained his secret, though Russell got an inkling of an attachment when he saw him taking off frequently for New Brighton.

They met some time in 1926. Whether Lowry met her family, and whether, like Tom Hardy's family, they were driven mad by his ukulele, is unclear, but from her letters it seems they contrived to spend time together in her bedroom at Thirlmere Street, and may even have come close to consummating their passion. Later, when he went to sea, he left a ukulele behind in her room, and her letters to him were full of remembered sweet nothings and mutual entwinings after twilight.

At the beginning of 1927, Lowry was still a seventeen-year-old schoolboy, and House sub-prefect under the benevolent eye of W. H. Balgarnie. Nevertheless, his position did at least allow him to indulge in one of his favourite pastimes, reading aloud. Now he read at bedtime to the juniors of West House, and later recalled how his reading of F. Anstey's *Vice Versa* caused so much hilarity that Balgarnie had to come and put a stop to the noise. The book duly turned up in the Consul's library in chapter 6 of *Under the Volcano* alongside Wodehouse's *Clicking of Cuthbert*, and *Peter Rabbit*. 'Everything,' says the Consul, 'is to be found in *Peter Rabbit*.'[28]

Songwriting with Ronnie Hill was working so well that they planned to continue it by going to Christ's together. McMorran was already there, and for Lowry, with a literary career in mind, Christ's also meant following in Hilton's footsteps. But just then he was more isolated than ever. By the end of 1926, Hardy, Rennie, Cook, Mac and Nick had all departed, though he still saw McMorran, who had digs in nearby Earl Street, and who was now himself sweet on Carol Brown. In February he sent her news of Lobs.

> The lad is sneaking out to lunch with me on the sly. I always thought it a crying shame he never had any lessons to help him with his dancing as he has an inborn sense of dance-rhythm. He and another boy, a little younger, have composed up to half a dozen dance tunes – mostly Fox-trots, one called "Charleston Girl" is now selling well and there are several on trial at different publishers![29]

'Charleston Girl' was *not* selling well, but Lowry, ever hopeful, was claiming that it was – a habit of anticipating success which he never quite shook off, to the confusion of his friends. What was true was that he and Hill had prised £100 each from their parents to pay for two songs – 'Goodbye Shanghai' and 'Three Little Doggone Mice' to be published in London.

Apart from seeming to offer him the best chance of self-fulfilment, he also hoped that writing would make him independent of his father, and craved the freedom of an adult to travel and to acquire material for his work. Even so, he continued to enjoy a few school activities – debating, acting, rough-and-ready rugby and robust hockey. More importantly, school still offered him an outlet for his writing. He read a paper on 'Walking' to the Literary and Debating Society that only added to his dotty reputation.

> C. M. Lowry's paper on walking was, as might have been expected, amusing. It mattered not whether the speaker had ever gone on a walking tour himself, or if he had, whether he had experienced the misfortunes he related. He was never dull. In particular he excelled himself in a description of a village inn on a Saturday night.[30]

Performing in another school play, Drinkwater's *Oliver Cromwell*, he was judged as having 'a pleasing vigour' as General Fairfax and being 'suitably diabolical' in another minor role. At an inquest on the production, with Frank Ives as 'Coroner', some of the complaints about 'masculine "females", unloverlike lovers, diminutive generals and turncoat double-rollers",' seem to have stung Lowry. In response, and speaking 'as a neutral', he proposed 'that this Society should attempt plays of a lighter and more boisterous character.' The *Fortnightly* complained that 'He judged authors by their private lives, and was somewhat indistinct.'[31] But indistinct or not, it was practically his parting shot at the school.

Hardly anyone knew about his plans, including Ronnie Hill, even when the two appeared in an end of term concert to great applause – unusual because the event was normally a dignified affair, Chopin piano pieces and, at the most, folk songs like 'The Farmer's Boy' or 'Cockles and Mussels'. Jazz with piano and uke was decidedly daring. Afterwards Lowry slipped away from The Leys without so much as a farewell fanfare.

The fact of his leaving must have been settled at least by early March, when he was still rehearsing in school plays and turning out on the rugger pitch. Now, rather than return to Inglewood, he escaped to London. McMorran told Carol on 21 March: 'Dear old Lobs (alias Malcolm) whom I consider as quite my best friend (male!) is going to put in a week with me after he leaves Leys for the last time.' However, as, Mac's sister reported, Lobs was not a successful house guest, too inclined to drunken excess for a genteel family like the McMorrans.[32]

Whether he planned simply to run away to sea to frustrate Arthur's plan to send him to university, or whether he intended taking a single trip just for the experience, is not clear. Like Ishmael in *Moby Dick*, for whom 'a whale-ship was my Yale and Harvard,'[33] he was determined on a different kind of education. There was the added attraction of following in the footsteps of Conrad, who also went to sea at seventeen – not the last such pilgrimage he would take in the footsteps of a literary hero. He may also have felt, as Hugh Firmin did, like 'a shipless buccaneer' . . . 'under a sad curse of futility because [he] had not sailed with [his] elder brother[s] the seas of the last war.'[34] Few chances to prove oneself existed for his generation. However, when Stuart learned what Malcolm intended, he knew his father would be opposed. He also knew Malcolm was both stubborn and cunning – he had insisted slyly that he wanted to be an AB before he became a BA.[35] Apparently it was Stuart's intervention which finally made Arthur relent. Stuart, at least, knew of Malcolm's hope for the trip because they had discussed it as they had discussed the wide world, books he was reading, and his ambition to write. He could also remember the sea-fever which had gripped his brother as a boy.

To Malcolm the sea always spelt 'escape', but here it was conditional on future imprisonment. His father was won round only on condition that he agreed to work for Cambridge entrance on his return, and once Malcolm had agreed, he very generously offered every assistance, including money. The easiest way to go to sea as an amateur in those days was as a carpenter's mate, but he refused this comfortable option, determined to 'rough it' and endure the same hell that Conrad's and O'Neill's sailors had before him. (It was O'Neill, he said, who sent him to sea.)[36] Despite high unemployment among seamen, Arthur, through contacts with J. Alfred Holt, arranged for him to be taken as a deckboy on Holt's Blue Funnel freighter SS *Pyrrhus*, due to sail for Yokohama from Birkenhead on 14 May.

Malcolm was keen for Russell to go as well, but he was too involved with Meg to want to ship out. Nevertheless, they read up about shipboard life together, boned up on sea-knots, and learned to recognize ships by their superstructures. Russell gave Malcolm a clasp knife as a parting gift and they composed a suitably appropriate sea song for him to take along.

> Marching down the road to China,
> You'll hear me singing this song,
> Soon we'll be aboard an Ocean Liner
> Sailing for Hong Kong,
> And when we've put these yellow faces
> In their proper places
> We'll be home once more,
> And I'll take my Alice
> To the Crystal Palace
> At the end of the China War.[37]

It would not be a hit on *Pyrrhus* with ten Chinese stokers on board.

At that stage, according to Russell, he had said nothing about basing a novel on the trip; songs and short stories were uppermost in his thoughts. And leaving Tessa must also have exercised his mind. He had already confided his plans and dreams of life at sea to her, and their parting was a suitably poignant and heart-wrenching affair. Having little feeling for his own family, she supplied him with a sailor's dream of home, and was as important to him on the trip he was about to undertake as his experience of the sea itself and his sense of escaping from an England blighted by industrialization and strangled by hypocrisy.

But as well as the romance, he had the mercenary idea of using his trip to gain publicity for himself as a writer. He contacted the *Liverpool Echo* who sent a reporter to Inglewood to interview him. Surprisingly, the reticent Evelyn also agreed to be questioned. Her son, she said, hoped to write short stories and foxtrots while at sea and would then go to Cambridge. The impression given to the reporter must have been that of a rich mother's boy going off to 'rough it' just for fun – not entirely true, but then not altogether false. Not long before he sailed, copies of the sheet-music of his two songs arrived from London. It looked most impressive, 'Three Little Doggone Mice' appearing as 'Just the Latest Charleston Fox-Trot Ever . . . Featured with Great Success by Alfredo and his Band' – an unlikely story. Alfredo probably took a slice of Arthur's hundred for the use of his name. The next thing was to publicize the songs and get variety performers interested in using them. Malcolm and Russell went around the local Merseyside music halls trying to persuade sweating variety performers, including the highly successful Two Leslies, to plug their songs, but without success.

Pyrrhus was to sail from Birkenhead on Saturday, 14 May, but the crew were required to sign on at the Company Office at India Buildings in Liverpool's Water Street three days before. She would sail for Yokohama via Singapore and ports along the China coast, with a crew of fifty-one men under Captain William J. Elford, a 51-year-old Lancastrian, returning by 26 September; a round-trip of twenty weeks. Having refused Arthur's offer of money to ease things for himself, he stood, as one of the two deckboys on *Pyrrhus*, to get 12*s*. 6*d*. for an eight-hour day, seven days a week. Only the Junior Assistant Steward got less, a miserly 10*s*.

CHAPTER V

SAILING EAST: SAILING WEST
1927–1929

> Why do I leave you and go to sea? It is because I want to die. I want to die because I am mad and want to write books and win the Nobel Prize. I want to be a real man and die gloriously. I want to be a real man and live gloriously.
>
> LOWRY (draft of *Ultramarine*)

On 20 May, the *Leys Fortnightly* announced that, 'C. M. Lowry sailed from Liverpool on Saturday as a deckhand in the SS *Pyrrhus*, which is going on a tramp voyage to the Far East, calling at Port Said, Shanghai, and possibly Yokohama.' This was not strictly true. *Pyrrhus* sailed from Birkenhead and was a regular 'Blue Piper' freighter on a set course of trade rather than a tramp which traded as it went. However, Lowry liked to call it a tramp – it sounded more romantic.

He left for the docks on the evening of Friday the 13th (not the most auspicious of days for one so superstitious). Coltman drove him to the dock gates in the Minerva en route to the Ferry to collect Arthur. He was not due to report until 6 a.m. on the 14th, but was obviously eager to get aboard. He had with him his trusty ukulele, with which he hoped to entertain his crewmates, and the notebook in which he planned to keep a diary of the voyage. He implied later that he was seen rolling up in the Minerva and that this was too much for the rest of the crew to stomach. The Liverpool *Echo* ran the story, which no doubt some sailors brought on board with them. One can only imagine their reaction to such blatant self-publicity:

> *Rich boy as deckhand*
>
> PREFERS 50*s*. A MONTH TO THE 'SILK-CUSHION LIFE'
>
> A Liverpool cotton broker and his wife from the quayside at Birkenhead to-day waved good-bye to their public schoolboy son, who is

sailing as a deck hand in the Holt cargo steamer Pyrrhus, for a wage of 50*s*. a month.

Malcolm Lowry, a curlyheaded lad of 17, is forsaking the comforts of home at Inglewood, Caldy, overlooking the River Dee, for a rigorous life at sea.

'No silk-cushion youth for me,' he said. 'I want to see the world, and rub shoulders with its oddities, and get some experience of life before I go back to Cambridge University.' . . .

Lowry had taken a ukulele with him and hopes to compose new Charlestons during the voyage.

'He is bent on a literary career, and his short-story writing is all to him,' said Mrs Lowry, when the ship had left. 'Of course he has taken his ukulele with him, and he hopes to compose some more Charlestons during the voyage.'[1]

The idea of Arthur and Evelyn waving from the dockside was journalistic licence, and quite out of character, according to Russell. But Lowry never lived down this news story. It got him off on entirely the wrong foot with his shipmates. 'Jesus, Cock, did you see the bloody paper? We've got a bastard duke on board or something of that'[2] and 'I hate those bloody toffs who come to sea for experience'[3] were the kinds of loud remarks he was intended, apparently, to overhear. It was not to be the story of a crew awestruck by the brilliance of a latter-day Walter Greenaway. It was to be a rough passage for the budding Conrad. Like Melville's Redburn he had 'the mildew on his soul', and, as one of the stewards, Joseph Ward, recalled, 'He was a lad lost.' Ward knew Wilfrid and introduced himself to Lowry. But Ward's friendship was no protection from the contemptuous hostility of the crew, and the steward himself came to join in the ridicule.

Lowry found *Pyrrhus* a great disappointment. Anyone who had read a Jack London novel, or seen an O'Neill play, knew that a ship had a fo'c'sle for'ard and a crew which drank, cursed, played cards and fought, and, rough though they were, were bound together by the brotherhood of the sea. But *Pyrrhus* had no fo'c'sle; its crew lived in quarters aft, and no sense of brotherhood was to be found. In fact, the ship was a hotbed of petty snobbery and hatreds. As Hugh, his youthful doppelgänger, recalls in *Under the Volcano*

if he had expected to leave British snobbery astern with his public school he was sadly mistaken . . . the degree of snobbery prevailing

> on the *Philoctetes* was fantastic, of a kind Hugh had never imagined possible. The chief cook regarded the tireless second cook as a creature of completely inferior station. The bosun despised the carpenter and would not speak to him for three months, though they messed in the same small room, because he was a tradesman, while the carpenter despised the bosun since he, Chips, was the senior petty officer.[4]

And Lowry/Hugh, as a deckboy and a 'toff', was probably picked on by his shipmates more than the other boys on their first trip. Behind his back they read his diary. His money was stolen and so were his dungarees, which crew members forced him to buy back from them. But they had difficulty knowing how to deal with him. One, it seems, even told him obsequiously, 'Do you realize, mate, you're working for us, when we should be working for you?'[5] But the clumsy, accident-prone Lowry was a poor apprentice sailor, and on occasion a veritable liability. Once he endangered the lives of the crew by pouring undiluted lime juice into the water-filter. He later included this incident in his story 'The Forest Path to the Spring',[6] but contrived to make it sound like a made-up story rather than a real event.

This incident did not help the youngster so desperate to prove himself a man like his literary heroes. Nor did his calling Chinese crewmen 'slant-eyed B's', or his singing the wretched 'Marching Down the Road to China', with its promise to 'put those Yellow Faces in their proper places' improve his standing. There was muttering about him 'taking a good man's job' and his 'having influence at the office', strong echoes of *Redburn*, through which obviously he came to filter some of his experiences. He was picked on by Banks, the quartermaster, and Spence, the bosun, and fell out badly with the cook, Andy Jepson, an Australian – a fatal mistake since a deckboy's job included fetching and carrying food from the galley.

Andy, made part-Norwegian in *Ultramarine*, takes an instant dislike to Lowry's hero Hilliot. 'You're just a bloody senseless twat,' he says, and Hilliot is made to understand that 'a man who went to sea for fun would go to hell for a pastime.'[7] The cook constantly refers to him as 'Miss', 'Your Ladyship' or 'Nancy boy'. And he is not the only crew member who picks on him. The 'fairy QM' makes sexual advances, and the bosun gives him a particularly hard time scrubbing, cleaning, hauling, and chipping rust from the hot decks in the Red Sea. According to Ward, Lowry threatened the QM he would write to the papers denouncing him, but was told if so he would get the same treatment back. However, he did denounce the bosun in a poem as 'Mr Facing Both Ways, / one green eye the mate's and one the men's,' who induced 'such fierce black loathing hatred and contempt / it lives on writhing like a Kansas whirlwind . . . '[8] On 24 May, reaching Port Said, his first whiff of the Mysterious East, he bought Tessa a present in a bazaar where he was importuned by an Arab hawker unable to resist the charms of this 'pretty' English boy. Later he told how the man chased him on to the *Pyrrhus*, staying on board after it had sailed, and trying to bribe him with a tray of 'real golden rings stolen off the mail boat', and was only got rid of at Dar es Salaam after the ship had left the Suez Canal.[9]

The journey through the Red Sea and Indian Ocean to Penang was broken only by a brief stopover in Perim. But this was not the perilous sea voyage so often celebrated by Conrad. There were no typhoons and Captain Bill Elford was no Captain McWhirr.

> I had expected the roar of the sea,
> and of tempest,
> not this sullen unremitting calm,
> this road of concrete to the Antipodes.[10]

And the more resentful members of the crew took every opportunity to humiliate him. 'On one occasion he received the full contents of a Red Lead Drum, and everyone aboard did the whahoo Indian dance at the spectacle of about 14 days of "Lobs" looking a real Indian brave,' wrote Joseph Ward.[11] On another occasion he was deliberately handed a pile of red-hot plates by his old enemy the cook.[12] Yet he did make some friends on *Pyrrhus*. The Scottish lamptrimmer, a quasi-communist, could not understand him wanting to dodge going to Cambridge, saying, 'If I were you I'd go to the poxing place. Get what you bloody can out of the set-up.'[13]

At Port Swettenham, their next stop, he had a chance to salvage his miserable reputation. But this, later a key event in *Ultramarine*, turned into yet another humiliation for him, as Joseph Ward recalled.

> Upon one occasion one of our unbidden passengers was a dove. 'Lobs' was fond of it, as indeed were all [the] sailors, but in Port Swettenham the dove fell overboard and could not rise from the water. 'Lobs' decided he had lost the chance to prove himself a hero by not diving after it, even though as we watched its struggles, there was a sudden

> skirmish in the water and the dove had become a meal for a hungry inhabitant.[14]

In the novel, Ward's dove becomes Norman the galley boy's carrier pigeon, which Hilliot is at first too slow to rescue from the masthead and later, when it falls overboard, too hesitant, because of sharks, to do what the heroic Walter Greenaway would have done without hesitation – dive in and haul it out.

Listening to the crew boasting of amorous times ashore and doses of VD contracted, he became both fascinated by the thought of the Eastern brothels and terror-stricken at the prospect of meeting the same fate as men like Norman, who had 'a bad dose of the clap'.[15] He tried remaining on board when the ship docked, determined to stay faithful to Tessa, or he hung about the dockside bars drinking heavily. In a draft of his book his alter ego laments, 'I am a coward. My habits are filthy. I am a syphilophobiac, and am shocked at the idea of fornication. I am a drunkard. My sleep is disturbed by erotic dreams . . . Yet I am a virgin, curiously enough.'[16] He heard from Tessa; the present was 'ripping' and she missed him like mad. 'At night I have pictured you tossing on the high seas and wondered were you ill or sad, did you need me, as I needed you. For I missed you so, at night, when the wind blew in a melancholy way and echoed round the house, and the lighthouse lamp flashed in and out of our window . . .'[17]

After Singapore and Hong Kong, the ship put in at Shanghai, where the Chinese Civil War had broken out. In his story, 'China', he recalls the thundering artillery, but 'the whole thing crashed over our heads without touching us.' And while the Chinese made civil war, a team from *Pyrrhus* and one from the British submarine, HMS *Proteus*, played cricket.[18] Later he boasted that it was there he caught a bullet, giving him the vicious scar on his right knee – the one from his boyhood cycling accident.

By 29 June *Pyrrhus* was in Kobe, and on 2 July she docked at Yokohama where she remained for just over two weeks. Throughout the trip Lowry wrote constantly to Tessa, eagerly collecting her replies at each port of call. Haunted by ghastly memories of the Anatomy Museum, he had resisted following the other crew to red-light districts ashore, but in Yokohama some of them got him drunk, dragged him into a brothel, then sat around to watch him perform. Joseph Ward witnessed this miserable ordeal: 'His reproductive organ was certainly in the back row,' he wrote 'it was a teeny-weeny object that disgusted a Japanese geisha girl to such an extent as to frustrate her into the most impolite abuse.'[19] Out of terror or because of drink, in front of a audience of scoffing drunks, he had been rendered impotent. Ironically, a letter from his mother had hoped that he was 'keeping *clean*' and would not be 'coarsened by a lot of hooligans'.[20] He toned down the brothel story in his novel but did confess all to Russell on his return

> Malcolm could still tell the truth when we were young and he did tell me this story well before it went into *Ultramarine*. The crux of the original version was his utter revulsion at the squalor of the place and his inability to understand how anybody could get 'turned on' . . . in such circumstances. Even, or especially, when drunk.[21]

Perhaps it was to distance himself from the philistinism of his persecutors that Lowry dreamt up his fictional doppelgänger, Dana Hilliot. The notebook was gradually filling, and by the end of the trip he had given up the idea of short stories in favour of a novel. He noted down scenes observed on the dockside – coolies fornicating in coal bunkers, names of bars, street signs, advertisements and newspaper headlines. He copied down old sailors' stories, noted games of poker, conversations and fragments of speech. He was particularly attracted to the infernal world of the fireman, the hellish stokehold where sweating slaves stoked the fires of Hades. However, the stokehold was forbidden to boys under eighteen.

On 29 July the ship arrived from Dairen at Tsingtao (Tschang Tschang), on the Yellow Sea coast. It was the day after his eighteenth birthday, which became the focal day of *Ultramarine*, on which Dana Hilliot stands on the very brink of manhood, groping towards an adult identity, torn between the poles of lost innocence and corrupting experience, between the fantasy of the past and the cruel realities of present and fearful future. Now old enough, he even may have spent a day or two in the stokehold; certainly he was to claim to have been a fireman on *Pyrrhus*.

The return journey took the ship through Foo Chow and Manila, then to Singapore where they took on a cargo of wild animals, most destined for Dublin Zoo, except for an elephant bound for Rome, who the sailors called 'Rosemary'. The animals were kept in cages on deck, or below the forepeak, and Lowry was detailed to help the keeper, watering and feeding them. Apart from shovelling coal, it was the one job on the ship that suited him. It also kept him out of harm's way. In his lonely state on *Pyrrhus*, he seems to have felt closer to the caged wild animals than to a crew trapped in its own petty class system. 'I once had a fixation on an elephant,' he wrote, '– the heart indeed is a lonely hunter, as someone says . . .'[22] Rosemary left the ship at Port Said after a month at sea, and *Pyrrhus* arrived at London's Victoria Dock on 26 September. There Lowry signed off, though not before the crew played the traditional trick of stuffing his case with dirty washing. The press was waiting to pounce, soliciting his verdict on life at sea. Four days later the *Daily Mail* carried a brief paragraph, but the Liverpool *Echo* gave it more prominence as befitted a story with local interest:

> *Seeing the world with a ukulele*
>
> Armed only with a ukulele, a schoolboy-composer sailed away from Liverpool in a tramp steamer last May to search for inspiration and to gather experience. He was Malcolm Lowry, the eighteen-year-old son of a Liverpool cotton broker. He was paid off yesterday, and today he described some of his experiences to the *Echo* . . .
>
> He told the *Echo* he wasn't anxious to go to sea again. At least not as a deckhand, for a deckhand was 'a domestic servant on a treadmill in Hades'. Nevertheless, he had enjoyed the trip, and he had found the rest of the crew a fine lot of fellows to work with – or, more correctly, to work for . . . 'Yet I am extremely glad I took the trip. I went for "atmosphere", and I got it. I have seen the world, and been paid for doing it.'[23]

Like Hugh in *Under the Volcano*, on his return from sea he rushed straight to Soho's New Compton Street to check on the sales of his sheet-music. Hugh, and probably Lowry, found thousands of copies awaiting collection but no attempt being made to distribute them. The feeling of having been had by the publisher must have been acute. As a result Hugh/Lowry briefly became fiercely anti-Semitic (the publisher was Jewish). In nearby Greek Street he discovered the Astoria, a sleazy hotel favoured by itinerant boxers and wrestlers which became for him a favourite London lodging place.

Now it was time to return home, full of strange stories and the raw material from which to start carving his sea novel. The first version Russell recalled as being just a plain unvarnished tale of the trip, and Tessa no doubt provided an adoring audience when he read passages to her in the deep voice she so loved. 'Do write and tell me what is happening to your novel won't you,' she wrote. 'I'm no end excited about it. The adventures of Hylyatt (don't know how to spell it) with

Hyliatt the 2nd!'[24] The name 'Eugene Dana Hilliot' was derived from Eugene O'Neill, Henry Dana, and T. S. Eliot. Early in the book the name is misspelt D. Heliot,[25] adding D. H. Lawrence to the combination. The doppelgänger Lowry began creating at sea was the focus of multiple literary identities. Hilliot's fear of venereal disease, and his psychological experience of the voyage, were no doubt essentially Lowry's own, but retrospectively his development would be viewed through a kaleidoscope of literary influences and allusions.

His transformation, however, was not just literary; in reality he had become more disillusioned and cynical. However, the first change Russell noticed was physical. Months of pulley-hauling and rust-chipping had given him massive shoulders and a deep barrel chest, emphasizing his rather short arms and lending a slightly comic air to the rolling nautical gait he slowly began to adopt. Having acquired this new tough-guy image, he decided to keep himself in shape. Stuart had brought a set of weights back from Dallas, and working out with them became a favourite recreation, along with drinking and brawling. He could no longer fit in at Inglewood with Evelyn's social snobbery and Arthur's humourless authoritarianism. Being a public schoolboy on the lower decks had brought only pain and humiliation, so if his class cut him off from one half of humanity, as a would-be novelist he had to abandon it. 'My sense of being déclassé has remained with me ever since,' he wrote some fifteen years later. 'I've never shaken off the point of view.'[26]

This new attitude was soon noticed by Russell. When invited to lunch at the Cotton Exchange he turned up in a sailor's navy-blue sweater with 'Holt Line' emblazoned across the chest. He began haunting the dockside pubs in Birkenhead, returning home drunk and obstreperous. According to Russell, 'Father was becoming frightened of going to his office because he didn't know when the telephone was going to ring to say Malcolm's just kicked Mother in the teeth.'[27] What Tessa thought of her 'reborn' lover is unknown. His attitude to women had changed. He had learned to speak of them in the cynical language of the fo'c'sle as whores, and soon this primitive misogyny would be rendered intellectually respectable by a man who would reshape his life even more radically than the rough diamonds on *Pyrrhus*.

His promise to his father to study for Cambridge entrance now had to be honoured, and it was arranged for him to be tutored by the old Leys master, E. E. Kellett, then living in Woodville Road, Blackheath. With his love of the theatre and cinema, and his liking for Soho, the prospect of living in London cannot have been too painful. Before going there in November, he visited The Leys to see Balgarnie and offer a poem, 'The Glory of the Sea', to the *Fortnightly*. It carried the dateline 'Yellow Sea, Aug. 1927'.

The tramp sailed grimly on her track;
A sickly haze shut out the sky;
The air was green, the sun was black;
The sea was calm like molten lead.
An engineer came staggering by:
'Another Chink gone west!' he said . . .

The owners lolled in office state;
The typist took her files away.
'Good business, Ephraim! How I hate
These rainy summers here, I guess!'
'My wife and I at Biarritz stay . . .
A coffee? Thanks, you've said it. Yes.'[28]

It suggests a more liberal attitude, towards the Chinese at least, and a stirring social conscience, but hints too at that fleeting anti-semitism. Whether he met 'Mr W. H. Barrelorgani' or not is unclear, but he did visit West House. In a sailor's windcheater, roaring drunk, playing his uke and singing at the top of his voice, he burst in on Ronnie Hill, who decided there and then that their songwriting collaboration was over. 'I was terrified. He'd moved into a man's world, and I was still a schoolboy.'[29] The thought of their being together at Christ's now horrified him.

Blackheath was certainly better for him than Caldy, but now, a few weeks after 'roughing it' with drunken sailors around the brothels of Yokohama he found himself 'back at school' studying with Kellett at his home in a genteel London suburb. Kellett was a pious and erudite old schoolmaster who looked back on the nineteenth-century public school with nostalgia. In agreeing to teach Lowry he was doing a favour, since he did not normally take private pupils. However, as The Leys' masters were poorly paid in those days, the five guineas a week Arthur was willing to pay cannot have been unwelcome. Kellett was a classicist, editor of the *Book of Cambridge Verse* and the author of books on Wordsworth, De Quincey, the Greek myths, and Icelandic sagas. He had a deep appreciation of Chaucer, though did not think too highly of Conrad.[30] So, however stuffy Lowry might have found life with an old schoolmaster with a reputation for firmness, he must have found 25 Woodville Road, with its bookish atmosphere, more congenial than Inglewood.

There were other compensations in Blackheath. London was there to explore in his free time, and there was a young daughter of the house towards whom he could turn his wistful attentions. Joan Kellett was fourteen when Lowry arrived as a paying guest, a small dark-haired girl then attending Hayes Court School near Farnborough, a short train ride away. Perhaps he hoped to attract her attention as a balladeer. If so he was disappointed, because, as she later told her husband, he 'drove the house mad' with his ukulele-playing. But he must have been lonely being so far away from Tessa, and it was a great chore to be swotting Cicero and Euripides, when he might have been exploring the taverns of Soho and writing his novel. But now he was faced with a three-part Cambridge entrance examination (the Previous Examination or 'Little Go'): Classical and Modern languages, English and History, and a compulsory paper in Maths and Science. Although he applied himself under Kellett's tutelage, at his first attempt, in December, he passed only the languages paper.

Back home in December something of great moment happened which changed the whole course of his life, for better and for worse. Perhaps because of Malcolm's recent sea-trip, Russell was avidly consuming nautical novels. A title which caught his eye at the public library was Conrad Aiken's *Blue Voyage*. He was reading it one day as he and Malcolm lay on their beds at Inglewood. Reaching a passage which read 'He saw gross Ronyans of the air, hairlipped and goitred, raped in flight By hairless pimps, umbrella-winged,'[31] he threw it across to Malcolm in disgust. 'Here,' he said, 'this is more in your line.' Malcolm picked it up and his fate was sealed. Here was an author who seemed able to articulate the inner anguish and inspired suffering which he felt gave his *Pyrrhus* experience its unique significance. And the book, apparently, was dedicated to him – 'To C.M.L.' Obviously it was a sign. Lowry wrote later of Aiken that 'his work first slammed down on my raw psyche like . . . lightning.'[32] Always curious about the lives of authors he admired, he found that Aiken was comparatively unknown in England, and so decided that he and *Blue Voyage* were his own discovery. This sense of possession was reinforced by his later discovering that not only had the book been panned in England, but written off as a poor imitation of James Joyce.[33] It was indeed its Joycean and Freudian pedigree which made it so innovative – rich in literary allusion, linguistically inventive and psychologically insightful; it was also racy, dark, self-flagellatory, and prurient. For Lowry, it was always a mystery how the immature mind of a boy of eighteen,

> could be drawn as by an irresistible teleological force toward an aspect of the mind or psyche of another much older, totally different in experience and nationality and outlook, and moreover, in *Blue Voyage* at least, with a philosophy and psychological *drang*. . . that he, the boy, did not understand, and had he understood, would have found thoroughly inimical – for sheer lack of sunlight and air and mountains if not blue water.[34]

What he saw in *Blue Voyage* was beyond his rational power to grasp. He not only read and reread it, and learned whole passages off by heart, but identified totally with its writer-hero. William Demerest, sailing from New York to Liverpool, is torn between lust for the available, sensuous Faubian and the lofty, unobtainable Cynthia. The action, in so far as there is any, switches from the flow of unremarkable external events on the ship to the anguished stream of consciousness of Demerest, between reality and the illusion of reality, the voyage slowly becoming a symbolic voyage of self-discovery. At times he feels 'as if driven by a secret feeling of being caged'[35] and regards his fellow passengers with amusement, when he is not tortured by savagely cynical self-reflection. '*Know thyself!*' he reflects, 'was the best joke ever perpetrated.' And what was he? 'A hurricane of maggots which answered to the name of Demerest.'[36] Beyond that is the self-sacrificial poet who sees himself as the lightning-rod, the man of suffering whose suffering is the world's suffering.

> I shall go mad someday. Yes. Etna will open, flaming and foisting, and I will be engulfed in my own volcano. I can hear it, on still days, boiling and muttering . . . I will weep. I will do nothing but weep. That is what I have always wanted to do – to weep . . . I will permit myself to be crucified. MY SELF. I will destroy my individuality. Like the destruction of the atom, this will carry in its train the explosion of all other selves. I will show them the way . . . I will show mankind the path by which they may return to God.[37]

Lowry's imagination was gripped. He was being offered an authorial persona with a lofty and noble purpose expressed through such 'phenomenal and magical use of language'. There were, moreover, a series of references which gave him the feeling that the book was directed specifically at HIM – the ship's heading directly for Liverpool, the self-loathing of Demerest, his feeling caged, a tormented childhood, his love of an unattainable one, a poker game such as he had recorded on *Pyrrhus*, references to clairvoyance and numerology, to the Duke of Clarence, to golf, to syphilophobia, to Melville and O'Neill, to ukuleles, and, oddly enough, to *Tilly of Bloomsbury*. Here, surely, was his literary alter ego, himself-to-be, communicating to him from some obscure time to come. It was, he wrote, 'a book of satanic and marvellous genius'.[38] 'I've never read a book that appealed to so many senses at once as that, including some not on the roster.'[39] Here, in fact, was a style befitting Lowry's own complex mind; a voice, or orchestration of voices, much as Lowry had begun to conjure from within himself in writing to Carol Brown. But here the technique had been raised to the level of high art. The problem for Lowry was that it was his own voice that he was hearing, yet is was not his own voice.

In *Blue Voyage* he also found the title for his embryonic book, in Aiken's reference to the ocean as 'the ultramarine abyss'.[40] The sea as a mighty abyss over which the vulnerable sailor hangs during his uncertain voyaging became an idea around which Lowry was later to organize his whole creative *œuvre*. According to Russell, Malcolm wanted to call his book *Ultramarine Blues*, but he persuaded him to call it simply *Ultramarine*.[41]

At first Lowry was unaware that Aiken was primarily a poet. In fact he was a contemporary of Eliot's at Harvard between 1907 and 1912, and had started visiting England in 1908, drawn there like Eliot by its poetic heritage. Unlike Eliot, however, he had been more attracted to English Georgian poetry than to French symbolism, and saw his prime role as extending American consciousness rather than adapting to an English one. To this end he became engrossed in psychology. 'I swallowed Freud early,' he wrote, 'and then pursued him in every direction.'[42] His attempts to produce a poetry corresponding to music met with a mixed critical response, and at times he became bitter and disillusioned with the hostility of some American contemporaries. After 1919 England became a welcome refuge for hard drinkers like Aiken in flight from Prohibition, and he took up residence at Jeake's House in Rye. But in 1927 he was in America teaching at Harvard and becoming embroiled in a messy divorce. When Lowry discovered his poetry he began consuming and memorizing it voraciously.

Another 'discovery' passed on by Russell was a passage from Chaucer's *Maunciple's Tale*, which he immediately adopted as a personal icon, and as an epigraph in *Ultramarine*.

> Take any brid and put it in a cage
> And do al thyn entente and thy corage
> To fostre it tenderly with mete and drinke
> Of alle deyntees that thou canst bethinke
> And keep it al-so clenly as thou may
> And be his cage of gold never so gay
> Yet hath this brid by twenty thousand fold
> Lever in a forest that is rude and cold
> Gon ete wormes and swich wrecchedness.[43]

It was yet another message apparently aimed directly at him. His commitment to authorship became Aiken's commitment – no longer simply to storytelling but to being a serious artist set apart, one chosen to inherit a sacred mantle. It was a step of enormous significance, and meant that *Ultramarine* would become a different novel from the one originally envisaged. He discussed his new-found vocation with Stuart, but faced with such depth of ambition Stuart admitted his limitations.

> I told Malcolm that if he wanted to be a creative artist there was a moment when he must be on his own – he would gain his own impressions. We were both getting older. As I grew older I would become old fashioned and he belonged to a new era. I was very sensitive myself about the new era because I'd seen most of my friends killed and I'd realized the tragedy of life ahead, and I believed that another war was coming. Malcolm did too.[44]

The visionary who foresaw new wars was already beginning to emerge, but he would have to look beyond Stuart for the guidance he needed, a lonely quest. 'My most intellectual moments,' he wrote shortly afterwards, 'such as they are [are] spent entirely alone.'[45]

The remaining Cambridge entrance papers now had to be worked for, first English and History, which he passed in March – an irksome distraction no doubt from the serious business of writing, and reading the poems of Conrad Aiken, which he did, he said later, on Hayes Common waiting to meet Joan Kellett at her school. By one of those strange coincidences which riveted Lowry, he discovered some eighteen months later that another pupil at the school was Aiken's own daughter, Jane.

The effect of 'discovering' Aiken is seen in 'The Cook in the Galley', a poem published in *The Leys Fortnightly* in May which showed that he had already acquired Aiken's ear, and some of his words too, for the music of the ocean. The following month, another poem, 'Number 8 Fireman', resonating with Aikenesque imagery, even included some familiar phrases from *Blue Voyage*:

> Jesus in heaven
> Counts sands on the seashore;
> The gulls that wheel, *Klio*,
> And mew round the funnel;
> The sharks and the dolphins;
> Red sponges, fiddler crabs,
> Snouted squids umbrella-winged . . .[46]

He passed the remaining Maths and Science part of the Cambridge entrance exam in June, but remained in Blackheath, presumably preparing for the entrance exams for Christ's, held in December. It was, however, a hopeless prospect. The Cambridge 'Little Go' was considered simple compared with Oxford's Responsions and not to pass at one sitting was thought a poor achievement. However, failing to get into a prestigious college like Christ's meant having to shop around, and prepare for more exams.

In September he was sent to Germany for eight weeks to study the language, supporting the idea that Arthur had a diplomatic career in mind for him. He went to Weber's English College in Bonn, which catered mostly for English public schoolboys. His memory of Bonn was of one long binge. He found the College head hostile and 'truly frightening' and later got his own back at him in characteristic fashion. 'I had to give his name at least if not his attributes to one of my villains in the Volcano, and revenge myself that way.'[47] Lowry's teacher, Karl-heinz Schmidhuis, had little to say for his unreliable, drunken student, who on one occasion was arrested in the street after celebrating victory in a hockey match in which he had played, and was fined even after buying the policeman drinks at the Hotel Kaiserhof.[48]

It appears he spent most of his time in bars, at hockey matches, or at cinemas hungrily consuming silent German Expressionist films later to supply his work with a powerful and haunting cinematic vision – *The Cabinet of Dr Caligari*, *The Hands of Orlac*, *Sonnenaufgang*. He said that the influences that had formed *Under the Volcano* were 'in a profound degree and largely German'[49] especially *Sonnenaufgang*, the seventy minutes of which had influenced him almost as much as any book, though he only saw it once. In October he went with a group to the

Schauspielhaus in Köln to see the first German production of O'Neill's *The Great God Brown* – 'the most imaginative wonderful production I have ever seen of O'Neill,' – and claimed to have delighted Schmidhuis by observing that O'Neill could not possibly have written it without the influence of Georg Kaiser, and then impressed him with his knowledge of Wederkind.[50]

It was at Weber's English College that he met a young Harrovian, Paul Fitte, who, like himself had been coached for Cambridge entrance privately. Fitte was the only son of a wealthy London company director. Charles Fitte was French, his wife English. The family fortune was in shoe polish, and one of the companies he controlled was Cherry Blossom. His eighteen-year-old son was tall, very slim, very blond, and very charming, and had been expelled from Harrow three years before under mysterious circumstances. As young as fifteen, Fitte had begun visiting illegal West End drinking clubs, and lying to his parents about the dates of school terms so he could spend nights alone in town. At Harrow he became bisexual, and came to enjoy the company of fast men as well as fast women, and at Mrs Meyrick's infamous Thirty-Three Club (at 33 Gerrard Street) he acquired a flighty girlfriend, apparently the mysterious 'Phonia' who was to feature in the dramatic events some ten months later. Despite his taste for the shady life and bizarre sex, those who knew him thought Fitte a most attractive, likeable and lively companion.[51] Meeting Fitte was to prove as fateful for Lowry as his introduction to Aiken. The latter would both inspire his genius and undermine his sanity, the former would sear his conscience in a way that would haunt him to the grave.

Having no luck finding a Cambridge college willing to take him, in February, 1929, he wrote a momentous and seductive letter to Aiken, beginning, 'I have lived only nineteen years and all of them more or less badly.'[52] Sitting in Lyons Corner House on the Strand reading *The House of Dust*, he wrote, he had become suddenly and beautifully alive, struck by the lines:

> I lay in the warm sweet grass on a blue May morning,
> My chin in a dandelion, my hands in clover,
> And drowsed there like a bee . . . blue days behind me
> Stretched like a chain of deep blue pools of magic,
> Enchanted, silent, timeless . . . .days before me
> Murmured of blue-sea mornings, noons of gold,
> Green evenings streaked with lilac . . . [53]

As he read on, he wrote, faces around him blurred, his tea remained untouched, his pipe went out, he walked down Villiers Street to the Embankment. With the sunlight roaring like the sea overhead and the ebb and flow of the wavering crowds, and the cry of the rag-and-bone man echoing in the streets, it seemed to him that fate was calling him to write to his new-found hero. He realized how presumptuous it was of him to write, he said; his letter might not interest, might even infuriate him. He signed off with a line from *Blue Voyage*, 'te-thrum te-thrum; te-thrum te-thrum; Malcolm Lowry.'[54]

Unknown to him, his hero was in Boston, where he had become infatuated with a young reporter, Clarissa 'Jerry' Lorenz (the CML to whom *Blue Voyage* was dedicated), and was now in the process of divorcing his wife. In September 1927, shortly after its publication, *Blue Voyage* had been banned in Boston, and in March 1928 he was fired from Harvard for 'moral turpitude' after students petitioned the President claiming that the author of such a book was morally unsuitable to teach the young. Lowry's letter was forwarded, but in the meantime he continued searching for a place at Cambridge.

Despite his rejection by such colleges as Christ's, Lowry, with a father willing to pay, was able to offer himself to poorer colleges with lower entrance standards. One such college was St Catharine's which selected students as late as March. Fortunately he had the support of teachers at The Leys. No doubt Balgarnie put in a good word for Camel, certainly Mr Gillard pulled strings,[55] and T. R. Henn, briefly a Leys master who had taught Russell, happened now to teach English at St Catharine's. He secured the offer of a place at the college for the following autumn.

Back in Blackheath on 11 March, the long-awaited reply from Aiken arrived. Greatly excited at hearing from a 'real' writer, he replied instantly, suggesting Aiken take him on as a tutee at five or, he would recommend, six guineas a week, although the last thing he would want was to be lumbered with any tutorial responsibility. In October he was going to Cambridge for three or four years to get an English tripos, but till then he was freelance 'and a perpetual source of anxiety to a bewildered parent.' He would make a perfect house guest, not getting in the way, and his appetite was satisfied entirely by cheese. 'All I want is to know why I catch my breath in a sort of agony when I read;

> The lazy sea-waves crumble along the beach
> With a whirring sound like wind in bells,
> He lies outstretched on the yellow wind-worn sands

Reaching his lazy hands
Among the golden grains and sea-white shells.'[56]

At home, he said, little was read other than the *British Weekly* and there were few books besides *Religion and Religions* by James Hope Moulton, though hidden in the furthest depths of the house might be found Donne and Chatterton, *The Smell of Lebanon*, Crabbe's *Inebriety* and, of course, *Blue Voyage*. 'When they see me writing anything serious they don't exactly discourage me but tell me that it should be subordinate to my real work. What my real work is, heaven only knows . . .'[57]

He enclosed some poems and an extract from *Ultramarine*, adding that the only thing that could be said in favour of his work and himself were that they were young and in need of much polishing. He pleaded for frank criticism. Did Aiken think that he had a style of his own or did he seem unconsciously to be imitating some other writer? 'I have been told by some that I have a tendency to rely on Whitman.' Artfully, the poems showed that if there was an unconscious influence, it was Aiken. On 18 March he returned to Inglewood and his 'bewildered' parent.

Having lost his Harvard job, and with an expensive divorce in prospect, Aiken found Lowry's offer irresistible. On 8 April he wrote to his children in England,

> A young man in Cheshire, who wants to be a poet, has asked whether he can come and live with me in Jeake's House, paying me six guineas a week for the privilage! . . . If he invites me to Cheshire, you may see the aged cahoun this summer: otherwise, I shall be too poor. He seems like a *very* nice young man.[58]

The idea of an unknown American at Inglewood would have appalled Evelyn, so Malcolm must have found it easy enough to persuade Arthur that he should invite himself to Boston instead. On 25 June, Aiken told his son, John, 'My young English novelist . . . is on his way here now from Liverpool.'[59]

He could have worked his passage, now having his seaman's ticket – No. R32237. But, even if Arthur had not objected – the publicity surrounding the last trip had been deeply embarrassing to him – he had no wish to repeat the miserable experience on *Pyrrhus*. In the event, as a passenger, complete with notebook and ukulele, he boarded the SS *Dovillian*, a Leyland Line freighter, outward bound from Liverpool to Trinidad, on 12 June. On the ship's list he was entered as 'student'; the only other passenger was a 54-year-old high-school principal bound for Port of Spain. By travelling via the West Indies, Lowry turned his trip into a wider literary pilgrimage taking him through seas where Ahab, Sard Harker, and O'Neill's tough stokers had preceded him. For six weeks before shipping north to Boston, he hopped from one island to another. After Trinidad he visited Montserrat, where he claimed to have 'altered geography books by climbing Chance's Mountain . . . in company of two Roman Catholics: Lindsey, a Negro, and Gomez, a Portuguese.'[60] In Barbados, birthplace of W. J. Locke, whose books so fascinated him at school, he played, he said, in a hot band in a brothel and spent the last of his money on a mulatto girl in Antigua.[61]

As a sign of the importance he attached to meeting Aiken, he timed his arrival in Cambridge, Massachusetts, for 28 July, his twentieth birthday. No doubt he considered this meeting a most significant one, one which would launch him into the literary firmament. As it happened, he turned up at Aiken's apartment at 8 Plympton Street, just below Grolier's Bookshop close to Harvard Yard, in the middle of a thunderstorm.[62] 'He arrived,' said Aiken, 'with a battered suitcase in one hand – a case containing the notebook in which he had started writing *Ultramarine*, and clutching a ukulele in the other.'[63] To Clarissa he described him as grimy and dilapidated, wearing dirty tennis shoes and carrying a broken suitcase.[64] However, they soon discovered a shared Rabelaisian humour. Aiken enjoyed filthy limericks and had helped Eliot compose the mildly obscene 'King Bolo' jingles. He was a compulsive womanizer who, even when married, patronized prostitutes. Above all, he shared Lowry's predilection for alcohol, though, with Prohibition at its height, he was reduced to drinking bathtub gin. They found they spoke the same language and to Aiken's astonishment Lowry knew *Blue Voyage* better than he did and could quote long passages by heart. Aiken suggested, ironically, that he knew the book so well he must have written it in another life, an idea which Lowry took most seriously. This degree of identification and hero-worship must have massaged Aiken's ego considerably and helped cement a close relationship which was to last almost until Lowry's death twenty-seven years later. To Aiken he was 'engaging and volatile and unpredictable', and of all the writers he knew, including Eliot, 'none among them . . . had been so visibly or happily alight with genius.'[65] It being Lowry's birthday, and Clarissa being away, there was every excuse for genius to enjoy itself, to throw a party and to submerge all sorrows in the alcoholic bathtub.

It was stunning for the young Englishman to find someone old enough to be his father with whom he could talk so explicitly about sex and matters scatological, and with whom he could happily drink himself unconscious. Aiken wrote to a friend shortly afterwards: 'Lowry is a nice chap, but incredibly dirty and sloppy and helpless. Writes exceedingly well, and undoubtedly should do something. Very companionable, too . . . though . . . a trifle vague.'[66] Clarissa, however, feared the worst. Conrad, she thought, needed a vacation not drunken orgies with a wild irresponsible young dipsomaniac.[67] Her fears were justified. On 1 August, four days before Aiken's fortieth birthday and four after Lowry's twentieth (and appropriately on Melville's 110th), a party was thrown at 8 Plympton Street. A week later, from his sick-bed, nursing a fractured skull, Aiken told what had happened:

> Last Thursday there was a wildish party, in celebration of young Lowry's arrival: Rob [Aiken's brother] and L[owry] and I. A wrestling match between L. and me, at one in the morning, for possession of the porcelain lid on a w.c. tank, (!) ended with me in possession, but unconscious on my hearth, having slipped, fallen, cracked my head on hearth-and-shattered-porcelain simultaneous-like; I bled for 48 hours. I've got a Christopher cross of some size on my brow, am dizzy as a fool, my nose has also changed its shape, and in general things are not too good. I shall have a scar, I fear, and am waiting for enough strength and stability to go and have an X-ray . . . There is an off chance that I have a piece of porcelain in my grey matter.[68]

It was, said Aiken later, 'the beginning of a beautiful friendship.'[69] To remind him of that evening, he carried a purple Y-shaped scar on his forehead for the rest of his life. Clarissa was less appreciative of the wild young drunkard who had invaded their lives so dramatically. Yet he did cut a romantic if dishevelled figure, and she happily agreed to photograph him outside the Harvard Bookstore at the top of Plympton Street on a spot where many famous authors had been snapped. The resulting picture shows him fresh-faced, innocently wide-eyed and cheerful.

With Aiken bedridden, Lowry became his rather ineffectual nursemaid, fetching milk and sandwiches from Grolier's while they worked together on *Ultramarine*. He also became Aiken's committed disciple, absorbing his ideas, not just about writing and poetry, but also about life. In the process he took on board much of his psychological baggage, an attempted metamorphosis which was to prove disastrous. It not only put an old head on young shoulders but also the disturbed mind of a complex man whose view of life, and especially women, was both twisted and malevolent.

Aiken and his friend George Wilbur had 'discovered' Freud together as Harvard undergraduates in 1909, and after reading *The Interpretation of Dreams*, recorded their dreams and practised psychoanalysis on one another. Aiken believed that it was a significant tool for the poet and writer, a means of probing character. He also used it for discomposing people he wished to manipulate. One friend recalled him leaning towards people saying '*I* know what's wrong with *you*!' followed by the pronouncement that they were neurotic or schizophrenic or sexually repressed.[70] He seemed to derive a perverse pleasure from this, as did Demerest in *Blue Voyage*, writing to a woman who has shunned him: 'If any smallest opportunity ever occurs, I will revenge myself upon you, "after no common action," with the deftest psychological cruelty: for I am a master of that art, I am by nature cruel.'[71] Lowry fell a ready prey to the older man's predatory impulse, an all too willing and suggestible candidate for psychological annexation.[72] Aiken suggested that he himself was a mere transmitter of ideas which would pass through the creative stream to Lowry, but soon began to discuss Lowry's psychological state, questioning his sanity. He pronounced him 'schizophrenic' and indicated that it was only a matter of time before he went mad, unless, Hamlet-like, he was feigning madness.[73]

It could have been Lowry's casual remark that *Blue Voyage* was good 'as far as it went' which prompted Aiken's diabolical plan to make him part of an even deeper exploration of himself than his novel had been.[74] According to his confessional autobiography, *Ushant*, he decided to experiment with Lowry, to make him into an extension of his own consciousness.[75] It would be putting his psychological powers to their ultimate test. The significance of this probably escaped Lowry at the time, but he had now met his Dark Angel. Meeting Aiken was deeply inspirational and he was immensely flattered by his encouragement and pronouncements on his potential genius. His portrayal of Abraham Taskerson in *Under the Volcano* shows how he recognized the importance of 'borrowing' Aiken's genius. What he could not have known was that in absorbing the poet's creative consciousness he would also absorb a damaged psychology obsessed with the dark, corrupt, feculent world of the unconscious which he felt himself destined to explore.

At the age of nine Aiken had all but witnessed the violent deaths of his parents. In the next bedroom, his father shot his mother and then himself in a fit of unbalanced jealous rage and the boy found the bleeding corpses. He blamed his mother for the tragedy, came to see all women as faithless whores, and spent the rest of his life revenging himself by callously degrading as many women as he could.[76] From his early days in London he patronized prostitutes and took every opportunity to seduce vulnerable women. *Blue Voyage* was a merciless piece of self-analysis, as he himself acknowledged. Demerest, Aiken's alter ego, is obsessed by lecherous feelings about every other woman he meets and his deepest sufferings centre on one who is socially out of his reach. In trying to take over Aiken's darkly inspired and introverted poetic consciousness, Lowry introjected much of his disturbed and cynical outlook. He was a victim of Aiken's experimentation, though not exactly an unwilling one.

One thing they had in common was a sense of alienation from their roots. Aiken's parents were dead, Lowry's he might have wished so. As Aiken taught,

> To be able to *separate* oneself from one's background, one's environment – wasn't this the most thrilling discovery of which consciousness was capable? and no doubt for the very reason that it is a discovery of one's limits, it is therefore by implication the first and sharpest taste of death.[77]

This must have been music to Lowry's ears, but the dark path Aiken pointed him towards led into the depths of human despair and cynicism. After all, in Aiken's view, misery was the essential state of mind for the flourishing of creative genius. But this was dangerous mental territory with which Lowry's fragile psyche would find it increasingly difficult to cope, and it took a long time for him to realize just how inimical the relationship was. When they met, Aiken was in fact at his most creative and unstable. Always fearful of having inherited his father's madness, he treated writing as a form of therapy, and regarded *Blue Voyage* as a courageous and ruthless exposé of his deepest fears, most diabolical fantasies and darkest deeds. His marital breakup had brought his deep sense of instability to the surface, and only his writing enabled him to hold on to a fragile sanity.

Henry Murray, a psychiatrist friend of Aiken's, was writing a Freudian biography of Melville, and this, added to Aiken's enthusiasm for *Pierre*, rekindled Lowry's interest in the author. But it was Melville's life rather than his work with which he identified, though he felt a strong attachment to works like *Billy Budd*, 'Bartleby the Scrivener' (who politely refuses orders saying, 'I would prefer not to') and *Pierre* (who disappoints his publisher by insisting 'I write what I please', whose parents had both died mad and whose childhood was spent partly in a madhouse). Melville's influence is immediately evident in the opening sequence of *Ultramarine*, where the dialogue of sailors signing on at the shipping office mirrors a similar sequence in *The Confidence Man*. He learned too about stylistic influences on Melville, especially Sir Thomas Browne, a copy of whose works he brought back to England. Melville was to be an abiding influence on Lowry, with whom, as with Aiken, he claimed 'an hysterical identification'.

What socialist tendency there was in Lowry would have received a setback from Aiken, a deep-dyed reactionary, but there were other influences at work on him besides Aiken. Despite his flattering obsession with *Blue Voyage*, unknown to Aiken he had acquired an English edition of the Norwegian Nordahl Grieg's novel *Skibet Gaar Videre* (*The Ship Sails On*), not published in England. If in Aiken Lowry had met his Dark Angel, in Grieg he stumbled across his Bright one.[78] Aiken's and Grieg's work were equally powerful influences. Less auspiciously, he found a story, 'What is Love?' by the editor and critic Burton Rascoe in an anthology, *The Second American Caravan: A Yearbook of American Literature*, which was to have a devastating effect on Lowry's entire writing career.

He learned a great deal very quickly from Aiken – about the Elizabethans, Swinburne, Henry James, Dante, Faust, Hart Crane, Emily Dickinson, and James Thomson, whose 'City of Dreadful Night' supplied him with his vision of the lunatic city, developed later in *Lunar Caustic* and in the urban deathscapes he came to see as so threatening to Nature. If he had not already discovered Thomas Mann (that year's Nobel Prize winner), he did so in America, where *Death in Venice* and *Tonio Kröger* had just appeared for the first time in English. He must have read the unexpurgated *Lady Chatterley's Lover* which Aiken was reading, 'eyes popping at the quaint four-syllabled words'[79] four days before his arrival, and latched on to Aiken's fascination with John Marston, especially *The Malcontent*. In America he also acquired a strong taste for Hemingway and Fitzgerald, and it may have been Aiken's close acquaintance with Eliot which led him to memorize long passages of 'The Love Song of J. Alfred Prufrock' and *The Waste Land*.

Another Aiken obsession Lowry came to share was William Blackstone, the seventeenth-century Cambridge Puritan who settled near Boston and went to live among the Indians, whose story Aiken had unearthed in 1925. It gave him yet another figure with whom to identify, as Aiken later recognized, 'for wasn't he destined . . . to be another rolling Blackstone, and from Cambridge, Eng., too? – moving to his own southwest and northwest mystical frontiers his own barrancas and estuaries of good and evil?'[80] At some stage, Aiken announced his plan to 'reinvent' Lowry, but Lowry replied that he would absorb Aiken even to the point of annihilation. This complex psychological game which Aiken initiated at Plympton Street was to have strange and bitter results just eight years later in Mexico.

Stylistically, Lowry learned a great deal from Aiken, who had commented years earlier on a play he was writing,

> I am trying to recapture the Elizabethan effect of the counterpoint (analogous also to the present movie technique) by rapid and frequent change of scene, always with the same or roughly the same setting. A few expressionist tricks thrown in also. In prose, but I seriously contemplate a little concealed or disguised poetry . . . it remains to be seen.[81]

Such a mixture of 'Elizabethan effect' and Expressionism, film, prose, and poetry, were taken up by Lowry, as embracing the modern without abandoning the classic. He had always considered Aiken, he wrote, a true descendant of the great Elizabethans, possessed of 'the supreme gift of dramatic and poetic language, a genius of the highest and most original order . . .'[82] Like them he was open to influences from the great dead poets, and from him Lowry learned to feel part of that creative brotherhood linking the dead to the living. Like them he, too, was ready to borrow ideas and phrases and even whole passages from the writers he admired. Consequently *Ultramarine* began gradually to acquire an Aikenesque flavour in moving towards what the poet called 'the first-person singular habit', but also moving towards what Lowry had told Carol Brown was the least socially harmful of thefts – plagiarism. And while Aiken scolded him about it he also tolerated this tendency for a long time.

When he was sufficiently recuperated, he took his pupil down to his house in South Yarmouth on Cape Cod – another pilgrimage for Lowry, for nearby was Provincetown at whose Playhouse O'Neill's plays had first been produced. Engrossed though he was in *Ultramarine*, and imbibing all he could from Aiken, he still had time to fall in love with a young Boston art student, Dolly Lewis, daughter of a friend of

Aiken's, no doubt egged on by the prurient poet. They went for walks along the beach, visited her studio, and talked about *Ultramarine* and art. He was not only thrilled to be in the land which he had previously known only through films, but now had met an American girl touched by that same magic. But Dolly found him too persistent and rather unappealing. Whenever he came looking for her she had a friend secretly warn her and she would hide in a barn.

In mid-August, after bad luck on the Stock Exchange, Aiken sold his South Yarmouth house, an occasion for another wild party at which Lowry and Aiken and Dolly ended up drinking bootleg gin from a bucket on the floor at midnight. Lowry stayed over afterwards at Dolly's, but failed, it seems, to make a favourable impression on her mother.

His departure was imminent, dictated by the need to be back in England for the start of the university term in October, and also by his wish to return on the SS *Cedric*, the ship on which Aiken had written *Blue Voyage*. He left New York for Liverpool on the *Cedric* on 16 September, and was soon writing to Dolly one of those involved letters of exaggerated passion of the kind he had once written to Carol Brown. However, now he had learned a few things from Aiken, and the unrequited lover was more mercilessly self-mocking. Also he had the added inspiration of a comfortable seat in a ship's lounge, and an attentive drinks waiter to keep his creativity well lubricated.

'Dear Mrs Goya,' it began, which, though sounding flattering (an allusion to her painting perhaps), had a cruel irony to it. In a dark visionary passage in *Blue Voyage*, a syphilitic family walks London's Portobello Road, and are banteringly referred to as Goya, meaning, Goya-like. Lowry's fear of women as both objects of lust and sources of disease can only have been intensified by his meeting Aiken, and he did later refer to him, in a story about a syphilitic sailor, called 'Goya the Obscure',[83] as subtly communicating to him his 'terrible mood'. The letter, however, began cheerfully enough. He ought to be happy, he said, having made 'violent and unintellectual whoopee' with four American architectural students bound for Rome, consumed 'Amazons of liquor' and kissed three pretty girls so far. 'But,' and this was a reiterated chorus, 'you do not love me'. While Aiken was sitting in America drinking bathtub gin, *he* was sitting in the exact smoking room on the very same ship on which Aiken wrote chapter 5 of *Blue Voyage*. But where was his heart? In Cape Cod, of course. What he did not say was that he was mimicking the style of a letter Aiken composed in

Blue Voyage to the unobtainable, aristocratic Cynthia, whose mother disapproved of Demerest/Aiken, as Dolly's mother did Lowry. And here, faced with the pure and unobtainable object of his affections, his obsessions with his physical inadequacies surfaced in an absurd hyperbolic protestation of love.

> I cannot kiss anybody else without wiping my mouth afterwards. There is only you, forever and forever you: in bars and out of bars, in fields and out of fields, in boats and out of boats . . . I would rather use your toothbrush than my own: I could wish, when with you in a boat, that you would be sick merely so that I could comfort you. Nor is there one ounce of criticism in this. I do not conceal in my heart the physical repulsion which, not admitted to oneself hardly, exists usually in the filthy male. I would love you the same if you had one ear, or one eye: if you were bald or dumb: if you had syphilis, I would be the same . . . You would have loved me after four hours chipping . . . Dirty, but strong: muscles bulging and the tallest man on the ship, with all the perpendicular inches god has given me, except the lamptrimmer. Christ how I would have kissed you then, till our lips were numb. You wouldn't? O and aye and aye and O: in excelsis Deo.[84]

Russell, with whom he had developed an equally hyperbolic form of humour for sending up their parents at Inglewood, would have been proud of him.

He was now engrossed in Grieg's *The Ship Sails On*. Although its hero, Benjamin Hall, lacks Demerest's intense introspective anguish, his suffering is directed outwards against a social evil the author is concerned to expose. The clarity and honesty of Grieg's prose appealed greatly to Lowry, as did the book's structure. Hall is no sophisticated lecher like Demerest, but an idealist. The story of his voyage as an ordinary seaman on the tramp steamer *Mignon* and the horror of the venereal disease among the crew was a *succès de scandale* in Norway when it appeared in 1924, and led to changes in the law to eliminate the squalid working conditions of Norwegian seamen. Lowry was struck, not only by similarities between Hall and himself, but also by the tragic theme, the fate of the sailors sealed up inside the ship, 'a Moloch that crushes the lives of men between its iron jaws, and then calmly turns its face to the solitudes as though nothing had happened'.[85] 'Everything perishes but the ship sails on, ever going forward . . . other lives will drive the ship forward to the rosy dawn and the sunset, and those of to-night will have gone under and vanished.'[86] And this is linked to a wider destiny: 'life perishes, millions of dead are buried every year, but our own home, the earth, is a star which goes forward on its silent, inevitable course.'[87]

On board this Moloch of Fate, Hall, the son of a shipbroker, in search of 'experience', is trying to remain true to Eva, the girl he has left behind, but is under pressure from the mocking crew to prove himself a man and join them in the dockside brothels. However, he sees the effects of syphilis on the others, and his desire to be true to Eva is reinforced by the fear of becoming himself infected. Finally he succumbs and, finding himself smitten by the 'vile disease', decides to commit suicide. Clutching the ship's sick and mangy dog, poised to throw himself overboard, as Hart Crane later did, he changes his mind and climbs back over the rail.

This book's effect on Lowry was as great as *Blue Voyage*. His identification with Benjamin Hall and his author, Grieg, were instant and lasting – 'this book about his experiences . . . were so like mine that they seemed to be about my experiences.' He felt his own book was futile by comparison. As he read it, almost every night for a year, he learned it by heart and it moved into his life. Some of its characters he came to love, Benjamin Hall in particular – 'not because he was like me . . . but because he represented to me the simplicity and goodness and frankness in the face of extreme trial, that I would have liked to have had'.[88] Certain of the book's images he adopted as his own – the ship as Moloch, the iron beast which consumes the lives of men yet travels to exotically beautiful places, the voyage as a journey of self-discovery, the stokehold as an image of hell, and the symbolic stray dog who just might follow one to perdition, which later shadowed him in Mexico and finally followed the Consul down the abyss in *Under the Volcano*. The simplicity, goodness and frankness evident in the book he assumed also to be qualities of the author, Grieg. *The Ship Sails On* offered him a straightforward structure for *Ultramarine*, even if it was Aiken's style which still bewitched him.

He arrived home with a mass of notes and ideas for revising his book, but torn between the frank, honest style of Grieg and the disturbed attachment to poetry of Aiken. However, having sat at the feet of 'genius' he was more than ever set apart from the prosaic folks at Inglewood, more than ever disdainful of their values, and ready to shock. He was pleased to inform Russell that his new-found mentor's mother was a whore and his father a murderer. Russell, by then a young man of business anxious to settle down and get married, was not amused. The direction he had taken as a result of reading Aiken was downwards and dark. As he wrote years later: 'I believe that Conrad's early work sent one even further down the drain than Eliot's, if possible. The trouble even with Eliot's kind of drain is that it reeks of sanctity, whereas Conrad's honestly and majestically stank. I see no reason why one should not be led down the drain: I believe it an important experience if the drain is fulsome enough.'[89]

CHAPTER VI

UP AT THE VARSITY
1929–1930

The road of excess leads to the palace of wisdom.

WILLIAM BLAKE, *Proverbs of Hell*

This is the first punishment, that by the verdict of his own heart no guilty man is acquitted.

JUVENAL

Lowry wrote that having left Cambridge once, returning there was like going back to school for three more miserable years, but feeling far too old to be a schoolboy.

> Cambridge was the sea reversed . . . the most appalling of nightmares, as if a grown man should suddenly wake up, like the ill-fated Mr Bultutide in *Vice Versa*, to be confronted not by the hazards of business, but by the geometry lesson he had failed to prepare thirty years before, and the torments of puberty.[1]

Aiken had no doubt warned him, however, not to alienate Arthur, especially if the Old Man could be coaxed into relieving him of the distracting necessity of earning a living. Indeed, Aiken himself, about to be all but wiped out in the Wall Street Crash of 24 October, would soon be faced with having to beg and borrow if not to steal to sustain himself as an independent writer. Given this advice, Lowry may have felt he had little choice but to turn up at Cambridge for the beginning of the Michaelmas term. And so he walked into the trap about which he later complained to his first wife. He had chosen to rebel, but made himself dependent upon the very people against whom he had rebelled. Now he had the great expectations of his parents to contend with. Evelyn especially was proud to have a son 'up at the Varsity', the first in the family. In his first week up she wrote to her 'darling boy' wishing him luck and saying how sure she was that he would do her proud. But if anything he arrived at St Catharine's in a dark and dangerous mood rather than one of excitement and high endeavour. The college matriculation photograph, taken on 4 November, shows him standing next to Paul Fitte. If Fitte looks bored, languid and detached, Lowry looks aggressive and morose; his head down, brooding, defensive, the man from the lower decks resenting having to mix with effete, genteel academics whose experience came mostly from books.[2]

St Catharine's College is just a few hundred yards from The Leys along the majestic Trumpington Street which meanders past Peterhouse and Pembroke. St Cats stands a little further along on the left opposite the ancient Corpus Christi and next to the magnificent King's. Beyond that stands Gonville and Caius, then Trinity and St John's. At 70 Trumpington Street, next to St Catharine's, Lowry and Fitte had neighbouring rooms, and Lowry attempted, reluctantly, to come to terms with a new routine in meeting his moral tutor, the Reverend A. J. Chaytor, and his supervisor, T. R. Henn, who advised him what lectures to attend and what books to buy. He did not, it seems, offer his sporting skills to the college, but in his second week turned out for the Cambridge Hockey Club, a town team. He and Fitte were invited to tea with F. M. Rushmore, Master of the college. It should, he thought, prove mildly interesting and the invitation was not without merit; indeed, not everyone was asked.[3] He bought recommended texts, and turned up for recommended lectures. He called, drunk and swaggering, on Ronnie Hill who did not encourage him to return, and made contact with his old literary rival Ralph Izzard, now at Queen's and heading for a journalistic career. There was also Pirandello's *Six Characters in Search of an Author* to be seen at the Festival Theatre.

His supervisor, Henn, along with Sir Arthur Quiller-Couch, George Rylands, Basil Willey, I. A. Richards and E. M. W. Tillyard, was one of the pioneers of the Cambridge English tripos. Henn was an Anglo-Irishman, the son of a judge, a distinguished scholar of Yeats and Ibsen, with a reputation among undergraduates enhanced by a war spent in the secret service. Lowry was not so readily impressed. Already he felt a degree of contempt for academics who, unlike his mentor Aiken, rejected by narrow-minded Harvard academics, were not themselves possessed of creative 'genius', and he came to sneer openly at 'the non-creative bully-boys and homosapient schoolmasters of English Literature.'[4] Having begun to absorb Harvard English circa 1909 by courtesy of Aiken, he was in no mood to be entranced by Cambridge

English circa 1929 by courtesy of anyone else. Henn was a man of rather exclusive literary passions who had no time at all for the likes of Joyce, Eliot and Pound,[5] and soon found himself temperamentally at odds with Lowry. He recalled him as 'a young violent person who, even at that stage, probably drank rather more than he should. He seemed to me very much like Eugene O'Neill's stokehole or forepeak character, the Hairy Ape. Very very tough. He wasn't the studious type.'[6]

In a book commemorating the quincentenary of St Catharine's, Henn proudly lists past students who had become successful writers, but makes no reference to Lowry whatsoever.[7] Privately, he acknowledged that, though academically idle, his awkward student was intelligent, original and pugnacious in argument.[8] For his part, Lowry said that Henn had discouraged his every creative instinct and every effort he made.[9] Although he got on badly with Henn and skipped supervisions, he did turn in *some* work. Kenneth Wright, a scholarship boy from the North East, was supervised with Lowry, and remembers them working together on essays, and others reported him attending lectures by I. A. Richards.[10] However, apart from once surprising Henn by holding forth on the subterranean life of sailors' ballads,[11] he was never going to impress his cultured supervisor, whose celebrated Tuesday evenings of sherry and poetry he probably attended no more than once. After a time he simply did not turn up for supervision.

Cambridge at the end of 1929 was dominated by certain key figures. Wittgenstein had returned the term before to start transforming philosophical thought, and his presence was magnetizing to many. Sir James Frazer was at Trinity College working to supplement *The Golden Bough*, and psychology and anthropology were the focus of intense intellectual interest, soon to be challenged by politics and economics. E. M. Forster was also at Trinity, as was A. E. Housman, the 'scholar poet', representing a Georgian tradition then under fire from young literary Turks more inspired by a rising generation of English teachers like Richards, whose *Practical Criticism* was published that year, and F. R. Leavis, a junior lecturer destined to make a profound impact on English teaching. Perhaps most fatefully, at the Cavendish Laboratory great experiments were bringing the nuclear age ever closer. The spirit of science emanating from the Cavendish seemed to permeate the whole spectrum of Cambridge thought, including literature, where it was finding its expression particularly in the kind of criticism Richards pioneered.[12] Some students of English had, like William Empson, started out in mathematics or science, and it was not considered unusual for a student scientist like Jacob Bronowski or Kathleen Raine to feel a strong commitment also to poetry and criticism.

From the mid-1920s, Joyce, Eliot and Pound, each an anathema to older scholars, were embraced enthusiastically by more analytically inspired younger teachers and students. In such a critical atmosphere, someone like Lowry, deeply romantic and seeing the creative psyche as the main driving force of his art, could only be marginalized, though he was not left unaffected by this intellectual ferment. Later he claimed that he had learned nothing at Cambridge except for a great deal of Eliot,[13] yet two of the books he retained from his student days when he went to America five years later were the poems of John Donne and Richards's *Principles of Literary Criticism*,[14] so influential upon his Cambridge generation.

The influence of a few of his contemporaries was in fact more lasting, and he certainly shared the enthusiasm for both Eliot and Lawrence. Yet as a student he was to plough a lonely furrow, impressing few of his teachers. Aiken remained his chief mentor, and what interested him interested Lowry. As at school, he declined to read what he was supposed to read or to address the questions he was supposed to address. However, his originality was recognized and promoted by the more far-seeing of his fellow students – a particularly distinguished generation of creative artists. Richard Eberhardt had only just left Cambridge and published his first book of poems; William Empson was about to publish his influential *Seven Types of Ambiguity*; Michael Redgrave, while considering himself primarily a poet, was already venturing into acting and reading poetry for the BBC; Humphrey Jennings, considered a man of 'prodigious intelligence' and an 'invincible' dialectician,[15] was painting a great deal; and Julian Trevelyan was destined to emerge as Britain's most important surrealist painter of the 1930s. Poets still at Cambridge included Kathleen Raine, her husband Hugh Sykes Davies, Julian Bell, and Robin Fedden. In due course Lowry would not only add his name to this list, he would add a legend.

Shortly after arriving at St Catharine's he was turfed out of 70 Trumpington Street for drunkenness, and moved to rooms at 2 Bateman Street, a short walk away. He moved in with his books, records and Stuart's barbells. His landlord was crippled, and Lowry decided he was syphilitic and refused to eat the food he prepared. At least that is what he told people, and for good measure, still identifying with Benjamin Hall, said *he* had syphilis, too. His new digs found their way into *Under the Volcano*, when Hugh remembers that at Cambridge he 'lived in a disgusting smell of marmalade and old boots, kept by a cripple, in a hovel near the station yard'.[16] Bateman Street had advantages for a man of Lowry's meandering intemperance and sense of not belonging. At half a mile from college he could more easily flout university regulations about being out late, being out without a gown and visiting banned pubs, though he was still at risk from the prowling proctors and their 'bulldogs', the university's own policemen with powers to apprehend. He was to collect more than his due share of 'gatings' and fines. On one occasion he was carted off to the police cells for being drunk and disorderly and, after various phone calls, the college chaplain arrived to bail him out. He was, supposedly, greeted by a cheerfully tipsy Lowry with 'Hullo, Chaplain. How the Hell did *you* get here?'[17] But at the very beginning of his university career he was overtaken by a traumatic event which left him guilt-ridden for the rest of his life.

Paul Fitte, like Lowry, unhappy about being at university, disappeared shortly after matriculation. It later emerged that he had gone to London, and then after some days, to Putney, where he told his father he had been in a car crash which had shaken him up and delayed his return to Cambridge. No doubt he had been renewing acquaintances at one of Mrs Meyrick's illicit establishments. He told his father he wanted to leave university and get a job, was also worried about having spent a lot of money, and seemed deeply ashamed about something. He returned to 70 Trumpington Street the same day, Monday 11 November. On the 14th he stayed in bed all day, not eating, and telling his landlady he was unwell. Lowry last saw him in his room that evening, leaving at midnight.

Fitte was discovered the following morning by his landlady, dead in bed from gas poisoning, his door and windows sealed tight with newspapers. There was an inquest at which it emerged that Fitte, on returning from London, had received a telegram signed 'Phonia' reading, 'Please send money without fail,' followed shortly afterwards by a second, seeming to confirm the theory that he was being blackmailed. While Lowry was still with him yet another telegram had arrived saying, 'Please send money tomorrow without fail,' and he had explained that it was all about some money he owed. Lowry told the inquest that Fitte had looked pale and slightly depressed and had mentioned suicide, but only jokingly, laughing and saying, 'I must get out of this altogether.' 'I think', said Lowry, 'he was so level-headed that it was the last thing in the world he would do.'[18] After the suicide verdict, the

Coroner took him aside and upbraided him for not doing more to save his friend.

This tragedy imbued Lowry with such remorse that he often thought himself to be the cause of other people's deaths. Of course, it provided him with the kind of horrifying personal experience which as a writer he sought, and his deep sense of guilt about Fitte may have been linked to his 'hysterical identification' with Benjamin Hall, Grieg's character, who feels personally responsible for the suicide of one of his crewmates. But there is a darker explanation for Lowry's reaction to Fitte's death.

What happened is still a mystery, but a convincing version of events can be pieced together from Lowry's writings and from what he told others, especially his first wife. He sometimes said that Fitte killed himself after he (Lowry) had rebuffed his homosexual advances, he being as fearful of homosexuality as he was of syphilis.[19] But he told his first wife, on two separate occasions, that while drunk that night he had actually helped Fitte seal up the windows and door of his room with newspapers and then said, as he left, 'Now do it!' In her novel *I Bring Not Peace*, Charlotte Haldane gives a version of that evening, doubtless related to her by Lowry, where two characters based on Lowry and the suicidal Fitte get drunk on gin and one tells the other that if he wants to gas himself he needs to seal his room off tightly. The Lowry character goes off to a pub for another bottle of gin, and tells the story to a bunch of undergraduates, one of whom says, 'Let the bugger die!' He returns and tells his friend that he would probably be better off dead. The truth seems to be that Lowry did go for a bottle of gin, which he and Fitte finished, and then, intoxicated beyond reason, sealed up the room before Lowry staggered home to Bateman Street at midnight. In a draft of his novel *Dark as the Grave Wherein My Friend is Laid*, Lowry helps clarify the story further.

> A friend of mine named Wensleydale . . . committed suicide, I knew he was going to do it – in fact I told him to – instead of sympathizing with him beyond a point . . . Only I, of course, know what happened. I was not blamed at the inquest, and even if I had told the more exact truth I don't see how I could have been legally implicated – it would have shattered even more lives than those that were shattered by it. Moreover it would have been hard . . . to tell the truth about Wensleydale, without making matters a thousand times worse.[20]

His heartlessness, he explains, arose from a quarrel in which Fitte/Wensleydale sneered at his literary pretensions after reading Aiken's

Blue Voyage and Grieg's *The Ship Sails On*. 'He hated them both and taking this as a spiritual affront upon myself led me to be hardhearted when I should have been compassionate.'[21] Elsewhere he hinted that he had tried to interest Fitte in literature to turn his mind away from perversion, but Fitte thought he had contracted syphilis and was so determined to kill himself that Lowry had drunkenly encouraged him, saying that it would not be death but rebirth and offering jokingly to sell him some real estate in the next world.[22] The full horror of what he had done and what evil genii had been let loose within him that night disturbed Lowry gravely. If, as has been suggested, he was symbolically helping to destroy the homosexual in himself, then one can well imagine the complexity of his sense of guilt. In different fictional treatments of the story he saw himself as effectively having murdered his friend. In real life, it would not be the last time that his near-murderous genie slipped out of the bottle, and he must have recognized and feared what he was capable of doing when drunk. Yet the agonies of remorse did not make him forswear the demon drink; quite the reverse. Nevertheless, thereafter he always referred to 15 November as 'that fatal day', and shuddered fearfully as it approached.[23]

He went home to pour out the whole story to Stuart and Russell. Arthur was also informed; for him this was the first of a series of hideously hurtful messes in which his youngest son was to embroil himself and which he was at a complete loss to understand. So began in earnest what Lowry later called the 'ghastly psychotic dance' with the Old Man. And from now on the figure of his stern reproving father would ever loom towards him out of the mists.

Back in Cambridge, he turned up at one of Henn's Tuesday nights at which Norman Jones, a fellow English student, remembered him reading a long poem in free verse about Fitte's suicide. He also began using the death to excuse his increasingly bizarre conduct. At a party he threw his glass through a window 'to let the air in', saying he was fearful of being gassed.[24] He told Maurice Hickin, a college friend, that he had to drink to keep awake because of the terrible suicidal dreams he had about Fitte, and said he felt guilty because Fitte had killed himself thinking he had contracted syphilis after Lowry had introduced him to prostitutes. He would bring a bottle to Hickin's room, and get so drunk he would be incapable of leaving and have to sleep on the floor. And he told Emile Marmorstein, another student, that he had given up dining in college because he could not enter without seeing Fitte sitting at his usual place at table.[25]

Occasionally he visited the Shirley Society, named after the seventeenth-century St Catharine's poet. In late November he took part in a reading of Georg Kaiser's play *From Morn to Midnight*, at a meeting also attended by R. C. Sherriff, whose *Journey's End* had just opened at the town's New Theatre. Sherriff's play, with its stark portrayal of trench-life in the war, caused great interest, and helped to swing public sentiment against the glorification of the conflict. Lowry had already had a distaste for war drummed into him by Stuart, and this can only have been reinforced by Aiken, who had been a notable American conscientious objector in 1918.[26]

With the Fitte affair behind him, if still haunting him, he set out to meet key members of the élite, the editors of student literary magazines, and it was said that he did the rounds with all the solemnity of one applying for membership of the French Academy.[27] Through Robin Fedden, who edited the *Venture* with Michael Redgrave, he met John Davenport, an editor of *Cambridge Poetry* and contributor to the more radical *Experiment*, edited by Bronowski, Empson and Sykes Davies. Davenport was a larger-than-life 'character', a self-proclaimed talent-spotter. Julian Trevelyan recalled him as 'Fat, witty, bibulous, charming, bawdy, with a vast warehouse of a mind.'[28] He had been at St Paul's School with Trevelyan and Arthur Calder-Marshall, spent his vacations in France, and claimed acquaintance with Joyce, Cocteau, and Cartier-Bresson.[29] Many of his contemporaries considered him a genius of great potential and he made himself the focus of Cambridge student literary life, parading for the part in Edwardian dress – velvet jacket and monocle, and, at one point, a large moustache. He had a cutting, often spiteful, wit, and a tendency to knock people down when drunk.

He lived over the courtyard at the Eagle, adjacent to Corpus Christi (where he was reading History), and invited Lowry to his rooms for a drink. Lowry later said he was afraid he was going to be offered tea, but Davenport produced a decanter of whisky and a friendship lasting twenty-eight years was born. They ate in Davenport's rooms and talked and drank till midnight, when he had to run back to Bateman Street to dodge the watchful proctors. Next day Davenport visited him at his digs where he found:

> a confusion of books, papers, bottles, gramophone records. There were a pair of barbells and a ukulele. Pinned on the walls were restaurant bills from many countries, photographs of pictures by Chagall and Rousseau le Douanier, and other objects, all of which I later

learned had some totemic significance. A mysterious order underlay the chaos.

In Lowry's library he noticed 'the usual Elizabethans', Joyce, Eliot, Knut Hamsun, Hermann Bang, B. Traven,[30] Grieg, the whole of Ibsen and Strindberg, e. e. cummings, Hart Crane, Wallace Stevens, Aiken, James Hanley, and heavily annotated volumes of Henry James, all of which, he concluded, revealed 'the eclecticism of the literary workman.' They also reflected many of Aiken's interests (the annotated set of James was almost certainly Aiken's – 'borrowed' from Plympton Street). Davenport recalled three novellas which he admired particularly – Mann's 'Tonio Kröger', Melville's 'Bartleby' and Ivan Bunin's 'A Gentleman from San Francisco.' All this reading, he discovered, was unusually integrated by Lowry into a scheme in which both Faulkner and Dante also fitted. He also had records by Bix Beiderbecke, Joe Venuti, Eddie Lang, Red Nichols and Frankie Trumbauer, and played them over and over on a small wind-up gramophone, especially 'In a Mist', 'I'm Coming Virginia' and 'Singin' the Blues', the Beiderbecke solo whose 'breaks' he thought so blissful and liberating.[31]

Davenport and Lowry discovered a common bond in shared feelings of hostility towards their respective mothers, something found in other of their contemporaries, like Auden and Isherwood. Like them they found in psychoanalysis a convenient excuse for blaming all their ills on their upbringing.[32] Of his mother, said Davenport, Lowry 'spoke . . . only with hatred,' and his own mother, the music hall artiste Muriel George, was to him an object of vitriolic contempt.

Lowry's exaggerated sea-yarns impressed Davenport who, though a year younger than Lowry, acted older and was himself a considerable line-shooter. He appointed himself Lowry's unofficial 'patron', and boosted Lowry's reputation by proclaiming his 'genius'. One who agreed was Charlotte Haldane, famous for her parties at Roebuck House, the large riverside Victorian mansion where she lived with her husband, J. B. S. Haldane, the University Reader in Biochemistry. There she bred plants, wrote novels, and entertained young students to afternoons of good food, good music and good talk. Some went because they shared her interest in music, others because good food was served, and others because they were curious to discover who Charlotte was currently trying to bed.[33] JBS never attended what he referred to as 'Chatty's addled salon'. Charlotte, not to be outdone, was wont to say about her distinguished husband, who unfortunately wore a truss, 'What can you do with a man who carries his balls around in a bag?' The Haldanes, unusually progressive, had survived a university scandal over their adultery and marriage. Haldane was a true iconoclast and educator as well as a brilliant scientist. Charlotte was dark and pretty, part-German part-American by upbringing, a woman of wide cultural interests, especially in European literature, and was at that time working on her second novel, *Brother to Burt*, about identical twins.

When Davenport first took Lowry to Roebuck House, Martin Case, a postgraduate student of Haldane's, was playing jazz on the piano. Charlotte brought Lowry over and said 'This young man has syphilis, or thinks he has.'[34] According to Martin Case, 'Malcolm talked about syphilis so much that Mrs Haldane thought he was actually infected.'[35] His fear of sex and painful shyness with women often left him isolated in mixed company, and he would withdraw to some corner with a bottle and his ukulele. But he did get close enough to Charlotte to share some of his deepest fears with her, and she almost certainly fell in love with him, recalling him in her autobiography as 'the most romantic undergraduate in Cambridge'.[36] She was so taken with him that in her next novel she based one of the characters on him. *I Bring Not Peace* was structured like a fugue for four voices, each chapter told from the viewpoint of a different character, a technique Lowry used later in *Under the Volcano*. It is a novel of expatriate life in Paris, in the racy style of Michael Arlen. Its portrait of Lowry, in the shape of the Rimbaudesque jazz-addicted American James Dowd, shows him at his disreputable best, and it includes a suicide closely based on that of Fitte, who appears as Dennis Carling. It gives a finely observed picture of Lowry through the eyes of a woman besotted by an exotic, wild, inspired youth.

> He was a light-heavy-weight dressed in old grey flannel trousers and a navy-blue jersey with pale-blue lettering across the chest. The jersey bulged, stretching tightly across the colossal pectoral muscles beneath it. Over the jersey was a thin grey jacket, of which the sleeves were too short. The peculiar slanting blue eyes, the yellow hair, the way he clutched the battered uke with one hand while the other impatiently dropped the rusty black hat on the floor, confirmed the impression: sailor – ashore and lost. S.O.S. S.O.S. A bright splash of blood dribbling slowly from his lip completed the spectacle of a powerful male animal at bay, temporarily dazed and out of his element . . . Comic creature, she thought, and knew herself susceptible to his clumsy masculinity.[37]

The book included several of Lowry's songs and references to many of his and Charlotte's shared enthusiasms: Proust, Goethe, Hemingway, Cocteau, Rimbaud, Chagall, Beiderbecke, Trumbauer, Louis Armstrong, and Lear's 'The Dong with the Luminous Nose', which Lowry preferred to render as 'The Nose with the Luminous Dong' in obscene honour of Gogol.

Robert Lazarus recalled him, at the beginning of every party at Roebuck House, strumming his uke and singing, 'I put cinders in Poppa's bed, Oh I put cinders in Poppa's bed,' repeatedly until asked to stop.[38] But he is generally remembered for his more accomplished compositions. One which Charlotte put into her novel included the line, 'My childhood broke through chords of music and of sound,' which she considered very beautiful. Unknown to her, however, he had lifted it cheekily from Aiken's *House of Dust*. When, in *Under the Volcano*, the youthful Hugh fears he is to be charged with plagiarism over one of his songs, his author knew what he was writing about. But now a legend was beginning to be constructed, the legend of Malcolm Lowry.

Among those Lowry met at Roebuck House were Empson, just deprived of his fellowship at Magdalene after a college servant discovered contraceptives in his rooms, and Martin Case, who became a lifelong friend. Case shared his passion for jazz, and they often played together round the Cambridge pubs, Case on piano, Lowry on the uke, which he now preferred to call the 'taropatch' or 'Hawaiian guitar'. These performances attracted fans like James Travers, 'a vague, amiable boozer, rather rich and languid, who worshipped Malcolm,' according to Davenport.[39] Travers was so enamoured of Lowry that he even adopted 'the Malcolm shuffle' – an exaggerated walk to the bar which his hero had perfected. Lowry told Case that he drank because consuming great quantities of beer helped flush out his constipated system, and tried teaching him to box, usually in pubs. These bouts, purely academic to begin with, inevitably degenerated into punch-ups, to the dismay of landlords used to a quieter type of customer.

Despite the inspired ruffian of the legend, however, he could appear differently when he chose, and Julian Trevelyan was surprised to find what he thought of as a tough, shy, Hemingway-type keen on Chagall. Kathleen Raine first met him in Davenport's rooms, shyly hiding under the table strumming his ukulele, and concluded that when he withdrew into himself and played like this, the uke spoke for him.[40] Much later in life he could still, when in company, withdraw into his own private world like this, much to the embarrassment of others.

In December he published his first student work, a poem, 'For Nordahl Grieg, Ship's Fireman', in his college magazine.[41] The influence of *The Ship Sails On* is evident; the poem is similarly concerned with the themes of fearful fate and lost innocence. The first stanza reads:

> Two Norwegian firemen, friends in the same watch,
> stand looking up at the ship,
> And what do they see? They see an iron moloch
> Securely waiting to swallow the lives of men . . .
> But the ship also visits lands of strange beauty
> Where broad leaves struggle against the sun.
> Yet there too dangers await the unsuspecting sailors.
> The girls laughing in linked quintets in the lamplight;
> A swarm of spirochaetes,
> Maggots hatching in the very pulse of love.

But also hatching are some 'warm fluffy' helpless chickens in a hen-coop on the ship, an affirmation of rebirth, a positive theme with which Lowry was always trying to lighten his generally doom-laden vision. It was included in *Cambridge Poetry 1930*, edited by Davenport, Sykes Davies, and Redgrave, which appeared the following May, and it was years later that Davenport discovered how much of the poem was lifted from Grieg's novel.[42] What he did not spot was that the last line quoted above was taken almost exactly as it stands from *Blue Voyage*.

Despite their closeness, the highly sociable Davenport did not find Lowry always easy to understand.

> His mind was very acute, and he had already felt and suffered deeply, but he presented the world with a persona of a drunken sailor in a dirty sweater playing a ukulele. Each was a true representation of himself. He soon had a number of friends, but he did not like them to overlap, preferring them to present a different image of himself to each. I was fortunate in being able to share more than one of his worlds, but the nameless misery that drove him made him often inaccessible. It is of course a commonplace that all men are essentially solitary. In Malcolm's case it was an absolute isolation. On its ordinary level it was simply a form of narcissism.[43]

This solitariness Lowry was perpetually to contemplate in his fiction.

By January 1930, he was ready to show *Ultramarine* to Davenport. He had done little to it since returning from America, and Davenport remembered it as a fairly straightforward account of the trip to China. Lowry later claimed that after reading Grieg's book he gave up *Ultramarine* on the grounds that it had already been written.[44] Another reason, no doubt, was the absence of Aiken, off whose encouragement he so obviously fed. It was probably Davenport who sent him back to the book by suggesting that he submit a part of the draft as a short story for *Experiment*.

This short piece, called 'Port Swettenham', was the story of the galleyboy Norman's lost bird. It begins with a quotation from the Book of Numbers about the Jews wandering through the desert on the journey from Egypt to the Promised Land. And now here is a young sailor Padraic Cleary, a wandering soul at sea, on a freighter in Port Swettenham, looking up at the tapering mast and hoping that one day someone would climb it and lose his nerve so that he could shin up and rescue him. Then how proud the captain would be of him. 'My boy, . . . you're a credit to the ship.' What Walter Greenaway did and Melville's Redburn did is what Cleary dreams of emulating. The galleyboy's pet carrier-pigeon escapes from its cage and ends up over the side in crocodile-infested waters. He remembers his third swimming colours from school and ponders whether to leap to the rescue. But, alas, he is too late, the bird goes under, taken by a hungry croc. A cigar-puffing agent comes up and announces that the bathing here is fine and safe at this time of year. The scene dissolves into a background of inconsequential talk, and Padraic is left trying to recall a story about a lark with a broken wing whose mate loses its power to sing, and wondering when he had read it.[45] The story includes some favourite Lowry symbols – the Wandering Jew, the caged bird who bids for freedom, the doomed escape. And he shows that he has acquired his own ear for the ordinary conversation of seamen. Apart from that the narrative is as straightforward as Davenport remembered.

Bronowski saw it and so did Hugh Sykes Davies, who was very enthusiastic. 'We published stuff of his above all because he wrote in prose . . . Mostly our contributors wrote stream-of-consciousness stuff of unutterable boredom – I cannot describe how shattering . . . Malcolm came along doing the same kind of thing, but his stuff was different.'[46] The story was published in the February edition of *Experiment*, and from then on, as *Ultramarine* was worked over and rewritten, it came more and more to include allusions to new experiences, acquiring the collage effect which he was to deploy later.

He got into the habit, begun at Roebuck House, of reading sections of his book aloud to anyone who would listen. He found a ready audience crawling round his favourites pubs, the Red Cow, the Bath, the Eagle and the Maypole, and would read a different chapter in each. One student recalled that as he progressed from pub to pub, each chapter read was discarded, so that next day he would have to retrace his steps, pub by pub, to retrieve his manuscript. By some miracle, the book survived these alcoholic perambulations.[47] This tendency to leave manuscripts behind persisted and was rivalled only by the cascade of bottles left in his wake.

After the Fitte affair, Kenneth Wright tried to steer clear of Lowry, thinking that he was rather a shady character. But when he discovered they were both living in Bateman Street, he invited him to spend an evening with him in late February. Wright found him so fascinating that afterwards he recorded his impressions of the evening and of his strange guest, who had once again been inventive about his past, saying that he had been at sea for three years since leaving school. After talking about Tom Henn and the theatre and cinema, Lowry sang one of his poems, accompanying himself on the ukulele, then suddenly asked Wright whether he believed in spiritualism.

> He . . . told me how he had been in contact with Fitte through the medium of his sister-in-law who had inherited powers as a medium. She did not know Fitte at all, but in her . . . transmission, of his voice she reproduced many of his characteristics. For example, his constant plea, she said, was 'Do not let them scorn me'. Lowry assured me that the word 'scorn' was often on his friend's lips and that he suffered from the inferiority complex. According to Fitte his soul was very miserable and quite isolated from all other souls. He was especially unhappy because he had not had the consolation of knowing that his body was nourishing the earth because he thought that, as he had committed suicide by gas poisoning, it would be poisoning the earth.[48]

They discussed religion and morality, Joyce and Lawrence, and whether the best and most natural life was that found in sating the passions. Lowry said that he had lived for three years in various states of promiscuity and intemperance, and was now more sane and a better man for having sown his wild oats, saying that he believed in the dictum 'Through excess to wisdom.' They discussed his artistic ambitions.

> Lowry is writing a novel dealing largely with the temptations of a seafaring life . . . [It is] rather unusual, consisting of four main

> chapters and three long interludes which play the part of a Greek chorus . . . I am perfectly convinced, now, that Lowry is genuine, and can be believed in.[49]

The novel finally settled into six chapters into which the interludes were integrated. And he talked about it as 'a prose fugue', much as Charlotte Haldane did about her novel, *I Bring Not Peace*.

Memories of his seafaring life were kept alive not just through his novel. Maurice Hickin recalled Lowry once turning up at his rooms with two sailors from the *Pyrrhus* in tow. The men who had subjected Lobs to initiation by red-lead and Yokohama geisha had come to pay their respects. He seemed to think that Hickin, reading English but aiming at the priesthood, was a suitable friend to whom to introduce his old shipmates. Presumably he was one of those Lowry kept well separated from more boisterous friends like Davenport, and another Old Harrovian, Tom Forman. Forman was the son of a wealthy Nottingham businessman, an eccentric scientist, who loved fast cars, and had pretensions to be an inventor, his pet project being a 'death-ray'.[50] George Northcroft, a medical student who had been at prep school with Forman, also became a staunch friend, and was to play a dramatic role in his life a quarter of a century later.

At the end of February he heard that Aiken was now married to Clarissa, the ceremony taking place at William Carlos Williams's home in Rutherford, New Jersey, with Williams as best man. Aiken had won the Pulitzer Prize for his *Selected Poems*, published the previous November, and in a fit of exhilaration decided to return to England. Lowry could now look forward to being reunited with his mentor and 'guardian'.

The coming of spring was darkened only by the news of the death of D. H. Lawrence – a death which shocked his literary contemporaries, Lowry not least. Almost a quarter of a century later Lowry remembered exactly where he was when he heard the news on 30 March 1930 – coming out of a Cambridge cinema which was out of bounds.[51] And he told his first wife, 'The sun went out the day Lawrence died.' However, to lighten things, there was swimming in the river from the garden of Roebuck House. Empson remembered being told by Lowry as they were swimming together that, had he not had his (Empson's) poetry to read, he would have committed suicide. 'I thought this was just the way to talk, and felt pretty sure no one had said it to T. S. Eliot.'[52] But in his expressions of taste Lowry was nothing if not extravagant.

His ironic poem 'In Cape Cod with Conrad Aitken'[*sic*], based on a dream which Aiken had told him about, appeared in the *Festival Theatre Programme* in March, and in May his poem about Grieg appeared in *Cambridge Poetry, 1930*. Its reviews, however, were not outstanding. *Granta* judged it 'interesting, though remote',[53] *Cherwell*, the Oxford student paper, called it 'sympathetic'. In the *Cambridge Review*, F. R. Leavis noted that 'Mr Eliot is still in the ascendant, though his authority is not everywhere accepted,' and thought Lowry's poem 'exhibits a curious mixture of Whitman and D. H. Lawrence, and is the kind of free verse that is hardly verse,'[54] a comment which cannot have displeased him entirely. At the end of May, the *Times Literary Supplement*, while noting that 'Sophistication has eaten far less dangerously into the undergraduate poets of Cambridge than of Oxford,' concluded that Lowry and the others 'are all in different degrees seeking for a form and imagery adequate to their mental and, at times, metaphysical originality.'[55]

In Aiken's absence, as *Ultramarine* began to grow and take shape again, Lowry needed to talk about his writing. He turned to Gerald Noxon, a second-year languages student, son of the High Commissioner for Ontario, and publisher of *Experiment*, whom he had met through Davenport. In his room at Trinity, he and Lowry listened to jazz, drank from the generous liquor supply Noxon's father laid in for him, and talked about films. With Stuart Legg and Humphrey Jennings, Noxon ran the University Film Society through which Lowry saw many foreign movies including the Russian films of Pudovkin and Eisenstein which he admired so much. He found Lowry pathologically shy; if anyone else came in he would leave. It was, he recalled, the technical problems facing him as a writer that Lowry was most eager to discuss. 'He seemed to know what he wanted to say, but he was terribly concerned with how he should say it.' He talked about the stylistic solutions offered by Joyce, Faulkner and Hemingway, and also about Aiken, Melville and Bunyan. He did not wish to repudiate the legacy of the nineteenth-century novel but felt that a purely realistic style was too arid for him, and said he found Hemingway too flat. However, he considered the personal shorthand used by Joyce and Faulkner made their work too immediately difficult for the general reader.

> For Malcolm it was necessary that his writing should have a perfectly wrought surface meaning, in the sense of the term established by Flaubert. A competent and thoroughly understandable narrative tech-

nique, however complex it might be in form, was a necessity, as was a sound dramaturgy of classical origin. And above all Malcolm knew that he had to use the full range of the English language as it had been given to him to know it and use it. And even in 1930 his command of the English language was amazingly authoritative.[56]

No doubt aware of his reliance on Aiken, he realized that he needed to create his own style in order to succeed as he wished.

Through *Cambridge Poetry* he had met Redgrave, and doubtless it was his suggestion that he submit his next story to the *Venture*. This was the strangely titled 'Goya the Obscure', also with its origins in *Ultramarine*, which appeared in the magazine's June issue, along with contributions from Empson, Anthony Blunt, and Julian Bell. With this story, he showed how far he had progressed stylistically since his previous story in *Experiment*. The 'Goya' in the title is taken from *Blue Voyage* (the 'Obscure' is an echo of Hardy). Lowry quotes heavily from *Blue Voyage*, as well as basing the beginning on the opening of an Aiken short story, 'A Man Alone at Lunch'.

A syphilitic nightmare, taken almost whole from chapter 4 of Aiken's novel, stands at the heart of this story, in which the smitten central character, punningly named Joe Passalique, is quite possibly his 'revenge' on Joe Ward for his humiliation in the Yokohama brothel – the lines 'Hullo, Joe . . . How go?' are said to both this Joe and to Joe Ward, openly named in *Ultramarine*. Joe, a sailor, has left the sea with a dose of VD; his wife is pregnant and he envisions the sordid end which awaits him and his family in contrast to the idealistic vision of what might have been. He walks the streets of Liverpool, finds himself at the Paradise Street Anatomy Museum ('Man know thyself') and ends up 'Walking and thinking in a vicious circle from which there could be no escape.' Lowry not only draws one whole passage from *Blue Voyage*, but prefaces it with a veiled accusation against his mentor for having corrupted his vision and feelings.

Hear me Conrad Aiken, Pyrrhus the red-haired, immolater of Polyxena, fiery Neoptolemus, obscene and cruel poet, sacrificer of Astyanax? Hear me imponderable and impalpable who beside me so subtly communicate your terrible mood . . .

He had also clearly absorbed Aiken's technique of switching from one voice and wavelength to another, from incantation and inner reflection to bald description, to bawdy sea-shanties and overheard disconnected speech:

> syphilis! that's what he's got, syphilis. Yellow-toothed the piano, Blüthner, which stood in a corner of the saloon in the Dolphin Hotel, Birkenhead Dock-road; yellow stained with pickles the plate at the glass-topped table at which he was sitting. Somebody approaching this piano grabbed a glass tankard, froth-ringed with stout, from the top, eructated and began to play a strange melody (on Merseyside long since mute) but in Singapore and still upon some Blue Funnel boats, known as Seraphina – 'Seraphina's got no drawers, I've been down and seen her, Ser-a-phina,' he sang . . . 'How go Joe?' somebody asked him, and 'Hullo there, how are yer doin?'[57]

What Lowry had found so admirable in Aiken was just this ability to switch between the objective world of the senses and the subjective world which the mind creates in response, but which he himself had groped towards, even as a schoolboy. The tough sailor is both in touch with the coarse sensual world of the lower deck, and yet stands above it all, as poet, to affirm his inborn superiority. This shifting between voices, from straightforward third-person narrative to songs, newspaper headlines, street cries, bird-calls, and interior monologue, illustrates how he was solving the problem he had discussed with Noxon of how to say what he wanted to say. His problem now would be how to distance himself from Aiken, which at this stage he had patently failed to do.

Reviewing the *Venture* in the *Cambridge Review*, Roy Pascal acknowledged something distinctive in this new young writer. 'Malcolm Lowry knows what he is talking about when he says "Talk of James Joyce in a bronchial voice." His voice is more various than the June's cuckoo. He is a master of styles, though he prefers the realistic and dithyrambic, he is lyrical and satirical, he is *very* literary; this all makes him very good.'[58]

In May, Lowry scraped through his first-year college exams with Third Class marks. His whereabouts after that are elusive, but he told Russell that he spent the first part of the summer in Scotland reacquainting himself with Helen Lindsay, who they had first met on holiday in Rothesay ten years earlier; his affair with Tessa Evans seems to have faded.

Back at Inglewood for his twenty-first birthday, Lowry must have felt keenly the kind of shock which Kathleen Raine experienced on returning to her suburban home after a year at Cambridge – as if she was becoming a different person, inhabiting a different world, acquiring quite new values. Home was a hostile and foreign country. After America with the Bohemian Aiken, and Cambridge with the progressive Haldanes and omniscient avant-gardists like Davenport, Inglewood must have seemed like a drying-out ward to a thirsty alcoholic. Here it was that on being asked by Arthur to say what he remembered of his childhood he replied that it had been one of perpetual suffering; for most of the time he was either blind, crippled or constipated. The response from Arthur was an icy silence.[59]

CHAPTER VII

PURPLE PASSAGES

1930–1932

Everything that is not literature bores me and I hate it, for it disturbs me or delays me, if only because I think it does. I lack any aptitude for family life except, at best, as an observer. I have no family feeling and visitors make me almost feel as though I were maliciously being attacked.

FRANZ KAFKA, *Diaries*

In August 1930, the Aikens arrived in England and Arthur took Conrad and Malcolm to lunch in London to discuss Malcolm's future. Arthur was no doubt reassured to find that Aiken was no wild Bohemian but a sober-suited middle-aged American of the sort he was used to doing business with, and agreed to pay him the usual five guineas a week to act as guardian and tutor to his difficult son during university vacations. He was also concerned, it seems, at having found a sexually explicit letter addressed to Malcolm from a homosexual friend.[1] Aiken is said to have reassured Arthur that it was not unusual for young males to write obscene letters to one another.[2]

On a sentimental trip to Mermaid Street in Rye, Aiken found his old home, Jeake's House, to let, and immediately took out a seven-year lease. On 26 August, Lowry helped them move in, and they were later joined by Aiken's children, Jane, then twelve, and John, sixteen. Jane recalled Lowry as a fresh-faced, jolly young man with whom she went for occasional walks;[3] John also found him a jovial character – 'rollicking, roistering, (and) rambunctious'.[4] There were long discussions about music and mathematics, energetic games of tennis, ferocious games of ping-pong on the refectory table, and musical evenings at the piano with Lowry twanging away at the inevitable uke and putting bawdy words to jazzed-up versions of hymn-tunes.

There were frequent drunken sprees to the Ship Inn nearby, where the landlord, Tom Neeves, kept a welcoming house and his wife served a delicious dish of bacon and rabbit. It was, wrote Aiken, a 'paragon of inns, pinnacle of blisses, helicon of delight, and only fifty yards away, hard by the river.'[5] There Lowry and Aiken would drink whisky by the quartern and, to Clarissa's annoyance, return late and drunk for dinner, and continually engage in horseplay and wrestling matches like the injurious one at their first encounter in Plympton Street. But at Jeake's too they would peer through the window across the sea towards Ushant, down the Channel off the Brittany coast, the distant invisible emblem, they decided, of their artistic goals.

While Aiken began sketching out a new novel, *Great Circle*, work on *Ultramarine* continued, with Lowry busily incorporating more and more from *Blue Voyage*, and its author just as busily cutting it out. Not that this prevented Lowry from putting it back again. After all, hadn't Aiken told him that *he* had written *Blue Voyage* in another life? Frustrated by these constant borrowings, Aiken suggested ironically that he call his book *Purple Passage*. However, his obsession with Aiken continued to inhibit the development of a personal style. Six years before, writing *Blue Voyage*, Aiken had told his American editor, 'My difficulty is to keep it from being too Joycish; I fear I am not doing so.'[6] Lowry could have said much the same about keeping *Ultramarine* from being too Aikenish and not doing so.

However, his dependence on Aiken was not easy to break, and Aiken was still intent on experimenting with Lowry and now more than ever dependent on Arthur's money. It was within this extremely complex relationship that *Ultramarine* took on its strangely hybrid form, absorbing Aiken (and, unknown to him, Grieg) but also weaving in new sensations and impressions. This, said Davenport, caused 'Proustian wrestlings' and explained why he worked so slowly. 'It was a ceaseless struggle to maintain an equipoise between past and present.'[7] And at the same time, Aiken raised the possibility of producing a multi-layered novel without beginning or end which embodied in its circular motion all the ideas and themes of a lifetime. The question was who would produced this prodigious novel first?

By chance, in September, Gerald Noxon was in Rye and bumped into Lowry – looking extremely well he thought – out shopping with Clarissa. He was invited to meet Aiken but soon decided that his relationship with Malcolm was an unhealthy one – the Rabelaisian humour, the perpetual drinking and childish wrestling bouts he thought tedious and bizarre, and he tried to get Lowry away when he could. They roamed around Rye and its many pubs, all of which Lowry seemed to know, and consumed large amounts of Sussex ale. They took long walks along the River Rother and swam off Camber Sands. There they sat smoking Balkan Sobranie No. 10s, while Lowry told Noxon the sad story of his life, the blind, crippled and unloved version, which Noxon took to be the source of his often strange behaviour. As he talked, Noxon felt himself in the presence of a truly brilliant mind – an extraordinary memory, great depth of knowledge, inexhaustible fund of funny stories and self-mocking humour.[8] He captivated Noxon as he did others, having come to recognize that 'genius' was, for those who believed in it, a blank cheque on which almost any kind of outrageous behaviour could be written.

But not everyone fell for Lowry's charm. Clarissa found his presence at Jeake's House ever more irritating, the scar on Conrad's forehead and his persistent headaches were constant reminders of the near-disaster of their first encounter. 'I associated Malcolm with catastrophe,' she wrote. 'He might set fire to his mattress, break a leg, or damage my husband still further. Just meeting him was a calamity, he admitted.'[9] Their pub crawls caused comment in the town, meals went uneaten, and she worried about the amount they drank. The sight of Lowry 'weaving over the cobbles, like a somnambulist, his striped blazer rumpled, hair tousled, a necktie holding up his white ducks,'[10] became all too familiar in the town. She wrote in her diary, 'How much longer will Conrad put up with this madman? . . . Between the two of them I'm fast going dotty.' When she complained about him, Aiken recited the Rabelaisian line that all good writers drank. 'A poet without alcohol is no real poet. Swinburne's personality disintegrated, and his creative flow was dammed up when Watts Dunton banned liquor.'[11]

Even so, by the end of September even he was anxious to be free of his roisterous student as his new novel began to press itself upon him. Lowry returned to Cambridge to find that Tom Henn, fed up with him, had 'handed him over' for supervision to the newly graduated Sykes Davies to prepare for Part I of the tripos the following May. Sykes Davies found him amenable enough, but only prepared to meet in pubs, which suited them both, and so began a very convivial tutorial relationship. They played golf together, went to the cinema and, when the weather was fine, went swimming in Quy Fen.

Sykes Davies was then married to Kathleen Raine, remembered by Julian Trevelyan as 'slight and beautiful as a flower' and the object of much admiration among male undergraduates.[12] Like Lowry, she and Sykes Davies had had Wesleyan upbringings, providing a bond of shared rejections, and she, like Noxon, remembered him being very shy, certainly too shy to converse with Empson and Humphrey Jennings. Bronowski also found him quiet and almost tongue-tied, ready to talk only about new literature with which he was very familiar.[13] For Raine, breaking from the Old Culture opened the way to new understandings, and Eliot and Freud and later Marx seemed to offer ways of thinking more in tune with their lives. She found Eliot's *The Waste Land* was *her* landscape, and, like Lowry, the 'discovery' of Freud enabled her to pin responsibility for early sufferings on her parents and their narrow religiosity. But Lowry never completely rejected religion as she did, and continued to affirm the imagination while the rest of young intellectual Cambridge genuflected before the altar of science. Empson was held in great awe because of his brilliance, but to Raine, Lowry was too intuitive – and puzzling because of his apparent rejection of 'civilized' Cambridge. If the others rebelled against classicism by embracing science, Lowry rebelled by embracing Romanticism. His heritage was not that of Einstein and Rutherford, but of Coleridge, Shelley, Swinburne, Rimbaud, Rabelais, and the Elizabethans.

Aiken had discovered a way of massaging expenses submitted to Arthur, and in October Malcolm thanked him profusely for 'shading, annotating, and connotating the disbursements'. Arthur had sent him 'a smoothly smiling sort of letter . . . which presages well for the future,' he wrote. But he was feeling ever more disenchanted with St Catharine's. The college buildings, he said, were like barracks, and the dining room like a mortuary. Nor had Cats produced any worthy literary figure as other colleges had produced a Marlowe or a Milton – in fact that very night he was dining at Pembroke in Gray's old room in the same block where Crashaw and Christopher Smart had lived. As ever, he preferred the world of fiction to that of sober fact. His letter to Aiken concluded with a parody of one from Arthur.[14]

> Well, my boy, I shall write you a long letter, dictated to my typist. Remember what I've said to you about drink and women. I don't want you to get mixed up in any – er – drinking bouts. I never did, and look what I am to-day. There's no need to talk about the other matter, self-abuse, of course not. I know you don't know anything about that. You won't even be tempted . . . None of the Lowry-Lowries of Inglewood-Inglewood have ever been drunk, or been tempted in any way whatsoever . . . Please give me careful account of everything you spend . . . I think you spend too much money on shooting, and repairing your gun – As ever

Davenport was still his closest companion. Sykes Davies saw them from time to time, usually drunk on 'some filthy stuff called Mousec'. Once when he bumped into them Lowry said, 'We're doomed. You're not doomed, but John and I – we're doomed!' His bizarre moods and fancies required a special kind of understanding and the eccentric Davenport seemed to have it.

> I had only three fights with him – horse[play] really. When drunk he would reach a psychotic stage of infantile self-absorption, and his monologues would become longer and more convoluted until finally he would fall under what I called a 'Malcolmspell', and fisticuffs would be the only cure . . . He would lock himself in his rooms for days with whiskey and sardines and read the novels of B. Traven until I could get him out for a short stroll. He was always making embarrassing gestures, insisting that we become blood-brothers with appropriate ceremonials, things like that.[15]

However, a new influence burst into Lowry's life with the arrival of Tom Harrisson at Pembroke. Another Harrovian and son of an army general, Harrisson was cheerful, aggressive, outspoken and handsome. He was as wild as Lowry and even more outspokenly contemptuous of university life. On one occasion they invaded a meeting of the Shirley Society, and Sydney Smith, a marine biologist, talking about a research trip on a North Sea trawler, found himself barracked loudly by Harrisson, claiming that you had not been to sea unless you had sailed as a stoker, like Lowry. They were both drunk and having delivered this broadside, left.[16] Harrisson was vigorously anti-establishment and thought education was not to be found in ivy-covered halls but out in the real world among real people, even if one sometimes had to sink into the lower depths to find it. He found Lowry attractive because he had already lived the low life. A keen anthropologist and amateur naturalist, he later made his reputation leading expeditions to the South Seas and helping Mass Observation. He left broke before being sent down after a year for printing an article critical of his college, once being set upon by a gang of hearties and projected fully clothed into the Cam. A year later he published his notorious *Letter to Oxford* advocating the philosophy of 'roughing it' to the priviledged students of Oxbridge. In his way of writing, Lowry embodied much of the spirit and method of Mass Observation - the noting down of observed detail, of places, persons and overheard conversations - and may have helped to shape the idea then germinating in Harrisson's mind. His notebook was his most constant companion and he had learned to write almost as fast as shorthand.[17]

Near the end of term Lowry wrote a wickedly cynical letter to Aiken.

> I am working hard here, mostly on the novel. Charlotte Haldane (the wife of J.B.S.) has offered me her body if I finish the revision of it this term. This is all right but I told her that I would masturbate after finishing each chapter in that case with the result that I would run out of semen before *la moment critique*. I think this is very funny. She is very pretty. I don't think I have ever seen anybody so pretty. I read the first chapter, revised and intensified and polished; and she was a bit drunk and fell down on her knees and wept; so I didn't have the heart to tell her that if there was anything good about it it had been copied from you. Christ what a breeze! . . . I drank a lot of whisky with . . . (her) . . . and was nearly sick into her mouth when I was kissing her. She says she loves me. This is rather awkward, but very gratifying . . . Three of my friends have Gonorrhea . . . I wish I had Gonorrhea, because that would mean I'd had had a good fuck which I haven't for a hell of a time. I'm all inhibited in that direction . . . and am having a bad time with masturbation.

Discussing his work with Charlotte meant discussing musical form as a basis for the novel, especially the fugue, echoing earlier discussions with Aiken.

He had also, he said proudly, been elected to the editorship of *Cambridge Poetry*, though this probably amounted to little more than being asked to read submitted poems. He concluded on a confessional note: 'My other ambition is to stop masturbating. Which is just bloody impossible. If there were a book on that there would be some sense in making me editor! I love everything, from soapdishes to medicine bottles.'[18] And he quoted Aiken back at him. Masturbation was 'the most poisoning of all illnesses. But we return to our vomit.' He told Clarissa that he felt deep guilt about masturbating and seemed to link this with a deep fear of homosexuality. John Aiken claimed that at Jeake's, fearing Clarissa would hear his bed squeaking, he went down to the public toilet at the bottom of Mermaid Street to masturbate.[19]

His sexual frustration was a source of constant misery, and following women in the streets was one way he seems to have sublimated it, just as he recalled doing after visiting Paradise Street in 1926. His syphilophobia probably stopped him having intercourse with prostitutes, but he was not averse to purchasing other sexual services, as Martin Case witnessed.

> One night late we were on our way back to Malcolm's digs from the Cambridge station. A hideous old bag – which meant she must have been thirty – waylaid Malcolm, and the two disappeared behind a shed in a builder's yard on Bateman Street. Later, he said it had been a marvellous experience being tossed off with a fur glove.

He was, however, finding it increasingly difficult to have normal relations with the opposite sex. 'He was terrified of girls,' said Case, 'except in the most idealistic, remote way.'[20]

Moved by his sad tales of a miserable home life, Case took him to spend Christmas at his home in Birmingham, where he met Case's brother Ralph, a medical student at Birmingham University. Their father was a director of Mitchells & Butler's Brewery and there was always beer on tap at the Case home, so the three spent many a convivial evening together without even going to the pub.[21] Discovering his hypochondria, Ralph looked him over and solemnly pronounced his slight beer-belly the first symptom of *adiposas dolorosa*, a condition associated with alcoholism. Lowry took this joke very seriously and required much reassuring before regaining his composure. They also found him irrationally fearful of authority figures, and once, in the toilet at the Birmingham University student's club, when he retired to a cubicle, Ralph began talking in a janitorial voice saying, 'I'm fed up with all these buggers coming in stinking of drink.' Terrified that some official was about to pounce, Lowry refused to come out, and was only dislodged when Martin told him that the pubs closed in ten minutes.

After a brief visit to Inglewood, he spent New Year 1931 in London with Davenport at his mother's house in Highgate. They headed straight for the pubs on the shadier fringes of Bloomsbury, and that night ran into a spot of trouble. Carousing at the Fitzroy Tavern, a hang-out for poets, artists and writers, run by the legendary 'Pappa' Kleinfeld, the drunk and pugnacious Davenport decided he wanted a fight. In the pub that evening was a group of small, insignificant-looking men, who he felt well able to take on. After he had insulted them in a suitably threatening manner, the parties adjourned to the street outside for what Davenport liked to call 'fisticuffs'. Unknown to him and Lowry, the small, unimpressive-looking men were Welsh miners up for a demonstration, who quickly wiped the floor with both of them. A few days later Lowry wrote somewhat sheepishly to Aiken, sending advance notice of his impending arrival in Rye. He had been beaten up, he said, in 'a Ulyssean brawl' outside the Fitzroy on his first night in London and was nursing injuries to his chin and lip, and the mirror told the whole miserable story.[22]

Aiken must have welcomed Lowry's return, however brief, if only because of the usual five guineas from Arthur. In his financially straitened circumstances he was no doubt deeply annoyed about how he had been hounded from his salaried post at Harvard. Spotting a news item about a history professor resigning from the Newcastle Literary Society because he thought planned lectures on Joyce, Huxley and Lawrence would pollute youthful minds, he and Lowry composed a poetic riposte, 'Those Cokes to Newcastle Blues', which appeared in the *Festival Theatre Programme* in February.[23]

Evelyn was still expecting great things of her dear curly-headed little boy. In January she wrote saying 'please write me again soon and tell me something thrilling about your own achievements.' But with Part I approaching fast, he needed more than chats in pubs with Sykes Davies if he was to pass. He had also been ejected from 2 Bateman Street, and in March he was writing to Aiken from the Globe Hotel. Still haunted by Fitte, he wrote of a persistent sense of despair and of not having been to St Catharine's for a whole term which, he said, 'reveals how little to myself Death ever leaves me.' Only the buttery sherry, or a sense of curiosity might draw him there. 'I am asking myself if I shall stay away for ever for the fear of this muddle about motives. An intricate tangle!'[24]

On 14 March, he was back for a five week stay in Rye, and he and Aiken were soon back at the Ship. One memorable evening, on April Fool's Day, exceedingly drunk, they decided to hold a javelin-throwing competition with some conveniently piled scaffold poles down at the water's edge at low tide. Aiken failed to let go of his and fell with it into eight feet of mud. Above him, Lowry, craning to see where his fallen comrade lay, pitched forward and followed him into the slimy depths beneath. Somehow they extricated themselves and crawled back to Jeake's House where Clarissa had been expecting them for dinner three hours earlier.[25]

Aiken's circle of friends in Rye now included Edward Burra, the surrealist painter. Clarissa did not much like Burra, a small, arthritic, sardonic creature with a waspish wit. He and Lowry had a rather strained relationship, tolerating one another only because of their mutual friendship with Aiken. Clarissa said the one thing the two had in common was 'an aversion to soap and water'[26] – Lowry's underwear was 'unmentionable'. When Aiken once remarked of his socks 'don't go near the gasometer, otherwise there might be another Neuenkirchen explosion', she remembered Malcolm's belly laugh echoing along Mermaid Street.[27] Some of the Aikens' friends were distressed to see what they thought a brilliant young man destroying his genius with alcohol. But with his hero and mentor as a model, there was little chance of Lowry signing the pledge. Nevertheless, he did work hard that Easter. According to Clarissa he seemed to work on several things at once, his room a mass of manuscripts, papers and books, and yet he seemed disciplined and kept sober for long periods.[28] Even so, he was still poaching, and took a particular liking to a passage Aiken had written for *Great Circle*, a dream sequence about a son eating his father's skeleton, which he promptly incorporated in *Ultramarine*. Aiken just as promptly ordered it out.

After Lowry told him how his involvement in Paul Fitte's suicide haunted him, Aiken told him that he was just 'a small boy chased by furies'. This prompted him to include in the book the first chorus from Aeschylus' *Eumenides* in the original Greek (Aiken had used Greek in *Blue Voyage*), which translates as 'and over the victim this lay, madness, madness, madness, hymn of the Furies.' (Lowry's translation goes, 'The Furies, singing over their victim, sending him mad.') That theme, too, began to haunt him, reappearing in his later work and giving his bitter pain a literary form.

Back in Cambridge, Lowry heard from Aiken that Arthur wanted a report on his chances in the Part I exams. What on earth, he asked, should he write? The fictional life spent with Aiken had been overtaken by the real world of A. O. Lowry. But before he could reply he was involved in a car crash. On 7 April, despite bruised hips and a banged head, he wrote telling Aiken the whole story. He, Davenport and Tom Forman had got 'pie-eyed' and decided to drive to Africa in Forman's car. 'We just sat on the accelerator for about twenty miles till the thing just overturned from sheer vexation.' Nobody was killed, he said, but personally he wished he had been. He felt he was in 'several kinds of shite', because of Arthur getting at him through Aiken, and suggested the answer he should give the Old Man.

> As far as I can judge from the papers of former years . . . they are often of a type which suggests that in preparation for them the student may well be blurred as to the real meaning, the sturm und drang of Literature, and hate it ever after; moreover the time is so limited for answering them that one has to have a mind like a sort of machine

> gun, you have no time . . . to let yourself go on something you really love! . . . Malcolm is a slow writer and . . . an abnormally slow thinker, which although not itself a fault makes him a bad examinee. I have done everything in my power to correct this for his exam but . . . have found [it] cannot be corrected [and] ought not to be – it might make him – tee-hee! – artificial and false in his reasoning in later life. The thought of failing . . . worries him on your account and he is quite capable of forgetting all he ever learned in a flash . . . I think, he is the sort of person who can never be tested adequately in the impromptu manner demanded by the tripos . . . I don't think he will fail, heaven knows we have worked hard enough! tchtch joke over – but if he gets in one of his unreasonable panics . . . he certainly will . . . I think a pass is all one expects for someone as temperamentally involved as Malcolm.

An honours pass, he should say, would not influence his final degree, which would depend on his next year's results. 'Don't tell him,' he ended, 'that all I know of the Life and Thought of any period is that people once wore tights.'[29] He implored Aiken to say nothing to the Old Man about the car crash, though he thought it might come in useful as an excuse if he failed.

In the spring edition of *Experiment* he had a new story – another excerpt from *Ultramarine*, a near-complete version of chapter 4, called 'Punctum Indifferens Skibet Gaar Videre', which shows a considerable step forward in his writing. The title, part Latin, part the Norwegian name of Grieg's book, meaning 'At the Point of No Return the Ship Sails On',[30] embodies that 'ceaseless struggle to maintain an equipoise between past and present.' It probably also reflects Lowry's reading of P. D. Ouspensky's *A New Model of the Universe* and J. W. Dunne's *Experiment With Time*, in which present time is seen to encapsulate all time. The hero is now called Dana Hilliot and the story revolves around his conflict with the ship's cook Andy. The poker-playing crew members act as a Greek Chorus, 'the Furies' commenting gloatingly on Hilliot's plight. Against this background of unstructured, overheard casual talk, Hilliot reflects on his personal agonies, his girl, his approaching confrontation with Andy and, in a sudden shift, putting his Shakespeare revision to good use, sees it all as a drama 'Tucket within, and a flourish of trumpets. Beware Andy! I move like a ghost towards my design, with Tarquin's ravishing strides . . .'[31] There is no obvious plot, the story is implicit in the overheard conversation and the inner monologue of Hilliot. Lowry's hero is now beset by Lowry's own problem, of failing to distinguish fiction from reality. His thoughts are littered with literary references and quotations, he is living in a literary world, viewing his condition through the language of others.

As this story was a sequence from his latest revision of *Ultramarine*, he must have hoped for some encouraging reviews, and was decidedly heartened when the London *Mercury* said that his story ('a sketch written in a mixture of Negro, Greek, American and occasional English') and a fragment from Joyce's 'Work in Progress' were the only things which lived up to editorial claims of breaking new ground.[32] Shortly afterwards the *TLS* judged it 'a kind of prose fugue with recurrent themes, effectively contrived.'[33] Within a couple of weeks he received a letter from Edward O'Brien, saying he had chosen 'Punctum Indifferens' for *Best British Stories of 1931*, which he edited in America. In a note to Kenneth Wright announcing this, he said proudly, 'I'm in the company of Tomlinson & Coppard. Wot ho she bumps. You can sell this letter!' He also sent the good news to Arthur to counteract the effect of possibly failing his exam.[34]

On 29 May, Lowry finished his final paper and celebrated by hitting the bottle. He then collapsed into two weeks of disorder and despair from which he was aroused only by a telegram from Aiken asking how he had done. A few days later came Lowry's reply on how he had fared in 'the tripeos'. He thought he had written a reasonably good essay on Truth and Poetry, quoting 'liberally not to say literally' from him (Aiken) as well as from Poe and a new book on Aiken's poetry, *The Melody of Chaos*.[35] He thought he had done well enough on the criticism paper and bluffed through on Literature from 1785 to the present: 'I knew my Keats better than I thought I did, for instance – on the whole I have nothing to complain about from the papers . . . and if I have failed, and that's on the cards, I was more stupid at the time than I thought.'[36]

His present despairing state, he told Aiken, was due to 'a complexity of melancholy reasons none of which are either particularly complex, melancholy, or reasonable'. He had made up his mind on only one point. 'I must, and as soon as possible, identify a finer scene: I must in other words give an imaginary scene identity through the immediate sensation of actual experience.' He might be accused of wanting to regress, of turning away from subtlety and sophistication rather than extending himself, of trying alternatively to kill Liverpool and himself – of being in *truth*, as Aiken had suggested, 'a small boy chased by the furies'.[37] Although he glossed over Aiken's perceptive judgement of

THE LOWRY FAMILY AT LEISURE.
Above: On holiday on the Isle of Man, in the summer of 1910. From left to right are Russell, Stuart, Wilfrid, and Malcolm in the arms of Miss Bell ('Bey'). *Below*: Arthur Lowry at the mast in Liverpool Swimming Club costume. Malcolm and Russell are in front; Helen Lindsay and her father are sitting behind.

HOME LIFE.
Above: Together – Arthur with Russell and Malcolm at Inglewood.
Below: Apart – Evelyn with Russell and Malcolm at Inglewood.

BOYHOOD'S BLOOM.
Right: The wounded soldier. Malcolm, in Caldicott uniform, with the cycling-accident scar on his left knee clearly visible; he later claimed to have acquired it in crossfire in the Chinese Civil War. *Below*: Beside the seaside. On holiday with his parents at Budleigh Salterton, 1923.

LIFE AT THE LEYS.
Above: The cast of *Tilly of Bloomsbury* – Malcolm is in the back row, sporting the cap. *Left*: 'Mr Chips' – W. H. Balgarnie, Lowry's housemaster and his first literary mentor. He had similarly encouraged an earlier pupil, James Hilton, who based the schoolmaster hero of his novels, Chips, on him. *Below*: Carol Brown, the girl who made Lowry completely forget the General Strike.

him, the worm of remorse had now eaten deeply into him, and following the Fitte suicide he always felt himself to be the persecuted victim of a vengeful fate. But he seems not to have wanted to admit as much to Aiken, and wrote, 'I prefer to think sometimes that it is because I really want to be a man rather than a male, which at present I'm not, and that I want to get from somewhere a frank and fearless will which roughly speaking does not put more mud into the world than there is at present.'[38] He added a final, self-mocking 'Nonsense' to that.

Whether Aiken knew it or not, this was an implied rejection of him and his wallowing in the world's muck and mire. It also indicated how intense Grieg's influence had become. For it was that 'frank and fearless will' which had so attracted him to *The Ship Sails On*, which he now sought. He wanted to dramatize the novel in the manner of O'Neill and have it performed at the Festival Theatre. To this end, he had written numerous letters to Grieg but sent none of them. So he decided to give his American 'guardian' a miss that summer, and seek out Grieg, as he had previously sought out Aiken. In his 'lost' novel, *In Ballast to the White Sea*, which he based in part on this pilgrimage, he implies that what was troubling his alter ego was:

> a stormy affair with an older woman, the risk of being sent down for pursuing it, the invidiousness of being a man at the University and yet treated as a child, a Dostoievskian brother, the ghoulishness of his contemporaries, the ideology of the English faculty, the feeling of hopelessness that overwhelms him about his choice of a vocation when now he figures he perhaps isn't a writer . . . by the fact that he can find absolutely no parallel in *literature* to his growing sense of identity with the character of [Benjamin Hall].[39]

To disguise his true purpose, he told Aiken also that he needed to take time to read more widely and find more writers who were amenable to him.[40] There is in this an image of the romantic Lowry trapped in the Symbolist world of the imagination, as described in Edmund Wilson's just-published *Axel's Castle*, wishing to break out, like Rimbaud, into the world of experience. Rimbaud, to whom Charlotte Haldane had introduced him, was another writer with whom he had come to identify – a poet who 'makes himself a *visionary* through a long, immense and reasoned *derangement of all the senses*.'[41] But he was to discover, like Romantics before him, that 'the reality never equals the dream.'[42]

With no Lowry and no money from Arthur, Aiken was feeling the pinch. He was also beginning to find his marriage boring and had complained to a friend in May that he had no sex life and was becoming increasingly irritated with Clarissa,[43] who in turn was writing to friends saying how much she hated Rye. The new book, *Great Circle*, was intensely self-analytical, far more probing than *Blue Voyage* and therefore far more unsettling. It was taking him back through the tragedy of his parents' deaths, hatred of his adopted parents, fears of inherited madness, and an obsession with the dark and degenerate side of existence. It was from Aiken's depressed and misanthropic vision that Lowry was anxious to escape, even if only temporarily.

In June he got the news that he had passed his Part I with a Third Class grade. His results, though modest, were a great relief. He had gained an Honours mark and Arthur and Evelyn must have been delighted. At least it seemed to justify time spent with Aiken and gave the impression that he was actually working. If he went home to Inglewood to give Evelyn the 'thrilling news of his achievements', it was only a brief visit. He planned to go to sea in search of Benjamin Hall, and somehow managed to obtain the *hyrkontract* necessary to sail as a fireman on a Norwegian ship bound for Leningrad and Archangel from Preston.[44] Like one of his later characters, his longing for the sea had 'emerge[d] into a longing for the fire of the stokehold . . . in which he sees himself purged and emerging as the reborn man.'[45] Although a trip to the White Sea would not take him to Hall's author Grieg, sailing with Norwegian sailors would give him background for the play he hoped to write; and there was always the chance of the ship putting into a Norwegian port eventually. He wrote explaining his plan to Aiken, who replied urging him not to go – it *would*, he said, be a form of regression. His father also disapproved, saying that Grieg would not welcome an uninvited guest disturbing his work.[46] However, there was no stopping him.

On 11 August, four days after the death at twenty-eight of his jazz hero, Bix Beiderbecke, and just two weeks after his own twenty-second birthday, Lowry sailed from Preston on the Nilson Niquist timber ship SS *Fagervik*, 'in ballast to the White Sea', with twenty-one crew members under the command of Captain Skaugen. A few hours out, off the north coast of Scotland, the ship's owners ordered it to sail instead to Aalesund on the west coast of Norway, a strange, dreamlike turn of events for Lowry, because a character in Grieg's book was called Aalesund, being from there. He later told Aiken he had very many happy memories of the ship, meaning probably that he was accepted by a Norwegian crew unfamiliar with the envy and spite of the English class system. *Fagervik* arrived at Aalesund on the 16th, and there being no deep harbour, tied up at a small island out in the fjord.

On waking next morning, Lowry found that most of the crew had been paid off and left the ship, but then the strange hand of coincidence took over. He checked into a hotel and went to a coffee shop hoping to buy some kroner. A customer who obliged, a teacher, happened to be reading a book by Grieg about his journalistic experiences in China in 1927, the very time Lowry was there on *Pyrrhus*. The cover bore the author's picture, his first sight of his hero, first evidence that he really existed. The teacher said that Grieg had been to his school and read his poems. He was, he told Lowry, a person 'right from the heart', who 'parted his hair in the middle'. He had a poem about him and promised to bring it to the coffee shop next day.

Meanwhile Captain Skaugen had been ordered to hire a new crew and head for Archangel, but told Lowry it was near impossible in a small fishing town like Aalesund. However, a collier from Danzig needed firemen and he would introduce him to the skipper that afternoon. In the coffee shop the teacher showed him the poem to Grieg which called him 'the hope of Norway' and was signed 'Nina'. He also told him that Grieg lived in Oslo 'somewhere in Bygdøy Allé'. Back at the wharf, his skipper took him to the collier, a rust-caked old steamer, but its master told him he could only take Norwegians. Lowry then saw the ship's name – 'Nina'. After two weeks in Aalesund (and meeting a girl there, he implied) waiting to see if *Fagervik* would be proceeding, he set off for Oslo. He went first by boat to Aandalsnes, then by night train to Oslo, missing out on the most beautiful scenery in Norway.

In Oslo he bought a new mackintosh and a bottle of whisky, and asked a taxi driver to take him to Bygdøy Allé, planning to drop off half-way and trust to luck that he would find Grieg. However, he was told that Bygdøy Allé, while an avenue in the city, stretched for some twenty or thirty miles beyond, out into the country. So he stopped the cab and asked the first passer-by, in English, if he knew where Grieg lived. Astonishingly the man said he knew him slightly, and he was living under an assumed name near to where he himself lived. Lowry offered him a lift home and there the man said he would take him to Grieg after making an urgent phone call. While taking him to Grieg's apartment the man said he was a shipbroker, and when Lowry mentioned the *Fagervik*, he said he had just been phoning about it and it was on his instructions that the ship had diverted to Aalesund. Asked his opinion of Grieg he said, 'Oh, a sloppy looking chap;' nor did he think much of his work, although some lines of his poetry did jump out at you, like 'Cain shall not slay Abel today'[47] or 'It is worse to betray Judas than to betray Jesus.'[48] Refusing a drink, the man led him to 68 Bygdøy Allé, took him up in the lift to Grieg's apartment, and left him at the door.

About to meet his Bright Angel, Lowry, filled with trepidation, knocked.

> The door opened and there was [Grieg], 'straight from the heart' and with 'his hair parted in the middle', just as the . . . teacher in Aalesund had said. Perhaps he was a sloppy chap too, but I was struck by his extreme kindness. He had in fact just got back from the mountains, and so it was very lucky that I hadn't called before.[49]

The experience, said Lowry, was overwhelming, and writing fifteen years later, he claimed to be able to recall everything Grieg and he had said and done in detail. They became friends and had a couple of whiskies together, but the meeting was brief (Lowry never even removed his mackintosh). Grieg was working hard on a new play, *The Atlantic Ocean* (*Atlanterhavet*) to be put on at the National Theatre that winter. His father had been right; his hero was a good host but did not like having his work interrupted. He said he was heading for Cambridge himself soon, to finish a book on Romantic poets who had died young – Keats, Shelley, Byron, Brooke, Sorley and Owen.[50] He said he was not interested in dramatizing *The Ship Sails On* himself and gave Lowry *carte blanche* to do with it what he could.

Lowry thought Grieg far more interested in the dramatic possibilities of *their* relationship, and remembered him saying that they should write a play about it. Lowry, he said, should have written *The Ship Sails On*, but he [Grieg] had, and, this being the nub of the play, he [Lowry] kills him. This was the theme developing between Lowry and Aiken, and perhaps Lowry transposed it from one Angel to the other. He later claimed that Grieg said the ship he had sailed on for his novel was called the *Henrik Ibsen*, the very name, he said, he had originally given to his ship in *Ultramarine* – thus confirming that strange powers had drawn them together. Now completely entranced by all the coincidences and his encounter with Grieg, and in a heavy storm, he walked all the way down Bygdøy Allé, stopping only to buy a Tauchnitz edition of Julian Green's *The Dark Journey*, yet another book that came to haunt him. They met again next day for lunch at Jacques Bagatelle on Bygdøy Allé, and shortly after they visited the Viking Ship at the Maritime Museum just over the Oslo fjord at Bygdøy, and afterwards, back in the city, dined together at the Röde Mölle (Red Mill), a restaurant popular with Oslo's artistic community. Like Aiken, Grieg was struck by how well his visitor knew his book, and, said Lowry, told him that he was just how he had imagined Benjamin Hall.

But mostly they discussed *The Young Dead*, which Grieg had been working on for six years. He was having difficulty completing it and planned to try finishing it in Cambridge, close to Brooke's Grantchester. The theme was what Aiken called the 'insidious doctrine, well-rooted in narcissism' which makes an early death an attractive prospect to the young artist,[51] an obsession which Lowry had absorbed from his mentor. At the time, Grieg was undergoing an acute identity crisis, and Lowry was lucky to find him so friendly. An unrequited passion for an Englishwoman, and a severe critical mauling for a book of poems, *Norway in Our Heart*, said to be pathetically sentimental and patriotic, had left him uncertain of himself. He was probably in no mood to spend time with a young man obsessed with a book written seven or eight years before by a self he was in the process of shedding.

However, on 8 September Lowry wrote from the Hotell Parkheimen a long intense letter to Grieg which sheds light on their conversations at Jacques Bagatelle and the Red Mill. Just in case he disappeared off to the mountains or to Bergen, he wrote (Grieg was from Bergen, a distant relative of the composer), and they were unable to meet again, he was offering him details about Brooke which he might not find elsewhere, and recommended his *John Webster and the Elizabethan Drama*.[52] His seemingly fluent grasp of Webster, Marston and the dark side of Brooke were pure Aiken, mixed alchemically with his reading for Part I and his own dark vision, to produce an immaculately self-possessed, almost delirious, letter.

Brooke, he wrote, had within him the germs of a metaphysical inquisitiveness which he was unable to develop before his death, and his biographers had missed 'the more terrible and bloody side – in a sense . . . the 'Skibet gaar videre' side of his nature', the side that recalled Webster (in Eliot's poem),

> much possessed by death
> And saw the skull beneath the skin;
> And breastless creatures under ground
> Leaned backward with a lipless grin.[53]

Brooke had been portrayed simply as the Great Lover. Yet it was he who appreciated more than anyone 'the far reaching importance of John Marston, the Elizabethan misanthrope who revived the old Senecan tragedies of blood on a subtler plane, and . . . more or less invented the *malcontent* character,' not just Hamlet,[54] Jacques and Flamineo but Daedalus and Demerest and Swann –

> not to mention all the ruthless women who foreshadowed Webster's flaming duchess, 'The Duchess of Malfi': and exhibited a clinical interest in satyriasis and nymphomania . . . in the dirt, mud, and blood of sex, in its eternal and ruthless power rather than in its sweetness and goodness – which is like Strinberg [*sic*] and O'Neill.

Brooke, he said, understood that Marston was 'one of the most sinister, least understood, figures of Elizabethan literature', who more than anyone gave that great creative flood what he had called, quoting Brooke, its necessary '*macabre* taste, like the taste of copper'. He thought that in identifying with Marston in this way, Brooke, who before he died saw his future as dramatist rather than poet, was '*approaching a Keatsean predicament*', but had not yet reached the edge of the abyss and had already shown signs of 'that most terrible of all fevers, spiritual ambivalence (I mean split mind, divided mind –) or schizophrenia . . .' The letter rose to an apocalyptic climax, suggesting a looming 'Keatsean predicament' in its author:

> Is it not at such times, sir, that one climbs, or attempts to climb Mount Everest? It is at such times that one roller skates to Saigon or Trebizond: or to the South Pole or Arcturus or Popacateptl [*sic*] . . . Or one goes to sea, or commits suicide; or delicately combines the two . . .

He wrote of the World War as a catharsis of such states of mind, and of how Stuart had confessed nostalgia for, as well as hatred of, fighting, much as they felt for the sea. In celebrating war, Brooke may simply have used it as 'a magnificent substitute, – or a ghastly compensation! . . . for the metaphysical danks and darks he would never absorb, *could* never absorb? . . . Was it not better to fall with Icarus than thrive with Smith? fall I mean in that international, unscenical, tragedy of blood which was the great war?' Keats was 'even delighted by the prospect of his own death; he died *consciously*: so with Brooke, the "Dark Self that Wants to Die" . . . was always present even when he himself was most happy and vigorous.'

He ended with the kind of flattery he normally reserved for Aiken. No one, he said, was better fitted to write about Brooke – it was a compliment to England and English Literature – but, with a dig at his own Faculty, added that no one at Cambridge would talk to him about Brooke, 'except as a picture postcard, as a sort of present from Grantchester!' Finally, he hoped they would meet again (quoting Webster) before 'the worm pierce [y]our winding sheet [and] . . . the spider make[s] a thin curtain for [y]our epitaph[s].'[55]

While awaiting a reply to this, Lowry explored Oslo, returning to the Parkheimen in the evening to read *The Dark Journey*. He went to Frognerseteran, a mountain resort just outside the city, reached by a tram which winds up through mists and clouds, and raved about the view.[56] To him the pure glacial beauty of the Norwegian landscape was symbolic of the rebirth he was seeking. And Grieg had doubtless taken him to the National Theatre where statues to Ibsen and Bjørnson proudly stare down 'Storlingsgaten', and he had visited the nearby National Art Gallery, drawing on the back of his letter to Aiken a copy of Edvard Munch's *The Scream*. He was drawn to the stark simplicity of Munch and wrote, that sombre though it was to be a Munch, his madness seemed both healthy and fructifying.[57]

These perambulations around Oslo duly went into *Ultramarine*, which changed dramatically after his Norwegian trip. Dana Hilliot's Norwegianness became more pronounced, and the girl he met in Aalesund was fused with Janet, who acquired a second surname, Trauhaut. Hilliot's ship, the *Nawab*, became Norwegian-built, and he and Janet are haunted by the recurring sight of a strange Scandinavian ship, the *Oxenstjerna*. Passages mentioning the lunar park at Aalesund, a visit to a circus, the Gamle Heidelberg restaurant and the Chat Noir cabaret at the Tivoli Theatre in Stortingsgata must have come straight from his notebook. But from a passage in chapter 2, it seems he also went up a winding hill out of the city centre to Oslo Cemetery. This was where he had all Dana Hilliot's little uncles and aunts interred, 'knocked for a row of milk bottles', the victims of congenital syphilis. The names are listed, Harald Wiers Hilliot, Brigit Eva Hilliot, Edvard Nikolai Hilliot, Mary Sarah Hilliot, just as they are, one name, one coffin, stacked upon the other in the family plots in the Oslo Cemetery. Probably he went there to visit the grave of Ibsen, and there, in its serene and peaceful grounds, discovered a substitute family. The dead, so much on his mind following his conversations with Grieg, were far less troublesome than a living family. And the great dead, like Ibsen and Bjørnson, were also family, for he saw himself as one of the company of writers past. A poem of his reflects the mood of that sojourn in the cemetery, and in it one captures his sense of meaningless disorder, the overwhelming complexity of existence, his readiness to embrace fear as a positive value, and his communion with the dead.

> As the poor end of each dead day drew near
> he tried to count the things which he held dear.
> No Rupert Brooke and no great lover, he
> remembered little of simplicity:
> his soul had never been empty of fear
> and he would sell it thrice now for a tarot of beer.
> He seemed to have known no love, to have valued dread
> above all human feelings. He liked the dead.
> The grass was not green not even grass to him;
> nor was sun, sun; rose, rose; smoke, smoke; limb, limb.[58]

No doubt because he was busy, had pressing personal problems and found Lowry's hero-worship too intense to cope with, Grieg to wrote him on 17 September saying, 'I am very sorry, but I have to work as hell these days. I have got no chance to accept your kind invitation, my nights and days are crowded with work. As a fellow writer I know you will understand and forgive.' A month later Grieg was in Oxford at the Bodleian Library trying to complete *The Young Dead*, and some of what Lowry had written seems to have rubbed off in what emerged. *The Young Dead* confirms Lowry's claim that Grieg was moving from darkness to light when they met. The book, he said, was written in desperation, and when it was finished, 'It was very good for me to come from the land of the dead to the land of the living.'[59]

The meeting with Grieg, said Lowry, changed them both. In his next novel (*In Ballast to the White Sea*), a visiting young English writer helps the confused Norwegian author he admires to choose life over death. The meeting almost certainly had a life-affirming effect on Lowry. Grieg could not have been more different from Aiken. He was a man of action and a man with a social conscience, a man who already, according to Lowry, recognized the dangers of the extreme right in Norway, including a man who until then had been *his* literary mentor, Knut Hamsun, later involved with Quisling. One side of him identified with the noble, self-sacrificial, idealistic Grieg, a Christ-like representative of Light and Goodness. The other side of him embodied the indulgent, self-obsessed Aiken, committed to exploring the sordid and squalid possibilities of the deep and treacherous subconscious – the Mephistophelean representative of Darkness and Evil.

The coincidences he had experienced, obeying a kind of Law of Series, were another important aspect of Lowry's trip, confirming his belief in the existence of an extra-sensory power. 'It shocked me into a new realization of the inexhaustible mystery of this life,' he wrote.[60] Fate had led him to Norway, to the coffee shop, to the teacher who knew Grieg, to Oslo and Bygdøy Allé, and to the shipbroker who had ordered *Fagervik* to Aalesund, and who in turn led him to Grieg's apartment. Doubtless it was fate, too, which took him to Oslo Cemetery, to Ibsen and the great dead with whom he found he could so readily commune. It was an affirmation of the world of imagination over that of cold reason. 'What a plot . . . a kind of Strindbergian Tonio Kröger by Maeterlinck,' he concluded.[61] It was to form the basis for *In Ballast to the White Sea.*

What happened after Oslo is a mystery. Somehow he got a ship home, and probably did not, after all, get to Archangel. In any event, he was back in Cambridge in time to vote for the first and last time in a British General Election, on 28 October, when Ramsay MacDonald's National Government was elected. He wrote later that he had voted Labour out of a sense of injustice rather than for the party, and for an independent candidate who supported the idea of a coalition.[62] This sudden interest in politics may not have been unconnected with his meeting Grieg, who was then beginning to flirt with left-wing ideas, as were many of Lowry's Cambridge friends. He had moved into a ground-floor room at St Catharine's, number two on D staircase, and because it meant being in before midnight or facing a fine, he kept a stock of liquor in his room. The college, however, was still haunted by Fitte, and he would often climb the stairs two floors up to Maurice Hickin's room, taking along a bottle of vodka, drinking to stave off the sleep which brought suicidal nightmares with it. Sometimes he fell asleep in a chair and Hickin would go to bed rather than disturb others by trying to get him downstairs. At other times Lowry would take his friend down to his own room.[63]

He tried to impress his old supervisor, Henn, by informing him that during the long vacation he had worked his passage to the land of Ibsen, but Henn was having no more of him. During this year it is said he was supervised by L. J. Potts of Queen's, but verification of this is difficult because records were destroyed in a flood. Certainly Henn no longer taught him, and he probably failed to attend anywhere for supervision. Also he had fallen back into his bad old ways, drinking heavily again, and friends noticed how out of shape he had become. He admitted that his alter ego in *In Ballast* became so grossly overweight that he was laughed at in the street and people called him Fatty Arbuckle. Also, he claimed, he now identified so much with Benjamin Hall that he went to prostitutes hoping that he, too, would contract syphilis, and thought something was wrong with him when he did not.[64] Maurice Hickin claimed he never heard Lowry use coarse language, but he did tell him that he spent almost all of his free time in pubs and brothels. His old drinking companion, Davenport, had departed prematurely and mysteriously from Corpus Christi in May 1931, the *Gownsman*, *Granta*'s rival, recording sadly that, 'The departure of Mr Davenport has robbed us of one of our favourite victims.'[65] It also briefly left Lowry feeling a bit deserted.

In November, O'Brien's *Best British Stories of 1931* appeared in America, with his story 'Punctum Indifferens Skibet Gaar Videre', renamed 'Seductio ad Absurdum'.[66] With his sometimes difficult son now well on his way to gaining a degree, and being published, Arthur seems to have been persuaded that Malcolm could make his way with the pen. He wrote to Evelyn from London to say that he had made a useful contact on the train up to town, a Mr Derry of Cunards. 'Also met Derry's son who is on the staff of the *The Times*. Derry Senior has been a journalist in London, and has promised to help me with regard to Malcolm when he leaves College.'[67]

In December Lowry visited Grieg in Oxford, where he was working at the Bodleian Library, and said later that he confessed to him his plagiarisms from *The Ship Sails On* but Grieg was just amused. They also talked about flying, a discussion which came back to haunt him thirteen years later.[68] He again spent Christmas with the Cases, and Martin generously typed a fair copy of *Ultramarine* for him. Afterwards, at Inglewood, Evelyn, still hoping for 'thrilling achievements', told him, 'Mawlcolm [she still had the false accent learnt from her elocution teacher], if you get a degree I will buy you one of these . . . er . . . Morning Roundabouts,' meaning a small car then popular, the Morgan Runabout.[69] It was an offer 'Mawlcolm' did not let her forget. But Inglewood stood for everything he was in rebellion against. In the evenings he took off to the pubs, once returning at six in the morning badly beaten up, having got into a brawl. He told Russell cheerfully that he should have been there. But the atmosphere between them was growing frosty as their interests and attitudes diverged.

Although he tinkered with it later, to all intents and purposes he had finished *Ultramarine*. It had taken him more than five years to write since returning from the *Pyrrhus* trip, and had undergone certain dramatic changes from that first straightforward description, as is evident in the short stories hewn from it for separate publication. Dana Hilliot had become more Norwegian, and Norway had been woven into the book, the shades of Aiken and Grieg in turn had leaned over his shoulder as he wrote, and he had dredged up from that photographic memory lines, phrases, and passages from many books stored there consciously or unconsciously, and patched them together in his own way to form a new and satisfying whole, a seamless web of shifting consciousness.

While wrestling *Ultramarine* to a conclusion he had badly neglected Aiken, who was so impoverished by New Year 1932 that he wrote to his Uncle Alfred, 'Funds are so low we've got to run.' Lowry, his old support in troubled times, had not shown up since the previous Easter, and was not just ignoring Aiken but also his studies. At the end of term he gave a reading from *Ultramarine* to the Shirley Society in the presence of a not very respectful Tom Henn. 'ML was not, as I remember, "in an advanced state of intoxication",' recalled one of those present. 'He had, of course, been drinking, but he was very lucid and coherent . . . In his slightly girlish lisp, with the top teeth just projecting on to the lower lip, he insisted that we should not identify the hero "either in love or liquor" with the author. But we did.'[70] Kathleen Raine read it and wrote a long, considered reply, revealing not only a strong sympathy with Lowry but an awareness that he was swimming against the prevailing aesthetic as well as commercial tide:

> It is a romantic poem, disproportionate according to the laws of mathematical form, because obedient to the laws of living form, in spite of your (possible?) intention about its kind and condition. To begin with, the kind of thought is poetic – the whole piece of experience that you deal with. Narrative or philosophic writing could never convey your meaning . . . The whole genius . . . is poetic, in the sense that the genius of Shakespeare is in prose passages (Lear for instance – Edgar). Sometimes the poetry clears itself of its chrysalid novel form entirely, and starts out naked . . . sometimes the balance holds . . . Sometimes, as in the last chapter, one has to make an effort to

> grasp the meaning – to say – 'This is a poem, and the conversation is to be read as poetry' – then it *will* yield its meaning, but not quite perfectly. On the whole, the symbols you use are what hold the book together – Janet, the Oxenstjerna, the uncles & aunts in the cemetery, the micky – . . . I think – there *is* greatness, and that can never be discussed, really. There was not one page that seemed to me meaningless or uninteresting. I hope you will not alter it any more for anybody – suspect the man who suggests alterations to the living organism.[71]

Arthur had been persuaded to hand over Malcolm for 'guardianship' to Davenport, and they took off for Hartland Point in North Devon. But instead of revising for his finals, as expected, they concentrated on finishing and polishing *Ultramarine* (cutting, Lowry claimed later, the material he had lifted from Grieg). The atmosphere was generally convivial. Davenport wired his friend Arthur Calder-Marshall, 'Bar opens 10 a.m., drinks all day to residents. Why don't you come down? Lowry père pays the bill.'[72] While in Devon, Lowry received a letter from Grieg. He got around to replying to this letter seven years later, though the reply was never sent.[73]

By the time he returned to Cambridge, two important events had occurred. In April, at the Cavendish, James Chadwick discovered the neutron, and from that time, as Robert Eddison observed, splitting the once indivisible atom became the ordinary occupation of the scientist.[74] The dawn of the nuclear age was that much closer, and must have been a matter of intense discussion in a circle which included the likes of Bronowski and would-be death-ray inventor, Tom Forman. When Lowry claimed later to have foreseen the advent of the atom bomb in *Under the Volcano*, it is very likely that such an idea was planted in his mind in his final term in Cambridge. Then, on 5 May, Charlotte Haldane's novel *I Bring Not Peace*, dedicated to 'Malcolm Lowry', was published. The Lowry legend, by now well born, was christened and confirmed in print. It would continue to grow, and was something Lowry enjoyed, working to extend and refine it, as he had with *Ultramarine*, and as he would with later work. Having acquired the fictional persona of doomed writer, it became a self-fulfilling prophecy, threatening gradually to overtake and destroy him. Aiken wrote, 'to have manufactured such a myth, and turned himself into it, was perhaps a feat of literary *trompe-l'œil* without parallel'.[75] Now more than ever he was living through literature, turning his own reality into a fiction, and his fiction into reality. As his letters to Aiken suggest, he was already having difficulty distinguishing between the two.

No doubt because he felt in danger of failing the tripos, he decided to invoke a rule allowing a five thousand word 'original composition' to be taken into account if a candidate fell between two degree categories. Lowry duly asked permission of Henn, as Director of Studies, to submit a section of his *Work in Progress*, and this was granted. On 20 May the English tripos final examinations began. How prepared he was is doubtful, and Sykes Davies recalled him racing up to the examination hall still reading Saintsbury's *History of Criticism*. The examiners found Lowry's papers unreadable, so they invited him to read his script aloud to them. However, he was unable to read his own handwriting. So the youngest examiner, George Rylands, was asked to take him aside and 'have a word with him'. Rylands came to the conclusion that Lowry was 'gifted' and so he was passed.

Before leaving Cambridge, however, and while awaiting his results, he gave one final performance as a songwriter. Davenport turned up to produce and write the script for the 1932 Footlights Revue, 'Laughing at Love', the first and, for a long time, the last one women were allowed to take part in. Lowry featured in it, appearing twice, and singing his own songs 'That's What I Mean' and 'Tinker Tailor'. Following the first night on 9 June, *Granta* reported: 'The music was above all excellent. Mr Lowry's ukulele turn was particularly outstanding.'[76] Until his results were known there was time to kill, keeping in shape with Stuart's barbells, and playing the odd game of tennis – he was once observed leaving the courts with Donald Maclean, later to distinguish himself as a Russian spy.

Not surprisingly, on his papers he barely scraped through. George Rylands is reported as saying that he would have just managed a pass had it not been for the submission from *Ultramarine*.[77] On the strength of that it was decided to award him a Third Class Honours. When he got the news he was free to return home to claim his Morgan Runabout. But before facing his family again, he decided to spend some time in Rye with Aiken, whom he had not seen for almost a year.

Although he was inclined to dismiss his time at Cambridge, he spent six years there as schoolboy and student, and was especially devoted to the Festival Theatre with its talented actors and directors, like Robert Donat and Tyrone Guthrie. And he did include in *Under the Volcano* a fond and haunting memory of the place, with echoes of Virginia Woolf's *Jacob's Room*.

> Ah, the harbour bells of Cambridge! Whose fountains in moonlight and closed courts and cloisters, whose enduring beauty in its virtuous remote self-assurance, seemed part, less of the loud mosaic of one's stupid life there, though maintained perhaps by the countless deceitful memories of such lives, than the strange dream of some old monk, eight hundred years dead, whose forbidding house, reared upon piles and stakes driven into the marshy ground, had once shone like a beacon out of the mysterious silence, and solitude of the fens. A dream jealously guarded: Keep off the Grass. And yet whose unearthly beauty compelled one to say: God forgive me.[78]

But there was also the painful sense of having had his creativity frustrated and having been a misfit, suffering what he called 'the profound inner maladjustment of the sailor who can never be happy on land.'[79]

Having apparently now gained his freedom he had resolved never again to allow his father to control him, and to live thereafter as a free spirit. He hoped to be able to make enough from writing to remain free and independent of his family. But Lowry was never able to support himself and Arthur would prove to have an extremely long arm. By now, discovering Kafka (a writer 'who strikes at the soul of man') was to become a source of solace to him, capturing as he did his sense of having to contend with anonymous powers beyond his control. Aiken had read and enthused about *The Castle,* just translated, and Lowry was especially taken by Max Brod's postscript to the book, where he quotes Kafka's line that 'though K's legal claim to live in the village was not valid, yet, taking certain auxiliary circumstances into account, he was permitted to live and work there.' He knew that his claim to live as a free writer at Arthur's expense was a dubious one – yet 'taking certain auxiliary circumstances into account' he was permitted to do so. It became one of his favourite expressions.

CHAPTER VIII

AN ILL-STARRED ROMANCE
1932–1933

> The writer's only responsibility is to his art. He will be completely ruthless if he is a good one. He has a dream. It anguishes him so much he must get rid of it. He has no peace until then. Everything goes by the board: honor, pride, decency, security, happiness . . . If a writer has to rob his mother, he will not hesitate . . .
>
> WILLIAM FAULKNER

Aiken had received an American offer for *Great Circle*, a book which embodies the savage and cynical misogynist vision which he for a time imparted to the impressionable Lowry.

> Love is cruelty. Love is hate. Love is a desire to revenge yourself. It's a bloody great butcher's cleaver, that's what it is. It has eyes of a ferocity known only to comets, its hands are red, its feet are claws, its wings are scythes of jealousy. Its will is destruction: it tears out the heart of the beloved, in order that its own heart may break. Love is murder. It's a suicide pact, and all for what? All for death.[1]

Maxwell Perkins, Aiken's editor, wrote, 'It's certainly not an "easy" book, nor a pretty one, but I think it's effective, myself, and a profounder thing than *Blue Voyage*.'[2] Aiken's agonizing efforts at self-analysis had apparently borne fruit.

When Lowry arrived in June he did not have him to himself. Aiken had taken on two students as paying guests, a Los Angeles poet and a girl from New Bedford called Ruth. Lowry reacted badly. To Clarissa he seemed 'a lonely, ostracized youth terrified of being supplanted or forsaken by his surrogate father.'[3] And when Aiken cast a final eye over *Ultramarine*, he had some harsh unfatherly words about what had been lifted from *Blue Voyage*.

Despite his dejection, Lowry attracted the amorous attentions of both Ruth and the Aikens' housemaid, Jenny, but was too preoccupied and shy to respond. Ruth, however, being American, lodged in his mind as a fantasy figure and was retained for later use. When Burra arrived, vying for Aiken's attention, Lowry's distaste for him was reinforced, and his drinking increased. He withdrew into a trance-like state, even shunning the usual ping-pong matches, bridge and parlour games, and when visitors came he retired with his ukulele to strum spirituals or Beiderbecke. To make him feel wanted, Clarissa would sometimes accompany him on the piano. But he was not the only one under strain. Aiken was also depressed and close to cracking when Lowry left at the end of July. Some six weeks later he attempted suicide by coal-gas poisoning.

With his examination results in his pocket, Lowry set off to spend his twenty-third birthday at Inglewood and to receive the congratulations of the ecstatic Evelyn. Bearing in mind her promise of a car if he got his degree, he managed to persuade her that his Third Class Honours meant that in fact he had come third in the whole university.[4] When he told her that Tom Forman had a car he would sell for two hundred pounds, she readily paid up. In the event he simply pocketed the cash for drinking purposes.

Arthur had had an upstairs room converted into a study for him, hoping he would pursue his writing career at home. After the charges of plagiarism in Rye, he now wrote Aiken a seemingly chastened, though subtly self-justifying letter about *Ultramarine*. Dana Hilliot, he said, was living in 'introverted comas', a man without feelings of his own, who is genuinely 'cuckoo', a poet incapable of writing now and maybe in the future. And in mitigation of his book being parasitic on *Blue Voyage*, however much a cento, having written it at all had given him for the moment a dominant principle. Acknowledging also the influence of *The Waste Land*, he inferred that since Eliot and Joyce revealed their influences openly, more freedom in this regard seemed to be permissible. 'Blue Voyage, apart from its being the best nonsecular statement of the plight of the creative artist with the courage to live in a modern world, has become part of my consciousness, & I cannot conceive of any other way in which Ultramarine might be written.' Yet reading it caused him such intense misery that he believed himself sometimes to be dispossessed – 'a spectre of your own discarded ideas, whose only claim to dignity exists in those ideas.'[5]

Although he felt uneasy about his novel, he wrote three short stories at

Inglewood – 'Tramps', 'China', and 'Enter One in Sumptuous Armour'. 'China' recalls the cricket match between *Pyrrhus* and HMS *Proteus* and again explores that land between dream and reality, for although Lowry had been there it now appeared to him as a kind of fiction, much as it was before he went. But 'you carry your horizon in your pocket wherever you are.'[6] 'Tramps' enables Lowry to express his love affair with ships, real or imaginary. Two sailors, tramps like their ships, sit on a pier and reminisce. Their conversation is intermittent and meaningless, and when they sleep the ships take up the conversation in their dreams, repeating exaggerated and pointless memories. One ship accuses the other. 'You're getting so you don't belong to anything. Just now you may have been lying about your nationality, just for fun, but soon you'll have difficulty remembering your name.'[7] It sounded like Lowry conversing ironically with himself. 'Enter One in Sumptuous Armour' is Lowry's homage to 'Stalky and Co.', and his other hockey friends at The Leys, centred around returning to school at the beginning of his final year having been asked to take care of a 'new bomb', who, though weedy, turns out to have a talent which ensures he is not bullied – a 'Pantagruelian' kick making him a potential star as a hockey goalkeeper.[8] All these stories show Lowry in retrospective mood – the past was beginning to weigh down upon him, like the father in *Under the Volcano* perched on the back of his own son.

Arthur's vision of Malcolm working quietly at Inglewood, however, was not to be fulfilled; he no longer fitted in, and was becoming more and more 'irregular'. He stayed out late, and returned home drunk. He would collect a meal from the kitchen and retire to the lavatory where most likely he would end up being sick, and Sarah would have to clean up after him. He was violent and threatening, and more than once had to be bailed out of gaol by Arthur, who must have wondered what had gone wrong for his dream family to have turned into a nightmare. To Malcolm, he had become a frightening authority figure embodying everything he was rebelling against, but this was a figure of his own invention, ever further removed from the ageing reality. Nevertheless, this was also the man on whom he depended for the one thing that mattered to him and without which existence was unthinkable, the income to enable him to continue as a writer. Now, having justified himself to Aiken, he dispatched *Ultramarine* to Chatto & Windus in London, and when he suggested he be allowed to live in the capital, closer to publishers and friends like Davenport, Arthur reluctantly agreed to pay him an allowance, but only on condition that he live in a temperance hotel and report in person every week to Buston's office in Mincing Lane for his stipend.

London, no doubt, was a refreshing change from the claustrophobia of Inglewood, the strained hothouse atmosphere at Jeake's House, and the restrictive academicism of Cambridge. But Lowry had a way of carrying his own hell around with him. And now, alone in the great metropolis, free of constraints, he was even more at the mercy of forces within himself. At first he stayed in Great Russell Street at the Kenilworth, a temperance hotel, as Arthur had insisted.[9] Ralph Case stayed with him briefly, and for the first time noticed something abnormal about his drinking – each morning at the crack of dawn, before dressing, he helped himself to 'a good snorter of whisky'.[10] Ralph's brother Martin had noticed something similar earlier that summer in Cambridge, when Lowry stayed with him for a while.

> He discovered two-and-a-half litres of a ninety-five per cent alcohol solution of limonene, an essential oil derived from lemon peel which I was using in some experiments. He was ecstatic. 'True fire water,' he called it, and proceeded to polish off most of it.[11]

He sought escape from his inner hell in the city's Bohemia, especially the pubs of Fitzrovia around Charlotte Street, skirting the more prestigious parts of Bloomsbury, where Cape and Faber had their offices and the literati of the Bloomsbury Group had their being. Fitzrovia, with its cheap bedsitting rooms, its scruffy pubs, its friendly restaurants, like Bertorelli's, where you could sit all day over a glass of wine, offered the ideal place to live the casually disordered life which appealed to painters like Nina Hamnett, Rex Whistler and Augustus John, and writers like Dylan Thomas, George Barker, and Louis MacNeice. MacNeice had no time for Lowry; Thomas became a close friend.

He did not last long at the Kenilworth and moved next to a bedsitting room, the first of many, in Old Gloucester Street behind Southampton Row, where George Northcroft, now a junior doctor at the London Hospital, found him. The room soon became a slum such as only Lowry could make – a permanently unmade bed, clothes thrown anywhere, cigarette ends and empty bottles strewn all around. There, too, were the ukulele, the books, the barbells and notebooks. Davenport recalled that all of Lowry's London rooms were extraordinarily squalid, usually unheated and unlit, one in Devonshire Place being particularly dismal. 'He'd got a terrible room and the door had got jammed – he could only get through by taking a panel out of it and crawling through – it was a grotesquely Dostoyevskian place.'[12] The effort to get along and collect his stipend was often too much, either because he was too hungover and preoccupied or because he felt that having to face the faithful scriveners of Buston & Co. was too humiliating a prospect. One day Davenport found him in a bar, unkempt, unshaven and in utter despair, claiming to be broke and too unpresentable to go along to Mincing Lane, where several weeks' money awaited him.

> He was forcibly cleaned up . . . and I accompanied him to the City. He walked into the office quite briskly, exchanged a few words with the chief accountant, and was handed an envelope which must have contained at least £70. Of course he enjoyed pretending to be destitute. It was another of his masks. He also enjoyed spending the money in forty-eight hours on the sad detritus of humanity that haunted London's Quartier Latin.[13]

Davenport saw this obsession with drink as no passing eccentricity. 'It was part of the whole thing of his life, part of this desire not to be born at all . . . Very Melvillian.' Sometimes Northcroft collected his money for him, and when he found him in a bar looking utterly filthy he would take him to his home in Harley Street to bathe and smarten up a bit.[14]

But there were good times too, in convivial Fitzrovia pubs. The Case brothers, when in London, would join him at the Marquis of Granby, the Plough, the Duke of York's or the Fitzroy, and while they hammered out their jazz on the piano Malcolm would accompany them on his uke. Often they were joined by that dedicated 'Malcolm staggerer', James Travers, now silver-fox farming in Devon, who shared Lowry's taste in music. And the legend continued to grow. Martin Case remembered walking with him past a cart-horse standing by the kerb. Just as they came level, the horse gave a whinnying snort and Lowry swung round, instinctively landing it a fierce punch on the jaw. The horse promptly collapsed, leaving Lowry consumed with remorse as usual. An angry crowd gathered, and Case and Lowry had to beat a hasty retreat.

He had come across another book which struck a deep chord with him – the story of a young, part-Norwegian, part-English actor, who runs away to sea, drinks heavily, gets into fights with bullying seamates, and finally dies in a car crash. It was John Sommerfield's *They Die Young*, a title uncannily like that of Grieg's book about dead poets. Michael Redgrave had panned it in *Granta* for its too self-conscious experimental devices, saying that it was 'essentially Georgian in feeling' but sprinkled with modern phrases, leaving out capital letters, and hoping to 'attract the modernist hangers-on as well as the conservative public.' Probably that is what attracted Lowry to it, because he was attempting much the same thing himself, and some of the devices Sommerfield used Lowry also came to adopt. One in particular he used later in *Under the Volcano*. Sommerfield placed his last chapter first, and the rest of the book was a life seen in flashback.

As he had with Aiken and Grieg, Lowry decided he must meet Sommerfield, and traced him to the workshop in the Old Kent Road where he was then employed as a stage carpenter. He was working at his bench when a scruffy-looking and slightly sloshed Lowry turned up and said that he had read his novel and wanted to talk about it. Sommerfield was quite pleased. 'Let's bugger off across the road to the pub,' he said, and they became immediate friends.[15] After that they were often in each other's company, usually on pub crawls, once sampling every brand of whisky sold at the Marquis of Granby and staggering out into the night to see elephants plodding through Soho leaving a trail of steaming dung in their wake.[16] Sommerfield was friendly but very tough, an early member of the Communist Party, later leading attacks on Mosley's Blackshirts, fighting in Spain and working for Mass Observation. He found Lowry uninterested in politics, but this did not prevent a fierce friendship growing up between them. Lowry wrote later that Sommerfield was 'approximately the best man I've ever met'.[17]

Davenport, whose genius as a contact man was flowering, introduced Lowry to Anna Wickham, the poet, who had probably already heard of him from Nina Hamnett, a regular at the Fitzroy, or from Charlotte Haldane, now in London and in touch with Wickham through a feminist group in Hampstead. Her large home at 68 Parliament Hill near Hampstead Heath (dubbed 'La Tour Bourgeoise') was open house for artists, and Lowry soon became friends with her sons, James and John, tall handsome boys who formed a music hall dance act together. James had understudied Noël Coward in New York, and toured with *Journey's End* the year before. They enjoyed Lowry's ukulele playing and considered him most professional, probably because whenever they met him he was sober and on form. However, they were not at all moved by his familiar yarns of suffering at sea. 'Get orf it, Malcolm,' they told him cheerfully. 'If you hadn't wanted to go to sea there was no goddamn reason why you should have gone.'[18]

With Anna he built up a strange creative relationship. She was a large, forthright woman, brought up in Australia; her husband, Patrick Hepburn, a lawyer and amateur astronomer, had died in a fall in the Lake District three years earlier. Her literary friendships were extensive, and she was a particular friend of Natalie Barney, whose lesbian salon in Paris was considered mildly scandalous. She and Lowry would talk about poetry long into the night, and she came to trust his judgement sufficiently to send him her work for comment. He tried adopting her as a mother-substitute, but she was disinclined to indulge him, writing to him with some of her poems in October, 'Concerning the difficult matter of parenthood, for the next hours I am your nice little daughter. So you will permit my performance.'[19] Aiken once found a poem she had written for him which read simply:

You'll sink
Through drink.

Ultramarine was being read at Chatto by Ian Parsons, one of their editors, and by Oliver Warner, the firm's reader. On 30 September, Warner sent Parsons a report which was enthusiastic, but guarded as to its saleability. 'This is an unsatisfactory work,' he wrote, 'because it is potentially so good and so original.' There was a lack of a sense of form but 'the man has a real flair for reporting, in which he is brilliant – he has an ear for conversation which is remarkable.' Despite the likelihood of it making no money and having mixed reviews, and their having to 'murder' the manuscript by excising the 'obscenities', it should be published because it was 'original, and poetic, without being obscure.' He concluded, 'He will never, I think, do four-square circulating library books, but his talent is one to be encouraged.'[20] However, on Saturday, 22 October, Parsons, heading off on a trip to Scotland, parked his sports car outside his office in St Martin's Lane to make a phone call. When he returned, his briefcase with the manuscript of *Ultramarine* was gone – stolen from the back seat of the car. He was not at first concerned – after all Lowry was bound to have a carbon – and so he continued on his holiday. On returning he reported the loss to his seniors, informed the police and arranged for a reward to be posted for the manuscript's return. In the middle of November, with no reply to the advertisement, he finally broke the news to Lowry. Only then did he discover to his horror that there was no carbon. Lowry's reaction, he recalled, was puzzling; he seemed to be invigorated as much as alarmed. Asked if he could possibly rewrite the book, he replied yes, given enough time.

Deeply embarrassed, Parsons offered to pay him a weekly stipend for however long it took him to complete it.[21]

However 'invigorated' he may have appeared, Lowry was now faced with the cruel fact that the previous six years work on *Ultramarine*, the sweat and toil, the personal anguish he had suffered composing it and the enormous personal capital he had invested in it, had all gone for nought. He fled to La Tour Bourgeoise and collapsed with delayed shock. He was quite distraught and threatened suicide. The whole fragile edifice constructed in celebration of his 'genius' had collapsed. Later he told Parsons that he first went home to try to reconstruct *Ultramarine* but could not work there. Then he toured the various places where he might have written or discarded portions of the book in the hope that it could be pieced together or be reproduced from memory in that way, but to no avail. In a final desperate effort to salvage something he went to Birmingham, hoping to find some notes or discarded drafts at Martin Case's home in Edgbaston. He phoned Case from New Street Station, in great distress, announcing that he was saying goodbye to all his friends before taking himself out of the world which had so disappointed him. When he quietened down, Case told him that after he had typed the fair copy of the book he had retrieved the carbon which he (Lowry) had blithely thrown into the wastepaper basket. The day was saved and Lowry was ecstatic. This (minus the amendments made at Hartland Point) was immediately submitted to a relieved Ian Parsons, who on 21 December wrote to say that Chatto had accepted it for publication.

Perhaps because of this near disaster, someone suggested he get an agent, and he asked the firm of John Farquharson to represent him. Farquharson examined the contract from Chatto and phoned Parsons suggesting he improve the author's percentage on sales and offer an advance on royalties. On 23 December, Parsons wrote agreeing to the improved conditions but refusing an advance, and Farquharson then recommended that the novel be sent to Cape, who had recently published O'Brien's *Best Stories of 1931*.[22] Lowry asked Parsons to meet him in a pub, where, after nearly half an hour of mysterious silence and numerous pints of beer, he told the whole saga of his hunt for the carbon and its final discovery. He then begged him not to feel obliged to publish the book because of what had happened, but only if he believed in it.[23] Given a chance to get off the hook, Parsons took it, and the manuscript was returned to Farquharson who sent it straight to Cape who accepted it promptly. Cape, then in a strong financial position despite the Depression, offered the same conditions as Chatto plus a forty pound advance. In the successful afterglow of near tragedy, Lowry set about fictionalizing what had happened. A paragraph in the *St Catharine's Magazine* reported the absent-minded genius leaving his manuscript in a taxi-cab; he told others that he had rewritten the whole novel in just a few weeks.

Shortly before Christmas he was evicted from his bedsit in Devonshire Street, owing almost a month's rent, and moved into La Tour Bourgeoise before paying his annual visit to Caldy to keep the Old Man sweet. With *Ultramarine* about to be published at last he had some 'thrilling news about his achievements' to give to Evelyn. But this time an event occurred which cut him off from a part of his past forever. He returned to his old habit of wandering around the Birkenhead docks gathering notes and visiting the pubs. Returning home very drunk late one night, he barged as usual into Russell's bedroom for a chat.

> He came in a thoroughly obstreperous mood, and I wasn't in that sort of mood. I wanted either to go to bed or write to my fiancée, or something of the kind . . . And so I told him to get out because he was a drunken young bugger and a bloody nuisance. And he wasn't pleased with that, so he hit me and I hit him, and we then proceeded to struggle all around the place. I chucked him out of my room and he eventually fetched up in the bathroom and fell into the bath . . . all very unbrotherly. The house was in absolute turmoil. Neither mother nor Father nor Mary nor Sarah batted an eyelid, and everything remained totally quiet, and nothing was ever said about it.

The two brothers practically never spoke to one another again.[24]

Although Arthur pretended not to notice, such behaviour had become all too common. He was fast approaching sixty-three and, because he had wisely extended the firm's business into insurance and commodities, Buston's was in good shape for the times. Now that he had sons able to run the firm he had thoughts of retiring to the Cotswolds. But as Malcolm became more and more of a problem, the prospect of a peaceful retirement gradually receded.

Back in London, Arthur Calder-Marshall finally got to meet Lowry, but by accident rather than design. Calder-Marshall, who had now had his second novel published, went one afternoon early in 1933 to a party given by the publishers Lawrence & Wishart at Gatti's Restaurant in Duncannon Street. Arriving punctually at five-thirty, he mounted the steep staircase leading to the restaurant. At the top, clutching the brass rail which ran the length of the stairs, appeared Davenport and a companion obviously very drunk. Calder-Marshall realized that the figure with Davenport must be Lowry and they greeted one another amiably. Davenport, however, insisted on leaving, telling Calder-Marshall rudely that he had no reason to talk to him, 'just because you've written two piddling novels, when I am with a writer of genius.'[25] When Lowry said they had a car outside and invited him to join them, Calder-Marshall said 'You can't drive a car,' to which Davenport replied, 'Are you going to stop me?' He and Lowry then piled into the car, and had not driven ten yards before being arrested. No doubt Lowry's fine was paid without question by the Old Man, who was still picking up unpaid bills from Cambridge. But on 12 January, Cape issued a contract for *Ultramarine*, and paid the first £20 of his advance.

Although later he claimed he had rewritten *Ultramarine* from notes, the version Cape saw was substantially the version typed by Martin Case a year earlier. It had developed from its earliest plain account, through one revision after another, into a layered, complex novel about Dana Hilliot's initiation into manhood, swinging from the external life on board the *Nawab* to the elliptical wandering of Hilliot's consciousness through past, present and future around the focal point of a single day on which his innocence is lost. If Lowry also used it to get revenge for his treatment on *Pyrrhus*, it was by including many members of the crew under their own names, knowing they were unlikely ever to read it. It also bears witness to Lowry's breadth of reading, and is indeed, as Lowry confessed to Aiken, a cento of quotations and allusions to the writers he found most impressive, especially Aiken, Grieg, Shakespeare, Conrad and Eliot ('I wish. I were – what? A pair of ragged clauses scuttling between two dark parentheses? Possibly I am.')[26] It was an achievement, but a flawed one.

Through Hamish Miles, his editor, he met Jonathan Cape himself for the first time. Miles was not sure that the passages of Latin and Greek in his manuscript were strictly accurate, and suggested that Calder-Marshall, also a Cape author and a Classical Exhibitioner at Oxford, should look at it. It was agreed they should meet, formally this time, as soon as it could be arranged.

Lowry had moved into his favourite Soho hotel, the sleazy Astoria, and continued to enjoy London, sampling the nightlife, visiting illegal drinking clubs with Innes Rose, now handling him for Farquharson's, as well as the familiar Fitzrovia pubs with all his old friends. Visiting La Tour Bourgeoise, he could now sit back and play the successful author, one of Anna's 'young men'. One day, with James and John,

sitting by the fire talking, Lowry picked up their young brother George's pet rabbit. He was stroking it when suddenly it went limp. He had broken its neck. When he realized what he had done he was terribly distressed, put it into a case and took it away.[27]

On the same day, Calder-Marshall had arranged a luncheon party at the Astoria for a few guests, including Hamish Miles, H. E. Bates, and Edward O'Brien. Lowry suddenly appeared at the door, and was invited to join the company. Miles enquired politely of his new author, 'What are you doing now?' and Lowry replied, 'As a matter of fact I've got a dead rabbit in my case and I don't know what to do with it.' Calder-Marshall went with him to his room and there was George's white rabbit. He suggested that if they called the waiter and ordered a couple of Guinnesses maybe he would take it away. Lowry thought this was a marvellous idea, but proposed that they order four Guinnesses instead. Later, over lunch, Hamish Miles handed Lowry a press cutting, commenting, 'Look, Malcolm, you're famous!' It was an article from the Manchester *Evening Chronicle* of 8 February, with the headline, 'Library Chairman Calls in a Book' and began:

> An intensive round-up by the library authorities of copies of a book to which objection had been taken on the ground that it contains an alleged 'obscene and revolting' story was made in Manchester this afternoon. All copies in the Manchester Public Libraries of 'The Best Short Stories of 1931' in which one of the stories is entitled 'Seductio Ad Absurdum', by Malcolm Lowry, were returned.

A Councillor had complained to the Chairman of the Library Committee that 'the language contained therein is deserving the strongest protest.' The article explained that, 'This action follows the ban by the Libraries Committee on a book in the children's section of a city library.' The reporter added that he had read the offending piece and thought that few young people would be interested in the story after page one anyway.

Lowry was delighted, and for days showed it off to friends around Fitzrovia, and composed a spirited and characteristically funny reply for Miles to use if he wished to respond.[28] He agreed, he wrote with heavy irony, with the Manchester *Evening Chronicle* that few young people would ever get past the first page of 'Seductio Ad Absurdum'. In fact, as he wrote it when he was nineteen he was practically a young person himself at the time, and some of the story's characters were even younger. There were, however, a few things worth knowing about it.

> It is the fourth chapter of a novel (Ultramarine to be published by Jonathan Cape in May) & as such it is consequent upon Chapter 3 & anterior to Chapter 5 . . . & both of these chapters are lyrical . . . containing no dialogue or 'censorious' material and 4 is . . . a contrast to these two – the idea being (a) kind of prose fugue, with recurring themes – Mr O'Brien has decided that it is a whole in itself . . . his idea being to put his finger on the pulse of living work wherever it can be found, of work, which . . . seems to him a criticism of life. He makes no claim that a criticism of life in 1931 is – a criticism of it in 1933, and [as] quite likely by now is my pretty story also, and all the bad words fallen out of use – into 'innocuous desuetude' in Manchester as well as anywhere else. *Conclusion* I do however agree that it should be removed from the children's section. But how in the name of Doodle Dandy & the public pool of shame did it ever get there? Leave them to Tristram Shandy and Don Quixote & Gulliver and the other schoolbooks.

On reading the proofs of *Ultramarine*, Calder-Marshall saw that Lowry had, as Miles suspected, indeed written the Greek wrongly, not knowing how to put on the accents. He also noticed that in the bridge game in chapter 4, which Hilliot overhears and which counterpoints his interior monologues, the bidding was all wrong. Lowry, however, refused to change it, saying, 'That's how I heard it. Let it stay.'[29]

At the end of February, not having seen him for over six months, Lowry decided to bare his troubled soul to Aiken. When he arrived in Rye, Clarissa thought him neater-looking but heavier, probably because he was drinking more beer. Their meeting cannot have been helped by the embarrassing fact that *Great Circle* had just been rejected by Cape, who were on the verge of publishing *Ultramarine*. When once more he found himself being upstaged by Ed Burra, now friendlier than ever with Aiken, he again became withdrawn, and his hostility to Burra intensified. However, he stayed on.

The proofs of *Ultramarine* arrived, and Hamish Miles wrote to say that the printers had raised the question of the indecency of some words. 'There are a few of the taboo words which crop up here and there, and I have ventured to make the customary modifications.' After the problems of a few years earlier with the Home Secretary over *The Well of Loneliness*, and perhaps with the Manchester ban in mind, Cape were taking no chances and *Ultramarine* was made safe.

Aiken, who was flat broke, was talking of a cheap holiday in Spain, an idea of Ed Burra's, who was anxious to visit Granada. He wrote complaining of strain caused by 'worries, illness, poverty, proof-reading, and the care of Malcolm Lowry, who has been with us for six weeks'. Also Clarissa's doctor had ordered her to have a holiday, so with the last of their bank balance they were off to Spain. He foresaw that they would go bankrupt and return to nothing but debts, 'but while we are actually there (since Malcolm goes with us) my wages from Mr Lowry will just support us . . . We plan to stay in Granada all the time we're in Spain, and to come back about the end of May.'[30] Going to Spain meant Malcolm missing Russell's wedding to Meg, some nine years after Arthur and Evelyn had forbidden them to meet. But the brothers' relationship had been strained beyond the breaking point by their fight at Inglewood, and they never met again.

On 1 April, the Aikens plus an overweight Lowry left Tilbury for Gibraltar on the SS *Ormonde*. Lowry took along his proof-copy of *Ultramarine*, his playscript of *The Ship Sails On*, a copy of *Ulysses*, and the inevitable taropatch. According to Aiken, on the voyage, during interminable alcoholic discussions, the strain imposed by his 'pseudo-guardianship' of Lowry began to turn from a friendly rivalry into something more sinister. They had long discussed the necessity for the 'son' to destroy and consume the 'father', and how Aiken's suicide attempt had brought his 'impending' death to the surface. The morbid yet tantalizing question of his creative dying when the sacred inheritance (of poetic consciousness) was passed on – which from Lowry's point of view was so desirable – seemed decreed by the nature of their hermetic relationship. What had begun partly as an experiment and partly as a game for testing one another's wits seemed to have become a more deadly struggle of wills. As events unfolded over the following weeks, this struggle was to have a fateful outcome for Lowry.

On the three-hour train journey from Gibraltar to Ronda, his ludicrous appearance – his over-inflated figure topped by a newly acquired ten-gallon sombrero – brought sniggers from the Spaniards. Aiken commented, 'It's a good thing he doesn't understand Spanish,' and Clarissa wondered how Lowry would cope with the barbed wit of Burra, who was to join them later.[31] His own record of the journey was written in notes for an unfinished story, 'Portrait of a Conquistador'.

> 'Cochinato!' / The word seemed to follow the train . . . He looked at himself in the cracked glass of the toilet window . . . He buttoned his grey double breasted suit, bought from a 50/- tailors 3 nights before sailing; if he held his chest in . . . / Cochinato? What did

> that mean, little pig. He was hurt to the bottom of his being. He saw himself as six feet two or 3 . . . He continually had to lie in order to live up in his own eyes to his conception of himself. / At Ronda he looked up cochinato. There could be no mistake: it meant little pig.*

Between Ronda and Granada, Lowry read *Ulysses*, sweated profusely and exchanged rude gestures through the window with the engine stoker. In Granada two rooms were reserved at the white stucco Villa Carmona, which was popular with artists; previous visitors had included Manuel de Falla, Herbert Read and John Singer Sargent. It enjoyed an idyllic setting close to the beautiful Generalife Gardens and the Alhambra, which had so enthralled Washington Irving. Climbing up to the Alhambra on their first evening, Aiken tossed coins over the parapet and listened for their ringing echoes. Lowry's fell noiselessly into space. 'No echoes, no answers. The story of my life,' he said.[32]

He went off on his own a lot, somewhat to Aiken's annoyance, and drew ridicule for his ungainly figure as he tried climbing the steep walk to the Generalife. Clarissa saw him being jeered and jostled as he lurched through Granada one morning, stolidly observed by Civil Guards.[33] To Aiken's disgust, he was bored by the sights that normally interest visitors to the city – the Moorish fortress, the breathtaking gardens, the gypsy caves and flamboyant dancing. He might as well have stayed at home. But he was confined inside his own country, the inner country of his mind, and in fact was at his most desolate. The Washington Irving Hotel and the American Pension turned his mind longingly towards America and the theme of rebirth. When he did write, it was to work on his play about the syphilitic Benjamin Hall, or make notes about the wretched poor he saw in the streets.

> Cripples dragged themselves through the street. A legless man on a stool used the stool for legs, & his heart went out to them. If I could reach them – their hearts! Only those who are low, down, down, only those who really suffer . . . the heat, the terrible heat, the suffering.

Lowry's Granadan landscape was not Washington Irving's, nor Aiken's, nor Clarissa's; it was the mythic landscape of symbols – the diseased man, the crippled man, the sense of being where the Conquistadors had

* The Spanish word for 'little pig' is in fact 'cochinito'

set out for the New World. His mythic America, on the other hand, offered some kind of hope, some sense of affirmation, the country of rebirth. In 'Portrait of a Conquistador' he reveals how these matters plagued him. He was torn, as ever, between his two identifications: with Demerest and Benjamin Hall. And he was still torn by nagging fears about the all too evident influence of Aiken and others on his book, a palimpsest in which the marks of his sources and influences had been not very clearly erased. The notable thing about it, he wrote, was not its genius but its plagiarism, and the only authentic thing in it was the sea. He still had the uncorrected proofs and so could refute it. But was that possible? The stitches must show. He agonized. If only it were possible for him to synthesize them away.

Aiken and Lowry were keen to visit the first bullfight of the season on Easter Sunday. In Spain, after a week of self-denial and religious festivities by tradition comes the pagan festival enacted in the bullring, the blood of the first bull symbolizing spring's arrival. Both men proclaimed themselves *aficionados*, and Aiken announced himself proud possessor of a signed photograph of Hemingway posed beside a bull.[34]

An odd visitor now joined them, in the form of I. A. Richards, a friend of Aiken's since he had favourably reviewed his *Principles of Literary Criticism* in 1925. Richards, one of Lowry's examiners for the English tripos, and well aware of his questionable reputation, was not happy to find himself and his wife sharing the back seat of a taxi with him on the ride to the bullring. The discomfort was mutual. Clarissa noted of Lowry, 'He felt *de trop*, even disliked, by his former examiner (and hero) . . . Head lowered, shoulders hunched, as if about to lunge, he had the menacing majesty of a bull.'[35] Back at the villa, Richards, en route to teach semantics at Harvard, was anxious to discuss the university with Aiken, but was further discomforted by Lowry trying tipsily to ingratiate himself. Aiken was furious.

Over the following days Lowry was riveted by a painting left behind by John Singer Sargent in payment of a bill, a portrait of Reine Ormond, the Cynthia of *Blue Voyage* – another haunting coincidence. There were musical interludes at a nearby wineshop, El Polinario, where Angel Barrios, the owner and guitarist friend of Manuel de Falla and Federico Garcia Lorca, played flamenco. They talked about Lorca, the local Granadan poet, already hated for his plays and his homosexuality, and destined to be shot there by fascists three years later, much as Lowry's Consul was to be on the Day of the Dead, 1938.

The arrival of the amusingly eccentric Ed Burra did not exactly improve Lowry's already strained relationship with Aiken. Clarissa noticed that when Burra took centre stage singing old music hall songs in a jaunty falsetto, Lowry was unamused, and whenever he joined Aiken, Lowry melted away. When the poet suggested that he show Burra the town, the overweight Lowry stalked moodily ahead with the tiny emaciated Burra dragging unenthusiastically behind. The Spanish jeers were doubled, Burra translating one remark as 'The big one is a German drunk and the skinny one is queer.'[36] When Burra caricatured Lowry as a sombreroed blimp, it was shown around the villa to some amusement. Incensed, Lowry grabbed it, drew a pipe in its mouth, tore it up, threw it in his tormentor's face then said to Burra, 'That was an unkind thing to do. The trouble with you is that people are too good to you,' to which Burra replied, 'Oh you don't know half the things they say about me.'[37] However, despite the tension between them, Lowry was often to be found lying with his feet protruding from beneath Burra's bed in the balcony bedroom they shared, strumming sadly on his uke while Burra worked on a rickety table.

Evening conversations with the Richardses were often spoiled by Lowry's drunken interruptions, and Aiken's patience was at breaking point. It must have been galling to be so dependent on income for the overseeing of this boorish delinquent. One morning while they were out walking, Aiken tore into Lowry, who returned to the villa looking flushed and deflated. He became even more elusive, and he was spied on at Aiken's instigation and repeatedly chased through the cantinas by Aiken and Burra. Clarissa recalled one report of his activities from a local spy: 'Thursday I see him in the Hollywood Café; he asked for three *aguardientes* and two señoritas.'[38] And Aiken was observing him not merely to avert him from trouble. He had chosen Lowry for inclusion in that great centreless and circular novel of his, which eventually turned itself into a confessional autobiography, *Ushant*.

There was unrest in Granada and talk of the impending overthrow of the Republic. The police were closely observing foreigners, and Lowry, who they knew as *el borracho*, was in constant danger of arrest. The tension in Granada foreshadowed what was to erupt in Spain two years later, and the Reichstag Fire in February and the burning of books by Nazis in Munich in May heralded the countdown to war. In Cambridge at the end of the year Julian Bell would be writing, 'We are all Marxists now,'[39] and university contemporaries of Lowry's, Maclean, Burgess, Blunt, Philby and Sykes Davies, not to mention the Haldanes, were to work more or less clandestinely for the communists as the struggle against Hitler accelerated.

On 19 May a glamorous young American girl, Jan Gabrial, arrived at the Villa Carmona, 'a beautiful and swift little creature,'[40] according to Aiken, with a striking line in picture hats and a presence all of her own. At lunch she had noticed the Aikens – Conrad 'red-faced and fleshy', Clarissa 'a tall slender Madonna-like lady' though 'rather colourless'. Conrad was ostentatiously reading a copy of the *New York Times Book Review* with a picture of himself on the cover, doubtless for her benefit. He claimed later that no sooner did he see her, 'clipping over the marble tiles with those absurd high heels of hers, and those fierce all-excluding eyes, under the ridiculous expanse of American hat,' than he 'had already embraced her all over. Known everything. By the time she had signed the hotel register and flashed up the dirty marble stairs.' She knew and admired Aiken's poetry, so was flattered when after lunch Clarissa came over and asked her to take an ice with her. She had already arranged to visit the gypsy quarter with some friends, so suggested that Clarissa join them, which she did. Most likely Aiken had put his wife up to approaching Jan with some lecherous purpose in mind, something he admits in *Ushant*. But that evening, a friend of Jan's, Calef, a Syrian from Tangier, whom she had met in Ronda and who was desperate to marry her, phoned to say he was coming to Granada next day.

Jan, born Janine Vanderheim in New York (in 1911), was the only daughter of Lion Vanderheim, a Dutch concertmaster, and his wife, Emily, an English teacher of German-English-Irish extraction. She had graduated from high school at fifteen, and her mother had wanted her to go to Radcliffe, the prestigious women's college at Harvard. However, she chose instead to go to the Academy of Dramatic Arts in New York, where she took 'Jan Gabrial' for her stage name. (It was based on numerology and was supposed to bring her good luck.) After a few years as an actress, she sustained severe facial injuries in a car accident, which also left her subject to attacks of claustrophobia, so she abandoned the stage for a writing career. For a year she had been on a Grand Tour paid for by her mother, which had taken her to Holland and Belgium to visit her father's family, and to Bavaria in search of her mother's. She had heard Hitler speak in Berlin, visited Mussolini's Italy and then Hungary before heading south to Algeria and Morocco, where she had been chaperoned among the Bedouin by Foreign Legionnaires. But her world was centred on Paris, where she felt close to the authors she most admired – Stendhal, George Sand, Gide, Colette, Cocteau and Raymond

Radiguet. Compared to France she considered America barbaric. She had made all her own dresses for the trip, and, with the help of friends from the Academy, a collection of hats which were a passion with her. When she arrived at the Villa Carmona that May, this colourful creature walked straight into the pages of *Under the Volcano*.

After breakfast the morning following her arrival, Jan invited Clarissa to go with her to the Generalife Gardens. She said she could not but suggested that her friend Malcolm Lowry might like to, as he had not yet been. The two were introduced by Clarissa, and that evening Jan wrote in her journal: 'Today seethed with romance,' and then took up the story.

> So off we started for one of the maddest, gladdest mornings of my life, and certainly one of the dustiest. Malcolm is almost 24, has been all over the world on tramp steamers, has just published his first novel, dislikes his wealthy family, and so lives with Conrad Aiken who is more or less his guardian and who receives an income from Malcolm's father for this stewardship. Malcolm is an odd blend of idealism and earthiness . . . Moderately tall . . . heavily built . . . with fine features and what can be when he wishes 'a commanding presence'. It happens that I read his 'Seducto Ad Absurdum' in Edward O'Brien's *Best British Short Stories of 1931*: it was later banned on grounds of obscene language. He was the youngest contributor to the edition. His mind is complex and brilliant and his conversation engrossing. We wandered through the strangest and wildest paths we could find, finally leaving the gardens behind us altogether, scrambling up and down through underbrush, falling into streams, getting scratched and filthy, and through it all we laughed so much we were practically breathless. The only flaw was the knowledge of Calef's arrival this afternoon. How was I to know I would be meeting Malcolm? After lunch, we walked some more and Malcolm avowed romantic inclinations . . . Believable? . . . Products of the moment? . . . I don't know and I don't think he does either . . . .But the end result of all this was that I arrived at the station too late to meet Calef. I made contact with him later and took after-supper coffee with him but insisted on returning to the pension early. Here I squelched progressive tendencies on Malcolm's part with the flat statement: 'I'm not going to bed with you,' . . . Clumsily done, but it served. Am seeing him again tomorrow morning. What do I do with Calef?[41]

Lowry was bewitched. He could not, he said, get over the fact that she had the same name as the girl in his novel. The hand of Fate was again at work; such correspondences could not be ignored. He told Clarissa '[I am] so much in love I could die.'[42] It was yet another rebirth; darkness had given way to light. Aiken, however, was infuriated. 'All this primping and preening is positively revolting,' he said.[43] Years later, Jan realized that Malcolm's complex, brilliant and engrossing conversation that day was fuelled by drink, but at the time he galvanized her by his magnetism and sense of fun. His eyes were clear and pure and innocent, and there was no sign that the day before he had been withdrawn and depressed. However, she did get the feeling that the Aiken party were getting on each other's nerves. Aiken's version of events was that he introduced the couple so that he could enjoy Jan vicariously.[44] There was a great deal of sexual jealousy in this fantasy; also the realization that now there was a competitor for the soul of his experimental subject and source of income.

Malcolm gave Jan his proof copy of *Ultramarine* and next morning she took it to the Alhambra Gardens and sat reading it until he appeared. In her journal she wrote, 'The book bowled me over. It doesn't seem possible its author is only two years older than I. Whatever qualms I may have about the man himself I am falling totally in love with the writer.' This was her last morning in Granada, so they walked down to the Hollywood Café where Lowry told her that he had learned that psychoanalysis was the best way for a writer to sum up people and understand character, and that he himself was schizophrenic; all this from Aiken's amateur analysis. He also told her that Lawrence and Joyce were his major influences, and dazzled her with tales of his travels to the Orient. As a passionate globetrotter she felt she had met a soulmate, a fellow traveller through life.

At the villa they had missed lunch, but just after three she finally met Calef and toured the town with him. Now she felt she had to choose. Calef was deeply enamoured of her. 'He loves me as Malcolm would never love me,' she wrote. 'Why am I so perverse?' That evening before dinner, she and Malcolm and two men from the villa went out for drinks and Calef joined them. After dinner he proposed, but she said it could never be a marriage made in heaven, and with much sighing and head-shaking he finally agreed.[45]

Although she was exhausted, Malcolm insisted on going for a long walk from which they returned at 1 a.m. He then asked to come to her room 'to philosophize about life,' but she told him sharply that what she needed right then was eight hours of undisturbed sleep. The rebuff worked and he sloped off to bed. But not to sleep. Instead he sat down and wrote one of his long passionate letters. Then, doubtless spurred on by Aiken's lecherous urgings, he crept back to her room at 5 a.m. But he was no smooth seducer. The creaking door woke Jan and the doorknob came off in his hand.

'He wore blue and white striped pyjamas and a brown suede wind-breaker,' she wrote later. 'He looked both rosy and rested, which was certainly more than could be said of me. I could have killed him.' Three hours of interrupted sleep was no prescription for passion. But he clambered into her bed and before anything could be brought to a conclusion he ejaculated prematurely. 'As I was disentangling myself from what seemed like a welter of tentacles, he confessed to almost complete sexual innocence. I bit back several obvious rejoinders and ultimately managed to head him back towards the door.' She read the note he had left her, and found it magnificant. 'I do adore the writer,' she wrote. 'Do I? Can I? feel equal devotion to the man?'[46] Later, thinking of Lowry's lack of inches and staying-power, she wrote, 'Strange how small slight men can be more favored by nature than larger, stockier individuals such as M.' His devotion to her was certain but, at that stage, probably illusory too. He was in love with America, a symbol of rebirth, and Jan seemed to him a lovely glamorous image from one of those Hollywood movies to which he was so addicted.

Their plans took them in opposite directions, the Aikens to North Africa, and Jan to Portugal and Majorca then back to France. They breakfasted together, and Lowry apologized humbly for what had happened. He said his experience on *Pyrrhus* had given him the distorted view that women were all 'wanton' and to be treated as such, the view also of the misogynistic Aiken. 'It seems to be my mission in life to make a mess of other people's lives,' he told her. But Jan thought he was just romanticizing, and was sufficiently enchanted by the writer to forgive him. They vowed to keep in touch by letter and to meet later in France or England. When she left with Calef, who planned to leave the train at Ronda while she went on to Seville, a disconsolate Malcolm waved her off at the station.

Afterwards Lowry and Aiken had a furious row. Lowry accused his guardian of not having his welfare at heart and only putting up with him for the sake of the Old Man's money.[47] He also accused him of trying to turn their father-son relationship into something vile with his perverted ideas about sharing Jan. Clarissa returned to the villa to hear Lowry bellowing, 'And what about incestuous Suzie?' referring to a character in *Great Circle*. And not for the first time he threatened to kill

Aiken[48] Alone in the Hollywood Café, Malcolm wrote an impassioned love letter to Jan, quoting Vachel Lyndsay, 'Darling, darling, darling, said the Chinese nightingale.'[49] Later, he said, he went into the Cathedral and cried. In a second letter he addressed her as 'Jan Gabrial Lowry' and quoted e. e. cummings, 'Nobody, not even the rain, has such small hands.'[50] Together, he said, they could 'knock Lawrence and Moses for a row of milkbottles as prophets.' Aiken had decided to wash his hands of his wild tutee and leave Spain rather than stay to the end of May as planned. On the train to Algeciras, Lowry came down with Spanish tummy and was lost with nothing to read, having left his copy of *Ulysses* behind in Granada. Rather than go to North Africa he opted to stay in Gibraltar, where he again wrote to Jan. She had given life to a dead man whose only gift, it seemed, was to make a mess of other people's lives, he said. Now he gave himself three months to 'clean the Augean stables of my consciousness with its fiendish cloaca of memories, fears, agonies, nightmares, rages & panics, most of them imaginary, which has reduced me to a state of "ceaseless nervous terror".' He urged her to share her sexual secrets with him. But then drinking got him into trouble again. On returning to Gibraltar, Aiken had to tell the police that Lowry was definitely leaving for England before they would let him out of gaol.

They embarked for home on the SS *Strathaird*, where Lowry found himself sharing a cabin with 'three Somerset Maugham colonels [homeward-bound from India] who were dying of the hiccups.'[51] Before sailing, he received a long 'confessional' letter from Jan and spent most of the voyage composing what Aiken called an 'immense "ship's log" ', that mythopoeic logarithm, of a letter imitating his own/Demerest's letter to Reine Ormund/Cynthia as incorporated into *Blue Voyage*.[52] Strangely, the tone of this letter Jan thought 'judgemental' and decided on no more 'confessions'. Aiken, obviously smarting that his plot for sharing Jan had misfired, told him, on a stroll round the deck, 'Keep a pair of scissors handy.'

Asked to explain this sphinxlike pronouncement he replied, 'I don't know. But I know enough to be able to say, when it does happen, I told you so.' On the first night, as the ship passed Cadiz, Aiken, still fantasizing about what might have been, had a disturbing dream involving all three of them. This gripped him so much that he saw it as the germ of that multi-layered flux-embracing novel which he had discussed with Lowry in Rye. Despite the strain between them, Aiken confided the dream to him. It somehow crystallized the notion of Ushant as the point towards which one projected oneself – itself like a multi-dimensional dream.

Jan, meanwhile, was in Barcelona where she had met and fallen in love with a young German. They went by motorcycle to Tarragon, and she only resisted consummating the affair because of the mesmerizingly beautiful letters Malcolm was writing to her. 'Christ Jan,' he wrote in one, 'even your name is the same.' The character he had invented, without whom he could not live, was herself. He dreamed of them living together in Rye, a seaport which has lost its sea, he said, and, already hinting at marriage, he quoted Baudelaire saying: 'You are more than my religion, you are my superstition.' Without those letters, she might never have bothered with him again.[53]

CHAPTER IX

INTO EXILE

1933–1934

Malcolm was very seductive – could take you over. There could be periods of great lucidity – then *Walpurgisnacht*!!!

JAN GABRIAL

Kenneth Wright, seeing news of the impending publication of *Ultramarine*, wrote of Lowry, 'He was the toughest man I ever knew . . . a great fellow, I hope he will not kill himself with whiskey.'[1] But back in England, Lowry was not feeling very tough and was avoiding whisky. He had toothache on top of his tummy bug, and back in Rye begged Aiken not to abandon him. But his adopted 'father' had had enough. 'My trip to Spain,' he told his brother, 'wasn't a holiday by a damned sight – I was in charge of a dipsomaniac, and was paid for it.'[2] Lowry in turn had written to Jan that he would never again share a place with the Aikens. He wrote urgently to her from Rye reaffirming his love and urging her to stay faithful to him. 'I want to hug you . . . to sink into you, as into the sand: oh, the comfort of you, my god the comfort & peace & calm after the seaweariness & blood & sweat . . .'[3] He returned briefly to London, but when Travers invited him down to Devon he went, despite still feeling ill. Travers had a silver-fox farm at Chagford on Dartmoor, and not long after arriving Lowry's condition worsened and a doctor was called. It cannot have helped his mental condition not to be able to write to Jan to keep her interest alive.

On 12 June, the day after Jan's birthday, *Ultramarine* was published. Ironically, on the same day, Lowry was admitted to Moretonhampstead Cottage Hospital suffering from 'dysentery' contracted in Spain, though Clarissa Aiken reported that he had gone in for drying-out. After four days of pain, and away from Travers and the temptation to drink, he got back to the serious business of wooing Jan, and wrote her a long passionate avowal of love, stressing the need to stay pure, and saying that he couldn't bear the thought that she would be giving to others what she would not give to him. When was she coming to England? They would marry, and working together would 'set literature ablaze'. The flow of language, she recalled, was 'allusive, poetic, urgent and intoxicating'. She was bewitched by his wild and whirling genius. When she wrote long letters about her travels he replied that he did not want to hear about places. 'Write to me about a pigeon perched on a lamp-post crying for its love.'[4] He had, he said, been found to have a 'sleeping bug', roused by the heat in Spain and the shock of first loving and then having to part from her. Did she recall how sometimes his hand shook with a drink in it? That was the bug. 'Well, thank god I can get rid of him, & all the bloody complexities & imaginary terrors he has evidently been responsible for all the while, in one, & be a fit man once more.'[5] Not for the last time he would greet an illness as an explanation for his haunting terrors and outlandish behaviour.

He hinted later that he was strangely threatened by the hospital physician, a Dr Dixey, who told him the authorities knew all about his conduct in Cambridge and elsewhere and were only waiting a chance to 'get him on the mat'.[6] On his release, Arthur arranged for him to stay at the Vernon Court Hotel in Torquay, where he could keep a check on him. Travers would come and pick him up in his smart red sports car, but still he felt doleful and weak and found Torquay unutterably dreary. Worried at having nothing from Jan for a while he wrote, 'And do you love me not & is chaos come again, do you peer at all my faults through a telescope . . . Meantime, beware the woman with the dark glasses, the humpbacked surgeon, & the scissors man.'[7]

He was haunted by what the doctor had said to him, fearing that he was being watched. Finally he decided that what he needed was 'a car like Travers, only better'.[8] He remembered the MG Magna that Forman wanted to sell and went to London (Forman decided to make him a present of it, however) and somehow got it down from London to Devon, no doubt with Travers's help. Back at the hotel the car was put in the garage, but although he took instruction from Travers, for a long time he was too nervous to drive it alone. Then his friend introduced him to Peggy Power, wife of a London advertising man, and, despite his obsession with Jan, he began an affair. Peggy, a well-endowed and attractive blonde, grew quite enamoured of him. Later he told a psychiatrist he was immensely inhibited sexually until his virginity was taken by a frustrated married woman in a cottage on Dartmoor – probably Travers's house at Chagford, a little tin-roofed bungalow perched on a tiny hill above the village.[9] Remembering Peggy years later he wrote 'his heart warmed to think of her – ah waiting all that time for him to carry her off – was she alive?'[10]

Travers also introduced him to Bob Pocock, a Metropolitan policeman and part-time Bohemian, and they were often together in Torquay. He had seen no reviews of *Ultramarine*, but finding a puff for it in a Cape catalogue in a bookshop, to Pocock's amusement he became as excited as if over a glowing review in the *TLS*. It was written by Hamish Miles.

> Mr Lowry's gift for taut, direct, photographic writing is impressive, and this first novel of his, if it does not resolve all the strange chords it evokes, is decidedly one of the most striking works of imaginative realism that has come my way for a long time . . .

At least it gave him an idea of what his editor thought of it.

He was disappointed to find very few reviews of his book in the London papers. However, the Liverpool *Post and Mercury* had brought news to Merseyside that 'Mr Malcolm Lowry is Liverpool's latest novelist.' The book, it said, was unusual and striking, but the hero was so highly sensitized that he 'should never have gone to sea in the circumstances . . . '

> The turmoil of his hero's mind and body gives Mr Lowry a great opportunity, and he uses it with a resource and exuberance that seem to blur slightly his intentions . . . The result I feel is obscurity . . . One has to recognize that [he] is a writer of unusual power . . . But [here] reality is lost in unreality, and . . . theme and method are out of tune.[11]

The Liverpool *Post* commented that the seed of Lawrence and Joyce was now ripening and Lowry was in the first harvest. Whether she read this or not, Evelyn was unimpressed. Lowry claimed that she locked the book away, scandalized by the language. No doubt if she had been on the local library committee she would have voted for a ban.

Unfortunately, James Hanley's *Captain Bottell*, another sea-novel, had been published in the same week, and was often reviewed in preference to *Ultramarine*. However, on 24 June, V. S. Pritchett gave it space, though few cheers, in the *New Statesman*.

> The curse upon the book is a strained self-consciousness, and self-conscious writers are metallic, monotonous and unrevealing. When he is not swinging the pendulum back into a number of unimportant

> memories of his schooldays, forcing a significance upon them which never justifies itself either in the story or as an illumination of temperament, he is reporting the fo'csle [sic] Hemingway dialogue. He is all nerves . . . Yet *Ultramarine* has a quality . . . When he has stopped straining eyes, ears and nerves and ceases to let the world hammer him so that he sees nothing but stars and fragments, he may do something good. His broken dialogue *in vacuo* bored me, but his direct and unevasive descriptions did not.

Simultaneously, Derek Verscoyle in the *Spectator* found the book 'disastrously mannered', and though some scenes were excellent and some individual episodes satisfactory, he thought the mixing of literary conventions produced 'no unity of impression.'

It was July before the *Bookman* gave it a short notice, but one worth waiting for. '*Ultramarine* is not at first "gripping" like the ordinary slick novel. It requires personal effort on the part of the reader, like good poetry. Once that effort is made, it sweeps one towards that satisfaction and inspiration which is the gift of great poetry.'[12] The *TLS*, whose review Lowry anticipated in the book, almost fulfilled his prediction, being oddly dismissive.

> *Ultramarine* reads less as a novel than as the first expansion of shorthand notes taken with a view to making a novel out of a new experience . . . The author's method of exhibiting the seamen as men of few ideas and few words is to report the words as they were spoken . . . The youngster's thoughts are set down with the same absence of selection as the talk of the men; it is as if they were reproduced from a recording machine. If the art of writing is imitation the author has mastered it . . .[13]

A satirical review in the *London Mercury* said, 'I dare say that Mr Malcolm Lowry's book will "ring bells" (as he hopes it will) with anyone who may have been through precisely similar an experience. But to the uninitiated the greater part of it is Greek.'[14]

No doubt because of the book's mixed reception he did not even send a copy to Jan, though he gave copies to Sommerfield, Martin Case and Davenport. In desperation he sent a signed copy to Richard Aldington, an acquaintance of Aiken's, who reviewed for the *Sunday Referee*, explaining the symbolism of the book. On 25 August, Aldington replied from the South of France, saying why he thought the book had not caught on with reviewers.

> A novel interests primarily through action, and the action must be successfully dramatised. Now, though I was interested in Hilliard's [*sic*] psychological conflict, I don't think it's sufficiently dramatised, it doesn't become externalised enough for the ordinary person. Again, while the talk of the fo'c'sle hands is excellently reported, the conversations don't get anywhere. Well, you'll say, they don't. But in a novel, it seems to me they've got to. You've got to give them a significance, and one so obvious that fatheads can see it. Do you see what I mean? From the selling point of view, you've got the material for a successful novel, rather than the novel itself . . . If I were you I'd call this book a miss in baulk and get on to the next. It's damned hard luck, but there it is. If a novel doesn't catch on in the first six weeks, it needs what your ABs call a bloody good unusual miracle for it to get going. Why not go and see Cape, and ask what he thinks about your having another shot at a novel. A success would revive this one.[15]

It took thirty years for Aldington's prediction to come true.

Although confined by Arthur to Torquay, Lowry did occasionally get back to London. In late July, staying again at the Astoria, he met Dylan Thomas at the Fitzroy. Thomas, just nineteen and looking, according to Pocock, a cross between Rimbaud and Groucho Marx, and to Davenport, 'an extravagant buffoon',[16] was on what must have been his second ever visit to London from South Wales. Thomas had also got to know Anna Wickham through Davenport, and he and Lowry met occasionally at La Tour Bourgeoise. Thomas said later that Lowry had encouraged him and talked enthusiastically about his poetry to everyone he met. Lowry also went up to London in August, hoping to interest theatre managements in his play of Grieg's novel.

Back in Torquay he kept up the bombardment of passionate love letters to Jan and she had replied to him from all over Europe – the South of France, Florence, Capri and finally Paris again. When she wrote to say that her trip to London might be delayed, he wrote back in great distress. How could she do this to him, he demanded. And again he cast his verbal spell over her so that she immediately agreed to come. He was delighted. He wrote urging her to travel by Channel Ferry to Plymouth, closer to Torquay. The ferry, the *Paris*, he told her, was most luxurious with a glass dance floor and a putting green.

One day in September, Travers invited him to Chagford for a pub-crawl with Pocock and telling him to bring the car along. The terror which the idea of driving inspired in him, he wrote, was akin to his terror of sex, but after several pints at a pub near the hotel, he felt he could drive anywhere, so he jumped into the MG and drove it happily the twenty miles to Chagford. Within a short time he and Pocock were completely drunk on rum and Lowry was under the table with his uke singing spirituals. After finishing the rum they retired to the Three Crowns in Chagford, Travers in his car, Lowry and Pocock in Lowry's, where they started on whisky. Then, with a supply of booze, they set off back to the bungalow, Travers leading the way along the corkscrew road from the village. Lowry failed to navigate a sharp bend and but for a huge flat rock, they would have plunged over a two hundred foot drop. The car was disembowelled and it took six farm labourers to lift it back on to the road again. The visit ended when, in the dead of night, Pocock and Travers were woken by screams. They rushed into Lowry's room to find him ashen-faced and shuddering. 'I'm being pursued by a salamander!' he said.[17]

Later they went swimming in Torbay and Lowry easily raced them to the centre of the bay and back. Afterwards he said, 'You know, they put a male nurse on me, to shadow me.' What on earth did he mean, they asked. 'He was there this afternoon . . . Out in . . . the middle . . . I turned over on my back to float, and there he was, swimming towards me.' Where was he now, they enquired. 'Oh, he's gone,' he said, 'he's like that. He just appears and he disappears.' The others were convinced he was becoming paranoid, but he had not told them about the menacing Dr Dixey, and it was not beyond Arthur to have hired someone to keep an eye on him. Now he had to pick up the bill for the damaged car and have it towed up to Liverpool.

Jan was annoyed at the suggestion that she come to Plymouth, and told Malcolm that she was not interested in glass dance floors or putting greens or in coming to Plymouth, but would meet him in London. Much chastened by the accident and her refusal, he replied quickly to say that he would meet her at Victoria Station and failing that she would find him at the Astoria. He added that now they had something else in common – a car crash.

He somehow managed to persuade Arthur to let him return to London. But the Old Man decided that his dissolute son, running up hospital bills and crashing cars, still required a 'guardian'. Lowry suggested Sykes Davies, now apart from Kathleen Raine and living in sin with the old Epstein model and self-styled 'Tiger Woman', Betty May. A meeting with Arthur was arranged and he was persuaded that Sykes Davies, having taught him at Cambridge, was suitable for the job.

Malcolm moved into a spare room at his Hampstead flat. Living with Lowry, however, brought people into contact with his more eccentric personal habits. One morning, Sykes Davies went into his room and there saw him pouring amber-coloured liquid from his shoe into a bottle. Was it a new way to distil liquor, he enquired, curiously. Lowry tugged on his sprouting blond moustache for a while and then explained.

> Well, Hugh, you know, not to put too fine a point on it . . . I notice that in this hot weather my feet smell. So I bought a large bottle of eau de Cologne from Woolworths. I put it in my shoes and leave it there overnight, and in the morning I pour it back into the bottle.

He was, said Sykes Davies, 'fastidious indeed on the one side, but handicapped on the practical side in carrying out a programme of fastidiousness.'[18] From time to time, Lowry would check into the Astoria because it was a more convenient base from which to drift around the pubs at night.

Jan arrived in London on 22 September, four months to the day after their parting in Granada, with every expectation that the hot and eager lover who had overwhelmed her with the most extravagant love letters imaginable would be waiting excitedly at the quayside. But he was not at Victoria Station; nor, as he had elsewhere suggested, was he at the American Express; and, after trudging through Soho, she found that he was not even booked into the Astoria. Finally she got herself a room in a Chelsea boarding house, just off the King's Road, once recommended by an English artist she had met. The artist, she found, was living there, so for the next three days he squired her around London, showing her the sights.

Then, four days after her arrival, while collecting her mail at the American Express, she found Malcolm waiting, full of apologies. He had been at the station but missed her; he had been at the American Express but had not seen her. (More likely he had been dallying somewhere with the eager Peggy Power.) Jan accepted his apology but their meeting could not have been more of an anti-climax. Instead of some great romantic gesture, he took her off on a pub crawl through Soho. Not until the pubs closed and he was fairly drunk did he become at all amorous, and abruptly asked her to marry him. But after this dreary amble through London's Bohemia, she was distinctly unimpressed and gave him a dusty answer. That night she wrote in her journal, 'What kind of writing-paper lover is he?' The last thing in the world she could conceive of doing was marrying Malcolm Lowry.

Next day she had arranged to visit the British Museum with a professor she had met in Berlin. However, early that morning, Malcolm rang to say they were flying to North Wales in Tom Forman's plane, so after meeting the professor for a short time, she left with Malcolm, Forman, and Forman's girlfriend Elizabeth Cheyne, for Heston Aerodrome, where Tom's plane was waiting. Bad weather forced them to fly instead to Reading and back, plentifully fortified with alcohol. Malcolm returned with her to Chelsea, equipped with the inevitable bottle, and it took a considerable effort to eject him from her room when, around midnight, he became demanding. He was more than attractive to her – magnetic, dynamic and utterly vital – but she was scared stiff of getting pregnant, having already had one or two false alarms during her time in Europe. Outside in the Chelsea street, Lowry, heading for the Astoria, climbed unsteadily into a taxi and waved goodbye.

Early next morning, Forman called her to say that Malcolm had disappeared. He was not at the Astoria, nor in Hampstead. It looked like the trip to Wales was off again. Then, in the middle of the morning, the lost sheep turned up. Instead of going back to the hotel, he had spent the night with the taxi-driver. In a short story, 'An Economic Conference', Lowry used that evening as the setting for a wild and meandering surrealistic tale of a brief encounter which develops into a night of over-exaggerated disputation between Bill, a Taximan, and Bill, his passenger, about the state of the world. He never, as he advised a young writer friend twenty years later, wasted any experience – it was all grist to the mill.[19]

Finally they took off for North Wales, though this time Elizabeth Cheyne wisely excused herself. After an emergency landing on Birmingham racecourse because of bad weather, and a brief meeting with Martin Case, they went on to North Wales by train.[20] When she remarked on Malcolm's heavy drinking to Forman, he told her it was due to sexual frustration, and that he would sober up once he got married. He took them to Pen-y-Pass on the Llanberis Pass, high up on Mount Snowdon. They booked into the Gorph Wysfa Hotel, which Forman had discovered a year earlier on a climbing expedition. Lowry was delighted to find in the visitor's book an amusing comment which he later inserted into *In Ballast to the White Sea* and *Under the Volcano*:

> 'Climbed the Parson's Nose', one had written, in the visitors' book at the little Welsh rock-climbing hotel, 'in twenty minutes. Found the rocks very easy.' 'Came down the Parson's Nose', some immortal wag had added a day later, 'in twenty seconds. Found the rocks very hard.'[21]

Although, according to Hugh in *Under the Volcano*, from the top of the Parson's Nose he could walk home to tea across the hills if he wished,[22] there would be no going home to tea for Jan; this was the nearest she would ever get to Inglewood. But Inglewood almost came to her. One morning, Malcolm told her his father was coming to the hotel and on no account must he know she was with him. She must hide in the bedroom. 'But I can be Tom's girl,' she said. He was, however, adamant and she could see just how afraid he was. The hotel had no central heating, the bedrooms were like ice and she had brought no appropriate winter clothing, so she stayed in bed shivering, and fumed. She already had a cold and felt generally wretched, all of which did not endear her to the man she had travelled so far to meet. Forman left and Jan and Malcolm stayed on for a few days. When he said he had to go home for some reason, she could not wait to return to London.

Back in Chelsea shortly afterwards, Forman asked her to look after his dog, but with the noise of barking and Malcolm's everlasting taro-patch, her landlady finally asked her to leave. The Astoria was full, but she found a room in Baker Street, where she met a wild South African girl, a mine of information about contraception, who taught Jan everything she knew. Perhaps because of this she began to be less nervous about Lowry's persistent advances. However, their relationship was becoming rocky. Once he and Sommerfield turned up drunk and late, after she had waited for two hours in pelting rain to meet him at the Dominion Cinema, Tottenham Court Road, so she left him. A few days later he waylaid her outside a theatre asking her to meet him at the Alhambra next day in symbolic remembrance of their meeting in Granada. Then, after he became drunk and noisy at Anna Wickham's, she left him again, and again he found her, coming out of the ballet, and again their romance was patched up. His strength of personality had come to exert considerable power over her. What really impressed her was his utter self-confidence in proclaiming himself a great writer who would leave his mark on literature, and it was difficult to forget those letters, each one a work of art. And at his best he was the perfect English gentleman with, to her American ear, a beautiful voice, as rounded and melodious as Dylan Thomas's became. This time their relationship picked up, and he took her around proudly showing her off to his friends.

She met Innes Rose, and they dined with Tom Forman and Elizabeth Cheyne, a quintessential English rose. But, according to Jan, they studiously ignored her, despite Malcolm's efforts to include her in the conversation. They met Pocock on his beat in Oxford Street and Travers drove them 'like a maniac' along the Strand at sixty miles an hour in his red sports car. Jan was now living in the Florina hotel at 63 Kensington Gardens Square, and wrote to her mother all about the man she was now eager to marry. Mrs Vanderheim, with a wickedly shrewd instinct, wrote, 'Tell me candidly, does Malcolm drink excessively, because if he does, don't have him for anything in the world because it doesn't improve with marriage.' However, if he was all she said he was, then he would be like her own son, and marrying someone of literary fame she might do as well as George Eliot. 'I am more satisfied that you should choose an Englishman than any other race,' was her final word on the matter.[23] Many Lowry-watchers have thought that Jan brought a radical left-wing ideology to the relationship, but in fact she, like her mother, was a true-blue Republican who had greeted Roosevelt's election the previous March with gloom. She found Malcolm very much to the left, and thought, correctly, that this was probably the prevailing outlook of his Cambridge contemporaries. And although he was by no stretch of the imagination an activist, being far too bound up with himself, his sentiments were anti-bourgeois and radical.

In October, he had a story published in *Story* magazine, edited by Whit Burnett and Martha Foley. 'On Board the West Hardaway' was yet another version of the tale of the drowning pigeon on *Pyrrhus*. In it, he takes up again Grieg's theme of the contrast between the vulnerable bird and the iron Moloch of the ship whose jaws crush the men within her, and the miracle of birth against the cruel inevitability of Fate. The carrier-pigeon is a messenger of love and, Janet, the girl left behind, seems to him remote – a figure in someone else's dream. The hero, now called Dana Hall (showing Grieg's continuing influence), dreams of proving himself a man to the crew, to himself, and to Janet; but torn between his desire to shine as a man and awareness of his fear of life, he is unable to act.[24] He ends with a sentence lifted from Grieg, 'Outside was the roar of the sea and the darkness,' a sentence also used at the end of chapter 5 of *Ultramarine*, and for the title of a set of later poems.

No doubt appearing in the prestigious *Story* magazine enhanced his kudos with Jan. For here was a regularly published writer – just what she aspired to be herself. By the beginning of November it had been decided that they would get married. Malcolm had proposed frequently, but Jan had always said 'No'. Now he had stopped proposing; but, after a certain time, marriage was just taken for granted, and they became 'engaged'. After the storm and passion of the chase, they seemed to have just drifted towards something more permanent. The only difference between them was that whereas Malcolm wanted merely to get married, Jan wanted to get married in Paris. However, fearful that he would be cut off if his father found out, he was quite happy to marry away from England. It was decided that Jan should go ahead to Paris to arrange things.

Before she left, she and Malcolm stayed alone at Sykes Davies's flat and there finally consummated their relationship. Jan recalled being very nervous about sex with Malcolm and this first time was 'not much of a much', no skyrockets.[25] He swore that he was all but a virgin – there might have been one woman – a maid, a barmaid, somebody in his father's house, he told her vaguely. They were exploring and experimenting. They shared a Rabelaisian sense of humour, and Lowry taught her roaring drinking songs, like 'The Bastard King of England' ('His hairy great dong hung down to his knees'), trotted out all of Aiken's filthy jokes and recited his favourite limericks ('There was a young man of St John's / Who wanted to bugger the swans . . .'). But when she suggested joining a nudist club he was adamantly against it, perhaps too self-conscious of his underendowment.

Davenport took him and Jan to the Café Royal for dinner just before she left for Paris. As usual, the more Davenport drank, the louder and more aggressive he became, this time giving vent, according to Jan, to a stream of anti-Semitic remarks, no doubt hoping to cause a scene. A man at the next table rose to protest and Davenport knocked him sprawling.[26] That night, Jan's last in London, she and Malcolm stayed with him at his Pimlico flat, so cold that they all ended up, à la Noël Coward's *Design for Living*, in the same bed clinging together for warmth. He gave her a letter of introduction to Julian Trevelyan whose Paris studio was a crossroads for British and American exiles in Paris. She left for France at the end of November, and Malcolm went home to get permission to draw his allowance in Paris. He told Arthur he needed to study at the Sorbonne, and, probably to keep his difficult son away from Inglewood, the Old Man agreed, on condition that he found a suitable 'guardian'.

There was time for one last fling in London. Lowry and Sommerfield crawled through the Soho pubs, rubbing shoulders with the passing parade of boozing Bohemians – Thomas, MacNeice, Sean O'Flaherty, Nina Hamnett, Charles Laughton and Elsa Lanchester. In the Scotch Pub they met Pocock, who irritated Sommerfield so much that he set fire to Pocock's tie. Lowry meantime was being written into Sommerfield's latest, and never-published novel, *The Last Weekend*, where he appears as the drunken novelist, David Nordall, named no doubt after the author of the book Lowry was trying to dramatize. Nordall needs to write in order to deal with his agonizing internal conflicts, but the easy way out he takes through drink is destroying the very talent that alone can save him. He delivers long psychoanalytic monologues, much like those Lowry had learned to recite from Aiken, and recalls a childhood of neglect and cruel nurses.

> David, whose hair is standing on end, is swaying about in his chair. When he talks he splutters, runs out of words, and everyone waits tensely for the end of his remarks; his pipe keeps on going out and he continually loses his matches. This, I imagine, is the way he conducts all the practical affairs of his life; now he burns his fingers trying to light a dead match at the gas fire; now Pat hands him a lighter, which he cannot get to function.[27]

He tells a 'long, very complicated story that, everyone felt sure, was leading to a tremendously funny climax, that continually receded behind a mist of parentheses',[28] and makes strange observations such as 'Regent's Park, like Dante's Inferno, is divided into circles.'[29] And when drunk he undergoes a Jekyll-to-Hyde transformation, a characteristic Lowry shared with his friend Davenport.

> David kept laughing, a wild laugh in which he bared his teeth and seemed to grin ferociously. There was something alarming, almost dangerous, about him when he was drunk like this. He exceeded the stages of comic or foolish drunkenness, but he didn't go through the sagging, slobbering, repulsive last stages of ordinary boozing. After days of hard drinking he became like this, only a little way from delirium, and his behaviour quite incalculable.[30]

His friend Martin Case, who, it was rumoured, had got into hot water over an affair with Charlotte Haldane, was heading for Kenya. That is how one of his friends interpreted Lowry's using a pub called The Case is Altered, to which the young Geoffrey Firmin repairs after being caught *in flagrante delicto* in the Hell Bunker, in *Under the Volcano*. Case received one weighty farewell present from Lowry – his prized set of barbells, perhaps thinking they would be out of place in a small Paris apartment. Whether he said one last fond farewell to Peggy Power is not known, but all those years later he wondered if she might still be waiting for him.

In Paris, Jan contacted Trevelyan, then working at Atelier 17 with W. S. Hayter and a group of like-minded artists including Max Ernst and Joan Miro. Tall, handsome, with light wavy hair, and a penchant for colourful clothes, Trevelyan was living in the Villa Brune off the rue Des Plantes with a beautiful New York artist, Louise Scherpenberg, with whom Jan struck up an instant rapport. Trevelyan helped her cut through the forest of red-tape necessary to get married in France, and put her in touch with the Irish writer, Kathleen Coyle, who was about to vacate an apartment in the nearby rue Antoine-Chantin. She found Coyle charming and took the apartment which was, she thought, delightful. Coyle also had a story in *Best Stories of 1931* – a good omen maybe. Finally Jan had the banns posted at the church of St Sulpice in the sixth Arrondissement.

After Christmas at Inglewood, Lowry headed for France. When he arrived in Paris on 30 December the city was looking its best under a blanket of snow. Jan met him at the Gare du Nord and took him to the Hotel Pas de Calais where she had reservations. There she gave him his wedding present, a gramophone and a set of Red Nichols and Beiderbecke records, found after much searching around the Left Bank. He wanted her all to himself, but she preferred to dance the night away; the New Year and their coming marriage were cause for celebration. But being no dancer, he was not keen. He asked her to write to his father, posing as his landlady in order to receive his weekly cheque. They could fiddle expenses and wring as much out of the Old Man as they could. Jan refused point-blank to start their marriage with a lie. Trevelyan, however, was happy to undertake the masquerade, and Lowry rewarded him with a copy of *Ultramarine* inscribed 'To My Guardian Angel'.

Having finally won his woman, paraded her proudly around London, and at last achieved some degree of sexual fulfilment, Lowry found in Paris a new and alarming sense of insecurity. Whereas Paris was home to Jan, he was on unfamiliar territory. She knew the city and had many friends there; he had been just once, with the school hockey team, and the only familiar face to him was Trevelyan's. His insecurity was only heightened when he found that rather than wanting to spend the next few nights tucked up in bed with him, Jan had accepted an invitation to a New Year's party at Trevelyan's studio. Lowry was emphatic. He did not want to go, nor did he want her to go.

On New Year's Eve it was snowing. They met Trevelyan and Louise at the Dôme, in Montparnasse, and sat outside drinking and warming themselves at braziers placed there. Malcolm sat withdrawn and aloof. Jan's attempts to cheer him up and include him in the conversation were fruitless. Then he disappeared, and no one noticed for a time. Finally someone asked, 'Where's Malcolm?' and Louise went to find him. After a while she returned, leading him by the hand. She had found him sulking in the gents. 'He just wants his mummy,' she said, and handed him over to Jan for comforting.

Trevelyan's party had attracted not only artists, but writers like David Reeves and James Stern, the twenty-nine year-old Anglo-Irish Old Etonian, ex-Sandhurst, ex-bank clerk, ex-farmer, just back from Africa and author of a well-reviewed book of short stories, *The Heartless Land*, then living with Ethel Mannin. The party was a lively affair, a farewell 'do' for a number of American expatriates returning home after the decline of the dollar. Lowry cared nothing for the others, wanting only to walk the snow-covered streets of Paris alone with Jan. The studio was packed, room for dancing was restricted, and close contact unavoidable. Jan, back in her favourite city and about to marry the man she loved, was in a gay mood. She wanted to dance, but Malcolm did not, and really could not. When a handsome English artist called Brockenshaw asked her for a dance, she readily agreed.

It didn't take Lowry long to react. As he watched broodingly his jealousy erupted. He dashed forward, pulled Jan roughly away from her partner, then turned on him. When Stern tried to intervene he spun round and fisted him hard in the solar plexus. As he went down, Lowry turned angrily towards the object of his hatred. Brockenshaw backed off and his brother, also an artist, came up to defend him. Lowry grabbed the brother, dragged him to the middle of the studio, and forced his arm on to the hot stove. As the man roared in pain, Lowry was dragged away by horrified onlookers. He shook them off and left. Jan followed, caught up with him and took him back to their hotel. It was not the most auspicious beginning to 1934. They moved into 7 rue Antoine Chantin three days later.

On 6 January, at 10 a.m., they were married at the Mairie of the fourteenth Arrondissement. Trevelyan was best man and Louise bridesmaid. Jan was dressed in a smart new suit from Vienna, and Malcolm for once wore a tie around his neck instead of his waist. He had forgotten to buy a ring, so they used an old one of Jan's. There were fourteen or fifteen couples packed into the Chambre des Mariages, and each in turn was called forward by the Maire. In England the story was that Malcolm, when asked, 'Do you take this woman?' replied 'Ça va, ça va.' It made a good story to have 'Monsieur Ça Va' answer in this way, but Jan remembered differently. He said nothing, but stood there dumbstruck. Finally, Trevelyan whispered 'Oui', and Louise whispered 'Oui', and thereafter the joke was that it was Julian who had really married Jan. It was only later that she realized why he had been tongue-tied before the Maire. He was terrified of officials, and became panic-stricken just going into post offices to buy stamps. As they left the Mairie, a figure came forward, hand outstretched, murmuring 'Pour les pauvres.' Lowry relaxed, broke into a huge grin, put his hand into his pocket and said, 'At last some words I can recognize.'

The wedding breakfast was held at Trevelyan's studio, a magnificent meal of rice pilaf and mock champagne. Malcolm gave Jan a couple of college sweaters and later a copy of Hemingway's *Winner Takes Nothing*, inscribed, 'This is for Jan Gabrial, author, 22, otherwise known as Starkey, with love from her husband.' Just a few of his friends were there. Some commiserated with her, genuinely curious. Why on earth had she married Malcolm? She was, she remembered, somewhat stuck for an answer. 'We didn't have a honeymoon, we didn't have a wedding ring, we didn't have wedding gifts. It was a very haphazard kind of marriage.'[31]

They settled into as domestic an existence as Lowry could take. He was keen to get *Ultramarine* published in France, and through Kathleen Coyle met Maurice Sachs from *Nouvelle Revue Française*. Sachs was an odd figure – a protégé and ex-lover of Cocteau, a Jew who Cocteau persuaded into the Catholic priesthood, a conversion long-since renounced. He was just back with his American lover, Henry Wibbels, from running an art gallery in New York. He was a translator of Poe and Firbank, and author of a book about the Lost Generation, *The Age of Illusion*. Now on the editorial board of the *NRF*, he was soon talking of *Ultramarine* being translated by Gide. Anaïs Nin described Sachs as 'a pale, tall and rather flabby-looking man with striking dark soft eyes.'[32] Jan remembered him as a lovable but clearly disreputable rogue. Lowry was so confident his book would be published that he wrote telling

Anna Wickham that it was due out. She in turn wrote to Natalie Barney, saying that 'One of the boys – Malcolm Lowry – has written a book, *Ultramarine*, which has been translated into French and has just appeared in Paris with an introduction by Paul Valéry.'[33]

Jan and Malcolm were beginning to discover one another sexually and were surprised to find themselves rather good at it. Lowry's main problem was premature ejaculation, but he learned to overcome it by singing the 'Star-Spangled Banner' to prolong matters. However, he told his psychiatrist later that sex with Jan did not really work for him; she was terrified of becoming pregnant and he could not function wearing a condom. Even so, they did discuss children and even chose names, including Hansel and Gretel.[34] As well as Starkey, Lowry's names for Jan were Rainbow Puss, and Lee.

Despite his optimistic claims, nothing had been settled about *Ultramarine*. He was having problems adjusting to marriage, and with his writing not going well began to drink and behave unpredictably, sometimes disappearing to brood darkly in obscure bars. When this first happened, after a row, Jan lay in bed wondering when he would return. Early in the morning she heard the creak of the old iron lift, and then the sound of the door opening. She lay quietly listening as someone entered the room and came across to stand silently over her. She lay there petrified, pretending to be asleep. Then came Malcolm's voice. 'Dormez. Le diable est mort.' Things, she felt, would never be quite so simple again. An element of fear had entered the relationship. Malcolm was determined to be in control; she was equally determined not to be dominated. A struggle of wills had begun. Sadly she noted that when he drank heavily Malcolm's face became red and swollen and he lost his good looks as well as his self-control.

This sinister, 'possessed' side of him emerged only gradually. Sometimes he would say, when they were considering what to do, 'I must see what the O. C. thinks.' This, he explained, was the 'Old Captain', Margot's grandfather, the old sea captain who had retired to Naples. 'Oh, is he still alive?' asked Jan. 'No,' he said, and she realized that her new husband was a spiritualist. In fact she found that he believed in all kinds of unorthodox practices – the ouija board, psychical research, occultism and tarot cards among them. Around his neck on a chain he wore an Italian coin, a gift from Margot, as his talisman. He identified himself with the Hanged Man described by Ouspensky in *A New Model of the Universe*.

> And I saw a man with his hands tied behind his back, hanging by one leg from a high gallows with his head downwards, and in fearful torments. Round his head was a golden halo. And I heard a Voice which spoke to me: "Behold, this is the man who has seen the Truth."[35]

(The influence of *The Waste Land* lingered on, it seems.) He referred to Jan as 'an old soul'. Who, she began to ask herself, had she married? This bizarre side of Malcolm was complemented by decidedly radical political views, and Jan found her Republican beliefs under challenge. She did not resist very fiercely. Having heard Hitler in Berlin, she knew enough about his ideas to realize, with her part-Jewish ancestry, that the Right was not really to her taste, and she was readily converted. In any case, in Paris at that time it was difficult not to take sides. The city was torn apart in early 1934 by street demonstrations of both the Right and the Left. On 6 February, right-wing rioters helped to bring down Premier Daladier, and six days later there were left-wing riots and strikes throughout the city.

But the Lowrys were more concerned about the Parisian literary scene. The old American expatriate community, centred around Sylvia Beach at Shakespeare & Company bookshop, had all but disappeared. The Wall Street Crash had depressed the dollar and by 1932 the most celebrated names had returned to the US. However, Beach's bookshop was still there in the rue de l'Odéon, and for Malcolm and Jan most days were incomplete without a visit. On 23 February, Joyce was down to appear at a meeting of Les Amis de 1914, but Malcolm refused to believe he would turn up, so Jan went alone. Joyce did appear but remained silent as Eduard Dujardin, to whom Joyce owed the interior monologue, paid homage to him, and there were readings from his work in progress, the embryonic *Finnegans Wake*.[36]

Afterwards, at the Café de Flore, Malcolm was more than usually withdrawn and it took Jan a time to get out of him the cause of his misery. While she was listening to Joyce, he had been reading her diaries, and was consumed with jealousy to read that she had had two affairs in Berlin before meeting him, and furious to read her comments on his lack of endowment and success in bed in Granada. They talked all of this out before making it up and setting off for Rouen where their reconciliation was so ecstatic that later when they quarrelled one would say 'Rouen' to remind them of how happy they *could* be. They stayed for a few days, haunting the riverside bars, touring the town on bicycles, and so liking it that they sent Jan's mother a picture postcard saying that this was the sort of town in which they wanted to settle.

They went to Fontenay-aux-Roses, and to Chartres, though the latter trip was preceded by a quarrel which Lowry incorporated into a short story, 'Hotel Room in Chartres'. The story concerns a nameless young man in Paris who has left the sea, 'no longer to endure the pain of its reality, as now without the presence of that reality he could no longer endure the pain of its illusion.'[37] Having quarrelled with his wife he reflects on the sweetness of their farewells when he went to sea. He is caught between two powerful urges – to return to Chartres, where they were once so happy, and to return to sea. But he fears that his occasional desire to hurt his love, like an angry ocean, will cast her onto the rocks and thus he will lose her. If they were more like the sea and the tide being summoned across the sand by 'the cool moon', they would be happy. On the train to Chartres he and his wife are joined by carousing sailors and when she leaves the compartment they accept him as one of them. On her return he is separated from them again. Only back in Chartres are they reunited in their love, as 'The moon drew softly the outgoing tide of the woman towards the calming sea of the man,'[38] an image reflecting his reading of Lawrence at the time. Being married to Lowry, Jan found, was like being married to lightning, he was so volatile. For a time everything would be fine, then suddenly '*Walpurgisnacht*!' But his creative energy was contagious. She, too, began gathering material for a book of stories set in Paris.

Then she became pregnant and Lowry panicked. Remembering his parents' opposition to his brothers' marriages, he did not want them to know about him and Jan. A child was unlikely to impress such stern Victorians already disturbed by his wayward conduct, and he felt sure he would be cut off. Nor was Jan overjoyed. Pregnancy was something she feared. She had had to face that fear before and had coped alone. But now she was married, and any decision had to be discussed with Malcolm. To her surprise he readily agreed to an abortion. He told his psychiatrist later that Jan had an abortion without his knowledge or consent, but Jan swore that he was most insistent. They agreed that they were too young to have children; they had plenty of time and lots of work to do before tying themselves down to parenthood. Jan had her pregnancy terminated.

As April approached, she had become anxious about her mother, who had paid for her travels. She had agreed to return after two years and the time was now up. In any case she wanted to see her before settling down for the writing life they envisaged. Malcolm agreed to let her go only with great reluctance. He said he would try to sell enough stories to bring her back for her twenty-third birthday, 11 June, or if not for his twenty-fifth on 28 July. Then they would move to Villefranche (where Somerset Maugham lived), sit in the sun, write and make love. This blissful prospect made the idea of parting more bearable, and a few days after the abortion they took the train to Le Havre where she sailed on the *Île de France* for New York.

Malcolm was left feeling, he wrote, like a tiger robbed of its cub, and he had run after the *Île de France* till he had lost sight of it.[39] He turned their parting into yet another story, 'In Le Havre', written for Jan as a sort of love letter, he said. Here a young wife, Lee, has just left her husband to return to America, partly because of an operation which has gone wrong, and because after two years of travel she has to return to see her mother. The husband is fearful of losing her, but wants to sort out his life before seeing her again. He talks to a hard-bitten American reporter over to report the Paris riots, and tells him that he has told his wife savagely, 'Oh, I don't love you; I never have loved you; it was just a caprice on my part. I married you to satisfy my own vanity, I was just getting one back at the old man.'[40] Jan and Malcolm made up that line in the train; it was never actually said on her departure by Malcolm, otherwise she might have left for good. However, in the story it is the reporter who leaves saying, 'Listen, the hell with you and your Lee. You only love your own misery.'[41]

Jan hoped to get Malcolm published in the US and took with her a copy of *Ultramarine* and several stories to show around. The best agent in New York, she was told, was Ann Watkins, and so she sent her the novel, a couple of stories, and an outline for a book ('a novel' he called it) of interconnected tales set in Europe called *So We Live Forever Taking Leave*. One of these, 'In Ballast to the White Sea' was to be expanded into a novel itself. Whit Burnett accepted 'Hotel Room in Chartres' for *Story* and Ann Watkins put Lowry on her books. At home, Jan discovered that her mother had raised the money for her travels from a loan shark, which only made her feel more deeply in her debt.

The flood of letters never ceased – the 'writing-paper lover' was back in his element. He quoted e. e. cummings to her – 'Nothing equals the power of your intense fragility.' When Jan's mother saw this shortly after she arrived home, she enquired anxiously if she was eating properly. His letters show him as deeply passionate about her as ever, yet disturbed as to whether he should have let her go alone to the States.

One he filled with Lawrentian 'sun and moon' imagery which gave his yearning for her a new lyrical depth. In another, he told her that in conceiving she had given him 'his manhood', and that he had had a fantasy about dominating and raping her. The independent-minded Jan did not find this prospect particularly alluring. He would try to write a new story every week to earn money to bring her back to France, he told her, and a little later said that he would come to America to bring her back himself.

Left alone it did not take Lowry long to hit the bottle, and within a few weeks he had reduced their beautiful apartment to a shambles. The gramophone and records, his wedding present from Jan, were smashed, chairs and carpet burnt, and other damage done. He was ejected by a furious landlady who brought legal proceedings, which ended with the Old Man footing the bill, as usual. After that he stayed wherever he could, mostly on the floor of Trevelyan's studio. One memorable evening he met James Stern in a bistro near rue Daguerre after which they meandered around Paris together for two days in various stages of intoxication, ending with Lowry collapsing into unconsciousness in Stern's flat.[42] He haunted the Grand Guignol near the Moulin Rouge, the Rhumarie Martinique, a favourite bar, and the café later compared by his Consul to the terrible Farolito – the Café Chagrin by the métro at Sèvres-Babylon,[43] a district of 'sinister bleak hotels and narrow dark medieval streets and alleys, with cocottes prowling singly or in pairs'.[44]

He next became involved with Maurice Sachs and Henry Wibbels. Through Sachs he met Cocteau, who kindly gave him tickets for two performances of his latest play, saying that to see it once would make it seem like a pantomime.[45] *La Machine Infernale* was Cocteau's fine modern version of the Oedipus story, played out in his own distinctive, bizarre style; a great tragic theme concentrated into a comedy of wit through the clever use of modern dialogue. Cocteau himself played The Voice, and he it was who intoned the fateful theme of the play: 'Observe, Spectator, wound up to the full in such a way that the spring will slowly unfold the whole length of a human life, one of the most perfect machines constructed by the infernal gods for the mathematical annihilation of a mortal life.'[46] And it was The Sphinx who articulated Cocteau's obsessive view of time: 'The time of mortals is that of "folded eternity".' The idea of the universe as an infernal machine and of time as a 'folded eternity' chimed with Lowry's own obsessions – Grieg's Moloch of fate and the time theories of J. W. Dunne and Ouspensky. He was riveted.

The theme of the infernal machine, of Fate and humankind's inability to escape it, was to be a central one in *Under the Volcano*.

As June approached, Jan waited in vain for her return fare. Malcolm's letters were becoming more and more confused. He longed to have Jan back, he wrote, but he could not send money yet because the *NRF* had given him two contracts, one for *Ultramarine*, which Gide was to translate, and one for *So We Live Forever Taking Leave* and he would have to wait for them to pay him. He had seen Joyce walking in the Luxembourg Gardens, he told her, had quarrelled with Robert McAlmon, back in Paris with the manuscript of his book *Being Geniuses Together*, and met Julian Green at a photographic exhibition in Montparnasse. Lowry assumed a life-long friendship with Green and over a number of years wrote him letters, all unsent.[47]

Then he wrote that he was leaving Paris. Trevelyan and Stern were trying to undermine him, he said; so was McAlmon. They were talking more and more about having to fight Hitler. 'Let them fight,' he wrote. 'You are the only one I would fight for. All I want to do is make love to you in the sunshine and live happily ever afterwards. I hope Jimmy Stern gets his entrails tangled up in barbed wire.'[48] Early in May he left with Sachs and Wibbels for St Prèst, a small village close to Chartres, where he took a walk across the cornfields and saw the spires of Chartres Cathedral rising up from the horizon, the walk which Jacques Laruelle recalls in *Under the Volcano* (where Lowry rechristens the village St Près), a memory evoked by his yearning passion for Yvonne:

> walking over the meadows from Saint Près, the sleepy French village of backwaters and locks and grey disused watermills where he was lodging, he had seen, rising slowly and wonderfully and with boundless beauty above the stubble fields blowing with wildflowers, slowly rising into the sunlight, as centuries before the pilgrims straying over those same fields had watched them rise, the twin spires of Chartres Cathedral. His love had brought a peace, for all too short a while, that was strangely like the enchantment, the spell, of Chartres itself, long ago, whose every side-street he had come to love and café where he could gaze at the Cathedral eternally sailing against the clouds, the spell not even the fact he was scandalously in debt there could break.[49]

He wrote telling Jan he had found the perfect place for them to live, the Hotel du Pont in St Prèst, but things were turning out badly. One of his two companions, he said, was romancing a landscape gardener, the other pursuing an oboe player. The exact nature of his entanglement with the sexually insatiable Sachs is unclear. It was undoubtedly through him that he had the promise of being published by the *NRF*. But Sachs was an unregenerate rogue who had stolen letters from Cocteau and was destined to become an informer for the Gestapo. More than likely Sachs was stringing him along for vaguely sexual motives, and after a violent argument when Lowry was drunk, lost interest in both him and *Ultramarine*. But as much as thirteen years later he was still claiming that he had a contract with the *NRF*, and had drunk the advance away on the very day he received it.[50]

His letters to Jan began to turn darker. 'I don't think we are the kind to live long,' he wrote, 'but it would be nice to think about growing old together.' Then came a letter saying that Sachs had stolen the money for her fare. There was no more talk of idylls in Villefranche. Jan was receiving such confused signals that she wrote asking, 'Exactly what is happening?' But his condition had deteriorated, and he was missing her badly. Sylvia Beach wrote to him in early June, reminding him that he had taken a book without paying for it. He sent an elaborate apology from St Prèst on *NRF* notepaper. He thought she had lent him the book, he had been terribly worried about his wife who had been much more ill than he had thought, and after she had left he had not slept for ten days. He never knew how much he loved her until she left, and should never have let her go – it had been hell without her.[51] Jan's birthday came and went, and there seemed no immediate prospect of her returning to Europe.

He decided to leave France, though it is unclear why. It might have been that talk of war added to his sense of missing Jan, and he might have preferred being with her in America now that the translation of *Ultramarine* was not materializing. He had had a love affair with America since visiting Aiken in 1929, and from the movies before that. America had become symbolic of rebirth, a world without the suffocating restrictions of British class snobbery (a feeling he shared with the shade of his hero Lawrence), a society where creativity was encouraged, not stifled (the tepid reception of *Ultramarine* still rankled). Probably, too, he thought he had more chance of earning a living from writing in the US after selling 'Hotel Room in Chartres' so quickly. He may also have had the idea of being like Aiken, a writer who spanned the Atlantic, whose soul was at home submerged in some Atlantis rather than on any known dry land ruled over by miserable humans. On the other hand, having had to pay for the damage he had wreaked upon the Paris apartment, Arthur could have ordered him home.

Returning to England gave him yet another story. 'Metal', is essentially a conversation between two Englishmen returning home. It is Lowry yet again conversing with his doppelgänger. Set ironically on the day of Hitler's Night of the Long Knives, it shows him more politically aware than is often thought. Bill Goodyear, its protagonist, reflects on how new metals allow mankind the choice of either constructing a world in which the human spirit will survive or developing weapons of self-destruction. It is a more elaborate expression of his remark about Stern and the barbed wire.[52]

He stayed briefly in London, back at the Astoria for one last time. Perhaps recalling Richard Aldington's advice, he had sent Cape some of his Paris stories and the outline for the full story-cycle, *So We Live Forever Taking Leave*. Cape had just acquired *Life and Letters*, a literary magazine which Hamish Miles was editing, to provide the firm's authors with an outlet for their shorter fiction. Miles took 'In Le Havre' for the July issue, and Cape, it seems, gave Lowry an advance for the full collection.[53] But he was still very upset and confused about his marital situation. Jan, in turn, was ever more uncertain of his plans. She wrote asking, 'Where are you? Your last letter was written in Paris but posted in London. What's going on?' He replied vaguely that all would become clear when he explained it to her in person. 'Don't worry, everything will turn out all right in the end.' This Micawberish attitude, she found, was one way he coped with the chaos he constantly created around himself. When he finally departed from the Astoria, he left his passport behind and his bill unpaid. Soon after, it became a nunnery and he liked to say that his passport and bill were immured inside along with the nuns.

He was still faced with having to break the news of his marriage to his father. It was to be their last meeting and they had already locked themselves for years to come into their 'ghastly psychotic dance' together.[54] Arthur was furious to learn about Jan. When Malcolm tried to convey a sense of the urgency of the times saying that there would be war within five years, he replied, 'What kind of a son are you to tell his father and mother that the world is hurtling towards disaster?'[55] He turned to Stuart and Margot, his only family confidantes, and told them that Jan had had a miscarriage. Even if the family had not put out the red carpet to greet the triumphant young author of *Ultramarine*, this, at least, was some proof of his manhood, something to be proud of.

In mid-July, Jan got a passionate, longing letter from him from Inglewood which included the plan of his work-in-progress, *So We Live*

Forever Taking Leave. He explained later that it was to be a book of linked short stories, plus a novel, *In Ballast to the White Sea*, divided into four themes – the four elements, water, earth, fire and air. He named the stories in order, with projected dates of completion. 'Hotel Room in Chartres', the first completed, was to be the final story in the cycle.

SO WE LIVE FOREVER TAKING LEAVE	
1 Bulls of the Resurrection	13 Nov.
2 English Tripos	15 Nov.
3 Zodiac	14 Nov.
4 Metal	Nte: 'Completed in England'
5 Café Chagrin	
6 Tramps	Nte: 'Completed in England'
7 A Goddam Funny Ship	
8 In Le Havre	
9 Hotel Room in Chartres	
10 An Economic Conference	16 Nov.
11 In Ballast to the White Sea	

OTHER PROJECTED STORIES	
12 An Ocean-Going Bachelor of Arts	
13 We Live Forever Taking Leave	
14 China	Nte: 'Completed in England'
15 A Tale You Couldn't Make Up	
16 The Poltergeist	
17 A Cage Went in Search of a Bird	

'Bulls of the Resurrection', reveals Lowry's sense of insecurity over Jan, and includes Aiken's warning that the relationship was doomed. It concerns two students, Rysdale and Sam, invited to Spain by another, Smith, to study for their finals. Sam has brought his girl, Terry, whom Smith seduces away. At a café in Granada on Easter Monday they discuss Smith's unfair advantage – money and 'a damned little secondary sexual characteristic of a car', stolen from his mother. As the errant pair drive off, Rysdale and Sam feel something terrible is going to happen – perhaps they will fail their exams – but even worse, Smith has hit a peasant and driven on, and the police may be watching them. They hope the loathsome Smith will be killed in his death-trap of a car, but they fear for Terry who is with him. 'They'll be paddling palms and pinching fingers,' says Rysdale, and Sam regrets being enslaved to so vile a passion as jealousy. Sam recounts a dream about Smith set partly in Granada and partly on Dartmoor. The dream landscape is like 'an El

Greco gone mad'. What corresponds to time expands and divides at will like a concertina. Smith is accused of a shooting and police take him on to the moor to re-enact the incident. He pleads that it was an accident but is beheaded at the bullring, and his head comes rushing through the entrance, alive and animated. Beheading had only enhanced his power. The two men discuss this dream and Sam senses that something extraordinary is about to happen which holds both the past and present in its meaning. Smith and Terry return then drive off into the snow-capped Sierras, and the other two know that something terrible will befall them. Does Sam know what his dream means, asks Rysdale. No, he replies, 'But I know enough to be able to say, when it does happen, I told you so.'[56]

The story shows Lowry at his most surrealistic and hints at how fearful he was of losing Jan to a more attractive rival. Using Aiken's cynical remark about him and Jan on the ship at Gibraltar underscores the part the older man played in planting the seeds of jealousy in Lowry's mind. But he wrote assuring her that he had fought a seemingly losing battle with drink and had won. He was back in training. 'When your body is perfect, see how your clear brain will reflect it.'[57] Towards the end of July, he sent her a revised order for the stories, but it was still uncertain when he would see her again. He had to sort things out at Inglewood first. Since Evelyn had been shocked by *Ultramarine* he promised to dedicate his next work to her, an uplifting book with a religious theme, to be named *Green Corners*. Clearly he was working hard to ingratiate himself at home.

At last Arthur made a decision. Malcolm was to join Jan in America and bring her back to Europe. He was prepared to buy him an expensive ticket which he could exchange in New York for two cheaper return tickets. He was at least to be put out of his lonely misery. However, instead of rushing off to find a berth on the first available ship, he studied the Transatlantic timetables. The *Berengaria* was due to sail for New York from Liverpool, but instead he chose the *Aquitania* sailing from Southampton. It meant a long train journey, but the fact that it was leaving on his birthday, 28 July, clinched the matter. If he was to make a new start with Jan, what better day to set out in pursuit of the holy grail of love, happiness and literary success than his own birthday? Again he was trying to conscript Fate for his own purposes. It had probably not escaped his attention either that this was the same ship on which Lawrence and Dorothy Brett had sailed for America in March

1924 en route to Taos and later to Mexico. He could also spend a few days looking up his old pals in London before leaving.

Arthur had booked his passage, bought him new clothes and arranged for him to draw his monthly allowance from a New York bank. He appeared on *Aquitania*'s passenger list as a 'clerk' in the pay of Buston & Co., whose country of future occupation was Britain; Arthur had temporarily written off his troublesome offspring as a business expense. As he sailed, Malcolm cabled Jan, telling her to meet him at the New York pier with her bags packed. They were heading straight off on a literary pilgrimage.

CHAPTER X

IN PURSUIT OF THE WHITE WHALE 1934–1936

If you go into exile you lose your place in the world.

JEAN-PAUL SARTRE

Of all tools used in the shadow of the moon, men are most apt to get out of order.

HERMAN MELVILLE, *Moby Dick*

He left England, he said, to get away from 'the non-creative bullyboys and homosapient schoolmasters of English Literature' and the like.[1] He had in mind not just the academics who had stifled his creativity and the critics who had failed to appreciate *Ultramarine*, but also the left-wing poets and writers who were in the ascendant in England at the time (as they were in France), who stressed writers' social and political obligations rather than their obligation to art. The Aiken in him was protesting against the Grieg.

When *Aquitania* docked in New York, Jan and her mother were there to greet him. Mrs Vanderheim was delighted by Malcolm at first sight. With those lovely deep blue eyes, the perfect white teeth, the mop of curly hair, the beautiful English accent and the apparently perfect manners, he seemed just the son she had always wanted. He liked to say that he arrived in New York with nothing but a football shirt and a copy of *Moby Dick*. In fact he arrived looking very spruce in a brand-new suit, with a brand-new set of luggage. Jan was equally thrilled to see him, especially seeing how her mother reacted. She had been careful not to mention his drinking, and Mrs Vanderheim had no inkling of the problem incubating within him. But for him, such encounters were always nerve-wracking. The first thing he did on arriving was to drop his wallet and passport. Jan retrieved them and from then on became 'Chancellor of the Exchequer'.[2] He may have hated what he called her 'terrible efficiency', but without it he would have been lost.

The excitement of being back in America galvanized him. Declining Mrs Vanderheim's invitation to go straight to her home on Long Island, he announced that he was in pursuit of his very own 'white whale', Herman Melville, whose frustrated and tragic life now possessed him to the point of 'hysterical identification'. He absolutely *must* see New Bedford, the Massachusetts whaling port from which Captain Ahab's *Pequod* set sail in pursuit of Moby Dick, and he *must* travel there by sea. They took ship immediately, to Lowry's delight having a top-deck cabin on a sidewheeler, the *Providence*, a most fitting vessel on which to embark on his new life with Jan. Later he was able to look back on the trip with a sense of retrospective foreboding. In his novella *Lunar Caustic* he changed Jan's name to Ruth, doubtless remembering the Ruth from New Bedford in Rye.

> They had paced the deck arm in arm. In the evening they had wandered around the ancient, lacquered ship, like a vast London hotel with its gilt stairways . . . They had listened together to that pulse of the ship he could hear now. What had they not learned about the world and each other in that cabin so high up in the ship? They had not learned that with all the beauty of the evening, the softness of the night, the tenderness of the blue morning, that every beat of the engine which took them nearer to New Bedford, nearer to Herman Melville, was also taking them nearer to their own white whale, their own destruction.[3]

But New Bedford was a great disappointment. Instead of the romantic whaling town he imagined, he found a bleak looking run-down modern industrial city. They did not linger, but took off immediately for Cape Cod, heading northwards towards Provincetown. On 10 August, they spent a short but felicitous time at a hotel in Martha's Vineyard, so felicitous in fact that the day became a byword for them, replacing 'Rouen' in its potency to cheer.

In Provincetown, they took a small summer cottage on the beach at 447 Commercial Street. Lowry was in his element, living by the sea with the ghost of one of his literary heroes in close attendance. They swam every day, and at night bathed nude; they went to midnight parties on the beach, and made passionate love afterwards. The uncertain past was forgotten, the slate wiped clean, the new start had begun. If the smallest cloud cast the smallest shadow, one of them would say 'August 10th!' and it vanished. Cape Cod was not only O'Neill territory, because of the Provincetown Playhouse, it was also Aiken country, and for Lowry it must have evoked haunting echoes of *Blue Voyage* and 'House of Dust' as well as fond memories of South Yarmouth and the delectable but elusive Dolly Lewis. Unable to resist, Lowry called Dolly from Provincetown inviting her to the house. She found Jan absent and Lowry drunk on the floor. Laid open on the piano was a piece of sheet music entitled 'My Dolly'.[4] It seems he still hadn't quite got 'Mrs Goya' out of his system.

Their stay in Provincetown was idyllic. The idea of returning to Europe was forgotten. Well away from a potentially strife-riven Europe and his increasingly bellicose anti-Nazi friends, he found, as Auden and Isherwood were to find later, a haven where free-floating artists could hope to create undisturbed by political turmoil. Work came easy to him on the Cape. He had brought along his Paris stories and the notes for *In Ballast to the White Sea* and worked on these steadily, discussing them at length with Jan. Without Aiken, Noxon, and Davenport, his past collaborators and critical confidants, Jan was conscripted to the role of literary interlocutor. And she too was working on a book of stories called *I'll See You in Paris*.

At the end of August, as Cape Cod became deserted, they planned to spend a short time with Mrs Vanderheim on Long Island, then head for New York. 'Hotel Room in Chartres' was due to appear in the September issue of *Story*, and they were invited to their first literary party on 24 September by its editor, Whit Burnett. Writing to accept, Lowry said he would like to enter *Ultramarine* for a novel contest *Story* was sponsoring, and offered to add a preface explaining the symbolism of the Tarot Pack and the pigeon.[5]

In Bayside he managed to conceal his drinking from Jan's mother and was at his charming best. Jan thought her mother was even more enchanted with him than she was. They stayed in Bayside for two weeks before heading for New York. Jan had found a small cosy old-fashioned apartment in Greenwich Village, at 99 Perry Street, and to Lowry's delight, just a few blocks south of Gansvoort Street where Melville had worked as Customs Inspector. It was a good base from which to launch themselves on to the literary scene.

As the season got under way, they met Burnett and his co-editor Martha Foley, Bennet Cerf, editor of Joyce's *Ulysses* for Random House, Donald Friede, publisher of Steinbeck, and Ann Watkins, Lowry's agent, still circulating *Ultramarine* to unresponsive publishers. They also met Harold Matson, Watkins's Vice-President, and his brother Norman. Lowry was drawn to the Matsons because of their Norwegian ancestry, and told them that he was half-Norwegian, half-Irish. But Norman was more impressed by something else, his utter confidence and commitment to being a writer.

Prohibition had been repealed the previous December, and there was now plenty of liquor for anyone wishing to drown sorrows, but as Lowry settled down to regular drinking his behaviour changed. He became bloated and lost his good looks again, and once, in a sexual frenzy, he bit Jan's breast, giving her an abscess which put her in St Vincent's Hospital for ten days. Left on his own, he went on a binge, never even visiting her, and leaving her feeling deeply hurt.[6] She found that he agonized a great deal about sex, especially about her affairs before she met him and slowly she was discovering just how emotionally immature he was and decided that what he was really looking for was, 'a mother who was a good lay', and that for him writing was a form of sexual sublimation.[7]

But something other than his relationship with Jan was bothering him. He revealed what it was in 'Portrait of a Conquistador'. He was fearful about *Ultramarine* being so derivative. It had not seemed a problem in England, but now he felt a sense of foreboding about it. He gave a copy to Jan's mother inscribed, 'To my mother, Emily Vanderheim with lots of love from the author, your son Malcolm. I wish the book were worthy of the recipient; I'll give you a better one next time.' But it seemed he *had* to be fearful of something. As he constantly asked Jan, 'Where would I be without my misery?' Misery, he had learned from Aiken, was a necessary condition of genius. His new 'mother', however, was soon to learn the sad truth about her beautiful new son. After one bad quarrel, Jan left him and went home. He followed her and arrived drunk so that Mrs Vanderheim had to sober him up. When he began to insult Jan she became very angry. '*I* can say anything I want,' she told him, 'but *you* can't say anything against my daughter.'[8]

At the end of the year Arthur wrote reminding him that he could, if he wished, exchange his return ticket for two cheaper ones and bring Jan back to Europe, but Malcolm never told her about this. It seems he had decided that he had better prospects as a writer in America than in Europe, and now had before him the prospect of a future in exile. But whether he would make enough from writing to become independent of his father remained to be seen. After their flight from Perry Street to Long Island, they stayed over the New Year with Jan's mother and gave up their apartment. Early in 1935, with Malcolm's visitor's visa needing renewal, they decided to go to Mexico. Jan had heard that not only was it very cheap but was one of the few truly barbarous countries worth living in. Malcolm jumped at the idea. He had read Lawrence's *Mornings in Mexico* and *The Plumed Serpent* and was eager to follow after his great idol. They decided, however, to stay in New York for a few weeks while he completed some work, and moved into the Hotel Somerset at 150 West 47th Street, near to Carnegie Hall and Columbus Circle just south of Central Park. As it turned out, they remained there for just over a year, according to Jan the most completely satisfying year of her marriage and a highly productive one for Malcolm. The hotel was close to everything. They lived in theatres and movie houses, took long walks in Central Park, enjoyed Manhattan's many restaurants, and spent hours each day in the public library. But the year began with another strong though grim identification for Lowry. During January, the Lindbergh baby trial was in progress and on 13 February Bruno Hauptmann was sentenced to death for kidnapping. The case haunted Lowry throughout this year and into the next.

Burnett had rejected the rest of his Paris stories. Not only were they uncommercial, often they didn't quite come off – too much talk and too little action. Two people meet in a railway carriage or in a café. Nothing happens but they talk, and as the talk unwinds Lowry yet again explores the themes which obsessed him – the power of Fate hanging over us, the sense of impending doom, and the search for signs, coincidences and correspondences signalling the existence of a reality and power beyond appearances. Ann Watkins advised him that to make a name for himself he needed to publish novels. Once established as a novelist, his stories were more likely to sell. So he decided to concentrate on *In Ballast to the White Sea*, cannibalizing some of his Paris stories like 'An Economic Conference' and 'A Goddam Funny Ship'.

By now Arthur seems to have become reconciled to Malcolm's remaining, at least for a time, in the US. Not only did he see that his allowance was paid regularly, but took a keen interest in his literary career. He would have preferred a son who wrote like Sir Philip Gibbs or John Buchan to one who produced such morally questionable novels as *Ultramarine*, but he very kindly had the *TLS* sent to him every week, and no doubt believing that tobacco was conducive to thought, regularly sent him his old, broken-in pipes. In return, Malcolm wrote kind letters to Evelyn, assuring her that he was busy writing that religious novel, *Green Corners*, dedicated to her.

In truth he was working on *In Ballast to the White Sea*, a far from religious work. It was a grim saga of his identification with Benjamin Hall and his quest for Grieg mixed in with the Fitte story, where a Cambridge student's behaviour leads to the suicide of his twin. It was now that he confessed to Jan that he had aided and abetted Fitte's suicide. She wondered if the story of *In Ballast* was not about the punitive heterosexual side of Malcolm wanting to kill the 'sinful' homosexual side.[9] It was clearly a work of expiation and like Aiken's *Blue Voyage* an attempt at ruthless self-analysis. It was as if he believed that by turning the tragedy into fiction, the horror could be expunged, leaving him free to be born again. And looming large once more is the sea (the symbol of escape), and a voyage of self-discovery, the ordeal to be endured before life may be reaffirmed.

In it Lowry took his state of mind in Cambridge after his Part I as a touchstone – his growing identification with Benjamin Hall, his stream of unsent letters to Grieg, his longing for the sea and the purifying fire of the stokehold, his heavy drinking, and his feeling that his work was worthless and that his life lacked meaning. Into this he introduced his relationship with Fitte, who appears as the narrator's (Sigbjørn's) brother Tor who is scornful of his literary ambitions and who commits suicide. Sigbjørn eggs him on to do it and then leaves him and runs off to his digs at midnight.

Behind this unfolds the story of their father, an authoritarian ship-owner, whose business is blighted by two *Titanic*-like disasters to his ships. It follows Sigbjørn's (Lowry's) journey to Norway 'in ballast', and the series of coincidences which led him to Erikson (Grieg) the writer he admires so much, and how their meeting realigns both men on the side of life. However, Sigbjørn is ever haunted by the thought that he is both a murderer and a fratricide.

This novel represented well the polar extremes of Lowry's nature and his world-view. The two brothers are clearly two aspects of the author. Tor is the Dark Angel affirming death and Sigbjørn is the Good Angel affirming life. Liverpool, where they were born, is a City of Dreadful Night; Norway, the home of their parents, is a Country of Light, a place across the sea where a human spirit may be refreshed and restored. This illustrates the keen struggle which Lowry saw within himself, between Good and Evil, between Life and Death, between Happiness and Misery, between Elation and Depression. It also gives a clue to the aesthetic which motivated him, the belief that only in the struggle from darkness towards the light could he find a theme profound enough for the great literature he wished to produce.

Appropriate to this design, his literary landscape has a Dantesque significance. Working in the public library he copied into his notebooks passages from his reading which illustrated the two competing visions: passages descriptive of the beauties of the Norwegian landscape, and dark, self-reflective passages like this from Kierkegaard's diary:

> Deep within me I knew myself to be the most miserable of men . . . As far back as I can remember I was quite certain of one thing that I must expect neither help nor consideration from others. Satisfied by all that had been granted to me in other respects I was full of longing for death my spirit craved for an eternal life.

Lowry still wrote letters to Grieg which he did not send, as he had at Cambridge. By now his Good Angel was a member of the Communist Party fighting Nazism in Norway.

Meantime, Lowry tried to keep in shape by visiting a gym and working out with weights, and on visits to Long Island he and Jan went horse-riding and he taught her to play tennis. In their room at the Somerset they worked on their books, she on her portable Royal, Lowry on her father's old Remington. To live with the noise, they pretended they were overworked journalists hacking away in a busy newspaper office. Sometimes, because they were long-stay residents, the hotel manager let them use a vacant room so they could work separately in silence. Afterwards, they would read their work to each other, and Jan would type fair copies on her more modern machine. Lowry wrote fast in his distinctive hand with the Greek e's, and after typing made few corrections, probably because of the plain social realism he was aiming then to produce. While he battled away at *In Ballast*, Jan was working on two projects simultaneously. One was her set of Paris stories, the other was a book about a mining disaster at Pécs, the Hungarian hometown of a girl she had met in Paris, to be called *The Dead Ride Hard*, which consumed her for much of that year. She had visited Pécs and believed, like Malcolm, that all worthwhile books came out of direct experience and nothing should be wasted. But it required research.

Lowry read insatiably – Hermann Broch's *The Sleepwalkers* and Mann's *The Magic Mountain*, both end of epoch novels, influenced him deeply. Seeking to explain the mysterious coincidences which he saw patterning his life, he explored the mystical writings of Swedenborg, and on discovering Charles Fort's books, *Lo!* and *Wild Talents*, on the bizarre and mysterious, he called it a red-letter day in his life.[10] After a morning at the Public Library he and Jan would visit the movies, cheering newsreels of Roosevelt, his wife and various labour leaders; booing Hitler, Mussolini and America's homegrown Fascists. In the evenings they ate out, and went to theatres or concerts by radical artists like Leadbelly and Paul Robeson. The only passions they did not share were jazz (Jan's musical education was classical), the ukulele (she hated it), and alcohol. However, throughout 1935 Malcolm stayed relatively sober. A photograph of him in their room at the Somerset shows him at his most handsome, relaxed in a dark shirt, smoking one of his father's old pipes and nursing a manuscript, no doubt *In Ballast* – the consummate image of the young genius in repose.

While Lowry was finding America conducive in many ways he did not, unlike many Britons living there, become Americanized. His mother wrote saying, 'Don't become too American; I don't like the accent.' She had not taken elocution lessons herself to see her children fall into slovenly speech habits. But she need not have worried; Malcolm would always remain an Englishman and an English author, even while married to an American. In pursuit of first-hand experience for Jan's book on miners, they hitch-hiked to Scranton, Pennsylvania to study mines at first hand. Afterwards they used the experience to write a story together, 'The Gift Horse's Mouth'. It was a socially conscious story, but, according to Jan, uncomfortably 'juvenile' because in a style unsuited to Malcolm.[11] It was the only thing they wrote together and to which they put both their names. Malcolm continued to urge her to make notes. He always had his notebook with him and if not would write on anything to hand – cigarette packets, match-books, and even, according to Jan, empty condom packets.

For his twenty-sixth birthday, Jan bought him Arthur Schnitzler's *Flight into Darkness*, inscribed: 'To Malcolm from Jan on July 28, 1935 as an introduction to a year even fuller & happier than the last. With all love.' Later he wrote, unkindly twisting this to suit a dramatic story, that the book had been presented 'with malicious intent' and presented 'caustically, and at a bad moment,' so that, in Grieg's words, 'another spiral had wound its way upward.'[12]

The bad moment to which he referred was indeed traumatic, and his contented life took a sudden dive into despair. Harold Matson, at Ann Watkins's, had sent *In Ballast* to Burton Rascoe, now an editorial adviser at Doubleday. He sent also the copy of *Ultramarine* offered by Jan the previous May, with favourable reviews pasted inside the cover. Reading *Ultramarine*, Rascoe became gradually enraged, detecting what he thought were serious plagiarisms of his story, 'What is Love?', which Lowry had read six years earlier when visiting Aiken in Cambridge. He decided that *In Ballast* was also highly derivative, and demanded a confrontation with Lowry at Watkins's office in Madison Avenue. Lowry was so traumatized that on the night before the meeting, he said, he paced back and forth across Brooklyn Bridge seriously contemplating suicide.[13]

Rascoe was a combative and acrimonious critic as well as editor, and a dedicated anti-communist. According to Rascoe, Lowry had lifted 'whole paragraphs, word for word, other paragraphs merely elaborations of effective lines from my texts, juxtapositions of poetic taglines [*sic*] which I had designed for sardonic effect, which, when I pointed them out in his own text, he could not identify the sources of the tag-lines.' Rascoe also charged that *In Ballast* was 'obviously an imitation of Charles Morgan's *The Fountain*, with derivations from Céline and Malraux and that he ought to start writing his own stuff instead of lifting and copying the work of others'.[14] He demanded that Lowry sign a confession in front of Watkins and Matson. In a state of shock he agreed to this, but then wrote a long letter defending his books. It was no longer sufficient to say blithely that plagiarism was the least socially harmful of crimes; he was faced by a man who had been dangerously offended. However, he said that *Ultramarine* had been lost by its publisher and had to be rewritten very quickly from memory. In the course of that, and in his semi-suicidal state, some passages from Rascoe's story must have strayed into it. He said that he had been writing stream-of-consciousness pieces as exercises for Aiken and his memory must have somehow absorbed this material and in the throes of composition unintentionally regurgitated it. Jan typed up the carefully drafted letter, noticing that at the top of each page he had scrawled 'Help me, O.C.!' invoking the aid of Margot's familiar. Rascoe was not placated, and Lowry signed the confession in front of his agents. In fact, what he had taken from Rascoe's story was minimal – a few Latin tags, quotations which Rascoe had himself borrowed. Rascoe might have had a better case against Aiken, who used the line 'What is Love?', followed by a cynical catalogue of hate-filled invective, in *Great Circle*. But Aiken, whom Rascoe knew and had clashed with, was probably now too eminent to take on. Lowry was Aiken's callow student, a much easier target, whose efforts to bury the hatchet were fiercely rebuffed.

Years later, Lowry wrote that due to his hysterical identification with Aiken and Grieg, *Ultramarine* was a form of 'plagiarism or disguised lampoon'. But, 'No writer worth his salt minds being plagiarised from or minds plagiarising if he can [be] sure of not being found out. It does no harm . . . but it can have a hell of an effect on the author involved.'[15] It certainly had a hell of an effect on *him*, and probably because of this he rewrote *In Ballast*. By October, a completely revised version had been typed and sent to Ann Watkins. Matson meanwhile wrote Malcolm a reassuring letter, and when he later left to set up his own agency, Lowry would follow him.

At the end of 1935, the Lowrys met an important radical figure in Waldo Frank, doyen of left-wing intellectual New York, whose studio on West 83rd Street was a centre of radical debate. He had written several books on South America, and was chairman of the Communist-dominated (and Moscow-controlled) League of American Writers. The couple's own leftish liberal views were further strengthened by contact with this group. Frank knew Mexico well and no doubt encouraged their plans to go there, talking of the new land reforms of President Cárdenas and the exciting artistic movement epitomized by the paintings of Diego Rivera. The sense that the future lay in more socialistic forms of society was infectious, and Lowry wrote to his friend Sommerfield in London saying that the only literature worth producing was socialist realist proletarian literature. The Lowry of *Ultramarine* under the influence of his Dark American Angel, Aiken, was being replaced by a more extroversive, stylistically economical and politically engaged writer, like his now overtly communist Bright Norwegian Angel. The dialogue in *In Ballast* turned ever more political.

The climate which encouraged Lowry's political awareness tended also to inhibit his poetic gifts. But although his stories were less elaborate than they had been under Aiken's direct influence, he could not abandon the intricate system of symbols through which he had come to interpret the world. Because of this his stories remained uncommercial. After 'Hotel Room in Chartres', it would be almost thirteen years before he had another significant work published. He offered his own explanation. Those 'non-creative bully-boys and homosapient schoolmasters of English literature' were as entrenched in America as they were in England.[16]

Christmas and New Year were spent on Long Island with Mrs Vanderheim. It was then she discovered Lowry's unhygienic habit of not wearing underpants and saw again his heavy drinking. In fact, by the beginning of 1936 events had begun to turn against them, and their idyllic hotel-based life came under threat. Friends met through Waldo Frank began taking them to Harlem jazz clubs, and often Lowry would go alone, so that Jan began to lose track of his movements. With his work seeming to go nowhere and his stories not selling, he began to complain of feeling hemmed-in by their living so close to one another. She, in turn, became more and more irritated by his lofty and drunken remarks to people, arguing against literature for art's sake in favour of socially aware prose. 'You bellboy people!' he once shouted, roaring off down the street. 'I will be famous long after you are dead!' And friends would ask her, 'What's wrong with him?' He was clearly torn between commitment and poetry, and alcohol released the Aiken who was trying always to burst out of him. In February, he took *In Ballast* back from Ann Watkins and began yet another revision. Clearly there was some 'overlaying' to be done, some 'decorating of the page', as Aiken discovered when he read it the following year.

Waldo Frank had edited Hart Crane's *Collected Poems*, and Lowry became deeply affected by Crane, the drunken sea-obsessed poet who three years earlier, returning from Mexico, walked to the stern of the ship, 'took off his coat, quietly, and leaped.'[17] Here was a man who had actually done what Benjamin Hall had thought to do but then stepped back. He quoted two of his favourite lines from Crane's poem 'The Tunnel' to Jan:

> And why do I often meet your visage here,
> Your eyes like agate lanterns – on and on . . .[18]

Crane's fascination with Mexico encouraged them to think about going south. Meanwhile he continued to explore and note the multitude of images which make up 'the numb brilliant jittering city'.[19]

Donald Friede, the publisher, who never concealed his attraction to Jan, read some of Lowry's stories. He judged them uncommercial, but told him that he was right to let his genius have free rein. They also got to know Frank's secretary, Eric Estorick. The 22-year-old Estorick, later biographer of Stafford Cripps and well-known London art dealer, was much taken with Lowry, never having met so committed an artist before. Lowry, in his turn, fell in love with Estorick's family, and liked nothing better than sitting in their kitchen eating chopped chicken livers and enjoying the exuberant warmth of a New York Jewish home. He was relaxed and articulate and the very best of company, having acquired yet another surrogate family.[20]

Less salubrious was Lowry's friendship with a Trinidadian novelist, Alfred Mendes, and his friend Tony Valleton, a 33-year-old Frenchman, who took Lowry to Harlem in search of hot jazz. Trouble between him and Jan began at a weekend party at Mendes's home on Long Island. The host's wife was away but he had moved in a girlfriend, a redhead, who flitted around inciting guests to relax to the point of abandonment. As the party grew wilder, and more orgiastic, Malcolm was, according to Jan, 'engulfed' by a woman in a flowing costume, called Nina, which led them to have a sharp quarrel. Here too, was the sinister Valleton, who was to cast a shadow over them shortly afterwards. The quarrel simmered on, and Malcolm embarked on another drinking bout leading to more drunken absences. In company he would attack Jan verbally in front of the others, and she would flee sobbing.

He was becoming more and more depressed, and at the end of March he wrote to Arthur saying that his desire to achieve was accompanied apparently by an unconscious will to failure. However, knowing the kind of thing his father liked to hear, he added that if one cultivated the tone of success and combined that with industry, there was every chance of achieving one's goals. Arthur replied that his problem was quite understandable; it was the same for him with golf – thus quite failing to appreciate the kind of pressure his son was under.[21] At the beginning of April, Malcolm told Jan that he felt so claustrophobic living in the same room with her that he must move out. They decided to leave the Somerset, and found two separate but connected rooms in an apartment house on 86th Street. They were hardly there a week when Malcolm disappeared, leaving Jan 'an icy little note' saying that he had moved out and giving a telephone number. The janitor told her that he and another man had been and removed his stuff. At first she was perplexed and worried, but eventually found him living in a squalid basement room below Angelina's restaurant in McDougal Street, Greenwich Village, where he solemnly announced to her that he had spent two nights with Tony Valleton, who was recovering from syphilis, so that he himself had now probably contracted the disease.[22] The 'horrible incident of Valleton & its relationship to B. Hall' excited old guilts, as did the verdict in the Lindbergh case: 'Hauptmann was executed & he felt worse because he not only believed him to be guilty (innocent) but when he looked up plagiarist in the dictionary he found it meant kidnapper.'[23]

Lowry, it seems, suspected his threatened illness was a punishment for the 'crime' of 'kidnapping' material from Rascoe, not to mention Aiken and Grieg. And there was also the idea that somehow his plagiarism made him responsible for the fate of the executed man. But at last, with syphilis a distinct possibility, he could complete his identification with Hall in reality as well as in imagination. He would have to have the usual blood tests, he told Jan, and until he was cleared he had best stay away from her. She did not want them to be apart, but her friends told her she would be crazy to stay if there was any danger to herself. Reluctantly she agreed, and soon thereafter moved out to an apartment on 68th Street.

Left on her own, she made contact again with two old friends from the Academy of Dramatic Arts, Teddy and Ann. For a dare and a story, she and Ann took jobs as taxi-dance girls. Jan planned to write articles about it for a newspaper, the *Mirror*, and Malcolm did not seem to object. Seeing that she was on to something, Jan decided instead to do a book which she planned to call *It's a Bawdy Planet*. But there were dangers to working in taxi-dance halls because men saw them as pick-up joints, and Jan found herself having to extricate herself from some persistent clients, including a gangster who finally gave up, cursing 'Educated Janes!' as he left in disgust.

With Lowry, drink had now begun to take its toll. He wrote later that

> New York . . . favours brief and furious outbursts, but not the long haul. Moreover for all its drama and existential fury, or perhaps because of it, it's a city where it can be remarkably hard . . . to get on the right side of one's despair . . . even hangovers don't seem the same in New York as anywhere else . . . the deceitful medicament being more easily at hand; which only makes it worse in the end.[24]

The brick-red swollen face returned – he was becoming his fat, deranged self yet again. Valleton had gone but later he depicted him in fiction as a secret homosexual in love with him, and 'such a powerful (character) that I'm not sure he's not the Beast in Revelation that pursues the Consul.'[25]

Distressed to see Lowry drowning his superb talent in alcohol, Estorick introduced him to a doctor from Bellevue Hospital, who advised him to get medical help. He discussed it with Jan and she agreed that it would do no harm, though she did not realize that it involved him going into hospital.[26] He entered Bellevue as a voluntary patient on or around 10 May, suggesting later that Estorick's doctor friend thought conditions at Bellevue disgraceful and had asked him to go in to write an exposé of the place.

He went in, he claimed, in the spirit of a reporter looking for a good story – it was 'an excursion into journalism (not madness, I'm glad to say),'[27] and went equipped with notebook and pencil. A bestseller he and Jan had read, William Seabrook's *Asylum*, tells of a well-travelled but alcoholic journalist who finds himself in a psychiatric ward, and deals with his ordeal while drying out and undergoing treatment. He includes an extract from a wildly surrealistic novel about madness written by a Rimbaudesque young English inmate, which may have given Lowry the idea of doing the same thing, only better. He may also have seen Scott Fitzgerald's *The Crack-Up*, which appeared in *Esquire* during February and April. Another important ingredient was his discovery that Bellevue, on 1st Ave and 27th Street, stood just three blocks east of the house where Melville died, at 104 East 26th Street – his last address. This intensified his 'hysterical identification' with Melville. Melville, too, had been a sailor whose grandfather was lost at sea, and his son Malcolm had (thought Lowry) just disappeared. 'His failure for some reason absolutely fascinated me and it seemed to me that from an early age I determined to emulate it, in every way possible.'[28]

Lowry was in Bellevue's psychiatric ward for not much more than a week or two. Jan was unaware that he was there, but when Estorick told her she was furious and rushed round to find him looking ghastly and shrivelled, dressed in a grey gown and obviously confused. He may have gone there in a journalistic spirit, but now he was feeling the effects of the institution and beginning to show symptoms of clinical depression. Not only was she shocked by his appearance but also because Bellevue was a public institution where patients were subject to periodic checks on their entitlement to treatment. Lowry was in the US on a visitor's visa and therefore entitled neither to a job nor to free treatment. He was in danger of being extradited. She quickly had him discharged. He too was annoyed when he discovered the danger in which he had been, and he, too, blamed Estorick and phoned him to say so.

Although not long in Bellevue, he emerged with a notebook crammed with observations, snatches of overheard conversation, and comments on his own situation with Jan. It was the first draft of what emerged as an important novella, at this stage called *Delirium on the East River*. It was a clear break from earlier work, and based on an experience through which he had begun to develop a sense of himself as both deviant and yet representative of suffering humanity. His notes depict his fellow inmates as souls with heightened consciousnesses. He wrote, 'I love my fellow men in a way I had not done before I was/had been sane.' Mr Horowitz (Kolowsky in the later *Lunar Caustic*), the communist Wandering Jew, and Garry the boy who has 'cut' a little girl with a broken bottle, and Battle the negro tap-dancer who sings fatalistically as he dances – are figures of sanity to contrast with the insane world outside. Against this are set his own discussions with his psychiatrist, trying to outwit him with enigmatic pronouncements like 'Return to the pre-sexual revives the necessity for nutrition,' and veiled accusations – 'Most of the nurses . . . are psychiatric cases themselves'. Nor can he help venting his spleen against American women, and '. . . their lousy heartbalms & alimony & Christ knows what & their heart-breaking beauty & their unprocreativeness & their general lousiness & bitter beauty & healthy striding shapeliness & inescapableness, they are hell, at least as far as I can remember . . .'[29] But whatever feelings he had for American women in general, he also noted, 'Jan & I soon together. Cupid & Psyche / the winged pig and parakeet / The American Express, Los Angeles: Our new address.' They had decided at last to go to Mexico. But Malcolm was being tested and treated for syphilis (with a mercury-based drug, Salvarsan or 606) and they decided not to leave until he got a clean bill of health. He moved into a basement on West 72nd Street, close to Jan on 68th, but continued to see Mendes. Soon after leaving Bellevue he cabled him: 'Must see you Monday afternoon Angelinas Restaurant. Terrifically important.' And quoting *Blue Voyage*, he added, 'While you were turning water into wine I was turning wine into blood.'

Delirium on the East River had by a Lowryan process of osmosis concentrated itself into a long story called *The Last Address*. The protagonist is a drunken journalist, Sigbjørn Lawhill, into whose story is woven Mr Horowitz, Garry, Battle and the psychiatrist, all imprisoned in the asylum. Through them Lowry had projected an apocalyptic vision of an urban wasteland, the lunatic city, reflecting the disintegration of modern consciousness. Into it he drew images from the Expressionist cinema and the rhythms of hot jazz to convey a sense of threat and the tempo of disconnected speech. In its more developed form he called it 'a masterpiece, or a potential one'.

For the three months he claimed to be receiving treatment and further testing for syphilis he and Jan stayed apart. It was not just a strain for her to be apart from Malcolm, but it was awkward because she was attracting admirers. However, they met for lunch every day, and occasionally went to literary parties together. At one they met the still-angry Rascoe who listened tight-lipped as Lowry told him how he had almost committed suicide the night before their confrontation. Jan continued work on her taxi-dance book, using the cover of freelancing for the *Mirror*, while Lowry sent a draft of *The Last Address* to Whit Burnett. *Story* was publishing novellas and Burnett accepted it, though he thought it still inchoate, and paid Lowry an advance of $45 to work on it. It was the first money he had earned from writing done in America, and must have encouraged him to hope that he might after all be able to live by his writing. The hope was short-lived.

On 18 July the Spanish Civil War broke out. Leftists now had a great cause, a challenge to their convictions, and, for young men like Lowry, a true test of manhood. But although he, like Jan, became an outspoken defender of the Republican cause, the idea of going to fight in Spain mobilized him only when drunk. Back in England his old friends Charlotte Haldane and John Sommerfield would go out there to 'do their bit', and Grieg went to report the war for the Oslo paper *Dagbladet*. Meanwhile, his Cambridge contemporaries, Sykes Davies, Maclean, Burgess, Blunt and Philby, Apostles all, were playing their own kinds of subterranean war games. Nevertheless, the war took hold of Lowry's imagination much as it did other members of his literary generation, for it was clearly a fight between good and evil, between the forces of light and darkness, as well as heralding the great battle to come. Spain began to feature in his stories and in poems he wrote soon afterwards in Mexico.

In August, Aiken appeared in New York. His marriage was now in shreds and his writing on hold after his last novel, *King Coffin*, had failed. His finances had not improved much since the trip to Spain, and at one stage he had turned to journalism, writing a 'London Letter' for the *New Yorker*. His mental state had also been unsteady, and he had undergone analysis after sending *Great Circle* to Freud, who, it was reported, now kept it in his waiting room, perhaps as a warning to those all too blithely indulging in amateur self-analysis.[30] On 22 August he wrote to Burra:

> Well, you'll never believe it but I found old Malc, living in a dreary cellar in 72nd Street West, of Central Park. I'd first found Mrs Malc living two blocks away, but she kept the door almost closed between

> us, eyeing me suspiciously the while, denied that Malc lived there, just gave me the other address. At 72nd Street a slattern in dirty white silk pyjamas opened the door, and when I said what I wanted howled down the dark stairs Mal! O Mal! And there sure enough was Mal, just finishing a short story. Such a basement scene, too, with laundry, negresses, cats, Mrs Taussig and a Stranger whom I wasn't introduced to. Subsequently I met Malc downtown several times, including a supper with Mrs Malc. Malc himself in very good form indeed – looks remarkably well, much thinner, cleaner, spotlessly dressed, punctual, much easier to talk to, less self-absorbed etc. Harper have taken his novel, comes out in Jan., and Story is featuring a novelette a month hence – which same is all about his visit to Bellevue Hospital for the Insane. O boy o Boy. Such conversations with blacks – I read a few pages which were superb.[31]

Aiken then claimed that Jan was being pursued by a 'quondam sweetheart' and that Malcolm had challenged him to a glass of beer in Times Square, and that the man had said 'It's time we met, for we have something in common!' That, wrote Aiken, was setting an all-time low in tactless truthfulness.[32] Again Aiken had to portray a woman in a bad light, implying that Jan had been having an affair. The so-called 'quondam sweetheart', she agreed was an admirer, a writer she had met at a cocktail party, but any impropriety occurred in Aiken's lurid misogynistic imagination. Lowry's imagination, on the other hand, was filled with anxiety to shine in his mentor's eyes, and he had once again pretended success. Harper's publication of *In Ballast* was as real as the French publication of *Ultramarine*.

His own account of Aiken's visit is rather more lurid. He was, he wrote, at not much past ten-thirty one morning typing in the basement kitchen, driven from his room by 'rare insects' and unshaven for four days, sitting in the midst of much washing and many empty bottles, the remains of a pinochle party, but which it looked as though he had himself just consumed. Just then, his thoughts were interrupted by his landlady's respectful whisper.

> 'Mr Kraken is upstairs, sir.' / 'What!' / '. . . Mr Kraken would like to see you, sir, and is coming downstairs now.' / It was indeed no less a person than Conrad Aiken . . . who finding himself in New York for a day had hunted up his old pupil in Columbus Circle, where . . . he had metamorphosed himself verbally into the famed Scandinavian sea-monster, in order, perhaps, to blend himself the more unobtrusively with my cavernous, indeed monstrous apparent

> circumstances which, hint[ed] to say the least of failure, if not the abyss itself.[33]

Innes Rose must have written suggesting he repay Cape's advance if the promised book of stories did not materialize, and Lowry penned a distraught reply, found later among Aiken's papers, so he may have been asked to deliver it and thought it too damaging to Lowry to pass on. He could not repay Cape, he wrote, 'I have a lot of damned difficult problems to settle . . . Please don't say "I'm a shit" – meaning me – for not writing more when you have dealt so kindly with me. It's just that my mind won't work.'[34]

Story, according to Lowry, changed its policy of including novellas, and so *The Last Address* did not appear, as expected, in the September issue. He wrote later that at the last moment the editors thought it too horrible to publish, but Burnett told Harold Matson that he thought Lowry had not yet got the story into good enough shape for them.[35] However, it must have been in this state of uncertainty and disappointment that Lowry turned to poetry again, perhaps as an attempt to break free from a sense of gloom. A poem called 'Peter Gaunt and the Canals' seems to date from this time – a poetic gesture in homage to Peer Gynt and his modern counterpart, Nordahl Grieg. Meantime Jan showed him what she had written so far on taxi-dance girls, but when he read it, uncharacteristically, he slated it so badly she abandoned it.

The syphilis scare now over (he was not after all infected), they prepared to leave for Mexico, with a loan from Ann Watkins towards expenses and as a sort of retainer. But before setting off, they stayed briefly with Jan's mother on Long Island, and here Malcolm wrote his will, leaving everything to Jan, and adding,

> It is my wish also that she try, in her own time, to make something out of the inchoate notes for the novel I have left behind on the lines I have sometimes suggested in conversation with her, and that while in England she see John Davenport about this: that also she make some effort to get my play produced, if and when she may have time for so doing. The same with my short stories.

He hoped she would visit Grieg and be treated like a daughter by his own family. All proof copies of his work and royalties from his posthumous works he left to Mrs Vanderheim.

Since arriving in the States, Lowry had heard several times from Davenport, but had rarely replied. Now he heard that he was in Hollywood under contract to MGM as a screenwriter, and he and Jan were invited to visit. In fact, through his much-despised mother, Muriel George, Davenport had been asked there by Robert Donat to work on a script with which he was having difficulties. He was now also married, to Clement Forbes-Robertson, an artist and granddaughter of the actor, Sir Johnston Forbes-Robertson. The prospect of Hollywood, the factory of the dream America with which he had been in love for so long, was immensely exciting to Lowry.

They bought a $35 Greyhound ticket, determined to see as much of America as they could on the way. The trip drew them together again, and 'These Foolish Things' became their song of reconciliation. The bus took them north through Buffalo to Niagara Falls where they did all the usual tourist things before deciding to cross over into Canada. They went through US immigration and customs and across the bridge leading to the Canadian border. There they were warned that if they left the US Malcolm would have to obtain a new entry visa before being able to return. They decided to retrace their steps across the bridge, and had great difficulty convincing the US immigration officers that they had not in fact entered Canada. Lowry's fear of officialdom was only intensified and crossing borders became a most terrifying experience to him. They continued via Chicago down to St Louis and across the great plains to Denver. In New Mexico they visited Lawrence's old home in Taos, to pay homage, having followed much the same route Lawrence took to get there in 1925 with Dorothy Brett.

At Los Angeles they put up at a dingy, flea-bag hotel near to the bus station. Next day Davenport and his wife Clement, then expecting her first child came and took them to their home, a lovely little Spanish villa on El Contento Drive just above Hollywood Boulevard. Although John was having no success with his scripts, he was winning money at shove-ha'penny, and spending it as fast as he could. He appeared to be buying up large numbers of modern paintings by Picasso, Hans Arp and Paul Klee. (In fact he had all these on loan from local galleries and stood to make a commission on any he sold.)[36] But he lived well, had a Filipino houseboy, dined at Musso Franks, threw parties for other writers, and ran an account at Stanley Rose's Bookstore. There Jan bought two books, Frances Toor's *Guide to Mexico* and her book of Spanish phrases, in anticipation of their forthcoming trip.

Malcolm showed *In Ballast* and some stories to Davenport, who wrote to Aiken that the novel was no good but some of the short stories were 'swell'.[37] He asked Davenport to find him a job at MGM, but he failed to do so and Lowry felt let down. Perhaps to annoy Jan, and echoing Zola on Sarah Bernhardt, Davenport told her that Malcolm had genius but no talent, and also made anti-Semitic, pro-Hitler remarks, no doubt in order to tease and mock her earnest anti-Fascism. The Spanish Republicans were calling for volunteers to fight Franco, and the Civil War was a major topic of conversation. He upset her again by borrowing $20 to put on a horse and then being surprised when she asked for it back. Money meant little to him, and when he left Hollywood just over a year later it is said he left behind debts of around $8,000.[38] The Lowrys, on the other hand, had barely $100 between them, and Jan was determined not to leave without her $20. Perhaps out of pique, Davenport wrote telling Aiken that the Lowrys had made their life a misery, consuming his whisky at the rate of a bottle a day. And it was not only Davenport who gave her trouble; one night a drunken Lowry knocked her down in the bedroom and raped her. After three weeks they left LA for San Francisco. As usual, Malcolm left some work behind, including, it seems, a copy of his story 'An Economic Conference', which Davenport produced again eleven years later, out of his hat like a magician, rather to Lowry's displeasure.

They spent a week in San Francisco where Lowry was intrigued by a city fascinatingly at odds with itself – Chinatown, the bridges, the cable-car and Sausalito – and which he called later 'the jewelled city', and which brought to his mind Lawrence's comment on life in general: 'The whole is a strange assembly of apparently incongruous parts, slipping past one another.'[39] To save money, they stayed at the Y, where Lowry wrote a long letter to Evelyn, waxing lyrical about the beauties of San Francisco and explaining the need to leave America in order to renew his visa. In any case, he added, travel was valuable to him as a writer. At the end of October, they returned to Los Angeles by boat, sailing out through the Golden Gate, and the following day set sail for Acapulco from San Pedro on the Panama-Pacific ship, SS *Pennsylvania*. The journey offered the chance of shedding the immediate past, the possibility of making a new start, the possibility of rebirth, the old theme reiterated.

CHAPTER XI

MEXICO: UNDER THE VOLCANO 1936–1937

> Mexico . . . is the most Christ-awful place in the world in which to be in any form of distress . . .
>
> MALCOLM LOWRY

> I was thinking . . . of my first arrival in Acapulco, my arrival indeed in Mexico, on the Day of the Dead 1936, the butterflies coming out to greet the *Pennsylvania*, and then . . . coming ashore in the launch, the difficulty of landing, then my first drink, 'where it had all started,' . . . over there by the Turismo. My first mescal had been the next day, after I had come back from swimming in Hornos – ah, how many memories were there, oscillations, deliriums, disengagements, all the foolishness of my youth and the Miramar – was it the Miramar that Ruth [Jan] and I had stayed at that first night?[1]

Here is Lowry, on a return visit to Acapulco in 1946, remembering his first impressions of Mexico. The images typify his sense of the place – the butterflies and the beauty, the Day of the Dead and the dark forces it symbolizes, swimming in the sea, the uncertainly recalled hotel, the first drink foreshadowing so many to come and the traumas and deliriums into which he was subsequently drawn in that mysterious and threatening country.

He and Jan arrived in Acapulco, according to Lowry's passport,[2] on 30 October 1936, but he always claimed it was on the Day of the Dead, a date with some dark and resonating significance. There are two Days of the Dead in Mexico: All Saints' Day, 1 November, when Mexican Indians believe the spirits of dead children return to spend a day among the living, and All Souls' Day, 2 November, is the day when adult spirits return. One of the first things Jan saw from the balcony of the Miramar was the funeral procession of a young child. The little white casket followed by merrily playing musicians gave it that strange mixture of the macabre and the joyful which catches the bizarre mood of the festival. Later they went to the crowded cemetery where they saw the sugar skulls and chocolate coffins and gaily bedecked skeletons, and listened to the strumming of guitars.

It has been observed how some of the beautiful short passages in *Under the Volcano* were probably begun as short prose poems and were later slotted into the main text as it developed. Their arrival in Acapulco became Yvonne's arrival, 'through a hurricane of immense and gorgeous butterflies swooping seawards to greet the *Pennsylvania*. . . as though fountains of multicoloured stationery were being swept out of the saloon lounge'.[3] And the child's funeral was also recalled:

> It came sailing out of nowhere, the child's funeral, the tiny lace-covered coffin followed by the band: two saxophones, bass guitar, a fiddle, playing of all things '*La Cucaracha*', the women behind, very solemn, while several paces back a few hangers-on were joking, straggling along in the dust almost at a run.[4]

Acapulco in 1936 was primitive and undeveloped. Living was cheap and Lowry's $150 a month was ample to live on. On the second day they went to Caleta beach, and at the Paraiso de Caleta Hotel, a dingy, dilapidated wooden hut with a few scraggy palm trees beyond,[5] Lowry bought his first bottle of mescal. Then they swam at Hornos, took the bus to Pie de la Cuesta 'with its atmosphere of the Belgian Congo, and its jungle and its roaring beach'[6] and on the bus he *drank* his first mescal. Perhaps because of the effect it had on him they spent the evening in a café discussing Jekyll and Hyde. Jan knew that it took little more than a couple of beers to transform Malcolm, but the effect of mescal was so much more dramatic, as was Mexico – on their first night Jan disturbed a thief in their room.

After a week, with Francis Toor's phrase book and *Guide to Mexico* at the ready, they set out to explore the country. They took the bus through the mountains, through Iguala to Taxco. There they met Alan, a young Spanish-American from California, and all three continued on by bus to Mexico City. They agreed to save money by sharing expenses, and through an advertisement at Wells Fargo found a Señora Baldwin with a house to rent in Cuernavaca, seventy-five kilometres south of Mexico City and five thousand feet above sea level in the Sierra Madre. On 18 November, they arrived in this pretty resort town, promptly fell in love with 62 Calle Humboldt, and took it. Malcolm was struck to find that the telephone number was Eriksen 34, Erikson being the name of his Grieg figure in *In Ballast*, and three and four adding up to the magic number seven. Then, not only was the immediate setting rich with bougainvillaea and other flowering tropical plants, but the view was breathtaking. Clear as crystal, dominating their horizon in those pollution-free days, stood the two great volcanoes, Popocatépetl and Ixtaccihuatl. As Jan recalled the scene:

> It really was a charming Spanish caseta – tile roof, huge grounds set back way from the street, with a pool . . . it was lushly lush and had lots of fruit trees, flowering trees, flowering shrubs, flowers . . . There were three bedrooms and a bath, and a huge verandah ran the full length of the house . . . with a magnificent view of the two volcanoes . . . really a stunning view . . . there was Popocatépetl and Ixtaccihuatl and in the evenings at twilight it was delightful to sit out there with one's drinks and look at the volcanoes and hear the humming of the insects from the garden below, and watch hummingbirds and just breathe the clear air and hear the clop-clop of horses . . . away in the distance at Acapatzingo because the air was so clear it carried sounds . . . There were quite lovely houses on the side on which we lived. The American Vice Consul lived next door . . . There were peacocks parading up and down behind fences. On the opposite side . . . were little Mexican casetas with dirt-floors . . . it was a lovely little street . . .[7]

Behind the house stood the great *barranca* across which, during the Spanish Conquest, a crossing by treacherous Tlaxcalans had helped Cortés subjugate dissident Indians at Tenochtitlán. This yawning gulf evoked a vision for Lowry, for here at his back door stood the great abyss, transformed in his imagination into a sexual, spiritual and occult image – 'the frightful cleft, the eternal horror of opposites', Marston's 'mighty gulf, insatiate cormorant',[8] Dante's eighth circle of hell and Malaboge, the cabbalist's 'awful unbridgeable void' between Chesed and Binah,[9] 'the enormous drop . . . that suggested . . . Kubla Khan'[10] and a 'general Tartarus or gigantic jakes'.[11] And above stood Popocatépetl, 'the Smoking Mountain'. and Ixtaccihuatl, 'the White Woman', symbolizing the perfect union between man and woman, each a Magic Mountain, the heights that all men must scale in order to achieve enlightenment. The world was indeed as Baudelaire said – 'a forest of symbols'.

Lowry's $150, paid on the first of the month through the Banco

Nacional de Mexico on Isabel la Católica in Mexico City, plus Alan's contribution, covered their expenses comfortably. The rent was $44 a month, including a gardener. A maid (Josefina) and a boy cost a further $42.[12] Now running a house, Jan found little time for her own work, though she had her portable Corona for typing up Malcolm's barely legible scrawl when required. He, a poor linguist, was utterly lost in Spanish, and she had but a few phrases from Frances Toor, so Alan, who was fluent, became their interpreter.

The city of Cuernavaca, their guidebook informed them, had a population of 8,200. Its old Aztec name was Cuahuahuac, an Aztec word meaning 'Near Wooded Mountains' but which the Spaniards thought meant 'Cow-horn', hence Cuernavaca. It was a favourite weekend playground for the wealthy of Mexico City, a city of bougainvillaea and gaily painted houses. Among its many hotels were the Bella Vista, facing the *zócalo*, the de la Selva with its disused casino, its tennis and jai-alai courts, and olympic-sized swimming pool, standing high up, half a mile from the centre of town, and the Cuernavaca Inn just off the newly built modern highway to the capital. Overlooking the *zócalo* stood Cortés's Palace with its famous Diego Rivera frescoes depicting the Conquest of Mexico. There was a sixteenth-century Franciscan-style cathedral, and the magnificent Borda Gardens laid out in formal Italian style in 1716 by Jose de la Borda, whose fortune came from the silver mines at Taxco. In the other direction, down the steep Calle Humboldt away from the town and off to the left, stood the ruins of the Emperor Maximilian's summer villa, also the love-nest to which Maximilian took his Mexican mistress behind the back of the unsuspecting Carlotta. The guide book made no mention of the model prison which stood at the town's edge, just visible from the high ground to the north.

The town, its hotels, the volcanoes and the *barranca* gave Lowry the topography of the fictional Quauhnahuac in which to set the story of the last day in the life of the drunken ex-Consul, Geoffrey Firmin. Calle Humboldt became the Calle Nicaragua and the street at the top which took you to the *zócalo*, Calle de las Casas, became the Calle Tiero de la Fuego. And it was around this town, from the Casino de la Selva to the north to the Acapatzingo (Alcapancingo in Lowry's Quauhnahuac) road to the south that Jacques Laruelle was to perambulate in chapter 1 of his book and that Hugh and Yvonne were take their horse-ride in chapter 4.

Almost immediately he arrived in Mexico, Lowry began to find it hard to continue with *In Ballast to the White Sea*. Gradually his mental picture changed from the bright pristine snowscape of the celestial north (the visionary landscape of *In Ballast*) to the dark, corrupting, surrealistic shadowland of the infernal south. But although the terrain was now so different, those high white mountain peaks still stood above, offering some symbolic prospect of hope to those striving upwards towards salvation.

He grew a beard and started to haunt the local cantinas, El Universal, Charlie's Bar and the Salón Ofélia, though to begin with he managed to limit himself to a few beers. As the mystique of the country began to take over, so his interest in it grew ever keener. The notes he had continued to make on *In Ballast* gradually gave way to observations, reflections and remarks overheard in cafés, on buses, and in bars.

One week a month they spent in Mexico City, collecting Malcolm's allowance, staying at the Hotel Canada on Cinco de Mayo, catching up with theatres, going to concerts and art galleries, loving especially the Rivera paintings at the Palacio de Bellas Artes, and visiting the American Book Store on Avenue Madero. There they met an Englishman, Teddy Wynn, a self-styled writer and traveller, whom Lowry liked but Jan considered a phoney and who was to reappear in Lowry's life only to confirm Jan's opinion. And not far from the hotel, he found the Church of Isabel la Católica where he could if need be offer a devout prayer to the Saint of Dangerous and Desperate Causes.[13]

Apart from Mexico City they visited Xochimilco, Oaxaca and Tehuacán. Lowry was constantly making notes, writing down signs, the names of towns, especially the Aztec ones – Mitla, Chiapas, Tlaxcala, Xiutepec – and of cantinas and pulquerias – El Bosque, El Amor de los Amores, El Farolito, Fleurs de Maguey – and delighting in amusing mistranslations by waiters of menu items – 'stepped-on eggs', 'divorced eggs', 'spectral chicken of the house'. And he continued to absorb the exotic richness of the country – at any moment, a wild-looking drunk, sombreroed and moustachioed, might charge on horseback down the Calle Humboldt flourishing a sabre or firing frantically into the air.

An event of great significance to Lowry happened on a bus ride to Chapultepec with Jan and Alan en route to Cuautla to see the bull-throwing. The bus stopped beside an Indian, apparently dying at the roadside. He may have been murdered or may have fallen from the horse grazing nearby. They left the bus with the others to look, but did nothing, as Alan advised them that Gringos were wise to keep their noses out of such things in Mexico.[14] But Lowry felt keenly the moral implications of doing nothing to help. It was not just the story of the

Good Samaritan. The Spanish Civil War was in his mind and he had friends fighting in it. He said later that he came to see the dying Indian as a symbol of suffering Spain, for wasn't the world standing by while Spain was bleeding? And wouldn't the whole world soon be dying by the wayside if the march to war was not halted?[15] And when a *pelado* robbed the dying man of a handful of bloodstained coins and gleefully showed them off to the other passengers, the seeds of a short story were sown, which ultimately blossomed into *Under the Volcano*.

In Cuatla they fell in with a Mexican film director and a couple of actresses, and for the first time in Mexico, Lowry dropped off the wagon. He again performed his 'reid-haird lowry' act – the cunning and elusive fox. Suddenly he disappeared, and Alan and Jan chased after him all day until they finally ran him to earth. Alan suggested a sedative, which had no effect, so they gave him another. He asked to lie down so they found him a bed. He would not sleep on springs so they placed the mattress on the floor and he seemed to pass out. When they returned he had disappeared. Later, on a trip to Taxco, he was picked up drunk in the gutter and carted off to gaol. In Guadalupe, in December, he disappeared into a huge crowd gathering to worship the Virgin and turned up next morning having slept the night on the floor of the basilica in a borrowed mackintosh – or so he claimed.[16]

His drunken behaviour failed to commend him to their American neighbour, a lofty character, who chose to ignore them. The scene with Mr Quincey in *Under the Volcano* was no doubt based on a brief encounter over the garden fence with the haughty Vice-Consul, who had no fewer than five gardeners compared to the Lowrys' one. Calling him 'Quincey' was ironic; that was the name of the man who bought the land of William Blackstone, the Cambridge scholar who escaped from claustrophobic Puritan Massachusetts and chose to live in the forest among the Indians. Lowry preferred his jungle to the carefully cultivated garden of Mr Quincey.

Jan had decided that Malcolm was more likely to get drunk if someone was staying with them. Left on their own he seemed able to control himself. So she decided to ask Alan, for Malcolm's sake, to leave. Their young boarder, however, had anticipated her and departed, leaving a note to say that he had come south to see Mexico and not to play nursemaid to a drunkard.

As the war in Spain gathered momentum, the Lowrys knew exactly where they stood, as did friends in Mexico City, Alfred and Marsha Miller, who worked for the Cárdenas regime. Mexico, one of the very few allies of the Spanish Government, became a haven for Republican refugees. In the past it had offered sanctuary to others from the left. B. Traven, author of *The Treasure of Sierra Madre*, having fled Germany, had been there since the 1920s; Trotsky, on the run from Stalin's assassins, found refuge there in January 1937. But there was also a pro-Nazi movement in Mexico, the Sinarquistas, not perhaps as violent as the Christeros whose atrocities Marsha Miller so graphically described to them, but dangerous all the same. The Lowrys kept abreast of world events through *El Universal*, a newspaper which carried reports in English.

After Alan's departure they settled into a quiet, productive life, succumbing to Jan's 'terrible efficiency', with a few visitors, mostly non-drinkers. As Mexico gradually exerted a grip on his imagination, the idea of expanding the story about the Indian into a novel also took hold, and any new experience was likely to be worked into it. When Jan came home one day and mentioned meeting a man called Forget, who lived in a strange tower with chevron-shaped windows at the top of Calle Humboldt, he gave the name instantly to the prototype of Jacques Laruelle, the film-maker-cum-Virgilian Prologue in *Under the Volcano*.

They swam daily in their pool, went horse-riding, explored the countryside around Cuernavaca, Cortés's Palace, Maximilian's summer villa, the Borda Gardens (where they carved their names on a tree),[17] occasionally entertained friends from Mexico City, and acquired two cats (Oedipuss and Priapuss). Despite the daily swims and relative abstemiousness, Malcolm developed a painful case of sciatica, variously diagnosed as lumbago, rheumatic fever, and infantile paralysis. He was later found also to have been suffering the onset of varicose veins, which were to trouble him a great deal, and he found it necessary to walk with a stick.

The absence of friends began to affect him, and he wrote to Davenport eagerly anticipating his promised visit at Christmas. But his letters went unanswered and he felt offended. As he wrote to him later, 'Our marriage got little ratification from any source. It would have been pleasant to think it had from you.' They had put other visitors off, expecting them right up until Christmas Day, he said.[18] Cut off from wider literary contacts, he wrote letters to writers he admired – Julian Green, Sommerfield and Grieg, though none were actually sent.[19] His sense of isolation is captured in a brief character sketch from his notebook, perhaps of a prototype of the Consul: '. . . a remittance man, a blot on some aristocratic family in England, paid to stay away . . . but what horror, or sinister discovery, had made him into the loveless creature he had turned out to be, I've no more idea than anyone else.'[20]

It cannot have helped his self-confidence as a writer to have received a letter from Evelyn just before Christmas warning him to remember what happened to rolling stones, and saying 'How much I would rejoice to hear of your success in life. Well! I shall just go on hoping.'[21]

By the New Year his story had grown into a novella, and he even began to conceive of it as part of a trilogy along with *The Last Address* and *In Ballast*,[22] an idea he may have picked up from Aiken's interest in Faulkner, or his own in Hermann Broch's triple novel, *The Sleepwalkers*. So far all he had was the incident of the dying Indian, but now, after another experience, he wrote a scene which so pleased him it remained almost unchanged in the final version. He had strayed one evening into El Universal, and there got *perfectamente borracho*, but not so much so that he could not take notes. At the bar he fell in with a group of other *borrachos* who attempted to talk to him in English while he tried to respond in Spanish. The result was so bizarre that he began to copy it down. Rather than getting annoyed by this the others seemed flattered. When Lowry staggered home that night he was met by an irate Jan, who complained bitterly about his drinking. He protested that he had gone to the cantina for purely literary purposes, adding self-righteously that out of consideration for her and at some sacrifice to himself he had decided not to bring the *borrachos* home to continue taking down their conversation throughout the night, an act of forbearance which might be costing him a masterpiece.[23]

Jan retired from the battlefield to bed, and Lowry, unable to sleep, went outside into the garden to retrieve a bottle which, Geoffrey Firmin-like, he had previously hidden there. He then sat down, so he later claimed, and wrote till six o'clock next morning, had some more to drink and then a swim, and, because Jan and he were not on speaking terms at breakfast, carried on writing until twelve. At the end he had the conclusion to his book – his hero, the Consul, is shot and thrown down the *barranca* followed by a dead dog. All that changed later, he said, was that he interspersed some letters which Jan wrote to him after she left him later that year.[24] The cantina was also changed from El Universal in Cuernavaca to be like a Farolito in Oaxaca and placed above a *barranca* in a place something like Chapultepec.[25]

In April, having now stayed for the six months permitted, they applied for resident cards. Soon after, Aiken wrote to say he was coming to Mexico to get divorced and remarry. 'We are chuffing down to see you in the land of the pulques and chinches,' he wrote.[26] In the meantime, the novel continued to take shape, and in order to provide some link with *In Ballast* he called his Consul William Erikson. He also took in more of the Mexican landscape. In April on a train ride to Oaxaca he began a poem, 'When Maguey Gives way to Pine', one of his first for some time, and noted that Cholula near Puebla had 366 churches. The poet was ever trying to get out, the accumulator of detail ever on the alert.

Lowry's commitment to the book and his belief in its prophetic power was intensified by an event which occurred early in 1937. At a café in Cuernavaca one day he and Jan read a newspaper story about a tourist who had been shot and thrown into the *barranca*, and who, unbelievably, had the same name as his murdered Consul, William Erikson. It was as if in writing of Erikson's death in his book he had somehow caused the death of the real Erikson. Lowry was both devastated and fascinated by this incident, and the book began to possess him in an almost supernatural way.

One day in the middle of May, Aiken called from Mexico City. He was with Ed Burra and Mary Hoover, the young artist he intended marrying after a quick Mexican divorce from the uncooperative Clarissa. Lowry was delighted to hear Aiken's voice again. 'You must stay with us,' he said, much to Jan's annoyance. The thought of having the hard-drinking poet in the house filled her with foreboding. She asked Malcolm what Aiken had told him about Mary. 'Conrad says she's marvellously inarticulate,' he said. She then asked what would happen to Clarissa (Jerry). 'Jerry,' he replied, using Aiken's words, 'was a bitch!' Jan protested that she had rather liked Jerry. Lowry shrugged. 'What do you expect when a man finds his mother killed by his father with a sad-iron?' 'I thought she was shot,' said Jan. 'Maybe,' said Lowry, 'but a sad-iron sounds better.'[27]

They went to the *zócalo* to meet Aiken from the bus, Lowry hobbling along manfully on his stick. In *Ushant*, Aiken remembered:

> the slightly absurd, but always altogether delightful, figure, advancing towards them with that stick of his – the tall sapling which he carried, because, he said, it helped him with his lumbago – advancing towards the *camión*, which had brought them over the mountains from Mexico City, his trousers knotted round the waist with a necktie, and looking as if they might fall off any minute; and grinning at them shyly, and

> affectionately, and a little drunkenly . . . A carelessly powerful and ingratiating figure, to which the curiously short arms, which he habitually thrust a little before him, lent an appealing appearance of helplessness.[28]

Seen from the other side of the camera, Jan thought the trio of Aiken, Mary and Burra, looked like a grotesque vaudeville act – Aiken an over-bloated, red-faced figure with sandy hair, Mary looking large and shapeless in a sweat-soaked dress, and the diminutive Burra hopping behind like a performing monkey. Lowry and Aiken hugged – 'two large florid-faced gentlemen embracing like wrestlers'.[29] But if there was to be any wrestling it was between Aiken and Jan, and the prize would be the soul of Malcolm Lowry.

Aiken hated Mexico and was already feeling unwell. 'Jesus what a climate, what a country, what a people,' he wrote to Harry Murray. 'We arrived more dead than alive – no sleep for three days – constant midnight and early morning changes at godawful little way stations . . .'[30] He had been struck down with stomach trouble, he said, and his insides had been coming out at both ends. But being invited to stay with the Lowrys was a godsend. 'We'll almost save the extra cost of the legal fees in the cutting of living expenses.' His mood was not helped by the fact that he had arrived in the middle of the rainy season. Not only were the days overcast and drenching, but the nights were torn apart by pyrotechnic thunderstorms.

The double bedroom opening onto the verandah was given to Aiken and his bride-to-be, and Malcolm and Jan took smaller separate rooms. Burra slept on a straw mattress on the verandah. This was Lowry's favourite perch during the day, where he liked to sprawl with his notes. Aiken later depicted him descending ever deeper into 'marital and alcoholic misery and despair . . . in that nest of old rags and blankets in which for the most part he lived, on the veranda of the villa.'[31] But the misery and despair into which Lowry was about to be plunged was the result of the sudden, and from Jan's point of view, highly unwelcome presence of the darkly brooding Aiken.

He soon put Jan's back up by ordering the maid off to a get him a bottle of *habanero*, and then carting Malcolm off to the nearest cantina. As it happened, Cuernavaca, as well as being a favourite resort for the wealthy, was a drinker's paradise. Cheap alcohol, which acted fast at the town's high altitude, and cantinas which opened at the crack of dawn and closed in the early hours, had attracted an alcoholic community of all nations. It was not the healthiest place for a man like Lowry to be coaxed off the wagon.

Aiken's bad mood was due not only to the country and the people. He was annoyed to find that Lowry and Jan were politically far to the left of him. He wrote in *Ushant* (in which Lowry appears as Hambo):

> Hambo had drifted pretty far, politically, towards something like communism: he had been through something like a social conversion, and clearly felt a need for some sort of fraternal joining and belonging: and D.'s [Aiken's] and Lorelei's [Mary's] more abstract political views were not calculated to make him happy . . . Revolutions were a waste both of time and human material; – you lost a hundred or more years only to find yourself just where you'd begun. A revolution was an attempt to freeze society on a particular level, and this was itself stultifying, no matter what that level might be. If the Nazis had frozen theirs on a slightly higher level than the Russians, with a shade less destruction of its living inheritance of culture, well, that made it a trifle less wasteful, but that was the best that could be said for it, and no excuse.[32]

To have as a house guest someone who had even a half-kind word to say for Hitler was something Jan found intolerable. Aiken's political views, she concluded, were 'somewhat to the right of Ghengis Khan.'[33] With two people of such different temperaments and such widely different views struggling for Lowry's soul, something was bound to give.

At dinner one evening, Aiken and Jan had a fierce argument. She proclaimed that a woman had as much right to sexual fulfilment as a man; Aiken said they didn't need it. When she argued with him he told her heatedly to shut up, that she didn't know what she was talking about. To Aiken women were objects of sexual pleasure, and little more. Lowry told her later that when at Jeake's House he once produced a copy of Van der Velde's *The Ideal Marriage* (a sexual New Testament to her and Malcolm), Aiken glanced at it, then said, 'For God's sake don't let Jerry see that!' Jan wondered what on earth Mary thought of her husband-to-be, but she was never to know. The atmosphere grew ever more icy. Still resentful of her lack of interest in him, and her taking away his most lucrative student, Aiken seemed determined to make mischief between them. Later he portrayed her as hard and wanton, her 'merciless and faithless heels' clacking on the verandah as she forever planned to go off and be unfaithful. What he may or may not have been aware of was that it was his presence that was driving a wedge between them. To Jan, Malcolm was warm, intuitive and charismatic, while Aiken was cold, logical and supercilious, and his politics obnoxious. She wished the visitors would leave. Malcolm, on the other hand, torn between respecting Aiken for his genius and being repelled by his views, just hoped in his amiable way that things would turn out for the best. But there was to be no escaping these daily confrontations. Aiken was determined to remain and so save money, come what may; he was also determined to express his views. Nor did it help when after a week he announced that he had just heard that the divorce would take another month.

If Aiken was using Lowry, Lowry was also using him. He claimed that his anti-revolutionary speech infuriated both Malcolm *and* Jan. But it was not wasted on Malcolm who later put it into chapter 10 of *Under the Volcano*. In fact the Consul would end up with more than an ounce of Aiken in his make-up. In an important sense he became Lowry possessed by his Dark Angel while the Communist half-brother Hugh was to be Lowry possessed by his Good Angel, Grieg. On another occasion, when Aiken watched a cat watching him, he said, 'He thinks I'm a tree with a bird in it.' This, too, went straight into Lowry's notebook for the novel, as did his comment on the jungle-like garden: 'I expect to see Rousseau riding out of there on a tiger.' And when Aiken told how a cat, which he had seen catch a dragonfly, was so amazed when it continued to fly in his mouth that he gaped and it flew away, that, too, turned up in *Under the Volcano*. Although he failed to win Lowry over politically, he easily won him over to alcohol once again. With him there, Jan found it impossible to keep Malcolm sober, and drink began to possess him almost to the point of no return. Finally he got to where he would drink anything he thought contained alcohol. Once he consumed a whole bottle of olive oil thinking it was hair tonic with a high alcoholic content. Finally he got the shakes so bad that he improvised a pulley system to hoist the glass to his lips.[34]

On 11 June, they were supposed to go to Mexico City and then to Lake Pátzcuaro in Michoacán to celebrate Jan's twenty-sixth birthday, but they had a great argument over Aiken's continuing presence. Lowry and Aiken stayed up drinking all night and next morning Malcolm was far too hungover to go anywhere. Jan decided she had had enough. These men were simply drinking her marriage into dissolution. She decided to leave alone, a scene which Aiken elaborated upon in *Ushant*, clothing it in prurient fantasy, and describing it with spiteful glee. He knew only too well, as he said in *Blue Voyage*, how to be cruel and vengeful towards a woman he wanted but who showed herself indifferent to him. There was what he called 'the pathetic episode of the earrings'. 'The faithless heels', he wrote, were obviously going away for a week to be faithless with two engineers at the silvermines. In Aiken, the self-confessed adulterer, who chose prostitutes when he could find no one else to bed, there was more than a strong whiff of hypocritical and lustful fantasy in his account:

> From the parting at the bus station, where they had all gone to see her off, they had done their best to avert their eyes. The stonily beautiful little profile avoided the anguished and hangdog gaze of poor Hambo, she was already looking ahead, over those propitious mountains, to the wealth of those silver-mines, and the promise of gay nights, and, as always on such occasions, the lavish and expensive gifts which awaited her there. And with this enthralling prospect before her, how could she possibly pay the slightest heed to the little gift which Hambo had brought, the little gift of silver earrings? They were for her birthday – he murmured – handing them awkwardly and shyly through the *camión* window: they were for her birthday . . . did she remember? But if she did, she expressed no surprise. She accepted them with a glance of repressed annoyance, thrust them almost angrily into her handbag – as if they were a sort of rebuke, and perhaps they were – and then the bus shot away, the usual cloud of dust whirling up from it, over the square and its baroque bandstand, and she was gone.[35]

Jan remembered it quite differently. Lowry saw her off with Aiken lumbering in their wake and Mary and Burra tagging along behind. After she was on the bus Malcolm handed her a note and a little pair of straw (not silver) earrings available cheaply in the market. She accepted them and put them in her bag as the bus pulled away. In the note he was full of remorse for his drinking and apologized for his friends who were so obviously troublesome to her. They would return to Europe together, and live in Chartres, as once planned, he said. The last thing she saw was Aiken with his arm around Malcolm, leading him away; heading, no doubt, for the nearest drink.[36]

The day after Jan departed, Aiken wrote that suddenly Cuernavaca had improved. He and Mary were 'lethargic, comatose, drugged with heat, but nevertheless enjoying ourselves in a queer primordial ophidian fashion, like a couple of amiable old snakes',[37] amid the ants, the lizards, the butterflies and the magnificent phallic fruits, 'one does feel that one has known this before, been in this slime, and it's enormously enriching.'[38] Mary painted watercolours, Aiken worked at an article about William Faulkner, and Burra, despite feeling unwell, made his savage drawings.

Lowry, on the other hand, was unable to work. If he had been hitting the bottle before Jan left, now he began to drink in earnest. The first night, in the middle of a thunderstorm, he returned very late and very drunk, and, trying to get in through the garden, slipped headlong into the stinking sewerage canal running behind the house. Aiken, hearing his cries, dragged him out. In an attempt to keep him sober, Aiken devised a series of difficult exercises in blank verse for him, stressing vowel and consonant control as well as caesura, but he only repaired to Charlie's Bar and mixed poetry with tequila. He would write them out and send them round to the house by hand. One of the lines which Aiken thought perfect was 'Airplane or aeroplane or just plain plane.' The rest were by no means perfect but show Lowry's obsessive fear and respect for alcohol and represent a return to serious poetry, for practically the first time since leaving Cambridge.

> Sir: drinking is a problem without doubt:
> Whether or not we like it, whether or not
> The goddam thing will put you on the spot
> With heebiejeebies hebephrene or gout . . .[39]

And so began in earnest the cycle of poems he called *The Lighthouse Invites the Storm*.

Three days after she left, Jan wrote from Michoacán. She had had to get away from the insufferable Aiken, she said, and would return a bigger brighter Rainbowpuss. He replied with a rather sad, yearning letter. Aiken was no friend, he said, despite pretending to be one.

> He is, in fact, a born chiseller – of everything, of his friends, & wives, & of verses . . . their constant wrong, hasty judgments, with occasional emasculated ejaculations from Ed – on practically all matters of importance, not excepting the aesthetic, make me feel even sicker than I actually am . . . Meantime as a gift horse one has the sense of being not only looked in the mouth but chiselled out of all one's teeth as well . . . For God's sake let's get close together again – as we were, & fundamentally are – & are – . . . I love you and long to travel with you again.[40]

The Faustian Lowry knew he had been persuaded to sell his soul to the Demon Drink by the Mephistophelean Aiken as a way of getting at Jan. He continued to drink heavily. Once he left to stay with a friend living in Cuatla, but wrote to Jan saying he had become dangerous and been carted off to hospital raving, suffering from syphilis caught from his maid. On 23 June, Aiken wrote to his brother that Lowry had been drunk for a week.[41]

One morning he materialized in Charlie's Bar looking more dishevelled and more in pain than ever. He sent a desperate note to Aiken. 'My host in Cuatla went nuts. Had to be held down & taken to hospital . . . & I'm glad Jan was spared the experience.' Then, in a fit of remorse at having blackguarded him to Jan, added: '(It suddenly occurs to me how much I love you both, you old Mephistopheles. Be happy, you two. I kind of feel you will.) . . . Come to Charlie's, where I am, soon: old Aggie's got the orrors somethink orful.'

Ever anxious to shine in the eyes of his father surrogate, he had proudly given him *In Ballast* to read and a forty-thousand word rough draft of *Under the Volcano*. Aiken was duly impressed. He wrote to Henry Murray,

> I'm reading Malcolm's really remarkable new novel, unpublished, very queer, very profound, very twisted, wonderfully rich – In Ballast to the White Sea. Gosh, the fellow's got genius – such a brilliant egocentric nonstop selfanalysis, and such a magnificent fountain, inexhaustible, of projected self-love I never did see. Wonderful. Too much of it, and directionless, but for sheer tactile richness and beauty of prose texture a joy to swim in.[42]

Despite being impressed by his protégé's novels, Aiken decided to confront him with the plagiarism there from his own work and bearded him in Charlie's Bar. They had had this quarrel before and Lowry had since had to face Rascoe's anger in New York. However, in this case he could argue that Aiken had actually invited him to become the son who 'absorbed' the father. According to Aiken's own account, Lowry was ready to admit the influence of Joyce, Dostoyevsky, Melville, and even Waldo Frank, but not his debt to Aiken because, he said, he was not so well known and his debt to him was greater. This brought to a head the great argument which had been brewing between them since they first met, and a titanic and convoluted psychological wrestling match followed. When Aiken announced to him in 1929 that it was the right of the son to consume the father he had in mind Lowry's becoming an extension of himself, but now the son threatened to eclipse the father.

> I shall wholly absorb you; I *am* absorbing you now. And it's your own wish, moreover – you said so. Am I not your son, in whom you are destined to be well pleased? . . . What possible escape is there for you from the logical and temporal sequence, as members of a series, by which it is your fate simply to become a better 'you' in me –? I shall become a better 'you,' and you will be dead.[43]

And Aiken revealed the bitterness he felt that this mad experiment he had instigated, had somehow backfired.

> Yes, it had been an astonishing conspiracy, in its way a conspiracy in lunacy, full of its own intentional ambiguities and low cunnings: an *agon*, to be played again and again between them, all the way from that first idyllic summer in Cambridge to Saltinge (Rye) and Granada and Mexico: and now, reaching its logical end in this delicious absurdity. Every angle of it had been studied in mirrors . . . each of them with an eye to making use of it first. And after all, in that so-long-elaborated symbiosis, who was to say just what was whose, and just which properties, of perception or invention, belonged to either?[44]

It was perhaps out of revenge that, Iago-like, he stirred Lowry's jealousy against Jan. After all, he had predicted the match would end disastrously when he told Lowry on board the *Strathaird* off Gibraltar, 'Keep a pair of scissors handy.' And so he spoke to his 'son' of

> 'The same brilliance, exactly, the finest nuances of apparently ingenuous charm, of gentleness, tenderness, and every note of it deceptive. Her eyes flying like birds after every male on the horizon – all of them. Cities of them – nations of them. Her infidelities –'
>
> 'More numerous even than yours?'
>
> 'Call it a dead heat.'[45]

All the same, he was perceptive enough to realize that Lowry, having purloined his William Blackstone myth, had himself chosen to escape from Puritan civilization and there in Cuernavaca on the edge of his *barranca* live among the Indians. And it was on the edge of the *barranca*, in that final chapter of *Under the Volcano*, that Lowry's Consul gave his name as 'William Blackstone', the very pretext his persecutors needed to accuse him of spying and then to murder him.

Shortly after this monumental argument Lowry wrote to Jan. Aiken now said that his divorce would take longer than previously thought and suggested taking rooms in the town, but he found it difficult to agree without giving offence.

> I think he's an extraordinarily evil person, capable of the profoundest harm to everything more human or with a more progressive nature than a cat . . . He pretends to the deepest friendship for me, to admiration for my work, but secretly he is jealous, unreasoning, or bitter, while the only real depth in our relationship is the extraordinary malicious extent of his hatred; but this is hatred for life too. It is wretchedness become evil . . . I can no longer bring myself to listen to the arid nonsense he talks. Ed is at heart an arid & contemptible fellow too. To hell with these degenerate, stupid people . . . It is only our admiration for genius even in its darkest flights that keeps us harbouring such a person as Conrad under our roof . . . you & I must at once simplify our lives & organize them – *alone*. . . away from such evil friends as these . . .[46]

Meanwhile Aiken was sitting like a cuckoo in the nest at 62 Calle Humboldt. As Jan saw it, having given so much of himself to Malcolm, he was squatting there, determined to 'collect'. But he had nothing very good to say about the place, complaining about the stench from the sewage canal and the food prepared by the Indian cook. All of them became ill, Burra seriously. He was so weak and ill that after seeing a doctor he decided to return to America, and Lowry was not sorry to see his old tormentor gone.

Aiken, however, had begun taking notes, and later wrote a novel based on his visit, *A Heart for the Gods of Mexico*, which shows evidence of his having read the *Volcano*. If Lowry could borrow from Aiken, the reverse was also possible. Here Lowry first appeared as the amiable if ludicrous Hambo.

Although writing every day, Jan suddenly wrote a desperately loving letter. She had met two silverminers in Guanajuato, and had been taken to see the fearsome mummies there. These so horrified her that she had gone off and had too many drinks. When she awoke next day she was so filled with remorse that she wrote to Malcolm stressing her love for him and her need to be with him. 'Let's start all over again,' she wrote, 'like we were at the Somerset – let's talk together, work together, discuss together. I need you more than ever, like in the old days.' Lowry later put lines from her letter into *Under the Volcano*: 'I want your children, soon, at once, I want them. I want your life filling and stirring me. I want your happiness beneath my heart and your sorrows in my eyes and your peace in the fingers of my hand . . .'[47]

Returning on 29 June, however, Jan found Aiken already weaving his fantasies, already turning her silverminers into lovers and the gift of a silver bangle from one of them into the sort of present that could lure her away from poor old 'Hambo'. There was now very little love lost between her and Aiken, and at his wedding that July, she and Malcolm were photographed together looking, in Aiken's words, 'like Sacred and Profane love', and in anyone else's 'glum'. Aiken put this down to the miserable incompatibility he had foreseen between them in Spain; in fact they were glum at being at the wedding of the man who had all but wrecked their marriage. When he left, of all the beautiful things he could have bought in Mexico, Aiken took as a sole souvenir some neatly scrolled yellow clay models of human excreta – a Mexican turd, a choice which Jan considered highly appropriate.

The strain of the past six weeks now began to tell. Soon after Aiken left, Lowry succumbed to malaria. However, he was soon back at work on *The Volcano*. The first short story version and first draft of the novel have long since disappeared, but the earliest surviving drafts show him still writing the economical prose he had been producing since his Paris stories, though this was being challenged all the while, as in *In Ballast*, by the visionary poet wanting to turn small incidents into large parables of the times. For example, the incident of the dying Indian was seen to embody the great struggle developing in Europe and about to engulf the world; the strange tower at the top of the Calle Humboldt was given, on its walls, an inscription from Father Luis Ponce de León, '*No se puede vivir sin amar*' ('One cannot live without loving').

Although he took notes as fast as a shorthand writer, in composing he wrote painfully slowly, writing several drafts before giving it to Jan to type. She found that even the apparently spontaneous love letters to her had been through two or three drafts before being sent. Once his work was typed he made few corrections, whereas later, his writing was to become more a dialogue, in Davenport's words, between Malcolm and Lowry,[48] more a form of self-analysis in constant revision.

The departure of Aiken had a therapeutic effect on his marriage. In early July, after seeing the Anatole Litvak film *Mayerling* in Mexico City, he and Jan wandered through the streets back to their hotel and enjoyed a night to rival 10 August 1934 at Martha's Vineyard.[49]

By now he was feeling deeply disillusioned with his friends. Davenport, he felt, had been less than welcoming in Hollywood, had not been helpful in finding him work with MGM, and had failed to show up at Christmas as promised. Now Aiken had all but destroyed his marriage. When Davenport finally wrote in August, he wrote back a rather hurt and bitter letter. His silence, he told him, had been 'eloquent', it was 'a silence between house and house' rather than between the two of them and this, he thought, deserved an explanation. Aiken, he added, despite his claims to friendship, was no longer a friend. ('Well, to hell with the old Medusa! A dirty, destructive, and excessively amusing fellow . . . I was well aware at parting I no longer thought of the pro-fascist Conrad as our friend.')[50] But he was mystified as to what had come between the two of *them*.

More cheeringly, there was a letter from Jan's mother saying that in a book about T. E. Lawrence, *Lawrence and his Friends*, she had seen that among the books in his library at his death was *Ultramarine*. Lowry was thrilled and built this small fact into another myth. Lawrence had thrown out all the books which meant nothing to him, and now, he claimed, his copy of *Ultramarine* was worth a great deal of money.[51]

Arthur Calder-Marshall had recently joined Davenport writing for MGM in Hollywood, and, laid off for six weeks in October, he and his wife Ara decided to have a holiday in Mexico. Before they left, Davenport said they must visit Lowry, who was feeling rather dejected just then. Equipped with a new car, they planned to drive to Acapulco, then make their way back to California along the coast. In Cuernavaca they checked into the modern Cuernavaca Inn, intending to stay just one night. The following morning, after breakfast and a swim, they drove through the rain to 62 Calle Humboldt. Calder-Marshall told his wife that she was about to meet one of the world's greatest drunkards. After Hollywood and the Cuernavaca Inn, the villa which Jan so loved seemed to them little more than a rural slum, something out of Somerset Maugham, approached along what looked like a shelled road in Flanders. The place seemed deserted but eventually Jan, barefoot and in blue denims, came to the door, and she called Malcolm.

Finally he emerged, bleary-eyed from his *siesta*, embraced Calder-Marshall and immediately fell to talking about old times. Jan was delighted to see them. To her they were 'beautifully and triumphantly British'. Arthur was a striking man, with the profile of a Greek god, and his wife Ara was widely regarded as one of the most beautiful English women of her generation. To Jan they epitomized what was best about Britain. Calder-Marshall at that time was one of the most successful young English authors. Since leaving Oxford six years earlier, he had published nine books including three novels and a book of short stories. He belonged to the Communist Party, and was one of the leading English advocates of 'proletarian literature'.[52] They talked about Spain and the fact that the Republicans were losing the Battle of the Ebro. Lowry must also have heard the news that Sommerfield had been twice reported dead in Spain, that Julian Bell and John Cornford really had been killed there, and that his friend Grieg was covering the war for an Oslo newspaper. They talked also about psychoanalysis, which Calder-Marshall had undergone recently and feared might have damaged his creativity. Malcolm, who had had a taste of it at Aiken's hands and then in Bellevue, seemed less fearful, but thought one could do it just as well for oneself.

Calder-Marshall got the impression that things were strained between the Lowrys, with Jan constantly digging at Malcolm for not being as successful as he seemed to be, a claim which she later denied. In fact she thought a writer could over produce. But they spoke eagerly about the healthy life they had led since Aiken's departure. When out, they limited themselves to a couple of beers, and kept absolutely no liquor in the house. They walked a lot and swam every day. But that did not impress Calder-Marshall, who remembered the swimming pool as 'about twelve feet by eight and . . . covered in dead butterflies and various insects;'[53] nor was this the prodigious drunk that Ara had been promised a sight of, so she whispered to Arthur, 'Do you think they'd be very shocked if we asked for a drink?' According to Calder-Marshall, when they did ask, Jan replied, 'Just one,' and they went off to dress up. At six o'clock they all took off for what Arthur remembered as the only nightclub in Cuernavaca, 'a tiny place overcrowded when ten people were in it.' Six hours later the one drink had turned into dozens, and Jan announced that she was going home, asking Calder-Marshall to drive her back. He suggested they *all* go back, but Ara wanted to stay – she was beginning to enjoy the drunken Lowry, who became more brilliant and amusing the more he drank. But when Jan said she was going home, he insisted on returning to the villa with her and Calder-Marshall to make sure she was properly tucked up. Then the two men returned to the nightclub, and Lowry said, 'Now the drinking can begin!' and pitched into the tequila. At 3 a.m. the visitors returned to the Cuernavaca Inn, leaving Lowry to carry on consuming.

Next morning at 8 a.m., not having been to bed that night, he was knocking on the Calder-Marshalls' hotel-room door, clutching his new novel and wanting Arthur to read it. Calder-Marshall had a roaring hangover, but it was obvious to him that Lowry would not leave until he had read the manuscript. He agreed with Ara that they could not go on that day to Acapulco, took a swim in the hotel pool, then sat down to read the book. He decided it was 'terrible' and there was nothing he could do with it because his and Lowry's minds worked so differently. However he did suggest sending it to Ann Watkins, who also happened to be *his* American agent.

Calder-Marshall had found an old newspaper, and said, 'Say . . . this is funny, here's an American chap (named Erikson) gets shot and thrown down a *barranca* too.' It was all that Lowry needed – to be reminded of the story which had so disturbed him earlier that year, to be reminded of a death for which he thought himself responsible.[54] Perhaps because of this or the fact that he had dropped off the wagon so dramatically, he now took off on an enormous fugue, disappearing and reappearing without notice before disappearing again. He scribbled a note to Jan saying, 'I am suffering from a mighty attack of insomnia. I love you and want us to be together, but I need to sort things out. Don't worry, everything will come out right.' She rang the Calder-Marshalls to say that although she had docked his money to try to keep him sober, he had run off to sell their alarm clock to buy drink. (He had stolen other things for the same purpose before.) After combing through the cantinas they finally found him sitting at a bar in a mackintosh he liked wearing, and from one of its voluminous pockets he produced the missing alarm clock. When Jan asked why on earth he had taken it, he replied, 'But my lovely, how else would I know the time?' Now Ara was certainly seeing the greatest drunk in action, and found him both delightful and endearing – good natured but like a fox ready to disappear in a flash to escape 'the ordinaries trying to sober him up.'[55]

After three days of this Jan had had enough and departed for Veracruz. They had planned to go there to see the setting of a film they had both enjoyed, Paul Strand's *Redes*, but Malcolm, caught up in this self-destructive alcoholic binge, refused to go. He was left behind to be tended by the Calder-Marshalls at the Cuernavaca Inn. A fleeting visit had turned into a nursing operation. Much to Lowry's delight, the doctor prescribed strychnine and brandy, and in the novel, Calder-Marshall administering the stuff to him in the hope of weaning him off mescal, became Hugh administering it to the Consul. However much Lowry enjoyed the idea of this bizarre medication, he was not that easily deflected from his present suicidal course, as Calder-Marshall discovered when the hotel manager complained that his strange patient had bribed the waiters and the chambermaids to smuggle bottles of tequila and mescal in to him.

One day he went back to the villa to change, and from there rang Calder-Marshall to say that the house had been robbed. But when the police were called they could find nothing missing. Finally, after a prolonged search of the house, Lowry said, 'There! There used to be one copy of *Story* here and now there are two.' The police left. A few nights later he managed to escape from the Inn and was traced to a cantina where he had got extremely drunk with a taxi driver; they were going to Veracruz, he announced, then by ship to Spain to fight Franco. Ara found this performance intensely amusing; Arthur found it more and more tedious. Two weeks after arriving in Cuernavaca, bored at getting nowhere with their capricious patient, they gave up and continued their drive through Mexico back to Hollywood.

What they found odd was that Lowry seemed to enjoy having been deserted by Jan. Like Lawrence's heroine, she had become 'The Woman Who Rode Away', and he now cast himself in a new dramatic role, the deserted husband. After all, misery was something he knew how to turn to creative use, it was an *experience*, it was hell and hell was the home of creative writers of genius as Aiken had long ago taught him, and as he had learned from reading Poe, Melville, Rimbaud, Thomas Mann, and Hart Crane. Jan had long noted how he loved to suffer, and liked to say, 'My misery is the hole in which the worm makes it home.' But, while drowning in despair he was aware of the comic side of things, and quite capable of suddenly grinning and misquoting a favourite line from Boswell, 'Cheerfulness keeps breaking in.'[56]

CHAPTER XII

'SOMETHING NEW ABOUT HELLFIRE'

1937–1938

> To conceive the horror of my sensation is, I presume, utterly impossible; yet a curiosity to penetrate the mysteries of these awful regions, predominates even over my despair, and will reconcile me to the most hideous aspect of death. It is evident that we are hurrying onwards to some exciting knowledge – some never-to-be-imparted secret, whose attainment is destruction.
>
> EDGAR ALLAN POE, 'Manuscript Found in a Bottle'

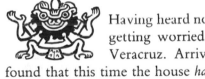

Having heard nothing from him since she left, Jan was getting worried and decided to cut short her trip to Veracruz. Arriving back at the Calle Humboldt she found that this time the house *had* been robbed. Practically everything was gone, including the carpets, her silver jewellery and portable typewriter. The cook was accusing the gardener and the gardener accusing the cook. Malcolm, whose frequent absences from the house had left it vulnerable, said meekly that at least he had saved their manuscripts. All that was left, unaccountably, was one suitcase containing some of Jan's clothes, but she felt that her whole world had collapsed. Malcolm departed for Mexico City and she stayed on to clean up before following him. The American Vice-Consul, their affluent neighbour who had never before deigned to speak to her, came round to say he had heard of their trouble and asked if there was anything he could do to help. When she told him she was heading for Mexico City he said he had to drive there himself, and offered her a lift. This developed into the myth put about by Malcolm of Jan going to Veracruz with the French Consul.

She joined Malcolm at their old haunt, the Hotel Canada, and there was talk of going to Acapulco and starting afresh. But he continued drinking and said he must go to Oaxaca where they made the best mescal, and could not be dissuaded. *Under the Volcano* had now taken him over and he needed to live certain experiences at first hand. He was looking for something – to live through more hell to share with his Consul. Jan, meanwhile, wrote to Donald Friede, now in Los Angeles asking about a job, and he replied that he was opening a script agency in Hollywood and offered her a job as editorial assistant. Malcolm, convinced that Friede wanted to take her from him, was furious but said, 'Take it,' so she did. She asked him to go with her, but he insisted he must go to Oaxaca and expected her to come, too. There was a huge quarrel in which he threw her out of the room in her slip and locked the door. She had to creep downstairs and ask the manager for something to cover herself.

Having decided to return to the States, she thought that if Malcolm was set on going to Oaxaca someone should keep an eye on him. She alerted a friend who lived there, wrote for advice to their old Vice-Consul neighbour in Cuernavaca, and talked to the Millers who took them for a meal at a German Restaurant, the Münchener Kindl, to discuss how best to help him. They brought along an American ex-union organizer, Harry Mensch,[1] just returned wounded after fighting with the Abraham Lincoln Brigade in Spain. He needed to get away to recuperate and lie low for a time, and agreed to go to Oaxaca with Malcolm, and look out for him.

There was still no definite sense of an ending to the marriage, but Jan was determined not to stay in Mexico with Malcolm if he continued drinking. She felt the country was bad for him, that the mystique and liquor were taking him ever further away from her. If she remained there with him she felt sure she too would end up an alcoholic. Nor did she wish any longer to be so dependent on him; one of his less endearing qualities was his constantly reminding her, 'Remember whose money it is we live on.'

During his last days in Mexico City with Jan, he said, he spent much of his time in brothels.[2] His fascination with prostitutes had never left him. He compared himself to Toulouse Lautrec and killed off his Consul only after he had performed a blasphemous act of blighted love with the prostitute Maria in the dark depths of the Farolito. Once, he left Jan in the Canada at 5 a.m. to find a cantina, returning very drunk and late with a stray dog he had picked up. He put it on the bed, and Jan, still drowsy from sleep, pushed it off. He was furious and walked out. Remorsefully, she borrowed the hotel typewriter and typed an impassioned two-page letter saying that if he gave up drinking *today* she promised not to leave Mexico. His answer was a categorical 'No'. It was, he wrote, 'the most purely destructive and negative decision he had ever made in his whole life.'[3] She found an advertisement in the paper from a man offering a lift to Los Angeles and showed it to Malcolm, who was deeply upset at the idea, but said bitterly, 'Call. You can even share a room somewhere on the way up there.' So she called. Their last dinner together before she left never happened because he got drunk with an Englishman he had met in a bar.

On 1 December, Jan left for LA with the young doctor whose advertisement she had answered. Before departing she pleaded with Malcolm to go with her as far as the border, but he was too hurt by her leaving and refused. There were last-minute hesitations and mutual recriminations, and thoughts of what might have been, which Lowry fictionalized later.

> 'But won't this be ruining your life?' she asked. 'You'll be sorry, you know.' 'If I am you won't know anything about it. Anyway, even if you stay, I'm going to Spain.' 'To Spain, huh!' she said contemptuously and turned away. 'But don't go like that,' Sigbjørn added. 'I'm sure you don't love me and never have. But goodbye, and God bless you . . . Farewell.'[4]

She wanted to hug him but he made no move towards her, and she left. He planned a story about their parting called 'Via Dolorosa', but then put it into *Dark as the Grave Wherein My Friend Is Laid*. Jan wrote her own version – 'Not with a Bang' – which, to Lowry's annoyance, later appeared in *Story*.

He went to the hotel restaurant and saw 'a man with a look like an executioner' dragging a pair of shrieking fawns 'to slit their throats behind the barroom door'.[5] One horror seemed to be following another. That afternoon he left with Harry for Oaxaca, leaving his passport for safe-keeping with Alfred Miller, and taking his notes, manuscripts, a book of Elizabethan plays and a copy of Cocteau's *The Infernal Machine*. Consciously or unconsciously his own drama unfolding ahead was that of Lawrence: when Frieda left Mexico in 1923 determined go back to Europe, they quarrelled in New York and Lawrence returned almost at once to Mexico, to Oaxaca. Malcolm wrote of the 'supernatural influence' of Mexico[6] which made it difficult to leave, and his sense of grief at being left alone at the Canada which made him go to Oaxaca with Harry.[7] He may even have persuaded himself in a drunken moment that he stayed in order, as he told Jan, to go on to Spain via Salina Cruz to fight in the Civil War.[8]

The city of Oaxaca is a handsome city of Zapotecan Indians close to the ancient ruins of Monte Albán and Mitla, and more so than Cuernavaca it lies under the two great volcanoes. Outside on a hill stands a statue of Juárez pointing away from the city, and saying, according to locals, 'If you don't like it here, leave.' Lowry and Harry stayed at the Hotel Francia, where Lawrence had written a celebrated letter to Middleton Murry in November 1924, and where Lowry had stayed with Jan on their earlier trip. This became the symbolic centre of a new maelstrom of disaster for him. He would sneak out at 4 a.m. to cantinas like El Infierno, or El Bosque, or El Farolito, whose name, meaning 'the little light' (he thought it meant 'the lighthouse'), became that of the cantina where the Consul is shot in the *Volcano*. There was a significant Sinarquista presence in the town, and someone like Harry, wanted in the US for fighting for the Spanish Republicans, would need to keep a low profile to stay clear of trouble.

From Hollywood, Jan, now working for Donald Friede, began sending passionate and yearning letters, pleading with him to join her and start afresh, but for a time there was no reply. She got in touch with the Davenports and Calder-Marshalls, hoping that they could help, but they had no ideas to offer. Davenport had moved to a new and grander house in the Hollywood Hills, and was living a thoroughly flamboyant life, still surrounded by paintings and spending money furiously.

The anxious and passionate letters Jan wrote to Malcolm he retained for use in his novel.

> It is this silence that frightens me. [It is] . . . as though you were away at war and I were waiting, waiting for news of you . . . but no war could have this power to so chill and terrify my heart. I send you all my love and my whole heart and all my thoughts and prayers . . . What is there in life besides the person whom one adores . . . ? For the first time I understand the meaning of suicide . . . You used to cry to me to help you. The plea I send to you is far more desperate. Help me, yes, save me, from all that is enveloping, threatening, trembling, and ready to pour over my head.[9]

Finally he wrote, but his letters were irregular and were never replies to hers. Even so, she wrote constantly trying to find out his intentions. 'Why don't you answer me? I can only believe that my letters have not reached you . . . I cannot, I will not believe that you have ceased to love me, have forgotten me.'[10] She came to think that her letters had been lost, until she saw them nine years later in the published version of *Under the Volcano*; these were the letters he wove into the final chapter of the book, where Lowry's side of the picture is captured when he wrote of:

> the horror of waking up in the morning in Oaxaca, his body fully clothed, at half past three every morning after Yvonne (Jan) had gone; . . . the nightly escape from the sleeping Hotel Francia . . . from the cheap room giving on the balcony high up, to El Infierno, that other Farolito, of trying to find the bottle in the dark, and failing, the vulture sitting in the washbasin . . . then – the escape! – drawing the blanket he had secretly brought down from the hotel room over his head, creeping out past the manager's nephew – the escape! – past the hotel desk, not daring to look for mail – 'it is the silence that frightens me'.

To Jan's annoyance he not only used her letters in his book but added the sardonic query: 'Had Yvonne been reading the letters of Heloise and Abelard?'[11] She had been pleading with him to join her, and his letters were muddled and confusing, much like his letters from France.

> Why do you not tell me what has happened? What do you need? And my God, what do you wait for? What release can be compared to the release of love? My thighs ache to embrace you. The emptiness of my body is the famished need of you. My tongue is dry in my mouth for the want of *our* speech. If you let anything happen to yourself you will be harming my flesh and mind. I am in your hands now.[12]

He was sliding ever deeper into his own dark night, sleepwalking into a world of hallucination and self-delusion. In the cantina he boasted of fighting in Spain, and high on mescal he 'saw' that vulture perched on his washbasin and an enormous turtle upended and bleeding to death in the street. Fear of his father's disapproval re-emerged and he dreamt of his life as a wasted voyage, and wrote, 'What I remember chiefly is that the wharf got nearer while my father grew larger and larger.' Also he recalled Aiken's remark in Gibraltar: 'All I know is when it happens, I said so.'[13]

He had few friends, besides Harry and Antonio Cerillo, the hotel manager. But his solitude was sanctified when, perambulating round Oaxaca, he stumbled across the Iglesia de la Soledad, the baroque church of the Virgin of Soledad, patroness of the state of Oaxaca, of all sailors and all who are lonely. She was Lowry's 'Virgin for those that have nobody with', who he adopted as his own, as Geoffrey Firmin does. He now replaced his lucky Italian coin from Margot with a medallion of the Virgin of Soledad. And he found this sense of isolation suited his tragic and poetic mood.

> For myself I like to take my sorrow into the shadow of old monasteries, my guilt into cloisters and under tapestries, and into the misericordes of unimaginable *cantinas* where sad-faced potters and legless beggars drink at dawn, whose cold jonquil beauty one rediscovers in death.[14]

Harry tried to keep an eye on him, but he was unwell from his injuries in Spain and unaware that Jan's letters were being ignored until Marsha Miller informed him. So he tried to keep him sober and persuade him to write. But Lowry resented this kind of thing, and turned awkward. At a pro-Franco bar, La Covadonga, drunk on mescal, he boasted of being shot down flying for the Spanish Republicans. He drew a map of Spain on the bar-top to illustrate his exploits and quickly came under suspicion, especially when he announced that Harry had also fought in Spain and was a Communist on the run, who, when caught, would be shot. Someone promptly tipped off the police, and when they came looking for the 'wanted Communist' and found Lowry without a passport, they arrested him. He was held in gaol and interrogated by the Police Chief, who, according to Lowry, was an obvious fascist. His room was searched and letters confiscated. They probably thought he was Harry, the Communist, and he claimed later that he played Sydney Carton for his friend. No doubt he had seen Ronald Colman doing his 'far far better thing' in the film of *A Tale of Two Cities*, a performance which accorded remarkably with his own tragic self-image. The police let him go while he was investigated, but kept him under surveillance. Antonio Cerillo bailed him out, and he wrote desperately to Alfred Miller in Mexico City, asking for his passport.

However, the fragile, tottering world through which he was drifting had collapsed. (Graham Greene pointed out in *The Lawless Roads* that, under clause 33 of the Mexican Constitution, foreigners thought undesirable could be expelled at twenty-four hours' notice without any reasons being given. Foreigners showing a particular interest in religion or politics were prime candidates for being 'thirty-threed'.) Everywhere he saw police spies in dark glasses watching him, so he, too, adopted dark glasses and was arrested a second time and thrown into a cell with a murderer and an alcoholic child of six or seven. The prison became important to his hellish vision. He had, he wrote, a Dostoyevskian fixation on the place. 'I have practically a pathological sympathy for those who do wrong . . . and get into the shit.'[15] Taking a risk, Harry visited him, and told him he was dangerous to be with when he got drunk, and he was leaving for Guadalajara.

At Christmastime, according to Lowry, all the political prisoners were let out except him. The police captain hauled him out of gaol and across the road to a cantina for a drink, and told him, 'We have found out, that you are a criminal and escaped through seven states . . . You say you are – ah, a wrider. We-ah read-ah your wridings and they don't make sense . . . You no ah de wrider you are de espider and we shootah de espiders in Mexico . . . and where are you friend? . . . What is he for? . . . You want ah to escape! Escape now!'[16] The captain, he thought, wanted him to escape to have an excuse to shoot him, and he told James Stern later, 'They tried to castrate me too, one fine night, unsuccessfully, I regret (sometimes) to report.'[17]

When Jan heard that Malcolm had betrayed Harry, and that he had had to leave, she was so shocked that her attitude towards him began to change. Personal disloyalty she could forgive, but disloyalty to the cause for which she thought they both stood was too much to take. And when Malcolm wrote saying that Harry was a phoney who had not really fought in Spain but had probably spent his time cowering under a truck, that was the last straw. She realized that she would have to try falling out of love with him because clearly drink was destroying the man she had once loved; the bottle was too powerful a rival to contend with. She wrote suggesting that it might be better for him to go to New York or return to England.

He was released finally when his passport arrived and his identity was established, but not before he had spent New Year's Day and his fourth wedding anniversary in gaol. In fact, he was very lucky not be 'thirty-threed'. He continued to haunt the local cantinas, and got into a dispute with José Cervantes, owner of El Bosque, over payment for a bottle of mescal, and ended up in prison again. However, he managed to get a note to a friend who got him out. He sent Davenport a suitably dramatic letter, but one which despite its urgency had clearly been worked on as piece of literature

> S.O.S. Sinking fast by bow and stern. / S.O.S. Worse than . . . the Titanic – . . . No words exist to describe the terrible condition I

> am in . . . I have, since being here, been in prison three times . . . Everywhere I go I am pursued and even now, as I write, no less than five policemen are watching me . . . This is the perfect Kafka situation but you will pardon me if I do not consider it any longer funny . . . For obvious and oblivious reasons I cannot write to my family; for reasons so obvious they are almost naked I may not write to my wife . . . I looked round in the black recesses of what use to be a mind & saw two friends – yourself & Arthur Calder-Marshall. I also saw something else not so friendly: imminent insanity . . . I can only send greetings from death to birth and go to pray to what in Mexico they call 'the virgin for those who have nobody with.' . . . Incidentally, I smell . . . It is possible I am leaving a heritage of destruction . . . Danger, both to mind & body, threatens from all sides . . . This is not the cry of the boy who cried wolf. It is the wolf itself who cries for help . . . I cannot see Jan now. But for god's sake see she is all right. I foresaw my fate too deeply to involve her in it . . . I fear the worst, & alas, my only friend is the virgin for those who have nobody with, & she is not much help, while I am on this last Tooloose-Lo(us)wrytrek.'[18]

Perhaps realizing that Jan's attitude had changed, he wrote remorsefully, to Aiken, telling him, no doubt with his 'hand me the scissors' remark in mind, that he had been a prophet. He had done his old mentor dirt, he said, but from jealousy and love. This note was never sent; nor, it seems, was this longer missive.

> Dear old bird,
> Have now reached a condition of amnesia, breakdown, heartbreak, consumption, cholera, alcoholic poisoning . . .
>
> All change here, all change here, for Oakshot, Cockshot, Poxshot & fuck the whole bloody lot!
>
> My only friend here is a tertiary who pins a medal of the Virgin of Guadalupe on my coat: follows me in the street . . . & who thinks I am Jesus Christ, which, as you know, I am not yet, though I may be progressing towards thinking I am myself.
>
> I have been imprisoned as a spy in a dungeon compared with which the Chateau d'If – in the film – is a little cottage in the country overlooking the sea.
>
> I spent Christmas – New Year's – Wedding Day there . . .
>
> Don't think I can go on. Where I am it is dark. Lost.
>
> Happy New Year
>
> Malcolm[19]

He wrote to Jan. 'I do not want to see you because if I did my suffering is such I should probably go into a fit which would only land me in prison again.' Like Toulouse Lautrec, he said, he wrote in brothels, and as for the future, 'I shall go into the mountains & work in a mine. I have a friend here – a Mexican.'

The friend (who had got him out of gaol) was Juan Fernando Márquez (who in *Under the Volcano* is both Dr Vigil and Juan Cerillo), a Zapotecan Indian he had met at La Covadonga. He was twenty-four and six-foot three, a trained chemist who was a messenger for the Ejidal Bank through which the Cárdenas government distributed funds to peasants to buy land. He and Lowry were drawn to one another and at Lowry's insistence became blood-brothers. The Indian called him 'Maker of tragedies' and told him 'Sickness is not only in the body.' Lowry delighted in recording his idiosyncratic English – 'Last night I got such terrible drunkness I shall need three full days of sleeping to recover myself,'[20] 'If you have not killèd yourself with drinking, I will resign my job,'[21] and 'Hullo, are you making more tragedies today?'[22] They discussed La Vida Impersonal, a philosophy of detachment expressed in such dictums as 'Throw away your mind.' Once he saved Lowry from a terrible fight between ten mescal-crazed drunks, after which he would say, 'But I owe you sixty pesos, Fernando, as well as my life.'[23] He was always on the point of resigning his job and the two men made grand plans to ride together down to Tehuantepec on the Isthmus.[24]

Juan Fernando took him proudly to see Monte Albán, and one Sunday, following an afternoon's drinking at the Farolito, they went with some students into the country for 'earth scratching', digging for fossils, and that evening at sunset his friend gave him another expression to recycle when he said, 'This is the hour I love . . . when all man began to sing and all the dogs to shark.'[25] They found fossilized skulls, including that of a syphilitic.[26] In a little public garden in Oaxaca he first noted the sign: ¿LE GUSTA ESTE JARDÍN? ¿QUE ES SUYO? ¡EVITE QUE SUS HIJOS LO DESTRUYAN! which in the Consul's 'hallucinatory translation'[27] reads 'You like this garden? Why is it yours? We evict those who destroy!'[28] But the question mark after jardín was wrongly copied and 'evite' does not mean 'evict'. He was only to discover the true meaning eight years later.[29]

Still dogged by police spies, some inside the hotel, he wrote to Juan Fernando asking why they persecuted a man who only wanted to write poetry? The poetry, when it came, reflected the darkness of the pit into which he saw himself having been cast, and the sense of suffering endured. As ever, words saved him. Writing was now more than ever his form of therapy, the thing that enabled him to keep a grip on his sanity.

> I have known a city of dreadful night,
> Dreadfuller far than Kipling knew, or Thomson . . . .
> In the dungeon shivers the alcoholic child,
> Comforted by the murderer, since compassion is here too;
> The noises of the night are cries for help
> From the town and from the garden which evicts those
>   who destroy![30]

Drink had made him fat again and he was again yelled at with contempt in the streets. A barber conned him out of a fine leather belt and in a pulqueria a bearded Mixtec Indian with two pistols walked off with his glasses and his copy of *La Machine Infernale*.[31] A worried Juan Fernando wrote to him, 'Did you keep out of drinking today? Is there no more remedy than cut our friendship if you are continuing on drinking?'[32]

On 29 January, Lowry sent Jan an SOS. He was desperate. She must come immediately to Oaxaca. And on 3 February she received a short frantic note hinting at an unspecified disaster about to overtake him. If she ever wanted to see him again she must come to his aid immediately. He asked her not to inform his father. Despite everything, he still loved him.[33] Rather desperate herself now, Jan wired him some money and cabled the US Consul in Oaxaca in the hope that he could find out what was amiss. And although Lowry had pleaded with her not to inform Arthur, she thought she should at least write to the British Consul-General in Mexico explaining his plight and her own inability to help, being without funds, and suggesting that it would help if he could be got back to England.[34]

Still feeling persecuted, Lowry decided to join Juan Fernando on one of his journeys into the mountains for the Ejidal Bank. According to Lowry, they went first on horseback to Cuicuitlan, where Lowry became ill again with malaria, and Fernando had to build him a bed in the bank.[35] Once he had recovered, they next left for Nichitlan to deliver money to the villages of Andoa and Chindoa, who were fighting one another across a ravine.[36] Here they were shot at from church towers by villagers fearful of buccaneers, and slept the night in the graveyard at Andoa.[37] While in the mountains he wrote to Antonio Cerillo at the Francia asking him to guard his papers and passport as he was about to return to Mexico City and thence to Jan. As they skirted the great Valley of Etla, Lowry became aware of the dangers facing Bank messengers, and heard how they were sometimes ambushed and murdered by right-wing assassins. They saw demon-dancing at Etla,[38] and once, when they were reduced to only one horse, his friend insisted that he ride it and ran beside him for twenty miles over rough ground.[39]

Fearful of spies, he was frightened to return to the Francia. His misery was compounded by news that Juan Fernando had been posted to Cuicuitlan, and at the beginning of February he said farewell to his friend at Parián station, last glimpsing him waving a bottle as his train pulled out.[40] Back in Oaxaca he found all his clothes had been stolen,[41] and all he had to wear was a white suit given to him by Juan Fernando as a parting gift.

Just as he prepared to return to Mexico City, he received a letter from Ann Watkins, who had just had a visit from Calder-Marshall in New York. Whatever he had felt about Lowry's novel in Cuernavaca, he had told her that it sounded like 'one of the most exciting books that has come down the line in a long time', but thought it would be some time before he finished it to his own satisfaction. She urged him to offer it to her rather than to Whit Burnett, as she was better placed to sell it. Several publishers were asking after him, she said, – 'the Little Brown crowd,' Bob Haas at Random House and Max Schuster – having been impressed by what they had seen of *In Ballast*.[42] If Lowry had not been in such dire straits this letter could only have boosted his flagging confidence.

By 9 February, Lowry was back in Mexico City at the Canada. He wired Jan saying that he had had a complete breakdown and was close to suicide. She wrote again to the British Consul suggesting he be induced to enter the British Hospital in Mexico City 'where he could be treated for acute alcoholism and be guarded against the possibility of suicide.'[43] She thought he ought to be got to New York or to England, perhaps with his father's help. His residency card would expire on 18 March and he might have to leave Mexico then anyway. On 19 February, however, he had fled the Canada owing some sixty pesos, with the manager threatening to call the police if ever he set eyes on him. By the beginning of March, the British Consul had informed Arthur that his son was in trouble, and he had immediately engaged a firm of Mexico City lawyers, Basham & Ringe, who hired private detectives to check on him and watch his every move.

The day Lowry's residence permit was due to expire, 18 March, was the very day Cárdenas nationalized foreign oil interests, and tension sprang up between Britain and Mexico. This may be why he hesitated to renew his card, or he may have been simply too drunk to remember. In any event, by not doing so he was suddenly in deep trouble.[44] As ever, he worked this experience into his novel, and it is against the background of diplomatic tension with Britain that Lowry's Consul became an ex-Consul.

Jan had decided he needed psychiatric help. She began to read up on alcoholism and lit upon Karl Menninger's newly published *Man Against Himself*. She thought his chapter on alcoholism fitted Malcolm so perfectly that she wrote to him and Arthur urging that he be professionally analysed. He replied that he did not need psychoanalysis – he could do that for himself. And in any case, he added, it would bring his father out from England, Aiken back from Cambridge, and himself back to the womb.[45] Arthur thought that Malcolm just needed to listen to his father and return to his wife, but finally Jan convinced him that her idea was worth considering.

At the El Petate, one of his favourite restaurants in Mexico City, Malcolm had met an American called John D. Bonsfield, and the detectives tracking him reported that he had moved with Bonsfield into the Hotel Carleton. At the end of four weeks he had run up a bill of five hundred pesos, mostly from drinks bought on account. The hotel management was keeping close watch on him, having given instructions to all shifts of employees to permit nothing to be taken from his room.[46] He was drinking very heavily and seldom in anyone's company but Bonsfield's; they would leave the hotel at 11 a.m. and not return until the early morning. Now he also met up again with Teddy Wynn and his current girlfriend, the Hollywood film actress and 'shimmy' dancer, Gilda Gray. Always dazzled by Hollywood, he was easily strung along by this pair, who found him a ready source of handouts.

Wynn was supposed to be in trouble and threatened with prison, but Lowry paid off a detective closing in on him, then went with him and Gilda to Acapulco. Bonsfield went along, and so did his 'ugsome' friend Stuyvesant. There Lowry came under suspicion for his drunkenness from Interior Department agents, and was spied on continually by a local police spy called Guyou. Events were reducing him again to a state of depression. Most of the time he haunted bars – the Monterrey, the Seven Seas, the Tropical Hotel, the Mirador – always running up higher and higher bills, always ready to pay for others, and sinking ever further into despair. Jan was blowing hot and cold, sometimes urging him to join her, sometimes suggesting he go to New York or back to

England. One day he decided to end it all. He swam out well beyond an island off Calete Beach hoping never to return. But then he was attacked by a barracuda and fighting it revived his will to live, if only because he wanted one more drink.[47] He was rescued in a boat by Gilda Gray, who got him safely back to shore and then promptly slapped him down. His rescue was another miracle and he was ready to start again. He wrote to Jan saying that he, Gilda and Wynn had built a house on the beach with their own hands, anticipating a dream he ascribed to his doomed Consul. He was also close to the sea and in his element.

Despite the sense of rebirth following his rescue, things soon went wrong again. He wrote to Jan saying that Wynn had robbed him of the money he had saved to bring her back to Mexico. He wanted her to go to San Diego, where Wynn and Gilda had skipped off to, to recover the money, but Jan refused to get involved. He began circulating stories of how his wife had deserted him, his marriage now replacing his childhood as the source of all his ills. Not only had she deserted him, but she was faithless and had destroyed his child. Jan began receiving letters from strangers demanding to know how she could possibly have brought such grief to so brilliant a young genius. But Lowry was carrying his own cross, moving towards his own personal Oberammergau.

He fell in with two young Americans, Peggy Riley and her husband. They found him in a bad state, drunk and penniless, but impressed by this inspired young Rimbaud, they took pity and decided to rescue him. They took him home, smartened him up and invited him to a reception at the US Consulate, from which he was ejected for being drunk. But before that, the Consul had asked to see his work, so he lent him his two manuscripts. He was obviously deeply smitten with Peggy Riley, and sometimes took her to the cinema. The Rileys, however, had an idyllic marriage. They were young, naïve idealists who played the guitar and sang romantic songs to one another. When they happily embraced Lowry he was too ready to mistake friendship for something more. At the Monterrey he wrote a sorrowful poem,

> Love which comes too late is like that black storm
> That breaks out of its season . . .[48]

What happened then is vague, but he wrote in an unpublished novel, *La Mordida*, that he took advantage of Riley's absence one day and attempted to rape Peggy, and he wrote to Jan boasting he *had* actually raped her, saying that she had enjoyed it. As usual, however, he was consumed with remorse about whatever happened, and it only confirmed his belief that invariably he caused damage to those he met, leaving a trail of desolation in his wake.

Once more cast adrift, and being watched by the Interior Ministry, he told Bonsfield he was in danger of being deported and had to retrieve his manuscripts from the US Consul; however, the Consul was away and he was desperate. Bonsfield said he would fix things and helped by the 'ugsome' Stuyvesant broke into the Consulate and retrieved the manuscripts. He then made sure that *In Ballast* was mailed to Ann Watkins, who received it in New York at the end of April. Lowry, however, saw Bonsfield, an extreme right-winger, as his latest evil angel just as Juan Fernando was his good one. In the *Volcano* Bonsfield appears as the sinister American Weber and in *Dark as the Grave* as Stanford, the man Sigbjørn Wilderness is fearful of meeting again.

The British Consul was also keeping an eye on Lowry, and on 12 May, Basham & Ringe cabled Arthur's Liverpool lawyer, saying that Malcolm was in Acapulco suffering from epilepsy – undoubtedly a false diagnosis; he was obviously drinking to excess. He was in debt to the tune of a thousand pesos and had been detained by the Immigration authorities both on that count and for having failed to renew his residence permit. By the 18th, having paid off some of his debts from his May allowance, he had been taken back to Mexico City by an Immigration official, the sinister Guyou, and was lodged at the Biltmore Hotel. He was treated rather roughly and may have been unaware of the deep unpopularity of foreigners following the oil nationalization.

On his arrival he was in a bad way, without presentable clothing, having to walk slowly because of rheumatism, and still owing seven hundred pesos. He now found that in future his allowance would be paid to him via Basham & Ringe, who had settled his outstanding bill at the Canada and retrieved his luggage held there. They feared that if he knew his father had intervened he might be resentful, so gave him the impression that it was Jan who had come to his rescue. A young member of the firm, Jesse Dalton, offered friendly help, and Lowry did not object, especially as he arranged some additions to his allowance, but said he was worried about his mother hearing of his plight. In fact Arthur had cabled extra money to pay for a set of new clothes, his bills in Acapulco, his fines for immigration offences, residence permit extensions and pay-offs ('*la mordida*') to various Interior Department officials. Malcolm expressed the hope that when Jan heard of his attempts to rehabilitate himself she would want to return to him in

Mexico. But Dalton wrote to Jan suggesting she get Malcolm to Hollywood, believing that the altitude of Mexico City made the effects of his drinking worse. She replied immediately outlining her plans for his treatment.

He returned to his old haunts, like El Petate, with his old acquaintance Bonsfield, and shortly afterwards moved back in with him at the Carleton. On 10 June he sat in the restaurant, as Bonsfield played 'Titipitan' on the jukebox, and composed a sombre poem on the back of the menu:

> Some years ago he started to escape;
> . . . has been . . . escaping ever since
> Not knowing his pursuers gave up hope
> Of seeing him (dance) at the end of a rope
> Hounded by eyes and thronged terrors now the lens
> Of a glaring world that shunned even his defence
> Reading him strictly in the preterite tense
> Spent no . . . thinking him not worth
> (Even) . . . the price of a cold cell.
> There would have been a scandal at his death
> Perhaps. No more than this. Some tell
> Strange hellish tales of this poor foundered soul
> Who once fled north . . .

The menu itself was reproduced as the one found by Hugh and Yvonne (plus the above slightly amended version of his original poem) at the El Popo restaurant, as they pursue the doomed Consul in chapter 11 of his novel.[49] When Bonsfield disappeared Lowry told Jesse Dalton he had left him with his half of the hotel bill. Dalton wrote to Bonsfield in California without success, but the hotel manager finally confirmed that Bonsfield's half had been settled before he left.

The lawyer found Lowry utterly confused about his future, saying that he had not heard from Jan for six weeks and this had so unsettled him he was unable to work. When he was urged to return to her in California, he flatly refused, saying that she could well afford to join him in Mexico. This stubbornness, Dalton concluded, was a matter of pride. He wrote to Liverpool saying that while Malcolm could not be forced to leave, his papers were in such a confused state he might be deported, though he felt that his firm could handle the immigration people. He had also written to Jan, but had no reply after three weeks, he claimed. Lowry had told him that if reconciliation was impossible he would not return to England alone, and had handed over his Cunard return ticket, promising to write to Arthur explaining what had happened and what he intended. Dalton reported that he no longer frequented bars so much, had borrowed books, hired a typewriter, bought paper, and was busily working again. However, it being the rainy season, he was bothered by a severe rheumatic condition and was developing varicose veins which impeded his walking.[50] He had hired a typist to retype *Under the Volcano*, and it seems that the original manuscript was then discarded.

Jan wrote to him on her twenty-seventh birthday, 11 June, a sorrowful reflection on their marriage and what it might have been. 'I left you six months ago,' she remembered writing, 'although we did not realize it at the time. We were idyllic in Cuernavaca for three months. I became your mother, now I am paying for it. You're a great writer, a great talent, the most gifted man I have ever known. You have it in you to become one of the century's greatest writers. But you need help, not band-aid. You say you can cure yourself with psychoanalysis, but you are not a professional analyst. You need professional help. Menninger and his brother have a clinic in Topeka in Kansas, and you should go to them.'[51] To this she received no reply.

Over the following month, Lowry stayed on at the Carleton working on *Under the Volcano*, typing single-spaced on both sides of sheets of yellow paper with few alterations.[52] When he later reverted to a richer, more elaborate style, he wrote copious insertions, but at this time he was writing still in a style close to that which he had adopted after Cambridge. But he was burning his bridges with England, and asked Dalton to cash in his Cunard return ticket which, having been purchased in Liverpool, could be redeemed only if he was not in the US where the ticket was some guarantee that the holder would not remain. In the meantime, Jan had persuaded Arthur to agree that in California Malcolm should be examined by three doctors – a medical practitioner, a neurologist and a psychiatrist, and then go to the Menninger Clinic, which had a special psychiatric programme for alcoholics.

Early in July, anticipating his imminent departure, Lowry moved from the Carleton to a nearby apartment. On 15 July he was granted a temporary US entry visa. Dalton had to arrange for his existing application for permanent residence to be ignored to get it through urgently, as he insisted, something he came to regret afterwards. Three days later he had a letter from Jan which he refused to show to Dalton, but which he assured him meant there was now no chance of a reconciliation between them. However, since his father had suggested he proceed to California and he desired to talk personally to Jan, he had decided to go to Hollywood anyway.

Dalton later reported that the Interior Department's case against him had been 'extremely serious' because of its handling prior to their intervention. He had been detained by Interior Department agents in Acapulco and the reports of the secret service men on his conduct had been extremely detrimental. Sorting out all this had been a time-consuming and very delicate matter, especially as secret service men had also been detailed to watch him in Mexico City.[53] Finally Dalton had persuaded them to let him leave, with the right to reapply for entry at a later date, if required.

A pullman ticket was booked for him to leave on 20 July, but at the last moment he said he was not ready to go – probably the wrong date for him. Finally, on 23 July, he got away, escorted to the station in person by Dalton to ensure he got on the train – 'a humiliating experience', he said later.[54] He was due to arrive in LA on the morning of the 27th, so clearly his plan was to arrive at Jan's apartment the next day, his twenty-ninth birthday.

Dalton had informed Jan that Malcolm was now in good shape, kitted out with new clothes, back in a working frame of mind and anxious to talk things over. She, in turn, had arranged for him to see three doctors as Arthur had agreed. But he must have kept her in the dark about his plans, because on his birthday she went to the movies with George Antheil, the composer, a friend of Donald Friede, and his wife, Boske. The film was *Mayerling,* which she had seen with Malcolm in Mexico City almost exactly a year before. That night she wrote about that memorable evening in her diary, recalling the sweet night of love which had followed. 'Where is he now?' she wrote, 'and with whom?' Next day, sunbathing outside her apartment close to Hollywood Boulevard, she heard footsteps on the gravel path. It was Malcolm, looking extremely unkempt and dazed; not the spruce new man she had been led to expect by Dalton, but the old disintegrated Malcolm, clothes dishevelled, face puffed up and bruised. He told her pathetically that he had been beaten up by the police – whether by the Mexican or the American ones he does not seem to have specified. But clearly something dire had happened to prevent him turning up on his birthday.

CHAPTER XIII

AN AMERICAN DIVORCE, A HOLLYWOOD LOVE, CANADIAN EXILE

1938–1939

The first thing we do, let's kill all the lawyers.

SHAKESPEARE, *Henry VI* Part 2

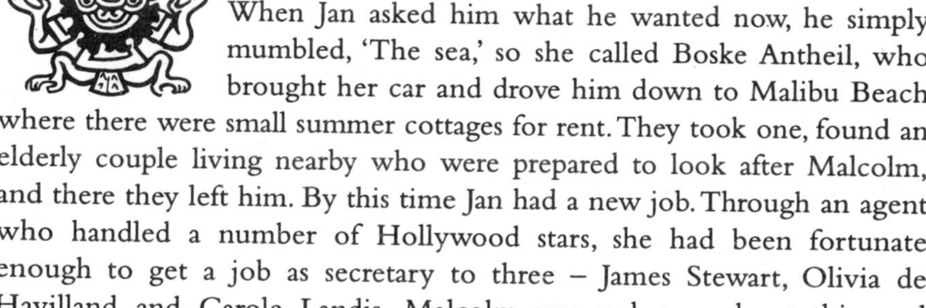

When Jan asked him what he wanted now, he simply mumbled, 'The sea,' so she called Boske Antheil, who brought her car and drove him down to Malibu Beach where there were small summer cottages for rent. They took one, found an elderly couple living nearby who were prepared to look after Malcolm, and there they left him. By this time Jan had a new job. Through an agent who handled a number of Hollywood stars, she had been fortunate enough to get a job as secretary to three – James Stewart, Olivia de Havilland and Carole Landis. Malcolm was unhappy about this, and warned her it would mean the end of her writing career. It also of course made her more independent of him. However, in accordance with her plan, she arranged for him to see three doctors. Their reports were then sent to Arthur, who agreed that he should go to the Menninger. But by 11 August, through one of his Liverpool lawyers, Arthur had placed him in the care of a Los Angeles attorney, Benjamin Parks, and from that moment matters took a different turn. Parks contacted Jan and, after listening to her story, said he would think things over before recommending action to his client.

The attorney, a large, humourless, heavy-jowled man, visited Malcolm at Malibu, posing as someone acting for Jan, then he cabled Liverpool – Malcolm was in a deplorable state due to continuous excessive drinking, and was temporarily separated from Jan. He had moved him to the seashore under supervision and rationed him to a quart of liquor a day. He seemed to be suffering from 'mental complexes' and in need of psychiatric treatment which would cost about $600. He had agreed to treatment but did not know that he (Parks) represented his father and he strongly resented the idea that his parents be told or asked to help him.[1]

Having taken credit for moving Malcolm to the sea, Parks set out to undermine Jan's plan for him to go to the Menninger. He informed her that what he needed was not psychiatric treatment but drying out.[2] He wired Liverpool saying that Menninger's treatment was a three-year programme at $700 a month and that he was informed that they achieved few permanent cures. He added that Jan was being uncooperative and he was putting Malcolm into a sanatorium. On 15 August, Lowry entered a clinic at La Crescenta for drying-out, something which Jan told Parks would be useless; he had gone through this before, in Moretonhampstead and in Bellevue, and it had never helped him. What he needed was in-depth psychiatric treatment.

By the end of August, Parks was able to report that the treatment at La Crescenta was having excellent results, but because of his client's infatuation with his wife, the doctor thought that, on his release, some psychiatric treatment was advisable. He also thought that Malcolm should be kept away from her and her friends because his past drinking was associated with her behaviour. He thought Malcolm was best advised to return home, and suggested that his father come over to collect him. But Arthur was not keen to have his alcoholic son back at Inglewood, so did not take up the suggestion. He was distressed by his plight and did not have the heart to abandon him, but he was determined to keep the bad news from Evelyn. On 1 September, Russell was finally made a partner at Buston's, and received a lump sum of £12,000. At the same time a trust of £12,000, known as the 1938 Settlement, was set up for Malcolm, and in future his allowance would be drawn from interest on this sum in trust. It seems unlikely that he knew of this for years, because he lived in constant fear of being cut off by Arthur.

Parks and Jan were like oil and water. Jan was radical, a Roosevelt supporter and internationalist; Parks was anti-Roosevelt, anti-New Deal and isolationist. His hostility towards her was reciprocated; she quickly formed as poor an opinion of him as he had of her. In order to discredit her to Arthur, Parks employed a private detective to investigate her. But Malcolm was still keen for them to get back together. From the sanatorium he wrote his last long passionate letter to her; it was his final throw of the dice, the last epistle from her writing-paper lover. If she did not come back to him, he wrote, he would have to find another model, suggesting that he was basing the female characters in his fiction on her. She replied that unless he had proper long-term treatment, like that offered by Menninger, she did not think they could get back together. She conveyed the same message to Parks, but cynically he wrote to Liverpool suggesting that Jan wanted Malcolm at the Menninger in order to get him out of her way.

In point of fact she went to the sanatorium to meet him when he left in mid-September, and found him looking much as he had on leaving Bellevue – pale, drawn and pathetic.[3] Parks moved him into Los Angeles, to the Normandie Hotel, arranging a brief course of psychoanalysis for him at the hands of a Dr Doyle. He was kept under close supervision, having to report every few days to receive his money in rationed sums, and the hotel manager was asked to report the first sign of his drinking. Parks seemed intent on showing he could get Malcolm back on his feet at minimal cost to his client. He proposed a regime of outdoor physical labour at a ranch owned by a friend of his. Meanwhile, Malcolm was in touch again with Jan, pleading for her to come back to him, but she told him she had been through one tunnel in Mexico and she did not intend to go into another. However, she did agree to continue seeing him and they met for a meal about once a week.

By early October, Parks was able to report that he was getting himself back into shape, swimming and writing and generally showing an improved mental state. He also passed on the results of his investigations of Jan. He had discovered that her father was Jewish, and informed Arthur Lowry of this as though it obviously threw important new light on the marriage. Furthermore, he had discovered that she was dating a Hollywood photographer, and suggested that she might soon be wanting a divorce. This seems to have convinced Arthur that the Menninger was unnecessary and that an attempted reconciliation might plunge Malcolm back into depression and heavy drinking. He would continue to send him his monthly $150, but if he wanted more he would have to earn it through his literary efforts.

Money was provided for him to buy a second-hand typewriter, but then to his fury he found out that Parks was acting for his father, not Jan, so he wrote to Arthur immediately trying to put a brave face on the situation. He was annoyed, he said, at having received help from him under the guise of it being from someone else, and was angry to have caused him further anxiety. No doubt he had been told that drinking was the cause of all his problems. If only it was! – but that trouble had been 'liquidated'. The real source of his problems, he said, were mental, but he refused to put him to the expense of psychoanalysis: 'It is possible with the aid of intelligence and a super-constitution to override these troubles . . . the keynote is fear, an appalling rooted terror sown somewhere in the dark of my childhood and only now breaking into its poisonous flower.'

He knew what his father had suffered on his account – he had been a father ('almost') himself. 'My own capacity for suffering is finite.' He mentioned Ann Watkins's letter about *Under the Volcano*, which he would send as proof of not having abused his trust as far as work was concerned. He was thinking of his mother and would write to her soon. He had had infantile paralysis in Mexico but was now cured and in A1 physical condition, but he would not blame him if he let him rot in the gutter. 'There is still, however, a fighting chance that I will come out on top with life, career, marriage, future, intact, and it gladdens me to feel that no one would be more pleased than you if I prove . . . that I can hold the Maginot line of myself.' He asked him not to write until he had first proved himself. If he had lied in previous letters it was only to avoid giving pain and because he simply did not know what was happening to him, 'so swift, ruthless and cruel was the destruction of everything I had built up'.[4]

He typed up his mostly Mexican poems (*The Lighthouse Invites the Storm*) and sent them to Jonathan Cape. Since the publication of *Ultramarine*, he told Cape, he had fallen on stony ground, and much of his recent work had been stolen or mutilated. Even so, he had three novels and a play (*The Ship Sails On*) 'on the shelf' as well as the poems. Cape, however, having failed to get the book of short stories he had proposed in 1934, was not prepared to make further advances, and sent the poems with a rejection slip to Innes Rose. Having been told about a book competition sponsored by a New York publisher, he wrote asking Whit Burnett for the manuscript of *The Last Address*, thinking that a re-worked version might be worth entering.

Parks felt confident a cure had been effected; Malcolm was settling down once again to his literary activities and keeping fit by swimming and having classes to improve his golf. On 22 October Parks wrote to Liverpool saying that soon his services would no longer be required. He calculated having saved Arthur $1,000 by foiling Jan's plans for Malcolm, and suggested a bill of between $1,600 minimum and $1,780 maximum. The treatment Malcolm had received, he said, had been at rock-bottom prices, and after he was living on the ranch he would need only minimal supervision at the cost, he suggested, of $100–150 a month. In reply, Parks was informed that Arthur was not, as Malcolm might have suggested, a bottomless pit of money, and he had already cost him far more than ever anticipated. The sum of $1,500 was agreed, but the idea of a permanent extra $100 to $150 a month for Malcolm's supervision could not be contemplated.

Parks's euphoria over Malcolm's progress was short-lived. Perhaps the prospect of living on a ranch far from Jan was too much to bear, or perhaps Parks had informed him that Jan was seeing someone else. For whatever reason, he slipped off the wagon again. The first time, at the end of October, he befriended someone at the corner drug-store, and took him back to the hotel with a quart of Californian wine which made him deathly sick. The manager called Parks, who immediately rushed over and dressed him down. The chance acquaintance had meanwhile picked his pockets and disappeared. When Parks refused to supply more money Lowry swore at him, so the lawyer then ordered that his money be withheld and the hotel supply him with meal tickets. Next day he apologized, and Parks told him he would be rationed to a dollar a day by the hotel manager, but only if he showed no evidence of drinking. When this was found to work, the daily allowance was increased.

On 11 November, Armistice Day, he fell from grace again. At about eight o'clock he was brought back to the Normandie by another chance drinking acquaintance. The hotel manager duly reported to Parks, but before he could call, Lowry himself phoned, explaining what had happened. He had been checking up on Jan, and claimed to have found that she had been living with another man and was being unfaithful to him. Hearing this, he had retreated to a bar (probably the Brown Derby – his favourite bar on Hollywood Boulevard) with a fellow who had been close to Stuart's regiment in France during the war. But after one drink, he said, the ex-soldier had slipped him a 'Mickey Finn' and tried to rob him. Parks refused to believe that part of the story and told him he was taking away all his money. For five days he was put back on to meal tickets. He tried borrowing but finally was forced to go to Parks who returned him to the dollar-a-day regime.

At this point the lawyer tried lecturing him. His father had spent a great deal of money on him. If he reported that he had been drinking he would probably be cut off, which would cause difficulties for him, being in a foreign country. Lowry tried to bluff, saying he had a written contract with his father and that he had to have six months written notice before his allowance could be cut off. Parks refused to believe him, and finally he capitulated and became contrite. Nevertheless, he was back on a dollar a day and being spied on by the hotel manager.

He then tried a more subtle tack, telling Parks that he had to haunt saloons to study characters in bars for his book, since it was only here that they showed their true natures. The prosaic lawyer told him that great writers did not have drunken characters as their subject, and a man with his weakness should confine himself to studying the abstemious ninety percent of the world. In any case, from here on he would have to choose sober characters, otherwise he would shut off his allowance. Lowry solemnly agreed, saying he would develop a new book along the lines suggested. All this Parks religiously reported to Arthur, adding that he had arranged for Malcolm to go to a ranch well away from bars and impossible to reach by car, and costing a mere $25 a week. When he asked Malcolm to show him his latest book, he was given *The Lighthouse* and surreptitiously had a copy made and sent to Arthur. He said he knew that sending Malcolm to the hotel manager for money was humiliating, but thought this was having a salutary effect on him. He then suggested that for $100 a month he could take on the supervision of Malcolm on a long-term basis, and Arthur agreed to this.

The passion for Jan was now cooling. Lowry informed Parks that 'with a great wrench' he had finally come to realize that she was not what she should be and he had decided to forget her. He had taken to dating a Miss Dionne, and by Christmastime Parks was able to report no further backsliding and that he was now writing quite industriously.[5] He had turned his attention to *The Last Address*, which he had received back from Burnett, and was anxious to enter it for the novel competition.

At about this time, in a mood of nostalgia, and because he still hoped to become independent of Arthur, he contacted James Hilton who came to the Normandie for a drink. As a schoolboy at The Leys, Lowry had aspired to Hilton's early writing success, first as a newspaper reporter, then as a novelist. Later that year, writing of their meeting, he drew several parallels between them – they were at the same school, both were editors of the *Fortnightly* under Balgarnie, and both shared the same London agent, Farquharson. But the differences between them could not have been greater. Hilton's style was simplicity itself and he worked very fast. *Goodbye Mr Chips* was written in three weeks flat in 1934. His greatest success, his 1933 novel, *Lost Horizon*, was filmed in

1937 from his own screenplay and put the term 'shangri-la' into the dictionary. In the same year he had written the script for *Mrs Miniver*, and was probably the most successful British writer (except P. G. Wodehouse) ever to work in Hollywood. When he met Lowry he was busily turning 'Chips' into a screenplay, too. According to Lowry, he promised to help get him into film-writing, but their evening at the Normandie turned into one of such heavy drinking that they forgot about it altogether.[6] More likely, Hilton decided, shrewdly, that Lowry was too keen on liquor to make a very reliable studio writer.

Aiken's Mexican novel, *A Heart for the Gods of Mexico*, was published in London in January 1939. A poor novel, it was savaged by Graham Greene in the *Spectator*. Aiken was himself rather ashamed of it, and Lowry probably never read it, but one book by a friend he did read was John Sommerfield's *Volunteer in Spain*, published in America in 1937. Sommerfield had been one of the first to join the International Brigades, and had been twice reported killed. In *Under the Volcano*, it was Sommerfield who had a dog called Harpo ('You probably wouldn't have expected a Communist to have a dog named Harpo – or would you?'),[7] loved vin rosé d'anjou and read de Quincey while holed-up in the University Library during the siege of Madrid.

Having withdrawn from close contact with Jan, he returned to his love of jazz and the beloved old taropatch, which Jan had disliked so much. In February, in a bookshop in Westlake, he got into conversation with a young jazz musician, Joe London, and his wife, Sheila, who were so attracted by this 'character' – unlit pipe clenched in his teeth, trousers held up with an old necktie, who spouted Dante in a well-rounded British accent and declared himself a writer – that they invited him home. London was a 'straw-boss' who organized and hired musicians for Ray Noble, the British-born band leader, and this naturally fascinated Lowry. He talked a great deal about Beiderbecke and said that he himself played the ukulele. He talked about literature and gave London a list books, saying 'Read these books, and you can consider yourself well-educated.'[8]

When Lowry next turned up at the Londons' Westlake house, he had with him not a ukulele but a tenor guitar tuned up like a uke. London quickly realized that Lowry was not much good, lacking any kind of professional background and unable to read sheet-music; and when he tried to play London's six-stringed guitar it proved to be too big for those small hands. Nevertheless the two men enjoyed each other's company and Lowry sang some of his old songs, like 'Rich Man, Poor

Man'. When, years later, he made the protagonist of his long short story 'The Forest Path to the Spring' an itinerant jazz musician, it was probably with Joe London and his wife partly in mind. When he invited his new friends back to the Normandie, they were astonished to find his room crammed with empty bottles, and the first thing they did was to go around picking them up off the floor, off the dressing-tables, out of drawers, out of the closet, from under the bed, and disposing of them. However, they thought this squalor only added to Lowry's charm.

One of London's bands performed on a gambling ship, the *Rex*, moored off Santa Monica, where it played gypsy music in the style of Django Reinhardt and jazz in the style of the Hot Club of France. Lowry was invited along and arrived, spruced up for the occasion, with a young woman, probably Miss Dionne, and afterwards invited members of the band back to the hotel for a jam-session. James Osborne, the eighteen-year-old bass player, remembered that Lowry had a very comfortable suite, and, as it was not uncommon to be invited for a private session in this way, they looked forward to a good evening of music, food and drink. There was music all right, and food, but no drink – for the band that was. Lowry had his supply of neat vodka to hand, but the band went without. What they did not know, and what he probably did not tell them, was that Parks had him on a very short rope and he could not order drinks inside the Normandie without being reported. As the band played, Lowry tried joining in. 'He would insist on playing this goddamn ukulele which was terrible,' Osborne recalled.[9] It was only because Joe and Sheila London thought so much of him that the band went along, but unlike his leader, young Osborne was not impressed, and when Lowry gave loud renditions of filthy Irish ballads he was quite shocked.

The group also played at Max Reinhardt's studios, so an evening was arranged for aspiring writers to come to the Normandie and read their work while the band improvised. As it turned out, the only writer there was Lowry, and an English friend gave dramatic readings of his poems to a musical accompaniment. Then, as they all sat around on the floor eating, Lowry launched into a long eccentric and rambling monologue about the great novel he was writing, and about the catastrophe that was soon to overcome the world. Osborne thought he was too full of himself and used his accent and command of English to seduce rather than inform. 'He thought the world was going to hell in a handcart, but he wouldn't say it in that plain American way. He would refer to "the violent storm that is brewing, the forces of evil destruction that are going to engulf everyone."' Surrounded by a captive audience bedazzled by his verbal wizardry, he was in his element, especially when drunk.

During the first three months of 1939, he was conducting himself well enough – or presenting himself to the hotel management well enough – to have his allowance upgraded to $7.50 a day. There was one small setback during March when he got drunk with a new ladyfriend, a Miss Auer, who worked in a Beverly Hills store, and ended up giving her a black eye. But he was extremely remorseful afterwards and Parks took Miss Auer aside and explained his history and situation, asking her to be sure that he never spent any of his money on liquor. She agreed, so this incident was not held against him. On 5 April, Parks reported to Liverpool that during March Malcolm had kept his expenses well down and was working hard. He had been reading a lot and had entered a competition sponsored by a New York publisher requiring two short novels to be submitted for a good-sized prize and guaranteed publication. Malcolm, he said, was working day and night to revise a book previously written (*The Last Address*) and was writing another (*Under the Volcano*). Miss Auer was helping with the typing and was quite enthusiastic about them, convinced of their unusual merit. He could not have read either because he added, 'I am sure that Mr Lowry will be happy to know that the subject matter of these books is on a little higher moral plane than his previous works, and indicate a much brighter outlook.'[10]

Not only was Lowry full of confidence that he would win the competition, but he was obviously happy and in control while working so industriously. He even told Parks that he enjoyed being checked up on and having his spending restricted, and promised to go off to that ranch once the books were ready for the competition's May deadline. But he was now seeing Miss Auer every evening and every Sunday, and said it would be difficult to leave her now. A *two*-novel competition sounds unlikely, and was probably invented to persuade Parks he was being especially industrious. Parks's restrictions must have been deeply humiliating for him, but he had made his pact with the devil and would find himself in thrall to such men for some time to come.

He spoke to Jan by phone occasionally, and although she had seemed to want a divorce earlier, she now appeared less anxious to do so. In reporting this, Parks remarked cynically that he thought this was because her current affair was coming to an end. However, Malcolm had told him that he could not think of getting back together with her now. One day Parks drove him and Miss Auer to Griffiths Park Observatory where he shot some colour movie footage of them and sent it to Arthur saying that if he did not wish Evelyn to know about Miss Auer, a Kodak representative could have the lady removed from the film by a very easy process. Although Malcolm was in good physical shape, the fact that he had fallen by the wayside a couple of times led him to suggest he undergo a glandular test, which Arthur gave permission to have done. No doubt both would have found a medical explanation of his conduct more acceptable than a fancy psychoanalytic one.

Evelyn, meantime, was kept mostly in the dark about what had happened. At Arthur's prompting, Malcolm wrote her a long-delayed letter in February, and when Parks handed him her reply, he put it into his pocket without a word. He kept it to use some ten years later in the draft of *Dark as the Grave*.

> My darling lost boy, I simply cannot tell you my feelings on receiving your letter three days ago . . . My heart has been pierced through and through by your apparent neglect of me and your failure to acknowledge my letter of Nov. and Oct. 1937, but 'never mind all that' – you are still my boy and while I cannot understand your mentality or your life you belong to me. Oh my boy, how different things might have been for both you and *we* – so far you have shattered our hopes for you, and had Daddy and I not been strongly individualistic and possessing courage you would have broken our lives – but you are my boy, and I have sometimes felt that I could leave everything and go to search for my prodigal son and bring him back to the fold carrying him on my shoulders like a lost sheep. Oh, oh, with my hands to my head, this has been my cry (metaphorically speaking of course) because others would not know of my hidden grief at any cost while Daddy silently and with stoicism bears all. I know you will not comprehend this sentiment but there it is and it is true. In you, because of your literary ability and my deep appreciation of it, I expected much that could and would have proved such a blessing had you willed it.
>
> Well, at last you have written me and still address me 'My very dearest mother', and if you really and truly mean this, I am more than grateful for your love.[11]

Not until mid-April did he manage a reply, sending it to Parks for approval and adding that he found it very difficult to write to his mother, as to all of his family, but he hoped that as he improved it would become easier. This optimistic note was premature, for the Furies were about to close in once again on Fate's chosen victim.

On 14 April he told Parks that Jan was talking about getting together again, but that he thought that was out because she had been unfaithful to him, and anyway he was now very much in love with Miss Auer. He begged an extra five dollars from his allowance in order to take her to the theatre and to dinner to relax after working so hard recently on his books. Because he had been so sober and industrious over the past weeks Parks gave him a cheque, but asked Miss Auer to see that he spent none of it on alcohol. At 9.30 a.m. on the following Sunday, however, she called to say that the night before he had got drunk, flown into a great rage and tried to kill her. Parks found her at her mother's apartment in a very bad way. Apparently Lowry had hit her with all his might on the left eye, which was now closed and swollen, as was her nose, and had then kicked her in the ribs as she lay on the floor. The whole left side of her face was bruised, swollen and turned black. She had also sustained two cracked ribs and was continually spitting blood.

How on earth, he asked, had Malcolm obtained liquor after her promise to see that he did not? She said that when he picked her up at the store he had already been drinking. A friend had cashed the cheque and they had gone to an Italian restaurant for a meal. They had had a little drink with their meal but were not drunk. However, Malcolm had got angry with her for trying to teach him to eat spaghetti the Italian way, by rolling it on a fork, and told her he had decided to go back to Jan. He took the five dollars from her by force, and walked out leaving her with one dollar to pay the bill. She followed him back to the hotel trying to reason with him, but inside his room he turned on her and started beating her.

She asked Parks to pay her doctor's bills and, since her store manager had told her not to return until her bruises had gone, to make good the salary she would lose. Parks said that any money Malcolm received was not his own but came from his father. Miss Auer's mother, who was there, was surprised and angry because he had given them the impression that he was a wealthy Englishman with his own income. She threatened that if money was not forthcoming she would bring charges of assault and battery against him. The result, if he was found guilty, would be a fine, imprisonment and possible deportation. Parks stalled, asking for a week to consider the matter. At the Normandie, the manager said that Lowry had come in late the previous evening quite drunk and had let Miss Auer into the hotel through a back door so she was unnoticed by the desk clerk. At 3 a.m. he came down, still very drunk, and said there was a woman in his room that he wanted to eject. When the clerk went upstairs he found that Miss Auer, also very drunk, had locked herself in and would not respond to knocking. Not wanting to disturb other guests, he got the pass key and opened the door. Lowry then said he could now handle the matter, so the clerk returned to the lobby. Almost immediately, he called down to say he needed help, and when the clerk dashed back upstairs he found him with his hands round Miss Auer's throat, beating her head against the floor and furniture while she screamed murder. The manager, who happened to have the room next door, then came in to find the battered girl partly undressed, clutching a half-empty whisky bottle and bleeding profusely. She was extremely drunk and refused to go home, so was put in a spare room and a doctor was sent for. It took him several hours to calm her down, and finally she was sent home in a cab.

The manager then told Lowry he was forbidden to have women in his room; any further scandals and he would be thrown out. Parks, in his turn, told him he was not to see Miss Auer again, and Lowry told him angrily to mind his own business. She had locked him out of his room, he said, and he was not going to stand for that. For a long time he denied being drunk, but finally admitted he had been very drunk. However, he said he had an absolute right to beat up Miss Auer because she would not get out of his room. As Parks reported to Arthur, he had then cried hysterically, saying he loved the girl and that was why he had beaten her up. Then his mood changed and he said that he had beaten her up because when he had told her he was going back to Jan she had threatened suicide, and if he had not beaten her she would have killed herself. His conversation was rambling and incoherent. Parks said he thought he was lying throughout, trying to put a different construction on what had really happened.[12]

The idea of paying Miss Auer's medical bills made Lowry angry. He told Parks he was fed up with him running his affairs, that as a grown man it was intolerable to be told whether or not he could see a girl. He also said that drink was not a problem for him and he was quite capable of handling his own money as he had done before Parks came on the scene. If he went to New York and got his book published he would be much better off. England was heading for war, and as he did not want to avoid fighting for his country, he would get his book published and then go back to England to be there when the war broke out. He demanded all the money Parks had from Arthur so he could leave immediately for New York.

The lawyer refused, but said he would put this plan to Arthur and ask for instructions. Lowry demanded his money and his freedom right away and grew belligerent, saying that if he did not hand over the money he would cable Stuart, who saw things his way and would help him out. Parks then said that he thought he wanted to go to New York not to see publishers but to escape from his restraining influence and that he was quite free to get in touch with Stuart, but that he would be writing to Arthur describing fully the previous night's events. This calmed him down and he pleaded with him not to do so, but Parks refused, saying that Arthur employed him and he must tell him everything. Lowry became so distressed by this that he forgot the money and promised to stop drinking if he did not tell his father or would at least delay doing so for a week. But Parks refused to make promises. The following day, he got a 'loving' letter from Malcolm to Evelyn, for forwarding to Liverpool. From this point onwards, however, Arthur made sure that Evelyn heard nothing about her prodigal son's ever-worsening conduct, and Stuart was the only one with whom he discussed the problem.

The day after his argument with Parks, Lowry began bombarding Miss Auer with telegrams protesting his love and saying he had cabled Stuart and would soon be leaving for London by way of New York, but must see her first. He then phoned her, drunk and barely coherent, saying that Parks had tried to discredit her to him, and he intended to fix him through Stuart. She then called Parks asking him to stop Malcolm annoying her further; if he did that and paid for one more visit to the doctor she would not pursue the matter. Parks promptly agreed. She then told him how Malcolm got money for liquor. He saved his 25 cents daily allowance for phone calls and car fares to spend on fortified wines costing only 50 cents a gallon. She also told him how he got the money for cables, by persuading the hotel clerk to add the costs to the phone bill. Parks went to the hotel to sort this out, and the manager showed him a cable which Malcolm had asked to be sent to Stuart and charged to his account. When he read it and saw the abusive way Lowry had denounced him – saying that he was a crook who was using him to cheat the family – he ordered her to cut off the daily 25 cents pocket money which he was using for liquor. Lowry was back on meal tickets.

Next morning he called Parks, demanding his pocket money be restored, but was refused. He accused him of double-crossing both him and Jan by putting it into his head that she had been unfaithful to him. Parks said that it was Lowry who had told both him and his psychiatrist that she had been unfaithful. Lowry then threatened that he would soon expose him, and Parks said that if he meant the cable, he had intercepted it and was going to send it to his father. When he realized that he knew what was in the cable, Lowry became apologetic, saying he had not meant it the way it sounded. He was a fine chap and had acted only in his best interests. He asked him not to show the cable to Arthur, and said he was sure he would send him enough money for six months to enable him to get to New York on the understanding that thereafter he need send no more. Parks said he would put that idea to Arthur himself, but Lowry objected and again became abusive, saying that he had sent another cable to Stuart which showed him in his true colours. If he could not get out of his hands, he would kill himself. Parks refused to believe in another cable, and, after more threats and pleas from Lowry, hung up, saying that he would talk to him when he was sober.

When he sat down to communicate all this to Arthur Lowry in a closely typed fifteen-page letter, he now cast serious doubt on Malcolm's sanity. This fortified wine seemed to be affecting his mind and altering his mental condition. When he drank his conversation was rambling and incoherent and the fits of rage which had led to his murderous attack on Miss Auer showed how serious the situation was and what was likely to happen again if he was not permanently restrained and kept from liquor. Had he not been stopped in time – he being so strong and Miss Auer being so weak – he could easily have killed her and now be facing serious charges. Miss Auer had told him that when Malcolm was drinking sometimes, he got into very rough fights, and he concluded that the venomous portrait of him in the cable to Stuart was also brought on by liquor and was an attempt to discredit him before the bad news of the near-murder got to Liverpool.

Malcolm, he thought, could do someone a serious injury or even kill while he was free, and needed to be kept away from liquor permanently, and probably should be declared 'incompetent by reason of alcoholism' and restricted in some way. Because he was British on a temporary visa, this was best done somewhere outside the US, preferably in a British possession, or in England, where he could be visited by his family. He would never agree to being restrained voluntarily, and compulsion would be necessary. His visa expired on 26 July, and he would then have to leave the country to have it renewed, Mexico being the most convenient country for this. It was advisable, he said, that Malcolm be accompanied all the way so that he did not break free and land himself in trouble again. In his opinion, no longer having a typist and having lost four or five days work, he would miss the novel competition deadline; in any case, he thought the worst thing in the world would be for him to win it because he would skip to New York with the prize money, get drunk and it would all be spent or stolen.[13] This, in all its gruesome detail, dropped heavily on to Arthur's desk a few days later, and Stuart was called into conclave to help decide what was to be done.

In trying to cope with this latest catastrophe, Malcolm wrote Grieg another letter destined never to be sent, beginning, 'Thanks for your letter of 7 years ago.' His identification with Benjamin Hall had eventually led him into mental trouble, he said, and much of *Ultramarine* was paraphrase, plagiarism, or pastiche of his work. He had finished dramatizing *The Ship Sails On* and thought the American theatre would be interested, but needed his permission to go ahead. He was feeling ill, reading short stories by Thomas Mann, and would probably die like Hermann Bang sitting upright in a Pullman car in Utah, without a country. Since they last met, terrible things had happened and he was but a skeletal shadow of his former self.

Despite these feelings of doom, he seemed to recover quite quickly from the Miss Auer affair, and was more than ever anxious to get his work to New York by the deadline, so he began urgently to search for a typist. Joe London mentioned that Jim Osborne had a 22-year-old sister, Carol Phillips, who was a typist. Osborne was not keen on his sister working for Lowry, whom he thought a dubious character. But Carol, divorced and living alone at Long Beach with two young children to support, needed the money, so finally he agreed to put Lowry in touch with her. She was delighted to find a job and readily agreed. Parks insisted on interviewing her first, warning her that the previous typist had been all but murdered, and asked if she still wanted the job. She was a small, tough, feisty woman, who had survived a violent first marriage with a lively sense of humour, and was herself aspiring to write. She thought the warning made the job sound even more interesting, and said yes. Having passed Parks's grim scrutiny she was given Lowry's room number and went along to the Normandie.

The room, she remembered, had a big rumpled bed on one side and a large gold-trimmed oak desk on the other, with a typewriter, and papers scattered around. Lowry sat in a golden rocking-chair smelling of cologne, with his pipe in his mouth – obviously trying to give the impression of a very English writer. She was immediately struck, as many others were, by his unusual 'cat-like' eyes. And although he was dressed smartly enough she noticed an open closet into which clothes had just been flung haphazardly. He asked her if Parks had given her any trouble, and she told him what he had said about him. 'Did that scare you?' he asked. 'Not at all,' she replied. 'Good,' he said, 'let's get to work.' Before they started, however, he showed her letters from various publishers about his work, one from Whit Burnett and one from H. L. Mencken; she was very impressed. She was, she told her mother, 'working with a PUBLISHED English novelist.'[14]

As she settled down at the typewriter to copy out a corrected draft, Lowry suddenly disappeared into his clothes closet. When he came out, he told her he had just been talking to Herman Melville, and that Melville often spoke to him from the top of the closet. 'Well,' she told herself, 'if he wants to play nuts he can play nuts,' and she paid no attention. A little later he tried unsettling her again, picking up the phone and talking into the wrong end of it. 'I'm speaking to Shakespeare,' he said. She saw that he was acting as if mad, trying to see what reactions he could get, but because she refused to react he stopped. He had chosen the wrong girl to try scaring – she had had far worse to put up with in her short life.

With little time left until the competition deadline he plunged straight into revising a twenty-five thousand word draft of *The Last Address*, hoping to get it finished and retyped within a week. His vision of the psychiatric ward as an embodiment of the lunatic city began to expand into one of the wider world about to plunge into the pandemonium of war. After work, he told Carol he was a member of the aristocracy whose family had all but disowned him. She was most impressed and quite in love with the idea of working for what seemed to her a mad, bad Byronic English poet with connections in the New York literary world. Within a week, *The Last Address* was finished and mailed off. But before she disappeared back to Long Beach, Lowry took her to dinner to celebrate, and said he hoped she would come back to work with him on his longer novel, *Under the Volcano*. He wrote her an enthusiastic letter of thanks. 'The Last Address is in the hat . . . or should I add in case I seem to brag / that thanks to you we've got it in the bag!'[15] Carol, in turn, wrote excitedly to her mother about him. 'His name is Malcolm Lowry and he is one of the British aristocracy and also a celebrated poet and incidentally he writes like the very devil.' He had, she said, looked at her poetry and would teach her to be a genuine poet. As a result, her verses had begun to include images of darkness and death, scarred ravines, graveyards, trapped and hunted foxes, and suffering nights. 'I am bestirring myself in the maelstroms of Hell,' she wrote, 'and being gloriously dramatic and insane and everybody is saying that I am truly a poet . . . I am . . . busy struggling with my inner dark angel.'[16] So, it seems, as always, was Lowry. On 30 April there was another rumpus when Lowry tried to smuggle Miss Auer and a man into his room while drunk. The visitors were ejected.

Carol had no phone of her own but a week later Lowry called her sister and left messages for her. By now, her brother Jim was convinced Lowry was unstable and an unsuitable person for her to get involved with, so the messages were not passed on. Finally he wrote, asking her to come to see him at the Normandie, which she did. He asked her to work with him on *Under the Volcano*, saying he could not afford to pay her now, but would pay her when the book was published. 'You write something out and I'll sign it,' he told her, 'and then we can go right to work.' How much did he want to give her, she asked. 'Twenty-five per cent,' he said, so she wrote out an agreement stating that she was entitled to 25 per cent of the income from *Under the Volcano*, when published. She wrote to her mother,

> Mr Lowry is utterly incapable of handling his affairs and all his money comes through a million lawyers who grease their palms well before passing it on. He is really suffering very real persecution and for that reason I am working for almost nothing so that I can help him. Of course, the value of the instruction he's giving me is priceless – I guess that you can see that in my poetry and wait until you see my prose.[17]

Over the next few weeks she worked on the book intermittently, because sometimes she got paid work or her sister could not babysit for her. But when she did come they started early and did a full day's work. She always found him full of ideas, as if he had been up all night thinking what he wanted to do. The manuscript, she remembered, was about a hundred pages single-spaced on both sides of the paper, stained with coffee and rather dog-eared, and work was slow because he wanted to make a lot of changes. He was unhappy because Yvonne was the Consul's daughter and Hugh her fiancé, and he wanted to change that, and he talked a great deal about the Consul being an Oedipal figure, reaching for something he could not find.

He would take her to dinner in the evenings and open up more and talk about himself, trotting out sad stories of his childhood and stirring times at sea. When he was young, he told her, his aristocratic parents had simply handed him over to servants to look after; when he misbehaved they just filled him with wine and put him to bed – an interesting variation on previous stories of abuse, more suitable as an excuse for the heavy and indiscriminate drinking. His father, he said, was dominated by his mother, and although he had been rejected by his family, he did not mind being supported by his father; if the Old Man was ready to keep him like this it seemed a pity not to take advantage of it.

As he grew expansive, he told her about his other work, modestly comparing *Ultramarine* with *Moby Dick*, and talking extensively about the ideas he was trying to develop in *Under the Volcano*. She wrote to her mother, enthusing about and producing what is probably the earliest written review of *Under the Volcano* as it then stood:

> I am truly fortunate in finding so willing a teacher. Honestly, his memory is phenomenal. In fact, the whole man is phenomenal. I know that without a doubt he is a genius . . . Good lord, he writes like nothing human. Such plots, and counter-plots and subterranean intricacies. The theme of this novel 'Under the Volcano' is first – Life against death, could anything be more gripping? Then man's inhumanity against man – that is the running thread. Then the actual story which all takes place in one day – that of a father and his daughter and her sweetheart – then the historical significance of revolution in Mexico – the general world unrest, the precipitation of war and rumours of war and general brutality, which is tremendous – the psychological by-play on the part of the father whose own love having been thwarted finds in his daughter's sweetheart a very menacing rival, the Oedipus complex, and the tragedy of Emperor Maximilian and Carlotta. How you like dose! Do you wonder that I sit at the feet of wisdom, struck dumb?[18]

She was dazzled by his supreme self-confidence; he told her he was writing the world's greatest story and once it was finished the world would recognize it as such. They discussed politics and literature and he gave her an anthology of poetry inscribed, 'From one afflicted to one angelic,' hinting that they would make a great partnership – two writers together.

It was while they were working on the book that he made a pass at her and so aroused her compassion with his sorrowful stories and protestations of love that she succumbed. She found Lowry a very assured, dominating and sensitive lover. He spoke earnestly of love and said that when he was free of Jan they should marry and have a houseful of children. But Carol was living on Social Security and needed to work to supplement her income to support her children, so had to leave for paid employment. Lowry promised to call, but her sister refused to pass on the messages, and when he failed to write she concluded that he had found someone else.

By this time Arthur had had time to digest the dire news about Miss Auer, and sent Parks a letter to be forwarded to Malcolm. 'It is with great difficulty that I bring myself to write this letter,' he began, 'for I have just heard the story of your recent behaviour in Los Angeles which has moved me almost to despair at your sanity.' His behaviour to those assigned to help him had been 'horrible', and he was in danger of causing revulsion in those he professed to love and bringing disaster upon himself. 'I can never believe that a state of intoxication is any help to the literary work of which you are always talking but of which we see so little, yet I feel that if you could only rid yourself of this failing you might do really good things.' He had kept this sad affair from Evelyn, he said. 'My heart you have pretty well broken. The effect that it would have on your mother I leave to your imagination.' For years he had acted against fatherly advice at the expense of his own character and *his* money. Now the time had come for a change. This could only be achieved by following his advice, determining to cut out drink and following the plans Parks had for helping him. He was no longer willing to send him money to squander on alcohol. He had *earned* his money and was under no obligation to hand it over to him. If he continued as he was his remittance would be cut. As to the future:

> Will you help yourself and me to a happier life by going into some institution in Canada . . . where you will be able to free yourself from this corrosive influence by submitting voluntarily to discipline and being deprived of the chance of letting your weaker side prevail . . . I yearn to save your soul – and *so do you now*, if you'll only be frank with yourself.

Just to ensure no further attempts were made to contact Stuart behind his back, he added, 'Stuart has read this letter and shares my feelings.'[19]

Parks must have been gratified at having outwitted Lowry and scotched his attempt to discredit him, but he decided not to show him this letter immediately, fearing a bad reaction. Arthur's lawyer wrote separately, making Arthur's point of view clear: 'Our client does not want Malcolm back in England, as he is apprehensive of what may happen and of the effect on his wife, from whom he has concealed her son's recent conduct.' He agreed with the idea of putting him out of the reach of drink, but in England it was difficult to get people institutionalized involuntarily. He should be induced to go to Canada, accompanied by a private detective, and enter a suitable 'medical or religious institution of the Protestant faith' under threat of being cut off.[20] Any shred of freedom he now had was about to be snuffed out; it would take all his cunning to outwit such alien powers.

His relationship with Parks remained stormy, and he was furious for a long time about him intercepting his cable to Stuart and sending it to his father. He was angry at being refused money to take Carol Phillips out to dinner, rowed with him about seeing Miss Auer and once tried to smuggle her into the Normandie again. But he did outwit him by concealing his amorous relationship with Carol. So sure was Parks that nothing untoward was occurring that he wrote assuring Arthur's lawyers that the relationship was entirely professional. He also told them that work on *Under the Volcano* was completed, and charged Carol's usual two week's fee of twenty-five dollars to his account, even though she swore she was never paid, which lends some credence to Lowry's charge that his father was being ripped off. Of course, if it were so, he was in no position to sit in judgement, having colluded in creative accountancy with his various 'guardians' ever since leaving home. Towards the end of May he wrote to Carol again. 'My soul has been standing still for a week – or is it a year or a thousand? – without you.' If she did not respond immediately it was because she had to work and because her brother Jim had warned her not to get involved with him.

But his life was forever taking dramatic turns. He was befriended by an Englishman also living at the Normandie, Jack King, who worked for Lilly Pharmaceuticals. He claimed that he had first met King in a bar in China in 1927, another improbable story which just might have been true; King, it seems, had travelled to the Far East for Ely Lilly, and could well have been in Foo Chow or Shanghai when Lowry was there on *Pyrrhus*. As he was at a low ebb and a loose end at the Normandie, King took pity on him and offered to fix him up with a girl. With Carol no longer available he was willing enough to go on the blind date which King arranged for him. Through his fiancée, King knew a Hollywood secretary, Margerie Bonner, an ex-silent movie actress, an attractive, sociable 34-year-old divorcée with a string of beaux, who would, he thought, be just the person to lift his friend out of his brooding melancholy. He called her at her home in Beechwood Drive, Hollywood, and told her he had a friend who was lonesome and in need of company. Would she join them to make a foursome? She wanted to know a little more before deciding. King said he was a well-bred Englishman and a writer. Bonner agreed to the date, but at the last moment Lowry phoned to say that, as they had no car, Jack had suggested that she drive down and meet them at the bus stop at the corner of Western and Hollywood Boulevard.

And so, on the evening of Wednesday 7 June, Margerie Bonner drove her car to the agreed spot and parked. Shortly afterwards, a bus arrived and Lowry got off alone. According to Margerie, 'Stars were floating. We were immediately in love.'[21] And she told her sister, 'I knew instantly that I had met my fate.'[22] She said, 'Malcolm?' and he said, 'Margerie?' and they fell into one another's arms. The clinch was a lingering one – it was a mutual embrace which was not to end for some eighteen years. In more ways than one Margerie Bonner had met her fate, and so had Malcolm Lowry. Shortly after falling into one another's arms they fell into one another's beds. The relationship was passionate and sexual from the outset. Parks noted that Lowry was behaving well, and when informed that his father had it in mind that he remain in the United States, he seemed quite cheerful and satisfied. The lawyer was not, of course, to know the reason.

'Marjorie' Bonner, born 18 July, 1905, was the youngest daughter of John Stuart and Emily Bonner, and at five foot one, the latest in the line of small, artistic women to whom Lowry was attracted. John Stuart Bonner, of Scottish Catholic descent, had been an adventurer and soldier of fortune, fighting in wars of independence in various South American countries, notably Brazil, and was fluent in both Spanish and Portuguese. After marrying in Washington in 1898, he wrote a newspaper column before moving to Adrian, Michigan, where his father owned the Adrian *Daily Times*, and there became head of the Foreign Department of the Page Woven Wire Fence Company. During the First World War he was a staff Colonel in the AEF and the family moved to Chicago. Although a Catholic, he never attended church, but Emily was a High Anglican and very devout. 'Marjorie' told Malcolm that some of her ancestors were MacGregors, agents of the Crown before the Revolution, so she was of pioneering stock. The Southern side of her family had made money from cotton plantations, the Northern side from the slave trade, and were bitterly divided by 'the War between the States'. John Stuart was a distant parent, 'awesome' to his daughters, and Emily was a closeted innocent who believed in fairies and was fascinated by astronomy. The two Bonner girls, Marjorie and Priscilla, who was six years older, were brought up to be loyal conservative Americans, reciting 'The Star-Spangled Banner' religiously at bedtime, and being encouraged to read serious literature by their grandfather, the newspaper owner. While still in her teens, Marjorie had read Shakespeare, Hardy, and Scott's Waverley novels, and was considered decidedly more precocious than her mother would have wished.

But it was Priscilla who did the unthinkable and at eighteen left for Hollywood to try to break into pictures. Within three months she had bluffed her way into a film, *Homer Comes Home*, starring opposite Charles Ray, and from there on starred in a long series of successful silent films, with actors like Jack Pickford and Will Rogers. Mysteriously, John Stuart had lost the family money, a loss which paralysed Emily, who never entirely recovered her equilibrium. In 1919, when Marjorie was fourteen, she easily persuaded her mother to let her quit school in Chicago and join Priscilla in Hollywood. When they arrived, Priscilla was expecting a kid sister in bobby-sox, but at the station, after her mother had got off the train first, she appeared dramatically on the platform at the end of the last carriage. She wore a paradise silk dress trimmed with black medallions, a large hat tipped over one ear with a long feather which seemed to encircle her whole face. She was wobbling along on very high French heels and smoking a cigarette in a holder. Taking a deep drag on the cigarette she said, in a studied drawl, 'Well, hello there!' She had arrived like the star she intended to become. Priscilla thought her hilarious, if not ludicrous.[23]

She refused to go to school and was impossible to control, insisting on accompanying Priscilla to the old Goldwyn Studios each day. Although she did finally get into pictures when she was eighteen, she played mostly minor roles, often no more than walk-ons, for which payment was minimal. She did become a good horsewoman and acted in a few westerns, but her movie career amounted to very little. Finally she stopped trying and took a job as an artist at the Disney studios, then worked on radio scripts for a time before becoming personal assistant to Penny Singleton, star of the Blondie movies, the job she was doing when she met Lowry. She had been married at nineteen to Jerome B. Chaffee, the scion of a wealthy Montecito family in the automobile business, seven years her elder. But Chaffee was a violent alcoholic, and she was finally rescued from him by friends who found her cowering under a bed as he rampaged round their apartment. She was not divorced, however, until she was twenty-five and shortly thereafter Chaffee committed suicide. (Subsequently she changed her name to Margerie.) Now she had met another violent alcoholic, whose saving graces were that he was not just the son of wealthy parents, but English and a literary genius. She had a strong literary bent herself, having tried her hand unsuccessfully at writing murder mysteries. Like Jan, she thought it was a relationship potentially as glamorous and enriching as Lawrence's and Frieda's. It was an illusion Lowry was never slow to encourage for his amatory purposes.

By now Parks had hatched two plots to get him out of the US to have his visa renewed. One plan, he told Arthur, was for him to leave the country and return on a quota and therefore permanently, which would have to be set up in advance but would mean just two days in Ensenada, Mexico before returning. This would be relatively cheap. Alternatively, he could be taken to Canada but would not get in if it was thought he was going in just to return on a quota. Furthermore, if they thought he was alcoholic he could be returned to England. There was, said Parks, only one place in Vancouver which treated alcoholics and it seemed better to find someone to look after him and his money, and, since a permit was required to obtain liquor in Vancouver, to make sure that he did not get one. A detective could take him up there at $15 a day, but he would probably object to going 'under arrest'. However, he would do the whole thing in eight days for $800, pretending that he had to go to Canada anyway and that Arthur had asked him to accompany him as a friend. This would not be difficult, he said, because Malcolm had been sober for a month and was trying to become friendly again. He did not want Arthur to think he was taking advantage of the situation to line his own pockets, but thought that *he* was best able to advise whoever took Malcolm on about his deceptive way of always appearing the victim of persecution, and about how dangerous he became when drunk.

After meeting him, Margerie had wanted to introduce Malcolm to her family, but her mother, who had been living with her, had become ill with pneumonia, and Priscilla, now married to a Hollywood doctor, decided she should in future live with *her*, and was too busy and in no mood to meet yet another of Margerie's many boyfriends. One of those boyfriends, Bob, was it seems very possessive and excitable, and inclined to bring out a gun when agitated. Both lovers, in fact, were living extremely complicated lives. However, that did not much matter to the happy couple, who were utterly consumed by each other. It

JOURNEYING.
Top: The 'tramp' that never was a tramp. SS *Pyrrhus*, the Blue Funnel freighter on which Lowry sailed to China and back as a deckboy in 1927. *Above left*: 'Alight with genius' and temporarily sober. Malcolm outside The Harvard Bookstore on Plympton Street in Cambridge, Massachusetts in the summer of 1929. *Above right*: In ballast to the White Sea, August 1931. Lowry posing beneath the Norwegian flag at the stern of a timber ship, SS *Fagervik*, of which he said he had happy memories. The ship was meant to go to Archangel but instead landed him at Aalesund in Norway. *Left*: Lowry's Bright Angel, 'straight from the heart' Nordahl Grieg. Lowry said that when he told Grieg he had lifted passages from his novel, *The Ship Sails On*, for *Ultramarine*, Grieg simply laughed.

CAMBRIDGE.
Above: Fateful friendship. Lowry standing beside Paul Fitte in the St Catharine's College matriculation photograph, 4 November 1929. *Below left*: Talent-spotter and poseur, John Davenport, in his rooms at Corpus Christi. He was almost certainly the first to proclaim Lowry a 'genius'. *Below right*: 'Chatty's addled salon' was J. B. S. Haldane's name for the circle that gathered around his wife Charlotte at their home, Roebuck House, for food, drink, music and good talk. Here in 1930, Lowry and other acolytes pose in the garden beside the Cam. William Empson is at far left, and Robert Lazurus and Charlotte Haldane are sitting in front of a pipe-toting Lowry.

MOVING ON.
Right: Lowry at Jeake's House, Rye, with Conrad Aiken and Catherine Freeman standing behind and John and Jane Aiken seated beside him.
Below left: Julian Trevelyan, Lowry's Best Man and 'Guardian Angel'.
Below right: John Sommerfield, 'approximately the best man' Lowry had ever met.

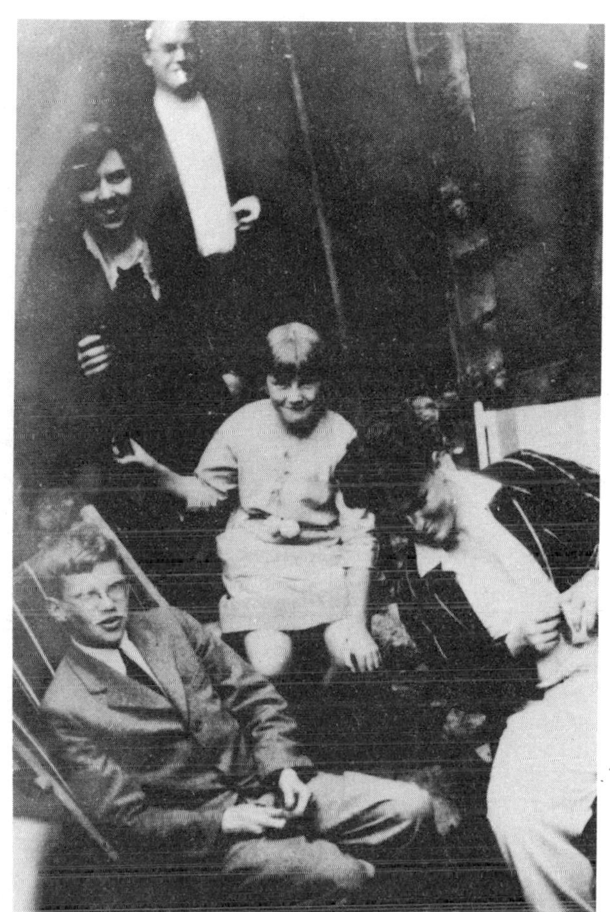

TO MEXICO.
Above: In the lunatic city, New York, the city in which Lowry said it was difficult to stay on the right side of despair. This passport photograph was taken in 1936 shortly after leaving Bellevue Hospital and before departing for Mexico. *Right*: Life transformed by art. Laruelle's Tower in Cuernavaca today, now a hotel, with the inscription 'No se puede vivir sin amar' painted on in imitation of *Under the Volcano*. *Below*: The happy calm before the storm. Jan and Malcolm at 62 calle Humboldt, Cuernavaca.

suited their equally histrionic natures to declare it a decidedly out-of-the-ordinary affair. Margerie was clearly enthralled by Malcolm's performance as the castaway and cast-out aristocratic genius, just as he was bowled over by her glamorous image, her past as a movie actress, and of course her enthusiasm for him. He was a past master at wringing the heart and evoking the maternal instinct. Jan had observed shrewdly that what he really wanted was a mother who was a good lay. Malcolm, it seems, had at last found such a woman.

The plan to take him to Mexico and bring him back on a quota had hit a snag. Parks told Arthur that a $30,000 trust would need to be set up in America (which he would be happy to administer) to persuade the authorities that he would not be a public burden. Money would need to be available from the principal sum, too, for emergencies like medical bills. That failed to find favour with Arthur – he was unhappy about Malcolm returning to Mexico, however briefly – but now the situation took a further dramatic turn. Malcolm was still meeting Jan once a week for a meal. They were frequently in touch by telephone and he had told her of the plan to leave and return on an immigrant quota. One day in mid-July she called him and thought he sounded unusually strained. Then in the background she heard what she described as 'a harridan voice' yell, 'Tell her to go to hell! Tell her to go to hell!' and immediately knew she had a rival. So in mid-July she decided to file for divorce, and the hearing was scheduled for 8 August. On hearing that Jan knew of their plans, Parks was sure the divorce had been filed for when it was known he would be out of the country. After some difficulty he traced Jan's lawyer, away on holiday (deliberately, Parks thought, in order to avoid a postponement), and was told that Jan was asking for $3,000 alimony. Parks was angry because he thought attempts were being made to outmanoeuvre him, and said Malcolm had no money of his own – anything he had told Jan to the contrary was untrue. He threatened to go to the Bar Association and bring a charge for unethical conduct and told the lawyer he would be lucky to get even his fee of $250. In a letter to Arthur's lawyers, Parks made much of Jan's lawyer being Jewish and said he calculated that any threat to his fee would bring him to heel. Jan had sued on the grounds of Malcolm being habitually drunk and as this would mean his not being readmitted to the US on any basis whatsoever, he undertook to persuade her to sue on different grounds. He managed to get the hearing postponed, and prepared an answer to Jan's petition. He took affidavits from Malcolm swearing he had no income or other money, and was not employed but supported himself entirely by voluntary contributions from his family, and promptly arranged to get him out of the country before his visa expired.

Meanwhile Lowry, unable to deal with all of this, had been drunk for four days solid until finally, alone, he had gone berserk, breaking the mirror in his room by throwing a bottle at it, breaking a chair and bedside lamp, and burning a chair and several blankets with cigarettes. It was a repeat performance, it seems, of an earlier experience in Mexico. His poem 'Delirium in Vera Cruz' certainly speaks for the drunken Lowry drowning in guilt-ridden nostalgia for Jan and what might have been:

Where has tenderness gone, he asked the mirror
Of the Biltmore Hotel, cuarto 216. Alas,
Can its reflection lean against the glass
Too, wondering where I have gone, into what horror?
Is that it staring at me now with terror
Behind your frail tilted barrier? Tenderness
Was here, in this very bedroom, in this
Place, its form seen, cries heard, by you. What error
Is here? Am I that rashed image?
Is this the ghost of the love you reflected?
Now with a background of tequila, stubs, dirty collars,
Sodium perborate, and a scrawled page
To the dead, telephone off the hook? In rage
He smashed all the glass in the room. (Bill: $50)[24]

The hotel manager had banned visitors to his room, but Margerie was smuggled in and they spent his last night in Los Angeles together.

Next morning he called Carol to the hotel urgently saying that he had to leave the country. In his room she found him in his overcoat, packed and ready to leave, with Margerie close by regarding her with cold suspicion. Malcolm, too, was cold, distant and businesslike. He asked her to take the half-completed manuscript of *Under the Volcano* home with her to finish, assuring her that she would get twenty-five percent of the royalties for her work. She saw that Margerie now regarded Malcolm as her territory, so she gave him a chaste kiss and left with the manuscript. When Parks arrived, he found him still drunk but with Margerie seemingly in charge and well able to cope.

On 26 July, the day his visa expired, and two days before his thirtieth birthday, Lowry and Parks left Los Angeles to drive up to Canada. If the fact that he now had another woman in tow registered with Parks, he did not consider it unduly significant, even though he had found him that morning drunk, having obviously spent his last night in Los Angeles in bed with her. They would have to live with the memory of that night for a while to come. As they drove away, Lowry leaned out of the open window of the car and shouted to her, 'I'll be back soon!' In fact it would be more than six years before he set foot again on American soil.

CHAPTER XIV

CUT OFF BY WAR

1939–1940

Hell is other people.

JEAN-PAUL SARTRE

At the Canadian border, they were held while Lowry was grilled for three quarters of an hour by a drunken immigration officer. Despite his British passport the officer said that Canada did not let just anyone into the country. Finally and grudgingly he gave him a three-month visitor's visa, which allowed him ample time to reapply for re-entry to the United States.

Once settled in Vancouver, he began bombarding Margerie with letters and phone calls. On 30 July he wrote from the Hotel Georgia.

> I don't know how I can smile till I see you again, or exist without your love and nearness and compassion: the sensation of underground bleeding, of being torn up by the roots like a tree by a big wind – do you feel that? God, I do! . . . Grrr. You have . . . spoiled all women for ever for me & I'm glad of it . . . My god let's make it soon when we can be happy again on a tousled bed and at peace in spite of the pain.[1]

Despite the familiar hyperbole there was a serious even optimistic note. He had spent the past five years predicting universal catastrophe; now he said war was less likely since the British Government had taken a firmer stand.

The men Parks had in mind as his guardians were Major Victor MacLean, a Vancouver stockbroker, and A. B. Carey, a retired English businessman. MacLean was forty-five and a war hero, a man of influence who had been in charge of organizing the unemployed in Vancouver, and Carey was his successor. He was fifty-five and a member of the Oxford Group, which was, Parks told Arthur, 'a philosophical semi-religious movement with high moral standards, but a very tolerant attitude toward sinners, especially alcoholics'.[2] He had himself had difficulty with 'liquor, and other things' but had overcome them to become 'an extremely fine and useful citizen, and his brand of religion has proved effective in the cure of alcoholics.' In fact Carey was a leading light in Moral Rearmament, the movement founded by Frank Buchman the previous year.

Lowry took to MacLean, an obviously brave man of action. The Major, however, thought Carey best suited to handle him, and at first the two seemed to get on well. Ironically, Carey offered Lowry an unsalaried post in the unemployment office, saying he would have plenty of free time for writing, that every unemployed man was a potential story and that the unemployment problem was 'a gigantic and epochal story' altogether. But working there, he would need to keep a clear head, avoid drink and always get a good night's sleep. MacLean said it was a tremendous opportunity for a writer, and this persuaded Lowry to accept. He told Parks,

> You know, I have always had a desire to get into some type of work with unfortunate people . . . this unemployment problem . . . could be one of the greatest stories of modern times . . . I have had a feeling of utter futility and uselessness for many years, and . . . this may be the solution of my problem. I also think that I am going to like the work.[3]

Who Lowry was trying to fool is difficult to say. No doubt he was keen to humour Parks, win his freedom and get back to Margerie. He told MacLean, however, that Carey's Oxford Group seemed too religious for his taste. The Major said he had never tried to force it on *him*, and, reassured, Lowry agreed to move in with him. But privately Carey told Parks he would put him with men of his own age who had been cured of alcoholism through the Oxford philosophy, and hoped this would keep him away from saloons.

MacLean and Carey then agreed to be responsible for him, and Parks put $200 into the Bank of Montreal, gave them power to withdraw funds on joint signatures, then left. Lowry had finally shaken off his old enemy, but was hardly in more liberal hands. Carey may have been careful not to thrust his religion at the influential MacLean, but saw Lowry as a sick soul, and the Oxford philosophy as his cure. That lost soul, however, despite expressions of good intention, was living in another world, a world of tousled beds and the glamorous Margerie Bonner, ex-silent film actress, drinking companion and lover. He said nothing of her to his new guardians, but continued flooding her with letters. Jan was being 'as murderous as possible', he told her, and if she managed to make her charges stick he would be unable to return to the US. Margerie had said that if he could not return and could pay her fare, she would come to him, and that at least was a straw to clutch at. Parks had departed, he wrote, and he had quit drinking. He sent Parks a letter to forward to Jan, and reported himself 'very fit' and his drink problem 'liquidated'. However, his future happiness, he said, depended on being free to return to the US to manage his own affairs and complete certain work. And he owed it to his family to give them no more trouble. Cunningly he added how glad he was they had parted as friends.

Soon he was showering Margerie with cables as well as letters. He would move the Himalayas to see her, would send money once properly free and was only awaiting permission from Arthur to return alone. While flattering Parks, trying to re-establish contact with Jan, and playing the writing-paper lover for Margerie, he sent a business letter posing as love-note to Carol Phillips. She must not forget him, he wrote. The truth was eternal. What was the state of *Under the Volcano*? Of course she would have her quarter. He was terribly lonely without her but he knew they would meet again. She was the grandest person he had ever known. 'You saved my life & I hope I can prove it was worth saving . . . I love you very dearly.'[4]

World events – trouble on the Polish border and in Danzig – revived his feeling that war was imminent, and the prospect of returning soon to Margerie was threatened. They could not marry for a year, he told her, but unless they acted, time would turn them old and grey. He would be getting $150 a month and in Canada, away from Parks, would be master of his own money – perhaps reason enough to remain, though if he were to succeed as a writer in the way he planned he would have to return to the States. He could not take a job in Canada but could make money from writing. He would remain an exile from his family, who would still control his money. Remarriage after one disaster would arouse their hostility; they would say that the money was for him and not for use on anyone else. If she came to him, he could pay more than Penny Singleton to type for him for several months, and it would help towards their future.

When the divorce came to court in Los Angeles on 30 August, Parks claimed that Lowry had no money of his own from which to pay the $3,000 alimony requested; Jan's lawyer then argued for a nominal monthly sum against future earnings. Parks opposed this, leaving it to the court to decide.[5] Two days later, as German troops invaded Poland, Lowry cabled his father for permission to come home via New York in order to enlist. He then cabled Margerie: 'Will see you first whatever happens,' and a week later, five days after Britain declared war on Germany, he said he hoped to be with her within a week. But Parks spiked this plan by also cabling Liverpool to say that Malcolm was 'using enlistment as a subterfuge [to] escape my supervision and see girl'. He thought he would not enlist if left to go free, and suggested that he should enlist in Canada or directly after returning to Britain.

Still wooing Margerie at long range, Lowry tried to persuade her to get rid of the gun-toting Bob, who had tried to dissuade her from joining Lowry unless he planned to marry her. Could she really be happy with a man who pulled a gun whenever his ego is afflicted, he asked, 'If you feel like breaking, think of all the . . . dreams unfulfilled, the children unseen, the books unwritten . . . the lost nights together . . . if you truly love me as I love you greet me as one come back from a long journey & who must go again, as I must.'[6] Even if he had no intention of enlisting he could still use the likelihood of going to war to dramatic emotional effect.

Canada declared war on 10 September, while Lowry was still awaiting news from England. Conscription now seemed a real possibility and he wrote to Margerie, saying that news from England was grim, and for all he knew half his family had been wiped out already. She must know that, without wanting to sound heroic, his allegiance was still to his country, 'grimy little island though it is'. He had his American visa, but could not use it, having agreed to await his father's approval, without which his income might be cut off. If the worst happened he might have to enlist in Canada.

Seeing the film of *Goodbye Mr Chips*, evoking memories of Balgarnie, seems to have revived his younger Cambridge self and he persuaded Carey to advance him the money to buy a ukulele, his first since marrying Jan. But his heroic talk of having to fight was no doubt little more than that. He had scorned the idea in 1934 and, despite his drunken boasts, had signally failed to volunteer for Spain two years earlier. Now, with a flame of passion to keep alive, he was more than ever determined to avoid what he thought would be a mindless slaughtering match. But he believed Parks or his family were hoping to force him to enlist in Canada, something he promised Margerie he would never do. As yet,

Canada was taking only the fittest volunteers, but going to England would mean automatic call-up.

Amid his anxieties about Margerie and conscription, he could still reflect on what this war meant to him and others, especially following the Nazi-Soviet Pact of 23 August. 'The bottom has dropped out of the world of my generation,' he wrote. Only she and his love of beauty kept him connected to life. He recalled ironically how his father had castigated him in 1934 for predicting a war by the autumn of 1939. 'I continued warning my family but they took no damn notice. Result: they'll probably not only lose all their money, but be killed, when they might have been living in Jerusalem'.[7]

At his urgent request, Parks cabled Liverpool recommending he be allowed after all to return to the States and from there to England to enlist. He also announced that the divorce had been settled on his terms, namely $265, Jan's lawyer's court fee. In fact the lawyer passed the money to Jan, apologizing for having handled the case badly, and that was all she ever received after the divorce, despite what Malcolm later told Margerie.

Just as he was able to return to the US, Lowry's patience ran out and he made a serious error. He later told Aiken[8] that Carey had read his letters, found out about Margerie, accused him of committing a mortal sin in loving a woman not his wife, and cut off his funds completely. He cabled Margerie for the money to join her, and she quickly obliged. On Friday 22 September he moved out of Carey's house, and next morning cabled Margerie: 'Thanks On My Way Bus Terminal Hollywood Eleven Monday.' At Blaine on the US border, he was refused entry – according to him for 'military reasons', according to Margerie for being 'drunk, reeking and saying all the wrong things', and according to the authorities, for being without funds and likely to be a public charge. (He later accused Carey of warning US Immigration that he had no money.) Stuck in Vancouver, he sent Margerie an SOS from the Dunsmuir Hotel, pleading with her to join him.

That same evening, drunk and despondent, in the cocktail lounge of the hotel, Lowry fell in with two other drinkers. They were taken aback by his dishevelled appearance, his sweatshirt and well-worn sandals, and wondered how he had been allowed into the place. But having found an audience, he launched into his equally well-worn yarns of life at sea. According to one of the men, Maurice Carey, an unemployed ex-Canadian Army Sergeant-Major, Lowry was all but broke but he and his friend readily stood him drinks. (Margerie's story was that what was left of the ticket money she had sent quickly disappeared into Carey's pocket.) After a long evening's drinking Lowry said, not surprisingly, that he felt disinclined to return to A. B. Carey's place, so the Sergeant-Major offered him a bed for the night.

Next morning, according to Maurice Carey, he began the day with a large Scotch, then said he must get back to work on a book. Finally he explained his situation – his status in Canada, his relationship with his father, how his allowance was doled out, and the moral pressure to abandon drink from Oxford Grouper Carey. The shrewd old Sergeant decided Lowry was worth hanging on to. He had an income and seemed very innocent – as gullible, he thought, as a young farmer's daughter who had never left the farm.[9] He proposed himself as guardian and Lowry quickly agreed. A man who frequented cocktail bars was much more to his taste than a moral fanatic constantly angling for a convert. Maurice claimed that he approached A.B., who was so impressed with his record as a Senior NCO in the First World War, that he agreed to hand Lowry over to him with the monthly $150 to be doled out at his discretion. However, the truth was that A.B. thought Maurice Carey an unsatisfactory character to supervise Lowry, and, while agreeing that he remain with him, refused to relinquish control of his money. But, having freed himself from the Oxford Groupers, Lowry phoned Margerie only to find that, on getting his SOS, she had taken leave from work, bade her puzzled family goodbye, and was about to take the train north to Canada. Her boats were burnt; now she would have to marry Malcolm or risk making a fool of herself. This was to be her big break, the part for which she felt she had been destined and which Hollywood had not afforded her.

She arrived in Vancouver on 29 September and went by cab to Lowry's new address at 595 West 19th Avenue. When the taxi drew up in the run-down suburb, she emerged heavily made-up and swathed in silken wraps to make one of her splendid Hollywood entrances. Maurice disliked her on sight and lodged them both in an upstairs bedroom, an unheated attic, according to Margerie. However, the need to keep her secret from A. B. Carey, from Parks and the Lowrys, put them firmly in Maurice's power. According to him, Margerie was snobbish, hysterical, and unable to control Malcolm's drinking. According to her, he was tall, dark, beaky and sinister – a card-sharper and a petty crook. Whatever her shortcomings, Margerie got Malcolm working, and got him to persuade A.B. to advance money for a typewriter. She also made him write to Carol Phillips for the manuscript of *Under the Volcano*, to

Ann Watkins for *In Ballast*, and to Whit Burnett for *The Lighthouse*. Meantime he got to work on *The Last Address*, and what short stories he had to hand.

News of Malcolm's dash to the border reached Arthur via Parks, who said he suspected a woman was involved and recommended his money be cut to break the romance. Maurice, egged on by Malcolm, wrote to Arthur directly, saying that he was now his son's guardian and that Malcolm had decided to stay in Canada under his control until able to enlist, and urging that his allowance be sent directly to him.[10] This plan was foiled when A.B. informed Parks that they disapproved of Maurice as a guardian for Malcolm.

For respectability's sake, Margerie informed Penny Singleton that she was getting married and would not be returning. But she worried also about her reputation with her family, so Malcolm wrote to her mother saying that he truly loved Margerie, wanted to marry her as soon as he could and would put off enlistment until the last possible moment.[11] Meanwhile, Arthur's lawyer wrote to Parks stressing that for Malcolm to come home would present his client with 'an even greater source of anxiety and danger to his family than at present'. Whatever its psychological basis, his unpredictable behaviour was due to indiscipline. His father would welcome his enlisting in Canada and would provide him with a regular allowance. Later perhaps he could see his parents again and rehabilitate himself in their eyes. If he could be encouraged to enlist, he suggested with unconscious irony, this would be 'a permanent solution of the real difficulty.'[12]

But Lowry saw another way out of his trap: his old friend and enemy Aiken. In a spirit of reconciliation, he wrote appealing to him 'to save my life'. He said that since seeing him he had written one book at least, which he thought mature, *The Lighthouse Invites the Storm*, but wanted to consult him before publishing it.[13] He regretted their strained relationship in Mexico and the subsequent silence between them. The Aikens were just back in Massachusetts, having fled Jeake's House and the war in England. Despite being broke and homeless himself, Aiken reacted generously, seeing that his old student was in a jam. He spoke to his agent, Bernice Baumgarten (who showed interest in him), and then offered to approach the Old Man on his behalf, adding, 'Avoid the army my dear fellow – nothing in it,'[14] an understandable sentiment from the man who had successfully argued to a US Draft Board in 1917 that poets served their countries best by not fighting.[15]

A. B. Carey and MacLean offered their 'permanent solution' also –

cut him off and make him stand on his own feet.[16] This idea was relayed to Liverpool. The reply was that if this persuaded him to enlist, then fine, but if not and there was a danger of his being deported back to England, then no. The trap Lowry was in was decidedly uncomfortable. Maurice, receiving just $15 a week from Lowry's money to board him, became unpleasant. Margerie said he pawned the typewriter so they had to hire another, which they could ill afford. He treated her like a servant and they were reduced to one meal a day. In November, Malcolm wrote to John Buchan, Lord Tweedsmuir, then Canada's Governor-General, asking, as a fellow writer, for help. When Tweedsmuir sent $50, Carey insisted they go downtown to cash the cheque, and then persuaded him to put it all on a horse, 'a sure bet', which lost. When he returned, broke and despondent, Margerie took him for a walk.

It was not quite dark and they walked for sixteen blocks while Lowry's state gradually worsened. Suddenly, on a street corner, he got into a wild, despairing rage, ran down the street, and disappeared. He had never done this with her before, and she had no idea how to react. Unable to find him, she returned for Maurice, but he began vilifying Malcolm, demanding to know why she did not leave him. Finally, late that evening, in the rain, she set off to search for him again. In a poor part of town she found the spot where he had bolted. Following the direction he had taken she came to a dingy old house. She felt sure he was there, and so he was. It was a whorehouse, and inside she found him lying drunk on a filthy bed. He had sold his clothes for liquor and had only his shorts left. He seemed in such bad shape, frozen and shivering, that she climbed in beside him to keep him warm, staying there all night.

Next morning, full of remorse and despair, he said, 'What can I do? I'm finished!' But she told him, 'We must go back to Maurice.' He protested but finally agreed. She threatened the owner of the whorehouse with the police, and he found Malcolm some clothes. Finally she got him out dressed in an old pair of shoes and threadbare suit. He then said he must have a beer, but they had no money, so he begged in the street for ten cents for a glass of beer while Margerie stood by. They returned to Carey's, where she nursed him out of his fit. After that they referred to Maurice as 'Papa Vulture' and began looking for a way of getting free of him.

In early November, one of A.B.'s young men, Thomas Rafferty, came calling, and reported to Parks that Maurice would not let him speak to Malcolm alone and was trying to supersede him as guardian.

He found Lowry in good health and spirits, but vitriolic when speaking of A.B. This, thought Rafferty, was due to frustration at being unable to return to 'an attachment' in LA. Maurice, said Rafferty, was encouraging this attitude and left a very unpleasant impression on him.[17] A.B., meantime, wrote to Parks, urging him against the greedy Maurice Carey and said that he would do all he could to ensure Malcolm enlisted.[18]

By now Lowry, however, was determined to avoid the war. On 8 November he wrote a careful letter to Parks hoping to put the matter to rest. He had been working towards enlisting, he said, when they had stopped taking recruits altogether. He had decided to carry on with his work and see what happened. He had already sent off three stories to his publishers and was just finishing another. But he was anxious to get *Under the Volcano* back from Carol Phillips and asked him to go to Long Beach to recover it personally if necessary. He confessed that, thinking he might be leaving for England, he had promised her twenty-five per cent of the profits, but he should say there would be nothing unless he got it and completed it.[19] At the same time he sent her an SOS asking for the MS and notes in whatever state they were, so he could prepare it for the publisher before going off to an uncertain future. He would not forget his promise to her, nor her share of the book's proceeds, but now he had the chance to work on it and publishers were eager to see it.[20]

In a long, rambling letter to Aiken, he opened his heart and appealed to him fervently for help. His situation was such 'a complexity of melancholy opposites', he wrote, that he would not attempt to explain it, then promptly did so. Upright citizen and Oxford Grouper, A. B. Carey, 'a dung-cart except for the straw which is in his feet', had held back his money, accused him of mortal sin, and betrayed him to US Immigration. Now he had fallen into equally dangerous hands. Maurice Carey, apparently sympathetic at first, had become intolerable. In return for secrecy from A. B. Carey and one meal a day and a bed if they were lucky, they were allowed $2 a week from the pittance he received from his guardians. The house was a bedlam which included a family of six, a loudspeaker, 'a howling wind which rages through the house all day,' twins, a nurse, and a fourteen-year-old boy, a dog, a canary, and a Cambridge-educated Hindu timber merchant who slept in the basement on a woodpile which he hoped one day to be paid for.[21] Bed was the only place where they found either pleasure or protection. Maurice had got them over a barrel, and was hoping to get control of his money. Margerie was now in Canada illegally and they feared she might be deported. He could not take work there, and the army was taking no more recruits.

He pleaded with Aiken to intercede with Arthur to get him to Boston, and proposed a set of persuasive reasons to use on him, stressing that he was unhappy and alone in an abominable climate and desperate to finish work for which it was urgent he return to America. He was in Canada against his will and had been refused enlistment there. He was willing to enlist if allowed to earn his fare with Aiken in Boston, but would at least like to regain his father's friendship first. If they decided to cut him off, why not give him enough to live on for a while in Boston to give him a chance of succeeding on his own?

Indirectly he continued to placate Aiken over what had happened between them and Jan. Margerie must be kept secret from the family, who would disapprove of his remarrying, but Arthur could be told that at least in Boston he would be thousands of miles from Jan, of whom he, Aiken, had disapproved from the beginning and whom he had continually warned him against.

> The only thing that ever went wrong with our . . . relationship was that you knew I was fundamentally unhappy with her, that I knew that you knew, that I resented that knowledge, and therefore took it out upon you practically to the point of betraying our friendship . . . I know now that all you really desired was my happiness: so, no Jan.

Margie, however, was just the kind of gal he had always wanted him to have, but he could not marry till the divorce became final and he wanted to avoid enlistment until then. He had arranged for his poems and *In Ballast* to go to Bernice Baumgarten, and would soon send *The Last Address* which was, 'among other things, about a man's hysterical identification with Melville'.[22] He enquired cryptically about 'the voyage that never ends' – alluding to the multi-layered novel they had discussed at Jeake's House and on the ship from Spain in 1933. It was a phrase he annexed as the title for the linked series of novels he had conceived of in Mexico, where *Under the Volcano* was linked back to *The Last Address* and *In Ballast*, an idea which would eventually evolve into an expanded version of Aiken's original concept.

Meanwhile, he said, he was heading for a Kafkaesque situation. Maurice, due to war injuries, had gone crazy and was threatening eviction. Should that happen they would be destitute in a strange, hostile and ugly country, without a home or friends. He enquired about a possible advance for a novel about his situation to be called *Night Journey Across the Sea*. As usual, he seemed to think that fictionalizing a disintegrating situation could somehow render it less threatening.

Aiken, now settled in South Dennis on Cape Cod, promised to write as ingeniously as possible on his behalf to the Old Man. But despite his readiness to help Lowry get to Boston, he expressed qualms about the prospect to Ed Burra.

> The idea is à la Granada, that I should again hold the purse-strings, and dispense ruin by the drachma or gram . . . I wouldn't, to tell the truth, do it at all if the old thing didn't sound so really down and out and (?) suicidal. Well, we shall see. I shall try to house them in Boston, if he does come, I think – I prefer a little distance.[23]

By the end of November he had Arthur's reply. Not only had he, too, been getting distressing letters *from* Malcolm, but also *about* him, and he had been a source of great anxiety for the past two years. He had been settled in Vancouver well away from the temptation of drink, where he could regain his self-mastery and now possibly join up. But since he found the place and people uncongenial, the army was no longer recruiting and he wished to be with Aiken, he agreed to the move to Boston. However, Malcolm might not be allowed into America, and getting money out of England was not easy. He stressed that Malcolm's troubles were of his own making, and if he did not reform and begin to produce the literary work of which he had heard so much but seen so little, he would cut him off.

Lord Tweedsmuir had recommended Lowry to the editor of the *Vancouver Daily Province*, which in December printed two articles by him. 'Hollywood and the War' shows how familiar he was with the City of Dreams and with film-making, and mentions actors like Charles Boyer being called to active service in Europe, as Laruelle is in the *Volcano*. If Hollywood was an unreal place of contradictions, he wrote, had the world not now become 'the ultimate UNreality'? In 'The Real Mr Chips', he reflected on the film and the fact that at the time Balgarnie retired, Robert Donat, who played Chips in the film, was starting out at the Cambridge Festival Theatre. Coincidences like this, he wrote, had a self-justifying logic all of their own.[24] Whatever small fees he got for these efforts were the first from his writing since the modest unearned advance from Whit Burnett to work on *The Last Address* three years earlier.

To oblige Tweedsmuir, the *Province*'s editor, McTavish, wrote in support of him to the US Consul in Vancouver. With such powerful friends it seemed he would have no trouble getting back to America, especially now that his father had approved his joining Aiken. If he could not get back, he would try to go East, somewhere like Montreal. In any case, with two of his manuscripts in Aiken's hands, he could enjoy the benefit of an honest, shrewd critical opinion of his work, something he had been lacking for the past two years. Aiken wrote that Bernice Baumgarten could not make head or tail of *In Ballast*, which she thought uncommercial. But her agency were 'pretty hardboiled' and 'anti-highbrow', so he should not pay too much attention to their judgement. For himself, giving a quick first opinion,

> It looks too confusedly elaborate, too circumambulatingly metaphysical and ego-freighted, to be effective. My own influence has been bad, as in the chapter on unwritten, partly written, letters . . . I think it's time you cut yourself adrift from all these here ghostly doppelgangers and projections and identifications and let loose some of your natural joy in swiftness and goodness and love and simplicity – put your complexity into reverse – and celebrate the sun. Some of your latter poems go that way – though your metrics *is* queer, blimey yes.

But Lowry was far too engrossed in the *Volcano*, on his journey through the dark night of the soul, to be able to take this kind of advice yet. As to the poems, Aiken betrayed his own fierce prejudices. He had been too influenced by 'the Complex Boys,' the 'adolescent audens spenders with all their pretty little dexterities, their negative safety, their indoor marxmanship'. What was wanted was 'something with a little more gush [illegible] guts, juices, blood, love, sunsets and sunrises, moons, stars, roses, – for god's sake let's let in the whole romantic shebang again, it's high time.'[25] His joy at the impending death of 'committed' poetry was clear, something probably not unwelcome to Lowry, who told Margerie he considered himself primarily a poet, and it was as a poet that he most wished to shine.

Anxious to assure Aiken how much he prized his friendship, he replied immediately. The copy he had of *In Ballast*, he wrote, was the one he had so liked in Mexico, and, although he had revised it as he had suggested, that revision was lost and he wanted to rewrite it again. As to his new novel, he felt he would approve of it. 'It takes the same things to town which you take in your general criticism of me and is the most mature thing I have done.' He complained about working in a vacuum and asked for more constructive advice, especially technical advice, on his work from 'the old maestro'. He needed to get something out soon so had to make the best of what he had. 'Telling me to throw away the whole boiling is, I submit, more moral, than technical advice. Ah, the whirligig of taste!' But he could reflect that, unlike some of his contemporaries, he had not taken up 'a position', which might now be his salvation as a writer: 'History has already made much of what I admired or pretended to admire during the last half decade quite senseless but since I *did* pursue a more or less middle course I think there is quite a lot I can restore, from the ruin in which I find myself . . .' As for 'Moonlight and Roses', even Aiken might find it difficult to write about the primrose at the old river's brim while living in fear of his life 'at the bottom of a stinking well in Vancouver!'[26]

With the prospect of Lowry turning up on his doorstep, Aiken wrote a stern fatherly letter to him expressing his misgivings.

> I don't want again to be accused, as in 1933, of being indifferent to your welfare, and only putting up with you for the Old Man's money. To hell with that . . . So now . . . No secret drinkings round the corner, eh? No disgracings of us with our friends, no scenes: and above all no continuous argument as to the amount of drink allowed: I'm to be the boss . . . a good brother: that's all: but let's have that agreed.[27]

He hoped that when he came it would be with good intentions: 'clean fingernails, a pure heart, a clear head, and prepared to be helpful and to work.'

On Christmas Eve Lowry composed a careful reply to this cautionary note.

> You probably expected me to arrive with a giraffe on either arm, to come howling and spewing into South Dennis and collapse in the Congregational Church. Then, later, the one shoe in the bathtub, the surreptitious vomit under the piano, the ukulele and the fractured skull.

But, he assured him, he was now genuinely 'striving for a Better Thing'. If he wished, he could, like Parks, take the OM's money and send him to a far-off place out of harm's way, though an occasional visit would be welcome – he had no desire to die off stage, like Mercutio. He reiterated his filial feelings, assuring him that his earlier Oedipal behaviour with its ungrateful accusations was now in the past. He had nothing to fear about his drinking or irresponsibility.[28] To this Aiken replied cheerfully that they looked forward to seeing them both and thought that at first they should all live together in Boston. He was obviously encouraged by Lowry's reaffirmation of poetry and his willingness to go along with his new mood. 'We'll all be showing them . . . a bengal light of a re-divivus yet. Up the moonlight! Up the everlasting rose! Up the sunset!'[29]

Arthur told Parks to apply for Malcolm to re-enter the US. This was duly done and Parks said he expected a result from Washington within a couple of months. The prospect of getting off the bottom of his 'stinking well' must have heartened Lowry, who now composed a piece of comic verse called 'Where Did that One Go 'Erbert?' for the Vancouver *Province*, a witty reply to a poem by A. P. Herbert, lampooning the pre-war Left, reprinted in the paper from *Punch*. It was his satirical farewell to the committed thirties and the 'indoor Marxmen' (he lifted Aiken's phrase) who might have been wrong about Stalin but who were now joining up to fight Hitler.

For Malcolm and Margerie, 1940 began in a state of uncertainty and unease. Malcolm wrote to Aiken thanking him for his help with the OM, but adding that his situation was grim; he was in the clutches of Oxford Group 'bastardos' and a virtual prisoner. When things started hotting up in Europe what his duty would be was unclear. But he would not be caught off balance by this war – if others were, too bad – but since he seemed for the time being 'a creature of luck', he was determined to get the freedom he needed to finish the work before that luck ran out. Parks had written that his family wanted him to enter America through Blaine, but he preferred Montreal, which would put him as close to him for supervision as he was now to Parks in LA. Getting free of Parks and Carey was important, as was the freedom to finish his work and make Margerie happy in what time he had left. But he was still eager to shine and report on his 'thrilling achievements' to Evelyn. 'I think that nothing in the world would give the OM and the mater a bigger bang than to have me have a few books accepted in the States in the coming year.'[30]

As important for him as returning to the US was the arrival in mid-January of the manuscript of *Under the Volcano*. Parks had finally done him one favour, going out to Long Beach and retrieving it from Carol Phillips. Now he had his manuscript, he and Margerie plunged straight into working on what he had every expectation would be a masterpiece.

He sent a carbon copy to Tweedsmuir, who wrote an encouraging reply which he showed around proudly as evidence of official recognition of his literary talent.

Deceiving Arthur about Margerie made Aiken unhappy and he urged Lowry to tell him the truth and ask permission to bring her to Boston for inspection.

> Also, and this is sort of hard to say, my poor Malc, but I think I'd better say it now – viz., you know, prolonged drinking *does* rot one's honesties, kind of – if you'll forgive me saying so you'd already become somewhat oblique when I saw you in Mexico – I gather from Parks you've since got worse, though of course I take it you're now very much better again: but the point is, I shall want to be shown.[31]

Stung by this, and sure that Parks was feeding Aiken lies about him, Lowry composed another of his extended self-justifying epistles. On the face of it, he wrote, there was no reason why the OM should not know about Margerie, but it would get back to A. B. Carey, who thought passionate love between a man and a woman was evil and who would put a dishonest light on it all. Parks would support Carey, who was a political cheat, a licentious sentimentalist, and a pervert who had contracted VD, from whoring or from boys, while married with children. He was not prepared to put Margerie's fate into the hands of such a hypocrite. Nor had he ever thought of Parks as anything but a crook to be outwitted. Compared to these two dyed-in-the-wool villains, he said, even Maurice Carey seemed like a good guy.

There followed a long account of his troubles in Mexico and LA. That 'little communist' Alfred Miller had started it, and others had tried to defame him to Arthur to extort money from him, calling him a communist (he was only ever 'the mildest pink'), saying he had diseases and had committed crimes. Many of his troubles as well as his wisest decisions were due to drink, but he was not, as Parks suggested, allergic to it. And upset by the charge of obloquy in Mexico, he reminded Aiken that he had done his best to accommodate him and Mary, had found him a more reasonable divorce lawyer, and helped send them off on their new life together. Also he was much more ill than was thought, having had something like infantile paralysis. The OM was told he had 'both epilepsy and WORSE.' Falsehoods about him had come from Jan, Parks, and a man called Mensch who he had helped out of a terrible jam at his own expense. Stories of him being in trouble with the police through drink were lies, and he could prove it. If Arthur found out about Margerie he would probably cut him off. Since they had tried with all their souls to make their relationship fine and honest, it would be a great pity if it were 'smeared by convention'.

More important than any of this was the fact that work on the *Volcano* had become a communal thing between them and they worked together on it day and night. He was, he implied, playing the Consul to her Yvonne.

> I feel that it is the first real book I've written. The certainty of war has let loose a hell of a lot of pent up energy and all played against the background of the false idealisms and abstractions of peace that we wasted our time with when we should have been thinking about living . . . All this is making for a real drama, something possibly first rate, within its limits. I'm more than glad I never got a chance to finish it without her because we too seem to be playing our parts within the drama.

In any case, he did not see how he could possibly finish it without her now they had introduced an entirely new character which was her idea.[32] Anyway, the OM was funny about marriage, having tried unsuccessfully to sabotage Stuart's, nor was he the first to have spies put on him, the same had been done to Stuart. He would never understand him remarrying. Now Aiken had the power to preserve it or wield the scissors he had once predicted he would have to use on him and Jan, but he swore there would be no 'dishonestness round corners, no drunken sailors smuggled in from the Navy Yard at night and above all no communistic talk under the banana trees.'[33]

Fear of being conscripted and the desire to complete at least one fine piece of literature in his life gave him a strong sense of urgency. His normally slow and painful method of composing gave way to a frantic race to complete *Under the Volcano* in time. Writing to Mary Aiken, Margerie told her that from the moment they woke till the moment they went to sleep they never stopped talking about it or writing; they were both thoroughly gripped by the mood and motion of the book. 'Malcolm is writing with flying pen and a gleam in his eye and turning out work that anybody would be proud of.' He had already written thirty thousand words of 'ebb and flow of stark narrative' unlike anything he had done before. If he were interrupted he might lose the feeling, enthusiasm and flow. Obviously the most important thing in his life was his work.[34] At the end of January he wrote to Tweedsmuir asking him to put in a good word for him with Washington, but whether he did is not known because eleven days later he died.

Aiken was both amused and nonplussed by his long letter of self-justification. 'What a deluge of Kafka-like elucidation, explanation, analysis, qualification, apology, reproach, everything!' he wrote, adding wisely, 'Every man his own Laocoon [*sic*] group, complete with the serpent.' 'The now quite alarmingly hyper-trophied Legend of the Lowry', which had been built up alternately by the Old Man, Parks, Margerie, and now Maurice Carey (who had written him a 'cracking' letter about him), out of what truths or lies he knew not, made no sense at all: 'it's the goddamnest farrago of inconsistencies I ever did see, and as hollow as a cream puff.'[35] To Aiken, the matter of his coming to Boston was settled, and although the final decision on his re-entry had still not come by the middle of February, Arthur wrote offering him $150 a month for Malcolm's supervision, apparently pleased that he saw some good in his son. Malcolm himself was keen to assure Aiken that his novel was being written in the new spirit which he thought should prevail in literature. 'It has blood, guts, rapine, murder, teeth, and, for your entertainment, even some moonlight and roses. And a couple of horses.'[36]

Doubtless pleased to have won at least one convert, Aiken wrote more flatteringly about the work Lowry had sent him: 'I re-read most of the *Lighthouse*, and with much increased interest, respect, and delight. If you could haul out some of the auden-esques, which are obvious and usually detachable by the unit, I think a small book might be put together, and good.' He had sent everything (*In Ballast*, *Lighthouse*, and *Last Address*) to Robert Linscott at Houghton Mifflin, thinking that his 'hard-boiled practical eye' might be useful. To date he had replied only that he thought that *The Last Address* was 'tainted with genius' but unpublishable, and thought he should use his talents more usefully, but was reading the poems with enjoyment.[37]

Two days later Lowry reported to Aiken that he had been refused re-entry to the US. 'The axe has fallen,' he wrote. His refusal had come, he was sure, because Parks and Carey had applied for his re-entry through Blaine. He could re-apply on 23 September, a year on from his last attempt to enter, but thought his chances were poor unless the war ended, which seemed unlikely. Now, however, it was all the more important that he finish his work.[38] Margerie added a frantic PS: a drunken Maurice had attacked her the night before, then turned on Malcolm, who, though wild because he had hit her, restrained himself knowing that he had a bad heart. Now a bruised right hand made it difficult to write. They had to leave to save themselves, and were thinking of going to Montreal, come what may.[39] Whether Maurice's drunken fury was because he, too, was disappointed that they were unable to leave soon for the States, she did not say.

This was followed by what Lowry called a 'self-conscious Wail of a letter'. They were not only writing *Under the Volcano*, they were living smack down in it, he wrote. He thought that if they dashed to Montreal, it could be squared with Arthur through Evelyn. Their needs were minimal – just enough to live on and work, but he could not work without Margerie, who was immeasurably helpful in cutting back his literary excesses. She had become an inextricable part of his work. Such a dependence might not be a good thing, but it definitely worked in their case, even though working in the dark. Parts of the book, he claimed, bore comparison to Gogol and Kafka, and together they could probably produce not just one book but a large body of work stamped with an individual imprint.

The tendency towards giantism, already seen in Mexico, had re-emerged. But how could he explain such vaulting ambition to Arthur, after so many dismal failures? Practical independence was his first priority, and he needed to take with him 'only . . . that necessary part of my psychic turmoils which are, to put it bluntly, saleable'. There would follow a rewritten *In Ballast*, *Lighthouse* and *Last Address* in accordance with Aiken's suggestions, a number of short stories and a new novel, *Night Journey Across the Sea* about his experiences in Canada. Their situation was desperate, he said, and he urged Aiken to butter up the OM further to free them from the 'Ibsenish A.B.' and 'Dostoievskish M. Carey'. They had had no square meal since Christmas, lived on a diet of bread, soggy potatoes and watery stew, and were allowed only one lukewarm bath between them every three weeks. Davenport, he complained, had been silent since last phoning him in Cuernavaca three years before, and he had heard that Grieg was on military service in Lapland, 'sent there as a punishment for defending Russia in the Arbeiderbladet: serve him right, perhaps; but what an ending to *In Ballast* . . . !'[40] On another haunting note, he had learned that *Pyrrhus* had been torpedoed and sunk with the loss of eight lives off Cape Finisterre, near to where Aiken had had his inspirational black dream in 1933.

In response to this, Aiken cabled Arthur informing him of the six-month delay and urging Malcolm's immediate transfer to Montreal, adding: 'Believe Vancouver environment unsuitable/accept full responsibility and arrangement agreeable yourself.'[41] Lowry meantime wrote Parks a conciliatory letter, blaming A. B. Carey for his failing to get re-entry to the US, but saying that he did not blame him for leaving him in the Oxford Grouper's clutches. As *Time* had said of Thomas Dewey, 'he was a man impossible to dislike until you got to know him well.' However his mother approved his going to Aiken, and it seemed senseless to enlist until his work was completed. He was now disinclined to drink, despite having more opportunity in Vancouver than in LA. So it was not for its dryness that he loathed the city.

> It is more the stultifyingness, the boringness, the Oxford Group, the women, whom I shall never forget you referring to as looking as though they had sore feet, the fact that I have been working hard – 45,000 words since January – and that both I, and the book, badly need a change of scenery – that puts Vancouver in the dog house with me.[42]

But Parks, stung by the charge that Vancouver was an unsuitable place for him, wrote to Arthur that he was reported sober and in good health there, and how could Aiken supervise him in Montreal, twelve hours by train from Boston? He advised against the move, saying he had in any case to obtain his re-entry permit through Blaine, where he was refused entry.

Under the Volcano, in Lowry's words, was rapidly reaching 'its last belch'. Evidently Margerie was already influencing it. The astronomy she had learned as a child from her mother she now taught Malcolm, who in turn passed it on to Yvonne (still the Consul's daughter, with much of Jan's sparkiness and character, while his wife, Priscilla, is absent in New York, having divorced him). As well as her stellar contribution, Margerie claimed credit for moving the chapter where Laruelle reflects on the death of the Consul (now called William Ames), from the end to the beginning, saying that nothing ought to happen in the book after the death of its protagonist. However, at this stage, it is Hugh with whom Lowry probably identified, and by and large the shape of the book remained unchanged by Lowry's high-speed frenetic rewriting. Some of the final book's celebrated passages are there, including the Consul's paean to the cantina in the early morning, the comic encounter with Quincey, the passage expressing disgust at Laruelle's nakedness, the scene on the Infernal Machine, the disturbing notice LE GUSTA

ESTE JARDÍN being misread by the Consul, and the final apocalyptic vision of the dying Consul as he falls into the gaping *barranca*. But connecting these oases of brilliance are long arid stretches of talk about books not always related to anything much. The novel is headed by a first chapter set three years later, after the outbreak of the World War, in which Laruelle, worried at the prospect of being conscripted, has a strange nightmare where its various themes parade themselves before his floating consciousness. The idea that the future can somehow alter the past is mentioned, and if, as Lowry liked to say, quoting Bergson, time is just a device for preventing everything happening at once, then the uncertainties of time are well represented.

On 7 March, Aiken sent the glum news that Arthur had ordained he must remain in Vancouver for six months and reapply to enter the US at Blaine. He thought this ridiculous and wrote asking Parks *who* said that a person refused entry must reapply through that same place? Seeing \$150 a month slipping away he hinted at having the case reopened in Washington. In any case, there was no reason why Malcolm should not go to Montreal until it was necessary to re-enter through Blaine. He wrote also to Arthur stressing the real interest in Malcolm's work from publishers, and urged Malcolm to get the novel finished *quam celerum*, keep up his spirits and look forward to 'at least six months of genial juice-swapping in Boston'.[43]

The prospect of Aiken taking over as Lowry's guardian did not appeal to Parks, who wrote asking him not to approach Washington before consulting him. He then wrote to Liverpool saying that he was convinced that Vancouver was good for Malcolm and that his complaints were really about being under restraint and not about the place. Vancouver was an extremely pleasant city, with a fine climate; he was living in a place of his choice, working hard and staying sober; in Montreal he could deteriorate. In any case if he was unhappy, it was his own fault. He was still unfairly blaming A. B. Carey. 'I rather feel that it will be good discipline and good training for [him] to have to suffer the consequences of his own acts.' And Rafferty had reported that his suffering was by no means acute. He asked that he be sent more money before it became completely impossible. Arthur readily complied, happy to continue paying to keep his son away from England, home and duty.

But Malcolm had not given up, and sent one of his long, self-justificatory letters to Arthur beginning, 'There is a side of the moon always turned away from the earth, and this is like an attempt to get in touch from that quarter.'[44] This was, he said, an important letter for them both. Vancouver was not what it seemed. He hinted at something 'dark', probably homosexuality, in one of his guardians (Carey). Parks had left him with people he didn't know himself. A.B. had confessed to having been to brothels while married and contracting gonorrhoea before coming to God. Was this a fit man to take charge of him? It was humiliating to be in the hands of such people. He had felt abandoned and had despaired, but he had stuck to his guns in spite of this uncongenial environment. The depth of his unrepentant loathing for Carey is seen in a sardonic dedication scribbled on a draft of *The Last Address* when his old enemy died a short time later.

> Dedicated to the eternal damnation of Archibald Carey of Vancouver, British Columbia, pseudo-demigogue and professional hypocrite, after his long unpleasant and painful illness, with love.

He was anxious to assure Arthur that, despite the squalid conditions at Maurice's, he had *worked* and not resorted to drink. He hoped they could bury the past, and re-establish the sincere and decent relationship they had once had – which would, he knew, make his mother happy. Just in case this would not wash, he added for good measure: 'I am yelling at you over a thousand miles of mine-infested Atlantic and 4 thousand miles of land. *I am co-operating with you. Will you help? Drink, follies, are a thing of the past. (This is the last chance.)*' The things Arthur wanted could not be achieved without a few changes being made. To prove that he was working, he enclosed his newspaper pieces and his prized letter from Tweedsmuir, who, he said, had made contacts for him in the East which he should have the freedom to use.[45]

But this last try for Arthur's support against his guardians failed. The Old Man wrote to Aiken on 3 April saying that the delay over Malcolm's entry to the US, though regrettable, was his own fault for disobeying orders and acting impulsively. He was not convinced that Vancouver was unsuitable for him; that was his own one-sided version. Perhaps it was time for him to suffer the consequences of his wilfulness, and he hoped Aiken would not interfere with Parks's efforts for him in Washington. For Aiken, that was the end of that, bad news on top of a poor reception for his new novel, *The Conversation*, which, he said, was 'being peed on, crapped on, spat on, sneezed on, coughed on, ejaculated on, died and rotted on, by all the critics from the Nation up.'[46] Yet another sad failure for Aiken.

Now Arthur gave his reply to his son's letter from 'the wrong side of the moon'. He was sorry he found himself living in lunar darkness, he said, but he did not put him there. Yet 'when you do manage to turn to me, as you often do, you get help, don't you?' His complaints against A. B. Carey he thought both unjust and exaggerated. If he was standing firm in a hostile environment, that was what we all had to do – take responsibility and make the best of our lives. We should not blame others, nor use the too easy excuse of saying that we could not help ourselves because this or that childhood tendency or experience went unchecked or uncorrected. Hard work was the only way to accomplish anything. No one – only circumstance – compelled him to stay in Vancouver. These were hard times and he was costing him a good deal of money he could ill afford; a move to Montreal could cost even more – he could go to Boston to enjoy Aiken's help in due course. He was pleased with the articles, and said he should be proud of the letter from Tweedsmuir. If he stuck to his guns all would be well.[47]

Following this burst of correspondence Lowry relaxed somewhat. There was now the hope of escaping from Maurice, who announced his intention to rent his home from 1 June. He wrote to Aiken about progress on his new opus. He was on the last chapter of the *Volcano*, 'a strange book' which made 'an odd but splendid din'. For once he had written a book which was not parasitic in some way on another or on Aiken's work, except for some of his wisecracks and political opinions expressed in Mexico. Clearly he felt the weight of his plagiaristic past and the need to warn Aiken before he stumbled across his own words in the book. He could not afford another Rascoe. He reminded him that they had talked once of doing a book about Mexico together but, apart from the wisecracks, the 'character' was not him.

However, he needed to be absolved in advance for any 'coincidences'. The trouble was that the character in question was pushed into a ravine, which might be construed as 'strange psychological goings on'.

> No, Conrad, the truth is the guy who goes down the ravine, disguised in dark glasses and a false beard, is partly myself, partly the little ghost of what was once bad between us, bad about me. There is also a bit of Margie's father, a bit of the guy who introduced Margie and I, and a bit of you, to account for the good parts. And of course the wisecracks the opinions (and how right most of them were!) an incident with my cat . . . I had to make the ghost an amusing fellow after all. But . . . I just wished . . . to ask you sincerely to regard my

> apparent similarities or nuances with a fatherly twinkle . . . Also . . . damn it, there *are* some similarities I can't help. The conflicts of divorce, conflicts of soul torn between England and America, the setting of Mexico itself, all these things are mine too; my anguishes and such, while again, my ancient doppelganger, I am, deep down in my psyche . . . damned like you.

The book, he told Aiken, was 'a gesture on the part of a grateful pupil to his master'. Every scene had been under the 'Aiken microscope', and it was the sort of book he would have wanted him to write.[48] Although they had got nowhere with the Old Man, he felt that in the efforts he had been making on his behalf something had been resolved between them. Aiken was intrigued, and wrote that he looked forward to his portrait of 'Aiken the old medusa' and his death in the *barranca* with his usual sang-froid. 'It seems a logical end! My portrait of you in *A Heart for the Gods of Mexico* (shat upon by G. Greene) was more kindly, I suspect!'[49] His next portrait of Lowry in his autobiographical *Ushant* was to prove less kind, and he did later accuse Lowry of failing to acknowledge the use of his 'wisecracks'.

The end of the book was proving stubborn, yet Lowry's sense of achievement was evident and he began to consider sending it to publishers. The extraordinary thing was that he should consider that something written so fast was ready to send off. He told Margerie's mother they had completed 100,000 words since January, and, no doubt inspired by all this literary energy, Margerie had completed a detective novel begun in Los Angeles. A pattern of companionate authorship and parallel writing had been established, the fortunes of which were to be distinctly rocky over the coming years.

In mid-April, he saw a story by James Stern in *Esquire*, and learned that he now lived in New York. He promptly wrote to him with news of his chaotic past, his new love, the encircling Oxford Group, and the novel. Exaggerating as usual, he said that besides *Under the Volcano*, he had three other novels not yet sold, as well as a long short story, *The Last Address*, his best piece of writing, except for some parts of his new novel. He asked him if, for a percentage, he could place it and his poems with *Esquire*. Stern was delighted to hear from Lowry, saying that Cape had been asking after him recently in New York. Having once been at Sandhurst, he said, he was uninterested in going to war, and was applying for US citizenship. He was doubtful about placing his poems and noted that in one, 'The Quartermaster', which he admired, 'You have a line there which I wrote in Africa 15 years ago . . . Odd.' He was amazed that Lowry had written so much and published so little. Novels, not poems or short stories, were the thing; but *The Last Address* was too long for any magazine except perhaps *Harper's Bazaar*.[50]

Margerie had completed typing the revised *Volcano*, but Lowry was still not satisfied. By the end of April he told Aiken it needed just two or three more weeks of polishing – that two or three weeks finally extended to two months before he considered it was ready to send off. Nevertheless, he was full of confidence. It was, he announced, something not unfavourably comparable with Kafka's *The Trial*. The idea of coming East was still on the cards. He had heard that he could apply to enter the US at any place he chose, thus refuting Parks's claim that he must apply through Blaine. That obstacle no longer existed, therefore, and with Carey planning to let his house, some change of address was necessary anyway.[51]

Being in touch with old literary friends was as much a tonic for him as having all but completed his novel. It gave him the stimulus to reflect on his art and where it might be leading him over the years ahead. He agreed with Stern about the greater importance of the novel over the short story, there being – for the true short-story writer – no satisfactory 'design-governing posture'. Nevertheless he thought that a good short-story writer was in the best position to write the best kind of novel – 'the shortish one perfect in itself, and without being full of inventories (like Joyce) or poems (like Faulkner) or conjunctions (like Hemingway).' He put forward a plan for a story cycle much like his plan for a set of connected novels.

> It is possible to compose a satisfactory work of art by the simple process of writing a series of good short stories, complete in themselves, with the same characters, interrelated, correlated, good if held up to the light, watertight if held upside down, but full of affects and dissonances that are impossible in a short story, but nevertheless having its purity of form, a purity that can only be achieved by the born short story writer.

(No doubt he had in mind the long-abandoned short story collection, *So We Live Forever Taking Leave*.) And the best kind of novel, he wrote, was 'something that is bald and winnowed like Sibelius, and that makes an odd but splendid din, like Bix Beiderbecke.'[52]

While writing to Stern on 7 May he got news from his father that the Government had stopped all funds going abroad, so added a frantic PS urging Stern to try placing his poems with *Esquire* immediately. He also had a story called 'June 30, 1934' (a rewrite of 'Metal') which could be ready in days. Neither he nor Margerie could work in Canada, and so did not quite know where the next meal was coming from. 'We progress from *Manon Lescaut* to *Crime and Punishment* to – possibly, shall we say? – "Two years as a scab lavatory attendant in Saskatchewan." '[53] The halting of funds meant that any change of residence was out of the question, but Arthur promised to try to borrow money from friends in America to keep him going. If he could justify his continued faith in him, he would arrange for $100 a month if possible. Once he had proof that he was capable of living a normal life he would try to get him to Montreal until he might return to the US.

On 10 May the British Government collapsed following the fall of the Low Countries and Norway, and a new coalition government under Churchill took over. The European war had taken a distinctly grim turn. Nordahl Grieg had escaped to England in romantic circumstances, and Lowry's old Norwegian ship, *Fagervik*, was sunk in the Battle of Narvik. Despite this chaos, Arthur was still ready to help the son who had so hurt and disappointed him, and was now living miserably but safely in distant Canada.

In the middle of May, Malcolm and Margerie managed finally to give Maurice the slip. Lowry had convinced Rafferty and A. B. Carey that he could save money by moving into a room of his own – $15 a week for rent and $10 for food and expenses would do him, he said. To his delight they agreed, and since Maurice was about to lose his lease anyway, he made little fuss when he found them gone. Rafferty reported $140 left in the kitty, probably enough to last until Arthur got more funds from the US. The only outstanding bills were dental ones, and there was the matter of $7.50 because 'Mrs Maurice Carey is having her mattress and bedding fumigated'[54] – the result, one supposes, of Malcolm and Margerie being afforded a bath only once every three weeks.

They had been taken in by a family of British Israelites called Smith, at 1236 West 11th Avenue. J. D. Smith, a six-foot-six tall Vancouver building contractor, and his wife, were moved by their sad tale of persecution. 'You look like nice people,' said Smith, believing that they were married. 'Separate a man from his wife, how can this be. I'll protect you.' Compared to Maurice's attic, here was luxury; they had a room, a bath, and use of a small kitchen. When A.B. came to inspect,

Margerie was concealed in the cellar with her suitcases and the Smiths were approved as landlords. They worked every morning on the book and in the afternoons got away to the beach. Lowry wrote excitedly to Aiken that they had 'swung a fast one on A.B.' and that the final version of the *Volcano* was being typed, about which he had received an enthusiastic enquiry from Whit Burnett. (But despite his air of confidence, the book was to take a little longer to complete having, as he wrote Aiken later, 'protruded some unexpected peaks'.)[55] Nevertheless, he was resigned now to staying put. Probably he could offer them no further assistance except 'by letting your genius storm into our spirits from time to time in these strange hours . . . As Haarlem burns and Joe Venuti swings.'[56]

Still haunted by the threat of conscription, and with his novel almost complete, he wrote to Burton Rascoe, trying to make peace with one part of his turbulent past. Rascoe never replied, and always remained embittered, especially when years later Lowry achieved the literary distinction which had eluded him. In the same spirit, he wrote to Juan Fernando Márquez. He would be glad to know he had given up drinking, and thrown away that part of his mind which he should have done. He remembered all his kindness, including the white suit. If ever he needed help, his home (even if only his shadow), was his to share.[57]

While in Canada, two letters had come from Jan to which he replied only briefly. According to Margerie, he never talked about Jan for fear of hurting her, but in June she announced that she was coming to Vancouver and hoped they could get together for old time's sake. Margerie was furious and, she claimed, Malcolm told her to burn the letter. But Jan had also sent a copy of a story she had published, inviting his comments. Instead of congratulations, he replied harshly that until the divorce was final, and even until the end of the war, they must regard one another as enemies. The story was better than others of hers he had seen, he said, but then accused her of lifting the theme of the dying Indian from him, though her story was based on a wounded black she had seen on an LA streetcar. She thought his letter uncharacteristically bitter and noted that, unusually for him, it was dated, and her name misspelled on the envelope. Later she realized that Margerie was there and had probably composed it for him to sign.[58]

Malcolm now felt sure that Arthur trusted him and in future would deal with him personally.[59] What he most wanted was to publish and so justify himself to make up for the years of exile. He planned to send his novel to Burnett, though he knew that Linscott also wanted to see it. Ideally he wanted *The Lighthouse* published first, so he could dedicate it to Evelyn as promised. Aiken suggested he send Linscott a duplicate, informing him that Burnett had first refusal. In any case, 'His idea was to consider . . . the whole bolus together, with a view to a *general* notion of some kind.'[60] Lowry was most taken with 'the whole bolus' and promptly made the phrase his own.

Arthur had contrived to get further funds to Parks, and Malcolm urged him to hand them over and free him from supervision by Carey. The evacuation of Dunkirk and the impending fall of France had led to local recruiting offices reopening, but Rafferty reported that he now said he was ineligible for enlistment because of varicose veins, and anyway he wished to prove himself first by publishing a book. Parks then recommended that all funds be turned over to him, and that he open a bank account because with large amounts on him he was likely to be robbed or persuaded to part with it.

By 22 June, the newly revised *Under the Volcano* was sent off to Burnett with a long covering letter making great claims for its literary stature. In writing about his work Lowry was not at all inclined to be modest. He hoped that it might be compared not unfavourably with Kafka's *The Castle*, though he realized that such books were rarely profitable, and to sell at all their author needed to be persecuted or dead. However, his book did set out, by taking a dime-novel theme, to have a wider appeal.

> But I have also tried to invest it with a certain quality which 'The Castle' possessed: 'Inexhaustibility'. I hope this doesn't sound too pretentious . . . And I feel something more, that I have perhaps been writing this book, as it were, out of Europe's 'unconscious' . . . As the last scream of anguish of the consciousness of a dying continent, an owl of Minerva flying at evening, the last book of its kind, written by someone whose type and species is dead, even as a final contribution to English Literature itself, the final flaring up and howling, for all I know – and other things pretentious – this book, written against death and in an atmosphere of total bankruptcy of spirit, might have some significance beyond the ordinary.[61]

He also enclosed his letter from Lord Tweedsmuir. Meanwhile, news came of the first daytime air raids on Britain. However, Lowry still expressed no great urge to return to defend his island home. He was far more concerned about new censorship laws banning US magazines from Canada, and that the *Volcano* might be affected. It was really an anti-Nazi book, he told Aiken, but various characters expressed frank opinions, and he was worried that he would not get another copy through the mail.[62]

Conscription in Canada was to be introduced on 19 August, so a sense of urgency now prevailed and he worked generously to help Margerie finish her mystery, *The Last Twist of the Knife*. To frustrate cross-border censorship, he wrote to Harold Matson, now with his own agency, asking him to handle *Under the Volcano* and his and Margerie's future work. They were, he said, 'a firm with a divided nature but a shared purpose'. With Rascoe in mind he assured him that 'It is "original" if you fear for past Websterian, not to say Miltonian, minor lacks of ethics on my part, nor is it drunkenly translated with a handpump out of the original Latvian. It is as much of my own as I know of.'[63] He had three books already written and presently Aiken had 'the whole bolus'. Aiken, who had just moved into a 'fine wreck of a house' in West Brewster on Cape Cod, now informed him that Gerald Noxon had arrived in Toronto from London, and sent on his address.

After sending off *The Last Twist of the Knife* on 12 August they decided to have a 'vacation'. Margerie saw a newspaper advertisement for a beach cottage at $10 a month at Dollarton, a deserted village north of Vancouver at Roche Point, where the Indian River enters Burrard Inlet. That same day she took the bus to the place, which stood on the water's edge, close to an Indian Reservation and a timber mill. She met the local storekeeper, Percy Cummins, who took her down the forest path to the rock-strewn shore below. The setting was idyllic, but the 'cottage' was a dilapidated old shack which she decided was unsuitable. A couple of days later they heard from Cummins of a better shack owned by a Scottish couple. When they saw it they immediately rented it for a month, and moved in on the 15th.

It was Lowry's first real house since Cuernavaca. There was one fairly large room, windows on three sides and a porch across the front; it was built just below the shoreline on high piles to withstand the sixteen-foot tides. There was a cook-stove with a stove pipe through the roof, a table with two chairs, a sink, and a bedroom with a small double bed. The rent was low because the shoreline belonged to the Harbour Board, so no city rates were payable. They had become squatters. Lowry named their new home 'The Wicket Gate', and they acquired a cat called 'Nunky'. Quite unexpectedly he had found his paradise garden. The world which had so disappointed him since childhood could have been a million miles away. If they wanted to conscript him they would have to find him first. Like William Blackstone, he had chosen to leave the oppressive purveyors of religion and 'civilization' to go, metaphorically at least, to live among the Indians.

CHAPTER XV

ERIDANUS: LOWRY'S WATERSIDE PARADISE 1941–1944

He was enchained by certain superstitious impressions in regard to the dwelling which he tenanted, and whence, for many years, he had never ventured forth.

EDGAR ALLAN POE, 'The Fall of the House of Usher'

There's nothing level in our cursed natures,
But direct villainy. Therefore, be abhorr'd
All feasts, societies, and throngs of men!

SHAKESPEARE, *Timon of Athens*, Act IV, Scene III)

Ironically, just as they found a suitably cheap home of their own their financial situation improved. Parks finally released the balance of funds held for Malcolm, who received $150 in August and $150 in September. He was to be paid $60 a month for the time being, with the promise of $100 a month as soon as more funds could be got to him. Aiken was at a loss to understand Lowry's sudden dramatic change of fortune. He was finally free of Parks and Carey, the novel he had always hoped to write was completed and he felt utterly confident of its success. He was living on an assured income with the woman he loved and so remote from Vancouver that they could live openly together without fear of discovery. Also he was well away from the world and its woes, and of course, from the dreaded recruiting office. And to cap all this, he found himself living in a setting of breath-catching beauty.

Dollarton originally housed lumber mill workers; many shacks along Roche Point had been jerry-built by the unemployed in the 1930s, and were now used as temporary homes by fishermen, or as weekend cottages by city folk. It had also become a resort area attracting people for recreation and sport. The wide expanse of blue water, which lay against a wooded shoreline with Seymour Mountain to the north, was perfect for swimming and sailing, and the rich animal and bird life was a delight for the would-be naturalist. The contrast with what Lowry saw as a sordid and sanctimonious city was immense. (Across the water, to remind him of the civilization from which he had escaped, stood a Shell Oil refinery; unobtrusive during the day, its flaming oil-jets were visible at night.) Dollarton gave him everything he desired – independence, escape and isolation amid the healing balm afforded by love and nature.

After a week in his new-found paradise, he wrote to Gerald Noxon, anxious for news of friends in England, of his 'generation'. 'I haven't seen a human face it seems in a decade, have snarled at no human beast in a year.' Who, he wanted to know, was dead, who in prison, and who had been interned. And what hopes did they hold about things? Defensive about not being in uniform, he said he had been refused by both army and navy and was confused as to where his duty lay. Typically he saw his situation in literary terms.

> I do not care . . . to live in a world where everyone cheats, so do not live in it, but rather, like Timon of Athens, on the edge of it: a shack on the sea in a deserted village . . . It is a fine wet ruin of a forest full of snakes and snails and terrific trees blasted with hail and fire. We dive from our front porch into a wild sea troughing with whales and seals. We have a boat, now diving at anchor. Everywhere there is a good smell of sea and timber and life and death and crabs.[1]

On Labour Day, 2 September, the holidaymakers departed, leaving the beach to the long-term residents, mostly fishermen. By now Malcolm and Margerie had decided to remain after their month was up. They negotiated a winter rent of $7.50 a month with the owners and moved their possessions out from Vancouver. It was as if nothing could go wrong for them, and early in the month Lowry wrote to Aiken joyfully, 'the authorities have told me, being a visitor, I don't have to, or rather can't, register.' The spectre of conscription was now well and truly laid.[2]

Aiken, having urged him to return to 'poetry', had spelled out this idea in an article, 'Back to Poetry', in the August *Atlantic*. For the last decade, he argued, poetry had fallen into the hands of 'social theorists, demagogues, snobs, pedants and schoolmasters anxious above all to avoid the "poetic", if only because to be poetic was somehow to be bourgeois.' They had been 'frozen by fear into a kind of chattering abnegation of self, an abject abrogation of the rights of the individual'. A romantic revival was long overdue, and it was up to poets to bring that revival about. What was needed was 'the poet once more standing, as he did in the Elizabethan age, naturally and vigorously at the centre of the world'. As the voice of the future he named Lowry's old friend Dylan Thomas.[3] Having read the article, Lowry told Aiken, he had caracoled,[4] and told Noxon that Aiken was a poet in the mould of Shakespeare and Keats and more of an influence on him now than when they had first met.[5] He was eager to get back to work and asked Aiken to return *The Last Address*, so he could start revising it 'full blast', promising to cut 'the dialogue *Great Circle* passage' – his conscience seemingly touched by yet another lifting from his old friend.

In mid-September Noxon wrote to say he was employed by the National Film Board of Canada as a producer. If they came East, he could probably find them congenial work in films. Lowry was galvanized, replying enthusiastically that he would take even the most menial job in movies. Excitedly he filled a sheet of paper with ideas about films and propaganda, noticeably ignoring Aiken's view about the need for art and poetry to unshackle themselves from politics. Good propaganda was good art, he wrote, and jotted down what he thought were good examples – the films of Feyder, Renoir and Duvivier, Paul Strand's *Redes*, Dovzhenko's *Frontier*, Eisenstein's *Thunder Over Mexico*. He could, he said, conceive a tempestuous *Thunder Over Canada*. He also noted, 'I have talked with Pabst who told me that he had "certain wisions of a film" . . . In fact Pabst is a character in my novel,' perhaps giving a clue to the origin of Jacques Laruelle. G. W. Pabst, the German film director, made a film about the lost continent of Atlantis, a theme which fascinated Lowry and which preoccupies the Consul.[6]

By now it would have taken at least a film job to prise the Lowrys away from the beach. They had only $200 to their name, but to them that was a fortune. Their rent was minimal, they cut their own logs, drew their own water, lit the shack with oil lamps and candles, and cooked on a wood stove. The lamplighting became a religious ritual for Lowry, and twilight the most blissful hour. It was, he told Margerie, their time to be alone, to light the lamps, draw the curtains against the world and be together.[7] They had a boat, 'My Heart is in the Highlands', and often braved the Inlet's strange currents – rowing fifty miles one Sunday to the mouth of the Indian River, returning by moonlight.[8] One could live like a king on barely nothing, he wrote – in fact far better than most kings, for that matter.[9] He found the best places to write were on a bench in front of the window, or standing up leaning on the table. Beside his bed he kept a Bible, James's *Varieties of Religious Experience*, a book of poetry and something by Dostoyevsky.[10]

By the beginning of October, having heard nothing about his or Margerie's novels, he wrote to Matson enquiring anxiously about both. Matson replied that Burnett had rejected the *Volcano*, Martha Foley writing that though they felt it was very unusual it seemed weighed down by the author's 'preoccupation with what might be described as the Dun (she meant Dunne) theory of time'.[11] It had been rejected also by Harcourt Brace and was now with Duell, Sloan & Pearce. Margerie's mystery was also circulating.

Lowry was upset and hurt by Burnett's failure to write to him directly and by Foley's rejection, and told Matson that never having read Dunn (sic) he could hardly be preoccupied with him (a complete untruth; *An Experiment with Time* possessed him). It was obvious that they had not read it carefully, and having kept it so long perhaps they were doing some experimenting with time themselves. In fact, unknown to him, they had rejected it six weeks earlier; it was Matson who had been slow to inform him. Then, sending it off to other publishers without consulting him meant he had broken his promise that Linscott would see it next. He felt acutely the problem of being so far removed from New York, but promised Matson that one day he would not be sorry for having borne with him for so long.[12]

He was right in supposing that neither Foley nor Burnett had read the *Volcano*, but he would have felt even worse had he seen the reader's report which prompted their rejection. 'The letter is good,' it began, with heavy irony, 'you might use it. But the book's another thing.' It was not really a novel and did not belong to the story or characters, 'but to some several quirks in the author's mind.' These were all right, but unfocused. His real interest lay in Dunne's theory of Time. 'He writes it as fiction, people at talk, begrudging like pearls before commoners. And his political ideas – a "communism".' His letter, however, was fascinating. 'I wish he'd write the book he describes in the letter: "the last howling; an owl of Minerva flying at evening: one cannot know what one must do, or whether a continent will stand from Wednesday to Friday." ' The author had gagged on his own portentousness, and the story was incoherent – too much talk, too opinionated. 'The comparison with Kafka is outrageous, & I think he doesn't know what he is writing.' The good parts were the landscapes and the symbolism. 'He makes such a good case for his novel, then writes so *impalpably*, that some may feel they can't be sure, maybe they missed something.'

The reader had hit on both Lowry's weakness and strength. The concept was too grandiose to justify the result; he knew he had a potentially great novel but had not yet acquired the skill to write a sufficiently complex work and had tried to produce it quickly when his natural pace was slow and painstaking. His strength was exactly that unpalpableness which lifts his writing at its best from the particular to the universal and scatters his texts with enigmas. Added to this was the brilliance with which he wrote *about* his work, a strength which made him one of the best letter writers of his age. Recommending rejection of the novel, the report concluded, 'Try a collection of his eloquent letters.'[13]

Marriage was now much on his mind, and no doubt on Margerie's, too. He had expected to be free to remarry on 15 October, but Parks wrote to say that he expected the matter would be final by 31 October, adding that Arthur had arranged for $110.44 (£25) to be paid to his bank account at the beginning of each month until further notice. As his account had shrunk to $25 it was doubly welcome. On 31 October, they celebrated Hallowe'en, the northern Day of the Dead. Malcolm set up a small firework display and Margerie carved jack-o'-lanterns from pumpkins, and this became an annual ritual for them on the beach. Still ignorant of Malcolm's plans to remarry, Evelyn wrote at the end of October saying that for the past few months they had 'lived on the edge of a volcano'. London and Merseyside had been badly hit in the blitz. So far Caldy had been unaffected, but six houses nearby had been destroyed and six people killed. She was 'so thankful', she added with unconscious irony, that his books were meeting with such success. Obviously, in his usual way of anticipating literary triumphs, he had been feeding her 'thrilling news of his achievements'. 'I am longing to read my book,' she ended, 'the one so thrillingly dedicated to me.' And doubtless she was praying it would be very different from that horrid *Ultramarine*. In fact the book he had in mind, *The Lighthouse Invites the Storm*, mostly poems about drunken delirium in Mexico, would probably have left her perplexed and shaken – for example, his hymn to his mistress, tequila:

> Most nauseous of all drinks, what is your spell?
> You are cheap, you are the whore of potions;
> You are the impalatable, you are the way to hell . . .[14]

Hardly lines for a good Methodist mother to show proudly to her friends.

His brothers had now been drawn into the war. Wilfrid was a Lieutenant in the Royal Artillery, Stuart in the Home Guard and Russell awaiting call-up. He must have felt well out of it and pleased that his plan to go home to enlist had been scotched, though he never knew the reason – Arthur's determination to keep his violent son at a few thousand miles' remove.

One sad piece of news from Evelyn was of the death of George Cooke, their old gardener. According to Margerie, on receiving this news Malcolm broke down and cried. He was moved enough to compose an epitaph beginning,

> Here lies George Edward Cook[e], a man
> Who to the world's wickedness added naught.[15]

When Noxon wrote to say that he was working with John Grierson, the documentary film-maker, now head of the NFB, and had mentioned Lowry to him, the prospect of a job in films seemed very real. Anticipating success as usual, and hoping it would get back to Arthur, he told Parks he was now employed on a small retainer by the National Film Board and was selling articles to the local newspapers. In mid-November he wrote to Linscott, who had by then received a copy of *Under the Volcano*, enquiring about Houghton Mifflin's annual Writer's Fellowship. His letter, however, crossed one from Linscott rejecting the novel, and quoting from three separate readers' reports.

> Interesting conversation, good background, an occasional vivid phrase about the characters but for the rest, static and a little dull. The characters don't really come off except now and then the Consul. As a whole it seems to me too literary . . . There are minor flaws such as a dull fourth chapter and an occasional sentence of extraordinary awkwardness . . . but above all, the pattern of the story fails clearly to emerge, lost as it is in meditation, description, and verbal pyrotechnics. I must confess to some alarm at the thought of trying to describe this book to a bookseller in such as way as to induce him to order it . . . A dream from beginning to end with these lovely, strange flashes a dream has and the horror and irrationality. It left me with a fuzzy taste.[16]

In a following letter Linscott said he thought the book could be sold but only to a publisher prepared to lose money on it. He said also that Fellowship applications had already closed.

Lowry was quite confident about his novel's ultimate acceptance, and in any case had his mind on other things. He thought and dreamt poetry all day long, he told Aiken, wrestling with the only form he knew, the one which Aiken had taught him. Nevertheless, 'nature poems, mature poems, hate poems, fate poems – all, but great poems – pour out', and he expected any day a visit from a man from Porlock. He sent one of his more accomplished pieces, hinting at the agony of composition.

> This wrestling, as of a seaman with a storm
> Which flies to leeward, while they
> United in that chaos, turn, sea-weary
> Each on his bunk, to dream of fields at home
> Or shake with visions Dante never knew,
> The poet himself feels, struggling with the form
> Of his quiet work.[17]

On 27 November he received his final divorce papers from Parks; he was a free man. Promptly next morning, he and Margerie dashed into town and applied for a marriage licence. Margerie gave her age as thirty-three, lopping two years off (she had lopped one off at her first marriage in 1924), and gave her status as widow, when in fact, like Malcolm, she was divorced. On 2 December they were married by S. Theodore Pagesmith ('a fine carrot-juice swigging Unitarian minister'), at 1009 West 10th Avenue in the despised city of Vancouver, witnessed by the janitor and his wife. Both gave their religion as Unitarian and their occupation as 'authorship'. Afterwards they celebrated in a tea-shop.

As a wedding gift, Malcolm gave Margerie a copy of *Field Book of the Skies*, an observer's book of astronomy. In it he found the astronomical and symbolic equivalent of his new-found home, the star Eridini (as the book called it), source of the great starry river of the constellation of Orion, Virgil's 'King of Rivers'. Its earthly equivalent was the great curving River Po, and its mythical origin lay in the story of Phaëthon, son of Helios (the book said Phoebus) and Clymene, whose desire to drive the chariot of the sun for one day against his father's will led to disaster. He was finally hurled into the River Po and his body buried beside the river by nymphs and wept over by his sisters. This story provided Lowry with a parable for his own life, for he too had been hurled from his disastrous path to land on the bank of a wide river. Dollarton was known thereafter as his 'Eridanus', his resting place after a stormy life.

It is difficult to know who exactly Margerie thought she was marrying. Malcolm had got so much into the habit of lying about himself that having told her numerous untruths when they first met, he never summoned up the courage to disabuse her of them. So she believed that Arthur owned oil wells and that Evelyn had lots of jewellery which would one day be hers. Who Lowry thought *he* was marrying is also difficult to say. Margerie seems to have exaggerated her movie career, and may never have told him her true age or that she was divorced not widowed, or that her first husband had been a drunken suicide. And if he still had dreams of having children she may or may not have told him that she had had a hysterectomy years before she met him. If the union began on a series of fictions it was to develop into a fiction of its own – a fiction both idyllic and Strindbergian in its complexities and ramifications. For the immediate future, however, everything looked rosy. No longer drinking heavily, swimming every day, rowing around the Inlet and taking long hikes through the forest, Lowry was probably as fit as he had ever been, and both were benefiting from the healthy but primitive life on the edge of the wilderness.

As a measure of his exuberance he sent Aiken a poem accompanied by the explanation of its genesis. He (Aiken) had once referred in a letter from Rye to the strange sounds emanating from his ukulele, and so aided by 'an introverted sensibility' he had composed his 'Epitaph'.[18]

Malcolm Lowry
Late of the Bowery
His prose was flowery
And often glowery
He lived, nightly, and drank, daily,
And died playing the ukulele.[19]

This was the poem Aiken liked best of those Lowry sent because it was 'formally complete'. The rest were too free for him. It was good that he was writing poetry, he said, but he needed to know more about poetic forms. 'Freedom comes *after* mastery not before.' He himself had a book of sonnets out, 'but nobody knows it, nobody reviews it, nobody buys it, nobody reads it – I'll send you one for Xmas'.[20] The great age which was to at last recognize and embrace Aiken's poetry had yet to arrive.

Their first winter in the Canadian wilderness was preceded by a 'freezing fall' which covered the forest in crystal ice. To prepare for the coming cold, they bought woollen slacks, flannel shorts, green and white lumberjack jackets, woollen socks and thick-soled boots. They sought advice from neighbours about coping with the hostile Canadian winter. First they met Jimmy Craige, a tiny Manx boatbuilder in his sixties, who had a large boat-shed along the shore, and lived in a cabin next to it. Craige, married to a half-gypsy descendant of Fletcher Christian, gave them advice on how to survive the winter on the beach and taught Lowry to chop and stack firewood, a simple activity he came to relish. He developed a deep attachment to Craige – 'a little homunculus in a fairisle pullover', he wrote – who taught them a great deal, and he in turn formed a close bond with Lowry and was mesmerized by Margerie, a glamorous figure strangely out of place among the simple folk living on the edge of the forest.

The fishermen living along the shore were at sea most of the summer and at times when the salmon were running. After the summer visitors had departed, they returned. One of these was 'Whitey', Miles Went, a Dane; another, Sam Miller, 'Sam the Fisherman', was one of the oldest residents on the beach. Once, to their horror, Sam presented them with a large bucket of live giant crabs which later they returned furtively to the water.[21] The other local they got to know well, though never to love, was store-keeper-cum-postmaster, Percy Cummins, a little Yorkshireman who thought very poorly of the beach squatters who paid no city taxes and spoiled the look of the place. He was happy to have their custom but resented having to fetch them to the phone whenever they got a call, and he was not always helpful over mail. However, the Lowrys depended on him for many necessities, although they had their own well of fresh spring water.

Over Christmas and New Year, Malcolm was engaged in what he called 'some hefty reading' all through English Literature, including Shakespeare, Jonson and Milton, and writing more poetry.[22] In January, Noxon wrote to say that all his plans had collapsed; Grierson had resigned from the NFB, and the prospect of jobs there had temporarily evaporated. (Grierson had been denounced as a Communist and forced to resign.) Obviously disappointed, Lowry replied with a poem about a previously frustrated plan, 'The Englishman Turned Back at the Border'. On top of the collapse of his film hopes, Matson wrote that *Under the Volcano* had been turned down yet again, and this time his optimism was shattered. According to Margerie, he fell into a deep depression, turned his face to the wall and for a whole month hardly spoke or ate. Finally she enticed him out of this severe state of withdrawal by sitting down to work on a new mystery, then asking him for help. Soon he was not only helping her, but turning back to his own work again. By mid-February he had recovered sufficiently to write a letter to Aiken praising both his flopped novel and book of poems.

A few weeks after snapping out of his depression he composed a letter to Matson full of new plans. Cheerfulness had broken in yet again. He was sorry to have given him nothing but disappointments so far with *Under the Volcano*. It was probably the hard circumstances under which it was completed that led him to confuse a moral triumph with an artistic one. He thought that perhaps after all the book *had* been far too preoccupied with time and the shape of the novel did not emerge from beneath it. Rather than embark on something new he was rewriting the whole book. To show him what he was doing he sent him a revised version of chapter 8, the story of the dying Indian, (later mistaken for the original 1936 short story from which the novel developed). In this Yvonne is still the Consul's daughter, though he is now called Jeffrey Ames. He had, he told Matson, 'cut and cut and cut' and was 'extremely proud' of the story, which he thought suitable for either *Harper's Bazaar*, *Esquire* or *Decision*. Recognizing for once his weakness for counting unhatched chickens, he wrote, 'I do not think the feeling is wish fulfillment this time that I have rung the bell.' He asked after *In Ballast* and *The Lighthouse*, which he thought also needed the kind of cutting he had dished out to the *Volcano*.[23]

Optimistically he settled into a new regime, rising with the sun, and, after a swim and a cup of coffee, getting straight down to work. In this mood he was quite unapproachable. Margerie would collect the mail and groceries at the store, then get back to work on her own novel. Sometimes they would take a walk through the forest, indulging their mutual interest in nature, especially bird-watching. They acquired a tin tub and on Saturday nights took their weekly bath. It was not an entirely abstemious life; they still had evening drinks, watered-down gin and orange, but there were no hangovers to disrupt the early start to each day's work. This moderate regimen was made easier by the fact that liquor was now rationed in Canada.

In March, Matson acknowledged receipt of the short story and announced that as well as Story Press and Houghton Mifflin, the *Volcano* had been turned down by Harcourt Brace, Duell, Sloan & Pearce, Alfred

Knopf, and Little Brown. But Lowry was now reconciled to his 1940 version of the book failing, and in a great burst of activity not only got on with his revision but helped Margerie finish her new mystery, *The Shapes that Creep*. Then in mid-April he sent off a new version of his school story 'Enter One in Sumptuous Armour', and promised Matson a revised *Volcano* soon, taking a recent volcanic eruption in Mexico as a good omen.

As he continued rewriting, he heightened the tension at the centre of the novel by combining the Consul's faithless ex-wife Priscilla with Yvonne, his daughter, and making Hugh into the Consul's half-brother who has had a relationship with her. In the process she became less like Jan, less spikey, and more like Margerie, more acquiescent about her one-time spouse's drunkenness. Now it is Yvonne, the wife, who is hoping for a reconciliation rather than the Consul. It is she who returns to Quauhnahuac, and meets Hugh, the optimistic man of the future, and is faced with choosing between him and the reactionary and pessimistic Consul. But there is no competition because the Consul wishes only to be left alone.

Having survived the winter they felt even more committed to life on the forest's edge, and at the end of March Sam the Fisherman reported a shack for sale under a wild cherry tree a quarter of a mile along the beach near a promontory called Dark Rosslyn Point. They bought it for $100 on 1 April. It was shingled, with two rooms, one long and rectangular with one end facing the sea. There was a sink and a stove in the living room, a peaked roof and an attic. It had a card table and planks and orange boxes for a desk. Other furniture they bought second hand, carting it down the forest path in a wheelbarrow. For a month they cleaned and mended it, helped by handy carpenters like Jimmy Craige. They painted the front door red, the inside white, and gave the windows yellow edges, then moved into the new 'Wicket Gate' on May Day. As a good omen, that same day all Lowry's manuscripts arrived from Linscott. A week later he wrote to Aiken, 'We have now *bought* a supershack on the sea – all paid for, no rent, no tax, but lovely, surrounded with dogwood and cherry and pines, isolated, and a swell place for work.' He thanked him for his help over the past difficult months and reflected on what his parents might be suffering in the Blitz, pleased at least that he had somehow made his peace with them, especially Arthur. 'The ghastly psychotic dance we led each other has come to an end.'[24]

His mood was buoyant. Margerie was working well on her novels, he had completed or revised three short stories and a stream of poems, as well as being hard at work on the rewrite, and was not particularly depressed when 'June 30th 1934' was rejected by four magazines, and 'Enter One in Sumptuous Armour' by six. There was also their first spring in the forest to enjoy, and the night sky to observe and record in his notebook.

> There was a silver line of surf on the beach. The night blazed with swords and diamonds. The moon was brilliant, and I saw my first constellation . . . Not till that . . . had I observed a spring. A year elsewhere of death./And then . . . Orion. Mintaka. Alnilam. The Pleiades. Eridanus. The stars were like splinters of ice in a sky of jet.[25]

Similar lyrical passages were stored away for use in his future fiction.

Yet all was not always well with them. Once he yelled at Margerie, 'Why don't you do something about those black circles under your eyes? Other women do!' But as ever he would be filled with remorse and leave an apologetic note for her to find. 'I am sorry from the bottom of my heart,' went one. 'I have no excuses. All I know is I'm going to do my absolute level best not to let such a filthy demon get hold of me again. And I mean starting *Now*!' Margerie put such childish rages over trivialities followed by deep remorse down to his loveless childhood and self-loathing. As to depressions, he had a ready-to-hand cure – a plunge off the shack porch into the icy waters of Burrard Inlet. It never failed. He called it his George III treatment.

While the isolation was a welcome escape from the cruel world, he missed the intellectual stimulus of people whose judgement he could trust. Fortunately, late in the spring, Noxon came west for the CBC and, to Lowry's delight, found his way to Dollarton. He had not intended staying the night, but they became so engrossed with *Under the Volcano* that they stayed up until morning discussing it. Lowry read long passages from it, anxious to know what Noxon thought.[26] In particular Noxon recalled that 'he wanted a first sentence of such extraordinary and monumental nature . . . that I told him this was simply unreadable the way he had put it down.'[27] The original long sentence they broke into three, relating Quauhnahuac to the rest of the world. The writing of that great wide-angled lens tracking shot into the opening shows that by now Lowry was bringing a cinematic dimension to the novel, which would result eventually in the inclusion of flashbacks, flashforwards and cutting between scenes and characters which would enable him to suggest later that it could be regarded as a film scenario. But right at that moment, what concerned Noxon was Lowry's tendency to work on several things simultaneously, rather than concentrate on one, believing that this would delay what was obviously a potentially great book. After he left, Lowry wrote saying how delighted he was by this visit from his 'first editor'.[28]

Now that his book was back on course, he felt able to write to Burnett and Foley, saying that he had been disappointed at their rejecting it because he had fooled himself by thinking it was great because of the effort he had put into writing it. But, on reflection, they were right. 'The issue *is* confused by Dunne stuff, by my own situation while writing it, and it isn't spherical and whole as a work of art should be.' Just as it was when they last met in New York, his life had been in 'a sad mess' while writing the book, but that was no longer the case. It seemed to him that work he had loaded on to them in the past was really notation for hard work to come, but he was grateful for their encouragement. He had sent a revised *Last Address* to Matson, and although he could not get money out of Canada to pay back Burnett's 1936 advance of $45, if he accepted this or any other stories he could put the fee against the debt. He was also revising *In Ballast*, he said, which they probably remembered also from 1936. Obviously he was not heeding Noxon's advice to concentrate on one thing at a time.

In revising *The Last Address* (retitled *Swinging the Maelstrom*, he said later) the tone had changed. Lawhill, the chronic alcoholic journalist, is replaced by Bill Plantagenet, ex-jazz musician, who is less self-pitying and more ironic. He has a greater sense of the injustice in the world, and as an ammunition ship (the *Mar Cantabrico*) leaves with arms and volunteers for Spain, he has 'the peculiar feeling that it was his ship, which would take him on his night journey across the sea'. Matson first sent *The Last Address* to Linscott, who returned it saying that it did not somehow add up. 'I'd say it was formless, meaningless, dreamlike, and unmotivated; that it lacked overtones or if it has them, they are imperceptible to this particular ear. At the same time, the writing and the minor characters are so good that one keeps on reading . . .'[29] He suggested more work be done on the structure to make it commercial.

After all these rejections he received a very small consolation prize. From a series of sea poems sent to the *Atlantic Monthly*, one, 'In Memoriam, Ingvald Bjorndal' based on a newspaper item about a letter in a bottle from a Norwegian sailor whose ship was sinking, was accepted.

While we sail and laugh, joke and fight, comes death
And it is the end. A man toils on board;
His life blows away like a gust of breath:
Who will know his dreams now when the sea roared?
I love you, my dear, but now I am dead,
So take somebody else and forget me.
My brothers, I was foolish, as you said:
So are most who place their fate in the sea.
Many tears have you shed for me in vain.
Take my pay, Mother, Father; I have come
A long way to die in the blood and rain.
Buy me some earth in the graveyard at home.
Goodbye. Please remember me with these words
To the green meadows and the blue fjords.[30]

He signed himself 'Malcolm Boden Lowry' and asked for any fees to go to a sailors' relief fund. Proudly announcing this sale (fee $14) to Matson, he told him to deduct his ten percent (a grand $1.40) from the next sale he made for him. It might have no meaning, he wrote, but on the other hand it might be the wedge he needed.

By the beginning of August he had now all but completed new drafts of both *Under the Volcano* and *In Ballast*, and was working over them, 'cutting mercilessly, while re-creating', he told Matson. And while he was staying close to the form and meaning of the book he was also trying to make them exciting as stories *qua* stories.[31] Also, having missed the date for the previous Houghton Mifflin Writer's Fellowship, he was determined to apply promptly this time. The prize was $1,500, and he planned to submit the newly revised *In Ballast*, and asked Matson for his formal agreement.

As a measure of his transformed fortunes, he had $500 in the bank by August and had high hopes of winning the $1,500 Fellowship money. He needed two letters of support and asked the Aikens to oblige, assuring Conrad that *In Ballast* had been thoroughly 'deplagiarized'. And a month or more after Hitler had invaded Russia and P. G. Wodehouse had been condemned in Parliament for broadcasting in Germany, Lowry could reflect that 'The world seems to have reeled away from one altogether into a bloodshot pall of horror and hypocrisy, a chaos without melody.'[32] Aiken, still amazed at Lowry's sudden affluence, said that *he* was $500 *in debt*!

September brought terminal news of the 1940 *Under the Volcano*, when

Matson wrote listing twelve publishers who had now rejected it. For the rest of 1941 Lowry toiled on, trying to place his poems and *The Last Address* without success. Klaus Mann, editor of *Decision*, wrote that he was hanging on to some poems,[33] and Edward Weeks rejected *The Last Address* as too esoteric and obscure. Lowry had anticipated this reaction because he pointed out to Weeks that much the same could be said of Dostoyevsky and Gorky, but Weeks replied that 'their characterization is capable of a compulsion and of a keen desire to know more, which I am sorry to say I find lacking here.'[34] To crown a year of failure, he was eliminated from the Houghton Mifflin Fellowship race.

Following Pearl Harbor and the outbreak of hostilities between Japan and the US, the war came a little closer to Eridanus, but Lowry's letters hardly registered the fact. His work now dominated him, and nothing was going to disturb his concentration. He tried to foster a close relationship with Margerie's mother, who shared his fascination with the occult, advising her to read Dunne, Ouspensky and Charles Fort.

So engrossed was he in rewriting his novels that he did not answer Matson's letters about the twelve rejections until 6 January 1942, when he and Margerie wrote jointly. The list of rejections over the past year had made them feel something of a liability to him, they said, and they had made a New Year Resolution to just keep going, despite all setbacks. Malcolm was determined to complete what he had worked and pondered on for so many years. *In Ballast* was finished and he was now engaged on a completely new and better version of *Under the Volcano*. Meanwhile, Margerie handled the public relations. Of the *Volcano* she told Matson, 'We know that within this matrix there *is* a novel which is not only truly good but saleable.' However, he need no longer feel under any obligation to represent them, and could return all their work if he wished. Malcolm suggested that he just chuck his copy of *Under the Volcano* into the furnace. Her two novels and *The Last Address* were all they needed returned.[35]

It cannot have helped Lowry's sense of failure to be sent Burnett's letter to Matson rejecting *The Last Address* and saying that although they had done a lot of work with him on the story and advanced him $45 for it (which he now wished to repay in stories), it was pretty hopeless to cram into his magazine at a time like this. If it had been brought into shape in 1936 the matter would have been quite different.[36] This waspish letter stung him and he wrote a detailed explanation to Matson, saying that in 1936 he had understood Burnett to have taken

The Last Address and thereafter looked for it in every edition of *Story*. When he had asked for it back in 1939 to enter for a competition Burnett had asked, if it did not win, to have it back when he had got it into 'the fine form which it deserved', and this rejection was the result. He may have thought he was trying to palm off stories rejected elsewhere to settle the debt, and Matson may have thought he was going behind his back in sending stories direct to Burnett, but he should have paid Burnett *and* the money owed to Ann Watkins when he could have afforded to. 'I have done a lot of things in my life up to the age of thirty which I find inexcusable and this was not helped by complete psychic disintegration. The way back over the acres of remorse is difficult.' *Under the Volcano* was almost rewritten, he said, and this time perhaps 'first rate'. But the idea for a linked series of novels had again taken hold. *The Last Address* was being rewritten, and *In Ballast* was ready for its final draft. These three together constituted one book, their themes being complementary – the first being, as it were, an inferno, the second a purgatorio, and the third a paradiso – 'an honest Baedeker, I believe, for he who would travel in hell'.[37]

Still hoping to keep his father happy, in March he wrote to his mother, listing all his ailments and how they must have been responsible for his previous delinquent behaviour. There was no reply for almost two months, when a letter arrived from Arthur. Even though their 'ghastly psychotic dance' had ended, for Arthur there was still a final reckoning to be had. He had read his letters to Evelyn, but was clearly suspicious about what he saw as a miraculous conversion without religion. Now he wrote demanding 'the simple plain facts'. Cambridge, London and France had left deep scars on his heart, and what followed had only deepened the wounds. He should read the parable of the Prodigal Son to where he says, 'When I came to myself.' He did not, he said, then try to justify himself, but said, 'I will arise . . . and say to my father, "I have sinned", and his father met him half way & *forgave* him.' But his own letters had shown more self-justification than true repentance. He demanded:

> (1) A frank statement as to your having seen the grave error of your ways, & an expression of sorrow for the harrowing and heart breaking agony you caused your father & mother, and . . . full assurance that you have turned your back upon those dark happenings, and . . . have turned to your father & mother & have sought forgiveness. (2) That your divorce has been made *absolute* and that there has been no

turning back in that respect. (3) Under what conditions are you living? (4) What are you earning? (5) What is your daily occupation & so on?[38]

He asked him in future to write to him at his office enclosing letters to his mother for forwarding. He also mentioned that returning from the Lake District at Christmas their car had skidded on ice and collided with a lorryload of cheese; Evelyn had suffered a head injury which had kept her in hospital for ten days, which was partly why he was writing in her place.

It might have been Arthur's obvious suspicion that his conversion to sobriety had some connection with the pleasures of the flesh which prompted Malcolm to reply swiftly and penitently. He expressed deep remorse for any suffering he had caused. As a rule, he wrote, he did not like wrongdoers who indulged in self-justification. 'However,' he continued slyly, 'as you know, lorries do tend to come along in life with their loads of cheese and side-swipe one, even if one was on the correct side of the road, even if that road was slippery, and be one going never so slowly and carefully.' He was not suggesting that Arthur had anything to explain away, he said, but he had simply supplied a convenient metaphor. His problem was that all too often he had been travelling on the wrong side of the road. He then launched into his most elaborate self-justification yet. The problem had not been drink but his failure to deal with it and that kind of 'organic cowardice' was uncharacteristic of him. He had had problems with his legs, now diagnosed as Grayson's Disease, what divers call the Bends, as well as possibly a mild form of poliomyelitis. Worse still, he had had 'a largely *streptococcic* multiple glandular infection', probably for ten years. In short, without knowing it he had been 'being slowly poisoned and undermined physically and mentally, for the best part of the last decade'. Drink aggravated but did not cause it, and it was more mysterious than a lorryload of cheese. But he was responding to treatment and would probably be cured within six months. This was not an excuse, nor was he blaming anyone, but he was claiming 'a queer sort of triumph' for the powerful constitution which he, Arthur, had provided for him. However, it did mean he would have to be out of the battleline for the time being.

On the touchy matter of his divorce he simply said that it was now absolute and that meant what it said. He was now living like a pioneer in a God-given house between sea and forest, which cost only a hundred dollars. He had a pier, built by himself, which enabled him to dive from his front porch into ten feet of salt water.

> It is magnificently beautiful, the Canadian Rockies tower across the fjord . . . Many townspeople of good families live in such houses for the summer, but I live here all year round. I don't like the city anyhow, but go there, twice a month now . . . My only luxuries are a radio and a gramophone.

However, he was in no way cut off from the rest of humanity, having a few simple though influential friends. He was also, he added, deputy ARP warden for his neck of the beach. It was the kind of life, reduced to the basics, which any writer, surrounded by his books, would love to work in. Illness had stopped him from earning, but he had had some articles accepted and was in touch with the head of the second largest broadcasting company in Canada. So, if stranded in Canada, with a slight change in his status there he could easily find work. 'I like Canada anyway,' he wrote. 'Who knows but that I might not become a Canadian Ibsen or Dostoievsky? [*sic*] They certainly need one. They haven't got any writers, at all: they all become Americans if they do well.' Cunningly he asked his father not to tell Evelyn of his illness as it would worry her, and said he realized now that he had acted in his best interests in handing him over to Parks. But he could not resist a final thrust at the recently deceased A. B. Carey, who had died, he said, of a similar disease to the one he himself had. 'The man recovered from the bite,' he wrote, 'the dog it was that died.'[39]

As the Pacific war began to turn America's way after the Battle of Midway in June 1942, it seemed that the Lowrys' fortunes were also changing. Matson wrote to say that Scribner's had accepted *The Shapes that Creep*. Lowry was as delighted as Margerie, but felt it necessary, in thanking Matson, to tell the sad story of his 'Bends' and infected glands to explain away 'some too apparent oddnesses and unratified irreliabilities on my part in the past, as well as the almost total fog in the *Volcano* as was'. The doctors, he said, were amazed that he had survived. Nevertheless, 'something really *good is* on the wing *this* time, *sans* self-deceptions, from this side.'[40]

In July, Noxon paid a return visit, staying for two or three days. This time Lowry read from all his work in progress – *The Last Address*, *Under the Volcano* and *In Ballast*, doubtless to give him a flavour of the Dantesque trilogy into which he was now trying to work all three.[41]

They went again over the opening of the *Volcano* and Noxon made detailed suggestions about the rewriting of chapter 2 which Lowry later acknowledged greatly improved the book. Again he urged him to concentrate on one thing at a time, but the tendency towards giantism had taken firm hold, and he found it difficult to create fiction which did not now conform to the grand design of his 'whole bolus'. Noxon's visit was a significant event for a man as isolated as Lowry, and his departure was painful. 'Thou leavest a gap in the woods, in the sea, at bus time and in our hearts,' he wrote, adding that since his departure they had been working extremely hard and by taking on board his suggestions had brought about a hundred per cent improvement in 'the early pachydermatous prose of the *Volcano*.'[42]

The symbiotic relationship between Lowry and his surroundings was at one level simple, at another quite complex. 'Nature is,' he told Noxon, quoting his friend Whitey, 'the most beautiful thing I ever saw in my life.'[43] But the haunting contrast between the idyllic rural setting of his childhood in Caldy and the grim urban landscape across the Mersey had developed into a symbolic contrast between Light and Darkness, between Heaven and Hell, and had become ever more entwined with his grand fictional design. William Blackstone's rejection of 'civilization' in the form of New England Puritans was being slowly transformed into conservationism. Every visit to Vancouver reinforced his hatred of the 'mechanical progress' so eagerly embraced by its inhabitants.

Margerie, awaiting proofs from Scribner's, was busy revising *The Last Twist of the Knife*, but already thinking of another novel based on an event in her own family's history, the rags-to-riches story of Daisy, a servant who unexpectedly inherited money and whose drunken father persuaded her to buy a racehorse which threw and killed her – 'a real Wuthering Heights', Lowry told Mrs Bonner. As a title he favoured *Horse in the Sky*. 'My talent for serious writing, after producing an initial success at 21,' he wrote, 'went fairly badly aground for several years, but was refloated with thanks to Marg.' However, it was she who had 'got over the bump'.[44]

Arthur finally replied to his letters of repentance, saying that he was specially heartened by his expression of sorrow at any grief and suffering caused to his mother – 'one of God's Angels', who had loved him devotedly with all her soul since he was born, and even before that had 'dwelt in the presence of God so that she might nourish you with His holy spirit – Concentrated her mind on beautiful things so that her dear baby might have beautiful thoughts – Nourished him until 9 months old from her own breast, so that he might have a beautiful mind & healthy body.'[45] If he reflected on these things he would find them deep down in his nature and realize that they were the most precious possessions of his life. So, just over eight years after he had left home, and five since he had sunk into gaol in Oaxaca, and almost four since he had practically murdered Miss Auer – finally, he had made peace with his long-suffering father.

By the end of 1942, Lowry had completed yet another rewriting of *Under the Volcano*. In this version, the Consul is now Geoffrey Firmin, a man whose self-pity is redeemed by self-mockery, and whose pessimism has given way to dreams of a new life with Yvonne (the life which he and Margerie were now living in Dollarton). Geoffrey is now a self-destructive Faust figure who makes his pact with the devil and whose tragic end somehow embodies the age. Yvonne has changed, too; she is more decisively in love with Geoffrey, but since Geoffrey dies, she too must die. She is killed by the bolting horse (Margerie's suggestion, she claimed), and the earlier description of her love-making with Hugh becomes that of her death agony. As the Consul reflected, 'How alike are the groans of love to those of the dying.'[46] Yvonne's death is identical to the death of the heroine of Margerie's *Horse in the Sky*. 'We swap horses and archetypes with each other all the time,' Lowry wrote later.[47] Now too each chapter is written from the point of view of one of the different characters enabling him to bring together some of the most densely and beautifully written passages exploring the Consul's alcoholic consciousness previously scattered throughout the novel. Geoffrey, as the ironic, doom-laden and self-destructive alcoholic reflecting upon a wasted and guilt-ridden life on his last day on earth, has now taken up his central position in Lowry's evolving masterpiece. The book's centre of gravity had shifted away from Hugh towards the Consul, no doubt reflecting Lowry's own change of consciousness, away from his old self towards something new, from being an optimistic 1930s-style of socialist towards what he called 'a conservative Christian anarchist'.

The coming year, 1943, was to further deepen Lowry's conception of Geoffrey as an inspired alcoholic, one who, through his suffering and vision, offered a path to 'Hidden Knowledge'. It was as if the ideas with which he had embarked on his writing career, diverted by politics for a decade, were now reasserting themselves, being concentrated together and finding their true expression in one book. And the Blackstone-like life at the forest's edge, now so important a part of his sense of his own existence, had become the Consul's dream, a Paradiso which he envisions whilst down deep in the Hell of Mexico:

> Between mescals . . . I seem to see us living in some northern country, of mountains and hills and blue water; our house is built on an inlet and . . . we are standing, happy in one another, on the balcony of this house, looking over the water. There are sawmills half hidden by trees beyond and under the hills on the other side of the inlet, what looks like an oil refinery, only softened and rendered beautiful by distance.[48]

Against this stood the clouded vision of the Consul's consciousness. According to Lowry, it was early in 1943 that he included one of the passages in the *Volcano* which he said anticipated the atomic bomb, when in chapter 5 he wrote, 'What did even the hierophants of science know of the fearful potencies of, for them, unvintageable evil?'[49] and included a reference in chapter 12 to the chemical elements. Such a claim of course was wholly consistent with a Consul who had become a visionary.

Noxon came again in early April, but this time for a change they discussed Margerie's novel and one Noxon was writing. In mid-June Lowry wrote to him that *Horse in the Sky* was finished and 'The Volcano smoulders to a finish in reverse.' He was brimming with ideas and was eager now to tackle the Paradiso part. Again sketches of small incidents were to find their way in some form into the novel. The grey smoke of a train going eastwards reflected in the water and the wash of a ship on the inlet 'like a great wheel, the vast spokes of the wheel whirling across the bay'.[50] And a poem written at this time captures his ecstatic sense of the beauty of nature, and the contentment which he then felt, living at Dollarton:

> Blue mountains with snow and blue cold rough water,
> A wild sky full of stars at rising
> And Venus and the gibbous moon at sunrise,
> Gulls following a motorboat against the wind,
> Trees with branches rooted in air –
> Sitting in the sun at noon with the furiously
> Smoking shadow of the shack chimney –
> Eagles drive downward in one,
> Terns blow backward,

A new kind of tobacco at eleven,
And my love returning on the four o'clock bus
– My God, why have you given this to us? [51]

More and more he had become dependent on Margerie's cooking, cleaning, typing, and keeping his life in order. 'Margie has gone to town for the day and there is major disorganization here: half a boiled egg in the sink, a shoe on the window sill, I have just dropped my cigarette case down the john, and I have been attacked by a pileated woodpecker.'[52] He became anxious when she was away, leaving little love notes in childish or mock heroic language for her to find – from El Leon to Miss Harteebeeste.

Horse in the Sky was sent to Mrs Bonner, who had supplied the original story of Daisy. But she was deeply upset by it, feeling that Margerie had inflated the story beyond recognition, and she blamed Malcolm for influencing her writing. Instead of capturing the proper period and letting the story speak for itself, she had first modernized it and then tried too hard to write a kind of *Wuthering Heights* – perhaps even finer than *Wuthering Heights*, Malcolm had written. She did not hide her disappointment and Margerie wrote her mother a furiously bitter letter. She found it very difficult to tolerate criticism of her and Malcolm's work. The myth of genius had taken hold and she believed him incapable of writing anything which was not great. With his guiding hand, she felt she could write nothing but successful books, touched by that greatness. It took a long letter of conciliation from Priscilla to smooth Margerie's ruffled pride.

To Noxon in September Lowry wrote to say that they had met and become acquainted with a magician.[53] This meeting was to have serious consequences for him and for his novel.

> It began to strike me that the Consul meant something more: was he not like man himself, like Faust, and in the position, as it were, of a black magician, and if so, had I not better learn something about what really haunted him? Fatal supposition! Indeed no sooner had I thought that than I actually encountered a strange personage in the forest here, who, ostensibly a canvasser for votes, was in reality just such a magician.

Well, not quite, he added, for the man was a benign white magician and no Amfortas.[54] This strange figure, in fact, was Charles Stansfeld-Jones, Frater Achad, magical child of Aleister Crowley. Lowry was convinced that Fate had delivered this odd character to his door, and the impact of the encounter was immediately felt in the book.

'Stan', as Lowry called him, was a Londoner who had become a student of Crowley's by correspondence in 1912, and emigrated to Canada in 1913. When 'the Beast' visited Vancouver in 1915 he decided that his young disciple was his magical son from whom he expected outstanding work. It is said that Stansfeld-Jones, when only a neophyte, swore the oath of the Master of the Temple and catapulted himself into the Abyss.[55] According to Lowry, 'My friend told me that a black magician who fell into the abyss was in the unenviable position of having all the elements in the universe against him. This is what . . . accounts for the recital of all the elements in Chapter X [of the Volcano] – written long before the atom bomb.'[56] It also accounted for the whole mystical side of the Consul.

Two days after meeting him, Stan returned with two books on the occult, *Q.B.L. or the Bride's Reception* and *The Anatomy of the Body of God*, and brought a diagram of the sephirotic tree, which so intrigued Lowry that he asked to be taught the Jewish Cabbala and then introduced references to it into the *Volcano*. In occult circles, Frater Achad was considered a significant author and teacher, later credited with announcing the dawn of the 'Age of Aquarius';[57] had Lowry wanted to learn about these things he could hardly have found a better teacher. Stan lent him a book about the 'sacred magic' of Abra-Melin the Mage, which laid down a regime of self-discipline and asceticism, the way to meet one's guardian angel and becoming a magus, a position of great power. This suited Lowry's mood – the road to hidden knowledge lying, so his new friend taught him, through contemplation of the occult and things magical. He needed little persuading to take all this very seriously. Margerie said that it was from reading Abra-Melin the Mage that Malcolm got his demonic voices for the *Volcano*.

Stan took the legend of Parsifal's quest for the Holy Grail as the key metaphor for the search for hidden knowledge. He introduced the Lowrys to yoga, i-ching, and astral travel, and they spent long evenings together, at the shack or at Jones's home at nearby Deep Cove, in magical practices. Those fictional demonic voices would move in and become real to Lowry later, and, as he wrote, 'It seemed that by merely looking upon these things I had involved myself with a far more intricate karma, not to say set of ordeals.'[58] From Stan's library of occult books Lowry took titles for the Consul's library, though for comic relief he concludes the brief inventory with *Peter Rabbit*. ' "Everything is to be found in *Peter Rabbit*,'' the Consul liked to say.'[59] He also took seriously several mystical sayings from Stan such as 'Fear is the lion on the path', 'What lies below is the same as what lies above', and 'Life is a luminosity between two darknesses.'

Meanwhile, Scribner's had decided to postpone publication of *The Shapes that Creep*, Matson was sitting on *The Last Twist of the Knife*, and *Horse in the Sky* was busily being rejected by a series of publishers, five by mid-November. Lowry, irritated by Mrs Bonner's dislike of it, continued to proclaim it 'a kind of classic', and told Noxon that though it was 'deceptively innocent', it succeeded in its intention and was 'a formally beautiful and complete work of art.'[60] But war novels were in vogue with publishers and Margerie was known as a mystery writer not a new Emily Brontë.

Nevertheless, Lowry's life was still idyllic, and few people intruded upon his Eden. Besides their beach acquaintances, they had just a few friends, like the local game warden, George Stevenson. In his notebook, Lowry recorded sunrises and the variable colours of the day, the tides, the density or luminosity of early morning fogs, woodsmoke against blue skies, the sighting of a solitary heron, the sun's struggles with grey clouds, strange shadows cast among the trees, the moon in various phases.

They spent Christmas Day with Stan and his wife Rubina at Deep Cove. Lowry was so committed to the wagon that he refused Christmas pudding when he was told it had rum in it. But winter on the beach was taking its toll. Barely recovered from his glandular trouble, he was struck down with flu over the New Year, and almost simultaneously Margerie also fell victim. When she recovered, having heard nothing about her novel, she decided to issue Matson with an ultimatum. Either he was interested in her work and would reply to her many letters rather than just send on rejection slips, or they should part company. Matson replied immediately affirming his continuing interest in her and Malcolm and pointing out that both her books lacked war interest and she should be patient until the climate changed. This only heightened her sense of their isolation. Quoting Lowry's line from Kafka, she told Noxon that Matson's letter made her feel increasingly like K. 'Due to certain auxiliary circumstances,' it seemed, she had had 'another cryptic message from the *Castle*.'[61] But Lowry told Noxon that he was up to his neck in the *Volcano* and at last there seemed to be blue sky ahead.[62]

Then suddenly something more than poor health and a gloomy spring cast a frightening shadow over him. In April he read a book about a drunk which had so much in it like *The Last Address* and the *Volcano* that it might even be the great novel about alcoholism he thought he himself had been writing so painfully over the past years. It struck him 'a shrewd psychological blow', he said, and made it difficult to continue working. He wrote asking Noxon, anxiously,

> Have you read a novel *The Lost Weekend* by one Charles Jackson, a radioman from New York? It is perhaps not a very fine novel but admirably about a drunkard and hangovers and alcoholic wards as they have never been done (save by me of course) . . . I'd like to know what you thought however, if it has seriously undercut my delowryiums.[63]

After reading *The Lost Weekend*, he wrote later, he had plunged off the pier and swum six miles out into the Inlet.[64] Jackson's book, the story of Don Birnam, a dipsomaniac writer, was to haunt him for years to come. There are, indeed, uncanny parallels between Jackson's book and both *Under the Volcano* and *The Last Address*, and also between Birnam and Lowry himself. Birnam is a committed writer like Lowry, living in New York, who believes in the inspirational power of alcohol. He is inspired by many of the same writers as Lowry (Keats, Byron, Chatterton, Poe, Dostoyevsky, Chekhov, Mann). He is at odds with his family, whom he considers philistines, but lives off his brother's money (on an allowance of a mere fifty cents a day), carries old letters in his pocket, is obsessed with mirrors, and is prone to quote Shakespeare in a self-mocking way. Considered a boy genius, he now contemplates writing a long short-story called 'In a Glass', to equal Mann's *Death in Venice*, about an alcoholic who ends up committing suicide to spite his wife. He sometimes has a whole story in his head but can't get it written down. His mother cannot show his books to the neighbours, and he engages in a constant battle of wits with brother and his wife to obtain drink and avoid their planned weekend on a ranch. His 'lost weekend' is spent in Bellevue Hospital Psychiatric Ward, and just to give the coil of coincidence one final turn, Birnam jokingly claims to have a son called Malcolm. If Lowry felt that his efforts of the past seven years to create a masterpiece (two, if *The Last Address* be included) had been torpedoed, can one be surprised?

CHAPTER XVI

A MASTERPIECE COMPLETED 1945

> Never wait for calm water, which never was, and will never be, but dash with all your derangements at your object, leaving the rest to fortune.
>
> HERMAN MELVILLE

The shock of *The Lost Weekend* was to be eclipsed by a catastrophe which overtook the Lowrys on 7 June 1944, the day after D-Day. For them it was no day of liberation. That morning Lowry got up to make coffee when suddenly he shouted, 'Something's burning!' He ran outside and found the roof ablaze. He ran to a nearby house in his underpants, shouting 'Help, help, help me!' and clutching his stomach as though stabbed.[1] Margerie meantime was hurriedly moving things out of the shack. Finding no phone at the house, Lowry rushed up to the store. He and Cummins grabbed pails and a pump and ran down to the shack where neighbours had rallied to help fight flames which had now taken hold. Fortunately most of their manuscripts were saved. According to Margerie, she rescued *Under the Volcano*, but when she went to return for *In Ballast to the White Sea*, neighbours held her back, although it was only six feet from the door. Lowry, however, desperate that *In Ballast* was still inside, dashed back into the flames, and had to be dragged out when a burning beam crashed down across his back. He received, said Margerie, 'horrible third degree burns', and the shack was reduced to a heap of ashes. Other work was also destroyed, including his extensive revision notes for the *The Last Address*, now called *Lunar Caustic*.[2] Most of their furniture was ruined, and they saved only a few clothes and Lowry's record collection, but not his wind-up gramophone.

He was at the point of collapse and had to be tranquillized and given first aid. He then wandered around as if stunned until he and Margerie were taken off by Stan to Deep Cove for the night, and next morning he and Rubina took them to hospital in Vancouver. Lowry's burns had become infected and his wounds had to be carefully and frequently dressed. For the next few days they stayed with George and Grett Stevenson, before Jimmy Craige's son-in-law Downie Kirk, a Vancouver schoolteacher, gave them use of his beach house for a couple of weeks. For months afterwards Lowry lived in a daze, haunted by memories of what happened. In his diary, he drew a line under 7 June and copied into it from Genesis the story of Adam and Eve's expulsion from the Garden of Eden. The event heightened his sense of remorse; the feeling expressed in *Ultramarine* and more powerfully in *In Ballast*, that the avenging Furies had caught up with him and were punishing him for past sins, and it suited well the mood of the Consul with whom he now so closely identified.

He contemplated the pathetic remnants of *In Ballast*, the work of some nine or ten years – a few tiny circles of charred paper. He noted that, mysteriously, on four of the remaining scraps the word 'fire' appeared.[3] Shattering as was the loss of *In Ballast*, it was strange to recall that he had promised Burton Rascoe nine years before that he would burn that manuscript. With his extraordinary memory, this bizarre correspondence cannot have escaped him. If so, he kept it to himself, and appears never to have mentioned the Rascoe affair to Margerie.

She had cabled her sister about the disaster and her brother-in-law, Bert Woolfan, wired them $100. Malcolm wrote to Noxon with the news, saying that he was badly hurt and broke into the bargain. Could he raise enough money for them to come east? Noxon immediately sent $200 for the train fare, and invited them to stay with him in Oakville, near Toronto. Despite being still dazed and crushed, he cabled back enthusiastically that they would be arriving in Oakville at eight-thirty the following Monday morning. 'Margerie unhurt myself fit though back fried no stiff upper lips or Nordic glooms . . . you are saints please do not dread'.[4] They left their books with Stevenson, the cat with Jimmy Craige, caught the Canadian Pacific train, and arrived at Oakville on the morning of the 26th.

Noxon recalled that when Lowry arrived he was in an appalling condition. Not only did he have serious back burns but he was in a great state of agitation which did not abate for weeks. The fire, he thought, was a terrible portent. He would pace up and down, apparently haunted by visions of the burnt-down cabin, and once turned on Margerie and blamed her for not saving *In Ballast*.[5] He wrote later to Aiken that the whole affair of the fire had been shattering and had driven them both slightly cuckoo: 'We had to live through the bloody fire all over again every night. I would wake to find Margie screaming or she would wake to find me yelling and gnashing my teeth.'[6]

The Noxon house, three or four miles outside Oakville on a Lake Ontario, was large enough for both couples to live in without being on top of one another. Betty Noxon was away, so Gerald took care of them and settled them down. After a week, Margerie wrote to Matson saying they were 'only a sleeper jump from New York', and suggesting that she come down to meet him to try to straighten out the business of her book with Scribner's. When she heard back from him she took the train to New York, carrying with her manuscripts of *Horse in the Sky* and *Under the Volcano*.

Without Margerie, Lowry began to pine; he sat down and wrote to her immediately she left. He worried about whether she would get across the border, and whether she would achieve what she wanted to in New York. He did not much like children, and without her Noxon's son and his friends pained him with their unwelcome noise. Margerie phoned every few days and they wrote daily. For Malcolm, each letter was a chance to explore some new experience and his innermost response to it, and because they were carefully crafted, often going through several drafts, he sometimes kept them for his book. Once, he and Noxon got up at 6 a.m. to meet Betty's train when she returned from Virginia, but, misreading the timetable, got to the station more than an hour early. The story of that wait in the early morning for Betty, the blonde Virginian, evolved into the strange memory sequence which opens chapter 10 of the *Volcano*, the memory of the Consul as he turns to mescal in the Salón Ofélia.

> It was as if . . . he stood . . . once more upon that black open station platform, with the cornflowers and meadowsweet growing on the far side, where after drinking all night he had gone to meet Lee Maitland returning from Virginia at 7.40 in the morning, gone, light-headed, light-footed, and in that state of being where Baudelaire's angel indeed awakes . . .[7]

But Betty, the daughter of a US Marine General, disliked Lowry and his drunken ways, and he knew this. In calling her Lee Maitland he combined his name for Jan with that of the prostitute in Samuel Butler's

The Way of All Flesh, indulging again his penchant for settling old scores in his fiction.

In the meantime work on *Under the Volcano* continued, but, after the silence and isolation of Dollarton, Lowry found the populous outside world clamorous and difficult to handle. He wrote to Margerie complaining that he was 'sweltering in a delirium of acoustics', and found this peaceful place by the lake the most absolutely bloody awful noisy haven he had ever struck and an almost impossible place to work. He was, he said, fighting against falling into one of his periodic moods of deep silence, which were embarrassing and hurtful to those with him, his soul was 'plunged in great chaos' without her. He was becoming even more dishevelled and disintegrated.[8] But experiences still crowded in on him as well as into his book.

> In the Oakville Inn sits an idiot: 'If you only kept quiet nobody'd know you're crazy,' someone said to him brutally, so I was kind to him. Now he says nothing but, when one comes in and periodically for the rest of the evening:
> 'I'm watching you.' or:
> 'I can see you.'
> 'You won't escape me.'
> (He doesn't know it but he's going into the Volcano.)[9]

Ever since the fire Lowry had buttonholed strangers and simply said, 'My house burned down.' He later told how Betty had a painting of a neighbour's house which she kept in the attic. The Lowrys liked the picture because it reminded them of their lost shack. One day, at home alone, he was in the attic studying the picture when in his imagination it kept bursting into flames; a week later the very house in the picture did catch fire, something that he claimed had not happened in fifty years on that rural route, and fire engines were unable to reach it. At the local inn he found fires a ready source of conversation. Everyone had a story – summer house fires in Oakville, where temperatures soared and houses were wood-built, were not uncommon, especially when people got drunk and fell asleep smoking.[10] Such stories obsessed him.

After Betty's return, he found life with the Noxons uncomfortable, the children around the house an irritant. He told Margerie that he felt he had nothing in common with them, or with anyone, 'save yourself, & demons & certain kinds of fish'.[11] He looked forward more than ever to her 'triumphal return'. After ten days she wrote from New York that Matson was sending *Horse in the Sky* to Scribner's and was reading

Under the Volcano. Also she had met Weber, her Scribner's editor, and received assurances that *The Shapes that Creep* had gone to press; proofs would be with her soon and needed to be back with Scribner's by the end of August. He had also expressed interest in *The Last Twist of the Knife*, which Matson had promptly sent him. She had found Matson tremendously keen on Malcolm, considering him 'one of the most terrific people he ever met'. She was sure that his ordeal of failure was over and the literary tide was now running in both their favours.

When she returned she found him already adding to the *Volcano*. It was as if he needed always to reinterpret his text as he reinterpreted his life in each new context. As his alter ego, Wilderness, says in *Dark as the Grave* about the agonies of creating and finishing the *Volcano*:

> Anything set down on paper ceases from that moment progressively to be true – we must consider what happens each morning when the artist is confronted with his work again. Has it not changed in his absence? Of course it has. Even on paper something has happened to it . . .[12]

He was now working on the book's last three chapters.[13]

He had just passed his thirty-fifth birthday when Fate struck again. Noxon, then working for the CBC in Toronto, picked up the news story that Nordahl Grieg had died when the RAF bomber in which he was travelling as a war correspondent had been shot down in flames over Potsdam on 2 December the previous year. Noxon recalled Lowry talking of Grieg and so casually mentioned that he was dead. This fell like a thunderbolt. 'This was another of this terrible concatenation of events which to Malcolm was starting to spell out doom.'[14] He clasped his head in despair and when Noxon asked why, replied, 'Here's another thing that's happened to me,' which he took to mean, 'Grieg has beaten me to it. He died young.'[15] On top of that, he had died on the third anniversary of his marriage to Margerie and six months before his shack had burned down. The news was riddled with occult significance, and Lowry was stunned by it.

Margerie's proofs had still not arrived, but she did get news that Scribner's had accepted *The Last Twist of the Knife*. She got a contract, a $350 advance, and assurance of publication by the fall of 1945. When she grew angry over the delayed proofs, Lowry and Noxon read to her from Kafka's *The Castle* to encourage her to 'take the long view'.[16] She received yet more encouragement when Noxon got her writing for

CBC schools' radio. This new source of income may have made them decide to stay in Ontario at least until the spring, when *The Shapes that Creep* was due to appear. Lowry's nervousness persisted, though he kept fit by swimming in the nearby lake, once in a thunderstorm. It was his 'George III treatment' and, Margerie said, he bared his chest to the storm, 'as if in tempest there were peace'.[17]

At the end of July the Noxons moved to Niagara-on-the-Lake, but arranged for the Lowrys to have a small guest house on the Oakville property rent-free for August and September. Then, much to Betty's irritation, after visiting them in Niagara-on-the-Lake the Lowrys began talking about moving in with them. She said the house was too small and they would have to find something of their own. To Betty's further annoyance a local doctor told them that a house nearby was for rent. When the same doctor called Noxon to ask about them, worried about what tranquillizers and alcohol taken together could do to Lowry, he replied that on no account should they be prescribed anything stronger than aspirin. But the doctor, it seems, did give them tranquillizers, probably because were both in a highly nervous state. Noxon was puzzled by their apparent poverty while they were in the East, and came to believe they had decided to sponge off him and his wife and save their own income.

In late August, Lowry spoke on the phone to Aiken. Although the conversation was rather garbled, Aiken gathered that Malcolm had finally come east, driven by fire. 'How did it happen?' he asked. 'Did you fall asleep smoking, or what? Or was it spontaneous combustion of a hot manuscript? or dirty work by the Japs?'[18] Possibly from this Lowry got the idea that he might have set fire to his own house, and he sometimes hinted that this had happened. Aiken was finally earning a modest income from his writing, and, more significantly, 'I ponder that three levels of reality novel which I dreamt of on the voyage back from Spain eleven bright years ago.'[19]

Lowry told Noxon that they were about to rent a house close to him in Niagara-on-the-Lake. Margerie claimed that the Noxons were pleased by this, but Betty almost certainly shuddered at the news, and secretly hoped they would stay in Oakville. Malcolm knew that his behaviour had embarrassed and exasperated Betty, and wrote to her, hoping he had not ruined her summer.[20] But he was still unpredictable. One evening, Margerie recalled, he returned from Oakville with an Indian to whom he referred as 'Chief of the Mohawks'; 'both drunk as skunks', on bootleg whisky. Malcolm was playing up to the Chief.

'Squaw get into the kitchen,' he told her. 'Squaw build good fire. Give squaw drink.' The party ended with a war dance and Malcolm passed out in the bathtub while the Chief went off to bring in a few friends. Margerie locked all the doors and windows and sat there in panic. Finally, when the Chief failed to reappear, she went to bed.

They planned to leave Oakville for Niagara-on-the-Lake at the beginning of October, but the lease on their new house did not start until the 15th, so they parked themselves on the put-upon Noxons for two weeks, much to Betty's disgust. Even when they moved into their rented house, they seemed to spend most of their time visiting, Lowry himself often in a drunk and disturbed state. On one occasion he just panicked and said, 'I can't think. All I can see is flames!' Noxon concluded that this behaviour was due to homesickness for Dollarton. One evening while they were visiting the Noxons, according to Lowry, the house next door to theirs went up in flames. Hearing the shouts and bells they raced back home thinking it was their place, and Margerie even rushed in and moved out their manuscripts.[21]

By December there was a huge and freezing snowfall and Betty was hinting that they were not exactly welcome any more. Finally they decided to return to Dollarton. Lowry linked their leaving to an event which happened to him just before Christmas. He was telling a local storekeeper of the catalogue of fires which seemed to have occurred around him since Dollarton. The man said, 'The element is following you around,' a remark which struck Lowry so forcefully that he took it as a sign that he must return to the burned out site and rebuild the shack. This would give the whole ordeal a meaning.[22] There was just one hurdle to overcome. One freezing afternoon at the Riverside Inn, an old pub by the lake, he suddenly threw down his pencil and exclaimed, 'I've finished it.' *Under the Volcano* was completed, and, while Margerie typed it all up, he sent a Christmas Card to Aiken: 'Just finished to-day after 3 years and 3 months revision 8 hours a day approx, soberly *Under the Volcano* . . .' He later claimed that he finished it on Christmas Eve, but in fact he would continue working on it for some months. He presented his working script to the Noxons as a Christmas present – an extraordinary document, a monument to the creative ordeal of the past three or four years of rewriting, a subtle piece of self-analysis, a soul and an age laid bare through a kaleidoscope of literary allusions. Occasionally at the top of a page he had scrawled a brief prayer: 'Dear St Jude please help me,' or simply, 'God help me.'[23]

He had heard that his father was ill, and sadly reflected in his card to

Aiken. 'The old man dying, Nordahl dead. *In Ballast* is no more . . . But keep working & keep your pecker up – the birds, as you say, endure.'[24] Margerie sent Jimmy Craige a card to say they would be back in four or five weeks' time to rebuild the shack and asking him to keep his eye out for useful lumber. She had written a few scripts for the CBC and Noxon proposed that she and Malcolm try dramatizing *Moby Dick* for radio. But, although they hung on into the New Year, the idea of returning to rebuild Eridanus had been written into Lowry's personal mythology; there could be no staying on, however tempted Margerie might have been. They had spent some seven months away since the fire, and during that time, despite being highly disturbed, he had managed to complete his masterpiece. Margerie was now buoyed up by the news from Scribner's that *The Last Twist of the Knife* was at the press, that she would receive galleys 'any day now', and that it was scheduled for publication in the fall. Lowry, meantime, completed a first episode of *Moby Dick* for the CBC, and got to work drafting a second.

They finally took the train from Niagara-on-the-Lake for Vancouver on 1 February and arrived four days later. For two days they stayed with Whitey and then managed to rent their original shack (a quarter of a mile from the ashes of The Wicket Gate), though it had fallen into neglect – 'stove falling apart, no towels, pans, or wood.'[25] Despite having a heavy cold, Lowry immediately began to think about rebuilding the shack, and was furious when he found that somebody had started building on the very spot where they had had their bedroom.

A week after arriving home, Lowry heard that his father was dead. True to form, the 75-year-old Arthur had worked until the day he died, although he had been ill for some time. He died on 11 February of cancer of the bowel, though Malcolm liked to pretend that his teetotal father had died of cirrhosis of the liver. Arthur Lowry was an honourable, industrious man, shrewd in business, but not in parenting, a humourless authoritarian who indulged his wife and never understood the children he paid to be educated beyond him. He was a Victorian out of tune with the modern world of which his sons were a part, a respectable citizen whose youngest son became a delinquent genius, a son he would have loved to be proud of, a prodigal son who never returned to repent. Noxon told Aiken that it would probably do Malcolm good. 'I formed the opinion that the father was a kind of an old man of the sea and that Malc was carrying him around a good deal of the time.'[26] Margerie said that on reading the news, Malcolm fell silent for a few minutes, then said, 'Let's go for a swim,' and promptly plunged into the ice-cold waters of Burrard Inlet. Although he had got that 'old man of the sea' off his back, he must nevertheless have felt cheated. His father would never know about the masterpiece which he had all but completed; in the Old Man's eyes he had always been a failure.

In March, Noxon wrote to Aiken dilating on Lowry's visit, these ever more frequent post-mortems only adding to the Lowry myth. His reaction to the fire, said Noxon, could be understood only in terms of his own peculiar inner world and its quaint logic, quite divorced from reality.

> I don't know how well you are acquainted with . . . Under the Volcano . . . but he has tried, with a great deal of success in my opinion, to put into it all the things which have happened to him since he was born and as a shape he has chosen the triple world of the Divine Comedy. Dante's conception has in fact become Malc's overpowering obsession and every single thing has to be worked into it somehow or other.

Dollarton had become his Paradiso, said Noxon, achieved after passing through his own Infernos. It was what he called his 'first home' and there he really got down to work on his book and achieved a great deal. Having all but finished the *Volcano*, the Inferno part, and having sketched out the Purgatorio and Paradiso sections, along came the disastrous fire. Fires in wooden shacks were not uncommon but for Malcolm it was something more. He had translated the whole thing into Paradise Lost and through some imagined fault of his, he and Margerie had been expelled from the Garden of Eden. 'When they got to our place they were in a monstrous turmoil and re-lived the whole fire incident every single night for weeks.'[27] Once he got working again on the *Volcano*, however, he seemed to improve, yet all the time he was trying to grasp the significance of the fire and to relate it to the peculiar world he had made his own. Returning to Dollarton was an effort to fight back against the gods who had dealt this blow to him, and rebuilding his Paradiso was a necessary condition of finishing off the whole Dantesque opus. Noxon had worried about this return to Dollarton and had tried to keep them in Niagara with the prospect of working for the CBC and dramatizing *Moby Dick*. But the news of Grieg's death, Margerie's nightmare saga with Scribner's, and Lowry's longing for Dollarton weighed heavily, and for all these things Lowry blamed himself. Returning to

Dollarton and rebuilding the shack was his way of coping. And out of all this had emerged *Under the Volcano* – 'in my mind,' said Noxon, 'a really important piece of writing that will stand the test of time'.

> It is very beautiful and also very frightening, packed with layer upon layer of meaning, so that as you re-read you uncover more and more. The danger is that Malc will want to keep on working at it although it is finished. In a sense he dare not let it get away from him. But I have lectured him on the necessity for getting it off to a publisher pronto and I'm hoping that Margie will be able to accomplish it . . . Malc's ability as a writer has developed tremendously and if he can only maintain his very precarious balance mentally, he will go on turning out great things.[28]

But he had caused Noxon a great deal of worry over the past eight months.

He had rediscovered that friends would forgive his delinquencies for the sake of his genius, and, perhaps sensing this, he had told Noxon that he still meant to return to the East, and had no intention of living on in his shack even when it was rebuilt.

Despite heavy colds and torrential rain, and despite some horrible characters with faces 'like uncooked biscuits'[29] constructing an enormous and hideous house partly on their site and cutting them off from the sun, by the beginning of April, with the help of Whitey, they had completed the basic platform of the shack. They pointed out to the interlopers a notice announcing their intention to return and tried reasoning then pleading with them, but the new squatters were in no mood to be neighbourly. Along the beach, other than among their fishermen friends, the Lowrys were not very popular. The squatters could not make them out and Lowry was thought to be slightly mad. Jimmy Craige's daughter Dorothy, married to a cockney immigrant called Charlie King, was friendly after a fashion. But the Kings were poor and Charlie deeply resented Margerie's grand, condescending, manner. Neither of them could understand why anyone would choose to live in such a remote place in a wooden shack. Once, when Dorothy came by with her young daughter, the child said, 'Some people named Lowry used to live here. Only some kid burned it down.' The child's remark struck a nerve. 'This scared the daylights out of me,' wrote Lowry, 'since I had, unnaturally as I thought . . . suspected the same.' And he also noted the hate-twisted faces of children he had seen on the beach the day before the fire.[30] 'Does God's dictum about the millstone round the neck apply to Canadian children. Whom can we trust?'

Lumber was in short supply but could be got at a price, as could second-hand windows, from the recently demolished Dollarton lumbermill, and Whitey and Sam had rescued some heavy pieces of timber floating past which were suitable for main posts. But by the spring the two fishermen were planning their summer trip to the Arctic and the Lowrys were thrown back on their own resources, plus whatever help they could get from Jimmy Craige. Margerie told Betty Noxon that there was lots they could do clearing the burned out site, rebuilding their steps and shoring up the pier they loved so much. They rose at dawn and worked till noon on Malcolm's book, then got to work on the rebuilding until they fell into bed exhausted.[31]

The final typescript of the *Volcano* was half-completed by the beginning of April, and at the last moment he began restructuring some passages of the Consul's delirium so that the prose should reflect the disintegrated state of his mind. By now it had been significantly transformed from the stylistically spare and straightforward narrative of the 1940 version into its highly complex, 'churrigueresque' final form.

After receiving both Noxons' accounts of the Lowrys' visit, Aiken sent the latest gossip to Ed Burra in Rye.

> No word has been heard from the Malc in months. G[erald] fears it means a return to the ever-threatening nostalgie de la booze. It appears that when the shanty burned down a year or so ago, (!) it was Margie's fault that the other novel, *In Ballast to the White Sea*, was not rescued, and burned, and now a dread shadow lies between them which of course is never mentioned.[32]

Back in Eridanus, however, Lowry was notably more relaxed and cheerful, and his sense of achievement was considerable. Margerie, too, had cause for satisfaction, if only partial; the proofs of *The Shapes that Creep* suddenly arrived in two batches, one corrected, the other not. Her man at Scribner's still seemed unable to get things quite right.

As a measure of the order newly restored to his life, Lowry began to keep a diary about the rebuilding of the shack, and once again sank back into the bliss of his surroundings so that accounts of makeshift carpentry are mixed with passages of sighing ecstasy over a sunrise or the strange shadows cast by the gigantic trees of the enclosing forest – good story endings, some of them, he thought. On 11 April, he wrote,

'Worked on Volcano all morning – pier and platform in after[noon]. (Obviously the work on the book and on the house are identified in some small measure.)' They picnicked in the ruins of their old house, enduring the sad memory of its passing and 'the terrible *smell* of disaster.'[33] And he was well aware of his own eccentricities. 'How I love just to stand in these wet woods listening to the moisture dripping, becoming like a tree myself, frozen – what if someone should see me standing there?'[34] They managed to salvage some thirty planks from the debris one afternoon, before Whitey rowed round to announce that Roosevelt was dead.

By mid-April the pier and platform were completed ('we build with the instincts of sea lions'),[35] and they threw a party, with home-made loganberry wine supplied by Whitey. There were hangovers all round and, Lowry noted, it was a day in their lives completely wasted.[36] But, now the *Volcano* was finished and the foundation of the new shack laid, Lowry was beginning to review his past. One night he dreamt that his mother was sawing off his arm, and cutting away rotten wood became a persistent theme. 'I try to cut away the rotten wood of Niagara experience again, with destructive results. That bloody B[etty] – I cannot forgive.'[37]

On 20 April, despite the many prayers entered daily in his diary, disaster once again overcame them. The second-hand lumber they had bought for the walls of the shack arrived from the dismantled sawmill, and, despite Malcolm's misgivings, Margerie suggested it be laid lengthwise along Dollarton pier. First he ran a nail through his sole, without injury, then she trod on one and pierced her foot. She managed to walk home and he tried in vain to call a doctor, but being a Saturday none would come, and he cursed Canadian doctors. Her foot was not bleeding so she decided to carry on helping with the lumber. By the end of the day she was in considerable pain and Lowry began to curse again. The Gods were once more punishing him for past sins, but wreaking their vengeance now on Margerie. That night she spent moaning with pain, but he hesitated to call an ambulance so far out of the city, and next morning tried again to get a doctor, still without success. A neighbour, Al Hopkins, operated on it with a razor blade and needle, covering the wound with a brown sugar poultice, and finally George Stevenson turned up and drove her in to North Vancouver Hospital. The wound was serious, and cellulitis and blood poisoning had set in. In some despair, and as some sort of penance, Lowry set out alone to walk the fourteen miles back to Dollarton.

For the next three days he made the same trip, Stevenson driving him in to the hospital, and he walking back home, blaming himself all the while. For his past sins, he noted, Margerie was now being made to suffer. At first she was on morphia and in some danger, and once, in her delirium, muttered, 'Blank pages, millions of blank pages.' Subconsciously she saw what the rest of her life with Lowry held in store for her. That day, on his walk home through Vancouver, he caught sight of Maurice Carey. Could he be an emissary from God? Lowry asked. 'I dodged Carey. I hope not God too.'[38] Without Margerie, he wrote, 'My life is an unimaginable chaos . . . I sleep in filth.' On the fourth day, Margerie announced that she would be out by the end of the week – a statement which proved as false as the report he heard on the way home that Goering had shot himself and his daughter. However 28 April brought news that she would be out of hospital the following day. As Stan drove Lowry into town that day he reminded him, by way of comfort, that 'Life is a luminosity between two darknesses, a space between two immensities.' 'What about life is a death between two immensities?' asked Lowry. Feeling rather more cheerful, he returned to the shack, collecting flowers on the way to brighten it up, spent the evening scrubbing and cleaning it for Margerie's return, and stocked up with food from the store.

Al Hopkins welcomed Margerie home with a short concert on his guitar. Although she was still weak, had to walk with a cane, and needed daily footbaths, Lowry was so delighted to have her back that he danced attention on her, running the house, cooking the meals and bathing her wound. In the wider world that first week in May, as Lowry noted, extraordinary things were happening to coincide with their private sense of exultation. Hitler committed suicide, Mussolini was hanged upside down in Milan, the *Wehrmacht* collapsed, and Margerie received a gift of flowers from a mysterious admirer. Her illness had again made him acutely aware of his dependence on her, and his anxiety to show his love and appreciation of her is evident from the notes he left lying around the shack, composed in their private schmaltzy baby-talk – drawings, poems, flights of absurd fancy, addressed to the timid but passionate Miss Harteebeeste from the macho but noble El Leon.

On 7 May, the first day of peace, Lowry noted 'a queer sort of stillness' in the air, and wrote yet again about 'a new start', but on VE day 'the horrors' next door tore up the Lowrys' flags and stakes and danced on their pier. On 13 May, in the middle of a great storm, he was reworking chapter 11 of the *Volcano* while Margerie typed out chapter 10. 'God deliver our house from devils,' he wrote. In an effort to catch up for lost time he began getting up earlier each morning. By the 22nd he could report that the *Volcano* really was all but completed. The 'horrors' were having a celebration and their children were throwing Lowry's lumber off the pier. When he rushed up to them angrily to protest they smiled, 'How do you like our new structure?' they asked, proudly surveying their monstrous construction. Lowry did not record his reply. As a break from composition he read some Hardy and John Gould Fletcher, and prayed for spring to arrive. Margerie meantime had the satisfaction of hearing her education scripts broadcast on the CBC over Whitey's crackling battery wireless when their own batteries failed.

On 1 June, 'after taking some thought', he sent the MS of *Under the Volcano* to Matson, following it with a long letter five days later, making the point that it was intended as the first part of a trilogy, and required a short preface and some notes. He thought he had done a pretty good job on it and eliminated the majority of the faults in the earlier version.[38]

The Lost Weekend, he added, was a 'considerable blow' to him and he did not know how far the success of that book would militate against the success of his: doubtless some would regard the *Volcano* as nothing but a pale reflection of it, but in fact nearly all the alcoholic part was written before he had ever heard of that book, and, having read 'the horrible thing' finally, he did his very utmost not to be influenced by it and even removed a quite fine passage because it seemed to possess something of the other book's rhythm. For himself he could say that *Under the Volcano* began where *The Lost Weekend* left off, and was of course about lots of other things as well. Even more damaging was the impact of *The Lost Weekend* upon the second part of the trilogy based on the novella called *The Last Address*. It was true that he was doing something fundamentally different and it probably would not matter, but he had somehow to overcome a not very worthy professional jealously over it. Matson acknowledged receipt of the manuscript on 22 June, saying that he was reading it and would submit it first to Duell, Sloan & Pearce.

The house now began to take shape. They started building a porch looking towards the mountains, and after work they swam or went for walks. Lowry particularly enjoyed walking to Deep Cove to visit Stan, and was making notes on a series of books about the occult. And on 16 July, Margerie's fortieth birthday (though he may still have thought she was two years younger), he made a special effort to please her. 'It was a glorious day,' he recorded, 'God be thanked . . . Feel very happy – a sense of life being renewed.' He decided to build a temporary barrier to shield them from 'the horrors' next door. In the mean time no word had come from the CBC about *Moby Dick*.

By the end of the month Matson replied that the book held a peculiar fascination for him but while he thought it had enormous potential, 'it needs a great deal of work to bring it down to size and proportion within the limits of its own worth. Perhaps I have become impatient with it and that may be the reason why this novel is much too long, and much too full of talk – for me.'[40] Cap Pearce, of Duell, Sloan & Pearce, had reported that he thought it ought to be placed in a 'sharper and more dramatic form', and doubted whether it would have much appeal as it stood.

This infuriated Margerie, who promptly wrote reprimanding Matson for failing utterly to understand what Malcolm was trying to do. Good books or even first-rate ones must come his way from time to time, but a book of the calibre of *Under the Volcano* was a rarity, she said. She had worked with him for five years on it and was well aware of his faults as a writer. For example,

> His astonishing awareness of the thickness of life, of the layers, the depths, the abysses, interlocking and interrelated, causes him to write a symphony where anyone else would have written a sonata or at most a concerto, and this makes his work sometimes appear dispersed, whereas actually the form and context have arisen so inextricably one from the other that they cannot be dissociated.

He was also hampered by having the equipment of a poet and so could never be a great writer of 'character'. But this book was a masterpiece, not just a thing of potentialities, and could be read a hundred times, each reading yielding yet more meanings. It could also be read with enjoyment at a surface level as the story of the last day in the life of a drunkard, and was frequently hilariously funny, and at one level, 'a sort of cosmic japes'. But the book needed to be considered on *all* its levels, which no doubt a man as busy as Matson was not able to do properly. The reader needed to be patient and to want his imaginative life enriched; he needed to want to seek out the author's intention, he needed to be someone who loved literature. To tell Malcolm the book was too long and full of talk, she concluded, was like saying the same thing to Joyce or Proust about their masterworks. He was being offered the opportunity to handle not just a good or first-rate book, but a classic; it was as much a milestone as *Moby Dick*, and must be handled in that way. The form was right and complete. 'Malcolm has found his style and come to maturity as an artist with it: it is finished.'[41] Although this bore Margerie's signature, the confident tone is Lowry's.

As far as they were concerned, Matson had failed them, and this letter was intended as a request for the return of the *Volcano*. They would now try to sell it on their own. It was probably at this point, disillusioned with Matson, that Lowry decided to send the novel to Jonathan Cape in London. He hoped, he wrote, that it might realize some of the promise he must have seen in him when he published *Ultramarine*. He knew he was still in Cape's debt, but his past lack of prudence was due to a breakdown and he hoped that in sending him the *Volcano* he would make some amends for his past behaviour. He suggested that Calder-Marshall, who had encouraged him at an early stage, might correct the manuscript if need be. The book was the inferno part of a Dantesque trilogy to be called *The Voyage that Never Ends*. The other two parts were almost ready when 'the theme stepped outside of my book and demolished my house by fire'. The book lost in the fire would be rewritten just as the destroyed house had been rebuilt, and he was writing on the very spot where 'the flames once raged the fiercest'.[42]

The completion of *Under the Volcano* was the greatest achievement of Lowry's life, yet at different times various other people collaborated in its writing. Aiken and Calder-Marshall read it and commented on it in its early form, and Jan Gabrial was his first model for Yvonne. The more telling involvement of Margerie and Noxon were clearly crucial to its final shape. And yet, even after the book had been sent off, Lowry would probably have been perfectly content to continue revising it. It had come to obsess him; the heart and soul of the man, and a variety of significant relationships through which he had sought to create an identity were in some strange alchemical fashion embodied in the book. In this eccentric, convoluted and visionary text he had accomplished a work of profound self-analysis and prophetic insight which could hardly be bettered. He came to regard it as the centrepiece of a grand fictional design, incorporating everything he had previously written and was yet to compose – the Proustian project mentioned to Cape but greatly elaborated. It is not always easy to understand the shifting nature of his metaphysic, nor to relate it very precisely to his view of the world or himself at any given time. However, as a running commentary on the conscious life of a man in tune with the times, a man whose central problems were of alienation, identity and exile, there can be few better achievements. The dropping of atomic bombs on Hiroshima and Nagasaki on 6 and 9 August he thought had somehow confirmed absolutely the book's apocalyptic vision.

With Margerie still hobbling on a cane, at the beginning of August Lowry cut off the end of his thumb while ripsawing and blood poisoning set in. In addition, he suffered from tooth abscesses, and had to take to his bed. His varicose veins were also giving trouble, and he had to soak his legs alternately in hot and cold water, lugged by Margerie in buckets from the store. While soaking his feet he composed tunes on his uke, but all work on the shack was stopped, and in September he wrote in his diary that it had been 'a disastrous more than month' for him.[43]

There was, too, the sense of the end of an era. As the Second World War became history, inflation began to take hold and there was talk of change in the post-war world. No sooner was their shack on the brink of completion and paradise regained, than a law was passed designating part of the forest for demolition to make way for 'Autocamps of the Better Class'. The news that their newly built home was under sentence of death, wrote Lowry, 'was finally too much for our sense of humour and my temperature went up . . . to 104'.[44] Aiken would soon write to say that he was returning to England before the trustees of Jeake's House sold it out from under him, and not realizing Lowry had already sent off his novel, he urged him to 'let it come out . . . (and) break the umbilical cord'.[45]

The house they had all but completed that summer, their third on the beach, was better than the previous ones inside but less attractive outside. It still lacked inside walls and the roof leaked, but there were windows on three sides, and two good-sized rooms, one a bedroom in which Malcolm had his desk. In October the waterfront was reprieved; the autocamps were not be built after all. They would not be disturbed for the next three years, after which they would be free to buy the land at a reasonable price. 'Thus', he wrote to Aiken, 'does your old Malc, if still a conservative-Christian-anarchist, at heart, at last join the ranks of the petty bourgeoisie.' As to his novel, it had gone off into the void, and he had had no intelligent comments or encouragement so far. He feared that *The Lost Weekend* had stolen its fire, but he was still confident. 'I'll learn 'em, as Mr Wolfe said . . .'[46] Feeling more than ever cut off, he asked Aiken to send any old literary journals he could spare, since all intelligent American magazines had been unprocurable in Canada for years, and all he had to read were copies of the *Illustrated London News* and the *British Weekly* sent from England by his mother. He also wanted to know of any American magazine which took short stories of an experimental kind.

But he was soon (on 2 November) to receive a delayed word of encouragement about the *Volcano*, from Jonathan Cape, who, while not offering criticisms, said that his reader (Daniel George) was greatly impressed and that it was a long time since he himself had begun to read a book with such hope and expectation. 'I will send you a cable when I have finished reading it so it is possible you may get a cable before receiving this letter.'[47] Excited by this, Lowry immediately replied saying he was dissatisfied with his US agent and asking Cape to act for him in America. He also said he would prefer to deal directly with him for UK publication, probably thinking that after failing to produce his book of Paris stories and not returning Cape's advance in 1934, Innes Rose might have washed his hands of him. The expected cable from Cape never came. As Lowry wrote to him later: 'I waited and waited in vain for that cable as you can only wait in winter in the Canadian wilderness, unless it is in Reckmondwike, Yorks.'[48]

In July he had received news that under the provisions of Arthur's will, his income of £400 a year (£33 *6s. 8d.* a month) would continue. Under wartime regulations he had been receiving only £25 a month since 1940, so he wrote asking if he could now obtain the accumulated balance due to him. According to Margerie they eventually received around $3,500. With this windfall safely in the bank, they decided it was time to travel, and in October Lowry told Aiken that they were considering taking off for six months into the sun, to Haiti or on a freighter to the South Seas.[49] Without inner walls to insulate them against the Canadian winter, anywhere warm was preferable. Lowry also felt that Margerie's health had suffered on his behalf and she deserved a change of scenery. Haiti he may well have dreamed of since reading William Seabrook's *The Magic Island* in New York, and in the South Seas he would be following vaguely in Tom Harrisson's footsteps.

In November, however, waiting patiently but in vain for Matson to return his manuscript and for that long-delayed cable from Cape, they decided, after all, to go to Mexico, planning to leave on 28 November, taking first a plane to Los Angeles, where Lowry was to meet his in-laws for the first time. With some trepidation he applied for an entry visa to the US, and was granted one valid for three months. (That day he took his first drink after a period of devoted abstinence.) They studied maps of Mexico and tried to learn some basic Spanish. It would be Margerie's first visit to a foreign country and she was extremely excited at the prospect, but Lowry was worried about leaving Dollarton and going off into an uncertain future in a country in which he had suffered so much. And, as he noted, November had always been a disturbing and unlucky month for him ever since Paul Fitte had committed suicide sixteen years earlier.

With Cambridge very much in mind, and perhaps with the idea of applying for a Fulbright scholarship, he wrote to Stuart, asking if his son, Donald, himself at Cambridge, could find out for him how to apply for an MA.

Doubtless, with the war over, he was wondering which of his old Cambridge friends had survived. Margerie, remembering that she had left a trunk of clothes with the Smiths, went back to pick her wardrobe for the trip, and insisted on taking with her her Arctic skunk fur coat. If she was going to travel she was determined to travel in style. They left during a typical Vancouver downpour and their last glimpse of the new cabin was through a curtain of rain. Ironically, the day after he left, Cape sent Lowry a conditional acceptance of his novel, but it would be the last day of the year before the letter caught up with him in Mexico.

CHAPTER XVII

MORE TROUBLE UNDER THE VOLCANO
1945–1946

Travel is a neurosis, so how should one expect that it would not make you neurotic?

MALCOLM LOWRY

According to Margerie, Malcolm was keen to travel but did not want to leave Canada. Those who knew them both said that it was Margerie who wanted to travel and that he preferred to stay in Eridanus, always fearful of leaving, especially after their eviction scare in the fall of 1945. They chose Mexico because Margerie was curious to see the setting of the book on which she had worked with him so diligently for the past five years. From his point of view, if he went, it was in the hope of meeting again Juan Fernando Márquez. There was also the advantage that Mexico was cheap. However, after Oakville, he was nervous about setting off into the unknown.

He took along a copy of *Under the Volcano* and the few charred remains of *In Ballast* as a talisman or a reminder of his fearful past, for it was still *that* month and the 15th was only just past. They both had notebooks, ready to record every experience. There might after all be another novel in this pilgrimage. His notes produced *Dark as the Grave Wherein My Friend is Laid*, an extended reflection on the nature of fiction and the role of the writer, trading back and forth between the worlds of reality and fiction.

On the flight to Los Angeles he was exhilarated to find himself flying over the border he was unable to get across in 1939, and, after a period of relative abstinence, began drinking – 'a little, not much', reflects his alter ego, Sigbjørn Wilderness, in *Dark as the Grave*, just 'to celebrate'.[1] But he also needed Margerie there to steady his nerves and make him feel secure. 'We're on our honeymoon,' says Primrose, Sigbjørn's wife.

'We're always on our honeymoon,' he replies.[2] Margerie certainly dressed for the part. Tired, no doubt, of the primitive life in Dollarton, and looking to a more exotic future, despite heading for sweltering Mexico, she was determined to travel in that beautiful fur coat of hers.

In LA ('that deathscape of bleary hoardings,' he wrote)[3] they were met by Priscilla, her husband Bert Woolfan, and her mother, Emily, and taken to their palatial home in Hollywood Hills. Priscilla was much impressed with the handsome, weatherbeaten, blue-eyed brother-in-law who stepped off the aircraft. Lowry in turn was thrilled to be part of a family and to meet Priscilla, who he said he had seen in movies and felt he already knew. In his tweed suit and smoking his pipe, he was on his best behaviour, playing the part of a typical charming Englishman in the best Hollywood manner. Margerie had never told her family about the spartan life they lived, but she told Priscilla it had been her karma to meet Malcolm, restore his self-respect and serve his genius. To demonstrate her feelings she fussed over him a great deal and said that he must have four meals a day, which was hard on Priscilla, whose own husband was very demanding.

As Malcolm felt unable to handle money, she was appointed 'Keeper of the King's Purse', and, one afternoon, when the two sisters emerged from the Pickwick Bookstore on Hollywood Boulevard, they found him waiting outside. 'Could I have ten cents for a Coca-Cola, please?' he asked. The Woolfans were eager to be hospitable, and had made plans to keep him entertained. Bert took him to a football match which thrilled him so much he talked about it non-stop at dinner that evening; they also dined out at Musso Frank's. But the high spot of the visit was an evening with film director Preston Sturges, reputedly the third highest paid person in America.

Sturges held Sunday evening parties for between forty and fifty people and, Bert being Sturges' doctor, the Woolfans were frequent guests at his home, a grand mansion with a sixty foot long reception room with a ping-pong table, and a bar which occupied the whole of one end of the room. On their fifth wedding anniversary, 2 December, the Lowrys were also invited. A US ping-pong champion was there challenging all comers. Lowry took him on and to everyone's surprise thrashed him twice over; all that practice on the dining table at Jeake's House had finally paid off. He was in good spirits and good physical shape, but had reverted to regular drinking, unable to resist the pressure to have his drink constantly 'freshened'.

At dinner he was thrilled to find himself sitting next to John F. Seitz, the cinematographer of such silent movies as *The Prisoner of Zenda* and *Four Horsemen of the Apocalypse*. But during the meal he learned that Seitz's latest film was Billy Wilder's *The Lost Weekend*, with Ray Milland playing the drunken Don Birnam. His sense of being pursued by Furies was only intensified by hearing it acclaimed one of the best films of the year, Milland and Wilder each winning Oscars for it. The parallels with his own work scared him. What, he asked, was the relation between Charles Jackson and Don Birnam, and between Malcolm Lowry and Geoffrey Firmin? To say these novels were autobiographical was too simple. His books were the outcome of a complicated life, so must Jackson's be. But this rival book had made him suicidal when he read it; now it was a great critical success. Meantime he and his book remained obscure and unpublished.

However, he was delighted to be part of a household, and followed Priscilla around like a puppy, asking if he could just watch her prepare a meal or do housework. Then, two days before they left, he gave her the manuscript of *Under the Volcano* saying sheepishly he would like her to read it. 'Margie says it's a masterpiece,' he said. At first she demurred. 'I'm not an intellectual,' she told him. 'No, but you're very sensitive,' he said. So, somewhat dubiously, she took it to bed with her. To begin with, she found the going heavy, but at the end of chapter I, she read the passage ending, 'Over the town, in the dark tempestuous night, backwards revolved the luminous wheel.'[4] She turned to Bert, engrossed in a medical journal, and said, 'Listen to this.' When she had finished, he said simply, 'My God!' Margerie was right, they decided. Malcolm *was* a genius after all.

Before leaving, they applied for Mexican visas, and were assured, he claimed later, that all regulations had been complied with and all was satisfactory.[5] They were given tourist cards valid for six months. Now, while terrified by the prospect, Lowry was ready to return to his own dark past and give Margerie a conducted tour of his Mexican Inferno.

Bert had quite taken to Malcolm, whom he found very innocent and trusting, and treated his varicose veins by injection. Privately, however, he noted that he drank rather more than necessary. Then over dinner, Lowry was expounding what the Woolfans thought were very left-wing views (there was a spy-scare on in Canada and he was unhappy about the political climate in America), when the conservative Bert began to argue with him. Lowry grew incensed, saying loudly that he was not prepared to be contradicted. After an embarrassed silence, Priscilla reminded him that he was a guest and that people at their table were free to speak their minds. The moment passed and on their last night there he was his old charming self, entertaining them, singing and playing his ukulele. But when they left finally for Mexico, a slight question mark was left hanging over him in the minds of his in-laws.

After just two weeks in LA, they flew to Mexico City. As a wedding anniversary gift, Margerie had given Malcolm a first English edition of Julian Green's *The Dark Journey*, and he wondered whether this was an omen of what was to come. Travel disturbed him: 'Travel . . . was the extension of every anxiety, which man tried to get rid of by having a quiet home.'[6]

He was full of fears – fearful of disease and death, of losing Margerie, of accidents and traffic, of fire and of 'the brutal boot-faced mask' of the Immigration Officer.[7] He was fearful of Mexico and memories of past disasters, and of mescal, of charges of plagiarism, and past untruths returning to brand him a liar. But the words of Juan Fernando came to comfort him: 'Are you making more tragedies? Throw away your mind.'

He was excited by 'the miracle' of his return, especially when Margerie spotted Popocatepetl, and Mexico City appeared below and they were told that their arrival coincided with festivities for the Virgin of Guadalupe. At the airport they had to pay ten pesos in advance for a taxi, and Lowry felt aggrieved. The profligate who had left Mexico seven years before had returned a miser. In the meantime they learned to say in Spanish, 'No we are not rich Americans, we are poor Canadians.' ('Nosotros no somos Americanos ricos, nosotros somos Canadianos *pobres*'.)

They checked into the Hotel Canada, where he and Jan had parted in 1937 after the quarrel which had 'chopped his life in half as surely as if he had done it with a meat cleaver,'[8] and he recalled seeing the fawns dragged off to have their throats slit in the restaurant kitchen. But Mexico had changed; the picture of Cárdenas in the hotel lobby had been replaced by that of Camacho. During the following week they visited the Palacio de Bellas Artes, Chapultapec Park, the Church of Isabel la Católica (Saint of Dangerous and Desperate Causes), El Petate restaurant where he had found the menu used in chapter 11 of *Under the Volcano*, and the Münchener Kindl he had once frequented with the sinister John D. Bonsfield.[9] And Margerie had her first tequila at a cantina called La Cucaracha.

Dark memories were stirring and Lowry began to think he was tempting fate by returning there. The prospect of finding Juan Fernando was reassuring, but the idea of going to Oaxaca to find him was terrifying. The country still had a supernatural influence over him, he decided, and therefore was perhaps a place to come as pilgrims, humbly, to find a meaning to their lives. Visiting the basilica of the Virgin of Guadalupe for the festival, something occurred which struck the 'first bass chord' and gave a sign of possible trouble ahead. After praying at the altar they took refuge from the crowds in a tiny cantina, when a drunk came by and set upon a blind woman carrying a dead dog, first beating her and then the dog with a stick. In the mêlée, Margerie's wine bottle was broken and the drunk then attacked them as 'Americanos', demanding they pay for the broken bottle, and they had to escape in the confusion. Clearly Americans were no longer popular in Mexico. 'We are not rich Americans,' they chanted, 'we are poor Canadians.'

From the outset Lowry had expressed anxiety about visiting Cuernavaca, fearing his distressful past would return to upset his delicately balanced psyche. But Margerie was eager to see the town on which Quauhnahuac was based, the initial setting of the *Volcano*, and so on 4 December they boarded the Flecha Roja (Red Flyer) bus and headed south. On the way, Lowry had 'the mysterious feeling that this road from Mexico City to Cuernavaca had something to teach him'.[10] Passing through the outskirts of the town he saw hideous buildings going up everywhere. The Cuernavaca Inn was changed, and the Terminal Cantina was gone. After checking their luggage (except Margerie's fur coat) at the bus station, they crossed the *zócalo* past Cortés' Palace to where El Universal still stood, the cantina where he had noted down the dialogue for his last chapter, and on which the Farolito was partly based. They sat drinking at a sidewalk table, hoping improbably that Juan Fernando would come by.

American tourists swarmed through the town casting money about, American cars circled the *zócalo*, and jukeboxes bellowed. Lowry wondered whether his old house in the Calle Humboldt and Laruelle's tower were still there. They took a room at the Pensione Vera Cruz, and next morning at the Café Bahia next to El Universal, they met Eduardo Ford, the Mexican-American proprietor, a shady but likeable character who told them of an apartment to let at 24 Calle Humboldt, at the Casa Maria. When Margerie went to check on it, she met the landlady, María Luisa Blanco de Arriola, and returned to say that Casa María was Laruelle's tower, chevron windows and all, now turned into apartments. The coincidence was too much to ignore; Fate again was playing a hand. Lowry had never seen inside the tower, only imagined it. They agreed to take it and moved in. The apartment was on the second floor with large windows facing east to the garden and the pool, the *barranca*, the town's outskirts, the bullring and a wooded valley rising to the twin volcanoes.[11] The dining room had windows on three sides looking down on the Calle Fray de las Casas – Calle Tierra del Fuego in *Under the Volcano* – and on the flat roof Malcolm set his desk and there they sunbathed and observed the town. There was a large garden, full of fruit and flowers, and a pool filled from a cool mountain stream. They found the radios, jukeboxes and barking dogs disturbing, and Malcolm took to wearing earplugs to deaden the 'maddening Aeolian horror'.[12] During the day he watched the mailbox from up in the tower, fascinated to see that the same postman, the one he had put into the *Volcano*, still delivered letters on the Calle Humboldt as he had in 1937. But would the cable from Cape ever arrive?

Another thing was making him feel uneasy. Living in the tower he felt in danger of becoming his own character, not Laruelle but the Consul, a feeling intensified when Margerie led him down the garden to peer into the *barranca* beyond. As he wrote to Priscilla, 'It gives us an odd feeling of living inside (!) a book, a kind of intra-dimensional life.' The town was preparing for the Christmas fiesta, the Nocha Buena, and that first afternoon they visited Maximilian's Palace along an overgrown path, and found the building deserted and crumbling, still a symbol of blighted love. On Christmas Eve they drank tequila together in the town and Eduardo Ford invited them for a drink. Lowry, realizing that alcohol had now reasserted its powerful presence in his life, prayed that Margerie would treat his drinking with the same toleration as Dostoyevsky's second wife had his gambling. And Dostoyevsky, too, he noted, hated travel. Over Christmas they visited the Cathedral, the Casino de la Selva and the Station from which Hugh departed after the Consul's death. Lowry had wrongly thought the old Aztec name Quauhnahuac meant 'Where the Eagle Stops' but now found that it meant 'Near the Wood' – most appropriate in view of his book's Dantesque echoes. But he was sinking more and more into 'a *barranca* of fear of he knew not what.' While Margerie was being renewed by the trip, he seemed 'to see nothing, love nothing (and) swayed away from her . . . into some agony of self, chained by fear, wrapped in the tentacles of the past'.[13]

They argued over his passion for drinking in the morning. 'Drinking before breakfast is like swimming before breakfast. A loathing of all respectable people comes over him, of all those who did not drink before breakfast, and before lunch.'[14] He always invited Margerie to join him, and she always said, like Yvonne in the novel, 'You have one . . . I'll cheer.' But gradually she began to drink along. 'They only had one drink, however, or at most two or three.'[15]

On New Year's Eve they took the bus to Yautepec, upon which same route he and Jan had seen the dying Indian; *Under the Volcano* and its ghosts were close at his elbow. Within him his daemon was writing another novel. On their return, there was the long expected letter from Cape. Lowry poured a glass of *habanero* and repaired to the bathroom to read it.

Cape wrote that he and also two readers had read the novel carefully, and he thought it best to show him one reader's report which crystallized what all three thought of it. If Lowry was prepared to make the suggested cuts, he undertook to bring it out within a year. If not, he would think again, but would not necessarily say no. 'We feel here that the book has integrity and importance . . . [and] . . . believe that it would be considerably improved aesthetically if the suggestions in the report are carried out.'[16]

The reader reported that the first quarter or third of the book was slow – a grave fault if the reader was not closely engaged – although, he said, he had later become more interested. It was, however, a novel of situation rather than action. All that really happened, he said, was that 'Geoffrey, Hugh and Yvonne spend the day roaming about, riding in a bus, visiting a fair, etc.; Hugh and Yvonne being mostly together and Geoffrey largely on his own. Eventually they lose him, he drifts into yet another cantina to booze, and in the end gets shot by a local thug.' All this was enormously elaborated by '(i) flashbacks of the characters' past lives and past and present thoughts and emotions; (ii) Mexican local colour heaped on in shovelfuls, and (iii) the mescal-inspired phantasmagoria, or heebie-jeebies, to which Geoffrey has succumbed.' The flashbacks were 'often tedious and unconvincing', the Mexican local colour was 'very well done and gives one an astonishing sense of the place and the atmosphere' and the mescal-inspired phantasmagoria were 'impressive but . . . too long, wayward and elaborate.' The book inevitably recalled *The Lost Weekend*. In sum, his objections included the initial tedium, weakness of character drawing, and the author having spread himself too widely. The book was overlong and over-elaborate for its content, and would have been far more effective if just half or two-thirds its length. 'The author has over-reached himself, and is given to eccentric word-spinning and too much stream-of-consciousness stuff.' The book's virtues were '(i) the astonishingly vivid and well-observed picture of Mexico; and (ii) the equally vivid and mostly impressive exploration of the tormented weakness of the drunken Geoffrey. (I question whether such a Consul would not have been sacked long before he got into such a state!)' It was well worth serious consideration but drastic surgery would make it more effective and worthwhile. He suggested cuts to the frequent over-long 'rambling, word-spinning passages' and to passages like those dealing with Hugh's past life, which were without much interest or relevance. 'Everything should be concentrated on the drunk's inability to rise to the occasion of Yvonne's return; on his delirious consciousness (which is well done); and on the local colour, which is excellent throughout.'[17]

The first reader, who advised publication, was Cape's chief literary adviser, Daniel George; the second, whose report Lowry saw, was William Plomer. To him, Plomer's report was worse than a rejection; it was an invitation to rewrite his book, and only added to his feeling of growing tension. The book had taken him nine years to write – 'time to grow up, time to die, time to fight three world wars in, time for a child to have grown up and become a drunkard.'[18] The reference to *The Lost Weekend* cut deep, and confirmed his fear that Jackson's book had sunk *Under the Volcano*. He experienced, he told Cape, 'one of those *barranca*-like drops in spirits peculiar to authors'.[19] Margerie [Primrose] tried to comfort him:

> You said yourself that English talent has all run to literary criticism. And that they're jealous of anything really good that comes out. And you said . . . that while [they're] always deploring the fact that your national literature has become so feeble when anything threatens that seems to be just the answer to their prayers, they'll do their damnedest to kill it.[20]

Eleven years after leaving England he still felt alienated from its prevailing literary ethos.

New Year was a good excuse to hit the bottle hard, Margerie joining him, and he noted ironically that finally he had persuaded her to drink in the morning like himself. On New Year's morning they were both drunk, and when Lowry left to buy two new bottles, Margerie was beginning to suffer mild delusions. It took them four days to sober up. On 4 January, they went out for the first time, walking to the church opposite the Borda Gardens by the Cinema Morelos. In the church they saw the effigy of a saint looking somewhat like Hamlet, but stabbing himself in the stomach with a pen. 'Undoubtedly,' wrote Lowry, 'another writer.'[21] And in the Borda Gardens he hoped Margerie would not see carved on a tree: 'Jan and Malcolm December 1936 – Remember me.'

Afterwards he settled at his desk on the roof of the tower and began to compose his reply to Cape. Despite his stressful state and sense of impending doom, he was about to produce one of his finest pieces of writing and probably the most subtle and revealing letter ever written by an English author about his work. He agreed with the reader's intelligent comments, he began, and might even have made them himself were he a reader in similar circumstances. But as an author, asked to make revisions, they left him at a loss. True, the book began slowly, but a reader would find it easier to navigate if it were in print as an established classic rather than in typescript, having 'the desperate look of an unpublished manuscript'. Much of course would depend on the reader's state of mind and his readiness to seek for 'the author's true intention' – a preface or suitable blurb might help, to give this mescal bottle an enticing label in order to attract the drinker. Was not *The Waste Land* attractive partly because of prior knowledge of it and the anticipation its reputation aroused?

The first chapter was necessary as it stood; it set the tone and mood of the book, 'as well as the slow melancholy tragic rhythm of Mexico itself'. In any event, the book was 'a good deal thicker, deeper, better, and a great deal more carefully planned and executed than [the reader] suspects'. The first and last chapters echoed and responded across the arch of the intervening chapters. Without the first chapter as it stood, the book would lose much of its meaning. While not wishing to defend his every word, he was pleading for a rereading. He recognized, he said, that the main defect of the book, and one which gave rise to many others, was the fact that the author's equipment was incurably subjective, more suitable for a poet than a novelist. He had tried to conceal these faults, but poems often had to be read many times before their full significance was grasped, and the reader had failed, in one reading, to grasp the full meaning of the book. As to the weakness of the character drawing, well, he was not attempting to draw characters in the normal way; the four main characters should be seen as aspects of the same person, of the human spirit. 'There are a thousand writers who can draw adequate characters till all is blue for one who can tell you anything new about hell fire. And I am telling you something new about hell fire.'

Perhaps he had 'overreached himself', spread himself too much, and if the book was 'too long and over-elaborate', 'given to eccentric word-spinning and too much stream-of-consciousness stuff', but without knowing the author's intention a reader was in no position to make such a judgement. Readers could overreach themselves, too, by reading too quickly and superficially. Any 'eccentric word-spinning' was 'in some way thematic', and most of the stream-of-consciousness 'stuff' was simply 'disguised, honest-to-God exposition'. The flashbacks may often be 'tedious and unconvincing'; if so he would be glad to make cuts, but in cutting, 'the whole churrigueresque structure' should be borne in mind. He was, of course, delighted the reader enjoyed 'the sense of place and atmosphere' through the 'local colour heaped on in shovelfuls' – but its significance had not been grasped. The effect had not been achieved through carelessness; the colour and atmosphere were there for a reason.

There was also, he said, a contradiction at the heart of the report:

> Here is my mescal-inspired phantasmagoria, which is impressive but already too long wayward and elaborate, – to say nothing of too much eccentric word-spinning and stream-of-consciousness stuff – and yet on the other hand, I am invited to concentrate still *more* upon it, since all this can be after all nothing but the delirious consciousness (which is very well done) – and I would like very much to know how I can concentrate still more upon a delirious consciousness without making it still more long wayward elaborate, and since that is the way of delirious consciousnesses, without investing it with still more stream-of-consciousness stuff: moreover here too is my local colour, and although this is already 'heaped on in shovelfuls' (if excellent throughout) I am invited to concentrate still more upon it and this without calling in the aid of some yet large long-handled scoop-like implement . . . nor do I see either how I can very well concentrate very much more than I have on the drunk's inability to rise to the occasion of Yvonne's return without incurring the risk of being accused of heaping on the mescal-inspired phantasmagoria with – at least! – a snow plough.[22]

He could hardly act on these suggestions without writing another book.

Jackson had obeyed the reader's (Plomer's) aesthetic and done an excellent job within the limits he set himself. But it should have been *The Lost Weekend* which recalled the *Volcano* rather than the other way round. The *Volcano* was begun in 1936, when he had also written *The Last Address*, set in the same hospital in which Don Birnam spends an afternoon. These had evolved with *In Ballast* into a trilogy, *The Voyage that Never Ends*, dealing with 'the battering the human spirit takes (doubtless because it is over-reaching itself) in its ascent towards its true purpose.' *The Lost Weekend*, with its 'desiccating' effect on him, and the fire which consumed *In Ballast*, he could only regard as a punishment. His past worst fault had been precisely lack of integrity. 'Youth plus booze plus hysterical identifications plus vanity plus self-deception plus no work plus more booze.' But just when he was about to offer something worthwhile to atone for his sins, 'it turns out that somebody from Brooklyn has just done the same thing better. Or has he not?'[23] He could not now turn his book into another *Lost Weekend*, as the reader seemed to want.

He would, however, suggest some of the book's deeper meanings and form, and its author's intentions. The twelve chapters were twelve blocks, each a unity in itself, all related and interrelated. Twelve was a numerically significant unit – for example the twelve labours of Hercules, the hours in a day (the time span of the book), the twelve months of the year, not to mention the symbolic importance of twelve in the Jewish Cabbala to which the deep layer of poetry in the book attached itself, and the Tree of Life atop which stood Kether, or Light, and somewhere above the middle an unpleasant abyss. The spiritual home of the Consul was probably Qliphoth, the domain of shells and daemons, symbolized by the inverted Tree of Life.[24] This was not important to an understanding of the book, he said, but was mentioned in passing to hint that, as Henry James says, 'There are depths.' He had to have his twelve because 'it is as if I hear a clock slowly striking midnight for Faust . . . I feel it destined to have 12 chapters and nothing more nor less will satisfy me.'[25]

The book, he continued, was written on numerous planes for all kinds of reader, and his approach was opposite to that of Joyce, trying always to simplify what originally may suggest itself as complex and baffling, rather than complicating the simple and straightforward. It could be read simply as a story, which could, if the reader chose, be skipped, though more would be got out of it if it were not skipped. It could be looked on as a sort of symphony or an opera, and even, if one preferred, a horse opera. 'It is hot music, a poem, a song, a tragedy, a comedy, a farce, and so forth. It is superficial, profound, entertaining and boring, according to taste. It is a prophesy, a political warning, a cryptogram, a preposterous movie, and a writing on the wall.' It could even be looked upon as a kind of machine – a machine which worked, as he had discovered. And just in case it was thought he meant it to be everything but a novel, he had better say that that was what it *was* intended to be, and a deeply serious one at that.[26] In Edmund Wilson's words about Gogol, it was concerned with 'the forces in man which cause him to be terrified of himself' and with man's guilt, his remorse, 'his ceaseless struggling toward the light under the weight of the past, and with his doom'.[27] Allegorically, it was the world, the Garden of Eden from which we were ever more threatened with eviction. The Consul's drunkenness symbolized at one level 'the universal drunkenness of mankind during the war, or . . . the period immediately preceding it'.[28] His fate was related to the fate of mankind. To lop off any chapter would distort what should be seen as a wheel with twelve spokes. Major changes would buckle the form, the motion of which could be conceived as something like time itself.

He then gave a chapter-by-chapter analysis of the book's symbolism, starting with Mexico, 'the meeting place . . . of mankind itself, pyre of Bierce and springboard of Hart Crane, the age-old arena of racial and political conflicts of every nature . . . where a colourful native people of genius have a religion that we can roughly describe as one of death' – a good setting for the 'drama of a man's struggle between the powers of darkness and light'.[29] The book needed re-evaluating on its own terms, stressing its severely classical pattern. It was essentially *trochal*, its form the wheel. At the end the reader should want to return to the beginning, where he would find again the Sophoclean epigraph, '*Wonders are many, and none is more wonderful than man,*' which should cheer him up. 'For the book was so designed, counterdesigned and interwelded that it could be read an indefinite number of times and still not have yielded all its meanings or its drama or its poetry.'[30]

Some critics have taken this letter as a blueprint for understanding *Under the Volcano*, for who can supply a 'true' reading if not its author? But a year later, Lowry commented ironically:

> The enterprise was doubtless a foolish one: to give all kinds of good esoteric reasons why the work should stay as it was in the beginning. Those reasons I have now almost completely forgotten . . . in all concerning his work a writer assumes the most extraordinary pretensions and is ready to justify anything.

And despite having stressed the importance of grasping the author's intention, he quoted approvingly Julian Green saying, 'My intention was – and has ever since remained to me – obscure.'[31]

The letter, written in some apparent mental turmoil, involved reliving the book's creation, and many of the memories he feared would come back to haunt him were evoked in the process. For seven days he wrote steadily and intensely in a mood of angry depression, determined to justify his book's every detail before breaking off to suggest to Margerie on the 9th that they take a trip to Zamboala next day for a change of scenery. She too was depressed, because *The Shapes that Creep* had still not appeared, and she had written to Scribner's threatening legal action for breach of contract. However, unknown to her, the book was due out on the 14th.

The day in Zamboala was a failure; they never got to see the lake they had gone to see; they were caught in a blizzard-like gale, glass cut their feet, and tempers were frayed. On the way back they brightened up, but at the Casa Maria, faced with having to complete his letter, Lowry again became depressed. Late that evening he brought in a bottle of mescal which led to a hysterical scene with Margerie. These mood-swings were very destabilizing, but at least he could go back to the letter clutching his comforting bottle. This time he became inordinately drunk and fell asleep on the floor beside his desk. Waking in the middle of the night, his memory had gone blank and he was full of self-hate. He sat strumming his out-of-tune uke, trying to pray but being able only to utter obscenities and feeling pathetic. The old fears had returned with a vengeance – fear of death and of dragging Margerie down with him. He was also drinking their precious money away. He sat on the floor and began to cut at his ukulele strings with a razor, then, mimicking a scene from *The Lost Weekend*, drew the blade across his wrist and watched the blood drip. The uke fell to the floor, waking Margerie, who rushed out and found a doctor. The superficial wound was bound and he was given phenobarbital. The next day, with a nurse in attendance, he stayed in bed, but soon went back to his letter, which was revised, typed and posted off on the 15th.

This prodigious letter into which he put so much was not simply a justification of his novel but also of his life up to that point. As he found with other intensely personal pieces of writing, composing it had a distinctly therapeutic effect, and now he was ready to return to Oaxaca. In his book the town stands for death, and the bus to Oaxaca was the number seven, but he had to go there to verify that mysterious sign which so haunts the Consul.

¿LE GUSTA ESTE JARDÍN?
¿QUE ES SUYO?
¡EVITE QUE SUS HIJOS LO DESTRUYAN!

More importantly, he felt he had to find again his friend Juan Fernando, whose words seemed more than ever appropriate. 'Sickness is not only in body, but in that part used to be call: soul.'[32]

Approaching Oaxaca, the past returned in memories of Juan Fernando – the trip to Etla, scratching the ground, the petrified head, drunk all morning at the Farolito, and the mountain ride for the Banco Ejidal. At the Hotel Francia, they found the old manager, Antonio Cerillo, no longer there, and were told there was only one very bad room vacant, one not usually offered to tourists. As Lowry had guessed, it was his old room, number forty, seemingly unchanged but for a broken window, and there was no vulture perched on the washbasin. It was here that he and Juan Fernando had drunk on the day he had 'saved' Harry Mensch's life, and where Juan had said to him, 'I get so horrible drunkness the next morning I fall off my horse.' The hotel was not much to Margerie's taste. She noted Lawrence's comment that the address would be good, and added, 'A [good] place to go mad in.'[33] But despite the disaster and near-madness which had overcome Lowry there, he could say that he had somehow conquered this fearful city by his art.

> Look . . . I have transformed, single-handed, my life-in-death into life . . . not an hour, not a moment of my drunkenness, my continual death, was not worth it: there is no dross of even the worst of these hours, not a drop of mescal that I have not turned into pure gold, not a drink I have not made sing.[34]

They managed to move to a better room and took a walk around town. Lowry was careful to avoid the Covadonga where he had met Juan Fernando and been arrested, but they found a quiet pub and drank *habanero*. Opposite, for the first time, they saw that fateful sign: ¿LE GUSTA ESTE JARDÍN? They tried to find Avenida Independencia, where the Banco Ejidal had been, but it was no longer there. Then, sitting at dinner at the hotel that evening, Lowry was shocked to see John D. Bonsfield, a bit beefier perhaps and balder, but looking ruddy and sunburnt, very much like nine years before. The man gave him the horrors, reminding him of the descent to the lowest point of his life in Mexico; he was 'a drunkard who never had the shakes, a debauchee who was never called upon to pay the piper because – who knows? – he was the piper himself.'[35] He symbolized death as Juan Fernando symbolized life. As he left, Lowry even recognized the sailor's walk copied from him, and recalled that it was to this man that he had sold Juan Fernando's suit for five pesos. Seeing him brought back such dread memories and feelings of remorse that he proposed they abandon the trip and return home the next day. But Margerie refused even to return to Cuernavaca until they had found Juan Fernando, the man he had mentioned almost every day since they married. Next day they found Cervantes's Salón Ofélia, now a drugstore, but found that the Banco Ejidal had moved to Avenida Juárez. Trying to imagine how it had looked, he recalled Juan Fernando standing outside the bank, his sword unsheathed towards the sun, and saying, 'I like to work them with.'

At lunch they again saw Bonsfield, hiding behind a copy of a newspaper, and afterwards set out to walk, as he had done with Juan Fernando, to Monte Albán, determined not to pay twenty pesos for a taxi. Now, unlike then, he had no pains in his legs and 'Rimbaud suspicions' about their cause, Bert's injections having improved them considerably. The climb in the heat was very tiring, but finally they got a lift to the summit. Below them in a great circular valley lay the countryside Juan Fernando had ridden through, taking money to poor farmers tilling the fields beside the river which stretched between villages to the far distant blue mountains. This was the Garden of Etla which Juan Fernando had helped to make flourish.

Monte Albán, the home of Zapotecan kings, with its deformed sculptures and indecipherable hieroglyphics, also spoke to him of his friend. The descent into one of the Monte Albán tombs – tomb number seven naturally – left both of them somewhat shaken. Afterwards they went to the Oaxaca Museum to look for the petrified head he had found with the Oaxaqueñian students, but found only the skull bored by syphilis. He then took Margerie to the church of La Soledad, 'the Virgin for those who have nobody with', and that night they drank *habanero* and Lowry had a bad nightmare.

While Margerie was showering next morning, Bonsfield knocked at the door and Lowry pretended to be pleasantly surprised to see him. The American was now married and owned a silver mine, and was amazed to see Lowry looking so well, remembering his wretched state when they last met. He had avoided the war and seemed defensive about it, much like Lowry. He asked about *In Ballast* and the *Volcano*, and Lowry told him one was burned, the other being rejected by publishers at that moment. Bonsfield said he had read *The Lost Weekend* and thought of him, which did not warm the atmosphere, and when Lowry reminded him that he had stuck him with his bill at the Carleton, he said he had paid both before leaving. As he departed he said, 'By the way, we're still *characters* in Acapulco,' which made Lowry shudder. Not for the first time he was being told he had become a character – no doubt one of his own, and the thought terrified him. With Bonsfield gone he felt better, even ready to go in search of Juan Fernando.

They found the new Banco Ejidal, at the junction of Avenida Juárez and Calle Humboldt. The manager's secretary said that Juan Fernando had been transferred. Lowry, not understanding Spanish, asked for his address, but the girl wrote on a piece of yellow paper, 'Juan Fernando Márquez – murió en 1939 en Villahermosa, Tabasco.' Still they did not understand. She began to cry, and Lowry now realized that 'murió' meant dead. The bank manager, a handsome man of fifty who Lowry remembered, came in. Juan Fernando had indeed died in Villahermosa in 1939 – in December, he told them. December! The month in which they were married, the month he had first met Juan Fernando, the month that Grieg was killed, he noted. Lowry explained that he had not known him long but regarded him as his best friend. He had, said the manager, been 'loco', crazily drunk on mescal, and was shot in a cantina after an argument. Shocked, and with Lowry in tears and inconsolable, they repaired to a little dirt-floored church nearby, and as they knelt in prayer to the Saint of Dangerous and Desperate Causes, a new horror dawned on him. His friend had died in the very same way his Consul had. Now, it seemed, he had written Juan Fernando's death, and as good as murdered him with his own hand. That evening, they passed the old Banco Ejidal building, where, in a back room, he and Juan Fernando had once fenced with sabres. It was partly flattened and now a profusion of flowers bloomed over the site. 'Independencia number 25 had become a garden.'[36]

Next day they visited the ruined burial city of Mitla, a place to think about those who die young, and returning to the hotel they skirted the old prison, now a convent, where he had spent Christmas 1937. That evening they returned to the church of La Soledad, lit candles and offered prayers for Juan Fernando. Mexico, he found, was drawing him into its churches, with their strange, haunted interiors. At about 4 a.m. next morning, Lowry stole out of the hotel to take once more his early morning walk to the Farolito, always somehow associated with freedom, and reflected that he had either wasted much time there or in some inexplicable way had grown from the experience. It seemed unchanged, was boarded up and a notice informed him that it too had 'moved to the Calle Humboldt'. He came back at 6.30 a.m. to take Margerie back to see it. They returned to the Francia for a last breakfast, and to pay their bill. Margerie had cracked a mirror. 'Seven years' bad luck,' said the manager.

The bus back to Cuernavaca wound through the Valley of Etla, and Lowry reflected that its new prosperity was due to the brave and generous work of men like Juan Fernando; it was a fitting epitaph to a noble man. Back at the tower, he felt that at last he had laid the ghost of Oaxaca, despite the sadness of his friend's death, and Cuernavaca had also lost its fears for him. He spent a few days resting and working on poems. A week later they set off again, this time for a happy week in Tlaxcala, returning via Mexico City and the American Bookstore, hoping to find that Margerie's novel had finally been published. No one had heard of *The Shapes that Creep*, but finally and triumphantly Lowry found a copy. There were celebrations and tears before they set off home. They stopped for tequilas and dinner at Charlie's Place, then went back to the tower, where Lowry sat watching a rainbow sunset, becoming suddenly homesick. Popocatepetl, still visible, linked him to Dollarton through the mountain chain running from the Sierra Madre to the Rockies, and then after dark, the Eridanus river of stars he saw overhead was the very same that could be seen up in Canada.

Although there was no news of *Under the Volcano*, Margerie was now a published writer and Malcolm could at least share in her pleasure. For the next few weeks they basked in her success. Their thoughts were turning more and more towards home, but Margerie was keen to see Acapulco, where Malcolm had first arrived in Mexico and, according to the tourist brochure, the place which most represented the magic of Mexico for the holidaymaker.[37] Malcolm was more anxious to return to Dollarton, but only when he knew that his book had been accepted. Also he wanted the holiday to be a success for Margerie's sake and, after all the drinking of the past few weeks, Acapulco offered an image of health and escape. As money was low, he wrote asking his Canadian bank to send $300 (1,500 pesos) to the bank in Cuernavaca.

They left by bus for Acapulco on 8 March, with overnight stops in Taxco and Iguala. But certain irrational fears had taken hold of him – he dreaded having to sign hotel registers, having finally to get off the bus, and seeing Acapulco again. After a jittery start they settled to enjoy the trip, but he was forever aware of what he thought were occult messages. At Ciudad Bravo, he spotted a torn newspaper in the gutter bearing an item on the excavation of Tomba 7, the same tomb they had descended into at Mitla, and then saw that their own bus was number thirteen – 'the number of Judas'.[38] Suddenly he felt that Juan Fernando was trying to warn against some impending disaster. On seeing Acapulco, however, Margerie became wildly excited and even Malcolm managed to recapture his sense of adventure on first seeing it with Jan nine or ten years earlier.

The town had been hit by a development boom. Hundreds of new or half-built houses in what he thought a stupid modern style had erupted along the beaches and up along the cliffs. The waterfront at Hornos, the poorer of the town's two beaches, was crowded with such buildings and hordes of holiday-makers, and he hoped the beach at Calete was not also spoiled. They passed a huge new liquor store called El Ciclón and noted it for future reference. When the bus stopped they negotiated the crowds of pimps and beggars and found one of his favourite old cantinas, the Bohemia, where they were served poor beer by a rude boy.

There was no sign of the Miramar, where he and Jan had first stayed, but they found the Monterrey, where he had written his sonnet, 'Love which comes too late is like that black storm . . .' Opposite stood the American Consulate from which his manuscripts had been stolen by Bonsfield and Stuyvesant. The owner of the Monterrey looked at him in a rather pointed way and they trotted out their usual litany: 'We are not rich Americans . . .' In fact, intending to stay no more than a week, they had brought only three hundred pesos, leaving most of their money and their papers behind in Cuernavaca. Two US warships stood offshore, and in the streets open hatred was shown towards American sailors, people squirting water, hurling abuse, eggs and rice at them. At his old drinking haunts that afternoon he refused to pay the sky-high prices, settling instead for beer at a peso a bottle. They passed the cinema where he had once taken Peggy Riley – another ghost returning to haunt him.

The following day they went to Calete Beach where he had had his first mescal – where his Mexican tragedy had had its beginning.[39] Its fine white sand was much the same, but there were new tasteless hotels and hot-dog stands giving it the air of Coney Island. He had found an expression which summed up his feelings about this. 'The abomination of desolation was standing in the holy place of Mexico.' The beach evoked memories of his suicidal swim, his encounter with the barracuda, and being slapped down by Gilda Gray. Margerie however, loved Calete and wanted to move there. They moved to the Hotel Córdoba, where a fat old Indian woman showed them around, flushing the toilet to prove that it worked, which it did not. 'What goes down must come up,' joked Lowry, 'ah, those old familiar faeces.'[40] Later, taking a moonlight swim, he recalled beating Riley in a race around the island. Riley had taught him the crawl, and he reflected how easily as a writer he picked up others' techniques.[41] He was disturbed when he thought he saw one of the stool pigeon cops from the Turismo who was so hostile to him in 1938, but they returned to the hotel to make passionate love, only to be kept awake for the rest of the night by chinches and mosquitoes.

They decided to move to the Quinta Eugenia, which resembled a stranded liner washed up on the beach,[42] and took a ground-floor room. Then the proprietor, deciding he liked them, offered them a better room on an upper floor. They accepted because it cost no more. Later, Lowry discovered to his horror that it was room thirteen. They drank only in the evening, mostly *habanero* bought in bulk at El Ciclón, and in general life at the Quinta Eugenia was so sweet and came so close to the paradisaical view of Acapulco in the advertisements that they decided to stay a little longer than planned. They booked the week ahead, paying in advance, then rose early to go underwater swimming and water-skiing, and on the 14th visited Pied de la Cuesta. Coming back, they were given a lift by two rich, flaxen-haired young Americans, the Heywoods, motoring through Mexico on honeymoon and staying only at the smartest hotels; they agreed that *they* preferred to live poorly and experience the 'real' Mexico at first hand.

After the siesta Lowry went for the same long swim he did in his suicide bid in 1938, and on his return was told there were some people to see him. In their room he found Margerie, just showered with her hair wet, having an argument with two men who were demanding to see their papers. They were from the Oficina de Imigración, with a detailed file about his last visit to Acapulco. 'We have a fine against you here for fifty pesos for over-staying your leave,' said one, and the file said he was forbidden to re-enter Mexico. Those pursuing Furies seemed finally to have struck. The Immigration man told him he had been ordered to put him in gaol but he did not intend to do so. Lowry protested. He had not overstayed his leave in 1938 – all bills had been settled by his lawyers, there was no outstanding fine against him, and anyway he did not have fifty pesos. All their money and papers were in Cuernavaca.

The men said they would wire Mexico City to check on their tourist cards. Meanwhile they must remain in the hotel. Lowry protested; they could not afford an indefinite stay and their rent in Cuernavaca was running on. They must stay or go to prison, he was told. Could they go swimming? Yes, but they must not leave Acapulco. He was aware that the matter could be cleared up simply by paying the fifty pesos ($10), but could not bring himself to pay, and they had barely fifty pesos left after settling their hotel bill in advance.

It was the weekend; everything, even the Consulate in Mexico City, was shut. They had $500 in Cuernavaca, but no means of identifying themselves at the bank to have it sent on. They were having 'the bite' put on them – *la mordida*, which also meant remorse. Lowry was quick to see the connection – 'the shadow of God's punishment' was in this. He foresaw deportation, not being allowed back into the US or Canada, and even the grim prospect of having to return to England in disgrace, something he always swore would never happen. He began to drink *habanero* like water[43] until Margerie started to cry in despair. They wondered how they had been found, unaware that all Acapulco hotels were required to send in names of guests to the Immigration Office. They quarrelled, each blaming the other for leaving their papers behind, and Malcolm telling Margerie that he would never have come back to Mexico but for her. She, in turn, accused him of being mad. 'You were mad when I married you,' she shouted. Then, just as suddenly, their mood changed. It was all rather funny and quite an adventure. There might even be a book in all this, thought Lowry.

Next day, the ides of March, they heard that two Americans had been robbed and murdered on the road to Chilpancingo. It was their friendly honeymooners, the Heywoods. Lowry went to the El Ciclón for two bottles of *habanero* and they both began drinking. When they visited the Turismo (the tourist office charged with helping tourists in trouble) Lowry saw the shifty-eyed stool pigeon he had seen the day before – maybe the man who had informed on him. Acapulco had no British Consul, only an unofficial acting one, a Mr Hudson, to whom they then went and told their story.

Looking for Hudson next day at the Immigration Office they met the aggressive Sub-Chief of Immigration, whom they dubbed 'Tojo', who waved a fat file under Lowry's nose. 'Borracho – borracho – borracho,' he shouted, 'Here is your life.' There were pages and pages – no doubt the damning secret service reports of 1938. 'It say you were always too drunk to do business,' said Tojo. Lowry glimpsed the name of Guyou, the official who escorted him back to Mexico City from Acapulco eight years earlier. His wife's name was given as 'Janine', and

Tojo would not listen when Margerie pointed out angrily that *she* was not Jan. Lowry also thought they had mistaken his original date of entry into Mexico, which might explain why they thought he had overstayed his time there. They had a pointless conversation in English which Tojo failed to follow, but said he had to go to Mexico City and would correct the papers for them himself.

The long weekend (Monday was a holiday) was spent in suspended animation. They went to Hornos, and again went underwater swimming. Temporarily they forgot their troubles and were happy. But by Tuesday Lowry was feeling tense. If Immigration's decision went against him it would mean a trip to Mexico City, and now he found the city and its traffic more terrifying than ever. He fetched a couple of litres of *habanero* from El Ciclón and passed the day drinking, underwater swimming, and surfboarding. An old freighter offshore revived his nostalgia for the sea, a 'wonderful soaring feeling of escape', but this time there was no escape.

On Wednesday the 20th they had a midday appointment at the Immigration Office. Tojo was absent but another officer they christened 'Fatty' was there in his place. He had little English and all they got from him was that there was no news for them. Lowry offered to pay for a call to Mexico City, to which Fatty agreed, but told them to return at four-thirty. Back at the Quinta Eugenia, they were again visited by an Immigration Officer (from the Oficina Federal de Hacienda) demanding over and over that they pay the fifty-peso fine. They kept telling him their money was in Cuernavaca and they were forbidden to go there. They said they would meet him at four at the Turismo. A friendly fellow guest offered to lend them fifty pesos, but foolishly Lowry refused. That, of course, would not just have been the end of the matter, it would have been the end of the adventure that was evolving into a possible novel.

At four o'clock at the Turismo, the Immigration Officer again threatened him with gaol if he did not pay up. When he refused, he demanded Lowry's watch as security and said that unless the fine was paid within three days he would go to prison. Lowry demanded that Margerie, on whom they had nothing, be allowed to go to Cuernavaca to collect their money and papers, threatening that otherwise she would complain to the US Consul and have him gaoled instead. The man then phoned his chief in Mexico City, who said they knew nothing about them. Finally he agreed that Margerie could go to Cuernavaca provided she returned within three days, by Saturday 23 March.

At the bus station there were second-class tickets only, and he worried about Margerie travelling alone at night on such a bus. As the bus pulled away with Margerie jammed next to a fat scar-faced Mexican, Lowry, half crazed with anxiety, went to a nearby cantina and came out with three bottles of *habanero*. Next day she cabled. 'Am in Mexico City trying to fix things this end with British Consul. Will wire again.' She had arrived in Cuernavaca early that morning, gone to the bank and collected a cheque for the $300, and set out to see the British Consul in Mexico City. Percy Hughes, the Vice-Consul, found their papers all in order, and advised her to return to Acapulco to pay the fifty pesos. He offered to see Tojo and sort matters out for her, promising to cable them if there were problems. She spent a sleepless night at the Canada before setting out for Acapulco on Friday 22nd. She arrived in Acapulco at 2 a.m. on Saturday morning utterly exhausted and got back to the hotel to find Malcolm deep in alcoholic slumber. She was furious. 'Get up, you drunken bastard!' she shouted. He was crushed. Any tenderness between them, he wrote, had disappeared and he felt more frightened of Margerie than of the threat of imprisonment.[44]

They had to report to the Immigration Hacienda to pay their fine that morning, and Lowry, terrified and still drunk, wanted another *habanero*, but Margerie refused him, and at 8 a.m. insisted that he go down to breakfast. He kept pleading for drinks and threatened to start on tequila if denied. She tried to get his mind off drink by telling him about her trip, but on the way into town he again demanded alcohol; without it, he said, he would be unable to sign the cheque she had brought from Cuernavaca. Anyway, he told her cruelly, if he went to prison perhaps he would have some peace. She refused to let him go for a drink, but let him buy two litre bottles of *habanero* at El Ciclón. When they found a bank, Lowry tried desperately to sign the back of the cheque, but the shakes made it impossible (a problem shared with Don Birnam of *The Lost Weekend*, which ironically was showing in Acapulco at the time). The horror of being unable to perform this simple act he put into a poem.

> Pity the blind and the halt but yet pity
> The man at the bank in the pitiless city
> The man at the bank who can't sign his name . . .
>   – Pity the blind and pity the lame
> But pity the man who can't sign his own name.[45]

As he sweated and wept in an agony of impotence, trying to excuse himself to the bemused teller by saying he had a touch of malaria, Margerie, at first angry, grew hysterical. Finally she dragged him off for that one drink he said would steady his hand, and there was a furious quarrel. She said they should have a joint account, and when he disagreed, saying he had to retain a modicum of authority in their relationship, she called him an 'infantile slob', and they repaired to the Bohemia for a beer.

In fact Lowry had several, watched by a contemptuous Margerie. He drank on past twelve, by which time the banks had closed; now they could not cash their cheque or pay their fine. He declared he was pleased to be going to gaol – it seemed a good way out of their present situation. Margerie then said that she had fifty pesos, borrowed in Cuernavaca, and hauled him off to the Immigration Office, where Hudson marched into the Oficina Federal de Hacienda, paid the fine, and demanded to know why they had been treated unconstitutionally. After eight years no one should be held liable for an unpaid fine, nor should Lowry have had his watch taken. The Chief of the Hacienda apologized and his watch was returned. They just wanted to get back to Cuernavaca and leave Mexico, but when Hudson asked if they were free to go, Fatty in the Immigration Office said 'No', they must wait for news from Mexico City and the office was closed until Monday.

For the next ten days, while they waited, Lowry withdrew more and more into solitary drinking, and Margerie felt that a glass wall had descended between them. They now had 1,500 pesos and their papers, but were imprisoned. Occasionally they checked the situation with Tojo and Fatty, but always they were told 'Nada', no news from Mexico City. Then, on Tuesday 2 April, an airmail letter arrived from Rodgers, the British Consul in Mexico City, saying the Mexican authorities had decided to deport him and enquired whether he had a re-entry permit and return tickets for transportation to the US. They tried phoning Rodgers but he was unavailable, and Hughes was unhelpful. That evening he went again for his 1938 suicide swim, far out into the bay, not caring whether he came back or not. Out in rough waters, however, he regained the will to live and battled his way back.

When he called Hughes in Mexico City, he was told that it had been decided not to deport him but to ask him to leave Mexico. They felt badly let down by the British Consul. The following day Margerie went to the Oficina de Migración alone and Tojo told her they could go, but then gave her a letter to be delivered to the Immigration Office in Mexico City within three days. They were free, if only temporarily, and back at the hotel they danced around their room with joy. One of the guests at the hotel suggested they write a story about a useless British Consul. At the Turismo next day they met the stool pigeon, Guyou, who Lowry was sure had betrayed them. 'Hello Lowry,' he said. 'Riley is here.' That, it turned out, was a cruel joke, and when Lowry asked after Peggy the man made a scissor-cutting gesture and grinned maliciously. 'Divorce!' he said.

On 5 April, just over four weeks after arriving in Acapulco, they boarded the night bus back to Cuernavaca. Equipped with a bottle of *habanero*, Lowry slept for most of the journey, catching a sleepy glimpse of the cathedral at Taxco where, he recalled, Hart Crane had rung the sad church bells. Back at the tower he slept till noon on Saturday morning. Shortly after he awoke, Margerie came bursting into the bedroom waving a letter just collected from Maria Luisa. 'Cape has taken your book!' she announced. He found it difficult to take in, but she was determined to make the most of this momentous news – the culmination of so many years of work and high expectations, and of what she had always known; she had married a genius. They rushed off to Eddie's to celebrate. That afternoon, when Lowry checked the mailbox, there was a letter from Matson. They thought they had dismissed him as their agent the previous August when Margerie informed him that he had not understood the book, but apparently he had continued sending it out. Reynal & Hitchcock, he wrote, had had the book since 18 February and seemed about to make a favourable decision. Only the president had to be convinced. They might want a few cuts and to see him in New York, but would pay all expenses. That was enough for Lowry. As he saw it, his masterpiece had been accepted simultaneously in London and New York, and the letters had been delivered by the postman he had put into *Under the Volcano* while they were living in Laruelle's tower – a set of significant coincidences signalling something profound. Margerie, still irked by Matson's reservations about the book, wrote to Noxon that he had *not* sold it, it had sold itself.[46] Lowry added, 'He had no belief in the *Volcano* had not even read it – we both told him to go to hell then he sold it.'

That evening they celebrated with Eddie and Maria Luisa at Charlie's, their joy tempered only by the knowledge that they must present themselves at the Immigration Office in Mexico City on Monday morning. Lowry wired Matson asking about an advance as they were in financial trouble, and Sunday was a day of suspenseful drinking.

There followed two days of frustrated trips into Mexico City, with Eddie along to translate. Their files were never available. Then they were told they must each put up a five-hundred pesos bond or be deported in two days. They protested; it was impossible to find anyone to underwrite such bonds. A sinister-looking Inspector then said they gave their occupations as writers and so needed work permits or to be approved as immigrants. Lowry said they were on holiday, not working. They might be taking notes but they were not earning. Nevertheless their papers were confiscated, passports and tourist cards included, and they were told to produce the bonds by Monday afternoon. Suppose, asked Lowry, they promised not to write another word in Mexico? But what if they walked in on them and discovered them writing, asked the Inspector. Couldn't they even write to their mothers, Lowry ventured. 'Posseebly es posseebly escribir in al escusado,' was all they got in reply.

That evening, Eddie offered to put up his little café, the Bahia, as security on their bond, but it being Holy Week no bonding companies were open. Finally, he arranged through a friend for the papers to be delivered for Lowry to sign. Over the weekend they drank heavily and Margerie was reduced to hysterics at one point. However, they did receive a wire from Matson confirming Reynal & Hitchcock's offer – $1,500 advance, plus $500 towards expenses for travel to New York.

They returned to the Immigration Office in Mexico City on Monday morning and handed in the bond papers, but the Chief Inspector, Corunna, refused to return their passports and tourist cards, and became incensed when Lowry tried to argue. The man, he decided, was the embodiment of evil. At the Bahia that evening they both became extremely drunk, and on Tuesday 16th Margerie felt she had come to the end of her tether, and wrote.

> This is the end . . . Why don't I kill myself? . . . but Malcolm without me will have no joy of his success . . . How can you love a man with all your being & be willing to be damned that he may have what he wants the most & still feel as I do – that he has outraged & insulted our marriage & himself so that I could kill him? And the stabbing, burning, unendurable agony of seeing the one you love reduced to a shambling idiotic dirty animal – I can't even pray any more.[47]

The following day the atmosphere was much lightened and on 18 April she wrote cheerfully to her family announcing the acceptance of the *Volcano* and saying they would soon be flying to New York to work on the book with the publishers. But the next day Matson wrote that

Curtice Hitchcock had decided after all that the alterations needed were not enough to justify a trip to New York; they could be handled by letter. He would now prefer to spend the travel money on extra publicity or to get them to New York for publication day. Lowry was thrilled that his book had been accepted almost as it stood by both publishers. Margerie wrote to her family about their change of plans. They would be returning home sometime in May and hoped to spend a week in LA. She waxed enthusiastic at the thought of the fanfare of publicity the book would receive, and Malcolm added a long PS, already uneasy about any such a prospect. He had no idea what she meant by fanfare, he wrote. 'What it probably will amount to is a few bad cocktails and some publicity the book and I would do well without.' He asked Bert to cable his family with the glad tidings, adding 'the book will probably kill my English mother stone dead if she ever reads it.'[48]

He cabled Matson for money, saying they needed help to get out of Mexico. They tried to enjoy the Good Friday festivities and went to the cathedral on an evening which culminated in a spectacular thunderstorm in which the cathedral dome was struck by lightning. Next day they got intoxicated with Eddie, and as Malcolm slipped deeper into drunkenness Margerie went home. Later someone slid into bed beside her. Putting on the light she found Eddie attempting to substitute for Malcolm. He was reluctant to leave until she produced a knife from the kitchen. Next morning, with Malcolm suffering a monumental hangover, Eddie bounced in as if nothing had happened, saying he had phoned Immigration and their papers were ready for collection. By Monday, the money from Matson had arrived and was being held at the bank for ten days. All they needed were their papers to identify themselves. A letter from Rodgers told them they were not to be deported and could return to the US on production of passports and travel reservations. The same day Lowry received a draft contract from Cape.

Back at the Immigration Office on Friday 26th, a bad-tempered Corunna told them he had no papers for them and began to insult Margerie when she demanded he hand them over immediately. When Lowry tried to reason with him, he, as if knowing nothing of their case, demanded their passports, the name of their hotel, and the date of their departure from Mexico. Hughes arrived and tried to help, but was told the papers were indeed in order but with another official who was absent. They should return *mañana* at 11.30 a.m. Wearily they made an appointment for noon with Hughes, who said they were lucky not to have been deported or locked up at the notorious building at 113 Bucarelli where those awaiting deportation were held.

On the journey to Mexico City, Lowry was 'eating phenobarbital from my pockets like lemon drops'.[49] It was a drug he had taken to control his shakes since Niagara, and again he had found a friendly doctor (the one who treated his cut wrists in January) to supply him. Corunna was no more helpful than before and Hughes was off-hand, probably exasperated with them. Finally Lowry persuaded Corunna to return his passport so they could at least get money from the bank. But it was only his old cancelled passport, which he carried because it bore his American visa. They were told to come again the following Tuesday. Back in Cuernavaca he managed to cash Matson's draft, and on the following Monday, finally drew the $300 from Canada.

On their next visit to Mexico City, they were photographed against their will by a seedy-looking Inspector they also christened 'Fatty'. They were kept waiting, then told that Corunna had gone and that they must report back on Thursday 2 May at noon with their baggage. When Lowry protested, Fatty said that if they were not there, Corunna would come to Cuernavaca personally to arrest them. The photographs made them look like desperate criminals, and Lowry feared they were being set up. That evening Eddie said that the bonding company had told him that the Government had cashed the thousand-peso bond and his café would be confiscated if he did not pay up. The following day a cable arrived confirming this, and Lowry duly handed over the thousand pesos to Eddie.

They set off early for Mexico City with their luggage on 2 May, leaving the carbon of *Under the Volcano* and some of their notes with Maria Luis, to be mailed to Dollarton. At the Immigration Office Lowry was told, 'You said bad things about Mexico and wrote – we know – we have it all.' Despite protesting, they were taken to 113 Bucarelli, the gaol for deportees, and left without their luggage in a filthy cell with a group of men waiting to be deported. After two hours they were taken out, put in a taxi and driven to the station; they were being taken to the US border. On the train, Fatty sat opposite, two guns on his hips. Margerie decided to get a bottle from her case but found that their clothes, the brandy and their camera had been stolen, which was why they were locked up without their luggage at 113 Bucarelli, they decided. But underneath a layer of dirty underwear they found what was far more precious to them – a layer of books and all their notebooks untouched. They could hardly believe their eyes.

Just before the train left, Margerie persuaded Fatty to let her off to get some Berrateaga brandy; she just made it and also brought what Malcolm wanted most with his brandy, a bottle of phenobarbital tablets. They spent two sleepless days and nights on the train's slow process to the border. At Monterrey, Margerie again got off to get Malcolm some drugs. Then at Laredo they were forced off the train into a taxi and taken to the Immigration Office. They were directly at the border. Outside stood a bridge over the Rio Grande. On the other stood Nueva Laredo in the US. Fatty then cross-examined them again. Why were they in Mexico? Were they writers? Why were they in Acapulco? They were then presented with a typewritten confession to breaking Mexican laws, saying they were going to be deported, which they refused to sign. Fatty became enraged and shouted at them incomprehensibly. Lowry accused him of deception, saying they could not be legally deported and demanding their passports and money. As he argued with him, and the clerk who had typed the confession pleaded with them, Fatty produced his pistols. Finally, intimidated, they signed under protest.

After Margerie had signed she was told she could go; Malcolm would be released the following day. She refused to leave him, however, fearing he might be shot out of hand or at least deported to England. Fatty refused to let them go to a hotel, ordering them to remain in the office until 7 a.m. next morning. It was his way of ensuring that Lowry looked dishevelled and generally undesirable at the US border next morning. Later, the kindly clerk agreed to let them go to a hotel provided they return before 6 a.m. Lowry still had enough money to pay *la mordida* this time. At the hotel they dosed themselves with phenobarbital and went straight to sleep.

Next morning back at the Immigration Office they thanked the clerk and sat waiting developments, noting sardonically a poster on the wall of a Mexican eagle tearing at a swastika flag bearing the title 'Mexico por la Liberdad'. At seven-thirty they asked if they could go, but were told to wait for the Chief to sign their papers. They were fearful the Chief might be Fatty but were reassured – he was not. At nine o'clock the Sub-Chief arrived, looking, to their relief, a kindly sort of man. Margerie pleaded with him, but he told her they were to be deported and showed her the order signed by Corunna.

When she explained their case, he appeared upset and agreed there seemed to have been a dreadful mistake, but orders were orders, he said. She continued to plead. As Englishmen could not be deported to the US, she and Malcolm would be separated. He said he had orders to hold them till Fatty returned and he dare not disobey an Inspector from Mexico City. He gave them coffee and said he would speak to his Chief when he came in. The suspense was acute.[50] When they returned the Sub-Chief told them they could leave at once. Fatty, in any case, was long overdue. Their papers were returned, they were put into a taxi and rushed through Mexican customs, with the Sub-Chief standing guard watching out for Fatty, and quickly crossed the bridge over the Rio Grande into America.

Their relief at being back in the US was unbounded. As they were negotiating American customs and immigration, overjoyed to be out of Mexico at last, they saw Fatty, who had actually followed them across the bridge in a towering rage at having been cheated of his victims. It was Saturday 4 May. Their Mexican adventure had lasted almost five months.

CHAPTER XVIII

JOURNEY TO THE MAGIC ISLAND
1946–1947

> Frankly I think I have no gift for writing. I started by being a plagiarist, then I became a drunkard. Then I became a hard worker, as one might say, a novelist. Now I am a drunkard again. But what I always wanted to be, was a poet.
>
> LOWRY (Haitian Notebook)

Relieved to be out of Mexico, they flew to LA. Lowry was in very much worse shape than he had been when last there. During the past five months of traumatic recall, having been drawn through the wringer of remorse, he had again taken heavily to drink. On the other hand, he was now to all intents and purposes the success he had always felt he could be. The Mexican trip had wrung him out, but he returned a hero with yet another harrowing tale to tell, the germ of yet another masterpiece, perhaps, if not two.

They arrived at the Woolfans' on 5 May. Bert presented him with a new typewriter to mark his success, and on 8 May he typed a letter to Matson, sending him a copy of his contract with Cape and asking how it should be altered, and said he would not sign until Matson had approved. The original and Hitchcock's cable, he would keep, he said, so he could brag to friends of Margerie's who were throwing a party for him. He then gave an account of their 'seven weeks of pure unadulterated hell' in Mexico. Their rights had been violated, they had been deported at gunpoint, and escaped the Consul's fate by a mere three minutes. The Mexican government was the evillest thing ever seen and apparently predominantly Nazi; he felt like turning Zola about it for the sake of others. His $500 loan had saved their lives, since all their other possessions had been taken.[1]

At the party given by Margerie's friends, he was lionized as a successful writer, and, at this stage, was obviously enjoying the admiring attention. He told one admirer that, 'You may have many inspirations when drunk but then you must look at it with a cold, sober eye and most of it will be no good.'[2] Asked how he had created such a book, he said, mimicking Lawrence, 'It is not I but the wind that blows through me.'[3] But despite such moments of lucidity, he was showing signs of being disturbed – drinking heavily and becoming more quarrelsome.

One morning at 4 a.m., the Woolfans were woken by a noisy disturbance and when Priscilla went downstairs in her nightclothes to investigate, there was Lowry, stark naked, having a loud altercation with their elderly black servant. She was furious and let him know exactly what she thought of him. By this time Bert had come down, and neighbours, also roused by the commotion, were hanging out of windows and over walls curious to know what was going on. Bert, who had a weak back and could not fight, tried to restrain Priscilla, but she was determined to put her uncouth brother-in-law in his place. Finally Lowry was faced down and left the room. 'Is that the way an English gentleman behaves?' asked Bert. 'He's no gentleman,' said Priscilla. 'He's trash and comes from trash!' There was a noise, and they saw he had returned and overheard this comment. He stared at them from the doorway for a moment, then went upstairs to bed. Bert now confirmed to himself that Malcolm was a chronic alcoholic who could be dangerous and who ought to be institutionalized. Next morning Priscilla told Margerie never to bring him to their home again.[4] But the diplomatic Bert suggested that as Mexico had obviously disturbed him, he should write a full account of the experience to A. Ronald Button, his lawyer, who would advise on any action he could take against the Mexican authorities. On 11 May he began another marathon letter, not completed and sent to lawyer Button until 15 June, long after his return to Dollarton.[5]

On 15 May the Lowrys set off by bus for Vancouver. In San Francisco, on the waterfront, Malcolm saw, or thought he saw, ships and shipping offices with names of good omen: Cape Friendship, Hitchcock Victory, Matson Line. Heading north again through giant redwood country, he began to scribble a revision for *Under the Volcano*. The Consul had misread the garden sign in Mexico. Now he could write in the error, and also the correct Spanish, as Hugh saw it. The misunderstanding was given a meaning.

Back in Dollarton, they found flowers growing on the burned site of The Wicket Gate. Remembering Parsifal, they took this as a good omen.[6] Stan, the real Parsifal expert, was so stunned by Lowry's

Mexican story that he wrote giving him a long magical explanation of why everything had gone so badly wrong – the golden rule being never to return to the scene of a past disaster. He would, he said, put the case in his Book of Accidents.[7]

A cable awaited him from Stuart congratulating him about *Under the Volcano* and telling him to write to the Praelector at St Catharine's College indicating that he wished his MA to be received by Donald, his nephew. This cheered him enormously, for while he felt alienated from his family he still wished to shine in their eyes. And it must have been a source of bitter regret that Arthur would never know of his success. Matson sent the Reynal contract, saying he had granted them certain movie rights believing that this might induce them to sell more copies. His letter ended with a bombshell. Curtice Hitchcock, who had been so keen on the book, had died suddenly from a heart attack. Matson did not think this would unfavourably affect its publication, but for Lowry it was yet another 'eerie coincidence', remembering the *Volcano*'s theme, 'Only against death does man cry out in vain.'[8]

The healing force of nature and the more congenial life of isolation wrought its magic. Now safely back in Eridanus a successful author, he took up his pen with gusto. On 28 May he returned the Reynal & Hitchcock contract duly signed, but was concerned that he had left his copy of the *Volcano* in Mexico, which might make it difficult to co-ordinate corrections or alterations with the publishers, something he was eager to begin. Two days later he sent a very lucid letter to Cape, showing how far he had recovered from his recent derangements. He explained that in asking him to act as his US agent he had not realized that Matson was persisting with *Under the Volcano*. Now, since he had sent them money to get out of Mexico, he felt bound to him. He was 'the best of agents' and a very old friend, and it would have been base ingratitude to turn away from him when finally he had sold something of his, having persisted even when he did not entirely believe in it.[9] It was a difficult letter to write, and he was able to pay Matson a compliment only in this rather back-handed fashion. He promised to inform Cape of any further cuts, and also to produce a thousand-word preface and a blurb of some two hundred words.

On 7 June he received his Cambridge MA. His old adversary and supervisor T. R. Henn, now Praelector at St Catharine's, had kindly 'supplicated' on his behalf and accepted the degree for him *in absentia*. Despite the harsh things he had written and said about Cambridge being destructive of the creative imagination, here, at least, was a sneaking admission that he owed more to his Alma Mater than he was prepared openly to admit. He wrote half-apologetically to Margerie's family, saying that despite his 'sloth-like manner' he had thoroughly appreciated their hospitality. Civilization, he complained, was now closing in on them, and a recently arrived Englishman who lived up a tree seemed to have discovered the best way to live. No doubt with the Consul in mind, he said that they might buy an island and live and work there for six months of the year and travel for the rest.[10]

Matson sent the (misleading) news that *Under the Volcano* had gone to press for publication in October; his proofs would arrive at any time and there would be very little work to be done as it had been decided to publish it practically as it stood.[11] The contract from Cape arrived back including all Lowry's suggested amendments and agreeing a £100 advance on signature. He signed and returned it immediately. On 16 June, he received his first letter from Albert Erskine, the Reynal & Hitchcock editor handling *Under the Volcano*. After expressing the admiration of all the editorial staff for the book, he said he was trying to impress its worth on their salesmen gathered for their biennial conference in New York, and assured Lowry they would do all they could to publicize it. The manuscript was now being copied for the printers and he needed help on certain points, though they were still willing to set it up as it stood, if he so desired. He made a few tentative suggestions including not framing the sign QUAUHNAHUAC, designating chapter 1 'Prologue' and heading it 1939 to indicate that it dealt with events from a year earlier, and rewriting certain passages which seemed obscure or unsyntactical. He suggested that chapter 12 be divided into two, and chapter 11 be inserted between them. In his reply, Lowry showed himself willing to improve his syntax for clarity, and to have his Spanish checked, but unwilling to make structural changes. To Erskine's dismay he sent six-pages of closely typed notes suggesting alterations and rewritings on various points he had raised.

Erskine had said he was extremely anxious to read *Ultramarine*, and asked if he could be sent a copy, a request which evidently alarmed Lowry and reawoke fears of plagiarism charges. The spectre of a wrathful Rascoe rising to denounce him again must have been terrifying. He had a copy, he wrote, but a book which he intended to be good had turned out 'an inexcusable mess' of which he had always been ashamed. The only real version of it, he said, had been lost and he had rewritten the whole thing in two months from notes found in a wastepaper basket and from a few published stories – the same exaggerated version of events he had given Rascoe in 1936. He had just one copy, he said, but would not like to send it without first expunging about half of it. He hoped to God that Erskine did not obtain a copy.

In the same nervous confessional spirit, a week later, having now received his carbon of *Under the Volcano* from Mexico, he began to reveal his sources to Erskine. He had, he said, thought of including a list of notes in the book to elucidate the deep layers of meaning woven into it so meticulously. The garden, for example, could be seen not just as the world, or the Garden of Eden, but as the Cabbala itself, and the abuse of wine could be identified with the abuse of magical powers, as it was in the Cabbala and in Byron's *Childe Harold*. It was also his intention, he added, thinking of *The Waste Land*, to acknowledge any 'borrowings, echoes, design-governing postures, and so on', as was once the custom with poets. The book, which had integrity, had been written with great care for detail, and his slight neurosis on this point was probably due to 'an Elizabethan unscrupulousness in my evil youth in other works mercifully forgotten save by the author's mediaeval conscience.'[12] The echoes to which he referred, he told Erskine, were mostly all in chapter 1 – a phrase lifted from a J. C. Squire story ('bangs and cries'); a couple of passages echoing D. H. Lawrence's *Letters* (references to 'personal battle', Laruelle's 'burden pressing on him from outside', and to 'secret mines of silver'); a thought borrowed from Julian Green's *Personal Record* ('there was always the abyss'); an image suggested by Virginia Woolf's *To the Lighthouse* (night sounds like the unbandaging of great giants); a favourite adjective of Faulkner's ('jonquil'); and a device used by Ralph Bates in *The Rainbow Fields* (the repeating of 'Compañero' in chapters 8 and 12).

This exchange of letters with Erskine began a long-term correspondence. A little younger than Lowry, Erskine was convinced that here was a great new author, and his approach was duly respectful. Flattered, Lowry outlined to him his further ambitions – *Under the Volcano* was the infernal first part of a Dantesque trilogy, and two volumes of poems, *The Lighthouse Invites the Storm* and *Wild Bleeding Hearts*, would also follow. However, since the fire, he was pretty well having to start again.[13] A pruned *Ultramarine* and *Lunar Caustic* could go into a single volume, and in Mexico he had blocked out a new novel (*Dark as the Grave Wherein My Friend is Laid*), 'potentially my best to date'. He and Margerie also had another up their sleeves, 'one of the best stories that ever came a writer's way only it was exceptionally dreadful to be in the middle of it'. This was the novel he called *La Mordida*.[14]

At the end of June, Cape's statement covering his advance arrived, and he found himself liable to pay nine shillings in the pound tax on it, so that after deductions, of the £100 agreed he received only £45. 'Someone,' he told Matson, 'forgot to enclose the cheque, which was kind of sad, unless it dropped out, which would have been sadder still.'[15] Margerie, meanwhile, had been brooding about her own career, her success with *The Shapes that Creep* having been eclipsed by the anti-climactic fashion of its appearance, with no advance notice from Scribner's or news of its critical reception, and now by the success of *Under the Volcano*. Anxious to keep her happy, Lowry trotted out to Matson the whole fiasco with Scribner's since *The Shapes* had been accepted in 1940. Someone should take it up with them, he said; he himself thought it would go better in England.

Erskine was surprised by Lowry's long lists of suggested changes and soon realized that the book would not be ready for publication by October. At the beginning of July, Matson informed Lowry that publication had been put off till the spring of 1947, and he panicked, fearing, correctly, that his letters to Erskine had led to the postponement. He wrote asking him to reconsider bringing it out in the fall. There would be few more changes and he hoped he was not losing interest in it. Erskine quickly reassured him of his intense interest, saying that postponement was good and allowed time to send out advance copies to various luminaries whose comments he intended to print on the back cover.

Lowry continued sending in corrections and modifications to his typescript, and the editor's decision to delay publication was almost certainly justified. In recognizing how close to a passage in *The Lost Weekend* the last pages of chapter 5 came, he worried that Jackson might be coming up behind with another book on the subject.[16] There were passages in chapters 5 and 10, he said proudly, which written in 1943, well before its advent, anticipated the atom bomb. Sensing that he had a highly intelligent editor who understood the book, his listed comments were as much a record of his own rereading of the book as they were textual corrections. He much enjoyed this 'hilarious, if scholarly, correspondence', he told Noxon.[17]

At the beginning of July, Erskine wrote, 'I now have so many letters from you that I cannot see or remember them all at once.'[18] Having digested two lengthy ones over a weekend he had found three more awaiting him on Monday morning. He hoped to have the book at the printers by the end of the month, and tried to calm Lowry's fears about

Jackson; he had not even read *The Lost Weekend*. As for the Spanish, he would consult both a dictionary and an expert. Some of Lowry's punctuation he found eccentric, but acknowledged that he seemed to be punctuating ' "for the sound or movement" of a sentence' which meant he could not really argue with him.[19]

Erskine must have been worried by his author's continually drawing attention to his sources. Here, said Lowry, there may have been an echo of Ralph Bates, there of Faulkner, Charles Jackson, Nordahl Grieg, and even Tom Harrisson. There was Hardy, too – the little pointing hand in chapter 11 he had taken straight from *Jude the Obscure*. (He said he had cut five of the better lines in the whole book from chapter 11 fearing they echoed too closely something from Katherine Anne Porter, not knowing that Erskine had once been married to her.) But Lowry's constant references to 'echoes' and 'liftings' show how deeply the Rascoe affair had affected him, and much later he told his psychiatrist that fear of exposure for plagiarism was what made him so hesitant to publish later on.

The shack was still without inner walls to insulate them against the elements, and once Lowry had finished his revision in mid-July, they got down to finishing it off. The faithful Jimmy Craige was there to lend a hand. He gave Lowry an eagle's feather found on the beach and fashioned into a quill pen, as a welcome home present. Delighted, Lowry decided for good luck to use it for signing important letters and contracts.

Matson announced that he had received the first $500 from Reynal & Hitchcock payable on delivery of manuscript, but wanted to clarify his tax position. If he was a non-resident alien he was liable for thirty per cent tax on any money from his US publishers, deductible at source. If he was a Canadian citizen he was liable to fifteen per cent US tax. As to future work, he proposed that if *Under the Volcano* was a success a pause of six months would be a suitable interval before the next Lowry work were submitted, namely for the fall of 1947. He also recommended that Margerie send nothing more to Scribner's. They had, however, sent a statement for *The Shapes that Creep* showing that it had sold over five thousand and gone into a second impression; she would receive a cheque shortly. On the other hand, *Horse in the Sky* had been rejected by nineteen publishers and he was at a loss where to send it next. Reynal & Hitchcock had rejected it, but in any case he thought a husband and wife should have separate publishers. He would send all three of her books to the A. D. Peters agency in England.

Lowry had not thought too deeply about his status in Canada. He had begun by hating the place, then grew to imagine he could give Canada a Dostoyevsky or Ibsen in the person of himself. Finally he formed a deep attachment to the wilderness in which unwittingly he found himself. In Mexico it had been useful to say they were Canadians because Americans were so unpopular there. But he was still essentially an English writer, drawing deeply on his Englishness and on experiences shared by other English writers who came to manhood in the 1930s. His political instincts, despite his claim to be 'a conservative Christian anarchist', were still to the left. And, although he sometimes had harsh things to say about Canada, he was never very complimentary about his own country, 'that great country that had murdered him with her ugliness so that had it not been for Canada he would never have known what it was to be happy.'[20] Now, however, his status would affect his financial position and it was important to him to sort it out. After all, they were talking about money he had earned himself, not money from his father.

He remained English, being in Canada only on a visitor's permit, he told Matson, although he could become a Canadian at any time he wished. However, he had been advised by the immigration people themselves that for tax purposes and ease of travel he was better off as he was.[21] He was hardly of a mind to swap nationalities, however, as he wrote shortly afterwards, 'This is a wonderful country to live, swim, work and bite trees in, but boy is it gloomy from a human point of view. I have yet to hear a remark that even deviated into humour. By their cafés shall ye know them, as Margie says.'[22] He was prepared to settle for the thirty per cent, and anxious to pay back $100 of the $500 Matson had sent to rescue them from Mexico. Margerie, he told him, was unhappy with Scribner's for charging her for corrections to her proofs which were never incorporated, and he was preparing himself to take up the cudgels with them on her behalf.

The memory of Mexico was slowly being softened by time and distance. He told Noxon that, dreadful as it was, it all seemed worthwhile now, for how often does one have the opportunity of being *inside* a novel as well as being its future author. He was full of praise for Erskine, who he felt was going to do full justice to the book and go to town on publicity. It still nettled him to remember that one of Cape's readers had found the book boring and in need of cutting. He felt that the thousand word preface he had promised Cape was probably important for English readers, and asked Noxon's advice about it. All his advice, he told him, had turned out to be right, and chapter 2 of the *Volcano*, which he had rewritten with his and Margerie's help, had been the strongest of all.[23]

Only now that the book had finally gone to the printers did he feel able to send news of his success to Aiken. He had been back at Jeake's House for some nine months now, and writing to him again stirred memories of those pre-war summers at Rye, not to mention Mexico in 1937. 'I hope to God you will like this work by your old pupil a little,' he wrote.[24] A month later Aiken wrote back of his delight that 'you've at last twanged the umbilical chord and cast off your Inferno off into the blue for weal or woe.' He and Davenport had heard about it on the grapevine.

Margerie's second thriller, *The Last Twist of the Knife*, was published at the beginning of August and the first that she knew of it was when she received a fan letter complaining about the ending. The murder had been solved but the murderer's motives remained unexplained. No proofs or advance copies had been sent. Evidently Scribner's had omitted the final chapter, and Lowry wrote urgently to Matson asking him to get them a copy. How was it possible, he asked, for two such different people as Erskine and Weber, her Scribner's editor, both to be in the publishing business?

Over the summer they finished work on the shack. Lowry swam, and made friends with a baby seal, and the only exciting thing that happened was that their cat got stuck up a tree and had to be brought down. By the end of an idyllic summer the house was completed and Lowry had received the first two instalments of his advance, $1,000 minus $150 in US tax. After eight years of silence an apologetic letter arrived from Davenport. Since they had last met in Hollywood, he had divorced Clement, and fallen on hard times, briefly becoming a schoolmaster at Stowe and working in journalism, 'my own 2½ years of total eclipse' he called them.[25] For a year or so he worked for the Crown Film Unit, and had remarried in 1944. Since the war he had lived with his new wife Marjorie in Chelsea, edited a series of literary magazines and worked intermittently on a biography of Norman Douglas. Lowry was delighted to hear from him. 'I never felt you very absent: & hence never very silent: & vice versa.'[26] Aiken and Davenport were almost certainly two of the people (apart from the great dead writers he admired) for whom he had specifically written his book, and whose good opinion of it he most hoped for.

With Margerie at a low ebb over her treatment by Scribner's, finally he wrote to the firm's senior editor, Maxwell Perkins. He wanted to draw his attention to 'a crashing and cynical injustice' for which his firm was responsible, he wrote, and then recounted the sad saga of *The Shapes that Creep* – the delayed launch, the missing proofs, the unanswered letters, the final and unannounced publication – and on top of that *The Last Twist of the Knife*, published without its final chapter.[27] Perkins wired back promptly: 'Horrified by what you tell me shall make thorough investigation and will do everything possible to meet situation.'[28] Margerie quickly rewrote the last chapter and Scribner's brought out a new edition, withdrawing the first from the bookshops. Charles Scribner sent Margerie a personal apology, explaining that her editor had had mental problems, and offered an additional $1,000 advance in compensation for the stress suffered.[29] This was in addition to some $800 which both her books had earned so far. She was not only delighted by this act of generosity but was heartened enough to revise *Horse in the Sky*, with Scribner's again in mind.

At the end of September, Lowry had another letter from Erskine. The Spanish in the *Volcano* had been checked by an expert, and the book was now due to go to the printers. There was much to discuss, he said, but letter writing was for him 'a laborious and unsatisfactory means . . . of communication.'[30] On 7 October – the real date of the death of Poe ninety-nine years earlier, Lowry liked to say – while waiting for the galley proofs to arrive, the Lowrys took a trip to Gabriola Island in the Straits of Georgia, a short ferry ride from Nanaimo on Vancouver Island.[31] As usual they took notes with a story in mind. It was to be a fateful trip, the beginning of a voyage into a creative maze from which Lowry was never able to extricate himself.

Galley proofs arrived on 24 October. For several days he found it hard to look at them, but a letter from Erskine stung him into action. He wanted them back with all corrections by 6 November, which meant mailing them on the 2nd (the Mexican Day of the Dead, Lowry noted). After that he worked furiously, often through the night into the next morning. Erskine had suggested cuts to Laruelle's biographical background in chapter 1, and surprisingly Lowry agreed, though he resisted other proposed cuts. 'One sometimes cannot be sure that one is not cutting the very thing that, upon reading it the first time, produced the final verisimilitude, and the compulsion to read it a second.'[32] When Cape sent him his proofs from London, he reported back ironically that he found himself making some of the very cuts suggested by Cape's reader, despite the noisy protests he had made at the time.[33]

By the time the second set of proofs arrived, Lowry said they were dreaming at nights of wriggling commas, colons like cannonballs, and ghostly galleys, but they were determined to speed through them as fast as they could. He asked that the novel be dedicated 'To Margerie, my wife.' The galleys were finished and returned by 11 November, and shortly thereafter, with Margerie's problems with Scribner's resolved and $3,000 between them in the bank, they began to think of escaping from the Dollarton winter to warmer climes again. Erskine had announced 19 February as publication date, so they made plans which would get them to New York in time for the launch. On 21 November Lowry told Erskine they were leaving for New Orleans within the week, planning to spend the next two months there before coming to New York. He said he would deal with page proofs down there.

After a couple of days in Vancouver, they boarded the midnight Greyhound bus for Portland, Oregon on 30 November. It was, of course, that 'fateful' month, but he had again survived the anniversary of Paul Fitte's death without any apparent harm. Margerie had packed her manuscript of *Horse in the Sky*, and Lowry had taken his copy of *Ultramarine* and the MS of *Lunar Caustic* for Erskine. Each had new notebooks, ready to record everything that happened on their next adventure.

Across the US border they celebrated by drinking sherry in a Seattle pub, then spent a miserable night on the back seat of a draughty bus taking them to Portland. The journey took them between the two great volcanoes, Mounts Hood and Rainier, and on through snow-clad forest country. They spent their sixth wedding anniversary at Boise, the capital city of Idaho, and the same morning passed through Salt Lake City, staying overnight at Cheyenne. As an anniversary gift, Margerie gave Malcolm a copy of Rimbaud's *A Season in Hell*, without comment. At the sight of Wyoming cowboys he lit up. 'Just like the cinema!' he said. Over the next three days they passed through Denver, Kansas City and St Louis, where, after forty-eight hours on the bus, they ended up at the Delmar Hotel, incredibly filthy, but with undreamed of hot water.[34]. Here, twenty years earlier, his hero Bix Beiderbecke had played in Frankie Trumbauer's orchestra at the Arcadian Ballroom. Lowry sent a postcard to Davenport. 'I am writing . . . in smoky old St Louis, drinking claret with my wife & eating Leiderkranze, in the middle of a coal strike, in a horrible beautiful hotel room'. For the next couple of months they could be reached at General Delivery, New Orleans.[35] But in a postcard to Noxon he said that after New Orleans they hoped to spend time in Haiti. They stayed the next night in Memphis where he was keen to see Beale Street. Here he was, after all, in the homeland of jazz, the cradle of Dixieland. In New Orleans they strolled down Canal Street, admiring the intricate ironwork on balconies in the old French Quarter, and there found a room at 622 St Ann Street, just off Chartres Street.

To Lowry's disappointment, 'thrice God-awful hillbilly music' had displaced jazz in the city's bars and joints, and he received a shock when he bought the fall issue of *Story* magazine only to find in it Jan's story, 'Not with a Bang', based on their stormy parting at the Hotel Canada in Mexico City. But whatever distress this may have caused him was forgotten on 17 December when he received a bound proof copy of *Under the Volcano*. He wrote congratulating Erskine on his editing, adding that New Orleans, beautiful and interesting though it was, was expensive and depressing them somewhat. They were thinking of going on to Haiti for a month, the only original thing about this being that 'we are going on a Liberty Ship carrying bauxite to Trinidad and which does not carry passengers'.[36] They hoped to get their work-in-progress in order in Haiti so they could discuss it with him when they met, he said, and wondered if Hitchcock's offer of travel expenses to New York for publication day still stood.

They took *Under the Volcano*'s page proofs to the backroom of 'a brawling New Orleans bar' close to the post office to work on while drinking fine beer out of copper tankards. But when they returned the following day they were thrown out by the barman. 'This is a bar, not an office,' he told them. 'We don't know what kind of a thing it is you're doing, and the boys are asking questions.'[37] Lowry decided that not much needed changing, and returned the proofs three days later. He sent Erskine a list of people to receive proof copies for pre-publication comment, including Stephen Spender, Jimmy Stern, Aiken, and Michael Redgrave, then in Hollywood filming with Fritz Lang. On 20 December, Stern, who had read *his* copy promptly, cabled to say he was 'consumed with excitement, jealous gratitude and indescribable praise'.[38] In his reply, Lowry acknowledged a phrase in the book, 'hangover thunder-clapping about his skull', borrowed from a letter Stern had sent to him years before.

They sailed on the Mississippi, visited riverside oyster bars and walked past Voodoo Square to the cemetery, where he copied down strange names from tombstones and they had to climb over the wall after being locked inside. In the dens of La Fitte the pirate they saw relics of torture, and Lowry was fascinated by the history of the steamboat *Robert E. Lee* in the local museum. They toured the Vieux Carré, and later, on a trip to the bayou country he was struck by the sight of the sinister parasitic Spanish moss draped across the branches of trees, leaving the forest devastated and ravaged beyond imagination. It was, he wrote, a symbol of creeping American civilization and of his own condition, where alcohol slowly came to threaten his sanity. 'This certainly was where Poe had put his terrible House of Usher . . . The slow accretion of Spanish moss upon the trees, is like the slow giving in to drink, once more, the stealthy inroads of madness.'[39]

They had no problem obtaining a Haitian visa and Lowry's re-entry permit for the US. The sailing date of that bauxite-carrying Liberty ship, the SS *Donald S. Wright*, was postponed till Christmas Eve, but after they attended Mass that morning at the cathedral they found the sailing again postponed because the crew were either drunk or had hangovers, and so spent a quiet day enjoying a book of Daumier reproductions, a Christmas present from Erskine. The sailing was postponed yet again until Boxing Day to enable the crew to sober up, but now it was Lowry's turn and when he went out to buy cigarettes, he returned so drunk he had to be poured into a taxi and carried on board ship. The next day he was visited by a classic hangover.

That week's *Newsweek* had items on Margerie's fiasco with Scribner's and the coming publication of *Under the Volcano*; they were becoming newsworthy. Aiken, finally about to return to America from Rye, sent the news to Davenport, adding that he hoped to get to New York for the launch. 'I suppose they'll shoot the Malc out of a volcano in purple-lighted champagne.'[40]

When Lowry began to resurface from his hangover, he looked over the ship. It was, he wrote, unlike any ship he had been on, with a superstructure evoking images of a huge centipede and the helmets of medieval warriors.[41] They were bound for Venezuela via British Guiana and Trinidad. The crew were dirty and slovenly and the ship had the general appearance of a railway station, though somewhat more noisy. The first day at sea, still hungover, he felt strangely inspired though depressed by the Gulf of Mexico, and could understand why Hart Crane had committed suicide there. In any other ocean, he wrote, there might be some hope of being picked up, 'but in this moonlit empty maniacal immensity none'.[42] In his notes he reflected on the deceptive belief that alcohol produced the inspiration he longed for. After the drinking and the hangover came the time to write. 'But by this time the thoughts are no good. The brilliant wild thoughts and inspirations have gone . . . that is another deception. The sea rushing through your soul in great cold waves of anguish.'[43]

They sighted the Cayman Islands, Jamaica, Cuba and Hispaniola. They saw Eridanus spread across the sky to starboard, and persuaded the mate to leave the bridge to show them the chartroom, upsetting the skipper who bawled them out, saying they had a million dollars' worth of cargo on board and were on one of the most crowded shipping lanes in the world, and they were just plain in the way.

He decided not to drink for the rest of the voyage and settled down to write the preface for Cape. It was a funny, ironic commentary on the long reply to Plomer's report on the book, beginning, 'I like prefaces. I read them. Sometimes I get no further . . .' The reason for the preface, he said, was because in a letter he had put up a considerable fight against the book being cut and had advanced all kinds of esoteric reasons in its defence. Slyly quoting Sherwood Anderson, he added, 'an author can grow fancy and learned and say almost anything' to justify his work. Summarizing the letter, he said that like Gogol's *Dead Souls*, the book was intended to be the Inferno part of a trilogy, and pointed up some of the underlying levels of meaning. He ended with a flourish: 'All applications for the use of this book by temperance societies should be accompanied by a case of Scotch whiskey addressed to the author. Thank you. Now you can put it back in the 3*d*. shelf where you found it.'[44]

Margerie, meantime, made copious notes as she drank with the captain, yarned with the third mate, and discussed literature with the second. Her notes were filled with all the excitement and anticipation of the innocent abroad. Haiti was sighted on New Year's Eve, and Lowry again wrote about impending rebirth. The crew warned, however, that it was a bad place, now under a dictator, and until recently boycotted by American ships. There was nothing but voodoo, bad food, shark-infested waters, and blacks and half-breeds running around. 'You'll get no protection there,' the steward said. American troops were no longer on the island. Port au Prince, Lowry noted, appeared to be 'a town of the dead', hardly any lights at night, the whole atmosphere one of veiled mystery and darkness. They celebrated New Year's Eve reading short stories, eating nuts and drinking icewater. Finally the New Year was marked by the firing of a single rocket from the ship's stern. Then, in the silent night they heard for the first time the terrifying sound of the voodoo drums beckoning them towards the island's heart of darkness.[45] 'I thank God and the Blessed Virgin,' wrote Lowry, 'and pray to her that the next year may be a real new year of goodness love and happiness for Margie and myself, I acting as a man and bring a real change of *character* for the better.'[46]

As dawn came, Port au Prince presented itself, and after an initial disappointing view of oil refineries and factory chimneys a town of beautiful houses with pointed roofs and church spires came into view, giving it the look, wrote Lowry, of Tewkesbury set against the 'rolling mysterious mountains of Oaxaca'. Like Mexico it exuded an air of infinite mystery not to be found in Canada, 'where what goes on is simply nature and scenery'.[47] Margerie noted it as a city of baroque architecture (houses with cupolas and pointed domes, with ornate pillars and fretwork balconies), its vegetation tropical and lush (hibiscus, poinsettia and bougainvillaea).

Before disembarking they had to undergo a cursory medical examination, an ordeal for Lowry, always fearful of authority, and an ordeal made harder when he had to return to the captain's cabin to sign the police papers a second time, his first signature being too weak to impress the carbon copies. A letter was waiting from Cape saying he was pleased he was making cuts in *Under the Volcano*, and that he would be in New York in February and hoped to see him there on publication day.[48] They checked into the Hotel Grand Olaffson, an ancient Victorian pile in the hills of Pétonville on the edge of the city, a hotel full of 'characters', where Dominicans in wide trousers mixed with 'loathesome Americans playing dice'.[49]

A group of sinister Dominican diplomats occupied the next room to the Lowrys, with bodyguards who slept on the floor in the corridor. On the other side was a cricket-playing New York newspaper editor whose house had burned down and who was suffering a nervous breakdown. But the food was good, there was a pleasant garden full of mangoes and banana trees, and a pool where Lowry swam every day. They went sightseeing, took photographs and, in Margerie's case, ever more notes. Lowry put the final touches to his preface for Cape, agonizing over its suitability. They soon grew accustomed to the voodoo drums from the hills across the valley and from the poorest part of town, which began in the early evening and continued until dawn.

Erskine, meanwhile, was beginning to receive comments from his selected writers on *Under the Volcano*. The first one, from his ex-wife, Katherine Anne Porter, was by no means encouraging.

> There is nothing wrong with the idea, the cast of characters, the writing is consistently good, it has the makings of a masterpiece (Dostoevsky on one hand, Hardy on another, would have known how) but it is a corrupt deathly book and – you know this letter is *only* to you – the corruption is in the mind of the author, the confusion is his, and if I had seen this in ms. I would have advised you not to publish it, because it is an evil book, in a way that no true work of art can ever be, because no real artist ever has such confusions . . . I really believe that this book will get along because it is the very expression of the kind of debased feeling and thinking that appeals to the public now more than ever. In another way, *Brideshead Revisited* is an example.[50]

Porter, whose marriage to Erskine had ended in bitter recrimination, may have written this to undermine his sense of having discovered a great new writer. Be that as it may, he spared his author the lady's severe opinion.

Not that it mattered; Lowry himself was receiving enthusiastic letters from friends. The New Year was obviously propitious for the novelist, Jimmy Stern wrote knowingly, closing as it did with a Seven on its rump, and its digits added up to twenty-one which was beautifully divisible by the magic number three. Literary folk, he said, were already asking after the mysterious author of the great new novel, news of which was humming its way around the New York grapevine. 'The city buzzes with your name.'[51] Though fearful now of what to expect in New York, he was enthralled by Stern's letter and kept it in his pocket for weeks, reading it over and over again.

To begin with the Lowrys were both drinking routinely, starting with a few rums before dinner, then a few afterwards. Neither could resist social drinking and on occasions they overdid it. On Haitian Independence Day, 7 January, they woke with hangovers and after a visit to the fiesta set off for the cathedral, where Margerie was anxious to pray. The drums had been going since dawn and the insistent rhythm was at times ravaging to the nerves. Later they watched the festivities from their balcony, and then at the hotel pool Margerie felt a sense of romance and hope, until she caught sight of Malcolm's face. Drink was beginning to take its toll, and she had a sense of no longer sharing the same experience with him.

Some American expatriates living at the Olaffson were scornful of her trumpeting about her husband's genius and her pleas to them not to offer him drinks. He clearly needed no encouragement, and the strange contrast between the nervous, slender, warily over-protective wife and the chunky, red-faced, tense and tongue-tied Lowry, became a subject of malicious humour. There was a mildly scandalous sensation when Lowry disrupted a poolside swimming party by staggering down a long flight of stairs with a glass held aloft, shouting to a man-eating American woman moving in on some handsome youth, 'Wait! I come!' When she told him to drop dead, he simply announced, 'You have killed my heart. I die!' and stepped fully clothed into the pool, still clutching his glass. Margerie screamed that the bitch had killed him and rushed to the rescue. He had to be dragged out of the water, having made no effort whatsoever to save himself.[52]

They made friends with two New Yorkers, Millie and Marian Tanner, who were waiting to move into a house near Port au Prince. When they did, the Lowrys were the first to share their exquisite views of the sea and across the valley to the mountains. They enjoyed several evenings just sitting on the porch watching the sunsets, sharing what Margerie called a 'precarious sense of luxury'. The Tanners introduced them to the young Haitian poet and novelist, Philippe Thoby-Marcelin ('Phito'), who, with his friends from the Centre d'Art was politically on the left, naïvely so, thought Margerie, but in the priest-ridden political climate of Haiti it took courage to be openly critical. Lowry began to spend time with Marcelin and his brothers, Pierre and Emile, and their friends Charles and Raymond Pressoir, seeing in Philippe something like a reincarnation of his dead friend Juan Fernando.

On 10 January he sent Cape his finished preface to *Under the Volcano*. He graded his effort gamma minus and thought it in places semantically and grammatically suspect. However, the beginning and end he thought rather good, though he was not sure it would do the elucidatory job he intended it to do. Perhaps Cape should let an 'expert' look it over before publishing it. Still wanting to conceal his second marriage from his family, he asked that the dedication in the English edition read simply: 'To Margerie'.[53]

On the evening of the 13th there was an impressive display of drumming and dancing. Chanting and singing white-clad dancers moved to and fro in a candlelit procession in front of the hotel. 'M[alcolm] is moved by the religious "supernatural" feeling,' wrote Margerie, 'I by the sudden, unexpected beauty.'[54] The weather, she noted, was too eerily perfect. It would have been only too easy for them to sit and let time and their money slip away. They joined Phito, the Pressoirs and Marian Tanner for trips around Haiti, well off the tourist's track. Once in a café they met refugees from Rafael Trujillo's brutal regime in

The Dominican Republic and a drunken Lowry rose dramatically to declare, 'My brother, I give you my shirt.' On a trip to Le Rivière Froid, he had a long discussion with Raymond Pressoir about voodoo, Baron Samdhi the Lord of the Dead, and demonic possession. 'The Gods are very much alive here,' wrote Margerie, 'and close at hand.'[55] By now Lowry was suffering the effects of drink, his face exhausted-looking and swollen, and Margerie mused sadly about the heartbreaking figure he cut and 'what might have been.' Their travels were not going exactly according to plan. She was gradually getting over her initial fear of so many black faces, but was overcome with a new fear – something dark and strange. Would they ever leave this place, she wondered.

It was a tragedy, she wrote, that Malcolm and Phito had such difficulty communicating, but Lowry got around this by first composing in French what he wanted to say to his friend. 'I believe in complete freedom of expression,' he wrote, 'but in a different society, one of true liberty.' They discussed Rimbaud and Céline, and Lowry approved of how Max Brod, asked by Kafka to destroy his works at his death, had preserved them. Phito read his poems and Lowry read his 'Letter in a Bottle', which Phito said he wanted to translate into French. He talked about *Ultramarine* being nearly translated once by Maurice Sachs, and of having met Cocteau and Jean Paulhan, editor of *Nouvelle Revue Française*. But half-writing and half-speaking French was a frustrating exercise, and he wrote of the agony of trying to communicate with Marcelin, as if across an abyss, and the feeling of love the man and the country evoked in him. Then, thinking of his novel, he added that there was something much greater in man than he had managed to convey, and 'This greatness alone can save the world from he who is living too close, I mean the devil.'[56]

His nervousness about the publication of *Under the Volcano* kept surfacing. On 18 January he sent Erskine a copy of his preface, and also the long letter he had written to Cape from Mexico a year earlier. This, he said, was sent on a sudden impulse, to impress him that he once did know enough about the book to think it worth expounding. He had crossed out the passage about Jackson and *The Lost Weekend*, about which he confessed he had also written to the author. Although he felt that certainly it was the best thing of its kind yet to be done, and 'a double-barrelled moral triumph', he had not liked it, and thought that it would bear reading no more than a couple of times, if that.[57] He was not feeling too well, he added, but thought he would recover. His and Stern's letters had done him good.

One day, after drinking heavily, he disappeared. Margerie and their friends searched the bars of Port au Prince for him for three days in vain. Then suddenly he simply turned up, looking pleased, and announced that he had spent time studying with a voodoo priest. When asked about this he clammed up and refused to elaborate.[58] Not realizing that he was now in a half-drunk and unstable condition most of the time, the Tanners invited the Lowrys to stay for a couple of weeks. Margerie was unsure about this, but Malcolm was keen to go. They had not been there long before he suffered a real breakdown. One night he had a fight with Phito and so hurt the Haitian's feelings that he ran out of the house. Fearing what might follow, Margerie told the Tanners that perhaps they should move out, but then a letter from Erskine temporarily raised his spirits. It also left him shaken. It contained a selection of the replies from the writers who had received advance copies of *Under the Volcano*.

Erskine was appalled by the effort he had put into the Cape letter. 'Great God, you could have finished another novel, or something, in the same amount of time (and perhaps of words).'[59] But he was glad that the preface had arrived too late to be considered by him. 'I think I'd assume a permanent blush if I acquiesced in our edition's appearing with such a preface.' He hoped Cape would not use it. The preface was a bad idea and references to *The Lost Weekend* even worse. It was not the book's fault that his English publishers had thrown that at him, but a letter to his publisher was different from a letter to the general public. He enclosed comments from Aiken, Stephen Spender, Robert Penn Warren and Alfred Kazin, which he was considering for the cover of the book, and which must have left Lowry dazed by the esteem and reputation he would now have to live up to. For Margerie, of course, it was yet more confirmation at the highest level of the genius she had nurtured for the past eight years.

After having great difficulty with the first page, wrote Kazin, he had been overwhelmed by the book, which 'obviously belongs to the most original and creative novels of our time . . . His ability to convey in a single texture the different levels of consciousness and the effect upon them all of the Mexican landscape as a stage of the human soul seems to me one of the most remarkable achievements in modern fiction.' In stark contrast to Katherine Anne Porter, he concluded: 'I think I understand as well that this is not only a profoundly sustained history of a man's disintegration, but also a positive statement in defense of basic human values and human hope: and that it is in the best sense a novel of the politics of men.'[60] Stephen Spender wrote, 'Malcolm Lowry's *Under the Volcano* is the most interesting novel I have read since Lawrence and Joyce.' Aiken was gracious, returning with interest the many compliments his pupil had showered on him since writing that first tentative letter to him in 1928. He managed, in passing, to include a sharp dig at 1930s social realism and three cheers for the return of poetry, the theme he had taken up with Lowry seven years earlier:

> Let us give humble thanks that we can once again, after a long long walk in the desert of contemporary prose, salute a novelist who can really *write*. Malcolm Lowry's *Under the Volcano* must be, for anyone who loves the English language, a sheer joy. Here it is, all renewed and alive again, a changeable shot-silk sun-shot medium of infinite flexibility, which can adapt itself to the subtlest shade of perception or mood, or suffuse with the bloodiest of horrors, or vanish upwards in air like the most mystical of rope-tricks. There is no contemporary writer who could not learn from this book: it should send us all scuttling back to our workshops. And I mean *all*!

Aiken, Erskine said, had wondered why Lowry had not written himself asking for his comments, and requested he write to him at once.[61]

But Lowry's condition was distinctly shaky, and it was made even more so by Erskine's flat rejection of the preface. He replied at once, but the letter was rambling and incoherent. 'Strange and even terrible, mystifying and wonderful things here,' he wrote, and went on about toy cemeteries and doves with ruby eyes and the mad American editor whose house had burned down, who wore a cricket cap and carried *Moby Dick* in his pocket. He was planning to go to the mountains to learn more about voodoo, he said, and raised again Hitchcock's offer to pay for him to visit New York, asking whether it still applied. In reply, Erskine asked whether he was seeking a further advance, and Lowry was quick to disavow this. However, it was evident that money was still a sore point with him and Margerie.

Soon afterwards he went right over the edge. According to Margerie, returning from shopping early one evening she found the Tanner sisters on the front lawn in a wide-eyed state of panic. They said that Malcolm was inside the house and was raving. She told them to fetch Phito, and dashed into the house to find him in the bathroom, swinging around, banging his head against the wall. Then he got down behind the toilet, screaming and having convulsions. Finally an ambulance arrived and he was carried out by two large Haitian male nurses and taken to Notre

Dame Hospital in the nearby suburb of Canapé-Vert, where he was given something to knock him out.

After a few days under sedation, he began to make disjointed notes, much as he had in Bellevue, but less coherent, more impressionistic. He was in a high room with a high bed and high grey open windows. On the wall were three small pictures climbing up at an angle, including *Lady Hamilton* by George Romney. The man in the next room, he wrote, had been castrated and mooed in pain, his bloodstained clothes piled in the bathroom with 'something like part of a human peeping from among them.' Phito stayed with him all of the first day, trying to assure him that his suffering would pass. 'And on the fourth day, sure enough,' he wrote, 'little pink grasses waving in the wind and bending so sharply caused me no pain.' One of Phito's friends came and they talked about Malraux. Then Phito brought his younger brother, 'a handsome hypnologist who once shot himself right through the body and felt fine ever after . . .' And Margerie came to talk about their eternally recurring theme – a new life. 'Perhaps this time we will win through,' he wrote. When Margerie visited him she found him fretting over Erskine's harsh words about his preface, now sitting on Cape's desk in London, and feeling insecure about himself as a writer.

With departure day drawing nearer, Margerie set out to smooth the path for the suffering genius. She wrote to Stern, taking up his offer to 'find a hole' for them to crawl into in New York. Unfortunately, she said, Malcolm was unable to write, being in hospital with 'a nasty cough'. Then, more honestly, she added that as publication day drew near he was becoming crazy and unable to do anything, even write a simple reply. They planned to sail to New York on a Dutch boat, arriving around publication day.[62] She wrote a similar note to Cape, now at the Gotham Hotel in New York, and about to be sent *Horse in the Sky*, mentioning that Malcolm had sent his preface to London, but no longer wanted it published; he was distressing himself because he had been told it was no good. If he used it would he have someone remove all reference to *The Lost Weekend*? She need not have worried. Someone at Cape had silently suppressed it.

Lowry's doctor, Dr Louis Mars, had written an essay on voodoo, and Lowry agreed to take his manuscript to New York, promising to put him in touch with Harry Murray, Aiken's psychiatrist friend in Boston. The grateful doctor allowed him out early on the 8th to go with the Marcelin brothers to a voodoo ceremony lasting two days and two nights. On the 11th, he wrote to Erskine that as a result of this he was feeling somewhat groggy from a combination of drugs and voodoo. 'The voodoo priest, perhaps recognizing a kindred spirit, has promised to initiate me by fire if and when I return . . . I really would like to be a voodoo priest.' He was right about the preface, he said, and had asked Cape to 'deracinate it'. As for the advance reviews of *Under the Volcano*, they scared him like hell and he had barely been able to bring himself to read them.[63]

Matson had sent his final $500 of the advance to be paid on publication, and somewhat cheered, he sent off a series of letters announcing their impending departure for New York. Haiti, he told Noxon, was replete with artistic genius and kindness, 'Truly a miraculous place in every respect.'[64] Stern had written to Margerie, alarmed at news of his illness. If he came to New York it was better he arrived fit, he said. What Erskine had in mind he did not know, but he saw no reason why he had to be there on publication day, 'Or is he prepared to be lionized, quizzed, televised, photographed, and sent shooting back into hospital?'

> He has nothing to worry about, except the prospect of being run down by fans in the street. Better keep him on beer & milk for a few days, I'd say. A lot of infirm & frustrated writers will want his autograph, a few of the hairs from his head or a fly-button or two. Let him be strong, silent and, when need be, savage. It's a vicious city, and many are vile. Malcolm Lowry will be about the most fortunate man in it. For that you need a sedative and good health.[65]

The prospect of all that literary junketing might have horrified Malcolm, but to Margerie it was something to revel in, proper recognition due to her own 'tamed' genius. There was also the prospect of impressing publishers like Cape with her own talent. *Horse in the Sky*, after all, had been compared to *Wuthering Heights* by the brilliant author of *Under the Volcano*.

Stern said he had booked them into the Murray Hill Hotel, not far from Reynal & Hitchcock's offices on West 40th Street. In spite of not having met him for almost thirteen years, the Irish writer was remarkably shrewd in knowing what Lowry would fear most in New York. What he could have known was his terror of someone (Jackson or Rascoe) suddenly appearing to denounce him as a plagiarist. But he need not have worried. The favourable reviews continued to come in and not one suggested that the book was that derivative. The film critic James Agee wrote 'I am particularly struck by his achievements in intensity and momentum,' and regretted he was too busy to review it for the press.[66] And Malcolm Cowley wrote, 'I dreamed about the story last night. I don't know any other book that makes Mexico so completely living in one's mind.'[67]

Parting from his Haitian friends was painful. Although there was a language barrier he felt a strong affinity for their radical aspirations as well as their attachment to poetry and strong magic. Before leaving he offered to help Phito and his friend Anthony Lespes by pushing their books in New York. When he left he took with him manuscripts from Phito, Lespes and the voodoo psychiatrist, Dr Mars. The plan to sail to New York was ditched and on 12 February the Lowrys flew to Miami, with a brief stopover at Camaguey in Cuba. Malcolm, wrote Margerie, was 'looking exhausted, dissipated and brave and shaking,' while she had a sinking feeling, a sickening sense of lost happiness, lost opportunities, waste and sadness.

They travelled by bus from Miami to New York, taking in places of literary significance on the way. Lowry noted down graffiti, signs, and tombstone inscriptions. On a lavatory wall in St Augustine, Florida, he found scrawled, 'dirty stinking Degenerate Bobs was here from Boston, North End, Mass. Warp son of a bitch . . .' In Savannah, Georgia, Aiken's birthplace, he posed for photographs in front of the fountains in Forsyth Park. When he saw these a few months later, Aiken wrote to Mary, 'I recognized Savannah before I recognized *them*. They both looked a bit liquidated.'[68] Staying over at the Argyle Hotel in Charleston, Lowry wrote warmly to Stern, thanking him for booking a room. They had some money, he wrote, but not a lot – 'enough for bottles but not for socks, if you understand me.'[69] He was still somewhat 'liquidated'. Leaving Charleston he caught a glimpse of what might come to destroy his Paradise in Eridanus – a sign reading: 'The Daniel Jenkins' Homes . . . Housing Project of the City of Charleston.' His single word comment: 'Horror'. They were, no doubt, 'homes of the better type', and someone's Garden of Eden was about to be devastated.

In Richmond he paid his respects to Edgar Allan Poe, and to his relics in the Valentine Museum. One of Poe's letters, written in February 1831, so struck him that he copied an excerpt: 'It will however be the last time I ever trouble any human being – I feel I am on a sick bed from which I shall never get up . . . I am wearing away every day, even if my last sickness has not completed it.' For a barely recovered, still rather 'liquidated' Lowry, the words could well have been his own. Poe and 'dirty Degenerate Bobs' were to find their way into one of his most subtle short stories, 'Strange Comfort Afforded by the Profession'.

HOORAY FOR HOLLYWOOD.
Left: All dressed up with nowhere to go. Lowry, spruced up and photographed at the Griffiths Observatory in 1938 by Benjamin Parks, the Los Angeles lawyer, to persuade Arthur Lowry that he had been reformed. *Below right*: Femme Fatale. Margerie Bonner, teenage silent movie actress. *Below left*: Carol Phillips, whom Lowry offered a quarter of the earnings of *Under the Volcano* for typing the manuscript, a promise on which he was to renege.

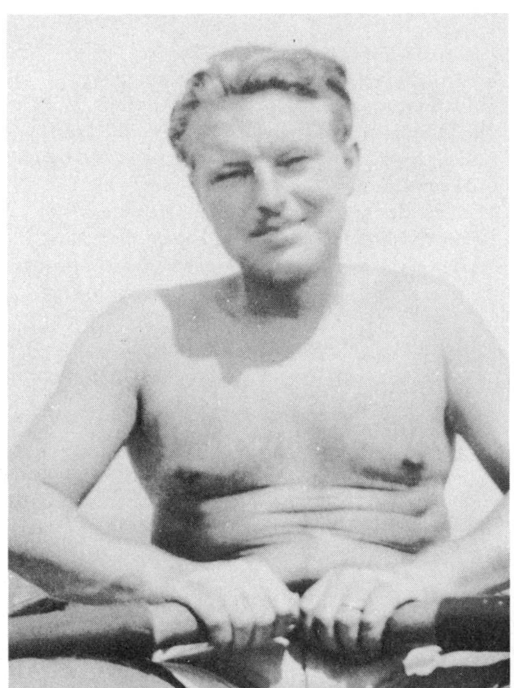

TO WILDER SHORES.
Left: The Ancient Mariner. Lowry, shortly after his marriage to Margerie in 1940, at the oars of *My Heart is in the Highlands*, his dinghy at Dollarton. *Middle*: The Wicket Gate, Mark III. The Lowrys' third shack, rebuilt after fire destroyed the previous one on D-Day plus one, June 1944. Margerie is standing in the doorway. *Bottom*: 'The Crazy Wonder'. The pier which Malcolm and Margerie built at Dollarton.

GETTING PUBLISHED.
Above left: With one of his first editors from his Cambridge days, Gerald Noxon, at Oakville, Ontario, November 1944. *Above right*: The *Volcano* about to erupt. Posing with the galley proofs of his book beside Burrard Inlet at Dollarton, 1946. *Below*: With his Random House editor, Albert Erskine, in Paris, September 1948.

MARGERIE ASCENDANT.
Above left: A day in 'Enochvilleport', as Lowry styled Vancouver. Margerie sports her much-prized arctic skunk fur coat, which she even took to Mexico. *Above*: A grim year in Europe. This passport photo of Margerie had to be taken in Paris in 1948 after Lowry had purloined and then lost her original passport. *Left*: A shining morning face. Margerie apparently enjoying life at the shack she ultimately became determined to leave.

On a postcard bearing a picture of Poe, he wrote to Phito from Fredericksburg, Virginia, telling him that he felt that in leaving them he had lost his whole family.[70] He also cabled Jimmy Stern and Albert Erskine announcing their arrival in New York the following day, 19 February, publication day for *Under the Volcano*.

CHAPTER XIX

'SUCCESS . . . LIKE SOME HORRIBLE DISASTER'

1947

> It was when thus haunted by publishers, engravers, editors, critics, autograph-collectors, portrait-fanciers, biographers, and petitioning and remonstrating literary friends of all sorts; it was then, that there stole into the youthful soul of Pierre, melancholy forebodings of the utter unsatisfactoriness of all human fame; since the most ardent profferings of the most martyrizing demonstrations in his behalf, – these he was sorrowfully obliged to turn away.
>
> HERMAN MELVILLE, *Pierre*

New York, Lowry wrote, was 'a city where it can be remarkably hard . . . to get on the right side of one's despair,'[1] and, when he and Margerie arrived there, memories of Jan and of his time in Bellevue must have been close to the surface. The city was in the grip of a snowstorm and they had only summer clothing with them. Their bus drew into the Manhattan bus station at dawn on Wednesday 19 February, and they huddled together nervously drinking coffee until offices opened and they could call Erskine. As soon as he heard they were in town, he took a cab to meet them. 'It was,' he recalled, 'a cold and ugly day and everything seemed to be a little bit off-key to me for some reason.'[2] It was an uncomfortable meeting. Lowry was tongue-tied and Erskine tried to put him at ease by enthusing over the advance reviews he had seen. The book would be a huge success and its author would be hailed as a bright new star in the literary firmament. If Margerie was thrilled, the new literary star was hardly ablaze; he found the celebration of commercial success all too unbearable. As he later wrote to Phito: 'all [this] may seem obscene to you and I, but . . . as you know [it] impresses publishers.'[3] He might have added that it also impressed Margerie.

Erskine took them to the Murray Hill Hotel, where Stern had reserved them a room. After a drink in the bar he left them to rest for a few hours. Later they had lunch with Erskine and Frank Taylor, his associate, who read out some of the encomiastic previews. In the atmosphere of celebration the editors were careful not to tell their strangely unforthcoming author that while Curtice Hitchcock had thought *Under the Volcano* magnificent, Eugene Reynal, the money side of the partnership, despised it utterly, and they had already had to fight hard to keep it in the firm's schedule.

Publication festivities were planned for the following day. When Erskine called to collect them, Lowry had equipped himself with a gallon jug of wine from which he took occasional sips, and which he took with him when they went to meet the editorial team at Reynal & Hitchcock. Margerie wrote to the Noxons, 'Malc . . . is nearly paralysed by triumph. The reviews are terrific . . . we are so overwhelmed with success we are chaotic.'[4] They hoped to see him in Niagara-on-the-Lake en route to Dollarton. Noxon replied promptly: they would be very welcome; Betty was in Washington.

That evening Frank Taylor threw a party for them at his home in Greenwich Village, and the wine jug came along, too. Erskine was surprised to find Lowry drinking, having gained the impression from his letters that he now disapproved of alcohol. For most of the evening he sat unexpressive and silent while the others tried to keep the conversation going. When Erskine quoted the opening of *Moby Dick*, hoping to provoke a response from Lowry, he suddenly awoke as if from a deep sleep and said, 'It's not right,' and proceeded to recite word-perfectly the complete first two pages of the book while everyone listened in awe. At this point he declared that he had to leave or 'terrible tragedy will strike this house'. That evening Taylor's son Curtice fell ill with cyanosis, but Erskine refused to ascribe Curtice Taylor's illness to Lowry's malign presence.[5]

Reynal was away when *Under the Volcano* was published, but on returning, wanted to meet the firm's new author. Lowry was unenthusiastic. Meetings with businessmen were not to his taste. Nevertheless, when Erskine pleaded with him, he agreed. On the day in question he had a haircut and a shave, and Margerie told him to be sure to be back in time for the lunch date. However, when Erskine called round he was still not back. They checked the hotel bar, then bars further afield. Finally, at 5 p.m., they gave up and sat down in the bar of the Shelton Hotel on Lexington Avenue to have a drink when in he walked, swaying slightly. He pulled himself up straight, looked at them, then said in tones of mock injury, 'My best friend with my wife – drunk together!'

Reynal was not amused at being stood up, but Lowry was even less keen to meet him, having gathered by now that he disliked the *Volcano* and had withheld money for its publicity. They finally met in Reynal's office, and were talking together when suddenly Lowry said, 'What am I doing talking to an office boy?' and left.[6] Reynal was, he wrote later, in fine hypocritical form, 'a (not very anonymous) member of Alcoholics Anonymous'.

But the reviews must have given Reynal pause. In *PM*, Dawn Powell saw parallels with *Look Homeward, Angel*, adding, 'But, in Mr Lowry, the noble fusion of senses, mind and heart is marvellously complete, which makes him a kind of angel in his own right.' John Woodburn, however, in the *Saturday Review*, featuring a front cover drawing of Lowry, gave it as passionately intelligent a review as he could have wished for:

> When I had finished reading this book for the first time, I could not bring myself to set down what I thought of it. I was so much within its grasp, so profoundly affected by the tides of its prose, the faltering arc of its tragic design, a design which gave me the feeling of wonder and beauty and fear, of melancholy and loneliness, the indescribable loneliness I have always felt at seeing a falling star describe its incorrigible curve of disintegration across the face of night, that I said to myself: you are this book's fool, it has stolen you and mastered you by some trickery, and you cannot appraise it tranquilly until it leaves you alone. It has not let me alone. In the street, in my room, where it has set its sorrowful music to the metronome of my clock, in the company of many or only one, it has been with me insistently. I have now read it twice, and the second time has bound me to it more tightly than before.

Woodburn emerged uncannily like the ideal reader Lowry had envisioned in his long letter to Cape, reading the book over again and recognizing its 'intricate, convoluted architecture' while responding to its 'sorrowful music'. He compared Lowry more than favourably to Charles Jackson, Wolfe, Hemingway and Joyce. 'He is Joyce's own child, there is no doubt, but he is also his own man, original.' His conclusion was positively rapturous. 'I have never before used the word in a review, and I am aware of the responsibility upon me in using it, but I am of the opinion, carefully considered, that *Under the Volcano* is a work of genius. Ladies and gentlemen: this magnificent, tragic, compassionate, and beautiful book – and my neck.'[7]

Parties were organized for him also by Jimmy and Tania Stern. As Stern had warned, he was in great demand. One such evening, probably on their first Saturday in New York, was recalled by Stern's friend Harvey Breit, when, after a small dinner, a whole party of people came round to meet him.

> We remember . . . the entering people coming up to him, saying sincere words of respect or admiration or congratulations, and Mr Lowry, feet wide apart as though on the deck of a storm-tossed ship, jaw bones working relentlessly, staring out of . . . very blue eyes, and saying nothing, not one single solitary syllable. Then the next person or people or group coming up, shaking hands, greeting him, waiting for his reply – and nothing. And the next, and nothing.[8]

Despite his great desire to succeed, Lowry had turned out to be a reluctant celebrity, no doubt fearing that the next hand offered would be that of a vengeful Rascoe or an accusing Charles Jackson. Among those he met at Stern's East 52nd Street apartment were Dawn Powell, James Agee and W. H. Auden. Powell took a great shine to Lowry and corresponded for a time afterwards; Agee became a life-long admirer. He also met Alfred Kazin, who was shocked by his drinking and would not be the last to be so on meeting him.

The Sunday papers were no less enthusiastic about the book. Mark Schorer in the *Herald Tribune Weekly*, also drew the parallel with Joyce, while noticing however the wider range of Lowry's influences. He was young with an exuberance of style, he wrote, and the delight he took in others' writing showed the difference between his and a more mature and integrated talent. 'But he has set himself ambitions of the Joycean order if not of their full complexity, and within the smaller frame of his novel, he has achieved them.' The book had left him 'exhausted and exhilarated'. In the *New York Times*, H. R. Hays called it 'an exciting and beautiful book' and concluded that '*Under the Volcano* may well be the best novel of the season.'

Stern took him to meet Djuna Barnes. 'She was painting some sort of semi-female male demon on the wall,' Lowry recalled, 'reproved me roundly for the success of the *Volcano*, generously gave me six quart bottles of beer, and expressed herself frightened by *Nightwood*, since when she said she had written nothing.' He could not make out, he said, whether her book was a work of genius or 'a disorder of the kineasthenia' and was probably both. 'All in all, I thought her him or It an admirable, if terrifyingly tragic, being, possessing both integrity and honour . . .'[9] Stern said that when they met, Lowry was very shy and withdrawn and hardly spoke[10] – one terrifyingly tragic being quietly observing another.

He did manage to take time off from drinking and partying to send a copy of the *Volcano* to Davenport. 'I have made an absolutely obscene success here with the book,' he wrote. 'It is just like a great disaster. My little wife is happy though . . .'[11] He also gave Erskine the manuscript of *Lunar Caustic* with notes on little bits of pink paper attached, and his copy of *Ultramarine*, which he handed over reluctantly and with many words of derogation. Erskine took him one evening to the Greenwich Village nightclub owned by jazz guitarist Eddie Condon, who came over and greeted Lowry like an old friend. It was a far cry from isolated Dollarton, and when they discovered Eugene O'Neill's *The Iceman Cometh* playing in town, the Lowrys got tickets, wired Noxon, and extended their stay in order to see it.

They made one trip out of town, to the Greenwich home of Harold Matson. The two had not met since 1936, a time overshadowed by the Rascoe affair. He talked at length about *La Mordida*, the novel he was planning about being deported from Mexico, a tale so grim in the telling that Matson suggested he was writing '*Under* Under the Volcano'. This so delighted Lowry that he adopted it as his own joke. Matson also suggested that he could well write a book about the writing of the *Volcano*, something Lowry had already conceived with *Dark as the Grave*, but upon which Matson's interest bestowed a blessing.[12] During lunch a large piece of wood fell from the fire, and, he got up, went across to the fireplace, picked up this burning log in his hand, put it back, then went back to the table and carried on talking as if it was the most normal thing in the world. Matson was convinced that Lowry had an extraordinary ability to handle fire without apparent injury.[13]

At another of Stern's parties he was found standing at the bathroom mirror, his nose pouring blood which he was smearing all over the walls. He was snorting with laughter, sure he had TB, and was quickly taken to a doctor,[14] where tests proved indecisive. But according to Margerie he put on a great death-bed scene with Erskine, Agee, Dawn Powell, Frank Taylor, and the Sterns in solemn attendance. At times he would cough weakly and say 'Well, you'd better get me a drink.' There was nothing wrong with him; he was simply enjoying the drama.[15] However, he was told to give up smoking, so he threw away his cigarettes and resorted instead to cadging from others.

Margerie was pursuing her own literary career. She told Erskine how 'nice' it would be if they were both published by the same firm and made sure that they both met Cape and Max Perkins, who was most apologetic about her bad time with Scribner's. He was immensely taken by Lowry. He had been editor of Scott Fitzgerald, Hemingway and Thomas Wolfe, and also of Aiken's *Blue Voyage*. Margerie recalled him being surprised that there seemed to be no competition between them, both being writers. He took them to lunch a couple of times and said he would never forgive Matson for not sending the *Volcano* to him. Dawn Powell told Lowry later, after Perkins's death,

> You exerted a spell over him and perhaps made him gloomier that the great writers were gone and moreover he was himself too tired . . . to do a good job on even a Lowry . . . He told me several times of meeting you in the Ritz bar and having drinks with you and also asking him for cigarettes because your doctor advised against your smoking so you dutifully never bought any yourself.[16]

By 24 February the first print run of *Under the Volcano* was exhausted. But Reynal had refused to order a second run earlier, and bookshops were running out of stock as the glowing reviews began to empty the shelves. If Reynal was surprised at the success of the *Volcano*, so was Cape, about to fly to Cuba to see Hemingway. He reported to his London office that it was getting important reviews and 'selling a bit (6,000 to date).'[17]

Aiken wrote to his old pupil from Rye, the letter which probably mattered most to him because it brought the homage of a master to his pupil.

> Your book is magnificent, magnificent, magnificent . . . I had some misgivings about the book qua *novel*: I think I still have, perhaps . . . But . . . as a piece of literature it is genuine bona fide first cut off the white whale's hump, godshot, sunshot, bloodshot, spermshot, and altogether the most aiken-satisfying book I've wallowed in for a generation. My god how good to be able to relish the english language again, to have it all vascular with life and sensation, as quiveringly alive shall we say as a butterfly on a dunghill –! It is all so beautifully and *easily* done – the elisions and transitions and ellipses and parentheses and asides, and time-notations and recapitulations and minatory fingerposts – how infinitely satisfactory to a writer to see

> all *that* so incomparably well done and understood! And that, only the beginning; for of course in the end it's the richness and perceptiveness of your observation that really feeds the book and makes it, the unsleeping eye and ear, whether inward or outward. O baby, o baby, o baby, it's marvellous Malc, and I hug it to my bozoom . . . the Consul you make wholly real and superb; even for me, who can see wheel and lever at work; yes, the great genial drunk to end all drunks, the Poppergetsthebotl of alcoholics! he will become famous.

Hugh seemed to him a bit functionless and Yvonne a little shadowy – her death a dramatic mistake, however well written, and the psychology was somewhat obscure – the reasons for the alcoholism and the infidelities – all of which weakened the sense of tragic inevitability. But the last scene was 'unforgettably splendid, genius in every page of it' and would make his name illustrious. 'You've been and gone and done it . . . Our very much loves to you both, and hail to UNDER THE MALCANO or POPPERGETSTHEBOTL!!!'[18] Despite this unfettered praise, Aiken was aware that here was something very much like that multi-layered, time-transcending novel of consciousness he had discussed at Jeake's House and had then dreamed, but which Lowry, not he, had finally achieved.

On 2 March, the Lowrys took the train to Niagara Falls, where Noxon met them and took them to his home in Niagara-on-the-Lake. If Margerie was sorry to leave the literary spotlight Malcolm was only too relieved to exit left pursued by Furies. The first night at Noxon's, he toasted his release from 'celebrity' with large amounts of brandy. Next day, heavily hungover, the two men went into Toronto to meet Noxon's friend, the radio producer Fletcher Markle, who had read the *Volcano* and was keen to meet the author.

They met at a Jarvis Street pub, and secretly he and Noxon counted thirty bottles of beer drunk by Lowry that day, leaving them well behind. Away from Margerie and the literati, he was at his relaxed best, and Markle was duly impressed by his display of English charm, his brilliant conversation and verbal pyrotechnics. Markle said he had been Orson Welles's assistant in South America, and had sent him a copy of the *Volcano* to read. Lowry was delighted, and hopeful that Welles might want to film his novel.

Back in Niagara-on-the-Lake, Lowry talked at length of his adventures in Mexico and Haiti. He read from a draft of *La Mordida*, which Noxon thought had far greater potential than *In Ballast to the White*

Sea.[19] But he was worried by his obsession with voodooism, feeling it could only threaten his delicately balanced mental state; having recreated his 'familiars' and 'Furies' in voodooistic form, they could only hound him towards madness.

After a week, Lowry was anxious to return to the seclusion of Dollarton. Betty had returned from Washington and no doubt he felt the atmosphere change. But Margerie was reluctant to go back to the wilderness after the excitement of her recent travels and the high society she had enjoyed in New York, and decided to remain for a while. Malcolm said he would return to get their little shack ready for her, an idea which Noxon found amusing, considering his condition. Nevertheless, on 10 March he flew alone to Vancouver and booked into the Sylvia Hotel (on English Bay), where he proceeded to get high. As when about to set sail on the *Pyrrhus*, he called the local press to announce himself a success. The *Vancouver News Herald* was unwary enough to send a reporter to the hotel and Lowry all too readily spun him a preposterous tale which duly appeared on 15 March.

> One of the year's most successful novels was written in a British Columbia shack without light, heat or water. The author is Malcolm Lowry, 38-year-old Englishman now back in Vancouver after a world-wide success that has brought him $250,000.

He had, said the report, received calls from Orson Welles and Hollywood film companies asking for film rights, and had written a new book, *La Mordida*. ' "It's horrible," said Lowry . . . "the history of a man's imagination. It's about Mexico." ' He then staked his old claim to be Canada's Dostoyevsky: 'Lowry thinks that there are only eight Canadian writers who are worthwhile. "There is so much to write about, and there doesn't [*sic*] seem to be the writers to do the job." ' He was unlikely to put British Columbia into any of his future novels, he said, though he intended to return permanently to his shack in Dollarton. He had made only passing reference to Vancouver in his novel, saying it was a city with strange licensing laws, 'where they eat sausage meals from which you expect the Union Jack to appear at any minute.' In Haiti, he told the reporter mysteriously but untruthfully, he had become a voodoo priest, adding: 'I believe I went through the ceremony . . . with flying colours.' This report on 'the new Hemingway' concluded by hoping that 'Lowry, a Cambridge man who has been compared to Joyce and Lawrence by national US magazines and became a voodoo priest from pure curiosity, might even one day write his own strange story.' What the reporter could not have known was that Lowry had been writing 'his own strange story' ever since *Ultramarine* and would continue doing so with almost everything he wrote. On his own once again, however, with no Margerie to embarrass him, it seems he was ready enough to bask in his success.

The newspaper story with its allusions to lucre quickly brought Maurice Carey, old 'Pappa Vulture', to the Sylvia Hotel. He found Lowry surrounded by empty bottles and the remains of unfinished meals, and about to be ejected for causing damage and a disturbance with a noisy drinking party of people brought in from a nearby bar. Now he was drunk and maudlin enough to embrace his old tormentor. 'Why may we not all be simple, Maurice?' he asked. 'Why may we not all be brothers?'[20] Carey took him home for an alcoholic evening and Lowry produced from his luggage the galley proofs of *Under the Volcano* on which he inscribed a drunken dedication dated 'The Ides of March' reading 'Remindful of old times – so to speak'. Next day, according to Maurice, after a book-signing at the Hudson's Bay Store downtown, he returned with a young female admirer who ended up having to flee the house in the early hours pursued by a stark naked Lowry.[21]

Margerie, meantime, was regaling the Noxons with woeful tales of his drunk, mad and intolerable behaviour. If Gerald listened with concerned tolerance, Betty enjoyed the quiet satisfaction of having her low opinion of Lowry confirmed. He had not been wrong about her hostility. A month later she wrote to Aiken, who quoted her letter to Davenport.

> Malc has indeed 'been on the bottle' for two years. Margie stayed on after Malc went back, and poured it all out – hallucinations, violence, 'misery, woe, agony of soul and body, near murder, proximity to death's door, something you need to hear to believe.' B adds also that Malc got a 'good grounding in voodoo while in Haiti, and you can imagine how neatly it fits in, especially with rum a dollar a bottle'. And a long saga of persecution, party political, in Mexico a year ago, with escape at pistol point, of which B says 'such as could only happen, if it *did* happen to them'. Of their success with the Volcano, she says they received it less with satisfaction than with an appearance of guilt.[22]

After three days of Margerie's confessions, the Noxons were looking forward to her leaving. Clearly something had happened to the Lowrys' relationship. What they had both been striving for, the success of the *Volcano*, had, of course, thrilled her; he, on the other hand, had not behaved as a successful writer should behave and had been a source of embarrassment to her.

She entrained for Vancouver on 13 March. Meantime, Lowry was again drinking whisky at breakfast, and the day before she arrived spent the afternoon bemusing the Careys with a strange psychical performance involving knocking poltergeists and voodooistic conversations with 'familiars'. On the day she arrived he was too drunk to meet her, so Carey went instead. According to Margerie, he told her that Malcolm was far gone and they should put him away and divide his money between them. She got him away from Carey fast, after first retrieving the *Volcano* galley proofs. Lady Harteebeeste was now back in charge of the roaring El Leon.

Not only was the shack not ready, but she was faced with having to sober him up, unpack everything and make the place shipshape. Among the stack of post awaiting him were excited congratulations from Priscilla and all in LA – Woodburn's encomiastic *Saturday Review* notice had had its impact in California, too. McClelland & Stewart, the Toronto publishers planning a Canadian edition of the book, were asking for biographical details, and ironically the *Ladies Home Journal* were seeking his opinion as 'a well-known man' on the 'controversial subject – when a man is most dependent on a woman'. Jimmy Stern sent him Nabokov's lectures on Gogol, inscribed 'Good Health and Good Writing . . . Don't forget: A nose is a nose is a nose,' and there was a letter from Carol Phillips reminding him of her promised twenty-five per cent of the *Volcano*'s profits on publication. Margerie made him throw it away.

Reynal had finally been persuaded by an angry Erskine and Taylor to get more copies of the *Volcano* printed. On 14 March they issued a press release claiming that the book's successful launching was due to 'one of the most thorough and successful pre-publication campaigns ever launched by Reynal & Hitchcock', illustrating the importance of teamwork and enthusiasm being transferred to those concerned with producing and distributing a book. Most re-orders were coming from bookstores, department stores and circulating libraries – a literary book in the best sense of the word was getting into more popular markets and was beginning to look like a best-seller. Indeed, on 23 March it edged into the *New York Times* bestseller list at number fourteen. Later Lowry claimed gleefully that for one week it was ahead of *Forever Amber*, but as that risqué romance had come out in 1944, it was hardly serious competition any longer. Immediately after ensuring a new run of the book, Erskine and Taylor resigned over Reynal's attitude to it. Lowry heard the news from Erskine's replacement, Chester Kerr; he was so shocked he promptly mislaid the letter. He felt he had lost the best editor he could ever have, and began to fret and could not settle down to work.

Margerie had got Max Perkins to read *Horse in the Sky*, the book rejected by every publisher in New York, including Scribner's, and by 18 March she heard that he had accepted it. He and Scribner were still eager to placate her, even if it meant publishing a novel they had previously rejected. But that did not worry her; it was her serious novel, her *Volcano*, and with its publication she could stand beside Malcolm as a novelist of substance in her own right. She received $400 in royalties from Matson and wrote saying that Malcolm would soon be back on top form. However, he was worried about losing Erskine, fearing that Reynal would let the book slide into obscurity and throw away its excellent start. Matson replied quickly with the reassuring news that the *Volcano* had been selected as a Book-of-the-Month Club's 'Special Members' Edition' for May, June and July with minimum sales of 2,500. Other book clubs were interested and Reynal & Hitchcock were about to get a further five thousand copies printed. Chester Kerr had assured him that he had no intention of letting the book 'slide off'. They considered it one of their most important books and valued him as one of their authors.[23]

Aiken and Davenport now had to face the fact that one of their company – in many ways the least likely one – had achieved a work of art which was being acclaimed a classic and a work of genius. To Lowry they expressed admiration, but to one another they wrote in a quite different vein. On 20 March, Aiken wrote to Davenport that from what he had heard from Linscott and Noxon, he and Margerie were suffering from

> a queer kind of co-operative hallucination: a dementia à deux. Margie aiding and abetting the Malc in his mystifications and self-mystifications, and all the lunar swings and roundabouts. But as Linscott says, perhaps Malc *does* do it with at least half a wink? Let's hope so at all events . . .[24]

By 23 March Lowry had shaken himself alive enough to write a funny letter to Stern on the profound and Gogolian subject of his nose, and again claimed that Orson Welles was after the *Volcano*. The truth was that a week after Fletcher Markle had given him a copy of the book, Welles had called up to complain, 'I've got to page 40 and nothing has happened yet!' That Welles was actively seeking the film rights was just another Lowry fantasy. Stern reported back that in New York Brentano's window was packed with the third impression of the *Volcano* together with a display of Mexican cloth.

Cheered by this, he finally wrote to Chester Kerr saying how 'desolate' and 'wrong' it seemed that Erskine and Taylor were no longer with the firm, but hoping that everyone would now be happy all round. He was hard at work on *La Mordida*, 'approximately 7 times as abysmal as the Volcano, though it has, or should have, a triumphant ending.' With conscious or unconscious irony, he said how much he had enjoyed meeting Reynal.[25] The same day, thanking Mrs Bonner for her congratulations, he wrote that his kind of success, 'may be the worst possible thing that could happen to any serious author'. Not that he had not enjoyed the adulation. That was the problem. 'All is vanity, saith the preacher.' This same sentiment produced a poem:

> Success is like some horrible disaster
> Worse than your house burning, the sounds of ruination
> As the roof tree falls following each other faster
> While you stand, the helpless witness of your damnation.
> Fame like a drunkard consumes the house of the soul
> Exposing that you have worked for only this –
> Ah, that I had never suffered this treacherous kiss
> And had been left in darkness forever to founder and fail.[26]

Of course, he did crave success, but it was the reverent celebrity visited on him by the New York literati which he had found so embarrassingly awful.

April began with the *Volcano* still at number fourteen on the *New York Times* bestseller list, just ahead of *Mr Blandings Builds His Dream House*,[27] and they were considered newsworthy enough to feature in Bennet Cerf's *Saturday Review of Literature* column.

> One New York critic has evolved an interesting theory in connection with . . . *Under the Volcano* and the fact that what is in effect an epilogue is printed as the first chapter of the book. It seems that author Malcolm Lowry's wife is herself a detective story writer of note named Margerie Bonner. Some months ago Scribner's published her newest

> book, *The Last Twist of the Knife*, and built up a very tidy advance sale for it. There was a minor imperfection in the first edition, however: the last chapter was left out entirely. A number of mystery fans, not to mention Miss Bonner, regarded the innovation with a jaundiced eye. 'Lowry himself,' explains the critic, 'decided to take no chances. *His* last chapter comes first!'[28]

Margerie's saga with Scribner's ended when a contract for *Horse in the Sky* arrived on 7 April. Following Malcolm's lead, she rang the *Vancouver Sun* who sent a reporter to interview her. 'Margerie Lowry, attractive wife of 38-year-old Malcolm Lowry, author of the current best-seller, *Under the Volcano*, does not stand in the shadow of her husband's fame, she writes books herself,' he reported. ' "I give all credit to my husband," says the slim, green-eyed authoress. "Before my marriage, everything I wrote was rejected." ' But with his help she had produced two mysteries, and a serious novel due out in October. Having a critical editor on hand was the greatest help to a young writer, she said, and although her husband did not like mysteries, he kept the peace between them by thinking her stories were good. She talked about the writing of the *Volcano* and near disasters to it, like the fire. Contradicting her later story of having rescued it herself, she said it was saved by Malcolm, who 'barely escaped with his life in rescuing the manuscript'. The book was in its fourth impression, coming out in five languages and about to be broadcast on the CBS national network, she said.

The broadcast was partly Noxon's doing. Fletcher Markle had persuaded CBS to launch their prestigious 'Studio One' series with a dramatization of the *Volcano*. He asked Noxon to put the idea to Lowry and then to write it. Noxon cabled Lowry[29] offering $350 for a single broadcast, saying that it would be excellent publicity for the book. How keen Lowry was is not known, but finally he agreed. Noxon then cabled a word of caution. 'Please understand we cannot do anything like justice to book on radio stop more like a movie trailer but will do our damndest to preserve integrity.'[30]

The book continued to be widely reviewed. The *Nation* thought Lowry had talent but the book had not quite come off, the prose being asked to do too much and buckling under the strain; *Newsweek* found it labyrinthal but rich, moving and powerful. Elizabeth Hardwick in the *Partisan Review* called it ambitious and expansive, its style reminiscent of Djuna Barnes's *Nightwood* and Yvonne of a Fitzgerald heroine.[31] Edward Weeks in the *Atlantic* compared it to *Brideshead Revisited*, concluding,

'Mr Lowry is a stylist of versatility and power. He has the gift of balancing the spoken word and the hidden thought; the facility of lighting up the inner life of those who are devoted yet opposed . . . Here at last is a novelist to enjoy, to praise, and to reread.'[32]

When the Canadian edition appeared, the *Toronto Globe and Mail* was not impressed. 'Told straightforwardly, the narrative might have been of novelette length. It actually uses 150,000 words to deliver the jumbled facts via the impressions of the consul's irresponsible mind.'[33] The *Vancouver Sun* gave it the headline, 'Turgid Novel of Self-Destruction'. Its prose, it said, 'occasionally ascends like a star shell and bursts into brilliant illuminating fragments and just as often loses its way in clouds of obscurity,' and though a unique and undeniably powerful novel it did not quite succeed. The country's Dostoyevsky was yet to be recognized. He became rather cynical about the book's reception in Canada, claiming that only one copy was ever sold there and that he had bought it himself. This, he wrote, was a country without many writers and what they did write went unnoticed or was unwelcome. Indeed, to say you were a writer in Canada and mean it, was to declare yourself a pioneer. 'It is not like saying you are a writer in Haiti or in Columbia or in other advanced countries where there are many writers. But British Columbia is the opposite of an advanced country and for it I am profoundly grateful.'[34]

Davenport (reporting Aiken about to sell up and return to Massachusetts, and himself now a director of a new London publishing house, Rodney Phillips & Green), wrote a long, sharp appreciation of the book.

> I love the contrapuntal clarity of it – no harmonic hunks; and apart from the arch of the whole grand plan there were for me innumerable exfoliations & escarpments to recognize – flowers on the railway track, Joe Venuti . . . Poor James Travers' Chagford; & even the ghost, mercifully transformed, of Charlotte Haldane . . . Also – but this is pure vanity – the blue lakes of B.C. had for me a personally evocative quality, for they reminded me of a long-forgotten 'dream' poem I sent you from Pimlico to Paris in 1933. The Astoria too poked a purple nose from its nun's coif. One strange thing: as I was reading UTV in a taxi going through Piccadilly I swear that each time I looked up from the page I saw a dead man walking in the crowd. Three: two perhaps more reasonably then the third – James Travers, Nordahl Grieg & Patrick Railton. Nordahl I met during the war in London: I'd have told you of it had I known your whereabouts.

His only criticisms were that the death of Yvonne seemed a bit too 'melo' and that Hugh seemed to have sprung too readily from the Consul's rib with some of his 'consular attributes'. But these were trivial points. 'You've begotten a great book of good & evil . . . The Fool salutes the Juggler. Hail!'

He followed this letter with another concerned that Lowry, having killed off one part of himself (the Consul) was fearful of what he had done. The book was 'an act of magic' and a 'tremendous act of contrition' but he must never stop 'or seven devils replace the one expelled'. He could see that the Consul and Yvonne had to be polished off, 'leaving Hugh free of these incumbrances of self and not-self', but he must not blame himself for a murder he had not committed. If he had not laid the ghosts he wished to lay, no matter. But it had a quality of absolution and he should 'take heart'.[35] Despite such admiration, the hints about plagiarism must have hurt, and his joy at receiving this good opinion was tempered by horror at news of the deaths of friends like Travers, whom he discovered had died in a blazing tank at El Alamein. He replied to Davenport that he hoped he had written the book for God and not for the Devil.[36]

The deaths of his friends and the question of his nationality which tax on his income had raised, concentrated his mind on the contrast between a 'decadent' England and a Canada whose people he found too materialistic. He noted that it was next to impossible for an Englishman to become a Canadian. With a peculiar lack of faith in the attractiveness of their own country, he wrote, Canadians believed that any Englishman coming to Canada must be there because he was a criminal, and there the English were a minority with fewer rights than an Indian or a negro. But it was not the Englishman who was the criminal. 'The criminal is the Moloch that has the soul of England like a young girl in thrall.'[37] A female soul it was not eager to embrace was Margerie's. Cape turned down *Horse in the Sky*, pleading lack of paper and a fuel crisis, and offered to send it on to any publisher Margerie named. Lowry suggested to Davenport that Rodney Phillips & Green look at it.[38]

Having made their personal obeisances to Lowry, Aiken and Davenport continued to dissect the 'genius'. Aiken wondered if he would write again. Ten years had gone not only *into* that book but *along* with it and the question was did he have anything left to write *about*? He complained at not having received 'a mumbling word of thanks' for his blurb. But, he added, there was 'a Guilt Thing' on Lowry's part because of the many liftings from him, both personal and literary, practically as vital as blood transfusions might have been; and their knowing this was a deep embarrassment to them both. Lowry had always found this difficult to face, he said. He recalled their fierce debate in Cuernavaca in 1937 when Lowry claimed the ultimate right to absorb him. It was all very subtle and sun-filled, and intoxicated in an amiable way, but Lowry had taken down everything he said, in note form, intending to use it in *Under the Volcano*. None of this now mattered nor detracted from the 'magnificence of the book', but he thought it left Lowry feeling unhappy with them both. He needed to acknowledge *him* as *he* had acknowledged Eliot to release him from his sense of guilt. The question was whether he was capable of doing so or even knew what he had done, the turns of opinions, observations, phrases he had lifted. He would, he hinted, be revealing all in a book called *Ushant*, his own attempt at that many-layered opus inspired by his dream on the voyage from Gibraltar in 1933.[39] He omitted to say that the idea of 'the son absorbing the father' was his own, raised on first meeting Lowry in 1929 and he had also forgotten that Lowry had acknowledged lifting his political arguments as far back as 1940.

But Davenport was quick to take the cue. 'Even I, a mere twin blood-brother of the sage, spotted 19 liftings in the sage's book . . . from myself.' That did not matter because he never published, but the debt to Aiken ought to be acknowledged. The first story he had shown him at Cambridge was 'a paraphrase of a chapter of *Blue Voyage*' and his poem, 'To Nordahl Grieg, Ship's Fireman', put into *Cambridge Poetry 1930*, he later discovered was 'a literal transcript of a page of Nordahl Grieg's *The Ship Sails On*.' If the debt was too large to acknowledge then at least some Act of Contrition was needed for everyone's benefit. 'Eliot's and your books of poems were available at . . . the same time; but on how many bookstacks displaying UTV are to be found copies of B[lue] V[oyage] and G[reat] C[ircle]? Guilt? I should say so!'[40] Aiken replied that his notes on the case-history of 'the Malcohol' were greatly appreciated. He thought he ought to call him his 'crypto-disciple'.[41]

By 20 April his crypto-disciple's book was at tenth place in the *New York Times* bestseller list, and the Lowrys had gone for a week's hiking and 'a rest from our leaking rooftree',[42] first to Salt Spring Island, off the BC coast, then to Harrison Hot Springs, 'a kind of swanky spa'. There he wrote to Erskine and Taylor, now both at Random House, saying he was hard at work on *La Mordida*. Having read *Ultramarine*, Erskine expressed interest in it, though the notes on pink paper appended to the MS of *Lunar Caustic* had not helped 'because they were of such a nature as to be available only to you.' The story he thought 'too patently charged with symbolic (even allegorical) functions', so that unlike the *Volcano* one saw first what lay beneath rather than what lay on the surface, and he preferred surface first.[43]

Belatedly, Lowry told Matson of the broadcast, due to be aired on 28 April. When Matson complained that permission had not been obtained, he said he had assumed Noxon had done so, and he himself had only heard of it incidentally over the CBS. On transmission day their batteries were flat, so Margerie called Stan's wife, Rubina, to ask if they could listen on their set. She was not keen to have them; Stan was away, one of her children was to be confirmed that evening and on his previous visit a drunken Lowry had called her 'a shit'. However, reluctantly she agreed.

They turned up with two bottles of whisky and she was none too happy to leave them alone in her house. When she returned that night the bottles were empty and there was no sign of Lowry. Margerie said he was in the bathroom, and there she found him, dead drunk, as she later wrote to Stan.

> I opened the door & there with his head wedged between the bath tub & the toilet, feet to the door, flat on his drunken back in a pool of his own leakage was 'The Consul'!!! britches half-off – mother of God! What price genius? I lugged him up & pulled up his pants, fixed his belt & Dee had to clean the floor, – Margy didn't do a thing. Noise – & except we were on the alert he would have ruined the place – he took 9 eggs out of the trug & ate them raw & the mess he made, he grabbed Bottles [puppy] & nearly squeezed the daylights out of the pup, but I told him I'd spoil his face if he really hurt the dog.

She got rid of them quickly and swore to Stan they would never enter her house again. 'I am viciously pleased to hear that income tax is getting them where it hurts,' she wrote to Stan, then away in Chicago.[44]

Ironically, Stan's radio had a defective valve and they had not heard the broadcast, despite sitting with ears glued to the set. Lowry was depressed, not only with a whisky hangover and from missing the broadcast, but also because Noxon had not alerted him. He wrote to Markle (who had cabled to ask if he would like a recording of it) to complain about their silence. It was like living in Siberia with a play coming off in Moscow, and hearing nothing until a commissar relayed a message from the producer six months later. He had, he said, been quietly piddling in his pants with suspense, and their silence made him think it had not come off.

In fact the play had been well received, and the critics felt that 'Studio One' was well launched. Squeezing a huge novel like the *Volcano* into an hour had left *Newsweek*'s radio critic gasping, and most impressed that Everett Sloane, who had played the lawyer in *Citizen Kane*, had been cast as the Consul. The *Herald Tribune* thought it 'ambitious and intelligent', but a strange choice. 'An hour of alcoholism is difficult even on the screen, where conversation is not always necessary. On the air, where a man must go to the dogs in prose, it's far more difficult.' But generally it was considered a success. Lowry, however, knew nothing of this until Noxon wrote on 9 May saying that it had been hard having to cut the book down so crudely, but 'it was an excellent show and has been acclaimed as such by all and sundry.' It had reached a vast audience and book sales would surely be affected. He was right: having slipped from the bestseller list at the end of April, it bounced back in May. He also mentioned that when they had left Niagara-on-the-Lake a man called from MGM, but, told that Lowry had no phone, he had said irritably that if he was not interested in $150,000 that was his problem. That week both Noxon and Lowry were featured in *Time* magazine.

Early in May, Davenport reported that Aiken was returning to the US and that Anna Wickham had hanged herself. 'A wickedly bad end to one who was only wickedly good. Deeps as well as danks & darks, she had,' he wrote.[45] In fact, this strange women had failed at her first attempt, sat down, wrote a poem about the experience, and then done it a second time successfully. Another chapter of friendship had ended for Lowry.[46] Again a doom-laden coincidence had foreshadowed the event: just two weeks before Margerie had bought a rare second-hand copy of Anna's poems for him in Vancouver.[47]

Confusion over the broadcast, and the sad news about Travers ('God rest him in his celestial silver fox farm') and Anna Wickham clearly disturbed Lowry. But more disturbing was Jacques Barzun's review of the *Volcano* in the May issue of *Harper's*. 'Mr Malcolm Lowry's *Under the Volcano* strikes me as fulsome and fictitious,' it began. Also he was 'on the side of good behaviour, eager to disgust us with subtropical vice'. This was shown by 'a long regurgitation of the materials found in *Ulysses* and *The Sun Also Rises*.' And, 'while imitating the tricks of Joyce, Dos Passos, and Sterne, he gives us the mind and heart of Sir

Philip Gibbs.' The characters were dull, even when sober, as was the language of their creator, who at moments had borrowed from other fashionable styles – 'Henry James, Thomas Wolfe, and thought-streamers, the surrealists.' The verdict was brutal. 'His novel can be recommended only as an anthology held together by earnestness.'[48]

The implication of plagiarism struck an exposed nerve and a shaken Lowry replied angrily to what he regarded as Barzun's cruelly unfair review. He had made no effort to get to grips with the book's form or intention. What 'tricks', he demanded, had he imitated? A young writer would naturally make use of what he read, and what Van Gogh called 'design-governing postures' were bound to affect technique on occasions. When another writer did get into the works he made every effort to 'sweat him out'. 'Shards and shreds of course sometimes remain; they do in your style too.' He imitated no tricks, and Joyce had once testified to his originality. He had never read *Ulysses* completely, had read little of Dos Passos, and never got beyond page one of *Tristram Shandy*. He had read *The Sun Also Rises* once, years earlier, but his book was begun in 1936 and any influences had been long absorbed. After a decade in the wilderness he had lost touch with fashionable styles. The comment about Sir Philip Gibbs, he implied, was just gratuitously cruel. If he read the book properly he would see that much of it was intentionally funny, a kind of self-satire. He thought he had created a pioneer work, and questioned Barzun's motive for so savage a review. He had heard its tone before; it was the same voice which had greeted Wolfe, Faulkner, Melville and James. He may well have absorbed a lot of wrong things, he said, but a good artist was led by instinct to what he wanted.[49] The jibe about Sir Philip Gibbs (a popular middlebrow novelist of the time) must have made him wince. It would be a cruel irony indeed if he had struggled so long against his family only to end up the kind of author his father had always wanted him to be.

Barzun replied promptly, clearly shocked by so pained a reaction from an author to one of his reviews. 'I wish I could feel differently about your novel . . . as I do about its author on the strength of this one letter,' he wrote. No doubt he had been too brief and too scornful, and he wished he had not found the book derivative and pretentious, but 'it is that combination of misdeeds that aroused my scorn.' However, his judgement might be at fault, and on Lowry's side there was a formidable array of critical talent which rendered his 'cavil' negligible. He would re-read it, expecting in the meantime to be assured of Lowry's powers by new work from him.[50] The letter failed to mollify Lowry. 'Barzun

I could garrot,' he told Matson,[51] and the barbed review duly went into *Dark as the Grave*.

Sybil Hutchinson of McClelland & Stewart put him in touch with Earle Birney, a keen admirer of the *Volcano*, then teaching at the University of British Columbia. Lowry invited him to the CBC studios where he was due to hear a record of the CBS broadcast. On 21 May, Malcolm, Margerie, Birney and his wife Esther, met at the CBC and heard a rather scratchy recording of Sloane's rendering of the Consul. Lowry found it disappointing, but Birney took them all to dinner afterwards, and he and Lowry became firm friends. In this poet-academic he found someone he could talk to about his work, especially his poetry, and he and Margerie were frequent guests of the Birneys over the following months, entertaining them with stories of voodoo and astral travel. None of his poems had been published in Canada, he said, and Birney, who edited the *Canadian Poetry Magazine*, undertook to see what he could do with them.

Until he met Birney, his only local intellectual friend was Downie Kirk, the languages teacher married to Marjorie Craige. Kirk, a tall red-haired Nova Scotian, admired Lowry intensely, and did all his translating for him at Dollarton. Now, through Birney, the Lowrys met the local literati, including Bill McConnell, lawyer and story writer, Einar Neilson, whose home on Bowen Island was open to writers every summer, Dorothy Macnair (Dorothy Livesay, the poet) and A. J. M. Smith, editor of *The Book of Canadian Poetry*. Lowry impressed them greatly. No writer in Canada had achieved the success he had, and they were anxious to claim him as a Canadian. In their company he was appreciated and tolerated, even when drunk and garrulous, for the brilliance of his conversation and the apparent scope of his knowledge. To them he expanded at length on his painful childhood and wild adventures at sea, his desertion and near-destruction in Mexico. Only Esther Birney, an Englishwoman familiar with pre-war literary London, was sceptical. She found him childish and at times tiresome. Earle, however, was convinced of his genius and determined to encourage his poetry and see it published.

Poetry editors like A. J. M. Smith came to see him, and encouraged by this he got Margerie to retype some fifty or sixty of his poems arranged into a three-part collection: 'Poems of the Sea', 'Poems from Mexico', and 'Poems from Vancouver'. Between summer and the end of that year, nine of his poems appeared in Canadian poetry magazines, Birney's included. Alan Crawley, editor of *Contemporary Verse* also took some, and Birney planned to include the *Volcano* in his university course. The academic love affair with Lowry had begun and he was now being reviewed by scholarly journals. In the *New Mexico Quarterly*, Vincent Garoffolo called it 'a novel of excellence', 'an exuberant and impassioned work'. Robert Heilman in the *Sewanee Review* stressed its poetry and many literary associations – Poe, Donne, Cocteau, Dante, Goethe. There was 'great power' in Lowry's 'solid world of inner and outer objects in which the characters are dismayed and imprisoned as in Kafka's work . . . Such a multivalued poetic fiction, with its sense of horrifying dissolution, and its submerged, uncertain vision of a hard new birth off in clouded time, is apparently the especial labour of the artistic conscience at our turn of an epoch.' The search was on for Lowry's sources. Like Joyce, he had made much work for future professors. Comparisons with Kafka, once thought outrageous, were now being made with scholarly equanimity.

Margerie heard from Rodney Phillips & Green that if she was prepared to rewrite *Horse in the Sky* they would reconsider it. Lowry leapt to her defence, again comparing it to a Brontë novel and accusing John Green of sneering at the book.[52] However, work had reclaimed him and he was deeply engrossed in *Dark as the Grave*. Margerie wrote to Stern saying that Malcolm was hard at work on his new book and that his groans and sobs were heart-rending to hear as he tried to get going. 'We swim in the cold sea, lie in the sun, walk in the woods, row in the boat, life is good & we are happy.'[53]

Aiken had returned to Cape Cod when Lowry finally got round to thanking him for his blurb and his 'supermarvellous letter' which had him 'purring yet'.[54] But evidently he had not yet forgiven him for his liftings, especially of the William Blackstone story. Asked for a dedication to his new poem, *The Kid*, based on the Blackstone theme, he wrote to Mary, 'I thought how neat to lay it at Malc's feet – so I did, This travelogue for Malcolm Lowry as from one rolling Blackstone to another . . . ! What fun we have.'[55] His obsessive links with Jeake's House and Rye had finally been severed; he had ended his exile and returned permanently to the US. Lowry's links with The Wicket Gate and Dollarton were as tight-bound as ever, and he had no desire to return to England or to see his family again.

Max Perkins died suddenly at the end of June, and a long sorrowful letter from Dawn Powell told Lowry how much he would like to have published him. She also said, having listened to the CBS dramatization, that despite what she called 'the phoney and confused acting' the power and tragedy of the book had come through 'with frightening force'.[56] Early in July, Noxon cabled to say he was taking part in a countrywide radio discussion of the *Volcano*, and when Birney took Lowry to a writer's convention on Vancouver Island, a *Globe and Mail* reporter, somewhat in awe of his presence, noted that he was said to have finished his next novel.[57]

Summer at the water's edge saw him in fine form. In mid-July Margerie told Erskine that he was 'tanned as an Indian, and working hard on *Dark as the Grave*, [of] which he has nearly finished a rough draft,' but adding that she thought that he should next publish *Lunar Caustic* and a revised *Ultramarine* in a single volume, mainly because they were not set in Mexico and could be done much more quickly. 'I know Malc and if he really gets going on this volume of *Dark as the Grave*, *The Wicket Gate* and *La Mordida* as he has planned it, well, my guess is two to four years at least. However, he has to work on what he wants to whether it seems "wise" or not . . .'[58]

The Wicket Gate, new to Erskine, was the beginning of a prose anthem to Dollarton and life with Margerie on the edge of the forest and the sea. It was later renamed *Eridanus* and finally emerged as 'The Forest Path to the Spring', a novella in the paradisaical mould with the themes of feared retribution and threatened eviction a powerful subplot.[59] Considering her unease at returning there after their high time in New York, Lowry may well have thought that by enshrining her in this lyrical piece and making it a key work in his grand design, he would give her a more meaningful place in the creative cosmos he was constructing around Eridanus.

In the same letter to Erskine she said that they had been discovered by certain local interest groups, and 'if the influx of admirers, newspaper reporter chaps with great flashing cameras . . . doesn't let up soon we're going to have to take to the even taller timber.' The reporters, it transpired, were not great 'admirers' but after a story. On 1 August the *Vancouver Sun* ran a picture story splashed across four columns, headed 'Wealthy Squatters Find Rent-Free Beach'. The angle was one of barely veiled hostility: 'A successful novelist who could write a cheque for thousands, is "king" of the beach squatters of Royal Row at Dollarton, ten miles east of Vancouver. Like hundreds of others in the Vancouver area, Malcolm Lowry occupies a tax-free house built on piling below the high tide mark.' Having gone there to find solitude for writing, it said, the housing shortage had brought people looking for cheap homes and the Lowrys' solitude was gone. They liked and respected their neighbours, but novels and neighbours did not mix and they were thinking of moving to a new solitude. Lowry was shown smiling and poised to dive from the rickety pier he loved so much.

To have dubbed him 'King' of the squatters was an unconscious irony, for apart from Craige, Sam and Whitey, few squatters on the beach had much liking for Lowry, who was seen as an eccentric drunk, if not a madman, about whom strange rumours circulated.[60] The unwelcome press publicity was a poor thirty-eighth birthday-present for a Lowry ever fearful of being cleared from the beach. It was yet another interruption to his work. To avoid such distractions they considered going to California for the winter.

However they did manage to take one break. Still searching for that 'new solitude' they went for the first of many visits to 'Lieben', Einar Neilson's home on Bowen Island, and by 13 August Lowry had finished a draft of *Dark as the Grave* and begun a second. He would, he told Erskine, deliver it when it was right 'in installments, unless my multiple schizophrenia gets the better of me and I decide I ought to revise *Ultramarine* and *Lunar Caustic* first'.[61]

Despite the local celebrity, Margerie was no longer happy to remain in Dollarton; there was, after all, a much wider stage upon which to play the wife of the successful author, and she began to talk of travelling again. This led to quarrels, and once Lowry became quite disturbed even at the idea of staying overnight at George Stevenson's rather than returning to the shack. Margerie talked it over with their GP, a Dr Rawlings, and later wrote down her thoughts on the matter.

> He cannot stay always in retreat hidden in Dollarton, that is not meeting the problem. Or do I deceive myself? Is it my own passionate longing & need that I rationalize? If he stays in retreat he has failed to meet his enemy and admits defeat? . . . he will have no material if he is always in retreat – but he *has* material now. More will only bewilder & confuse him. We should stay here. But his problem is not that of just an alcoholic or even just that of a psychotic – he is a genius. God help me to understand & to help him.[62]

He in turn realized the consequences of digging in his heels. In a draft of his story 'Through the Panama' his alter ego Martin Trumbauer thinks, 'if she gives up the desire to travel, gives dramatically in to [his] wish to stay and work . . . in Eridanus she would equally make it impossible for him to work by nagging him all the time about what he had deprived her of . . .'[63] Margerie's wish to travel and Malcolm's to stay put was to tear at any tranquillity in their increasingly complicated relationship, a complication intensified by a growing sense of their competing with one another. Nor may she have realized just how much travel now evoked his painful past.

The weight of a tragic past was, of course, a key theme in the book, which itself was now part of Lowry's own past, and weighed down upon him with equal force. If he felt imprisoned, as he told Phito, like a character in Kafka's *In the Penal Colony*, for the crime of being a writer, he could never escape having written the *Volcano*. If Aiken wondered whether he was not entirely written out, the same thought must have haunted him. In beginning on *La Mordida* and *Dark as the Grave* he was using again a familiar symbolic landscape, Mexico. The lyrical Dollarton novella *Eridanus* was just to set off the other two. But, as Margerie knew, he would wrestle with them for ages while *Ultramarine* and *Lunar Caustic* were all but ready for publication. Fear of Rascoe doubtless made him hesitate over *Ultramarine*; fears of American attitudes to anything critical of America made him hold back *Lunar Caustic*. But his fears about Mexico were fears of himself. With *Dark as the Grave* he was raking over a painful past there and reliving the writing of his book, and he worried about 'getting buried under its rather Pirandellian masonry'[64]

Margerie, too, was feeling jittery – about her own book's coming publication. To take her mind off things, he got her to work with him on a couple of stories set in British Columbia. In doing this he abandoned his earlier judgement that the scene was unsuitable for him. One, 'Gin and Goldenrod', is a slight tale of a husband and wife setting out to pay off a debt for bootlegged liquor at a local Indian Reservation, and becoming suddenly conscious of the encroachment of 'civilization' upon the blissful solitude of their forest home. The other dealt with their search the previous year for that 'new solitude', when fears of eviction were in the air. It was a plain tale, simply told, called 'October Ferry to Gabriola'.

Letters from Davenport and Stern, then in Paris, and the prospect of foreign editions of the *Volcano* appearing, focused Lowry's attention on France. Early in September, they received a substantial amount of *Volcano* royalties, and learned that an advance for a French edition was being held for him in Paris by the French publishers, *Revue Fontaine Mensuelle*. The plan to go to California was abandoned in favour of Europe; Margerie, it seems, had won the argument about travel. If and when they did go abroad, it made sense, she decided, to keep their money in US dollars; she told Matson, 'We are at the moment very seriously considering jumping on a freighter here and going off to Europe for a few months,' and asked him to keep the money in their New York account and supply them with funds as needed. They sent 'October Ferry to Gabriola', Lowry suggesting it as suitable for *Harper's Bazaar* or even a mass market audience.[65] He also thought it could be published in Canada along with *Lunar Caustic*. Birney, however, told him it was wiser and more profitable to publish in the US,[66] but he was happy to bring out 'Sestina in a Cantina', a fragment of a verse play, Lowry's first poem to be published in Canada (excepting his 1939 jingle).[67] Alan Crawley printed five more in *Contemporary Verse*. The poet trapped inside Lowry for so long had finally been let out.

He wrote to Cape saying that as they had now been declared 'Landed Immigrants' and had to pay tax in both countries, he and Margerie had appointed Innes Rose as their agent in England. Matson had been very quick to sell translation rights, and Cape, left with no more than UK publication of the *Volcano*, did nothing unusual there by way of advanced publicity, and publication day, 15 September, was greeted with neither fanfares nor cocktail parties. However, its first serious British review, in the *Times Literary Supplement* was quite laudatory. Despite its theme of the last day in the life of a dipsomaniac, said the reviewer, it was neither morbid nor of minor significance.

> If there is morbidity here, it is akin to that of Elizabethan tragedy, born of an involved and passionate interest in the secrets of the fall of man. So strong is the light which the author directs upon his central character that the shadow it casts is one of tragic dimensions.

Lowry's success, it said, lay in the lucidity and originality of his presentation of the Consul. 'He writes with the eloquence of one under the spell of his subject, and, though his manner is sometimes perplexingly elliptical, his central character has the living quality that only great imaginative power can give.' The reviewer, despite his measured terms, judged the book as something formidable. 'He may have set out to write a complex love story, but he has done better: he has created a character in whose individual struggle is reflected something of the larger agony of the human spirit.'[68] The next day in the *Observer*, Lionel Hale wrote that 'by comparison, *The Lost Weekend* has something of the placid contentment of a milk-bar.' The setting was wild and Lowry's style was correspondingly wild, but it was a controlled wildness. The action was:

> seen through a glass darkly, a darkness shot with vivid gleams of beauty and sudden shafts of poetry . . . It is hard to convey how close-packed is the imagery, how intense the concentration, of the Delirium Tremens. The prose is Hemingway-plus-lava, with an added pictorial sense that can be horridly reminiscent of Hieronymus Bosch, if that macabre master had included among his devils the Demon Rum.[69]

A week later, Evelyn sent Malcolm a copy of the *Illustrated London News*, pointing out an article by the historian Sir Arthur Bryant, but failing to mention a review of the *Volcano*, by K. John, one of the most perceptive it received in England, recognizing well the book's ambiguities and contradictions, and ending with a remarkably apt, Lowryesque metaphor – 'You look down; the bottom is never reached, but the reflections are fascinating.'[70]

The weekly reviews gave the book a mixed reception, as if not quite able to accept that they were dealing with something extraordinary. In the *Spectator*, D. S. Savage wrote that, considering the scope of the book, Lowry's treatment of the individual lives of his characters was inadequate. Nor was he impressed by his style. 'Mr Lowry writes rather prolixly; a slight thread of incident carries too heavy a burden of reflections and perceptions.' However, he considered it 'the most interesting, the most perceptive and the most promising novel it has fallen to my lot to review so far this year'.[71] In the *Listener*, P. H. Newby found it 'overloaded'.[72] Not until December did the *New Statesman* review it. There, Walter Allen spotted 'reminiscences and quotations' from Marlowe, Raleigh, Donne, De Quincey, Baudelaire, Tolstoy and Dostoyevsky, and characters which had previously appeared in the novels of Djuna Barnes and Conrad Aiken. So much symbolism, concentration upon the tragedy and other factors of method and style and characterization 'makes also for an inescapable impression of pastiche . . . how much happier one would feel about this novel, impressive though it is, if one were not so conscious on every page of its literary sources.'[73]

This rather mixed reception has been put down to the prevailing literary climate favouring novels of social realism or suburban intrigue. A work of such poetic richness and conceptual grandeur was not calculated to make a great impression in a Britain gripped by economic blight and general post-war malaise.[74] Burra wrote to Aiken in November: 'I don't think anybody took any notice of the Volcano. [A]s it isn't a beautiful little subtle-psychological piece about a bunch of Bloomsbury cook-housekeepers letting down their hair in a lovely prose and he isnt here to log roll how could you expect anybody to notice it much.'[75]

In late September Cape sent news that of 5,000 printed, 2,700 had been sold by the end of the first month. He had forgotten the shortened dedication requested by Lowry, and, as in America, the London edition was dedicated, 'To Margerie, my wife.' If he still hoped to keep her hidden from his family, the cat was well and truly out of the bag.

But now they both had Paris on the mind. Never having been to Europe, Margerie was extremely keen to see a city of which Malcolm had spoken so much. And although he would have preferred to stay and work on his trilogy, he was anxious to please her, and the work could be taken along. He told Stern he had gone into training like an Indian wrestler to get fit for his new book. The autumn was superb and they were the lone inhabitants of the beach; when the tide was high he could dive from the window into the sea. They planned to visit France and possibly Morocco and Italy, he said. They had 'quite a lot of cash', but needed to know the cost of living in Paris, the best cheap hotels, and whether Sylvia Beach and other old friends were still there. Fortunately they had Canadian 'Landed Immigrant' status so were not covered by UK travel restrictions, and he would not be going to England precisely because he feared it would be difficult to get out again.

By mid-September there were contracts from France, Switzerland, Denmark and Norway, as well as Germany. They planned to leave in December, after publication of *Horse in the Sky*, and *after* November, the month with such grim memories for Lowry. Aiken sent a copy of his *The Kid* and, in congratulating him, Lowry missed the sardonic edge to the dedication – 'To Malcolm Lowry. From one Rolling Blackstone to another' – or pretended to. The opus he was at work on, he told Aiken, three interrelated novels, two set in Mexico, and *Eridanus*, a Canadian intermezzo, read in part like 'the bizarre concatenations and symbol formations of dementia praecox, noted by Herr Jung'. He was 'really down among "the catacombs of the live" with a vengeance'. However, it ended on a note of triumph and seemed to break new ground, even though that in itself, if true, might not recommend it. Despite a poor reception in England the *Volcano* was due to come forth heralded by a great fanfare in France, whither he and Margerie intended to sail in a freighter and remain for a time over Christmas.[76] *Horse in the Sky* appeared on 6 October with little or no fanfare. The lack of any coherent response to her 'serious' book rankled with Margerie for years, and Malcolm continued to urge it on all and sundry as 'a classic' comparable to *Wuthering Heights*. No one else saw it quite that way, and it was the last novel of her own Margerie would ever publish.

They acquired French visas and passages on a freighter, due to sail on 1 December. Meanwhile he began work on his Canadian novella, 'my little erudanus [sic]', hoping to complete a first draft of the trilogy[77] and pack all his notes into a briefcase to take with him.[78] He read a lot, too, telling Alan Crawley he was being 'driven nuts' by discovering that much of Heidegger's thought paralleled what he was doing in *Dark as the Grave*, 'a virtual psycho-analysis of the Volcano itself among other things'.[79]

Birney wrote announcing that he was including the *Volcano* in a University course on 'The Novel', along with *Lord Jim*, *Ulysses* and *Mrs Dalloway*. 'This is the sort of thing you will have to get used to (wait till the doctoral theses begin, if they haven't already; "Lowry, The Dollarton Period", or "Meat and Drink in Lowry").'[80] Between work and planning to leave, he read Pushkin and dwelt on the death of artists. They were dithering with anxiety about *Horse in the Sky*, and at the same time Lowry was becoming more and more agitated about his tax position, finally acquiring an accountant and leaving him to sort matters out.

Having had no further contact with Reynal & Hitchcock, Lowry now addressed Erskine as his publisher-in-waiting. He was writing, he told him, what could fairly be described as a good, if sinister book, which he would receive in driblets. 'We progress towards equilibrium this time instead of in the opposite direction, and the result is considerably more exciting, if not even more horrible, more "inspiring" is probably the word.'[81] The idea of sending his novel in driblets probably arose from a sense of uncertainty about what he was doing. It seemed very good to him, but he needed Erskine's confirmation. In fact the offering of 'driblets' was postponed, but Lowry seemed to expect Erskine to help him through the creative process. What he needed was a Noxon to tell him to finish his work and send off only complete manuscripts. But he had a wife eager to travel, and was about to up anchor again and set off into uncertain waters.

They heard on 1 November that their sailing was cancelled, and were offered instead the SS *Brest*, a French freighter leaving within the week. This of course was Lowry's unlucky month. It did not bode well, though the ship would sail on a numerologically significant date, the

7th! They were asked for a quick decision, which Lowry was unhappy about. But there was no holding Margerie and a decision was taken; they confirmed their booking, and Birney agreed to look after the shack in their absence.

An offer for Italian rights meant that Italy was now added to their travel itinerary. They were less than happy, however, to hear that *Harper's Bazaar* would reconsider their jointly written 'October Ferry to Gabriola' only if it were 'recast'. Margerie wrote angrily to Matson. They certainly would not recast it; they liked it as it was. Malcolm bet $25 he would be including it in a volume of prize stories one day, and his judgement, she said, was almost always right.[82] But his confidence was high. He wrote to tell Erskine that he was working eight hours a day on a book which was coming along fine. He was planning to take it with him on the ship. Working on it was really enjoyable and he was writing it almost with self-adulation.[83]

On the 4th came a letter from Stern, packed with good 'Chesteronian' advice on what to do and who to meet in Paris. He said that he would inform a good friend, Joan Black, that they were en route. The fact that they would have a thousand US dollars in a Paris bank would help hugely with costly train travel and with currency problems. Davenport also wrote to say that he would be in Paris to celebrate Christmas with them. Margerie replied, 'I am so excited I can't eat or sleep. Suitcases, letters, books, clothes, notebooks, are piled or tossed in a frenzy all about but we'll make it yet.' On top of the American money, they were now allowed to take a thousand Canadian dollars, too, she said.[84]

Before leaving, Lowry was pressed into one last duty. He wrote to scores of literary editors urging them to review *Horse in the Sky*. It was, he told Linscott, 'a work of genius . . . an Aeschylean tragedy of hatred and revenge, and it certainly deserves some notice'.[85] In what replies came, however, editors were far more eager to comment on the *Volcano* than on Margerie's offering. The *Brest* would be calling at LA before heaving down the coast of Mexico and through the Panama. When Priscilla heard they were coming, she arranged an apartment for them to stay in. She had no intention of having Malcolm in her house after what had happened on his previous visit.

CHAPTER XX

'THROUGH THE PANAMA' TO EUROPE
1947–1949

How right was that historian he must one day read: success invites self-neglect; by means of self-indulgence.

MALCOLM LOWRY, 'Elephant and Colosseum'

As they set out, Lowry again affirmed the beginning of a New Era. He assured Margerie that his drunken misbehaviour of the past two years was behind him and he would make that extra effort to be less selfish and more considerate. News had come, too, that *Horse in the Sky* was a Book-of-the-Month recommendation, so despite the absence of reviews she could go to Europe feeling that she, like Malcolm, was an author to be taken seriously. She began taking notes as soon as their taxi left for the docks. They went aboard equipped with a bottle of rum, and were seen off at the dockside by their friend Neilson, who had travelled from Bowen Island for the purpose.

The SS *Brest*, a five-thousand ton American-built Liberty ship, being French and the crew mostly Breton, was unfamiliar territory for Lowry and he was worried that he might accidentally tip an officer. Nevertheless, they were excited to be at sea, and delighted when the Captain invited them to his cabin for a Benedictine. There Lowry got the idea that he had been insulted and became upset, but finally they retired to their cabin to drink rum and sing old sentimental songs; some of the crew overheard them and joined in.

Next morning they passed through the Straits of Juan de Fuca past Cape Flattery. Lowry noted its 'whale geometry' – 'finny phallic furious face of Flattery'.[1] He pondered on their 'dark sailing' and noted that they were only eight days away from the 15th, that 'fatal' November day in his life – this one the eighteenth anniversary of Paul Fitte's death in Cambridge. 'Turn this into triumph,' he wrote: 'the furies into mercies.'[2] Again he was plagued by irrational fears – 'the inerrarable inconceivable desolate sense of having no right to be where you are – the billows of inexhaustible anguish; haunted by the insatiable albatross of self'.

Despite all the talk of a New Era, Margerie was worried. Malcolm's mood worsened, and at times he seemed determined to spoil the trip for her, then at evening a drink or two would cheer him up again. He wrote to Davenport, looking forward to meeting him in Le Havre around Christmas Eve. The ship was being followed by three albatrosses, he wrote, and for the first time he was finding himself intimidated by the sheer size of the sea.[3] On 10 November they sailed under the Golden Gate Bridge past Alcatraz into San Francisco Bay, and next morning, a customs officer drove them to the Palace Hotel where Margerie was determined Malcolm should meet some important people. She telephoned Joseph Henry Jackson, literary editor of the *San Francisco Chronicle*, and arranged a meeting that morning at his office, then called Mark Schorer at the UC campus at Berkeley where he was a Professor of English, and he came to the hotel later. With Jackson, she noted, Malcolm was 'perfect and on top form'; the interview with Schorer in the afternoon was 'more chaotic . . . but successful'.[4] Obviously he had made a great effort not to spoil things for Margerie. 'How happy we are!' she wrote, as they sailed out of San Francisco that evening. But she then became fearful, noticing storm signals in his behaviour, and began to think they should not have come.

On the morning of the 13th they arrived in San Pedro, Los Angeles, where Mrs Bonner and Bert Woolfan met them at the ship and took them home. Priscilla joined them later and they all spent an evening together. Ronald Button came, along with some fans who had read Woodburn's encomium in the *Saturday Review* and were anxious to meet a real 'genius'. Perhaps remembering the midnight scene on his previous visit, Lowry was nervous. However, he was ready with authorly answers to their admiring questions. Asked by Priscilla, 'Aren't you proud of the Volc?' he replied, 'I'm proud before men but humble before God.' And of his reception in New York he said, 'They overcame me with catastrophic endearments.'[5] The Woolfans parked them in an apartment at Normandy Village, according to Margerie, an uncomfortable 'goldfish bowl' looking out onto a vacant lot. The curtains would not draw nor would the windows open, and it rained for most of their stay. But she did not criticize Priscilla for not having them, believing that she had problems enough of her own. Bert, a little ashamed perhaps of their lack of hospitality, gave Malcolm a supply of Vitamin B to keep him going if his appetite deserted him when he drank.

Margerie noted on 15 November that he was restless and sad, and after a day when she felt 'fear, triumph, excitement [and] unreality', they returned to the ship, Lowry praying that they would not sail on 'that fatal day'. But they did, and that evening he got plastered on whisky they had brought on board with them. There was a new passenger on board, the ominously named Norwegian Consul for Tahiti, Charon.[6] Such correspondences were unnerving simply because, he wrote, his novel was about a character who becomes enmeshed in his own novel, as he had in Mexico, a character 'Joyced in his own petard'.[7]

His drinking gained momentum. Margerie noted that he now drank a cocktail before lunch, and pre-dinner cocktails started as early as 3 p.m. 'Now begin the signs I really dread: drinking before mirrors – the retreat into the blue lagoon, the excuses [for] some – any! emotional crisis, the alternate cruel & cold, shifty & calculating looks with fake affection which infuriates & sickens me. But still I hope.' But hope for the New Era was growing fragile. On the 17th, off the coast of Baja Mexico, they woke with grim hangovers and pitched into a terrible quarrel lasting all morning and making them late for lunch. He employed, she wrote, every 'sly dodge' and 'bitter fake promise' to try to fool her, and finally she agreed to give him two days to quit drinking himself. But it was soon evident that he had no intention of even trying to stop.

> When I remember the New Era I am in such pain I nearly jump overboard [she wrote] . . . Perhaps he is not truly evil but only weak – but I cannot love & live with someone I neither trust nor respect – *nothing* is worth that shame . . . how happy & lucky we could be if only . . . But the sight of a man who is – or can be – as good as great as Malc shaming & demeaning himself is pitiable to anyone . . . [8]

As in New York he refused to conform to her image of a celebrity. He played the drunken imbecile to spite her, then suffered remorse for having done so. Unknown to her, too, he was trying to drink away the dreadful memory of Fitte's death and of Mexico, now approaching on the port bow.

The two days were a charade. The first morning he rose at 3 a.m. to start drinking and, when his stumbling around the cabin woke her, told her he was drinking water. Sickened by his pathetic lies, she went on deck till breakfast-time. He then showed up looking dirty and dishevelled, his face flushed, and when he bragged to the chief engineer about his book, she felt ashamed and later dissuaded him from going to lunch, feeling everyone was pitying her. Later he joined her on the deck, sweating profusely in a woollen shirt and trousers, his face hideously swollen.

> To watch the self-destruction of a man, to see him disintegrate like this, as so often before is so shocking & disgusting I cannot face it. If it were the high romantic evil he thinks it that would be fascinating but what he will never realize is that . . . if I leave him . . . it will not be for the cruelty or suffering but that which too much suffering finally produces – boredom.[9]

The threatening proximity of Mexico, the French atmosphere on board, and the haunting rhythm of the ship's engines combined in Lowry's mind to produce a recurrent theme – 'Frère Jacques, Frère Jacques, dormez-vous, dormez-vous?' which began to crop up in his notes signifying something fearful, relentless and inevitable. (As ever he found refuge inside his own fictional 'selves', Sigbjørn Wilderness, the displaced protagonist of *Dark as the Grave* and Martin Trumbaugh, from early drafts of that book and from *La Mordida*, debating the question of the multiple 'I' and the life of authorship.)

As he emerged from his drunken fugue, he had a fearful and deathly nightmare – 'a vaudeville show with horrors of every kind' – Grand Guignol mixed up with Paul Fitte and some lurid Freudian imagery . . . 'A vagina with teeth that snap tight on entering,' beyond which waits . . . Death –

> a hideous looking red-faced keeper of a prison, with half his face shot away, and one shattered leg whose shreds are still left 'untied' . . . He is the keeper of the prison, and leads him or me through the gates, beyond which is St Catharine's College, Cambridge, *and the very room*. . . but Death, although hideous, has a kindly voice, and even sweet in his gruesome fashion: he says it is a pity I have seen 'all the show' . . . this meant I was doomed, and gave me 40 days to live.[10]

He felt devoid of ambition; he was in such a state of sorrowful abjection that it would need a miracle to pull out of it. He played both his alter egos – Wilderness and Trumbaugh. 'In spite of having spent the night wrestling with the torments of the d.t.'s, Martin Trumbaugh put in a remarkably good appearance at breakfast, looking bronzed and hearty,' he wrote. But Mexico was close by, and he became obsessed about seeing Popocatepetl. Also, somewhere to the north, across the Gulf of Tehuantepec in Villahermosa, lay the grave of his (and Wilderness's) friend Juan Fernando.

Off Acapulco, he thought he could pick out Calete Beach, Manzanillo, and even the Quinta Eugenia. Two days later, off the coast of Guatemala, Margerie had produced the cure he had come to address in mock-Shakespearian tones, 'My faithful general Phenobarbus, treacherous to the last?' His sudden transformation delighted the ever-optimistic Margerie, and an invitation onto the bridge for 'a snort' with the Captain seemed to confirm a new start. Approaching the Panama, forms had to be completed for the Immigration authorities, prompting old fears. 'Over the freedom of all people hangs the shadow of the Immigration Inspector,' he wrote. And the arrival of an albatross on board prompted thoughts of 'The Rime of the Ancient Mariner'.

SS *Brest* reached Panama at noon on 26 November. After a day of quarrels ashore, he and Margerie were barely on speaking terms. Then they learned that, because of new passengers expected at Christobel, they might be put into separate cabins. This idea was so unbearable that they bought a bottle of Martell from the steward, followed by several quarts of pinnard, and Lowry began to fret about not being invited to the bridge for a drink again. The passage through the Canal, recorded in a set of impressions in his notebook, became a metaphor for rebirth. He was passing from the New World back to the Old, the two cultures between which he was caught reflected in the competing identities which so confused him.

They were still in the same cabin as the ship entered the Caribbean heading towards Curaçao in the Dutch Antilles. There he sent news of their progress to Davenport, and was shocked to receive a second letter from Carol Phillips reminding him that she had his promise of twenty-five per cent of earnings from the *Volcano* in writing, and threatening action. His notes show him searching for a meaning to the voyage, noting his sudden obsession with cleanliness, cleaning his teeth ten times over and washing his feet for the first time in four months. The writer, Sigbjørn Wilderness, was observing Martin Trumbaugh, author of a book about a book which threatened to enmesh and kill him. 'In spite of stars, wind, and sun, Martin had almost foundered in some complicated and absurd abyss of self, could only pray for another miracle to get out of it . . .'[11]

On the morning of their seventh wedding anniversary, Margerie woke feeling sad and despairing, but determined to be gentle and sweet-natured. He, too, though looking dreadful, tried hard, making her a present of a lighter. However for most of that morning she was frightened, depressed, and tearful. When the captain and ship's officers presented them with a cactus in a pot with a message reading, 'Bon anniversaire de mariage', they were so touched they took it and placed it on the table at lunch for all to see. Later, at the bow of the ship, huddled under a winch, Margerie took Malcolm through a 'ceremony of the ring' in which they pledged their continuing love. Appropriately enough, perhaps, they had just entered the wide Sargasso Sea. The second engineer put a notice on their door reading: 'Don't Disturb. Just Married. L'amour c'est l'éternal printemps,' and they invited people to their cabin for 'snorts'. The chief steward provided cream puffs, and after dinner there was a sing-song in the *salle à manger*. They sang opera and sea shanties and there was much banging on the tables. That evening Margerie wanted love, but Malcolm was drunk and incapable. She wrote, 'Malc and I struggle and founder in our passions like this wretched badly built unseaworthy ship until I do not know which I fear the most; to go down and die in this ocean or to land in France with him as he now is.'

He, too, recorded his feelings, but his notes were scrappy. He found the sea worse than before for him. 'Well do I understand, now, Joyce's fear of the sea.'[12] The captain lent him an old *Harper's* with an article on Thomas Wolfe. 'Wolfe', he wrote, 'was in a hurry, knew he was going to die, like N[ordahl] in same sort of hurry.'[13] And the third mate lent him a copy of Waugh's *A Handful of Dust* which reminded him of 'the emptiness of life in England' and why he did not want to return there.[14]

Entering the Atlantic next day, there was a great storm to leeward which made Margerie nervous – 'I am afraid of this boat thrown together in wartime by makers of washing machines.' Malcolm was drinking rum and she was so dejected by his duplicity that she felt dragged down by the experience herself. 'Is it conceivable that a man's weakness can be so strong, that such evil can overpower me & exhaust me to the point that I become evil too?' On 5 December, she confessed her deepest feelings to her notebook:

> Altho he makes a great pretense of working (nothing has been written) & of exercising & tries his best to fool me it is too obvious he is drinking all afternoon . . . I had thought when I adored him as tho

> he were a god that love could survive anything but I begin to think that there are certain insults to *human dignity* that one should not survive . . . I have stopped thinking of myself as an artist because the last years my whole consciousness has been so completely absorbed by Malc & his immediate desires & storms . . . when he is too drunk to be potent, or is stinking & bloated & his breath disgusts me, I am rendered exasperated & furious & frustrated & sick. But . . . when he looks at me with his eyes with that look so infinitely innocent & appealing . . . my whole being dissolves before its appeal & I would, & do, surrender all I am – even my final dignity? . . . & what of the spiritual significance of all this; the 2 people who are doomed to love one another to mutual destruction?[15]

This remarkable if melodramatic passage conceals the fact that it was she who had suggested buying the pinnard from the steward when the Los Angeles whisky ran out, but gives a glimpse of how she saw her role as keeper of the great genius. She felt fated to spend the rest of her life with him, and he helped her to get her own work published and gave her a special kind of love. But the price was heavy. Bert had warned her that in one of his moods he could kill her, but she took little heed of such warnings. If he offered her violence it was her *karma*, something she was destined to bear.

They were still good enough to make the literary gossip columns. On 7 December the *New York Times* reported:

> Ex-seaman Malcolm Lowry, author of 'Under the Volcano', and his wife Margerie Bonner, author of 'Horse in the Sky' (just published by Scribners), departed . . . for France on a slow (forty days) freighter. Slow enough, Mr and Mrs Lowry hope, for Mr to complete the first draft of a new novel and for Mrs to get one under way . . .

In his Christmas list of the ten best novels of 1947, the editor of the *New York Times Book Review* rated the *Volcano* third of the five top works of fiction. George Mayberry in the *New Republic* placed it first out of five, above Sartre's *Age of Reason*; and Joseph Henry Jackson, whom they had met at the *San Francisco Chronicle*, rated it the year's second best novel. It did not feature in Jacques Barzun's list in *Harper's*.

The weather had deteriorated and a violent squall descended with great hammers of thunder and lightning, which delighted Malcolm, and his mood brightened considerably; he even remained playing games with the crew in the *salle à manger* after dinner. For the following three days they had to weather a huge storm, the ship rolling wildly, buffeted by seventy mile an hour gales. For two nights they had little sleep and the *Brest* seemed to be making no headway. On the 13th, with the wind at Force 10–11, the Captain told Margerie, 'Well, there's now nothing I can do. But if you like, Madame, you can pray.' Lowry was reflecting that they were in a storm over Atlantis – below them lay an unknown and unknowable world. Next day the sun shone and the sea was tranquil. They were two days out from Bishop's Light. The storm was weathered, the ordeal survived.

The prospect of land ahead lightened the atmosphere and the ship was filled with singing and laughter. At midnight on the 16th they went on deck to see the Bishop's Rock lighthouse flashing. Next day in the English Channel they learned that in the storm the ship's steering gear had broken and the crew had worked all night to repair it. They could have foundered; they felt proud to have got through. At 5.30 a.m. they were hoping to see land, but poor visibility meant they missed the Lizard, Eddystone lighthouse and Start Point. The English coastline was shrouded in fog. After a thirteen year absence, the Ancient Mariner was to be denied a sight of his homeland.

They reached Rotterdam the next night, and the following morning they set foot for the first time in post-war Europe, and were horrified by the war damage. Margerie made detailed notes, like a good tourist; Lowry noted, 'Fear and horror in Rotterdam: cannot look at the bombed flattened buildings, the cadavers of churches.'[16] At the art gallery, he found himself riveted by two 'mad pictures' by Hieronymus Bosch, one of St Christopher carrying Christ on his back and one which he took to be the Pilgrim's Progess but was, in fact, the Prodigal Son. He made detailed notes on them for a nightmare sequence in *La Mordida*, but it eventually developed into a separate story based on their voyage, 'Through the Panama'.

They disembarked at Le Havre on 23 December. There was no sight of Davenport and Lowry reacted badly. They took the afternoon train to Paris on a grey misty day, travelling first class via Rouen. They went to the hotel recommended by Stern, the Hotel d'Islay on the rue Jacob behind St Germain des Prés. Finding they had spent almost half of the three hundred francs bought on the ship, Malcolm went out next day with the last of it, intending to change some more dollars, and did not return. Margerie spent the whole of Christmas Eve not knowing what had happened to him, scared to leave the hotel and without food and drink. On Christmas morning, after a night of miserable anxiety, she was still alone. In desperation she drafted a telegram to Joan Black,

Stern's friend, saying that Malcolm had disappeared with her money and passport. But at 3 p.m. he showed up wretchedly drunk and refusing to explain his absence.

Davenport announced he would be arriving on New Year's Eve and Margerie hoped that he would take Malcolm in hand. The weather was dreary, overcast and raining, and it took her a few days to get him sober and free of the shakes. But, unknown to her, Davenport had come to Paris anticipating a great binge to celebrate the New Year; after all, he and Lowry had not met for eleven years and had a lot of drinking to catch up on. He arrived with no money and they said he could sleep in their room. They had dinner in a good small restaurant, then Margerie left them alone and went back to the hotel. She was woken after midnight by Davenport saying that Malcolm was downstairs and too heavy to lift. They went down and solicited the help of a passing soldier and together they carried him up to the room. Margerie wrote that Davenport's arrival was where everything went wrong for them in Europe. What she may not have realized was how much Paris, like Mexico, was full of ghosts for Malcolm; after all, this was where he had married almost exactly fourteen years earlier. But of Jan he never spoke to Margerie.

All three set off next day for Chartres to do the walk across the cornfields from St Prèst which Lowry had taken in 1934 while staying with Maurice Sachs and Henry Wibbels and which Laruelle remembers taking in the *Volcano*. Having trouble over train times, they spent the morning at the Cloiserie des Lilas in Montparnasse, arriving in Chartres only in the early afternoon. The Lowrys had talked so often about doing the walk from St Prèst, but when they got to Chartres they got no further because Lowry and Davenport preferred to sit in a café and drink. The great reunion ended when, after one noisy drunken orgy at the hotel, the police were called and the Lowrys were asked to leave. They moved to a hotel on rue San Benoît, nearer still to the Boulevard St Germain and its cafés.

Before leaving, Davenport introduced them to Joan Black, who loved *Under the Volcano* and enjoyed the company of writers, even drunken ones like Lowry. They were invited to stay at her house at Vernon, some fifty miles north-west of Paris, and were happy to accept. The house, La Cerisaie (The Cherry Orchard) was close to Giverny, where Monet had lived, and to Rouen, where Lowry had once been so happy with Jan. Joan was a tall, rather imperious Anglo Irish woman who had bought the house in the 1930s and spent the war years in the (for a time) Vichy-controlled south until the Liberation. It was a charming Normandy house with a large garden, and was 'open house' to English writers living there during the summer. The French housekeeper, a formidable widow, Julienne LaPierre, took instantly to Lowry. She was, according to Joan's sister Leslie, 'a force of nature', a lover of food and good wine, a proud housekeeper and a marvellous cook with a wicked sense of humour and a great roaring laugh.[17] She obviously thought Lowry amusing, tolerated his odd behaviour and ensured he had a regular supply of wine which secretly she diluted. According to Margerie, Malcolm and Julienne were often together and she would say to him, 'You are my bad egg, but I love you.' One day, returning from market they went into a church to pray. Inside they tripped and fell on the floor together. While they lay there laughing the priest entered. 'I am disgraced for life,' she told Margerie afterwards.[18]

At the end of January, Lowry phoned his French publishers, Fontaine, offering help with the translation, and found the translators only too happy to accept. The many strange and hidden allusions, cabbalistic references and half-disguised quotations from Dante and other sources had often left them baffled. Numerous potential translators had read the book, shaken their heads and declined. Now the task was being undertaken mostly by Clarisse Francillon, a middle-aged French-Swiss novelist, later to be joined by Stephen Spriel, a young scholar from Martinique. Lowry invited Francillon to come to Vernon to work with him, and rather reluctantly she agreed.

When they met at the station he said nothing but bundled her into a taxi and took her off to La Cerisaie, she sitting beside him quite tongue-tied. At the house, Joan and Margerie greeted her and drinks were poured. She tried to take in the man whose book she and her colleagues at Fontaine were struggling to translate. He stood at the fireplace clutching a glass of whisky, observant if withdrawn – obviously an eccentric. Later, alone with the two women, she asked if this was *le Consul*. Indeed it was, she was told, and the novel was based on his life. While writing the book he had managed to stay sober, but now drink had overtaken him and he was unable to write. Helping with the translation could be his salvation. It was an invitation too romantic to refuse. Regularly for the next two months she visited the house to work with him at the library table – he, with little French and permanently high on diluted wine, she, with limited English, struggling to comprehend the nuances of the book he had written when sober.

The Lowrys still visited Paris, Margerie hoping he would pick up past contacts with Cocteau and the *NRF*. He found Cocteau unobtainable, now too famous to be walked in on, and when Margerie tried phoning Maurice Sachs, the *NRF* office was closed. Later they met Sylvia Beach who told them that Sachs was dead. He had turned collaborator during the Occupation, tried to play both sides against the other, and was arrested by the Gestapo and sent to a camp in Germany. In 1944, inmates were forced to march west before the advancing Russians, and Sachs was shot by an SS officer and left in a ditch at the roadside. (An alternative version has Sachs being shot by the Resistance as a collaborator.) Here was yet another of his old friends who had been shot. The literary resonances did not help his stability one bit.

He also spent time in Paris alone with Clarisse, at the offices of Fontaine in the rue Gozlin and at her apartment at 23 rue Gazin. She found him fascinating but hardly helpful in trying to understand the book's very English humour, as in the Consul's reading of the menu at El Petate, or his conversation with Quincey. He was often drunk, yet, even when gripped by the shakes and apparently distracted, he could suddenly pick up a complete Shakespeare, turn quickly to a scene he wanted, and read out some apposite speech with unexpected brio and appropriate accompanying gestures.

On occasions, especially when Margerie was with them, he performed his old vanishing trick, disappearing at the drop of a hat for hours or days at a time, haunting the dimmest bars in the most obscure backstreets. One day Clarisse found him discussing his book in inadequate French with the bemused patronne of a café, the *Perroquet*, asking her earnestly how best to translate the title. Paris seemed not to interest him; his main obsession was the next drink. While they worked at La Cerisaie Clarisse never saw him sober. She noticed that he chose to work indoors, never looking out of the windows, and seemed disdainful of Joan Black's carefully cropped lawns and blooming flowerbeds. Although in Julienne and Joan he had company that was *simpatico*, it took very little to make him plunge off on a binge. Upset by the assassination of Gandhi at the end of January, he disappeared for a day into Rouen.

The Lowrys now found themselves well off. They had had a twenty-thousand franc advance from Fontaine to add to the dollars they had brought with them. There was money due from Matson, they were paying no rent, and on 25 January the French franc was devalued, thus doubling the value of the dollar and so offering the prospect of cheaper travel. At the end of March, Davenport was due to visit La Cerisaie but when Lowry, who had a touch of flu, injured himself while drunk, he volunteered to go into a nearby nursing home run by nuns, knowing that 'Davvy' would only carry him off on another binge and fearing that he might suffer a complete mental collapse. Margerie was pleased because drink was making him more and more violent, and at least he would be safe among the nuns. Davenport was annoyed to find him in hospital and blamed Margerie for his poor condition. He brought news that his publishing career had ended and he was now working for the BBC. In the care of the nuns, Lowry managed to write a long flattering letter to Aiken and draft a reply to Carol Phillips, explaining why she would not be getting her slice of money from sales of the *Volcano*. It was not legal to transfer money from France, he said, and he did not see she had a right to it, which was not to say he would not have helped her out if he could have and if she was in trouble. The letter was never sent.

While Lowry was being ministered to by the Sisters of Mercy (who secretly fed him red wine, he claimed), Clarisse and Margerie discussed his volatile mental condition. Clarisse suggested an analyst in Zürich, Dr Meier, who had been a *mitarbeiter* of Jung's, and Margerie wrote to him immediately describing Malcolm's symptoms and enclosing a copy of *Under the Volcano*. Meier replied that he would be very interested to treat him, but Margerie was then faced with having to overcome his antipathy to psychoanalysis, and his belief that he knew enough to administer it to himself. Then Joan Black suggested they go to Cassis, a village on the coast between Marseille and Toulon, where she had friends. Lowry was keen to live by the sea again, so they took the train south, and early in April were ensconced there at the Hotel de la Plage. They found a picturesque seventeenth-century fishing village with Roman and Moorish origins beginning to be disfigured by ugly new villas, much like Acapulco. The sea was cobalt blue and the sunsets magnificent against a backdrop of red cliffs. However, the rocky descent to the sea was not to Lowry's liking, and after being badly burned by the sun while floating on his back, his pride was hurt when he slipped and fell on the rocks. He spent the rest of the day complaining about 'the beastly Mediterranean' and refusing to go back in.

Before long he was drinking heavily again. One morning, after being ejected, fighting drunk, from the bar of a nearby luxury hotel, he turned on Margerie in their hotel room, grabbed her by the throat and tried to strangle her. Her cries brought hotel staff running to their room and they managed to pull him off. They were told they must leave, but then out of pity for Margerie the manager and his wife gave them a reprieve.

Joan's friends had left, and Margerie had no one to turn to. In despair she suggested getting Stuart over to help him, and surprisingly Malcolm agreed. She wired Stuart, but since it was all but impossible to get funds out of England, and difficult to travel abroad, she offered to pay his fare, and he promised to try to get away. If the family had not known of Malcolm's second marriage, they knew now. While waiting for Stuart, Margerie told him about Dr Meier, and her plan to ask his family to fund his treatment, and he seemed quite compliant. He tried swimming again, but had to be dragged from the water by Margerie and a young Englishwoman when he collapsed. On 16 April she wrote in her diary, 'This morning I have had an incredible conversation with Malc which shows me he has gone completely off his rocker.' She feared Stuart would arrive too late.

When he did arrive he brought Margot, who spoke better French. They were not impressed with Margerie, whom they found theatrical and unreal. Margot later told the family about her, waving her arms with bangles jangling, and stating dramatically, 'He has the word of God!'[19] But Stuart was distressed to find his brother in such a sad condition, staring and withdrawn, and seemingly unaware of him. He said he must see a doctor, but Margerie objected. If he got violent, he could be deported or committed to a hospital with little hope of ever being released. Stuart insisted, however, and a local doctor came. He said he could do nothing and that Malcolm should be taken back to England. That, said Stuart, was impossible, as was the suggestion that the family pay for treatment in Zürich – money of that kind simply could not be got out. He suggested to Margerie that they see the US Consul in Marseille and get him admitted to the American Hospital in Paris.

Left alone, Lowry brightened enough to pen a note in verse to Erskine:

> Albert the Good: Sorry I haven't written.
> Maybe I am a bit berausges-himmer,
> I don't eat my food and in my bed I have myself geshitten,
> Anyhow I am living here.
> In a comparative state of mundial fear –
> Also give my love to my dear Twinbad the bailer
> I mean dear Frank Taylor.
> This is written on the night of April 18th

Anyway or the other, there is no rhyme
Unless you can think of one above.
Save love
Malcolm[20]

Two days later he was sufficiently *compos mentis* to write an irate letter to Matson complaining of his apparent neglect of a Hollywood offer for *Horse in the Sky*.

The American Consul in Marseille arranged for him to be admitted to the psychiatric ward of the American Hospital in Paris and, since he had improved slightly, Stuart and Margot decided to spend what little time and money they had left on a brief holiday before returning to England. Margerie felt deserted; she would have to get him back to Paris alone. On 26 April, with Malcolm under sedation, she managed to get him on to the train. There was no one to meet them in Paris and he began to get worse so she dared not leave him to phone the hospital. Finally, a young American offered them a lift. Lowry was expected and was admitted immediately. After about ten days, by some act of willpower, he had pulled himself together and was soon discharged. When Margerie asked the doctor's advice, he told her, 'Leave him. Get out from under right now. He's going to kill either you or himself.' When she replied: 'That's the most immoral thing I've ever heard in my life,' he said, 'Well, that's my advice.'[21]

They returned briefly to the hotel in rue Saint Benoît, and picked up their mail at the American Express on the rue Scribe. There was a letter from Erskine announcing his impending arrival in Paris, which may have panicked Lowry, still not fully recovered, into a diplomatic retreat. He decided it might after all be a good idea to go to Zürich to be treated by Dr Meier, or even by Jung himself – Margerie's dream. Then, surprisingly, he suggested they leave the comparative peace and tranquillity of Paris and their friends there and go to Italy, where *Under the Volcano* was also supposed to be being translated. Their planned route, through Florence, Venice and Naples to Capri, looked like a further pilgrimage in the footsteps of Lawrence. Perhaps he wanted to make things up with Margerie after the Cassis disaster. From Joan he got advice about places to stay and an introduction from Davenport to Norman Douglas on Capri. Once again, he vowed to behave and to refrain from excessive drinking.

When they set out on 15 May, things went badly. A promised lift to the station did not materialize and they missed their train by ten minutes.

But Lowry was in a jovial mood and they spent the time waiting for the midnight train at a pavement café close to the Gare de Lyon discussing, appropriately enough, Jekyll and Hyde. They finally crammed into a train full of soldiers, miraculously found an empty compartment, had a snack of hard-boiled eggs and wine they had brought along, and fell asleep. Next day they were speeding through Switzerland enjoying the scenery, and Lowry was taking great gulps of air and saying how good it was to get out of France. Margerie, meantime, was recording every peak and lake and valley in her notebook. After a slight panic about Malcolm's passport, they reached Milan and there took the train to Florence where they arrived on the 17th.

They got a room at the Pensione Niva overlooking the Piazza della Indipendenza with views of the Duomo, the dome of San Lorenzo and the square tower of the Campanile. Lowry slept every morning and they went out in the rain in the afternoons. They toured the usual sights – the Ponte Vecchio, the Uffizi – then stood quarrelling in the Piazza della Signoria because Margerie refused to look at the statues. They tried to contact their Italian translator, Luigi Berti, without success. After three days, Margerie noted in her diary that Malcolm was extremely bored and becoming cantankerous. He had, she wrote, 'no sense of history & says why the excitement over things that are dead?' But, she reminded him, Shakespeare was dead! His riposte, if any, went unrecorded. She wondered if his lack of interest was because he was European and used to old things. It did not occur to her that he might have been reacting to her excessive enthusiasm. One day he remained behind in a trattoria and failed to return to the hotel for dinner. Wondering whether to search for him, she noted 'A glimpse of my old tired wrinkled face in the mirror,' and saw it as a record of their stormy relationship. Finally she went out and found him leaning against a stone pillar in the piazza.[22] A few days later he disappeared again. This time she found him in gaol for drunkenness and had to get him out. That evening in a fit of despair she threatened to jump from the hotel balcony, but he held her back. Nevertheless, next day she had recovered enough to be able to fill her diary with details of paintings and statues they had seen.

They went by bus to Rimini and hated it because of the 'horror' of its luxury hotels. They settled finally at the Pensione Adriatica in Cattólica, a small seaside village, where Malcolm swam daily from a pleasant sandy beach, and where they were practically the only visitors. But the blare of the jukebox from a nearby bar disturbed them, and within days, despite promises, he reverted to heavy drinking. By 28 May he had become so quarrelsome that Margerie was reduced to tears. The day ended in a long walk during which it began to rain. Malcolm stuck out his chest enjoying the soaking; Margerie was distressed because of the state of her hair and feeling that she was looking like a hag. With her forty-third birthday approaching she was becoming ever more conscious of her fading looks. And the rough outdoors which Lowry loved was less and less to her taste.

Her swings of mood were now matching his. She wrote happily at the prospect of seeing a real castle for the first time. A guide took them to a castle called Malatesta and Lowry was intrigued by the sight of the dungeons and the tales they were told of clandestine love and torture. Margerie was overwhelmed by the idea of centuries of suffering and agony associated with the place. Malcolm, however, grinned with delight and all the way back talked endlessly about torture while she was trying hard not to be sick. He had found yet another way to tease and discomfort her. Nevertheless, the impression on her was so great she decided that the stories the guide had told them would form the basis of her next novel.

Moving on to Venice, they stayed for about a week at a run-down hotel on the Grand Canal. From there they toured the city in a gondola and visited the Doge's Palace, where Lowry insisted they be shown the dungeons, despite Margerie's protests that she found such places claustrophobic. The subterranean labyrinth included a cell where Byron had been imprisoned. 'What a wonderful place to work,' said Lowry. In Venice he drank very little and was relaxed and in good spirits. He loved the place and was reluctant to leave, and when Margerie insisted they stick to their schedule and go on to Rome, he became first anxious and then deliberately got drunk.

Of all the places they visited in Italy, Rome made the greatest creative impact on him, and was the setting for two of his best short stories, 'Strange Comfort Afforded by the Profession' and 'Elephant and Colosseum'. On 2 June they checked into the Hotel D'Inghilterra on the Via Bocca di Leone near to the American Express, and Margerie went to change some money. When she returned, she was stopped at the desk. Malcolm was in the bar, drunk, screaming and raving, and had attacked another guest. Hotel porters hauled him struggling up to their room where he was locked in, and a doctor summoned. They heard him running around inside, banging his head against the walls and screaming. When the doctor arrived he managed to calm him with a sedative, but said that he needed immediate medical help; he had obviously had a breakdown and could become dangerous. He was taken to a sanatorium just outside the city, and given a room costing $50 a day. Margerie moved into an adjoining room, but, as none of the nurses spoke English, she felt unable to help much. In view of his dangerous condition a guard was placed on her door, but that night, when the man dozed off, he burst in on her, leapt on the bed and attempted to strangle her. The guard, woken by her screams, managed to drag him away, and he was again sedated.

Within a week he had regained his senses and was discharged. Because of the high sanatorium bill, they had to move to a cheap, awful, noisy little *pensione* just off the Via Veneto. Next morning, Margerie wrote of the man who a week before had attempted to strangle her, 'Malc, the angel, woke me at 7.30 & didn't even murmur at the stale bread & one half cup of coffee. He was sweet but sweet & strange & spoke hesitantly & his remarkable blue eyes withdrawn. I have never seen him so subdued.'[23] Whether he was still sedated is unclear, but she had long got into the habit of feeding him phenobarbital at night when he got drunk and threatened to be disruptive. From time to time she substituted the Vitamin B Bert had prescribed in Los Angeles, but he came to blame that for his being ill and looked upon the phenobarbital as a benign and helpful drug.[24]

Despite having just survived a murder attempt, Margerie doggedly pursued her sightseeing schedule and continued making her notes. They visited Keats's house in the Piazza di Spagna across from the church of Trinità dei Monti. The room where he died was lined with books, prints, portraits, and paintings of the poet and his friend Severn and of Shelley's house and the Bay of Spezia where Shelley drowned. Here was a shrine to the young dead of whom he and Grieg had talked with such intellectual passion in 1931 and among whose company Grieg now was. Lowry took notes from a letter from Severn about the poet's dying: 'for his knowledge of internal anatomy enables him to judge of any change accurately and largely adds to his torture.' His knowledge of his internal workings as a writer largely added to the torture of creating, yet it was only in creating that he had his being and could contain his sanity. However, since leaving Dollarton, Lowry had written next to nothing.

They threaded their way through ancient streets crammed with screaming trolley buses, motorscooters and horse cabs. They climbed the Capitoline Hill and wandered among ruined arches and temples until they reached the Colosseum, where Lowry's recorded comment was, 'It looks like the Albert Hall in a dentist's nightmare.' At the Mamertine Prison beneath the church of San Giuseppe dei Falegnami, Lowry was again fascinated by the dungeons, and copied down the nicely ambiguous note from a guidebook: 'the lower prison is the true prison.'

Before entering St Peter's to see Michelangelo's *Pietà*, he insisted on putting on his tie and touching the fountain water, declaring that it was undoubtedly holy water. Two days later at the Vatican he was even more mischievous, teasing Margerie for her earnest pursuit of culture. In the Sistine Chapel, she noted down details of the interior, the lighting, the magnificent paintings, and as they lay on their backs on pews beneath Michelangelo's great frescos, Margerie gazing up in breathless wonder, Lowry nudged her and whispered, 'Margie, do you remember when we painted the ceiling of the shack?'

After the Pantheon they visited the Borghese Gardens where Lowry claimed he again encountered Rosemary, the elephant he had looked after twenty-one years before on *Pyrrhus*. There was something of *Tarzan of the Apes* about it, he wrote, not to mention Kipling, Rider Haggard and Stephen Leacock.[25] He wrote to Davenport that the Italians were most enthusiastic about the *Volcano* and were bringing it out soon, excellent, he said for his ego – another wild anticipation: it did not appear till 1966. Rome, he said, was 'the happiest & loveliest city I have ever seen, full of lovers, motorscooters & monks.'

His feeling for Rome was founded on its strong associations with writers he admired. Here Gogol had written part of *Dead Souls*, and here had lived at one time or another Mann, Ibsen, Mérimée, and Schiller. He thought too of Fitzgerald in the Forum and Eliot in the Colosseum.[26] But despite loving Rome, there was Margerie's ruthless schedule to be kept, and on 13 June they set off for Capri, heading first for Naples. There they stayed at the Hotel Patria, a commercial hotel overlooking a crowded narrow cobbled backstreet, with people hanging out of windows watching the passing parade. He sought out the old medieval part of the city and found a Dostoyevskian scene – a maze of filthy, foul-smelling slums swarming with ragged children, diseased beggars, women nursing babies, and men playing cards.

Compared to the Romans, the Neapolitans seemed grim and surly. Lowry's dormant socialism was stirred by the sight of such poverty and he and Margerie had an unresolved argument over it. But it was also, Lowry reminded himself, the city which drove Boccaccio back to Florence and where Virgil had written the *Aeneid*.

It was wholly appropriate that they set out to climb Vesuvius – the Consul and Yvonne eventually getting to climb the volcano. Margerie, in her black suede Parisian sandals, found her feet being burned by hot cinders, but still paused long enough to note down their progress and describe the view across the Bay of Naples. At the summit she was disappointed they could not climb down into the crater, but the guide pointing to a wide crack in the trail said, 'Last week . . . she geeva the beega shake,' a line Lowry adopted gleefully for appropriately ridiculous occasions. Two days after climbing Vesuvius they toured Pompeii – the setting for yet another story, 'Present Estate of Pompeii'.

After a week in Naples they moved on to Capri, where they found a hotel, the Hotel Belvedere e Tre Re, on the beach at Marina Grande, not the smartest place, but within their means. Lowry was delighted when the Lithuanian artist-proprietor told him his father had been a bosom pal of Dostoyevsky's, and he wrote to Erskine in Paris, 'Papa reported that Feodor was an awfully nice fellow but sicka in the head.'[27] At Tiberius' Villa he copied down names scratched into the walls and Margerie wrote mysteriously in her notebook on 22 June, 'Pursuit in a sort of way, of O[scar] W[ilde]. Ridiculous, yet good & courageous . . .'[28] Next day she noted that in the morning 'M. tries to work on U[ltramarine], but can't.' After lunch they went to Anacapri and visited San Michele, Axel Munthe's 'dream villa', now a museum. They bathed at the Piccola Marina and Lowry swam in the 'blue' grotto. But after receiving no mail for several days, he began to fret.

They hoped to meet Norman Douglas, but he was difficult to contact. This upset Lowry and led to quarrels. Finally a friend of Douglas, Cecil Gray, the Scottish music critic, got in touch, and when they met on 3 July, Gray seemed to like them and was charming (so much so that he found his way into *Dark as the Grave Wherein My Friend is Laid*). He arranged a meeting with Douglas and next day they met at a terrace café overlooking the Bay of Naples and took wine with him. Lowry had long admired *South Wind*, and was excited to meet the old sybarite, now approaching eighty. He recommended some cafés to them, Piene No 13, the Bishops and Pepinella's Cave. Margerie thought him 'a darling'.[29]

Now they were broke and wired to Paris for more money. But when it arrived on 6 July it had been mistakenly sent to a bank in Naples, which meant an awkward journey to retrieve it. The day was unpleasant with a cold high wind, and Lowry was out of sorts. When he met Douglas again that afternoon they had what Margerie called an 'unfortunate encounter' which put Lowry in 'a furious temper'. He and Margerie then quarrelled violently and he disappeared for the afternoon. She found him later, drinking in a vineyard which he had stumbled into on the way back to the *pensione*.[30]

In spite of the 'unfortunate encounter', the Lowrys met Douglas once more, but by now Malcolm was anxious to meet Erskine in Paris, and on 8 July they decided on the spur of the moment to return to France, cabling him their time of arrival. Lowry slept for much of the journey back to Paris, and they arrived at the Gare de Lyon on 10 July, but there was no sight of Erskine. They phoned his hotel and finally met him and his wife Peggy at a café called the Madison. Erskine was shocked by Lowry's befuddled state – worse, he thought, than when they had last met in New York. Over lunch a book of matches exploded in Erskine's hand, badly blistering his fingers, and a shaken Lowry was convinced that it was the element still following him around.[31] From Erskine he heard that Harcourt Brace had taken over Reynal & Hitchcock in December, so they now held the copyright of *Under the Volcano* and first refusal of his next book. But he was determined to go to Random House and again have Erskine as his editor, and Erskine was just as keen to win Lowry for Random House.

Afterwards, Malcolm dragged Margerie to the Grand Guignol, for which he had developed a taste as a schoolboy in Paris in 1926. She hated it, but went along in order not to lose track of him. They were back at the hotel in rue St Benoît, and he was back into his old ways – permanently drunk and disappearing at intervals, only to return wrecked and hungover. Clarisse offered to take him off her hands over Bastille Day, so on the evening of the 13th he went to stay with her at 23 rue Gazan, where he quickly discovered a bottle of rum she had carefully hidden. When, in exasperation she told him to hand it over or she would never speak to him again, he grinned and said, 'Oh, you'll speak to me; you love me too much not to.' She was intrigued by his phenomenal memory, his ability not only to quote an aphorism from Nietzsche but to take in and retain the small details as you sat talking to him. 'By what miracle did both types coexist in Lowry?' she wrote. 'The first memory vivifying the second, one supporting the other, made for an extraordinary verbal inspiration, not unlike that of Rabelais.'[32]

Fed up with chasing him around Paris, Margerie asked Joan Black if they could come back to La Cerisaie, and she said they would be welcome. They moved there on 21 July, and Julienne LaPierre, pleased to see her 'bad egg' back, laid on her usual supply of watered wine for him. From then onwards he seems to have been in a permanent state of intoxication. On 23 July, Erskine phoned to say goodbye before leaving for London. Margerie took the call, even though Malcolm was in the next room, and then wrote to him: 'The tragic fact is that Malcolm is losing his mind & . . . is becoming actively dangerous: first to himself & me but now more savage towards everyone who crosses him in any way.' She thought the only hope was to get him to Jung in Switzerland, but found it difficult to get him to agree. It would take one or two years and she hoped the Lowry family would help financially. One possibility, she thought, was to leave Malcolm in Switzerland and get a job, and she had already applied for work with the Marshall Plan in Paris. She asked Erskine if there might be a publishing job for her in New York, and told him that Malcolm's main problem was that he saw everyone as plotting against him and could become dangerously angry.[33] She told him Malcolm did not know she was writing to him, but he did and added a knowing PS: 'Mad one might go but certainly everybody has not jumped overboard.'[34]

A number of Joan Black's friends were now in the Giverny area for the summer, and were frequent visitors to the house, notably Allanah Harper, Eda Lord, Esther Strachey Arthur and Nancy Cunard. Cunard, editor, poet, writer, a celebrated figure in Bohemian society between the wars, then fifty-two, had taken rooms at an inn at Giverny with her 25-year-old bisexual boyfriend, William Le Page Finley, and was often at La Cerisaie. The evenings were always gay, with the guests dancing to Radio Andorra late into the night. Lowry, hopeless with a partner, danced alone, taking occasional sips from his glass of watered wine. Cunard, just back from Mexico and deeply impressed by *Under the Volcano* and its author, composed a poem specially for him.

Lowry had often expressed hostility to homosexuals, but had had homosexual friends, like Fitte and Valleton. And in certain moods he was game for any experience, it being the writer's sacred duty to expose himself to everything, and if he could shock others at the same time, all well and good. Le Page Finley, 'very thin with beautiful eyes'[35] clearly found Lowry attractive and knew his weakness for strong liquor. One evening at La Cerisaie he 'liberated' a bottle of gin from a cupboard and persuaded Lowry to escape to an empty bedroom where they could enjoy themselves.

> We were finally discovered by Nancy followed by the other guests & a disagreeable scene followed. The gin was confiscated & they left

> us alone. The next morning at dawn feeling very guilty we crept out of the house & made for the inn in Giverny picking up a bottle of cognac on the way. We locked ourselves in Nancy's room as it was larger than mine, stripped & went to bed with the cognac. By noon Nancy & Malcolm's wife Marjorie [*sic*] were at the door & we refused to open. I said, 'Can't you understand when two men want to be alone together?' They went below to the dining room & sent up a platter of food. When we finally unlocked the door Marjorie got her husband dressed & took him away. Joan Black never forgave me for this incident & I was barred from the house. It seemed best at this point to return to Paris where we ran into Malcolm & his wife again . . .[36]

It may have been this event which prompted Margerie to urge him again to see Dr Meier or Jung in Zürich. She asked Clarisse, about to leave on a visit to Switzerland, to try to fix an appointment, and then, with Joan Black's help, tried to persuade him that this was his only salvation. The problem would be the cost. Meier's fee was thirty francs an hour, but treatment could last two years and their money was running out. They had some US dollars left, a Swiss publisher and Fontaine owed them money, and Margerie was still hopeful of getting a job in Paris. There was also Malcolm's income, which might be switched to Europe, but her greatest hope was the Lowry family, who she thought bound to come to the aid of the family genius. On 9 August, Malcolm struggled close enough to sobriety to write a sad little note to Erskine, regretting their all too brief meeting in Paris.

> I have to confess . . . that I am going steadily & even beautifully downhill: my memory misses beats at every moment, & my mornings are on all fours . . . in a nutshell I am only sober or merry in a whisky bottle . . . I have now reached a position where every night I write 5 novels in imagination, have total recall . . . but am unable to write a word. I cannot explain in human terms the incredible effort it has cost me to write even this silly little note.[37]

Allanah Harper recalled the brilliance of his conversation and storytelling, including a dramatic account of having accidentally killed George Hepburn's rabbit. She also remembered him disappearing for days at a time to Paris or to Rouen, but Margerie seemed not to bother; by this time she was used to his absences and knew that eventually he would turn up. She tended to stay in the background at La Cerisaie, perhaps feeling somewhat outnumbered by the English. One day, when Allanah was there for lunch, screams suddenly issued from the Lowrys' bedroom; Malcolm was drunk and beating Margerie. Eda Lord ran upstairs and banged on the door until he appeared, only to charge down the stairs and out of the house. Margerie was left in an appalling state and had to be tended for cuts and bruises.

In September they returned to Paris and Malcolm was spending more time with Clarisse at the Fontaine offices. He tried dictating to her from memory his 'Preface' to *Under the Volcano* composed for Cape on the voyage to Haiti. According to Clarisse, he never gave her a complete version, being too incoherent for much of the time, and the preface which did appear in the French edition she composed from her notes of his dictation. When it became clear to his translators that his presence was not making their job any easier, they asked for an extension to their deadline, and Lowry agreed without consulting Matson. He was worried that the vitamins he was taking were having a bad effect on him, and Clarisse took him to her doctor, who he visited on several occasions. Perhaps it was his name which attracted him – Dr Courvoisier.

By the end of the month Margerie again had itchy feet and was wanting to travel. It was decided not to go so far this time, so on 2 October they travelled to Brittany. They went to St Malo where Lowry drank cider and ate oysters, and they visited Carnac and Mont Saint Michel. He sent a postcard to Jimmy Craige describing the quicksands and 48-foot tides. The swimming in Dollarton was much better, he wrote, and asked the old boatbuilder to guard their precious house and pier for them.[38] Back in Paris he heard from Downie Kirk, who had read *Horse in the Sky* and considered it 'fine', and asked after the fate of their story 'October Ferry to Gabriola'. Birney also wrote to say the shack was in good shape except that the pier was on its last legs and he was worried about possible break-ins.[39] All this must have tugged Lowry more towards Dollarton and literary evenings with Kirk than towards Switzerland and Jungian heart-searching with Dr Meier.

Margerie, however, was determined on Switzerland. But then they learned that the Swiss publisher who owed $750 for German translation rights of *Under the Volcano* had gone bust and had skipped to New York.[40] With that money gone, she decided to go to England and, leaving Malcolm in Clarisse's care, set off hoping to persuade Evelyn to pay for her son's treatment in Zürich. In London she contacted Davenport, who took her to meet William MacAlpine, friend and patron of Dylan Thomas, who lived in Richmond, in the hope that he could do something for Lowry. She met Thomas and his wife Caitlin, and Thomas told her about first meeting Malcolm in Soho and how kind and encouraging he had been, telling his friends about him and reading his poems to them. But this friendliness was not matched by an offer of aid from MacAlpine, who was already helping to support one indigent poet. Margerie then set off to try her luck in Caldy. She may have had another interest, the hope of catching a glimpse of that expensive jewellery, especially diamonds, which she thought would be hers when Evelyn died.

Stuart met her train at Liverpool and took her to Caldy. She later told Priscilla that she was put on her own in the living room at Inglewood to wait for Evelyn, Stuart warning her under no circumstances to sit in a certain chair. When asked why not, he replied, 'That's where her spook sits.' Not realizing that Malcolm's mischievous sense of humour was shared by all the Lowry brothers, she took him seriously and decided that this was a very weird family indeed. Evelyn welcomed her in a kindly but vague sort of way. Margerie showed her the American reviews of *Under the Volcano* and told her that Jung was so impressed by it that he had offered to treat Malcolm for nothing. All they needed was the money to live in Zürich for a year. Evelyn, it seems, embraced her and cried, but she was far too canny to make any commitment about money. In any case the family thought Malcolm too far gone to waste good money on, and Margerie was regarded with tolerant amusement when she spoke so dramatically of his genius. She returned to Paris empty-handed, having concluded that Stuart was 'nuts' and the whole family simply scared to death of the bugaboo of insanity. What she did not know was that since returning from Europe, Stuart and Margot kept suitcases permanently packed by the door just in case she and Malcolm turned up asking to stay. They would then say, 'Oh, what a pity, we're just off on our holidays.'[41]

Malcolm meantime was working intermittently with Clarisse on the translation. But Fontaine was in danger of going out of business and Le Club Français du Livre contracted to bring out a limited edition of *Under the Volcano*. They paid him half of their advance of forty thousand francs on signature, which would at least see them through for the rest of their time in France, and there were others interested in Lowry, too. He met Maurice Nadeau, literary editor of *Le Combat*, who suggested they might serialize the book. As usual, Lowry took it for granted that it would appear, and so informed friends.

Once, at Clarisse's invitation, a journalist, A-J Frédérique, came to interview him at her home for the journal *Liens*. There he found Lowry drunkenly strumming a guitar 'borrowed' from an office next door to

Fontaine. Asked, 'Why do you write?' he replied, 'Out of despair. I always feel desperate, so then I always try to write, I write always except when I am too despairing. If I should write again, I would write Under, Under, Under the Volcano . . . I write because I am a humourist. King Lear also was a humourist . . .'[42] Asked by another journalist about *Ultramarine*, he said he hoped no one would ever see or try to revive it, though Gide had translated some of it. He mentioned his play of *The Ship Sails On*, implying that his own novel was 'bad because derivative' of Grieg. At some point he showed Clarisse his manuscript of *Lunar Caustic*.

When Margerie returned and told him his family would not pay for him to go to Switzerland, he was, according to her, angry with Stuart; more likely he was pleased because the alternative was to return to Canada, where he was mentally more at peace. However, he still wanted to please her and she was still anxious to stay in Europe and find a job after she had parked him in Zürich. Her other idea was to try to publish her novels in France, and she had given copies to Clarisse in the hope that she could find a publisher.

When they heard that Julian Trevelyan was in Paris, they arranged to meet him for dinner. Trevelyan was shocked because Lowry, although well dressed, was drunk and would not eat, and to his embarrassment Margerie kept putting spoonfuls of food in his mouth. After dinner she said, 'Well, take your boyfriend out, but don't let him drink too much and then bring him back to our hotel.' When they left, Lowry wanted to go to the Grand Guignol, sampling every bar on the way. 'Well,' said Trevelyan, trying to limit this excess, 'every *other* one.' He was struck by the way Lowry spoke about himself, as if he were not there (much as his old hero Walter Greenaway had done). After the melodrama and eye-gouging they ambled back to the hotel bar for a last drink, and Lowry said that Margerie wanted to send him to be analyzed by Jung. Trevelyan, despite his Bohemian manner, was typically English and sceptical of such mumbo-jumbo. 'I don't think there's much wrong with you,' he said. 'When you want to write a book you clear the decks and write it. I don't think any psychoanalyst will do much with you.' He then took him back to his room, rather proud that he had brought Malcolm back in one piece and not too intoxicated. But there he said, 'Julian thinks all this psychoanalysis stuff is rubbish,' and Margerie, having spent the last six months persuading him to her point of view, was horrified. 'Oh, Julian,' she said, 'you've undone a lot of good work.'[43] Trevelyan judged her a very ambitious woman, but now her ambition to leave Malcolm in Zürich and find a job in Paris had come to naught. He had completely changed his mind.

It was probably at this point that she realized they would, after all, have to return to Dollarton. But Lowry wanted still to help with the translation, so it was decided to hang on until after Christmas. He carried on drinking steadily and Clarisse and Stephen Spriel found him of little use, and all too often he crept away to sit alone in dark obscure bars. He had been told never to return to Les Deux Magots, so found a drinking hole in the little *zinc* at their hotel in the rue San Benoît. There he was found one day by Norman Matson, Harold's brother, whom he had last met in New York in 1934. Matson and his wife were living in a house in the rue Cels in Montparnasse, and the Lowrys were duly invited to tea. Malcolm, however, being drunk, felt unable to meet anyone and repaired to a nearby bistro. Margerie suggested to Norman that he join him, and he found him there, drinking rum in the company of only a hostile madame, irritated, among other things, because he found her café 'uniquely interesting' and funny. He took Matson to a curtained arch at the back and dared him to peer into the alcove beyond. There, in a dusty gloom was suspended the life-sized effigy of a hanged man. The place was like no other, he said. It even had an aquarium. And indeed there was, with a herring too big for the tank inside. 'I find places like this, dark small places with their own meaning, everywhere,' said Lowry. 'Sometimes I think I first imagine them, see them in a nightmare and then find them actual and existent in the world. But the herring was special, wasn't it?'[44]

The Lowrys spent Christmas and New Year in Paris with the Matsons, drinking champagne and whisky and visiting the flea market,[45] before preparing to return to Canada. Clarisse was sad, in a fashion, to see the back of Malcolm, and insisted on hanging on to *Lunar Caustic* which she was keen to see translated into French. Just before they left, Lowry went for a last visit to Dr Courvoisier who provided him with a paregoric – something to soothe his nerves on the long flight ahead.

CHAPTER XXI

HALLUCINATIONS AND SHADOWS

1949–1950

> Tis we, who lost in stormy visions, keep
> With phantoms and unprofitable strife,
> And in mad trance, strike with our spirit's knife
> Invulnerable nothings.
>
> SHELLEY, *Adonais*

The realization that there was no future for them away from Dollarton must have been hard for Margerie to take, but at least there Malcolm could behave as he wished without bringing authorities, police and doctors down on their heads, and upsetting too many people. William Blackstone, having sampled civilization once more, was ready to withdraw again into the depths of the forest – to live among the Indians.

On Friday 14 January, they boarded a plane for Montreal with a stopover in London. Davenport arranged for a few old friends to meet him at the West London Air Terminal in Cromwell Road. As well as Davenport there was Arthur Calder-Marshall, the writer Randal Swingler, John Sommerfield, Innes Rose and John Green, the publisher. Calder-Marshall remembered Lowry being 'absolutely pissed', and with four hours to kill (their flight was delayed sixteen hours altogether), they repaired to a pub and ordered beer. Margerie, looking very worried and rather dramatic, said beer would be all right for him. In the pub he showed off his varicose veins and leg ulcers, announcing that he had the same illness as the King,[1] and when Calder-Marshall asked what he was working on after *Under the Volcano*, he replied 'Under Under the Volcano.' Then in the toilet he produced a large bottle of brandy from his hip pocket; beer was not enough. Calder-Marshall decided that Lowry was unlikely ever to finish another book.[2] He was probably not alone in thinking this. Since landing in France more than a year earlier, he had written nothing more than a few scratchy notes and a handful of disjointed letters. The manuscript of *Dark as the Grave*, and the copy of *Ultramarine* he had brought with him, remained untouched.

In London he had the shakes, which he blamed on Courvoisier's paregoric, and thereafter took three or four sonoryl a day, and continued for the rest of the journey in a semi-drugged condition. Next day, after a breakfast of coffee, bacon, potatoes, brandy and sonoryl they took off at dawn for Montreal, via Shannon and Newfoundland. However, the weather was so foul that after Shannon they were diverted to Reykjavik. On the flight to Iceland, he wrote, he had drunk countless whiskies and brandies while taking sonoryl, and yet had not become intoxicated. At the same time, he had eaten with a growing appetite.[3] At Reykjavik a blizzard kept them grounded for three more days. On the second night someone smuggled in drink from the grounded planes and Lowry consumed just over a pint of whisky. On the third day, back on the plane, he promptly ordered and drank six straight whiskies before settling down for the flight to Newfoundland. This time, however, they were diverted to Labrador, arriving at 3 a.m., when Lowry, his appetite miraculously restored, consumed vast quantities of turkey and vegetables, a quart of milk and a large amount of fruit juice. He followed that with three whiskies at the bar and more sonoryl at the airport.

After taking off for Montreal they had to return with engine trouble and Lowry slept a sound and prodigious sleep, as if catching up on what he had lost in the whole past year. Next morning he shaved with a steady hand and ate an enormous breakfast. Finally en route to Montreal he slept deeply but had nightmares.[4] In Montreal he drank cocktails and ate heartily, and on the flight westwards he and Margerie got through half a bottle of whisky together. In Vancouver they went straight to a pub, ordered beer and poured the rest of the whisky into it, had an enormous meal, then bought two more bottles of whisky and took the bus back to Dollarton where Lowry put himself to sleep with sonoryl. They were lucky to have made it; a US B29 following them to Iceland crashed in Scotland killing everyone on board.

They woke to a freezing morning, in what was in fact the worst winter in Vancouver's history. Despite the arctic conditions the shack was safe and dry, though Lowry's much-loved pier had been damaged. He built a fire, made breakfast, consumed sonoryl and the remainder of the whisky, and fought his way up the snow-clogged path to Cummins's store to buy provisions. He was amazed by his own sense of co-ordination. He had intended catching the bus at the store and going into town to buy more whisky, but suddenly – and this perhaps was a psychological turning point, he wrote – he returned to the shack and went for the rest of the day without drink.[5]

The following morning, 21 January, a week after leaving Paris, he felt as if he had never been away, and immediately slipped back into old habits, lighting the stove, making breakfast, doing the chores around the shack and now vigorously shovelling snow. Margerie had bought some gin which they polished off, but for the following two days he drank nothing. However, having run out of sonoryl he switched to allonal, a sleeping drug prescribed for Margerie. He began by taking one at night and one and a half during the day, but by the Thursday of that week he was taking nothing. It was as if he had never been ill. His need for drugs and the craving for alcohol had gone. The return to Dollarton had cured him.

> For the last year I had averaged 2½ litres to 3 litres of red wine a day, to say nothing of the other drinks at bars and during my last 2 months in Paris this had increased to about 2 litres of rum per day. Even if it ended up by addling me completely I could not move or think without vast quantities of alcohol, without which, even for a few hours, it was an unimaginable torture . . . I have waited in vain for the shakes, in vain for the D.T.s, or even worse horrors.[6]

As soon as he had settled he got back to work on *Dark as the Grave* and *La Mordida*, but his creative flow had been seriously affected since leaving for Europe fourteen months earlier. Also 'the King's problem', his varicose veins, were still troubling him. Soon after returning, he went to a new doctor in Deep Cove, Dr McNeill, who was instantly struck by his odd appearance and demeanour, his slurred and hesitant speech.

> 'I am a writer,' he said, 'but I have to dictate. My wife takes down what I say . . . Most embarrassing. Sometimes I have been in places where I was supposed to sign my name and when I pick up my pen my mind goes completely blank. My wife . . . does all the business. This has even happened to me in the bank.'

Margerie explained that he dictated standing up. 'He leans with the back of his hands on the top of the desk. Sometimes he will stand that way for what seems like an hour thinking of the proper word. At the end of the day his legs are all swollen and aching.' When the doctor examined his hands, he was surprised to find hard calluses on the back of the first knuckle of each hand. They were. he pronounced, 'anthropoid pads' – apes developed them from leaning and dragging the backs of their hands on the ground. Lowry was delighted. They lived the simple life as squatters on the beach, he said, but he did not know he had regressed back to the apes.

The doctor saw that his varicose veins stretched from groin to ankle, and suggested that he wear a surgical stocking, or dictate lying down or walking around. Lowry said he could only dictate standing still leaning the backs of this hands on the desk. An operation which meant a few days in hospital with three or four weeks convalescing was the only alternative, and he opted for that. When he was dressing, Margerie had to remind him to put on his socks, and in doing so she gave the doctor a knowing look. Here he thought was a man who required a great deal of looking after. It seems to have occurred to neither of them that the mischievous Lowry was acting the Consul, who makes his entrance in the *Volcano* minus his socks.[7]

Having had to relinquish the idea of a life in Europe free of Malcolm for a while, Margerie now had to settle back in the forest with a man whose mental state was, to say the least, unreliable. Probably as part of the deal for remaining there, he proffered her (or she extracted from him) a declaration which, anthropoid pads or no anthropoid pads, he wrote out for her to witness.

Resolution of the Higher Self

TONIGHT

Try *not*, under any circumstances, to get tight; at the first sign of any obliviousness take a spirits of ammonia instead of a drink.

Do not provoke any arguments or *lose temper*. Be sympathetic to dear Margie but try to finish work.

Get off will and a note at a sober moment.

Do *not* argue about having more drinks when suppertime comes.

Try to enjoy, also so far as possible, *use* drinks, all this with leading the whole drink business to some real and wise *lasting* solution, such as that you may reach a position shortly where it is not *necessary* to drink, where you may abandon it altogether without feeling it to be a problem, or subsumed with guilt, or handle it without its using you or your feeling afraid of it. This has to be done sooner or later: why not NOW? Both for Margie's sake and your own.

NO GUILT![8]

This was pinned above his desk, a ready reminder that Margerie's tolerance had its limits. As a further measure of his insecurity about her, he began a flood of little love notes from El Leon to Miss Harteebeeste which he left lying around for her to find, and there was always one waiting when she returned from shopping trips to Vancouver. The 'love' for her which he had rendered into fiction had become part of the fiction of everyday life.

The Italian translation, he heard, had after all been delayed and Cape wrote to say that the book had not quite clicked in England, and just under half the five thousand printed remained unsold. To this Lowry replied that, despite its poor performance there, the book continued to be heaped with praise in America and was required reading in at least ten American universities. In Canada sales had been poor, but it would soon be out in France as the main selection of Le Club Français du Livres. He had been sent a passage from the *Encyclopaedia Britannica Year Book 1948* reading, 'The year produced no new voice as commanding as that of the Canadian, Malcolm Lowry, in Under the Volcano, to presage a major movement among the younger writers of fiction.' His pride in this was unconcealed. It must, he told Cape, be a rare distinction for that august volume to give a writer from Canada precedence over any from America as a source of literary influence.[9] And thereafter he took every opportunity to quote this to anyone he wished to impress.[10]

Indeed Lowry was still a name to conjure with in the US. Erskine wrote to say that someone from the *New York Times* had phoned to ask what truth there was in the rumour that he had a new Lowry novel up his sleeve. Speculating on who had started the rumour, he wrote, 'I hope it was a major prophet.'[11] Lowry had informed Eugene Reynal, now with Harcourt Brace, of the *Encyclopaedia Britannica* accolade, and to his surprise got the reply, 'Books like *Under the Volcano* are very few and far between.' The fact that it had sold well had presumably changed the money man's mind about it. His mother, however, was still awaiting her complimentary copy. 'I should love to read one of your books,' she wrote, but appears not to have made the effort to order a copy.[12] In his reply, he told her, 'I am writing a comparatively optimistic book. It is even rather religious.'[13]

While working on his damaged pier in early March, he received letters from Erskine at Random House and from Frank Taylor, now working as a producer for MGM in Hollywood. Erskine wrote that Signet Books were publishing a pocket series of abridgements of books at twenty-five cents a copy, and wanted to know whether Lowry would be prepared to see an abridgement of *Under the Volcano*, with him doing the abridging. Erskine said he was 'a little horrified' by the idea himself, but Signet had recently done Joyce's *Portrait of the Artist*, and two novels by Faulkner. He had replied that it would be a difficult book to cut and there would be 'screams of anguish if anybody walked off with an adjective'.[14] Later, he said, he had had second thoughts because several hundreds of thousands who otherwise would not read the book might be enticed by reading only part of it into trying the real thing, and also Lowry might need the money. On balance he did not think it such a bad idea, but wanted Lowry's opinion.

Surprisingly enough, he was not averse to the idea of making changes, including a 'brutal cut' in chapter 1, a 'whopping cut' in chapter 6 as well as the guidebook extracts in chapter 10. He even suggested cutting some of the 'muddy Lowromancings' from the final chapter.[15] He must have been getting a bit desperate for money to agree to an abridgement of the masterpiece which three years earlier he had defended sentence by sentence so fervently to Cape. As to work in progress, he told Erskine, he was working hard on another book – 'at the moment like a dark belittered woodshed I'm trying to find a way around in with a poor flashlight.' But when he had got it into shape a little, he said, he would send him some of it.[16] The idea of sending his work to Erskine in bits and pieces had surfaced again.

Taylor wrote to say that under Dore Schary, MGM's head of production, he was working on a screen adaptation of F. Scott Fitzgerald's *Tender is the Night*, something Hollywood had been attempting for thirteen years. It was magnificent film material, he said, and they were creating a fine script. He had been surprised that so few Californians had read *Under the Volcano* and he was remedying this by handing out copies, including one recently to John Huston. 'He, too, is such a Mexican at heart, I'm sure he will be thrilled by it.'[17] (Ironically, it was thirty-five years later, in 1984, after over sixty screenplays, a long string of directors and false starts, that Huston finally got round to filming Lowry's book.) Taylor hoped he was well into his next novel, but Lowry was having difficulty picking up where he had left off.

The man then doing most to promote Lowry in Canada was Earle Birney, publishing his poetry, teaching his book at the university, and broadcasting about it. On 5 March the Lowrys went to 'an evening' at Birney's Vancouver home, where the poet read from his nascent novel *Turvey*. Lowry thought it excellent and funny, comparing it to *The*

Good Soldier Schweik and *Dead Souls*. Later, Birney sent Lowry his students' reviews of the *Volcano*, which delighted him. He valued Birney's friendship and encouraged him to look for a shack on the beach so they would be close.

Although resigned to the *Volcano*'s relative failure in England, it did not help his self-confidence to hear from Cape that the public had not responded to his book. If interest picked up, there was the possibility of issuing the 1,600 unsold copies in a cheap edition, but, he wrote with an unconscious last twist of the knife, there seemed to be a general idea that it was very much like *The Lost Weekend*, and sales that year had been negligible.[18] This on top of his varicose veins operation left him feeling low, and it was not until May that he next wrote to Erskine saying that he might have some instalments of his new novel for him in a month or so, and asking for a letter to cheer him up.[19] Erskine replied promptly, saying how pleased he was that he was writing again and that he wanted to see anything he could send him, but would, of course, keep it dark from Reynal at Harcourt Brace. 'Whatever the legal, proprietary, contractual, and what not machinery of publishers, etc., I want to see these parts, and I do hope you're working steadily and well. I don't have to tell you, and I couldn't, the degree of my interest in it, and faith.'[20] With luck, he thought, Reynal would let the *Volcano* go out of print, and he could buy back the rights at a reasonable price and sell them elsewhere. The implication was that he and Random House would be first in line for it. For that reason Lowry regretted having sent Reynal the *Encyclopaedia Britannica* plaudit, thinking it might encourage him to hang on to the book longer.

Birney had taken a shack just down the beach from The Wicket Gate, and gave a party for a group from his creative writing class calling themselves 'Authors Anonymous', to which the Lowrys were invited. Birney again read from *Turvey* and Lowry hypnotized all present with a reading of 'Sestina in a Cantina'. He found such occasions difficult without a drink, but tried hard to stay sober because of his recent operation. However, that evening one of the young guests goaded him into a drinking match and soon he was roaring drunk. Margerie, too, became tight, and by the end of the evening was sitting on the lap of one of the students while Lowry declaimed, 'Take her! I have had many children by her.' Finally he had to be carried home over the shoulder of the would-be seducer with Birney calling after him, 'Come down off your cross, Malc!'[21] He did, however, enjoy his friendships with the young writers, one of whom, Norman Newton, impressed him so much that he invited him to help with his long-delayed dramatization of *The Ship Sails On*. Birney's wife, Esther, was not as keen on the Lowrys as he was. She had been offended when Margerie marched in on their first day at their shack to say, 'Now, you're not to come and disturb Malcolm. No unannounced visits.' She had replied. 'The same goes for you. Earle has to work, too.' Nevertheless they did visit one another and Birney was able to observe Lowry both at work and at play.

> He was a man who was a spree drinker and he was a spree writer, too. He did things in great bursts of activity of one sort or another, and he would build up a head of steam. He would start – he wasn't an early riser particularly, most of the time – he'd get up about the middle of the morning and first thing off he might go for a swim. And then he would do a little reading, and the reading would start getting him thinking, and he'd begin to turn that reading into something he was writing. And he would start [writing], and he might go on then right throughout the evening and right on through the night, and he might still be working the next day. And if he ran out of paper he would use anything in sight, and if there was nothing left, just because it was coming out of him, he would start writing over sideways on top of what he had already written, until he would stop out of sheer exhaustion. Or he would get a blockage and then he would take a drink and then he might pass from writing to drinking.[22]

The strain of the past eighteen months finally caught up with Margerie, who was found to have a low blood-count. Early in July, she heard that her mother was ill, and decided to visit her in LA for a while, hoping at the same time to get Bert to examine her. Malcolm alerted Frank Taylor, suggesting they get together. They were probably not just thinking that they might interest MGM in filming their own books, for they had both read *Tender is the Night* since hearing of Taylor's interest in it. His own new book, Lowry said, was Pirandello in reverse – authors in search of their characters, but he was worried that the philosophical implications might prove fatal.

Margerie flew to LA on 6 July planning to stay for a week. Four days later, Lowry, lonely and lost, and thoroughly intoxicated, walked out on to his pier, and, forgetting that the tide was out, dived, jumped, or fell on to the rocks below. So much for his Resolution of the Higher Self. He lay in great agony for hours until someone heard his cries and came to his aid. Dr Victor Drache, who had a summer cottage along the beach, was called out, put in a boat, and rowed round to the shack. A group of people stood around Lowry as he lay on his back shouting with pain. The doctor recalled,

> We got him off the sand and he was roaring like hell. And we got him up to a balcony and into his room. And from what I saw, not knowing the man, not knowing how seriously injured he was I suggested he go to the hospital, and he roared at me, 'Not me! I'm not going to any hospital!' And he didn't. So I spent some time with him, and I think he had a few pills to relieve some discomfort. And he wouldn't go to hospital. He wouldn't. He roared and roared and roared. And so I left.

At least from his preliminary examination Lowry's injuries did not appear serious; he was not paralysed.

Next day the doctor was phoned and told that Lowry was still in great pain. However, he refused to go again to be roared and cursed at, so instead sent an ambulance which took Lowry to St Paul's Hospital, which was run by Catholic sisters, where he was admitted on 11 July. When the doctor saw him two days later he was told that he had yelled and shouted continuously from the moment he was admitted and was so difficult that the sisters threatened to eject him. On the evening of the 13th he had calmed down enough to be visited by Jimmy Craige, but next morning he suddenly became very disturbed and unruly and was put in a room with bars where, according to Dr Drache, he simply stood by the door and bellowed. The sister in charge threatened that if he were not removed he would be ejected and the doctor would lose his hospital privileges, too. So Lowry was moved that afternoon to the Vancouver General Hospital, which had a ward with a padded room where he could be properly contained. A psychiatrist was summoned and he was kept off alcohol and under restraint.

It was not until the 12th that Lowry sent a cable to Margerie telling her of his accident. She was lunching with Frank Taylor at MGM when she got a call to say that Malcolm was in hospital. She hurried back home on the 14th, where a message at the airport directed her to the Vancouver General. There she found him not only trussed up in a straitjacket in a padded cell in the psychiatric ward, but in a disordered mental state, claiming to have experienced 'the most incontrovertible psychic phenomena that has ever occurred on this plane . . . in broad daylight'.[23] Most likely he had suffered an attack of delirium tremens due to alcohol deprivation coupled with sedatives, but Margerie, though sceptical about the psychic experience, thought his hallucinations had probably been brought on by misprescribed drugs, and stormed into Dr Drache's office complaining loudly. 'She shouted at me, "Do you know who my husband is?" I said, "I don't give a goddamn who he is. Get off my back!" So she started telling me who he was. She said, "My husband wrote *Under the Volcano*." ' But the doctor, who had all but lost his hospital privileges at St Paul's because of Lowry, remained unimpressed. In any case, it appeared to him that she was drunk and he concluded that the Lowrys were 'a pair'.[24]

Because her attempt to impress Dr Drache had failed, Margerie called Bert Woolfan and asked him to talk to him, which he did. Woolfan was, among other things, an orthopaedic surgeon and Drache felt he was someone with whom he could deal, so sent him the result of Lowry's back X-ray. 'There appears to be a very slight wedge of the fourth dorsal body indicative of compression fracture here, with slight depression of its anterio-superior margin,' he wrote.[25] Both agreed on the phone, however, that he needed not just medical attention; he was a psychiatric case.[26]

After a few days in the Vancouver General, Lowry was fitted with a back-brace and discharged. Dr Drache, glad to see the back of both the Lowrys, chose not to follow him up. For the next six months, he had to sleep on a board and wear the brace into which Margerie laced him each day. If from the doctor's point of view the case was closed, for the patient the experience had been and continued to be apocalyptic. He had suffered and seen visions. He quickly began to make notes about the experience which he would eventually expand into another story, at first entitled 'Atomic Rhythm' and later *The Ordeal*. James Travers, he was sure, had tried to contact him from beyond the grave, and it troubled him deeply. Getting all this down at length, of course, again disrupted work on his trilogy of novels for Erskine. It had a further, more far-reaching, effect – it extended in his mind the idea of a trilogy to something more ambitious and extensive, a project which would have taken a lifetime to complete.

The Ordeal was never developed much beyond a sketchy first draft, but encapsulates many of Lowry's enduring obsessions. This time, Lowry in the guise of Martin Shriven, experiences a psychic (or hallucinatory) encounter with Travers and other figures from his dissolute past. Shriven is a writer writing a novel about writing a novel, (here *Under the Volcano* becomes *The Valley of the Shadow of Death*). He is a characteristic Lowry hero, seen in a hall of mirrors. Remembering how he sought out Juan Fernando, on whom he had based two characters in his Mexican novel, and found that he was dead, he recalls that he himself was made into a character, James Dowd, in the novel of a woman he calls Roxy Anne (Charlotte Haldane) while at university. In hospital, undergoing his psychic experience, Martin overhears Anne talking alternately to James Travers and Ralph Izzard, both of whom sneeringly refer to him as a sexual obsessive and plagiarist. He fears homosexuality and syphilis and women, the creatures of passionate agony who bring death to this world in a 'vicious circle of pleasure and abortion, of ecstasy, fear of disease and perversion and murder of souls'. It shows that Lowry continued to be strongly influenced by Aiken's misogynistic vision in *Great Circle*.

He wrote to Taylor of the 'grotesque' experience he had undergone at the hands of the malevolent nuns of St Paul's, and how the staff of Irish Catholics had decided to take out their spite on a Protestant Englishman, especially as it was Irish Day and he was the odd man out. It was, he wrote, 'a little island of super super English hating and bigotry set in a gasworks Canadian sea.'[27] Even the stretcher-bearers had stolen $40 and walked off with Margerie's binoculars. At the hospital they had fed him drugs which produced horrifying hallucinations, yet he argued that 'over sedation does not necessarily destroy the validity of a supernatural experience such as that: from a Catholic point of view however such a thing pertains to the devil . . .'[28] As a direct result, he added, the ward was closed 'for cleansing and exorcism'.[29]

More disruption had arrived in the form of the screenplay Taylor had commissioned for *Tender is the Night*, which Margerie had brought back from Hollywood and about which he wanted Lowry's opinion. It was, wrote Taylor, 'on the shelf', but could be taken down again if someone came up with 'a new twist'.[30] It was an invitation Lowry could not resist. As ever, the prospect of film work found him ready and eager to cast everything aside, and since Margerie was itching to be creative herself, they were soon reading and rereading Fitzgerald's novel and anything else of his they could get their hands on. In August, Lowry wrote to Taylor that despite the fact that both he and Margerie had been into hospital and in spite of his bad back making it difficult for him to search for notes or work on his novel, he was devoting himself to the problem of *Tender is the Night*. Although they thought the screenplay had 'possibilities', its writer seemed to have misunderstood the novel or its cinematic potential, and his invention was often applied at the wrong moments, moreover he had failed to understand the influence of cinema on Fitzgerald himself. The best thing he could do, he said, would be a précis much as Fitzgerald himself might have done, without playing up the incest motif. He thought it would make an absolutely first-rate film 'qua film', and said that he and Margerie would do a treatment.[31]

The back-brace inhibited work on his novels, but did not hinder him in other ways. For example, it did not stop him plunging off his pier for a swim still laced up, nor from correcting, with Downie Kirk's help, the proofs of the Club Français du Livre edition of *Au-dessous du volcan* which Clarisse had sent from Paris. Kirk enquired yet again about the Canadian story 'October Ferry to Gabriola', and it was his continuing enthusiasm, Lowry said later, that rekindled his own interest in it. It also gave Margerie something to work on with him in tandem, and in the fall she wrote to Matson to say that he could soon expect to receive a new version of it.[32]

Although work had been suspended on the Mexican novels and the 'intermezzo' *Eridanus*, by September Lowry reported to Taylor that considerable progress had been made with the film treatment of *Tender is the Night*. 'I believe as we are distilling [it], it offers a general and sometime particular architectonic of a great film,' he wrote, and he had not felt so creatively inspired since producing the best parts of the *Volcano*. He saw it, he said, as one of the greatest and most moving films of all time in the great tradition of movies which should combine the emotional impact of *Broken Blossoms*, *Isn't Life Wonderful?* and *Citizen Kane*. To this Margerie added that they thought they had an inspired new slant on the novel. Malcolm's genius was working joyfully and at full thrust, and in taking this one apart and putting it back together he was learning a great deal about 'the Novel'.[33]

A month later Taylor replied expressing delight that the Lowrys felt inspired by the project, which the studio could still take up if someone could add that new and exciting twist. Realizing perhaps that he had diverted Lowry from the fiction he was writing for Erskine, he warned that he was not commissioning them and that they continued working on the script at their own risk. 'You, of course, must decide whether or not you wish to take this kind of speculative chance.'[34] It was a chance they were well prepared to take and the work came to consume their creative energies almost completely. Lowry made it clear to Taylor that, unlike some writers who despised the movies but prostituted themselves to Hollywood, if he wrote a screenplay it would be something of worth and integrity because he thought highly of film as a medium.[35]

However, the creative idyll was disturbed when a local Town Planning Commission, aided and abetted by Percy Cummins, now a North Vancouver councillor, recommended in September that fifteen acres of land at Roche Point be set aside for a park and that plans be drawn up for future roads, walks, playgrounds and promenades. The threat of eviction had again become real. Equally unsettling was the announcement on 18 September that the pound sterling had been devalued by 30.5 per cent. Lowry's UK income shrank accordingly, and for the first time for several years they were threatened by financial difficulty. Once the position became clear, Margerie wrote to Matson explaining the problem and asking how much money of theirs he held and what royalties had accrued from sales of *Under the Volcano*. She also suggested he offer her mystery novels to Signet for their twenty-five cent abridgements.[36]

In Paris, Davenport had asked Lowry for poems for *Arena*, a new literary magazine he was editing with Randall Swingler and Jack Lindsay in London, and, in the first issue in the summer, he had included three of his Canadian poems and his story 'An Economic Conference' retitled 'Economic Conference 1934', and billed as 'a passage from an unpublished pre-war novel'. This story, published without permission, had apparently been left behind at Davenport's house in Hollywood in 1936. Lowry was angry at him printing this old story, but forgave him, it seems, for old time's sake.

The screenplay of *Tender is the Night* now absorbed them utterly; Margerie blocked out the scenes, Malcolm did the detailed writing and she then commented on his drafts, much as she had in the writing of the *Volcano*. They kept it secret from Matson and Erskine, partly because they did not want the news to get to potential competitors, and partly because the agent and editor were expecting a new novel from him. In November, however, he dropped a heavy hint to Erskine suggesting that his plans for the three-novel book had been effectively altered by his hallucinatory experience in hospital, and that he was 'working on a kind of enthusiastic deviation from usual work'. Margerie meanwhile wrote to Matson about two short stories, including the imperishable 'October Ferry to Gabriola', dropping never a hint about the screenplay. Having had no answer to her letter about their financial crisis, she followed this up with a further request to know what money of theirs he held and to enquire about selling her mysteries for abridgement.[37]

Just before Christmas he received news from France that book club orders for *Under the Volcano* were building up quickly, the arts review, *Liens*, had given it enthusiastic advance publicity, and the first chapter had been published in *Mercure de France* in November. These stirrings from continental Europe foreshadowed an interest in Lowry there which was to rival the initial enthusiasm he had met in America.

Winter on the beach was again ferociously cold and they put hot bricks in the bed for warmth. In a Christmas letter to Aiken, Lowry said that they were still living in the same old shack, but in frighteningly tough conditions that winter. Floods had destroyed neigbouring houses, but theirs still stood, and they were both happy and working hard. Despite a broken back he had swum until mid-December, even though just north of them temperatures were fifty-three below zero.[38] Work on *Tender is the Night* continued, interrupted only briefly when the page proofs of the Club Français du Livre edition of *Au-dessous du volcan* arrived from Paris, which Lowry had generously dedicated to Philippe Thoby-Marcelin as well as to Margerie. Fontaine were about to go out of business, and the book would now be published first in France by the Club. Margerie gave him for Christmas a copy of Kafka's diaries, a writer he enjoyed because he fed his heightened sense of persecution.

But at least they would stay put in Dollarton for the winter, however severe it was. Lowry probably realized that by involving Margerie with the screenplay he was keeping her lust for travel in check, and even her desire to leave him. The year ended on a note of high optimism, buoyed up by the forthcoming French publication of *Under the Volcano*, and the growing feeling that their script of *Tender is the Night* was developing into an important piece of creative work. The back injury was a thing of the past and in the new year he would finally throw off the hated back-brace. His sense of the ridiculous about the accident did not desert him entirely. What happened? 'I broke it . . . falling . . . off one of my own erections,' he told Aiken.[39]

Au-dessous du volcan was published by Club Français du Livre in hardback on 17 January, and Clarisse wrote to say that there would be a book launching party at the end of the month, and Correa would publish the paperback reprint for a wider readership later in the year. She added the news that in October Joan Black had married Lord Peter Churchill. Margerie was thrilled that a friend of theirs had married an English lord.

Although their financial plight was worsening they persisted with *Tender is the Night*, despite having no definite prospect of payment for it. The project had come to obsess them. They believed they were producing a masterpiece that MGM would find difficult to resist. Nevertheless, their situation was grave enough for Margerie to write a blistering letter to Matson demanding to know why he ignored her letters about money owed to them and about possible cheap editions of her mysteries. The pound's devaluation had 'knocked a great hole' in Malcolm's income, the situation was critical, and 'this time you've simply *got* to answer and right quick too.'[40] To this Lowry added that they were not exactly dying, though close to freezing, and attempting to get by on a hundred dollars a month. He hinted at their working on something secret which eventually he would be delighted with, but the work was 'conceived in love' with not even a shred of a financial motive, yet there should be no pity for their money trouble, because 'no one asked us to do it and it is our responsibility.'[41]

Matson cabled an immediate apology, saying Margerie's letters had never arrived. He also sent a cheque, temporarily relieving their financial worries. She replied that Scribner's had told her that her books were out of print and the plates destroyed, so could he, she asked, enquire about buying back the rights and selling them elsewhere. In view of the *Volcano*'s success in France she urged him to find the book a German publisher, and to get the latest news about a possible abridgement for Signet.[42]

Hope of selling a few short stories soon faded. Matson failed to place even one of Margerie's, and she wrote asking to have 'October Ferry to Gabriola' back for revision, while Malcolm urged him to try selling *Horse in the Sky* again, quoting a late review which said it was 'a wonderful book . . . far better than National Velvet'. But these feeble attempts to make money were mere distractions. They were still deeply engrossed in the screenplay and trying to survive an even worse winter than the last. Blizzards and freezing temperatures kept them more or less housebound. Outside their window great icebergs drifted past down the Inlet, and inside their typewriter iced up, the ink in Lowry's ink-well froze, and he even managed to get one hand frostbitten. When the thaw came there was the threat of floods and torrential rain.[43] But to Lowry there was a satisfying lesson to be learned from all this. It was a source of dismal satisfaction, he said in a letter drafted to Philippe Thoby-Marcelin, that one of the worst winters on record had brought civilization to its knees.

> No trains got through, the trams stopped running, the electric power gave out, the water was all but rationed. Yet our well remained full;

our oil lamps burned & we had no modern conveniences to go wrong: none the less it was hell, and we could not take off our clothes for nearly six weeks.[44]

Despite that hell, on 14 February they informed Frank Taylor that their *Tender is the Night* scenario was all but finished. Taylor was delighted and replied immediately, saying that shortly before he had been reading passages from the *Volcano* with Christopher Isherwood, 'rolling it on our tongues', and the same day had met Fletcher Markle, also now at MGM.

Strange coincidences still inspired Lowry's sense that hidden powers control our destinies. A copy of *Au-dessous du volcan* arrived on 24 February and the same day Charles Stansfeld-Jones died. He told Clarisse that the old magician had turned Catholic and died. Significantly, he said, someone had shot Stansfeld-Jones's old dog, his companion for fifteen years, on the very same day. Hopefully he would lead him across the river and not down the abyss. 'His last words to his wife were, "Do you know, I'm not really here, I'm beginning to function on a different plane already – it's quite an extraordinary experience, old girl –" '[45] This, according to Stan's wife, Rubina, was pure fabrication,[46] but Lowry's humorous version of his friend's demise fitted better his belief that truth lay on another plane of existence. It was all 'mysterious and eerie', he wrote.[47]

French acclaim for the *Volcano* was deeply gratifying, and Clarisse had now written asking for other work. He told Matson that the French considered *Lunar Caustic* a masterpiece, adding with ill-concealed pleasure, 'Should I be the one to disabuse them?'[48] He had also been delighted to hear that *Combat* definitely wanted to serialize the book, because Julienne LaPierre read it, and as for the translation, he told Clarisse, it was often superior to the original, and the lack of ambiguity in the language gave it greater depth and range of meaning as well as beauty of style. He gave her permission to publish *Lunar Caustic*, but said it was incomplete, and he had many ideas for revising it. Perhaps he felt that the translation to French could only improve it. He asked her to 'smuggle' a copy to Cocteau in the hope that it might inspire a play in him.[49]

Spring came early and spurred him to even greater industry, determined to see the screenplay finished. The success of the French *Volcano* also helped sustain him, and he wrote to Downie Kirk, 'They have decided that it is the writing on the wall, that your amigo is everything from the Four Quartets (which he has never read) to Joyce (whom he dislikes) – finally relating him to the Jewish prophet Zohar (of which he knows nothing).'[50]

By early April the screenplay really was all but finished and he was close to meeting his self-imposed deadline, showing that he could, when sufficiently enthused, work to order. His problems began with his own fiction, so highly personal that it readily became an endless form of self-analysis. With this screen adaptation he (and Margerie) had to keep in mind Fitzgerald and also the camera, a triangular relationship within a co-operative medium which worked against self-obsession. However, the script is studded and inter-woven with experiences from Lowry's own life and allusions to his work, published and unpublished, including echoes of *Ultramarine* and *Lunar Caustic* and passages taken from notes later developed into 'Through the Panama'.

Hearing that Dylan Thomas was coming to Vancouver on 6 April to give a broadcast and a couple of poetry readings, the Lowrys duly trooped in to the evening performance at the Vancouver Hotel. Afterwards they all met in a nearby pub and then went off to a party thrown in Dylan's honour. Thomas did not much like Vancouver, 'a handsome hellhole', he wrote to Caitlin. 'It is, of course, being Canadian, more British than Cheltenham.'[51] He was horrified that the pubs served only beer and that the hotel had bars segregated by sex. However, he was obviously cheered by Lowry's presence, and the small, cherubic, unkempt Welshman and the short, pink-faced, dishevelled Lowry must have made quite a couple in their respectable surroundings. They left the party for a talk with the Birneys and a young woman who had attached herself to Thomas. Later the woman invited everyone to her house. Finally the Lowrys went along and fell asleep on a couch, and when they woke next morning they were all alone in the house. They returned to the Vancouver Hotel to say farewell to Thomas, and found him in bed with, according to Margerie, 'the gal hanging over him'. He simply said, 'Won't somebody do something with this pest?'[52] Once 'the gal' had departed, the two men reminisced about their days together in Fitzrovia and at Anna Wickham's, and about old, dead friends, like James Travers. George Robertson was one of a group sent to get Thomas on to his plane for Seattle.

> We entered Thomas' room expecting . . . to find these people who'd been drinking all night laid out on the floor. Instead we found a most calm and sober group of people: Dylan Thomas was sitting on the

> bed cross-legged; Malcolm and Margerie were sitting on the floor with their backs to a wall; they were all still drinking . . . Malcolm was describing a hallucination he had in a hospital while taking treatment for the DT's. He said he was walking down a hall and arms and legs *burgeoned*. . . from the walls like plants or growths – a very striking image.[53]

The 'burgeoning hands' Lowry likened to those in Cocteau's film, *La Belle et la Bête*, seen at the local film club. The other Cocteau film which made a profound impression on him was *Orphée*. When he first saw it with Stan Fox, who ran the club, he sat riveted and immediately asked for a reshowing. It is not surprising that it should have stunned him, being perhaps the film which echoes his life most closely. A poet accused of plagiarism and pursued by the Furies and leather-clad motorcyclists heralding Death must have gripped Lowry as the realization of his own deepest fears. Orphée complains that his life is threatened by success. He has a love affair with Death and his relations with women are cursed. His guide to Hades is the shade of a young student who has gassed himself and who is called Huertebise. Finally he is shot and driven away in a chauffeur-driven Rolls. The film piles one Lowryesque image and fear upon another – death, the loss of a wife, mirrors, plagiarism, the inspired poet. It explores the territory of the dream, of the myth, of suffering and despair, of threatened and doomed love, the poet beset by and haunted by the Furies. This was the world Lowry had lived in for years. Across those years, the author of *La Machine Infernale* spoke to him again.

The screenplay, over four hundred pages long, was completed and duly dispatched to Taylor in Hollywood. Maybe it was overlong, wrote Lowry, 'but . . . we have left enough out for an opera by Puccini.' His version of *Tender* was idiosyncratic to say the least. The incest theme was cut out, he invented scenes not in the book, including a transatlantic voyage from his Panama notes, scenes from his own times in Paris (even the herring, transformed into a carp, from the dingy Paris *zinc* got a look-in), and newsreels à la *Citizen Kane*. The script suggests a strong identification with Fitzgerald and his hero Dick Diver on Lowry's part, and also perhaps with his strangely self-destructive marriage. The end of the story is given a positive emphasis – with Dick dying in an Atlantic storm helping a wounded captain of a sinking ship. The script was also meant as a commentary on the American film and on America, using Dick Diver as 'a sort of protagonist of the American soul'.

If Dick represents the heroic soul of America, Nicole, the schizophrenic wife, stands for the 'divided mind of the world', which America symbolizes. Lowry aimed at producing 'pure cinema' – much as in his fiction he attempted to explore his protagonists' consciousness (the camera eye of the interior) in all his motives and movements. It was, as he recognized, a dangerous road to go down – especially as potentially unbalanced as he was. But he hoped that it would fire Taylor's imagination, he said, and be regarded as 'an adjustable blue-print for an inspiration for a great American film'.

Perhaps because Margerie was his co-writer, he seemed happy on this occasion to sever the umbilical cord to the point of renouncing ownership. The screenplay, he wrote, could no longer be conceived of as theirs, and was now Taylor's property to dispose of as he saw fit.[54] Taylor wrote straight back to say he was immersed in their script. 'It requires my most careful attention and I don't wish to speak or think lightly of it, but even the most superficial glance staggers me with your brilliant, cinematic conceptions.' Despite being busy with another film, he was 'in a state of exquisite dazzlement everytime I pick it up. I think you have done an extraordinary job.'[55] But they would have to bear with him for a fuller reaction. Meanwhile, as if a leaf had been turned, and still charged with creativity, Lowry had returned to his novels.

Au-dessous du volcan was published in paperback by Correa on 10 May. Copies were sent to Phito, Cocteau and Gide. However, the serialization in *Combat* had been dropped, Correa fearing it would stop people buying the book,[56] a sad loss because serialization would have meant money up front. Their funds were getting perilously low, a situation only underlined by news from Innes Rose that Cape was disposing of remaining copies of the *Volcano* in a cheap edition. A statement showed earnings from Cape of £3 17*s.* 5*d.* for the second half of 1949. Lowry sent Rose an account of his 'vision' at St Paul's, and his 'visitation' from Travers. He asked whether Rose knew the address of Travers's mother whom he felt should be informed of her son's presence in some limbo between this world and the next.

As if on cue, Taylor wrote to say that he continued to be haunted by the enormous richness of their screenplay and once he had worked out a way to present it at MGM, they should ask for a flat fee for the script plus a weekly fee for any additional work required. He had, he said, discussed it with Jay Leyda, co-founder of the Museum of Modern Film Art, who was eager to read it, and with Joseph Mankiewicz at Twentieth Century Fox.[57] Just over a week later, Leyda wrote 'a fan letter' saying that Lowry had not wasted his time in 'putting an amazing film on paper'. Taylor, he added, was determined to take it on, though he also hinted that MGM were rather antagonistic to the novel. Lowry replied that they waited 'on hooks'.

As he turned back to his post-*Volcano* trilogy again, he was invited to write an article about Mexico for the *United Nations World* in New York. It was easy to accept but very hard to write, perhaps because he chose ground he had worked over already in *Dark as the Grave*. He called it 'Garden of Etla' and in it distilled from his experiences in and around Oaxaca something of that 'Higher Self' he found so difficult to live up to, even in Dollarton. 'Some people undoubtedly feel drawn to Mexico as to the hidden life of man himself; they wonder if they might not even discover themselves there,' he wrote. Having found his own 'Higher Self' there in the form of Juan Fernando Márquez, he drew a generous portrait of him under the name Fernando Atonalzin. According to the Oaxaqueñan, 'Every man was, in a sense, his own Garden of Eden. To this extent others could be seen as spiritual modifications of oneself. This was evil, but not wholly an illusion.' What was not an illusion was that you either found yourself inside this symbolic garden or were evicted from it. Overblown self-esteem was the surest way to expulsion, and then excessive remorse or sorrow for what was lost ensured one could never return. The ideal was Fernando's borrowed philosophy of La Vida Impersonal. He wrote of the Banco Ejidal and its mission to give even the poorest peasant a place of his own in the Garden of Etla, and of discovering that his friend was dead. In dealing with his sorrow he sought comfort from Bergson's saying that 'The sense of time is an inhibition to prevent everything happening at once.' The Garden of Etla was the perfect place to reflect upon this.[58]

For this article Lowry received a much-needed $75 and a letter from the editor calling it 'a little masterpiece'. He later told Stuart that in the interests of international co-operation he had resisted telling a few home truths about Mexico.[59] If he was nervous about Mexico, he was deeply concerned about anti-communist feeling in America, intensified when Senator McCarthy had launched his particular crusade in February. He vowed never to return to the United States while McCarthyism prevailed there.

America, however, still brought him the acclaim he sought. On 12 July, Isherwood wrote from Santa Monica about his 'wonderful script'. He had been greatly impressed by his bringing out new meanings and the greatness of the novel, which was a new sort of masterpiece with every right to be called *An American Tragedy*. 'I wait to see it filmed of course – but equally I wait to see your full script published with all your notes and comments . . . It *ought* to be printed as well as played, because much of it is for a mental theatre like Hardy's Dynasts.'[60] After Spender's letter of praise and Auden's congratulations on the *Volcano* three years earlier, a commendation from Isherwood meant that he had now been applauded by the three most prominent English writers of his generation, and he was quick to reply. Having written something sufficiently good to evoke praise from him, he wrote, was certainly a high spot in his life. 'I've often felt like writing to you in regard to your own work; I never thought I'd see the day you wrote me first.' What no one – Taylor, Leyda or Isherwood – had been impolite enough to say, however, was that the script was quite impractical, both too literary and too detailed, leaving little or no room for a directorial contribution. It was the script of a cinema-inspired novelist, not of a film-maker.

Although he needed the $75 from the UN, in an impossibly scrupulous gesture, he sent Matson $7.50 – the ten per cent he had not earned, and then in reply to a brief note from Erskine, brought him up to date with the launching of *Au-dessous du volcan*, and broke to him the news that he and Margerie had 'something' (the screenplay) about which they had to be 'enigmatic' for the time being – 'It is a case of not crossing one's bridges before one's chickens are hatched.'[61] Innes Rose sent Lowry's munificent £3 17*s*. 5*d*. from Cape, and, on his 'visitation' from Travers and his wish to contact his mother, advised him to 'let sleeping dogs lie', as this kind of communication could bring added distress to the family.[62]

The extent to which they had gambled on their film script bringing them a rich reward is evident from a letter Malcolm wrote to Stuart, who was himself being unhelpful about money. He hinted that he had something ambitious brewing. If it did not come off they would be 'in the soup' financially. Yet, if it did, 'soup may well start running out of our eyebrows in the form of dollars. But we can't count on it.' To ingratiate himself with Stuart he said that the state of the world made him rather conservative and he had ceased now to believe in 'progress'. He cited the loss of their old clockwork gramophone in the fire as a case in point. Clockwork gramophones were now unobtainable and if they bought an electric one they would need electricity installed and that would mean by law having to clear away part of the forest around their house, which they did not wish to do. Margerie had finally managed to replace the old gramophone with a second-hand one, but he did not consider the material progress of the mechanical age anything like worth the candle.[63]

Discovering José Ortega y Gasset's lecture on Goethe in the *Partisan Review*, he plunged into his philosophy. A passage from his *Towards a Philosophy of History* struck him, especially his distinction between the 'zoological' life of man – his biological existence – and his 'human' life' – the one he invents for his own well-being.

> Have we heard right? Is human life in its most human dimension a work of fiction? Is man a sort of novelist of himself who conceives the fanciful figure of a personage with its unreal occupations and then, for the sake of converting it into reality, does all the things he does – and becomes an engineer?[64]

This passage acted to catalyze a number of ideas which he had been exploring in *Dark as the Grave*. As he told Kirk,

> I can see something philosophically valuable in attempting to set down what actually happens in a novelist's mind when he conceives what he conceives to be the fanciful figure of a personage, etc., for this, the part that never gets written – with which is included the true impulses that made him a novelist or dramatist in the first place.

Pirandello had seen all this in *Six Characters in Search of an Author*, but Ortega had turned it into a theory of history. 'Man is "what has happened to him".' Compared to Sartre's Existentialism, Ortega's philosophy 'gives value to the drama of life itself, of the dramatic value of your own life at the very moment you are reading'.[65]

In the same letter he disapproved of Soviet Communism because of its restrictions on freedom of expression, and because he realized that an artist had no future except when free to express himself. His true enemy was totalitarianism, whether of the left or the right – hence his growing alarm at the intolerance sweeping the US. 'There is more hope and life in Europe than meets the eye, and that its liberal tradition – which extends over here – will eventually save the day.'[66] His mind had been further concentrated on this issue having also read Orwell and received a strongly anti-communistic letter from Stuart.

That 'liberal tradition' did not extend, however, to the case of capital punishment in Canada, something Lowry opposed with passion. When an eccentric, probably schizophrenic waterside dweller, Frederick Ducharme, living close to Dollarton, was found guilty of the 'sex murder' of a young girl and sentenced to be hanged, he wrote impassioned letters to the press opposing the death penalty as barbaric. Hangings in Vancouver were carried out in a disused lift-shaft and the gruesomeness was intensified by detailed, almost gloating reports of executions carried by local newspapers. To Lowry these practices were obscene and he made a collection of news items about murders and hangings, and the horror of capital punishment became a theme he was to explore in a future work.

The European interest in him continued to grow, and by now he had received foreign editions of the *Volcano* from Norway and Denmark as well as France. When one of Matson's assistants wrote in July to say that a German publisher was keen to do a translation, he was eager to explain for the Germans that he was not 'a one book author' but was busy with a larger project for three novels linked to the *Volcano*, the overall title for the four to be either *The Ordeal of Sigbjørn Wilderness* or *The Voyage that Never Ends*. He hoped to have parts of these novels published, but completing the whole project would take a very long time.[67]

However Europe had provided no money since their return from France and the coffers were getting low. On 17 July, Lowry finally took the humiliating step of asking Matson to loan him $200 (preferably $300). Prices, he said, had risen 1,100 per cent and his income had dropped to $90 a month. He thought it also an appropriate time to confess 'the Great Secret' that, entirely on spec, they had spent six months slaving over an elaborate film adaptation of *Tender is the Night*. He could not say exactly that Taylor had initiated this, he said, because a full script was not what they had been asked for, and they had done it entirely at their own risk. However, he added, it was of course understood that Matson would handle the business side of things. Nor was it just a Hollywood Dream. The reports on it had been so staggeringly complimentary they could hardly take it in. Nevertheless some misgivings had arisen in their minds. No doubt, he wrote, they were unwise not to have involved him until they were 'staring the Grocer in the face', but they had wanted to surprise him with a full-blown success and had not wanted to look foolish by promising something which finally came to nothing.[68] But a Hollywood Dream it still was. They had tried to be prudent by setting their own deadline to their speculative screenwriting, but now they were reduced to begging for money.

Lowry suggested that his Mexico article could be sold to the *Readers' Digest*, and perhaps Harcourt Brace could be asked for an advance on

Dark as the Grave. It was based on Matson's own idea that, 'A book could be written about writing the *Volcano*.'

> That is the whole point, what I have set out to do, bearing in mind . . . E. M. Forster's dictum that no one has yet written the history of the human imagination. The result – parts of which ought to be eminently saleable meantime – ought to win us the Nobel Prize or at least a free trip to Chinatown and a visit to Helzapoppin.

Of course, if the Hollywood thing came up and he were working on that he would not want to be tied down to a novel deadline. He wondered also how he could get out of his Harcourt Brace contract so that he could send his next novel to Erskine at Random House.[69] Matson immediately cabled $250. Thanking him copiously, Lowry replied that there was still no news from Hollywood, but even as he wrote there might be a letter or telegram awaiting them at the post office.[70] There was no telegram, nor any letter, except a bright one from Evelyn 'thrilled by his literary successes' and a gloomy one from Stuart about the threat of communism following the outbreak of the Korean War in June.

By the end of August, Matson sent terms of the German contract and Lowry then hinted that *Lunar Caustic* might be available for them next. He had already given permission for it to come out in France.[71] However, the need to make money led him to offer a short story to the Canadian Bank of Commerce, whose magazine included short fiction. He called it 'Sooner or Later or So They Say', a seven-page version of the later novella, 'Elephant and Colosseum', based on his encounter with Rosemary the elephant in the Rome zoo. It is about Harry Wilderness, Canadian author of a humorous novel about a cargo of wild animals, unknown in Rome except by Rosemary the elephant, who had been part of the experience which inspired the book. As the saying goes, 'If you sit here long enough, sooner or later, so they say, you were certain to meet someone you know.' Looking at it, he thought the story had 'dropped straight out of heaven', and sent it to the bank.[72] To Lowry's annoyance and disappointment, it was turned down as too long and unsuitable for them, and he wrote angrily that it was a comic and inoffensive story which could be shortened. He liked it and thought it 'first-rate of its genre'.[73]

If Lowry was again frustrated at not getting published in North America, in France he was being greeted as a major new literary figure, as reviews sent by Clarisse showed. Pierre Hambourg in *La Rouge et le Noire* wrote that *Au-dessous du volcan* might have been written by Baudelaire, and made complimentary comparisons to Verlaine, Valéry and Poe. Gilbert Sigaux in *La Table Ronde* admired the way he had created his own language and universe, and Paul Gadenne in *Cahiers du Sud*, found it rich and powerful.

Despite the bank's refusing his elephant story, Lowry completed another one set in Rome, 'Strange Comfort Afforded by the Profession', a subtle story put together from a series of notes which he happened to find in the same notebook. On a visit to Rome, Sigbjørn Wilderness, an American writer on a Guggenheim Fellowship, visits Keats's house and makes notes on the various relics kept there, including Shelley's marriage certificate to Mary Wollstonecraft and the letter from Keats's friend Severn about his illness and death. In his notebook he also copies the sign found in the Mamertine Prison, 'The lower prison is the true prison', and makes notes on the house where Gogol wrote part of *Dead Souls* in 1838. Rereading these notes, he reflects on the sinister line from Severn's letter on Keats's death – 'On Saturday a gentleman came to cast his hand and foot.' The shades of the many writers who had visited Rome haunt him. He then sees at the other end of his notebook observations recorded in America – graffitti like 'Dirty degenerate Bobs was here from Boston,' and notes from a visit to Poe's house in Richmond, Virginia, and passages from Poe's letters there. Their tragic tone reminds him of a letter he himself sent from Seattle to a Los Angeles lawyer in whose charge his family had placed him to be kept on twenty-five cents a day. This links him to the great brotherhood of dead romantic writers, and their presence in death affords him the strange comfort which the profession provides. Lowry had once cynically noted that Canadian stories did not sell in America and if he changed Vancouver to Seattle it would make all the difference. He had made this change, now he sent it to Matson with a recommendation that, since it was 'a decidedly literary story', it be sent to the *New Yorker*.

With no word from Hollywood, he said, they had been working something like ten hours a day at stories similar to 'Strange Comfort', though that was the only one completed. If it came off it would be encouraging because he needed to make some money if he was to get back to his novel in a whole-hearted fashion. And parts of that might also be saleable.[74] Not only had work on *Tender is the Night* disrupted work on his novels, but waiting for news of it kept him away from them still longer. It was need of money that had forced them almost in desperation to short-story writing. At the end of September, he wrote to Aiken, now occupying the Chair of Poetry at the Library of Congress in Washington: 'We are working hugely so finances may improve, with a rush.'[75] It was three and a half years since the *Volcano* had been published and its sequel was stuck firmly on the rocks.

In early October the eviction scare returned briefly, but he was more worried by the pound's devaluation, which had further worsened their finances, and he hoped desperately for an advance on the German translation. Matson had written to say that 'Strange Comfort' was not right for the *New Yorker*, but the spate of short stories continued. He was working on as many as four of them simultaneously, he wrote, so they might soon have enough money to pay off all they owed him. In the meantime he wished that his daemon would stop tormenting his mind sometimes. 'I suspect him darkly of having been trained in the school of Torquemada.'[76]

The daemon, however, was persistent, and on 14 November he announced a list of half a dozen stories which they needed to sell before 1 December. With price rises of 270 per cent and a costly false alarm about Margerie having a brain tumour, they would be broke within two weeks.[77] The stories, in their probable order of arrival, were 'October Ferry to Gabriola', now entirely rewritten by himself, 'Venus and the Evening Star', a Mexican story by Margerie, then 'Present Estate of Pompeii'; 'Homage to a Liberty Ship'; 'Deep Henderson', about a dying jazz musician travelling to Haiti; 'The Course', a story about Hoylake; 'A Heartwarming Episode' about an American playwright visiting a puritanical English home, which dealt with the cultural debt England owed to America; and 'Gin and Goldenrod'. He acknowledged having been 'flawlessly wrong' in predicting the saleability of his work, with the exception of the *Volcano*, but had now mapped out *Lunar Caustic* as a novel to be part of his 'whole work', *The Voyage that Never Ends,* which, he said, he could not wait to begin working on.[78]

Worries about her health and the prospect of another freezing winter at Dollarton led Margerie to hope to spend the winter in California, where they could get assistance, financial and medical, from Bert. But Lowry was determined to avoid the US while the McCarthy witch-hunt continued. Reluctantly she agreed to stay on, but in return he made an extra effort to promote her writing. Over the coming three years, he told Matson, they were aiming to make him and themselves a great deal of money. 'It is my prophesy that this will be done.' Not just cheerfulness but unrestrained optimism had broken in. The German contract was signed on 14 November, and Lowry felt that at least one more important cultural victory had been won.

Hoping to liberate some of his English capital he had written to the lawyer administering his trust, asking for help, but received no reply. So in October he had written a long, rambling letter to Stuart describing the tribulations of life in the wilderness – fighting the elements, coping with ill-health and the threat of eviction, and having to endure 'the crucificial position of a writer in Canada'. There must be some provision in Arthur's will to cover such a crisis. If all else failed he might write directly to Evelyn. 'Damn it, I shall always remember she once gave me a threepenny bit.'[79] But Stuart was not much more trusting of him than his father had been. For obvious reasons, the Trust had been set up to ensure that the capital could never be touched, and having seen Malcolm almost committed to an insane asylum, he could hardly be expected to want to alter things. When nothing came of this, Margerie, who already felt let down by Stuart in France, decided that Malcolm's brothers were against them, and probably persuaded Malcolm himself to much the same view.

The news came from Stuart that Evelyn was dead. She had died, aged seventy-seven, of diverticulitis, peritonitis and heart failure on what Lowry claimed was her birthday, 7 December.[80] This, he told Downie Kirk, had thrown him 'emotionally out of gear somewhat'. Perhaps he was taken by surprise that he did not react with any overt display of sorrow, but seems to have felt it necessary to justify not doing so and to read some meaning into it. In such circumstances, the effects were not always outwardly visible, he said. One was pitched into a spiritual crisis, caught 'between the deathward wish that unconsciously wishes to follow one's mother into the grave, and the lifeward one that is striving once more within the conditions of birth itself, towards a rebirth.' Characteristically, he then found some universal significance in this and in so doing made one of the most remarkable prophecies anyone could have made at that time.

> Grim though the picture seems, it doesn't seem half so hopeless as it did in 1939 – or even 1938. Even if communism were temporarily victorious it doesn't carry with it such a hopeless *teleology* of tyranny – even if tyrannical in its present phase – as did Nazism. In short anything [that] is a revolution must keep moving or it doesn't revolute: by its very nature it contains within it the seeds of its own destruction, so by 1989, say, everything ought to be hunky dory, all of which certainly doesn't make it any easier to live in 1950.[81]

He refused to take sides in the Cold War, thinking it tragic that a peacemaker like Nehru got so little hearing. Evelyn had died intestate, so Arthur's money was to be divided equally between his sons. Stuart wrote that as chief executor of the estate he was now able to offer some immediate help, and that Malcolm's financial prospects were greatly improved (though it would be some years before he got his hands on what was termed 'Malcolm's Settled Share'). So, any sadness he may have felt about Evelyn was tempered by a sense of joyful release from the fear of poverty, and there was no great note of sorrow in any of his letters, no suggestion of mourning. He seemed more concerned about painful calluses on his fingers which made it difficult for him to write.

CHAPTER XXII

THE VOYAGE THAT NEVER ENDS

1951–1952

Out of the trunk, the branches grow; out of them, the twigs. So, in productive subjects, grow the chapters.

HERMAN MELVILLE, *Moby Dick*

They had to turn down several New Year invitations because Margerie was suffering from neuritis and Lowry had a 'heavy heavy' hanging over his head, he told Neilson, because of his mother's death – though the more likely cause was his financial position and the lack of news from Hollywood. Once Margerie felt better they resumed their social life, though Lowry, as ever, found it difficult to cope with company. Faced with the ordeal of meeting people, he took phenobarbital, not a drug to mix happily with alcohol. A couple of days after a party at Kirk's he wrote, 'I am . . . told I used bad language in front of your wife . . . this is utterly inexcusable of course . . . But I was not so aware and here you must believe me. I am deeply sorry.'[1]

He was cheered when Phito, now in Washington and hoping for a Guggenheim scholarship, sent him a copy of his newly published novel, *The Pencil of God*. But towards the end of January the weather deteriorated and they were again beset by blizzards as well as debt. With their radio still out of action they were more cut off than ever, something Lowry accepted and Margerie endured for his sake. By the end of the month Cummins was getting awkward about credit, and Lowry asked Matson to speed up payment of the $150 for the German translation rights, as 'on its expectation we are . . . practically dependent for something to eat . . .' All this made writing no easier, even though there was now the prospect of some family money following his mother's death. However, they could only promise Cummins that money was 'on the way'.

Impatient for news of their screenplay, Lowry wrote to Frank Taylor, who was now with Twentieth Century Fox. Taylor replied that the atmosphere there was more encouraging than at MGM. He had given their script to Joseph Mankiewicz, and although he was very busy, what he had read so far had 'aroused him'. Also, Arthur Mitzener's new biography of Fitzgerald had created a fresh interest in the writer, and he had sent a memo to 'the front office' about him and his work on *Tender*.

If at that their hopes shot up 'like a rocket',[2] a letter came in early February which gave him pleasure of a more substantial sort. Clemens Ten Holder, engaged by the Stuttgart publisher Ernst Klett to do a German translation of the *Volcano*, wrote saying that it was already half done, and added, 'I consider it the most important novel that has been written in our time or can be written.' However, he complained, the book 'struggles against being put into German',[3] the principal obstacles being the poetic language and the musical rhythms. He sent a list of questions, and among other things, was perplexed by the Consul's reading *double entendres* into the menu in chapter 10. Lowry asked Kirk to translate this letter and in return promised to dedicate the German edition to him. How, he asked, could he explain the obscenities of the menu if the translator were a woman? He would have to reply in English because, 'I could scarcely elucidate a point in German that depends upon mistakes being made in English by a Tlazcaltecan [*sic*] translating from a misprinted menu in Spanish and French.' Perhaps prompted by Ten Holder's letter, and his current concern with short-story writing, he added that he was trying to learn more economy of style.[4] The ideas he wished to explore in his stories, however, were not always capable of being expressed in such pure and simple language.

On 12 February, Matson sent the depressing news that their stories had all proved unsaleable, and that the advance of $150 due for the German edition had been postponed. He suggested approaching Harcourt Brace for an advance on his next novel, though it would mean agreeing a deadline. Lowry, however, wanted a different publisher. In desperation he wrote to Erskine, asking for an immediate loan of $200, explaining that over the past six months, although they had worked hard, they had used up all their capital and were now scraping along on a devalued monthly income. The store was about to stop their credit and Margerie was in constant pain from a growth affecting her teeth and he could not afford her X-rays. 'This is a callous and barbarous country in many ways . . . Not Maxim Gorky himself could dream up any worse privations than we, and especially she, have had to suffer this winter.'[5] Stuart's promised help had not materialized and eviction still threatened. They were near to despair and worry was preventing them writing the stories which could save them.

Despite Matson's Harcourt Brace suggestion Lowry affirmed his loyalty to Erskine, but was anxious that this together with his request for a loan should not be seen as moral blackmail, and gave a hint of the grand project he was brewing. 'I have unsmugly worked out an unsmug project in my mind which, if of huge proportions, would more than live up to your expectations of me, if only I can find a chance to begin to execute it.' Because so much work was lost in the fire, he had been unable to recreate it or get it and his Mexican experience into proper focus until now, and since Erskine's departure he had felt that he lacked a publisher and had been somehow excommunicated as a writer. But as to the projected multi-volume novel, he assured the editor, it should go on earning money for its publisher well beyond its author's death. The package also, he added, included the *Volcano*.[6]

With nice timing Erskine cabled $200 on 19 February, the fourth anniversary of the publication of *Under the Volcano*, and was quite hopeful that Lowry would be able to leave Harcourt Brace for Random House. Lowry was buoyant. He truly believed, he wrote back, that his failure to make headway with the novel was an uneasiness about being without Erskine. 'It must be obvious by now that I'm not going to write anything for Reynal Harcourt Brace, yet I have never in my life felt or been more creative.' Once Matson had got him free of Harcourt Brace he could discuss the entire immense and intricately conceived project with him.[7]

Two weeks later Matson forwarded the $150 due for German translation rights. There was good news for Margerie, too; her toothache was found to have been brought about by her grinding her teeth, and was curable simply by knowing its cause. But then she went down with 'flu and Lowry's time was taken up nursing her through it. The flow of stories slowed because he depended on her typing drafts and his own typing had fallen out of practice. Stuart, in the mean time, sent word that money would be coming at the end of March, and sought Malcolm's permission for Inglewood to be sold.

On 20 March he informed Matson that he had discussed his plans with Erskine and, 'So complete was his understanding of . . . creative sympathy with my work that psychologically and in every way it seems to me unthinkable that I could ever have another editor.' He had been told in utmost confidence that Random House would be delighted to have him, and there was even the possibility of a contract enabling him to follow Erskine if he left. He thought that without Erskine to discuss it with, his work was somehow not going right. He then announced that he had written in longhand 'a sort of whole first draft' of his new novel but it would take three months to have it typed up. It was not, he added, just one novel but three, and not three but six (including the *Volcano*). Three of these were short, including *Lunar Caustic*; another was a short intermezzo. 'The whole fills me – and I hope will you, eventually, with the wildest enthusiasm and in fact consumes me day and night.' Without Erskine, however, he could not begin even to speak about it in practical terms.

As to his short stories, 'Themes from the novel keep getting into mine and giving them elephantisis. Then again, there are parts that will be part of the novel . . . '[8] What Lowry was highlighting was the difficulty he had in finishing a single work. Already he had, in various stages of incompletion, *Lunar Caustic*, *Dark as the Grave* and *La Mordida*, not to mention the aborted *Ordeal*. It looked, in some way, as if he had suffered a great loss of self-confidence since the publication of the *Volcano*, as if he felt it an impossible achievement to follow. Even the *Tender is the Night* screenplay was completed only in tandem with Margerie. The new project, *The Voyage that Never Ends*, was perhaps one way to justify to himself this erratic way of working – the several novels on the go all became part of a gigantic web of stories centred on an over-arching theme. But he had had difficulty enough finishing the *Volcano*; trying to complete a giant project like this would be six times more difficult. He was happy to see *Lunar Caustic* published singly in French as it was, but as part of the whole scheme he meant it to achieve a new level of perfection, and that would take time and freedom from distraction. It was as if the whole grand design had been conceived in such a way that it could never be fully completed to his satisfaction.

As if confirming this he wrote to Erskine, 'The short stories that have nothing to do with the novel I tend to be schizophrenic about, to the detriment of the stories themselves. The ones that have something to do with the novel sometimes seem to suffer from not being bona fide chapters.' But he had never been more creative, he said, and was determined to send off as many of the stories 'disciplined to their form' as possible over the next two months. His problem was that being so continuously creative he hardly had time to get down a quarter of what he wanted to write.[9] To Margerie he explained, 'It's all written down on the walls of a dark room and what I have to do is walk around and see it – and copy it down.'[10] At some times, it seems, the room was darker than at others.

The arctic winter suddenly gave way to spring, further raising his spirits. In a burst of energy he wrote a closely typed twelve-page letter to Ten Holder. It was an expansive and confiding letter, introducing himself to his German alter ego, discoursing on himself and his life, before addressing his questions point by point. He tried to explain the intricate web of allusions and cross-references down to the level of 'sub-sub-sub plot of the novel', and the play of voices overheard, as if a doom-laden counterpoint were being played against the major chords and melodies of the narrative. He discussed the irony of the people in dark glasses in chapter 2 really spying on Hugh while the paranoid Consul thought they were after him. The book could be seen as 'a shadowy filmic fiction of M. Laruelle', and Hugh and the Consul were doppelgängers but also 'separate breathing human beings' and not merely symbols. He tried to explain the menu, which he had been told was now 'famous', though, he said, the success of the book had always been 'at a great distance' from him. Then painfully slowly he went through every humorous connotation of every item on the menu until the meaning and double meaning could not have been plainer, and in so doing showed his exuberant enjoyment in word associations and playing with meanings to the point of absurdity. The inadvertent and deliberate misreadings were linked, he said, to the Babel motif at the end of the book. The letter was an extraordinary exercise in deconstruction of his own creative process, akin to the analysis through which he so often put himself, and has since been seen as a gift to academics wanting to understand his creative process or catalogue his literary associations.

By the end of the first week in April, almost a year to the day that the *Tender is the Night* screenplay was finished, they heard from Frank Taylor that Darryl F. Zanuck, in charge of production at Twentieth Century Fox, was unenthusiastic about Fitzgerald. However, Fletcher Markle and John Houseman at MGM were preparing a script of the novel hoping to get Dore Schary's approval, with Markle's wife, Mercedes McCambridge, in mind for Nicole, and Ray Milland for Dick Diver. He suggested Lowry try to interest Markle in taking their script for MGM.[11] If the rocket of hopeful expectations now fell to earth again, their spirits were soon raised by a friendly note from James Agee, who had just finished the screenplay of *The African Queen*. He had seen their screenplay and what he had read he thought great – 'because besides every accomplishment of insight and atmosphere, you're of course one of the maybe dozen really original, inventive minds that have ever hit movies.'[12] Yet that original and inventive mind was making next to nothing from his writing. In May he received his Cape royalties for the second half of 1950 – £2 8*s.* 6*d.*, which, minus commission, amounted to £2 3*s.* 8*d.*

By now they had lost a number of their friends. It was not long before they parted company with the Birneys. The end came for Esther Birney when the Lowrys came to dinner and Malcolm drank so much that his talk began to veer out of control, his sentences growing longer and more elliptical, often punctuated by long silences, before returning to the complex ideas he was trying to articulate. Birney noted the way his drunkenness progressed from talkativeness towards intoxicated inspiration.

> In its earliest stages it was marvellous to behold because he would become very eloquent and tell stories and the stories would then move into the room and things that he was imagining at one moment the next moment would be real for him. The corners of the room would be peopled with familiars, invisible to us, and he would be going over and talking to them, and not just talking to them – pleading with them, sweating. You could see the sweat coming off – really in a horrible state, and what would follow would be a stage in which he was trying to say something and couldn't say it any longer – the words would be choked in him. He would be trying to talk about something so mystic that he couldn't express it.[13]

But as Jan had noticed years before, Malcolm enjoyed sounding enigmatic – the more mystifications he uttered, the more people were impressed. Often he would be caught glancing at his audience with a cheeky grin as if to see the effect he was having. But on this occasion he went too far and announced loudly, 'Earle is only cultivating me for the use of my name.' Esther was outraged and told Earle that she did not want the Lowrys coming to her house again. He laughed and said, 'Oh, Malc was drunk when he said it. He didn't really mean it.' He, like some others, was prepared to tolerate him because of his genius, but that evening marked a parting of the ways with the Birneys, who finally sold their shack and moved away. Lowry had also lost touch with Noxon, had heard nothing for over six months from Aiken and Davenport, and even the good-natured Marjorie Kirk was no longer keen on his visits. But he was still in touch with A. J. M. Smith, who brought the American poet Theodore Roethke to see him that spring.

Perhaps it was a sense of growing isolation which led him to respond so readily when a young New York postgraduate student, David Markson, wrote to him in June. 'I am 23, a foetal novelist . . . I have to do a thesis and have convinced my adviser that *Volcano*. . . merits consideration.' In preparation for this, he said, he had been rereading Joyce, Dante, Djuna Barnes and Faulkner, and, worried by his own limitations in tackling the thesis, asked for Lowry's attitude to the book seven years after its completion.[14] He almost spoiled his chances by asking after *Ultramarine*, claiming a fetishistic curiosity about first novels. Here was the first thesis being written on the great book, something Birney had warned him would happen. But he was flattered, and sent a brief note offering to help; 'If I can do anything to lighten such a grim chore for you in a hot summer I certainly will be glad to . . . '[15] He thought, too, that a letter from Columbia University to British Columbia addressed to himself was a mystic sign he could not ignore: 'My name means "Servant of Colomb" and we have two Columbias in the address.' Moreover, Markson's address was 60 Forest Avenue, and Lowry lived on the edge of a forest – more signs.[16]

Within two weeks, having been delayed, he said, 'by certain auxiliary circumstances', he wrote a friendly and much more detailed reply to Markson. As a matter of fact, he wrote, 'I too seem to have been reading a bit of Faulkner hotly pursued by Djuna Barnes, Dante, Joyce, etc., and feeling frightened by *my* limitations.' Repeating his standard advice to young authors, he recommended taking his limitations to Palembang – 'after all they can be among the most valuable cargo one has, those limitations.' He enclosed the preface to the French edition of the *Volcano*, saying this best expressed how he felt about it. He was writing 'the history of someone's imagination', but, he had had some setbacks. He warned Markson not to be misled by references in his preface to the Cabbala, which played only an incidental part in the book, and approved Joyce, Dante, Barnes and Faulkner, believing they were writers who in youth reacted against a ready-made tradition foisted on them by teachers. It was the writers the writer discovered for himself which were the most valuable. He had only recently discovered what a 'tremendous writer' Faulkner was. But *Ultramarine* was an 'abortion' – 'of no interest to you unless you want to hurt my feelings.' It had never been printed as it had been meant to be and would have to be rewritten. He mentioned *Lunar Caustic*, and hinted at a larger plan of which it would be a part. He got in his ritual reference to *Horse in the Sky*, wrote warmly of

Aiken, and ended by recommending their 'sunfilled and seay life' on the beach, inviting Markson to visit them.[17]

Early in June their financial position improved. A slight rise in the pound against the dollar increased their monthly income to $98 and they received a lump sum of $560 from Arthur's estate. Now the most pressing worry was the fear of eviction. An American company had bought up the surrounding land and Malcolm's only hope was that they would be more humane than the Canadian authorities. But as ever he thought the experience could be useful to him as a writer. Their intermittent eviction scares provided 'a situation of some universal significance' he had always intended to work into the novel, he told Erskine. And he was still gripped by his old lurking fear, that somehow his life was being controlled by his own writing. His work had been inhibited recently by these anxieties – 'the more so since it has been as if the plot of the novel, which gets into all the short stories too, were catching up with me.' What they had been going through would give their work a sounder quality.[18] All suffering, he suggested, was improving to the writer and the work.[19]

He asked Erskine to consider Margerie's new short novel (though most of his own time had gone into it recently) *The Castle of Malatesta*, completed in 'a real burst of creative genius', and 'quite one of the most remarkable short novels, or stories of passion, ever written by an American woman'. She wanted above all, he hinted, to be published by the same firm as him. Aware that this put Erskine on the spot, he stressed that she wanted it published only on its own merits, suggesting that she knew exactly why Scribner's had published *Horse in the Sky*.[20] After that book's poor reception, she had decided to change her *nom de plume* from Margerie Bonner to Margerie Lowry, hoping that the name now would work some kind of magic for her.

Their relationship was by now extremely complex. Malcolm could not function without her and when she went into Vancouver he would wait for the bus at 4 p.m. looking frantic and anxious. When she arrived he would always say, 'Thank God, thank God!' The bus driver was fascinated. 'I've never seen anything like it,' he told her. 'He's always there and always the same. Look at that face!'[21] He was still scattering love notes from El Leon to Miss Harteebeeste about the shack, though there is little evidence of similar notes being sent in reply. It was as if he remembered only too clearly her intention of leaving him in Switzerland to seek her own destiny, and was fearful that she would walk out on him without notice.

Some sense of the idealized life he felt he lived with her at the water's edge can be found in the long lyrical story 'The Forest Path to the Spring', which he announced to Erskine in June was 'more or less finished'. In it, Margerie features not as a component of an ambiguous character like Yvonne, but as the more recognizable figure of the doted-upon wife of an ex-musician. If Lowry was fearful of losing her in the real world at least he could lock her up as a character in his fictional one. This story, he told Erskine, was part of the intermezzo segment of the great design to be called *Eridanus*. It contained, he said, some of the best things he had ever written. The theme of rebirth is uppermost in 'Forest Path', which is an anthem to Eridanus, the paradise which the Consul had dreamed of in *Under the Volcano*. In terms of his Dantesque trilogy this forms the paradisaical part. The first person narrator, the ex-jazz man and composer, reflects upon an unhappy past and is composing an opera about Eridanus where he has found peace and the chance of a new start. But even in the idyllic present he has to confront and deal with a sinful past in order to rid himself of guilt and avoid self-destruction. On the forest path to the spring he meets a cougar – a mountain lion – and this meeting takes on a mystical significance, for 'Fear is the lion on the path,' and by reflecting on that encounter he is able to face up to himself and his past. Now, through art, his and Lowry's past sufferings can, like his fear of Mexico, be conquered and transformed.

'A kind of log jam', he told Erskine, had prevented *The Voyage that Never Ends* from getting written or even blocked out. He thought that writing up the plan would take some four months and since he was fearful of losing it as he had *In Ballast*, suggested depositing what was done so far with Erskine. He also worried that his creative drive was waning, or that something else might divert or delay him. Eviction or another fire would finish him. So he had to get started as soon as possible: 'ideas seem to be escaping all the time, but perhaps it's merely "ripening".' *The Voyage* was beginning to possess him. He told Erskine of having a long and happy dream about it, which included an interminable but fruitful discussion with him.[22] It was as if he feared embarking on his ambitious project alone, unsure whether he could ever achieve what he had with the *Volcano*. In *Dark as the Grave* and *La Mordida*, he had clung to that novel, and by enclosing it in *The Voyage*, he could hope that the rest would shine in its afterglow. He was, he told Markson a few weeks later, in an 'interrogative stage' and his work might take him 'anywhere'.[23]

However, despite an unusually hot summer and the threat of forest fires, he got down to completing some unfinished short stories, notably 'Elephant and Colosseum' and 'The Forest Path to the Spring'. Another important story was also taking shape, 'Through the Panama', based on the diaries he and Margerie had kept on their voyage to Europe. Of this Lowry said, 'it reads something like *The Crack-Up*. . . but instead of cracking the protagonist's fission begins to be healed.'[24] Each story, like *Dark as the Grave* and 'Strange Comfort', continued an interior monologue he was conducting, not just about his own psychological state, trying to achieve an integrated identity linked to his past, but the process of creation itself and the author's engagement in the world of fiction with which he surrounds himself. Two of the three stories are about writers reflecting upon themselves, their relation to writers now dead, their present status and their entanglement in their own works of fiction. 'Through the Panama' comes partly in a raw state straight from notebooks, but is coupled with reflective themes and commentaries, a comingling and orchestration of voices – Lowry conversing with his familiars – and just as the journey through the Panama is punctuated by transitions from lock to lock, so the highly subjective, somewhat dislocated text is punctuated at its margins by an objective account of the Canal and its construction, and the passionate instability of reflective consciousness comes up hard against the concrete reality of dispassionate historical narrative. This gives way to the reiteration of a marginal theme hinted at early in the story – that of the Ancient Mariner. So, while the rhythm of the engines (Frère Jacques, Frère Jacques) serves as a reminder that some hidden Fate awaits the troubled Sigbjørn Wilderness and his intrusive character Martin Trumbaugh, the Mariner finally 'beholdeth his native country', and as the ship comes safely through the life-threatening storm, he is resolved 'to teach by his example, love and reverence to all things that God made and loveth.'[25]

The rocket of hopeful expectation about their screenplay spluttered into life again in August when Fletcher Markle wrote that he had read and been astonished and enormously impressed by the script, and was trying to figure out a way of getting MGM to do it. They had the rights but were reluctant about it following earlier abortive screenplays.[26] The effect of this was probably to keep Lowry's novel-writing on hold for a bit longer. He did, however, write long letters to Ten Holder and Markson. Ten Holder had been sent a copy of *Horse in the Sky*, with a view to a German translation, and Lowry felt it necessary to dilate upon its history, sing its praises (a work of 'genius' with a form comparable to Aeschylus) and relate it to Leavis's Great Tradition. He had been reading Jung's *Modern Man in Search of a Soul*, and implied that the archetypal symbolism of the horse and the mother also gave the book an importance akin to the *Volcano*.

The letter to Markson was a marathon effort, taking Lowry almost a month to compose. In it he not only responded to earlier enquiries at length but adopted a manner more father-confessee than father-confessor. Markson's letter, he said, led towards 'the primeval forces of creation' and the answer could take him twenty years to write, but he would speak like a parent, though not always so austerely. He wrote of his relationship with Aiken and said that what he would say would be more use to him as a writer than for his thesis, and could lead into intensely personal and psychological areas. He was anxious, however, to point out the pitfalls of identifying too closely with another writer. He obviously had no desire to experiment with this young man's consciousness and enmesh him in such a peculiarly complex relationship as Aiken had with him. If he wanted to sway his mind, he wrote, it was 'towards A Better Thing'. On the question of psychic phenomena, although he had dismissed the Cabbala, he saw the value of such supernatural systems to the creative artist. Joyce was a very superstitious man, but being superstitious did not make one 'mystical'.

He showed his continuing distaste for academic critics by advising Markson to ignore Joseph Frank and Mark Schorer, from whom he planned to take his critical framework. But he noted with 'the purr of a fellow artisan' that his approach showed the predominance of the artist over the critic. Evidently he preferred to write to Markson the writer than to Markson the academic.[27] He generously recounted at great length the plot of *In Ballast to the White Sea*, and in the same spirit sent the young admirer some fragments of an early draft of *Under the Volcano*.

Having unburdened himself to Markson, he settled down to one of those work sprees noted by Birney. He was in fine creative form and fitter than ever. On 2 October he sent Matson 'Elephant and Colosseum' (an expanded 'Sooner or Later or So They Say'), 'a comic classic, or at least a masterpiece of nature', he said, though he recognized that the magazine did not exist which would print a story longer than *Heart of Darkness* in one issue. His original plan had been to publish this alongside 'The Forest Path to the Spring'. As far as he knew it was 'the only short novel of its type that brings the kind of majesty usually reserved for tragedy . . . to bear on human integration . . . I'm mighty proud of it.' The author of the humorous novel *Ark from Singapore* is now Kennish

Drumgold Cosnahan, an exiled Manxman visiting Rome. The success of his novel was due to clever publicity which left him feeling discomforted, and he hopes that in Europe, without the American hype, his work will be taken more seriously. His creativity has been inhibited since the publication of his book, but a chance encounter with Rosemary the elephant reminds him of the healing power of humour and of magic, and offers a hope for his future as a writer.

Of these stories, he told Matson, 'The Forest Path' was merely 'an adumbration' of a longer novel, *Eridanus*, part of his six-novel scheme which would include the *Volcano* – not the best, for *Dark as the Grave* would be 'ten times more terrible'. The final novel, *La Mordida*, would throw the whole thing into reverse and the sequence would end on a note of triumph. He thought that the ordeals and disappointments of the years since the *Volcano* was published had prepared him spiritually for the great task he had set himself, and he now saw the truth of what he was getting at. 'All that remains is to get myself into a material position where I can consummate the ordeal by the further ordeal of writing it.'[28]

Margerie had made it plain that if they could not get to a warmer clime, they must move into a heated apartment in town away from the arctic winter. His recently completed stories he hoped would be enough to win a contract with Random House and enough money to survive the winter. They formed a collection to be called *Hear Us O Lord from Heaven Thy Dwelling Place* – the title of an old Manx fisherman's hymn in the Methodist Hymnal. This, he told Matson, would include 'Through the Panama', ready in about a month; 'October Ferry to Gabriola', now grown into a novella, on the theme of eviction; 'In the Black Hills', a tragi-comic story, not as slight as it appeared; 'Strange Comfort Afforded by the Profession'; 'Elephant and Colosseum' and 'The Forest Path to the Spring'. More might follow, and 'as a matter of fact I could go on completing short stories till all is blue.' But he wanted to call a halt to story writing and, whether this cycle was saleable or not, intended to get on with the novel project.[29]

Erskine had quickly rejected *The Castle of Malatesta* as being too short. Margerie then suggested to Matson that it be offered with *Horse in the Sky* and another story as a single volume.[30] She told Erskine how they were 'racing the wolf neck and neck' as Christmas came on, but how well Malcolm was working on his stories, clearing the decks before starting on his six-novel project. 'He hopes with this collection to get out of his contract with Harcourt Brace and fly to you at Random

House.' They hoped for a deal which would give him enough to get started on his 'Life Work' for which he was now psychologically ripe. 'He says he now knows what he is getting at, what it adds up to, and what he wants to say and how to say it, and we are both mad with impatience to begin.' He already had 'trunks full of notes, first drafts, etc.'[31] Still hankering after the same publisher as Malcolm, she attached her proposal for a three-story volume of her own.

On 1 October, a fan letter from a 25-year-old unknown writer called Allen Ginsberg arrived, comparing him favourably to Melville and Faulkner, and he quoted this at length to Erskine. Even more exciting was the arrival of *Unter dem Volcan* published by Klett in Stuttgart in mid-September. Klett wrote applauding his 'outstanding novel' and praising Ten Holder's 'fine translation'.[32] Ten Holder's wife, Hildegaard, wrote to say it had been well received at the Frankfurt Book Fair and that Klett, at first lukewarm, was now bursting with pride over it.[33] Anticipating a warm German reception, Lowry told Matson that Hesse was 'the writer to whom I feel I bear most inner resemblance',[34] and indeed he had once signed himself 'Malcolm Von Steppenwolf'. He asked Frau Ten Holder to send Hesse a copy of his book, bearing a personal dedication. Lowry's passion to be involved in movies was reignited by a letter from Ten Holder saying that Klett wanted to make a film of the *Volcano* with Peter Lorre as the Consul and would be writing soon for permission. He was anxious that if a film was made the translator would not go unrewarded.

Margerie quickly informed Matson that Klett would be referred to him and that she and Malcolm would want a hand in the script; but she had learned to be cautious over movie plans, so added that quite likely this was the last they would ever hear of it.[35] Lowry in turn wrote eagerly to Klett. He had always thought it had great possibilities as a film and, having followed German films from his youth, if it were to be filmed, Germany was the country in which he preferred it to be made. He had long thought about it for the cinema and had lots of first-rate ideas for transferring it into that medium, and felt strongly that he should be the person to write the treatment.[36] He told Ten Holder they would be very happy if it were done in the best German tradition of films like *Caligari*. 'Nor has anything I have read influenced my own writing personally more than the first twenty minutes of Murnau's *Sonnenaufgang* or the first and last shots of Karl Grüne's *The Street*.'[37]

He explained to Markson that he was busy trying to get a contract for a book of short stories before the winter was out. He had, he said, also 'sprouted Zola's whiskers' and had been preparing an objection to the proposed hanging of a sixteen-year-old boy for a rape he had not committed. The penalty had been commuted to life imprisonment to please Princess Elizabeth, then in Canada, but, he said, it was a thing one could not leave alone:

> if you had studied the evidence, the feeble and neurotic protests, the bloodthirsty cries for revenge, and you were the only writer in the community, much as one hates to risk one's position in it, even if one hasn't got one, and what is more does not care whether one has or not.

He stressed the importance of magic to the writer, recommending he read Yeats's *A Vision* (but not to forget Joe Venuti) and remember 'that priceless possession, the author's naïveté.' There is a celebration of naïveté in another story he had just completed, 'The Bravest Boat'.[38] This lyrical love story, intended as the first in his collection, is set in Vancouver's Stanley Park. Sigurd Storlesen, aged ten, son of a lighthouse keeper, has cast adrift a tiny boat bearing a message close to Cape Flattery in Washington. Twelve years later it is found by a seven-year-old girl on a beach in Canada, and ten years after that the two are married. They recall this story and reflect on the beauty of the scenery which somehow reflects a dream of life, while at the edge of this vision is the encroaching horror of modern civilization – sawmills swallowing up the forests and the creeping blight of suburban Enochvilleport (Vancouver). It is Grieg's fluffy chickens and the hideous Moloch of the disease-ridden ship all over again, but now embodied in a Lawrentian image of an idyllic marriage. 'But ah, the storms they had come through!'

These stories were enfolded along with much else in *The Voyage that Never Ends*, the outline of which, entitled *Work in Progess*, he sent to Matson on 23 November, hoping he would send it at once to Erskine. The first offering would be *Hear Us O Lord*, his story collection, now all but finished, which he thought would run to some 330 pages. He was not concerned if they were unsaleable, he said, because he genuinely thought they were masterpieces. The long delay in getting his work out was due to the loss of *In Ballast*, which had obliged him to tackle 'all the subject-objective problems all over again' and some had yet to be solved. Nevertheless, he was extremely confident about the whole thing. 'I am convinced that *The Voyage that Never Ends* will be a great book if it is found I deserve grace to finish it.' 'The whole bolus' was organized with the *Volcano* at its centre, the book from which, like his umbilical, he was reluctant to sever himself.

Work in Progress

THE VOYAGE THAT NEVER ENDS

The Ordeal of Sigbjørn Wilderness I

Untitled Sea Novel
Lunar Caustic

Under the Volcano — The Centre

Dark as the Grave Wherein My Friend is Laid
Eridanus
La Mordida
} — Trilogy

The Ordeal of Sigbjørn Wilderness II

Hear Us Oh [*sic*] Lord From Heaven Thy Dwelling Place — Tales

The Lighthouse Invites the Storm — poems

(Other Tales, poems, a play, etc.)

Hear Us Oh Lord, said now to be stories and three short novels, was to be linked to *Eridanus*, a novel whose setting was the forest shore. He also mentioned a story called 'Battement De Tambours' to be based on his and Margerie's Haiti Notebooks. The aim of this grand design, he said, was to give chaos a meaning, delirium a form.

He had once told Jan never to throw anything away. Now he was practising what he had preached. The scheme included almost everything he had ever written. But what he had done, by reworking and recycling themes from the *Volcano* throughout the wider scheme, was to lay himself open to the charge of being a one-novel writer, in the same sense that Proust has so been described.[39] Unlike Proust, however, the dream was to remain a dream, the great elaborately conceived castle in the air to remain just that, turrets, crenelations, spires, and all. There was a centrepiece and some half-constructed and abandoned ruins – but the reality would never emerge complete from the fictional design. Naïveté, as Lowry said, could be a writer's most precious possession; it could also be his downfall.

There was still no news from Markle and presumably he was having the same problems with *Tender is the Night* as Taylor had had before him. Lowry, however, was still excited about a possible German film of the *Volcano*. He was distinctly keen on the idea of working on both film and fiction in Germany, and insisted to Matson that he and Margerie be involved. This would not interfere with *Hear Us O Lord*, he said, because Margerie could do a treatment while Ten Holder translated it. At least it would get them out of debt, and in Germany Ten Holder could also start translating the stories. As the money situation was becoming critical he was eager that Harcourt Brace be bypassed or persuaded to let him go to Random House.[40] Erskine also knew about *Hear Us O Lord*, and *The Voyage*, of which it was a tangential part. As to the order in which these works should come out, *Hear Us O Lord* could be followed by *Lunar Caustic*. Much of the work was done, he said, though in note form only, making samples of it difficult to submit. If only he knew his work was wanted he was capable of working ten times as hard.[41]

Having got this Work-in-Progress off to Matson and informed Erskine of his plans, he sank into a lethargic uncertainty which came of not knowing where he was with any publisher or whether his work was wanted. He wrote later that between mid-November and the beginning of January he was unable to work at all.[42] What he meant was work on his fiction. He did manage in November to compose a letter to Seymour Lawrence, editor of *Wake*, who was planning an edition devoted to Conrad Aiken. When it was published, Aiken considered Lowry's letter to be the best contribution of all. In it, he paid his usual gushing tributes to his old mentor – 'as Winston Churchill might say – never has such a great author been for so long recognized as such by so many yet seemingly so few!' And although some of his work was of 'an appalling savagery', he had always thought him 'one of the truest and most direct descendants of our own great Elizabethans, having the supreme gift of dramatic and poetic language, a genius of the highest and most original order . . .'[43] It was as though he felt that finally acknowledgement was due on the large, though publicly unadmitted, debt he owed him, the lack of which Aiken had bemoaned to Davenport four years earlier.

Hopes of a German film faltered when Klett indicated that he preferred to deal directly with Lowry rather than through Matson, the deal being fifty-fifty, with Klett keeping control of the script. This he wished Lowry to sign and return.[44] Lowry immediately informed Matson, stressing that he would deal only through him and that he must insist that control of the script remain in his hands. However, he did hope that Lorre could be interested independently because he was one of the greatest actors ever and the part might have been written for him.[45] But

Matson had not even acknowledged receipt of his manuscripts and he was worried lest Erskine had read his material and not liked it. There was also the problem that without much money they were unable to escape the approaching winter, something Margerie had vowed she would not endure again if possible. She, of course, with the various illnesses which had threatened (including false alarms), stood as a constant reproach to him for living so far from the civilization he despised and she now yearned for.

The hope of making an easy switch to Random House was dashed when Harcourt Brace refused to relinquish the right of first refusal of his next work, insisting that they could match any offer, and Matson felt obliged to send them the stories and his Work-in-Progress. Lowry was not happy about this, and to his dismay, Robert Giroux, Harcourt's Editor-in-Chief, wrote back to Matson enthusing about the package.

> I have been very much impressed by the manuscript of Malcolm Lowry's stories, *Hear Us O Lord From Heaven Thy Dwelling Place*, which you have been good enough to let us see. 'Through the Panama' and 'The Forest Path to the Spring' are excellent, and so are the two Roman stories. 'In the Black Hills', which one might call a 'Western', is one of the best stories I've read in a long time. Altogether it is an admirable collection, and one which whets the appetite for the dozen or so additional stories which Mr Lowry describes in his notes at the end.

The Voyage that Never Ends, he wrote, promised to be one of the most important literary works of the decade. He would like to see the almost completed *Lunar Caustic*, and said they were ready to work out a publishing and financial programme for all six novels.[46] Matson, reporting on this, said he had no preference between Harcourt and Random House, but that Giroux might make him just the offer he hoped for. He asked whether *Lunar Caustic* was available and what kind of financial deal he would like.[47]

Ironically, considering he had not published a book for almost five years, Lowry's disappointment was intense. He wrote telling Erskine that Harcourt Brace's refusal to release him from his contract was melancholy news to him and seemed to leave him no option in the matter. He had thought for weeks that the manuscripts had been with *him* while all the time they were with Harcourt. However, without the *Volcano*, for which Harcourt still held the rights, the centrepiece of his project would be missing, and anyway Erskine might not like the new material.

He recognized, however, that in wanting to stay with Erskine he might be being perverse; had he not been there Giroux would have been a happy enough choice. However, he felt like Judas Iscariot, he said. Without him he felt 'like Germany without Bismarck, not to say Enos without Fruit Salts, or Johnny Walker without the whiskey'. He pleaded that they might stay in touch.[48]

What he seems to have dreaded most was having no one to whom he could confess his persistent self-doubts and fears about his writing. 'I am frightened by the appalling meaning of some parts of the book ahead and the character of some of the demons who have to be turned into mercies . . . Anyhow I hope you will still let me share some of its burdens with you.' He felt he had acted contrary to his Higher Self, especially in view of Erskine's readiness to help them with a loan. 'Alack. Thank you. Alas. Blast. Damn it.' Then it seems to have occurred to him that he just might have bitten off more than he could chew. Perhaps, he said, it would be better for Erskine, too. 'For all God knows by the time I got to the end of the benighted work you may have returned to Brace and even be running it.'[49]

If he was disappointed at being kept to his contract, Giroux's letter must have heartened Margerie, being further confirmation of Malcolm's genius. It may have given her the fortitude to remain in the shack despite being snowed in, with only $50 in the bank, and no immediate prospect of being able to afford an apartment in Vancouver. The weather was a real problem. As Lowry wrote to Matson on 20 December, he had just one copy of *Lunar Caustic*, on which Giroux wanted to judge the whole novel sequence, and being frozen made it impossible to get it retyped until they could move into warmer quarters in town. He again asked for a loan, assuring him that he would be able to pay him back soon, when his family money came through and when the half million francs ($700–800) due from Correa could be got into the country. *Lunar Caustic* needed both retyping and extending to novel length by adding a hundred pages and strengthening the motivation.[50] He was sad about Erskine, but at Random House the sequence would appear without the *Volcano*.

Erskine realized that Matson had thought it unethical to show him the work before offering it to Harcourt. In the circumstances, he told Lowry, it might have been better to have sent it to him directly, then only *his* ethics and not Matson's would have been involved. However, if Harcourt turned it down he would work to ensure that Random House was receptive to the proposal.[51] Yet even this failed to cheer

Lowry. On Christmas Day he was at his most dejected, sitting over a bad whisky in front of a tree decked with just two presents and composing blues on his ukulele. Two days later Cummins informed them that $100 wired to them had been waiting for collection since the 21st. It was an advance from Giroux sent on by Matson. Lowry had now been placed on a monthly retainer of $200 by Harcourt Brace, pending a contract, and this was the first half-month's instalment. The storekeeper had just not bothered to tell them it had arrived.

They began searching for an apartment, but found that even the hotels were all full of lumberjacks there for the festive season. It took them until New Year's Eve to find a vacant hotel room, and until 6 January to find what Lowry called 'a practical hole to crawl into'. This was Apartment 33 at 1075 Gilford Street, close to Vancouver's Stanley Park, which became their home until the end of March. Here, he claimed, they had their first civilized bath in three years. Nevertheless he found 'civilization' uncomfortable. The steam-heating drove him mad, and, though grateful for the warmth, apartment living made him feel like a wild animal put into a zoo for the first time. On top of that, they now had to pay rent and this produced a diatribe against the evils of landlordism. Alcohol, despite its pains, brought some pleasure, but rent was nothing *but* pain.[52]

Once settled into the apartment, Margerie began retyping *Lunar Caustic* and Lowry wrote a long letter to Giroux. He was obviously pleased that Giroux thought highly of his work, and set out to write the kind of letter he often wrote to Erskine, full of hopes, fears and anxieties, detailed anecdotes and castle-building, but the effect was muddled and over-confidential. He began on a fairly practical note by stressing the need to complete *Hear Us O Lord* before starting on the novels, and asking him to suggest how many stories he thought the volume needed. Later, he showed himself obsessive and confused, hardly the competent, professional author likely to impress a prospective publisher. Because he was prone to certain disasters, he said, he owed it to him to submit as quickly as possible 'a copy of even imperfect drafts or half intentions to cache away', and he would send two versions of *Lunar Caustic*, neither of them final. He mentioned his attachment to Erskine, how painful it was to part with him, and how much he owed to him. Then he rambled on about his life in Dollarton and how after three years in the wilderness away from all conveniences, 'civilization seems almost as strange to me as if I were Alley Oop.'

It was not easy for him to rework old ideas in a new place, he said, and yet the dramatic events of the last month might compose themselves into one of his best stories. 'I am one of those fellows who when not deeply engaged in work immediately find themselves on the receiving end of some twenty works.' (And of course he had been, over the past months, often working on several stories at once, no sooner having begun on one than another suggested itself – through an encounter, a memory, a paragraph in a newspaper.) These, he said, rather weakly, were some of the things which perplexed him. But he needed to know to whom it was that he should address himself, and even to whom, as his editor, he should 'unburden' himself. For he must speak at length, he said. Just after he mailed this letter to Giroux (dated 11 January), Matson wrote saying that Klett's film offer looked unproductive to him, but he would contact Peter Lorre directly to see if he was interested.[53]

Markson's thesis had arrived and Margerie thought it 'marvellous'. Lowry wrote to him saying that he was 'touched beyond measure' and it was obviously marvellously documented, but because he had (partly echoing Grieg's words from 1931) to 'work like hell day and night' he dare not look at it. 'I cannot let [my mind] be stimulated when trying to concentrate on something else. Please understand and forgive.'[54] Having set himself a great and complicated task, he was already beginning to have doubts (sometimes to the point of panic) about whether he could do it. He could not read Markson's thesis for fear of being distracted. He knew his weakness only too well.

What he was 'working like hell' on was a twenty-page letter to Giroux to go with the two versions of *Lunar Caustic* which were sent off on 21 January. It was a convoluted apology for the material submitted. The two versions were *The Last Address*, written in 1936, and *Swinging the Maelstrom*, the same MS 'worked up' in 1939, 1940 and 1941.[55] He asked Giroux to read *Swinging the Maelstrom*, bearing in mind that some material from *The Last Address* needed to go into the final version. It must all have seemed oddly muddled to an editor thinking of granting an author a long-term contract. It was as if he were willing Giroux to lose interest. He later told Markson, 'I seem to have been somehow unconsciously determined to stick to Erskine, even while knowing that it was an impossibility, unless I wrote something deliberately bad for H & B & so caused them to drop the option.'[56]

He expounded to Giroux his conception of the two pieces, explaining their evolution and assessing the effectiveness of each version. Then, having discussed them at length, almost as a footnote he said he was thinking of recasting the protagonist as a suicidal English aristocrat and jazz musician, whose American wife has married him only for his title – thus throwing the whole thing back into the melting pot. If Giroux had not realized how improvised *The Voyage that Never Ends* was, trying to draw into one net everything Lowry had written, and might write, then this letter must have brought the message home. No sooner had an idea coalesced into one shape, than, amoeba-like, Lowry began to transform it into another.

Having dispatched this weighty missive to the editor, he sat down to read Markson's thesis. He soon wrote to say what excitement and pleasure he found in reading it. It had, he said, told him a lot of things about his book which, if he had not read it, would certainly have encouraged him to do so. It was the only thesis he had read which had a feeling of dramatic excitement about it. No creative writer, he said, wanted to write 'a goddamned thesis', and he was scornful of 'the gradual creative declension of something like the Partisan Review . . . into a kind of incestuous gobbledygook,' which was, he argued, a case in point. Nevertheless he had made it 'as thrilling as a drama of the unconscious' of which he felt unworthy. Even so, he asked that Markson send him some fiction or poetry. He was polite about the thesis, he was flattered by it, but what he really looked forward to from him was something creative.[57]

He broke off long enough to send a note to Aiken, who replied by announcing that finally, after a long gestation (and doubtless spurred by the publication of the *Volcano*), he had given birth to that multi-layered work which they had so often discussed. It was an experimental autobiography, more brutally honest in its self-analysis than either *Blue Voyage* or *Great Circle*. He called it *Ushant* after the point on the French coast lying beyond the horizon from Jeake's House which he and Lowry had taken to symbolize the perhaps unattainable goal of their artistic strivings. He pronounced it 'You Shan't!', because it attempted to record a consciousness experiencing the liberation of the id, essential to all creative artists, but often so damaging to those around them. In it, thinly disguised acquaintances of his appear, including Eliot as Tsetse and Lowry as Hambo. By exposing poor old plagiaristic Hambo, he claimed back all the work which Lowry had purloined from him. 'Frankly,' he wrote, 'I don't know what to think of it. It grew, all by itself, into a New Shape, its own, a spiral unwinding of memory into a spiral projection of analysis: it has a design, and yet it would be hard to say what it is.' He hoped his old student would forgive him for it.

Some three weeks after Lowry dispatched his monumental letter and two versions of *Lunar Caustic*, Giroux had still not acknowledged their receipt, and Lowry was beginning to fret. Margerie wrote to Matson, who had just sent them a further $375 retainer from Harcourt Brace, expressing concern and explaining that, having been wrenched away from Erskine, Malcolm had felt it important to establish a close relationship with Giroux, but now felt very isolated. To send letters off from such a distance and receive no reply, and so be ignorant of what was happening, she said, was a truly 'glum' experience.[58] This, added to worry about the shack, which had been heavily pounded in the bad winter weather, made it impossible to complete 'The Forest Path to the Spring'. Margerie, however, worked on, typing over two hundred pages of notes for *Dark as the Grave*, while Lowry composed another self-reflective story about a writer, 'Ghostkeeper', set in Stanley Park, thought by some to be one of his best.[59]

Not until 6 March, more than five weeks after Giroux had seen his material, did a cable arrive from Matson with the bad news. 'Brace decided today no more advance on basis of work available.'[60] Lowry would not be held to his contract after all. Margerie claimed later that Giroux was keen on the material but unable to persuade colleagues, including Lowry's old enemy Reynal.* Probably the confused letter of 21 January also had raised doubts with Giroux about Lowry's ability to complete his ambitious plans in anything like a reasonable time. Despite not having wanted to go to Brace in the first place, as always he took rejection badly, and was utterly despondent. But Margerie wired Erskine jubilantly. Their prayers had been answered. If Random House wanted Malcolm, he was free to come.[61] In fact Matson had already contacted Erskine, who immediately wrote to Lowry saying how delighted he was, that Matson had passed on all his material, and he would prepare a report for 'one of the main wheels' (Robert Haas) at Random House. He asked him to be patient while he worked things out. Embarrassed by Harcourt Brace's rejection and again short of money Lowry cabled Erskine,

> Brace failed answer letters even acknowledge manuscripts received meantime kept me in abyss though heartsick honestly tried cooperate albeit delighted things went wrong cannot believe Giroux fault probably office boy again find committed apartment Vancouver till April first therefore financial difficulties . . .

* A claim born out by Giroux himself – in his youthful naivety he had enthused wildly before ensuring he had the backing of his boss, Reynal, in the endeavour. He did not.

Erskine dispatched $50 on the 12th, but, by another of those accidents which forever befell Lowry, it was wrongly addressed and delayed. Fate, he felt, was at work again. 'I shall almost suspect witchcraft, that Satan does not want me to write the book or something,' he wrote.[62]

In a long rambling letter to Erskine which took four days to compose, he ranged over all his current plans and anxieties, saying that he felt he had been beguiled and forced by Matson and Giroux into the situation with Harcourt Brace. This may be why he came to discuss his creative and personal problems with Erskine rather than Matson, and to regard the editor more and more as his special friend and confidant. He had tried to make the transference to Giroux and had written to him fully and from the heart, but had had no answer. Perhaps, he speculated, Giroux had 'declined the psychological gambit', meaning probably that he was unprepared to act as editor-analyst, the price to be paid, apparently, for having him as an author. Perhaps Giroux had concluded that he was 'an untrustworthy bastard' but he felt that the *Volcano* underwrote that. And maybe Reynal, the office boy, had got into the works; maybe *Lunar Caustic* was just too gruesome. He had not meant to be 'a demanding author', he said, but thought that in view of his achievements he deserved at least a contract for *Hear Us O Lord*.[63]

When Erskine cabled assuring him that a cheque for $50 had been sent, it provoked the pathetic response. 'Last night a night of grief and suspense – you do not say "love" to us on wire.' If he had given up on him, no one could blame him, but now they were living in dread of his next letter arriving or even not arriving. The following day he wrote of 'a hell of a tension within, worst thing I have ever been through . . . worse than the Consul, and it is not an alcoholic hell. It is the abyss itself . . .'[64] On the 16th, now quite broke, the tone of the letter to Erskine became even more gloomy. Margerie's eyes needed attention, her nerves were wrecked, and they could not obtain credit for groceries – he felt set apart from others by his ill fortune. Terrible mischances and coincidences, like the continual returning of cheques by Cummins, had bedevilled them – 'but I believe . . . that you are – with Margie and the house – a link with the world of light and the powers of light and goodness.'

By Monday the 17th, as he continued writing, his mood was suddenly changed by the arrival of Erskine's $50. There was the prospect of security once his father's estate was settled, he wrote. Correa owed them $800, and Taylor still had their screenplay masterpiece which might yet make them rich and famous. And, in any case, all the disasters which had occurred since they left Dollarton were material for yet another story which he had cooking, called 'In the Abyss'. He even asked Erskine to retain his letter because that, too, was material for the story.[65] Anxious not to lose him as they had Giroux, they sent him Markson's thesis, the French, Norwegian and Danish translations of the *Volcano*, a set of favourable French reviews of the book, the news that it had earned over a million francs for them so far, and the story of Peter Lorre's interest in a possible German film.

The inclination to excuse Giroux disappeared when Lowry received a painfully apologetic letter from him, explaining that it was not the quality of his work which led to them dropping him. He thought well of *Lunar Caustic*. 'There is fascinating material here, and it is clear that the place of the finished book will be important in your long work-in-progress. Financial considerations, rather than literary ones, have led to our decision.' The time the project would take did not seem to justify the expenditure. He thought they would have worked well together and hoped there would be no ill-feeling on either side. 'I shall always be an admirer of your work, and in every way a well-wisher.'[66] But Lowry was in no mood to accept Giroux's good wishes. He felt he had been strung along and then betrayed, and was clearly angry. It was, he told Erskine, an 'astonishing' letter, the first and last he had received from Giroux, and sent it for him to read.

As the time for returning to Dollarton drew near, he began to worry that the inadequate postal service to this far-flung outpost and the practical demands of living in the shack would intrude upon his work. He also worried about the safety of his manuscripts in Dollarton, hit by flood and tempest during their absence. To safeguard against disasters, he bundled off all drafts of *Lunar Caustic* and all his short stories to Erskine for safe-keeping, and proposed sending some of his poetry, too.

He told Erskine he would write to him every day in the hope of supplying ever better reasons for Random House to take him on. On 30 March and the day following, he wrote bitterly of Giroux's betrayal after first insisting on keeping him to his contract and talking of financial arrangements, a crime only worsened by the long delay to which he had been subjected. He felt this was his last chance to persuade Erskine to take him on and he worried that he might half-wish to get rid of him. If so, he would dash with all his derangements at his object, and leave the rest to fortune.[67]

Harcourt Brace, he thought, might now be in the mood to relinquish rights to the *Volcano* and Random House could gain possession of the centrepiece of his grand design. Giroux's betrayal gave him a moral lever to get the book from them. Yet he still had doubts about his own grand scheme. Maybe the whole plan seemed over-ambitious, he reflected, and he worried that Erskine, like Giroux, would dislike the project or be overruled from above. The whole thing was driving him nuts. Brace's conduct in this matter, he wrote, amounted to moral dereliction because their promise had prevented him from earning money by some other means over that period.[68] He also felt badly because Margerie had put her own work aside to type up his. But come what may, he said, he would hang on, like a man on a storm-tossed ship, 'so that the adverse winds turn fair and the furies turn to mercies.'

Money, as ever, was a problem. He began to worry that he would have to repay the $500 advance received from Harcourt Brace. The rent in Vancouver, he told Erskine, was 'killing'. However, the editor sent him another $50 on 21 March, so that any immediate crisis was overcome. Also worrying him was Margerie's health, about which she complained increasingly. The strain, she told him, was getting to her, and had she been English and not an American with a tough pioneering ancestry, she would have been 'carted away' long ago.[69] The fact that they were approaching the anniversary of Erskine's acceptance of the *Volcano* in 1946 was significant to Malcolm. The situation seemed like a repetition of their Mexican ordeal in Acapulco – the Kafkaesque experience he had begun writing about in *La Mordida*.

Having worked up a head of steam over Giroux's 'betrayal', he composed a long letter to him, berating him for causing them so much anguish and saying that his letter had been a complete rejection of himself as well as his work. The whole thing was 'inexcusable' and 'a tragedy of misplaced ethics'. He then meandered through his recent past and all the vicissitudes which he and Margerie had suffered, and, after concluding on a note of high moral indignation, graciously assured Giroux of his continuing friendship.[70] This letter was put aside and never sent, partly because Margerie was unwell and unable to type, and partly because, as Lowry put it to Erskine, 'The Case was somewhat altered.'[71]

The altered case was encouraging news from Erskine, who had now read the material sent by Matson. There was a great amount to delight him, he said, and doubtless, as with the *Volcano*, that would increase with familiarity. However, 'There are also things I don't quite understand, "get," and also a few things that I don't on one reading approve of. But there is enough already here to maintain my faith in what you can do and will do, and to cause me to hope that the management will think so too.' Some of it was now with Robert Haas, vice president and part-owner of Random House, and he hoped for a decision soon. However he added a note of caution about his own taste in literature and how that affected his judgement of what he had read. He had long felt that relationships between writers, editors, publishers and critics were rarely interesting or fruitful subjects for fiction, and felt much the same about fiction about writers and writing.

> I have some misgivings about the outcome of writing a book about a man who had written a book about writing a book . . . etc., especially since I've thought since you once sketched the skeleton of it for me that La Mordida would be a terrific thing without any reference at all to Under the Volcano or any of its characters.

Nevertheless he was sure these doubts could be dispelled and Lowry should concentrate on the fact that his editor believed strongly in what he could do and would do everything he could to get a contract and financial support for him. 'You can even make writing about writers interesting – it is only that I wouldn't want to see you devote yourself to it exclusively, or nearly so even.'[72]

Erskine's serious reservations about Lowry's central concern – the writer writing himself – hardly made for a propitious beginning to a publishing relationship dealing with a great sequence of books in which 'man, novelist of himself' was a central theme, and which was designed to have *Under the Volcano* at the centre of its mystery. Erskine no doubt expected, not unreasonably, another *Under the Volcano*, perhaps more than one. But Lowry had moved into an even more innovative mode than before, and was less concerned than he had been as a young writer to ensure that what he wrote was accessible to the general reader, except when he wrote short stories with a view to selling them. The point of getting a long-term contract was that it might free him from commercial pressures on his work. Kafka and Joyce were probably more of an influence now than such earlier mentors as Mann, Conrad and Broch, and any surviving attachment he had to Poe and Melville was for the dark cast of their lives as much as for their formal literary qualities. He wanted to innovate, and liked to say of his work, 'I think it is an original work and a classic of its kind,' or 'This work requires something different from the stock response.' When others rejected him, like Giroux and Reynal, he thought they had simply not read his work properly. What he seems to have forgotten sometimes, was that editors have to make commercial judgements as well as literary ones, and often attempt to read, as William Plomer had read the *Volcano*, with the general reader's reactions in mind.

On 25 March Erskine sent his report on Lowry to Robert Haas. He greatly admired Lowry, he said, and he had never been associated with a book which gave him more satisfaction than *Under the Volcano*. He found the unfinished 'Forest Path' and 'Elephant and Colosseum' the most impressive of the short stories; they grew better on every reading, his very experience with *Under the Volcano*. He found that *Lunar Caustic* also grew on him at each reading, and suggested Lowry be given a contract and an allowance for two or three years. He was the kind of writer who deserved their interest and support, and a well worthwhile risk.

> Malcolm Lowry is certainly, as you can see from the evidence, an innovator; and offering innovations to the public is a risky business. But he has already been accepted by an international public, and this fact reduces the risk a great deal. There are a lot of people who already regard him as one of the important writers of our time (as I do), and I think there will be more such as time goes on.[73]

When Erskine's letter arrived, Lowry would not open it, fearful of what it contained. Finally, Margerie glanced at it and assured him that it was hopeful and encouraging. When eventually he allowed himself to read it he promptly wrote yet another lengthy reply to convince Erskine that a novel about writers could be viable, original and exciting. (While writing the *Volcano* he had been told a novel about a dipsomaniac would not work.) But he did not think this prejudice was widely shared, for inside everyone there is an artist, a poet, and so the poet is a universal figure with whose struggles anyone can identify. Being entirely against such novels would put one pretty well against most autobiographical fiction. He was after a new approach to reality itself, and works which had treated this tragically or philosophically rather than romantically had often failed for that reason. Pirandello's *Six Characters in Search of an Author* and Chekhov's *The Seagull* were cases in point. Most people seeing *The Seagull* would forget completely that it was about writers and their art in some fashion. But what would strike them was that a talent misused could destroy the artist, and they would apply the sad lesson to their own lives. His novel sequence was not about a man or a writer so much as man's unconscious. Much of the irony of *Dark as the Grave* would be lost if Sigbjørn Wilderness had not written the book which now threatened to take him over. But Wilderness was not a novelist in the ordinary sense. He was a kind of underground man, Ortega y Gasset's man creating his own life in the process of living it and trying thereby to find himself. 'What he suspects is that he's not a writer so much as being *written* – this is where the terror comes in.' He was less of a Faust than a latter-day Aylmer, the water diviner in search of his lost soul. 'I'm damned if I don't think him an original fellow, not to be confused with the ordinary novelist . . .'[74]

That week, it seems, the Lowrys put to sea (probably on a trip to visit the Neilsons on Bowen Island), and on 28 March they almost foundered in a typhoon in Falmouth harbour. Margerie was so shattered by the experience that she was unable to type for the rest of their stay in Vancouver, and on the 30th they returned to Dollarton. It was Jimmy Craige's birthday and he had 'celebrated' by making the shack ready for them, drying out their soaking mattresses with hot bricks and chopping wood for them.[75] They missed by one day the cable which arrived at Gilford Street on Monday the 31st. 'Am authorized to discuss contract with Hal and have accordingly begun to. Am overjoyed. Letter soon. Love to you both. Albert.'[76]

CHAPTER XXIII

THE LIFE OF FICTION
1952–1953

God keep me from ever completing anything. This whole book is but a draught – nay, but a draught of a draught. Oh, Time, Strength, Cash, and Patience.

HERMAN MELVILLE, *Moby Dick*

On 1 April Margerie was called to the store to have Erskine's telegram read to her over the phone. 'Margie came whooping through the woods with the best news I ever heard in my life,' wrote Lowry. When the cable itself arrived shortly afterwards they pinned it on the wall to remind themselves that their dream had come true.[1] Lowry wired his joy to Erskine and two days later wrote him a letter beginning '*Hooray*, Albert!' A rather gloomy letter he had begun to Aiken now ended with a triumphant postscript carrying the latest news: 'Random House and the Modern Library people are taking me in tow with a large advance and contract upon the wing.'[2]

Dollarton had been devastated by winter storms. Some shacks had been badly damaged, others washed away. Four uprooted trees had been swept down the Inlet and got jammed under the piles of the shack, but they were delighted to find that the house 'built with their own hands' had withstood the winter onslaught and that the pier – Lowry's pride and joy, also built with their own hands and nicknamed 'the crazy wonder' – was still standing. And not only had Dollarton taken a battering but its population was reduced to just four: the Lowrys, Craige and Whitey. Yet Lowry's world was intact and he was further buoyed up when Random House's contract arrived on the 4th. With the prospect of a new life before him, he got down happily to cleaning and repairing the shack, and to his usual routine chores, even if they affected his work. He had spent the whole of the previous day salvaging a huge log from the shore for fuel and so had been unable to write, he told Erskine on the 5th.[3]

The contract was extremely generous. It ran until the end of 1956, with deadlines for various parts of *The Voyage that Never Ends* in November 1953, May 1955 and November 1956. It offered $5,000 to be paid over two and a half years at $150 per month ($110 after tax); this way the overall tax bill would be kept down. This, together with his regular $90, would more than double his monthly income, and their financial survival would be assured. But he was worried at having to deliver two novels and a book of short stories in two and a half years, as specified. He could finish *Hear Us O Lord* and *Lunar Caustic*, he told Matson, and had a book of poems ready any time, but could not promise another novel. If he did get a work finished in time it might not be his best. *Hear Us O Lord* could be delivered within a year, but he preferred a flexible arrangement which would allow him a chance to exceed rather than fail to meet expectations. However, he rewrote a lot, and did not want to submit anything less than his best. The fear of being interrupted by ill-fortune also haunted him, and he asked Matson to insert a clause enabling him to draw up to two or three hundred in the case of an emergency such as an accident. He also wanted a means to suspend the payments if any film work came up. Even though the offer was generous, he said he could not settle down to work and feel happy until everything was signed and sealed.[4]

His fear of being unable to deliver in time also surfaced in a letter to Erskine; he had, he said, a terrible case of stage-fright over it. He was worried, too, about the enormous amount of notes and drafts needing to be transcribed before he could start work on his novels, so said he would concentrate first on getting *Hear Us O Lord* into shape. Nevertheless he was 'speechless with gratitude' and standing at the barrier waiting for the bell.[5] On his fears about the three books Matson reassured him, saying that he thought Random House would be quite flexible on the point, and in case of interruption by such matters as making a film in Germany, monthly payments could simply be suspended.[6] And although nothing was heard from Klett, Lowry did have some flattering news from Germany. Frau Ten Holder wrote that Hermann Hesse had been reading *Under the Volcano* and after only 120 pages, had returned and affirmed his dedication to him.[7]

But the question of the book deadline continued to nag him, and he wrote again to Erskine on 9 April saying that *Lunar Caustic* could be finished in time and possibly *The Ordeal*. Alternatively, perhaps he could finish *Dark as the Grave*. He hoped that he would not think that he was 'beginning to hedge or chisel on the contract'; he did not want to be a 'difficult' author in that way. On the contrary, once he got going he might even exceed expectations. Yet he was evidently unsure of being able to deliver. Almost pathetically, he suggested his poems for one of the books, and even, with a sudden inspiration, the screenplay of *Tender is the Night*, which he had dropped his novel to write and from which he had got nothing but 'three years of heartbreak'.[8] It was as if he had given up hope of completing his three even before he began. But then, worried that he might have undermined Erskine's confidence in him, he offered to send him a batch of foreign reviews of the *Volcano*. A week later he sent another letter, anxious that there had been no reply to the first, and wrote to Matson, worried that the contract had been sent but was lost in the mail. In his mind, beyond the forest lay a Kafkaesque world where events were determined by 'auxilliary circumstances' and letters ended up in the dead letter office of Bartleby the Scrivener.[9]

What would have released him from the need for a contracted income would have been the money due from the Lowry estate, but probate was proving a long and tangled affair. In time, he had heard, his annual income would be about £1,000, but that would be subject to UK tax. So as things stood, the Random House deal seemed the best way to be free to write over the next few years. Anxiety over the delayed contract, however, was preventing him from working, the weather was miserable and he had to spend time hacking fuel from the forest every day.[10] Worried also about the $100 he owed Erskine, he asked Noxon to send Margerie's CBC money (returned by Cummins marked 'Addressee unknown in Dollarton') directly to the editor. Showing his present lack of self-confidence, he added, 'We only wish to God we were lucky enough to have your counsel at the moment in regard to Work in Progress.'[11]

Struck down with a chill towards the end of April, and still paralysed by concern over the contract, Lowry sat down to read right through *Ulysses* (a present from Erskine as editor-in-chief of the Random House Modern Library) for the first time. On the 28th he was cheered by a cheque for $200 from Matson in anticipation of moneys to come, and, feeling more confident, got down to finishing off his Rabelaisian story 'Present Estate of Pompeii'. An earlier version had yet another writer-protagonist, but, in deference to Erskine, he changed him into a schoolteacher based on Downie Kirk. It is yet another tale of exile, yearning, and 'the abomination of ruination'.

Roderick MacGregor Fairhaven, a Scots-Canadian schoolteacher, is sitting in a restaurant reluctant to tour the sights with his impatient wife. Was there any reason why he should choose to visit Pompeii rather than sit in the Restaurant Vesuvius? Yet if he *has* to go he is anxious to extract some universal significance from the visit.

> This, pre-eminently, is where you don't belong. Is it some great ruin that brings upon you this migraine of alienation – and almost inescapably these days there seems a ruin of some kind involved – but it is also something that slips through the hands of your mind, as it were . . . and behind you, thousands of miles away, it is as if you could hear your own real life plunging to its doom.

He thought of the shack and the paradise left behind. He should not be visiting the great cities of Europe, he should be in Eridanus. Pompeii was 'a bit like the ruins of Liverpool on a Sunday afternoon,' or Vancouver after a catastrophe. Reflecting on the 'abomination of desolation' which the modern city has become, he observes that, 'the difference between the man-made ruins and the ruins of Pompeii was that the man-made ones had not for the most part been found worth preserving . . . Partly it was as if man built with ruin in view.' Nonetheless there was something deeper and the soul of William Blackstone continued to stir within him. 'What was this instinct which made men herd together like partridges, like sardines in tomato paste, this cowardly dependence on the presence of others?'[12]

Fears about meeting his deadline were further complicated by a suggestion from Erskine that it was better to publish *Lunar Caustic* before the book of stories. He wrote explaining the difficulties. On the face of it, he agreed, this seemed a better and more financially rewarding plan, but he had been working on the assumption of the stories coming first and had a good chance of completing them ahead of schedule. This would mean that in eighteen months time he could have the stories finished and *Lunar Caustic* near completion. There was also a practical problem. In the cramped shack, with Margerie typing up notes and drafts, it was not easy for him to work on a novel; the set of stories were easier to write, being less intricately related to other works – although that was shaping up 'less like an ordinary book of tales than a sort of novel of an odd aeolian kind itself . . . more interrelated than it looks' (like the idea he had put to Stern in 1940 and the stories planned in 1934). They were not being written with money in mind and might not sell – the contract had relieved him of having to polish them up to sell individually. Rather, they were being written as training for 'the Popos and peaks ahead' and because he hoped it would be a worthy book. But he feared his 'greedy daemon' which had to be prevented from plunging him into the danks and darks to which he was naturally attracted and which awaited him in *La Mordida*. Not until he had *Dark as the Grave* and *La Mordida* transcribed and stored, would he rest or feel confident about meeting his deadline. The trouble with the daemon was that he had no sense of time, nor was he concerned about his problems in the outside world, like his fears of eviction – which had surfaced again because of the post-war boom and a forthcoming election in British Columbia.[13]

The Random House contract arrived on 10 May, and for the time being all fears and anxieties evaporated. With the contract signed, he felt able to get to work on *Hear Us O Lord*, which he still hoped to publish first. But the weather then turned foul and he had to get out into the woods for more fuel. Life at the shack never ceased to offer problems, he told Matson – a bit like trying to get the *African Queen* downstream.[14] And when he did start work his daemon quickly took charge and became unpredictable, though he was able to sound positive about it to Erskine. Against that, *Dark as the Grave* had taken a premature and amazing forward leap, and he and Margerie were working in top gear.[15] By the end of May he was valiantly struggling to get back inside his work after so many diversions, interruptions, delays and paralysing attacks of anxiety.

When summer arrived, both Lowrys were working flat out. On 14 June, Malcolm informed Matson that they were well ahead of schedule. 'Work is going marvellously – to date more than 500 (!) pages typed of drafts of *Dark as the Grave*.' However, that unpredictable daemon was clearly at work, too, altering and extending. '*Hear Us Oh Lord* [sic]' was, he said, 'shaping up as something completely new . . . the whole book completely plotted out, and interrelating itself better every day.' Within that whole, 'Present Estate of Pompeii' had grown from short story to novella, thus repeating an established pattern in the development of his fiction, and foreshadowing difficulties ahead. To Erskine he reported that 'Pompeii' was 'a riot,' and was to be included as the last but two story in *Hear Us O Lord*, which now included 'October Ferry to Gabriola' as the penultimate one before 'The Forest Path to the Spring'.[16] In mid-July Margerie wrote to Marie Moore, Matson's assistant, saying that the story collection would be completed by the spring, six months ahead of schedule.[17] But a book he had long ago said was all but finished was, in good Parkinsonian style, expanding to fill the time available for its completion.

If Lowry still felt English rather than Canadian, it was due mostly to his isolation, his feeling that Canada did not value creative artists, and his dislike of the material urban civilization represented by Vancouver. However, he was the amused spectator of both local and national politics. On 14 June he wrote to Matson announcing that they now had a Marxist, though he was pleased to say not a communist, government in BC.

> It is a kind of loggers' Ruritania and tomorrow one expects to see Ezra Pound enthroned in the White House at Victoria or a royal reception for King and Queen Tito given by a procession of Colonel Blimps headed by Viscount Alexander, Raymond Massey and the Duke of Edinburgh to represent the fireman's union. Meantime Margie and I live in a sort of self-governed ruggedly individualistic sub-proletarian super-Kashmir that seems to have no relation to it at all.[18]

Seymour Lawrence, now editing for the *Atlantic*, wrote asking for a new prose work, and Lowry suggested a selection of his 'much travelled stories', from which he could choose. There were also 'October Ferry to Gabriola' and 'The Forest Path to the Spring' on which he was then working. At the end of July he reported to Matson that 750 pages of *Dark as the Grave* had been typed and were to be deposited in a bank vault. There were strong hints, however, that *The Voyage that Never Ends* was proving tyrannical and he was having difficulty bending his work to the shape demanded by the scheme. *Hear Us Oh Lord* [sic] was progressing excellently but was proving difficult to integrate into the overall plan. 'The Present Estate of Pompeii', 'October Ferry' and 'Forest Path' formed a trilogy in themselves and would bring the story cycle to 'an astonishing close', or even make a separate volume together. The Pompeian story was very good, very bawdy in parts and therefore unsaleable except to a magazine like the *Partisan Review*; consequently, he was 'grappling . . . for the umpteenth time now' with 'October Ferry'.[19] By now he had got the message that Erskine preferred to see completed work rather than unfinished sections. Margerie meantime was typing notes for *La Mordida* and had completed a hundred pages of *Eridanus*, the intermezzo in the grand scheme, which he was having to be careful not to mix into 'October Ferry'.

Newcomers had arrived at a nearby shack; Harvey Burt, a Vancouver English teacher, and Dorothy Templeton were looking for a summer hideaway. On the day they moved in Margerie arrived with a bottle. Over a drink she told them, much as she had Esther Birney, 'Now don't ever come over here in the morning because Malcolm works.' They never did go – they were looking for seclusion not company, but the Lowrys, seemingly lonely, were forever dropping in. Dorothy decided that their extravagant expressions of love disguised a great deal of mutual hostility, and she was horrified at Margerie's apparent lack of concern when Malcolm was overdue from a long swim after dark – as if she did not *want* him to return. They found Malcolm endearing, but like a child who had become too dependent on its mother.

David Markson had been working at a logging camp in Oregon when the threat of forest fires closed the camp. He wrote to say that he was hitch-hiking to Dollarton, and by coincidence, at the end of his journey he met Margerie on the bus-ride from Vancouver. At the shack he found Lowry very shy at first, but was promptly offered a drink. It was a day to celebrate, an occasion to note – 28 July. He had arrived on Lowry's forty-third birthday. Faced with his literary hero, he was both impressed and shocked. He found him extremely warm and hospitable, but even at midday he appeared to be drunk, and remained that way for the whole of the week of his stay. Margerie was full of zest and charm, clearly delighted to have the company of the good-looking young student whose thesis they had both found so flattering. In the heat of the summer Lowry was rarely out of his bathing suit and Markson was struck by his curious physical appearance.

> In a bathing suit [he had] an appearance of squat but massive strength. He had inordinately short arms that seemed inept . . . His front teeth protruded slightly. He was handsome enough, but his eyes had a kind of Scandinavian cast, a certain whiteness up there in the pigment . . . but there was a glitter, a gleam in his eye either of madness or genius, or a touch of both . . . [and] . . . there would always be a lock of hair down the middle of the forehead, too.[20]

As Lowry overcame his shyness and began to talk, Markson was astonished by the way his conversation moved, the strange verbal connections he made, the puns and allusions. 'He could start to tell a story . . . and there would be so many digressions, interruptions, jokes, so many turnings, circlings back as it were – well he himself called it "contrapuntal thought".'[21] He later realized that these strange perambulations, with their many asides and excursions into the occult and invented anecdotes about writers, were the result of alcohol, and closely resembled the

Consul's thinking in the *Volcano*. Clearly he inhabited a world of his own creation, peopled not only with the shades of dead authors ('As old Melville might have said if he'd been here, and perhaps he is . . . '), but by powers from beyond. He told Markson that one day a bird had flown into the shack and circled several times before flying off. He had said to Margerie, 'Someone is trying to get in touch,' and that day Markson's first letter had arrived.

Lowry, he recalled, swam every day – 'bellowing like a whale' – in the icy waters of the Inlet, and Margerie proudly read 'The Forest Path to the Spring', while Lowry sat listening and nodding his approval. Jimmy Craige came around and they sang sea-shanties, and drank a great deal. One day Lowry decided that Markson must see the nearby town of Port Moody, so they set off in his dinghy – 'Around the Horn to Valparaiso!' he declared. What should have been an hour's trip became an expedition of four hours with Lowry describing every part of the shore as they rowed along. They passed below enormous freighters and oil tankers moored out in the Inlet before finally reaching Port Moody. In his exuberance Lowry had somehow managed to toss his trousers overboard, and so had to enter the tough waterside saloon at which they finally arrived dressed in his bathing trunks. Markson was struck by how popular he was with the other drinkers. He was obviously well known in this particular tavern – which perhaps explained his lengthy absences on those long swims. After some hours and in pitch darkness they returned, and to Markson's alarm seemed to get lost out in the vast Inlet. There were no lights to guide them and from a far-off lumber mill came the menacing high-pitched whine of a circular saw, at which Lowry remarked, 'That's old Kafka leading his orchestra.' Then he added, 'You know, I prayed to Kafka once and he answered my prayer.' In some uncanny way he knew the direction, and sometime after midnight they arrived back at the shack, guided in only by a flickering oil lamp placed in the window by Margerie. Her only comment on their late return was, 'Oh, I knew you two chaps would have some adventure or other.'[22] It was around two in the morning; they had set out at around two in the afternoon.

Just before Markson left, heading back to his logging camp, Lowry took him outside and shyly gave to him his medallion of the Virgin of Soledad. 'Don't tell Margerie,' he said.[23] It was a generous gesture from a man for whom such trinkets could have talismanic significance. Perhaps there was a sense that the torch of genius taken from Aiken, his 'father', was now being passed on to Markson, his 'son'.

Margerie's $100 radio fee had finally arrived and had been sent on to Erskine on 9 July. Having had no acknowledgement, Lowry wrote on 5 August, anxious to know if he had received it, adding that seven hundred pages of a draft of *Dark as the Grave* had just been lodged in a bank vault.[24] A week later, with still no reply, he wrote again in case Erskine thought the material should have gone to him. He had not sent it, he said, because it was unfinished, but would send 'suitable selections' if Erskine wanted them. 'October Ferry to Gabriola' was giving him trouble because it tended to overlap with other, completed work and had to be kept consistent. 'I don't feel I've earned my hire for the last month despite a more or less sizzling (though still imperfect) "Pompeii".' And perhaps in the light of discussions with Markson, he added that he felt sorrowfully ignorant of the world of contemporary fiction. Yet despite these anxieties, the work seemed to be getting done[25] and he wrote to Norman Newton, who had returned the play of *The Ship Sails On*, which he had had to abandon. 'I have written (900) pages of present book, and Margie has typed 250 of the one after that, 750 of the one after that, and another 250 for the one after that which is only 1/4 finished in 1st draft.' That, he said, gave some idea of the size of the undertaking, and on top of that he was working to a deadline. 'Obviously I shan't be able to keep to the time schedule but I've got to produce enough to impress them that no man could.'[26]

Work was held up again in late August because Margerie had the flu. But there was good news from Germany of earnings totalling $340. The days of penury seemed to be receding into the past. However, they still owed $200 to Erskine and a similar amount to Matson, not to mention an old debt to Noxon and a $100 borrowed from Neilson in April. Hearing the Canadian Government was offering Arts Fellowships worth a tax-free $4,000 for a year in France to men of distinction over thirty, Lowry applied. The only likely snag was that he might not be considered a Canadian, but it was worth a try. The prospect of paying off all debts at once was too much to resist, and being in France would enable him to help Clarisse translate his stories. Moreover there was an even more pressing case for a year in France. He was worried that his work was developing its own momentum. A year off the Random House pay-roll might enable him to get the daemon back under control. By now *Hear Us O Lord* had grown into something different from the original concept; the last three stories had grown into a trilogy of short novels, each a hundred pages long. Erskine wrote him a generous reference for the Fellowship, affirming that the *Volcano* was one of the most extraordinary books he had ever read and that his current work in progress promised to enhance his considerable reputation further. 'Mr Lowry is a slow and careful worker, and the work that he has done has been under difficult economic circumstances.'[27]

While Margerie was ill, Malcolm wrote to Clarisse who was eager on Correa's behalf to know what he was ready to have published next in France. A translation of *Lunar Caustic* was already in hand and he had also sent them 'The Bravest Boat', and poems, which he thought best discussed when and if he got to France. She also enquired about *Ultramarine*, but again he dismissed it as 'that wretched book'. He said he was very proud of the version of *Lunar Caustic* being translated, but then revealed his fear of publishing it in America. In the present intolerant climate there, a story exposing the grim conditions in a New York psychiatric ward could be construed as un-American. He was even worried about 'The Bravest Boat' which included a passionate attack on Vancouver, and criticism of the materialism of which most Canadians were so proud. He was biased on the side of the country versus the town, Earth versus World, and the dispossessed versus those in possession. In this regard the tale was 'almost completely reactionary, and as it were conservationary.' And although 'to a certain kind of immigrant . . . Canada is heaven . . . to a certain kind of artist it can be hell too.' He was trying to express the viewpoint of the victims of industrialization rather than its beneficiaries, he said, but was worried because the story was a sideswipe at the *Vancouver Sun*, which had first attacked the Dollarton squatters, and rousing their ire might lead to eviction.[28]

Perhaps to disguise his fears about being unable to deliver the books promised, he was eager to impress Erskine with his industry. On 9 September he sent him a progress report on a postcard. Margerie had typed a hundred pages of *La Mordida* and the end of 'October Ferry' was in sight. As with the *Volcano*, there would be twelve chapters in *Hear Us O Lord*, though the narrative movement was in the opposite direction, 'towards the stars and the sunrise not the *barranca*', and concluded with the protagonist of 'Forest Path' drinking from a forest spring. 'October Ferry' was a 'terrific story' and the two preceding ones, 'Present Estate of Pompeii' and 'Henrik Ghostkeeper', were 'finished in a second draft'. These four were each as long as chapters in the *Volcano*, which was why they were proving so hard and time-consuming. Nevertheless, he wrote, he was still ahead of schedule, though he added a warning note: '*Hear Us* is becoming an anomaly since last three chapters make a novel in themselves, as I've probably said. It is damned exciting though & makes the [most] beautiful & splendid noise, though I say it.'[29]

Late that summer, Aiken sent him a copy of his newly published *Ushant*, inscribed, 'For our beloved Malc-Hambo-Blackstone with all affection from Conrad.' Three weeks later he sent his bruised but admiring reaction. 'Ushant is a knock-out – ow, how it hurts!' (the last part echoing a dire warning displayed in the Paradise Street Anatomy Museum). It was, he said, a masterwork. So far he had read it turning the pages a bit like the wind in the garden, expecting to find his own pants down on the next page, that was to say he had not read it dispassionately. 'Meantime there are wonders of prose, profound perceptions and apperceptions and complexities expressed in miraculous limpidity . . . It possesses a similar genius [to *Blue Voyage*].' Again he was portrayed as Hambo, but this time more cruelly as a drunken though endearing cuckold and plagiarist. He recognized the ruthless honesty with which Aiken had anatomized their relationship, but hinted that he might perhaps have treated their friendship with a little more respect.

> It is a bit hijeous (as our old cook used to say) from the existential point of view, to think that at those few moments one actually did imagine one was being truly helpful – however intolerable – or sharing in some mutually sacred or secret drama that one was in fact . . . being eyed (as Strindberg might say) as a rabbit for vivisection.

Then graciously he affected to see something generous in the insults. 'When I think what gobbets of Hambo you might have chosen for display I can only affirm that in the manner of forbearance Clive of India has nothing on you.'[30] In spite of this, he kept the book well away from Margerie.

By the end of September, he was engrossed in completing 'October Ferry to Gabriola', having set himself a 1 October deadline. Margerie could hear periodic sniffing and groaning as he groped for inspiration. She, meanwhile, struggled to type twenty-five or more pages of *La Mordida* each day from a variety of notebooks and off backs of envelopes, every scrap of writing considered sacred. Markson had written to say he was suffering from writer's block; Lowry's problem was the reverse – his stories were forever expanding and threatening to turn into novels. However, he was encouraged by the reception his work got when read aloud to Canadian friends, who always found his well-modulated voice and powers of dramatic expression compelling.

The necessity of avoiding another punishing winter became a matter of urgency as autumn drew to a close. They were aiming to go to California if he could get through Customs, he told Markson.[31] However, he was still nervous about McCarthyism, now deeply entrenched in America. Even Charlie Chaplin had been labelled a 'subversive' in the oppressive climate that had been generated, and now the witch-hunting Richard Nixon was on Eisenhower's ticket as a possible vice president in the forthcoming elections.

His German translator, Ten Holder, was ill and Lowry wrote to tell him he was praying for him to God and St Jude, a saint known for his powers of intercession for those in desperate straits. He also wrote to Klett (now enquiring about future work) on St Jude's name day, 28 October, asking hopefully about the proposed film, and saying that he was working to a contract but the book he had hoped to have finished was still only three-quarters complete. He was being handicapped by lack of news from England and 'the continual shadow of eviction'. 'Here today they are voting to turn our Paradise into a garden of iron and steel – no unique story.'[32]

It was probably the news that Eisenhower had been elected president and Nixon vice president on 5 November, that decided Lowry against going to California for the winter. So they now considered moving into Vancouver again before the bad weather set in. By mid-November he reported to Erskine that 1,600 pages of *La Mordida* and *The Ordeal* were about to be lodged in the bank, to join *Dark as the Grave*. It would take many more months to get it into shape, but something else was growing. 'October Ferry' had expanded into a short novel of some 160 pages, and was occupying more and more of his time. '*October Ferry* in this present form wasn't on my itinerary but since it developed so well I persevered and am persevering.' There was some cutting and rewriting to do, but,

> The rest of *Hear Us* has been building up too. It should be finished well in time . . . though not quite as soon as I thought, partly because of going up and down on this ferry so many times. Anyway, it's one of the world's best stories, though I say it who ought not.[33]

So the concluding trilogy in the short-story collection had become a quartet, and a hint of panic now entered Lowry's letter to Erskine.

'Please send a word, for my recasting of Gabriola and the delay caused by the last month have given me a bad case of the "At my back I always hears". In point of fact, the amount accomplished . . . has been very great.'[34]

Amid growing fears about the way his work was developing, one piece of comfort did come his way. A cable from Liverpool told him that more money would soon be due from the estate. Shortly afterwards, in mid-November, they moved into the Bayview Apartment Hotel at 1359 Davie Street in Vancouver. It was, he wrote later, 'less a place to invite a friend than ambush your worst enemy and even that's an understatement: misery-grisery'.[35] They had been there just a few weeks when he heard that Clemens Ten Holder was dead. It was as if he had lost yet another close friend. 'It seems to me, I, also have died; with Clemens,' he wrote.[36]

If he had had the idea that he could work with his editor on drafts of his text as he had with Noxon and Aiken, he was soon disappointed. Even though Erskine was impressed by news of the truckload of material deposited at the bank, he wrote to say that he would like to see any stories in roughly final shape, but it would be a waste of time to work on piecemeal rewritings by post.[37] But Lowry was beginning to worry about his work from another perspective. He wrote later that he was uneasy in case 'the whole work itself was in places not consonant with the best mental health and spiritual economy of its benighted author.' He had taken some weeks off to read nothing but psychology, and what he had learned about himself was not very encouraging.[38] Yet he seemed to emerge unscathed from his psychological pessimism, and by the end of November, Margerie reported him hard at work once more. On 3 December, Marie Moore of Matson's wrote that New American Library were interested in his stories. He was duly cheered and replied that he hoped the novellas he was working on would interest editors, too.

Moving into Vancouver meant paying rent again, and there was much agonizing over money due from England, from France, and from Klett. The German money did arrive, but a mere $66.66 instead of the $340 expected, and there was a sorry little $11.55 from Harcourt Brace for the *Volcano*.[39] For Christmas they went to the Neilsons on Bowen Island, Lowry taking along *October Ferry* to try on a new audience. Neilson wanted to record him reading 'Strange Comfort Afforded by the Profession', but he became so drunk it seems he imagined himself to be talking to a crocodile, and no recording was made. On Boxing

Day he was hungover and Margerie fell ill with stomach pains, so they returned to Vancouver, Lowry not unusually leaving his 'Strange Comfort' manuscript behind. Margerie took a week to recover, but was well enough a few days later to write an apologetic thank you letter to which Lowry added the ironic postscript, 'The crocodile is doing well and has already learned to sing Life gets tedious don't it.'[40]

There was good news at the beginning of January when *New World Writing* accepted 'Strange Comfort Afforded by the Profession'. It was only the second story he had published since 1934, the first since Davenport's unbidden publication of 'Economic Conference 1934' over three years before. He had every reason to be pleased, but, typically, even this modest success found him unprepared. He had revised this story, he told Matson, but might have to revise the revision.[41]

The work in progress – all notes and drafts – had now been typed and stored in the Vancouver bank, except the intermezzo, *Eridanus*, which was being cannibalized by *October Ferry*. The latter had obsessed and delighted him for months, but had now burgeoned into a novel. It was not proving easy, he told Matson, but he was getting there 'not too far behind schedule'.[42] By the end of February the completion of the story, still considered by Lowry as a part of *Hear Us O Lord*, hove into sight again and he told Erskine to expect it within a few days. That would be followed by 'Ghostkeeper' and 'Pompeii' at monthly intervals. 'Am not far behind,' he said, '– or am I in front?' As an afterthought, and with a hint of foreboding, he added that *October Ferry* had almost slaughtered him, but he hoped that Erskine did not hate it.[43] It had changed greatly from the simple story of two people seeking a new home on Gabriola Island which he had written with Margerie in 1947. By the end of 1950 he had done a longer version and since October 1951 had redrafted and revised it. Upon signing his contract he had picked it up again and it had expanded into a novella. Its narrator, Ethan Llewelyn, a lawyer like his friend McConnell, having failed ingloriously to defend a man on a murder charge, retires to Eridanus, but is threatened with eviction. He and his wife Jacqueline travel to Gabriola in search of a new home. The journey, like so many in Lowry's stories, offers him the opportunity to reflect remorsefully on his past, constantly reminded of it by sights of advertisements and by intrusive memories. A chance meeting with an old client, whom he *had* saved from a murder charge, brings him face to face with his past guilts, and enables him to face up to the future. Although Eridanus is reprieved, the need to find a new home, and a new start, is more important than ever.

Some money from England seems to have arrived towards the middle of March and he was able to pay off his debt to Neilson. But that happy event was soon overtaken by a sequence of disasters which was to have a devastating effect on his whole programme of work. News came that Margerie's mother was gravely ill, possibly dying, and Malcolm insisted that she go home at once. When she arrived Bert urged her to have a medical, and tests suggested that she might need treatment for a blood condition. Left alone, Malcolm began to neglect himself. Without Margerie to type his work, he began drinking. Finally, he abandoned the apartment and found a room in a seedy hotel in Vancouver's downtown skid row. After a few days of alcoholic squalor, he called Norman Newton, drunk and distressed. Newton and his wife Gloria immediately went to find him and when they did he seemed to them to be disturbed and hallucinating, doubtless suffering from DT's.

They took him to the coach house they were renting and put him up on the living-room couch. He would not eat, refused to stop drinking and was occasionally sick. The DT's continued and when he had a nosebleed Gloria wanted to call a doctor, but he refused to let her. He talked constantly in his own strange disconnected way, sometimes to himself and sometimes apparently to the Newtons, who began to find his presence exhausting; his state was pitiful and he was obviously terrified of being left alone.[44] He was drinking gin and tomato juice, so Newton began to cut down the gin in every succeeding drink. Lowry, he decided, knew his drinks were being doctored, but had to go through the charade of 'having a drink' to be happy – a kind of oral compulsion like thumb-sucking, he thought.[45] He had long hero-worshipped Lowry, but now began to regard him as pathetic. When he returned from work on the second day, his one-time hero lay stiffly on the couch, giggling like a child, and he concluded, not unlike Aiken, that he lacked an adult personality, was somehow empty, as if never having lived at all.[46] They got Margerie's phone number from him and called her in LA. She said she would return as soon as possible, but did not, it seems, make haste. Her family had discovered how she was living, and told her she should be living a far better life as the wife of a successful author, and it took less persuading than it would have a few years earlier to convince her of this.

Finally, finding him too much to cope with, Newton rang friends who suggested he be taken to the Neilsons. Next morning Newton shaved him, and a friend drove him to the ferry and took him across to Bowen Island. To help him recuperate, the Neilsons got him reading.

In a copy of *Atlantic Monthly* he read an article by Thomas Mann, on the theme of the passage through the Perilous Chapel in search of the Holy Grail in *The Magic Mountain*, which led him to start rethinking his novel. Anxious about Erskine, who was expecting soon to receive the first book in his contract, he brought him up to date with the latest setback. The delay over *October Ferry* was, he said, due to 'serious difficulties of sickness' and sudden and tragic happenings. But now Margerie had returned, and everything depended on when she could get back to the typewriter. He was on a cliff's edge on Bowen Island, he said, trying feverishly to complete *October Ferry* alone 'in a beautiful perilous chapel belonging to a great mutual friend' and ought to be able to send him a final version soon, whatever might happen. He hoped that Erskine would be patient with him.[47] Margerie in fact seems not to have been eager to see him until he had recovered himself, and spent a week in early April going back and forth between Vancouver and Dollarton preparing for their return to the shack.

By 11 April they were back in Dollarton and Lowry was able to resume work. But the disruption of the past weeks was now to be transformed into ultimate disaster. He had a new conception of *October Ferry to Gabriola*, and found he had to reconstruct the story entirely. Added to this, Margerie was still unwell and his conscience was being torn, both over his inability to fulfil his promises to Erskine and the feeling that by overworking Margerie he was responsible for her illness. He had more reason than ever to offer prayers to the charitable St Jude. 'You wouldn't think I had troubles about religion but I do,' he told Markson, 'and especially with my conscience which races like an overheated engine sometimes.'[48]

Her family having insisted that she deserved more than life in a shack, Margerie now began to complain that Dollarton was simply not good for her health. This plus the constant threat of eviction was uppermost in Lowry's mind when he replied to a sympathetic letter from Erskine. It was a theme with which he was deeply engaged in *October Ferry*, and living the experience was an important part of writing the story, so he was in no mind to think about leaving. If they were Swedenborgian angels, he mused, they could take the place with them, embracing joy, in Blake's sense, as it flies. But at this critical point he had discovered from Mann that his hero was probably searching for the Holy Grail and this gave a tremendous fillip to his imagination while he was going through a Perilous Chapel of his own. So, instead of finishing the book as planned he had written 'another long & horrendous scene which I'm not quite sure now belongs – even though this, despite all my efforts to make the thing behave otherwise really does make it in[to] a novel'.[49] So there it was. Erskine had asked for a novel first, and Lowry seems to have decided that he would get one, but it would be *October Ferry* rather than *Lunar Caustic*, which he feared would get him into trouble in America.

In a PS to his letter, Margerie added the prophetic words,

> Malc is engaged in a life & death struggle with his bloody story, which seems to have turned into a novel, & he's determined to get through to the end [of] this work before it kills us both . . . *October Ferry*. . . is going to be first rate Lowry. At the moment it is, to me, a vampire, a tiger, a merciless tyrant but I *think* we are going to survive & defeat the goddam thing after all.[50]

Lowry had decided that his novel was to be a moral parable with deep religious significance. The journey to Gabriola was a pilgrim's progress in search of redemption. It concerned 'the tragedy that man is not an angel'. Writing it had become a matter of 'personal salvation . . . a matter of life or death, or re-birth, as it were, for its author, not to say sanity or otherwise'. Ethan's journey with Jacqueline was now to be beset by further obstacles, he was to be confronted with new ordeals and indictments – for past lies, for failing to help save a young boy condemned to hang, for having all but murdered a college friend, Peter Cordwainer.

The introduction of the Cordwainer character, based on Fitte, seemingly prompted by the image of the gassed student in Cocteau's *Orphée*, reveals the still crucifying effects on him of what happened in 1929. Eviction is linked in Llewelyn's mind to the feeling that he too is fated to kill himself. Not only is he incapable of defending a murderer, he is unable to control the murderer within himself, a monster rooted somewhere in his childhood. As a result he is pursued by furies, and threatened by encroaching civilization and hostile elements, like fire. He is not just an exile but an outcast, like the Wandering Jew or Heathcliff, searching for redemption through contact with the simple craftsmen on the beach at Eridanus, through the powers of magic (his wife is a magician's daughter) to counterbalance the irrationality of life, and through submission to ordeals that might thereby purge him of sin. He is both self-analyst and father-confessor at the same time. The reconceived novel was so personal that it is not surprising that he feared for his own sanity in writing it, though he may have hoped for the opposite effect.

Towards the end of April Erskine asked for a progress report and, no doubt driven by that overheated engine of conscience, Lowry replied with 'a Pantagruel letter' which was never sent but which revealed the complex psychological state into which he had sunk. Margerie was again ill, he said, this time with worms, and work had ground to a halt because she could not type and he could not spare the time to learn. Both he and the work had suffered, but not necessarily to the work's detriment. *October Ferry* had cost him far more pain than the *Volcano*, and he was suffering because it had thrown him completely off schedule. Yet even now he hoped it would still fit into *Hear Us O Lord*. He had had to write two new passages to include the Perilous Chapel theme and to take account of his hero's state of mind. He hoped thus to engage the reader in wondering what experience the author was passing through to be able to recreate such a deliberate disintegration of consciousness; Lowry now saw the book as a challenge to his 'actual personal salvation'. In other words, it had become a means of self-analysis, the logical conclusion of the approach to creativity taken from Aiken, who had also come to rely on writing to maintain his mental stability. It was a risky business, but 'perhaps miracles may be wrought with the pen even while actual catatonias seem to vampire the mind'. One nightmare told him that he should have taken Erskine's advice and got straight down to a novel. The stories were originally done for money, but one was becoming unwieldy. And yet he knew that with a little work the cycle would be shown to have both a beautiful form and to make a beautiful sound when taken together. 'But at my back I always hear Time's winged chariot changing gear.'

Moreover he sometimes had the terrible thought that Erskine might not like *October Ferry*. He would be glad, he said, of a comforting word. His daemon was still in charge. 'I have not yet learned how to master that bugger.' It had transformed 'an innocent and beautiful story of human longing into quite the most guilt-laden and in places quite Satanically horrendous document it has ever been my unfortunate lot to read, let alone have to imagine I wrote.' Its one saving grace was that in places it was very funny. Yet he believed his book would be 'a psychological triumph of the first order'.

> True you have not been paying me to achieve psychological triumphs of the first order, for my own benefit: but here the challenge seemed – and seems – ultimate, a matter of life and death, or rebirth, as it

> were, for its author, not to say sanity or otherwise: perhaps I overstate the case, but my love for this place and my fear of losing it, nay actual terror, has begun to exceed all bounds.

It would be a bitter pill to swallow if he had to return his advance and to have to admit that the office boy, Reynal, had been right all along. Meanwhile they seemed under a special providence as the bulldozers crashed everywhere else but in Eridanus.[51]

There were still delays in getting his money from England and he found Stuart's legalistic letters hard to fathom. He was also pessimistic about an Overseas Fellowship, since to be a landed immigrant was now no longer enough to count as a Canadian; one had to swear a loyalty oath and forfeit one's British passport, something he was not prepared to do. If Canada wanted artists to stay there, he thought, they should not try to bribe them to renounce old loyalties with Fellowships. With freedom of speech under threat in America, and semi-fascist parties, like Social Credit, close to taking power in British Columbia, the old blue British passport was to him a symbol and guarantee of freedom. Even the more Marxist CCF party he regarded as quasi-totalitarian in an Orwellian sense and bad news for creative artists. He also disliked what he saw as a tough, intolerant attitude among some Canadians and thought the tendency to use informers and the power of the ubiquitous Mounties were inimical to freedom, which did not mean to say he did not love the country. He and Margerie talked about maybe moving to the sterling bloc – somewhere like Barbados, or Majorca, where Robert Graves lived, or even to Sicily, where Lawrence had once been.

Finally he resisted sending this breast-baring letter and instead sent Erskine a précis of the more optimistic points, adding that he was on the wagon, living an ascetic but healthy life, and their position on the beach was reassuring for once. *October Ferry* had taken him over and turned into Grand Guignol, but would end in triumph. With 'The Forest Path' and the two other novellas from *Hear Us O Lord* it could make up a good single volume. 'So I am behind – or ahead of – schedule: I can't be sure which.'[52] It was now confirmed that he had been turned down for an Overseas Fellowship, so there was no escape to France and therefore no way out of that looming November deadline. Forgetting Erskine's preference for finished work, he asked whether he would like to receive *October Ferry* serially, recalling how enjoyable it was sending *Volcano* proofs to him in instalments.

He had reverted to his old punishing schedule of working fifteen-hour stints late into the night and leaving Margerie to type the results next day. He still worked standing up, moving between notes and drafts scattered around the shack – the working method somehow patterning Lowry's observed conversational style – shifting and moving off at tangents before returning to the mainstream. The danger of this *modus operandi* was that any interruption could mean losing the thread that held the whole multi-layered contraption together. He also found it personally painful and taxing trying to grapple with the growing monster that was *October Ferry*.

The arrival of a copy of *New World Writing* containing 'Strange Comfort Afforded by the Profession' should have stiffened his wilting self-confidence, but although he supplied the editor with a list of people around the world who might be sent copies, he was also seized by his ever-lurking fear of charges of plagiarism. He said that he had just found, in a literary magazine left in the shack, an article linking Poe and Keats in a way which made it appear he might have lifted the idea for his story. He was anxious to assure the editor that it was not plagiarism since it had first been written in 1949. And he continued to be plagued by what he saw as threats to artistic freedom in North America. As if to confirm his worst fears, on 19 June, American anti-Communist hysteria reached a crescendo with the execution of the Rosenbergs for spying. If Margerie still wished to go to California to escape the Canadian winter, she would again have to go alone.

His debt to Erskine was finally repaid on 26 June and he promised to send him the first instalment of *October Ferry* the following week. But it was not to be. That evening they entertained George Robertson with poetry and gin, and the following afternoon another old student of Birney's, Gene Lawrence, now an architect, arrived with the customary bottle. This time the drink flowed more liberally. At one point Margerie sent them off to get water from the store, and on the way Lowry said he would show Lawrence the spot where he and Margerie had envisioned Yvonne's death in the *Volcano*. As they climbed the path, Lowry caught his foot in an upraised tree-root and fell, breaking his leg in several places and dislocating his ankle. After receiving first aid from their neighbours, Harvey and Dorothy, he lay in agony all night. Next morning Margerie decided to get him to the hospital.

She climbed the path to the store only to be set upon by Cummins's large black guard dog, and her right thigh was severely mauled. Although she was bleeding badly, she called the hospital, returned back down the hill to tell Lowry that the ambulance was on the way, and then climbed back again to guide the ambulancemen down. When they saw her they insisted that she needed treatment too, and so they both went along.

Lowry's condition was complicated by his varicose veins, but after a week they returned home, Lowry condemned to wear his leg in a plaster cast for three months. Now he had to try picking up where he had left off and explain to Erskine why his work had not been delivered as promised. Having told him so often that he was on the wagon he could hardly say that his accident was caused by drink, so he said that the root had been a snare raised by children. Hospitalization and the break from work, he confessed, had caused him a problem: the thread of what he had written recently had gone. On reading it through, however, he was impressed by its power and originality; it reflected the discipline he had achieved before the accident. He would not take time to convalesce, being determined to finish 'the flaming bloody thing' despite considerable pain. Then rather ominously he added that none of his Grand Guignol experiences in the hospital would be wasted, and he had had the presence of mind to keep his pencil at the ready. So here was something else to be worked into the book, by now a means of absorbing and dealing with all present agonies and private torments. Despite the pain, he said, he was working in bed, and Erskine could expect the first instalment within the week.[53]

Since Erskine's replies to his long letters of excuse and exposition of his albatross of a novel were brief, he and Margerie had somehow created a world in which his genius could do no wrong and *October Ferry* could only be the best book he had ever written. Erskine would therefore understand the endless promises, assurances, delays and excuses. A week after promising him the manuscript he was writing again to excuse its delay. Margerie had had no time to type, his cast had come loose requiring a further visit to the hospital, he had difficulty working for more than twenty minutes at a stretch, and in his cast he could not work in his usual manner, moving from draft to draft around the room. However, he was optimistic about the original plan of *Hear Us O Lord*, though he would now need Erskine's advice on how to encompass the short story which had turned epic.

On his forty-fourth birthday, he was photographed by Margerie on his crutch, sporting a beard grown in hospital, he said, as a gesture against the conformist world.[54] November was still the deadline in mind as he slowly resumed work. Margerie wrote to Erskine, 'Malc really *needs*. . . reassurances from you, not to mention editorial advice, at this point. He's worrying himself into a STATE . . . the November first date . . . now looms like a black giant with teeth and claws taking a step nearer every day.'[55] The problem was that *October Ferry* was only an offshoot of the work he really wanted to do, but having got so far he felt he could not go back. He was depressed about possibly missing the deadline, and illness – his accident and her dog-bite – had simply made things worse. By November they would have to find somewhere to live away from Dollarton, and eventually hoped to move to southern Italy for a year to finish the whole *Voyage that Never Ends* there. She suggested that monthly payments might be halted until he caught up lost time, but first of all he would like to deliver something worthwhile and publishable 'as an earnest of things to come'. She asked Erskine to send him a word of comfort, and enclosed a letter from him which he had been unable to finish. Now in some desperation they were both appealing to him no longer as an editor but as a friend. It seems not to have occurred to either of them to ask Matson to negotiate an extension on the deadline.

To celebrate the removal of the cast from his right leg on 21 September, Lowry plunged into the inlet in a deep dive. 'Getting up,' he told Markson, 'was another thing.'[56] Five days later he made a will, leaving everything to Margerie, and his income in trust to his widow after his death as long as she remained his widow, a form of words seemingly embedded in Arthur Lowry's own convoluted will and to which he was chained. Margerie was also chained by this, meaning that if Malcolm died she would inherit his income only for as long as she did not remarry. Harvey and Dorothy acted as witnesses with Stuart Lowry named as executor. (Malcolm later told Dorothy that Margerie had bullied him into leaving everything to her and into putting their joint account entirely in her name.)[57] Now, as he still refused to go to California and they were too poor to go abroad, they were both thinking again about Vancouver for the winter.

Before moving, however, Lowry finally sent Erskine the first hundred pages of *October Ferry to Gabriola*, suggesting keys to its interpretation. There was still some way to go to a final draft, he said, but the book would come in batches and the final text would be about three times as long as the first batch sent. There were overlaps with other things, and he had not entirely abandoned his original plans, but he would need Erskine's advice on this. Eighteen months after signing his contract he was little nearer to producing what originally he had promised to produce, namely the full short-story collection and *The*

Voyage that Never Ends. To say he needed Erskine's help was one thing, but to get back on track he needed help from someone closer at hand, someone like Aiken, Davenport or Noxon, with more literary perception than Margerie, who was too involved to give detached opinions or advice. She kept reminding him that *Under the Volcano* had begun as a short story about a bus ride and she believed that this book was just as great if not greater. Isolated as he was, Lowry's judgement had suffered, and, extraordinarily enough, he asked Erskine after reading it to pass the first batch of manuscript to Frank Taylor and David Markson.

As a further excuse for the delay, he said his leg had been worse than originally thought, that Margerie was ill with 'one feminine trouble after another', and as he could not type or contemplate life without her he would have 'a hell of a problem' trying to meet his 1 November deadline. Probably he could not do that anyway because the book simply would not stop growing.[58] He was still worried at having no news of his money from England, and began to suspect that Random House might cut him off. He was caught, he said, between optimism on the one hand and panic on the other – fearful of being unable to continue working if he missed the deadline and his payments were stopped, and if no money came from England. He put in a plea for some sort of reprieve. Could they not find a way to penalize him short of 'absolute excommunication', or devise a compromise of some kind? Meantime, he felt certain of being able to send in more of the novel by 1 November. It was a good, original book 'in its hildy-wildy way', and at least it was not about a writer. 'The hell it's not,' he added, wryly.[59]

Erskine acknowledged receipt of the manuscript on 22 October, saying he was reading it and would reserve an opinion for later. Lowry meanwhile sent off another batch, assuring him that the book got much better as it went along.

> Brother you just wait till that old tide starts a'coming in, a'roarin' and a'growlin' and it does too, a bit: in the next batch, and then what rugs and jugs & candlelights; and corpses and last judgements and perilous chapels; I suppose I ought to tell you for your peace of mind that I *do* get my bloody hapless characters off the bus eventually and *on* to the ferry.[60]

In order to explain what he called 'the magic of Dr Lowry's dialectical-Hegelian-spiritualism-cabbalistic-Swedenborgian-conservative-Christian-anarchism for ailing paranoiacs [*sic*]' he drew a diagram show-

showing how the relationship between the three parts of the book had their geographical counterparts on terra firma:

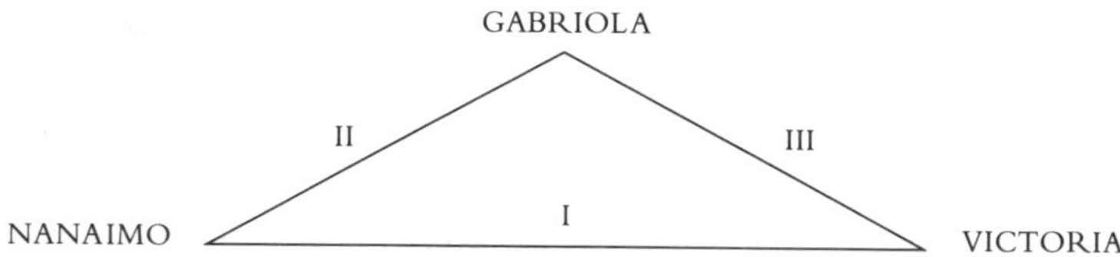

He was now enjoying writing the book, unlike a year earlier when every page was covered with invocations to St Jude and it took him three months to produce as many readable pages. A few days later he was writing to say that the next batch had been held up because Margerie had criticized part of it and he had thrown it out, and was now grappling with overhauling a previous final draft of the book in an earlier version. It must have seemed to Erskine all ominously muddled.[61]

A decision to climb on board the wagon lasted only briefly and was abandoned on 11 November when Harvey Burt brought the news that Dylan Thomas had died in New York's St Vincent Hospital. With an enormous sense of grief, they drank his health in gin and poured a libation on Lowry's verandah before ritualistically chopping down a dead tree which was threatening to fall on the shack. On the same day, the news arrived from Marie Moore that 'The Bravest Boat' had been accepted by the *Partisan Review*, and that 'Strange Comfort' was to appear in an Italian anthology of English stories.

They moved into Vancouver on 15 November (the twenty-fourth anniversary of 'that day' – Paul Fitte's suicide), this time to Caroline Court, a seven-storey apartment block at 1058 Nelson Street, where he was greeted by an inspiring letter from Maurice Nadeau from *Les Lettres Nouvelles* in Paris, enclosing the latest edition of the magazine which contained a translation of 'The Bravest Boat'. 'I would be very happy, dear Malcolm Lowry, to publish any new story of yours which you might choose,' wrote Nadeau. 'I would be equally happy to know if you have a manuscript ready for publication in a volume for the library in the same collection as *Under the Volcano* appeared.' There was, sadly for Lowry, no similar letter from Erskine.

Indeed, as November wore on and there was no news from Random House, he descended into a Gothic gloom, put his head down and ploughed on with *October Ferry*. Then, just before Christmas Eve, he received a terse, businesslike letter from Erskine: 'I have been reminded by the Keeper of Contracts that we are now six weeks beyond the first delivery date (November 1, 1953) called for in your three-book agreement and in the middle of the 90-day period by which the contract allows that date to be extended.' He asked for a progress report and some idea of where the story was going. He needed to know in detail because there was to be an 'official review' of the situation.[62] (He had sent a personal letter separately to soften the blow but it was delayed in the post.) Considering the urgent request for reassurance from Lowry two years before when Erskine had failed to put 'Love' at the bottom of his cable, this official-sounding letter, signed simply 'All the best', must have driven an icicle into Lowry's heart. He said later that 'the killing tone of [that] letter made us want to fall out of the window rather than take anything off the Christmas tree.'[63] The signal was clear: the party of self-indulgence was over, and, friend though Erskine was, he was also an editor who had put his reputation on the line by backing Lowry.

They were bound for Bowen Island to spent Christmas with the Neilsons and there the condemned man found time for a cheery last meal and plenty of drinks before the hanging. When he had recovered from his festive hangover on the 27th, Lowry began composing, in his own way, the 'clear and brief' update on his progress which Erskine had requested. He seems to have thought that he was now having to defend not just his book, but his whole sense of himself as a writer. His 'clear and brief' reply ran to over three closely typed pages, and must have seemed anything but 'brief' and decidedly 'unclear'. It gave an insight into the state and condition of his increasingly complex relationship with Margerie, where tensions and suppressed hostilities lurked behind a façade of extravagant love and devotion.

He had, he said, just completed forty new pages (the chapter entitled 'The Element Follows You Around, Sir!', based on his experiences of fire in Niagara) which were ready to be dispatched, making him about half-way through the 400- to 450-page novel. There would, he hoped, be a further hundred pages by the extended deadline, 28 January. In its untyped and unrevised form it was complete but for possible hitches or inspirations. 'Where it insists on growing I must give it its head.' Of course, it might be finished earlier, and, as to the story's direction, there was an excellent and sinister reason for its apparent failure to move forward. 'It turns out that both characters are potential suicides. Each one had become afraid that in a fit of hysteria or drunkenness one may murder the other.' So it was not easy for the protagonists, Ethan and

Jacqueline, to see any meaning in the present or future. And that was the whole plot of the novel – getting to Gabriola was like Kafka's K not getting to the Castle. Both, it turns out, are 'hopped up to the gills' and Ethan is unaware till later that he is hungover from secretly swallowing the barbiturates he has been filching from Jacqueline. (All strangely prophetic; but he was sticking limpet-close to his own experience.)

He was better equipped to write it than to describe it, he told Erskine, but it was bloody good, though not meant to slot into any specific category or conform to any usual rules for the novel. The hero, now a complete misanthropist, was able to keep himself from a complete breakdown only with the help of barbiturates. He had had to 'psychologically' renounce his attachment to Eridanus (an infantile one) and face up to a terrible truth about himself. He was too mentally ill to remain there. But more:

> It is he and no one else that produces the so-called coincidences and disasters that happen to them: himself, as it were, the paranoiac black magician of their own lives. He has to face the fact also that he actually is – or has been next-door to, a murderer and criminal himself in the case of Cordwainer: though it's time he stopped punishing himself – he's had 20 years of penal servitude already – and others for it.

Cordwainer appears in a dream to inform Ethan that he has been prevented from settling into his lot as a suicide in the next world by Ethan's continual self-punishment for his murder, which has kept drawing him back to this world. 'If Ethan should kill himself he would thus be turning Cordwainer's spirit into Ethan's murderer.' Because of this Ethan has to renounce Eridanus, his destructive life and alcohol. The end, said Lowry, was a kind of *Volcano* in reverse, presumably meaning his furies were turned into mercies. It was as if he had taken his own life by the scruff of the neck, ruthlessly analysed it, and, playing novelist of his own life, was writing a happy end for it to conclude this part of his therapy.

Of course, he added, the book lost something by not being in the company of its fellows, 'The Forest Path to the Spring', 'Ghostkeeper' and 'Present Estate of Pompeii', with which it formed a quartet within *Hear Us O Lord from Heaven Thy Dwelling Place*, which he could quite easily finish now. He must have thought that with this one novel and the story collection he was close to having two books ready to deliver.

Meantime he had sent an SOS to England for his share of Evelyn's money, and hoped soon to be able to buy time from Random House, realizing they might be dissatisfied with *October Ferry*. In fact he half-expected to be told his monthly payments were being suspended. If payments had to be cut off, he told Erskine, he would find some way to keep going. Then, in a proposal which revealed how unaware he was of quite what impression he had produced so far, he added that if *October Ferry* could not be finished by the extended deadline, he could abandon the rest of *Hear Us O Lord* for the time being and ask Erskine to consider *October Ferry* as a novel on its own. It would not be difficult for him then to revise *Lunar Caustic* by the following deadline.

In a postscript, he recast the book in psychological mode, which might, he said, cast doubt on the author's sanity, but the thing can be read thus as an abreaction or cathexis and the news that the Llewelyn's Eridanus had been spared and they are not to be evicted acts like the news of the armistice on shell-shocked soldiers, and the past with all its suffering is thrown off. 'The future, once accepted in this case, imposes its own teleology . . .' Then, in what seems a darkly confessional mode, he wrote,

> Both protagonists lie to themselves, perhaps they will have to continue to do so. Our expression is the ancient psychiatric one that it is nobler to do so than to make a suicide pact, and the meaning widens on the reader's soul as he realises what I mean by eviction.[64]

When Erskine had looked at the first batch of *October Ferry* he thought it the most tedious thing he had ever read.[65] He was now on the spot. He knew that once Bob Haas saw it Lowry's money would be stopped, and so resolved to withhold it for as long as possible. Then, after reading Lowry's letter of 27 December, he decided he could do so no longer. When Haas had read it he sent Erskine a note. 'A. E. Is this about as confused as anything can be, or is it just me? Anyway, what do you suggest we do now?'[66]

On 4 January, back in Vancouver, Lowry heard that £500 was on its way from England. Apart from the money held in trust under the 1938 Settlement, boosted since his mother's death, over the next month he received £8,000 after tax (in cash and securities) as his share of Evelyn's estate. This was no doubt much less than Margerie expected from Malcolm's stories of oil and cotton riches and jewellery, and the idea of a large amount being held in trust she must have found irksome. However, to her it meant they now had enough to travel away from Dollarton; to Malcolm it meant the possibility of buying time from Random House and putting off that dreaded deadline.

He wrote immediately to Erskine saying that he was now able to do what he had long wanted, namely to ask for temporary suspension of his payments to give him time to deliver *October Ferry* and to indicate the shape of work to come. He was anxious for his book not to be judged on what had so far been sent in. Its form was necessarily bizarre and would go on getting more bizarre. Moreover the next chunk of manuscript received might be in the wrong place and might need editing. He hoped he had not put Erskine in the awkward spot of having to write to him saying that payment had been suspended or something worse, and that their letters might cross.[67] The informal letter Erskine had sent separately had said he was anxious that he not be cut off and was doing all he could to prevent it. When it arrived late, Lowry replied hoping that he had not embarrassed him too much.

But Haas and Erskine had come to a decision already, and on 6 January, Erskine wrote suspending payments. They felt uneasy about where his book was going, he said. While he had made it sound interesting and exciting, they were worried that its themes were not being clearly conveyed and that it lacked the surface drama and pure narrative to draw the reader in. If it could be done they were sure he could do it, but unlike the *Volcano*, with its many beautifully orchestrated levels, this book seemed overweighted with ideas which it could not bear. He apologized for the decision but said that things might change once the book was read in its finished state. He had told Matson, who understood and seemed in accord with the decision.[68] In a separate private note, which arrived later, he added that Haas had taken a 'dimmer view even than mine, perhaps because more objective'.

For Lowry here was a doom-laden echo of Giroux's rejection two years earlier. He was crucified, barely able to believe that Erskine could write such a letter. He had treated him more as a friend than as an editor, had confided in him rather than in Matson his troubles, fears, and ambitions. In return he was being treated in a cold, formal and business-like manner and though he had expected that payments might be suspended for lateness (for all that he had until the end of January on an extended deadline), and had himself requested this suspension, here he was being cut off because the material was judged unclear, unexciting and narratively undramatic. He was mortified, and felt keenly the loss of face at what he saw as both a punishment and a reflection on his work. His sense of identity as a writer – perhaps the only one he had – was being undermined, and this could, if it got out, seriously damage his reputation. He felt very bitter, especially when Erskine failed to acknowledge his own letter proposing that payments be suspended. He realized the letters had crossed (it was one of those wretched accidents to which he was prone) but he thought that Erskine should have acknowledged that he had requested suspension first. He told Neilson that 'an unconscionable amount of misery-grisery and anxiety' had descended upon him.[69] Yet the story of Hemingway surviving two plane crashes which he cut from the *Vancouver Sun* may have reassured him that he was in good literary company where disasters were concerned.

CHAPTER XXIV

EVICTED FROM THE PARADISE GARDEN

1954

> Two books are being writ, of which the world shall see only one, and that the bungled one. The larger book, and the infinitely better, is for Pierre's own private shelf. That it is, whose unfathomable cravings drink his blood.
>
> HERMAN MELVILLE, *Pierre*

A sudden change of weather, when the worst blizzards for four years cut Vancouver off from the rest of the world, can only have heightened Lowry's sense of misery and isolation. By the time he heard from Matson in mid-January, confirming Random House's position, Erskine had still not acknowledged his letter requesting suspension, and evidently had not told Matson of it. By now regretting having sidelined his agent, he wrote to Matson on 25 January putting his side of the story and apologizing that a sense of loyalty to Erskine had inhibited him from keeping his agent informed of the situation. It had arisen partly because Erskine had been 'tepid' about *Hear Us O Lord*, and preferred a novel first, so he had let *October Ferry* develop into 'a full-dress novel'. Despite his accident he had never asked Random House for emergency money as he might have done, because such accidents sounded 'too much like clairvoyance', 'too . . . psychologically suspect'.

He pointed out that he had warned Erskine in September that he might be behind, but was told not to worry, he had three months' grace, until 1 February. If it had seemed an urgent matter he would have got Matson to deal with it, and would have anyway, except that he needed the monthly payments because his accident had been so costly. He thought it unfair to judge his work on just 159 pages of the book. 'It appeared I had not only laid a Great Auk's Egg, but where, even, was the Egg?' He complained of Erskine's failure to acknowledge his letter, implying that he had cut him off *after* receiving it, so giving the firm a better chance of reclaiming their money. The cutting off was distressing and mortifying, and the way of doing it implied irresponsibility on his part when in fact he had been writing to Erskine about it for months. It appeared to be both a punishment and an impugning of the work itself. But this novel would not admit of stock responses, it was something new. Most likely they were right and it was not a 'good' book. It wasn't, nor did it set out to be one. Rather it considered itself to be a classic.[1] He did not impugn anyone's powers of reading, but in the same situation identical criticism might have been levelled against the *Volcano*, which Haas had once turned down. He sent Matson 'The Element Follows You Around, Sir!', the chapter written in five days just before Christmas, as a sample and to prove that the book could move horizontally as well as vertically. This was shrewd because it is undoubtedly one of the strongest sections of the book, and quintessential Lowry.

He realized that he had made several bad mistakes. He should have kept Matson informed at every stage and asked him to rearrange payments and deadlines, he should not have assumed that he could depend on Erskine as a friend when Erskine had his own job to do and his own reputation to uphold. He should either have insisted on Random House publishing *Hear Us O Lord* more or less as it stood when he signed his contract or finished off *Lunar Caustic*, which Erskine liked, first, and he should not have fed material through in batches, but sent only finished material. Two weeks after receiving Erskine's letter, Lowry replied to him, obviously still much distressed and angry.

> My God, you old rapscallion. I don't mean that I'm really distressed by the set-back, am not over sensitive (like hell I'm not, as you once observed, in fact my throte is only cutte unto the nekke bone) but if it was all going to be done as rapidly as that, and *like* that, couldn't *you* have called *me* somehow, so that I would have been given more of a chance to call myself, been given credit at least for trying to move hell so to do, and then, in fact, finally for doing it, which I morally did, for my letter was posted on Jan. 4, yours to me on the 6th: or if not for doing it at least acknowledgement that I'd done it, or . . . at least some to Hal, who writes me on the 11th, and is still in the dark, though I can see opposing ethical obliquities there that might have prevented you.

Erskine should have seen this situation approaching and given him a way out, a way to 'save face' – it was unfair to judge him on unfinished work before the agreed deadline. He accused him of not having his 'reading cap on' and if Haas had taken a dimmer view of it he must have 'borrowed the Consul's dark glasses in order to read it'. He was worried about possibly having to return the money, and of Erskine feeling that he had 'backed the wrong horse'. He enclosed 'The Element Follows You Around, Sir' and hoped it would make him even now change his mind; 'auxiliary circumstances' had prevented it being typed earlier. Despite his hurt and angry tone, he tried to keep things sweet. 'For the rest I hope (a) the tone of injured innocence (b) facetiousness of this letter, will not blind you to the fact (a) I'm deeply sorry I've put you in this situation (b) deeply grateful (c) your friend (d) more than ever on the job.' However he thought Random House had not acted in a very businesslike way. For instance, it seemed not to have occurred to anyone that, with *Lunar Caustic* almost completed, it would have been easy for him to have fulfilled the minimal terms of his contract by simply submitting that for the deadline. It does not seem to have occurred to Lowry either. (Margerie then interpolated a few angry sentences, for which he apologized. By cutting Malcolm off in this way, she wrote, they had no idea whether he could afford to finish the book, or did they think the shock of the letter would inspire him to finish it overnight? 'As for you, brother, let us have less stock responses. Get out of your rut. You sound like Mr Reynal.') The main casualty of all this, wrote Lowry, would be the book itself, adding, with hopeful bravado that he would love to see his face if eventually he discovered himself including *October Ferry* in the Random House Modern Library.[2]

Erskine's letter had left him shocked and humiliated, for in rejecting his novel he had also rejected him and his world. His self-esteem had been shattered, and he must have been worried about Margerie, who had married and clung to him believing in his genius, and here were two distinguished publishers telling him that his work was not worth paying for, and the identity he claimed as a writer was worthless. All the anguish he felt about this had gone into his reply. After mailing it off together with the next batch of the novel, he went to bed and collapsed.

This letter obviously incensed Erskine, who replied the following day. He was sorry not to have answered his last letter, he said, but since the letter's intention had been to save him having to send the unpleasant news, he had thought a reply unnecessary, and had informed Haas that

BACK IN, AND OUT OF, MEXICO, 1946.
Above: Looking relaxed on his hotel balcony in Tlaxcala. *Left*: 'Expelled at gunpoint!' Arriving in Los Angeles, having just been deported from Mexico.

FICTION OR AUTOBIOGRAPHY?
Above: 'The Consul' beneath the Ferris wheel, which is likened in *Under the Volcano* to the Wheel of the Law. 'Over the town, in the dark, tempestuous night, backwards revolved the luminous wheel.' *Left*: A journey to nowhere. Lowry aboard the October Ferry to Gabriola, 1947.

OPPOSITE:
DRINK AND OTHER DAEMONS.
Top right: Looking boisterous, even somewhat 'liquidated' with Einar and Muriel Neilson on Bowen Island, Christmas 1952. *Top left*: Voodoo and alcohol dominated Lowry's visit to Haiti, and so did his friendships with Haitian writers like the Thoby-Marcelin brothers, Pierre (left) and Philippe, pictured with him here in January 1947. *Middle*: At La Cerisaie in the summer of 1948. Joan Black is on the left; next to her, Eda Lord. Julienne LaPierre, the housekeeper, is standing beside Lowry, her Bag Egg, whom she kept well supplied with watered wine. *Bottom*: Dylan Thomas and David Markson in a New York bar, 1952.

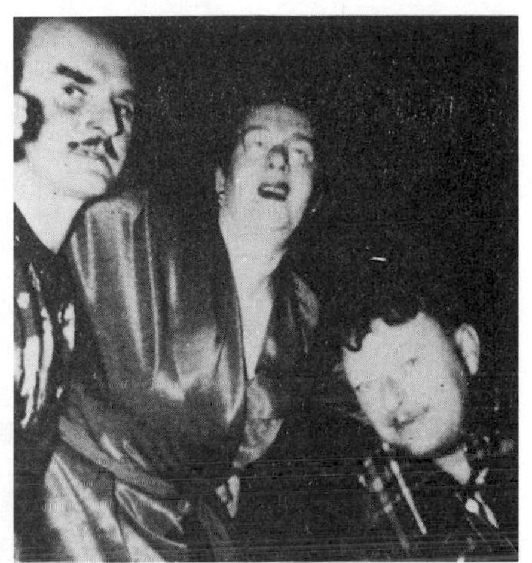

... FOREVER TAKING LEAVE.
Left: Under Etna, Sicily, 1954. *Middle*: Close to the end. One of the last photographs of Lowry, taken in the Lake District in May/June 1957. *Bottom*: The White Cottage, Ripe. Lowry died in the first-floor bedroom on the left.

their letters had crossed and that Lowry had suggested payment be suspended. He thought talk of 'face' was 'juvenile', as were the references to his 'stock responses' and sounding like Reynal. As for his reading cap and dark glasses, he could read with only the equipment he possessed and if that was inadequate there was nothing he could do about it. He was still hoping as he read on that something would break through to him to justify the book's beginning.

> Do you want me to say I understand and love it when I don't? Is flattery what you want? Don't bother to answer these questions. I don't get the whole business, but I know I'd prefer not to get any more letters like this last one, or for that matter, please, any further references to it (the letter, I mean).[3]

When Margerie read Erskine's letter she decided to keep it from Malcolm; he had been ill for the past five or six days, unable to eat, and so desperate that she was becoming frightened. She dashed off a quick reply: 'I'm afraid the tone of his letter – half jocular, half angry – has misled you as to his real feelings. Now you may think he's "taking this too hard" or making a mountain etc etc & so may I. But he is *how* he is & can't help it.' He felt disgraced and cast aside, like Falstaff cast out by Prince Hal, to have not only his ability as a writer questioned but also his sense of responsibility. 'But finally & most importantly he is so despairingly *hurt* & heartbroken it would move a brass mule to compassion.' Isolated as they were, letters of encouragement from Erskine meant a great deal. He did not want flattery but faith and encouragement.

> You've never seen him in the throes of creation, feeling his way, unsure, (even while sure in the long run) & super super sensitive about everything. In the later stages he will take, & ask for, criticism, & he is an unsparing & brutal critic of himself. But at this point, criticism, or above all a *lack of enthusiasm*, or discouragement makes him literally sick.

This might be immature on his part, but he was so extraordinarily proud and touchy that he could not endure humiliation, whether real or imagined. She begged Erskine to write an affectionate letter, without feeling he had to say he liked what he did not.[4]

Erskine, having cooled down somewhat, duly obliged with a more conciliatory letter, admitting it was wrong not to have answered his letter suspending payment. Perhaps he had been insensitive, but to him it had been merely a matter of economics. He had not lost his admiration for him or his work and still hoped to understand *October Ferry* as it grew, but it did no good for him to say he understood what he did not and anyway his judgement was not infallible. He was sorry the letter had caused such distress, but in any case, since their letters had crossed, technically speaking it was he who had initiated the suspension; and even if he had not, nobody's 'face' was at stake.[5] He played down the fact that he did not like *October Ferry* – the thing that had upset Lowry much more than the suspension of payments.

Being turned down was a blow to his carefully constructed self-image as a writer, perhaps the only one which had any substance. Yet, devastating as Random House's rejection of him was, there was a part of him which responded to failure. However, he was worried that if news of this disaster got around his literary reputation would suffer. Sending birthday greetings to Markson, he joked about besetting discouragements and thinking of 'throwing in the sponge', though he urged his young admirer not to be discouraged himself. Nevertheless, he also promised that he would soon present him with something 'that will make the top of your head blow off.'[6]

If Lowry had ever reconsidered taking out Canadian citizenship the idea was abandoned when a Social Credit Government was elected in British Columbia. The shadow of McCarthyism, he felt, had now fallen across western Canada. The new government, he told Markson, was a fascist one; they had threatened to burn library books and had banned the film *The Wild One*. The thinking behind this was all too obvious, he said. 'McCarthy is their hero (though even Ezra Pound wouldn't have recognized these Strong-armed Stinkweasels – they are Social Creditors.)'[7] His sense of persecution intensified when the owners of the apartment complained about him feeding pigeons and attracting mice and vermin. However, he may have been heartened when at the end of February, McCarthy finally over-stepped himself by attacking the US Army, and incurred Eisenhower's displeasure. McCarthyism was at last on the slide.

He was further cheered in March by *Harper's Bazaar* asking for a travel article, by a letter from Marie Moore admiring 'The Element Follows You Around, Sir', and by the arrival of the Italian contract for the *Volcano*. But shortly afterwards yet another accident brought him and his work to a halt. He had begun drinking heavily again, and one day at the apartment, trying, he claimed, to free a pigeon trapped in the ventilator shaft, he slipped in the bath, struck his head on the soap-dish and broke a blood vessel. When Margerie, hearing his cries, came running, he was spurting blood. She tried calling the hospital but the phone was out of order; she rushed out to the elevator and got stuck between floors. Her yells finally brought someone who freed her and then called an ambulance. At midnight Lowry ended up back in St Paul's, among the Irish nuns in black habits.[8] When he returned to the apartment, after having his wound bound, he suddenly doubled up in pain – he had broken several ribs. This time, he walked back to St Paul's, where X-rays were taken and drugs given to relieve the pain. 'I ought to have been writing this, not living it or dying it,' he told Markson a week later.[9] And he was not the only one under the doctor. Margerie continued to suffer from strep throats and complained more and more about life on the beach. She was, after all, approaching fifty and still had her own unfulfilled literary ambitions. Before leaving Vancouver to return home, she went to the Italian consulate and asked about visas and ships to Italy.

By the beginning of May, they were talking more and more about leaving. 'We are bound for Sicily, or at least the kingdom of the 2 Sicilies' he told Markson, 'there to live, if not in turn like that old Typhoeus, beneath Mount Etna.' They planned to come east to New York in late August or September and take a passage on a freighter from there. First of all, they planned to visit his Italian publisher in Milan and offer to assist with the translation, then head towards Sicily. He asked if Markson could put them up in New York before they sailed, 'not for financial reasons, but rather from love'.[10]

The return to the beach coincided with 'The Bravest Boat' appearing in the *Partisan Review*, alongside Saul Bellow and Robert Lowell.[11] No doubt this helped restore further his faith in himself as a writer of worth. When Markson wrote despondently about his emotional and creative problems, Lowry urged him not to ignore his unconscious needs – 'the absolute necessities . . . such as a few stars, ruins, deserts, cathedrals, seas, forests, ducks, ships . . . uncharted waters and undreamed shores, even indeed other cities. And above all perhaps a swim when you want it?' He worried that he had been a bad influence on him, as he thought he might have been on Juan Fernando, and as he felt Aiken had been on him. It was best that he threw out the *Volcano*, he wrote. He could keep the book as a symbol but now he had to try to transcend it. He suggested that he and his girlfriend come to Italy where they could live near to one another and discuss work in progress. A certain amount of despair was actually necessary for people of their peculiar temperament, he said, but that did not make suffering any easier. He then hinted at the complex tussle he and Margerie were having over leaving Dollarton: 'Margie suspects me sometimes of suffering without there being any proper "objective correlative" for it: as I her: but one overlooks the fact that the most hellish kind of suffering of all can be simply because of that lack – the Waste Land type.' It was possible to suffer because one was unable to suffer, because 'to suffer is to be alive'. They had done some pretty energetic suffering recently, and he knew just how Markson felt when he implied that nobody cared about him. He had sometimes felt this, too: 'none of my own brothers – though they expressed themselves pleased to hear of its success in the US – has ever said a word, intelligent or otherwise, about the Volcano; (my mother kept Ultramarine locked up in a drawer, which was perhaps the best place for it) . . .' And his advice when Markson said he had been offered a $3,000 advance on a novel seems as much a comment on his own recent history: 'Don't try *proving* you have any talent . . . that way you can overreach yourself.'

Margerie continued to protest her love of the beach but also to complain that the present life was inimical to her health. 'There's nothing but a sort of heartbreak here: we love the place too much, and that's to be, alack, in the devil's clutches,' he wrote. Although they had avoided eviction so far, on almost every other beach notices to quit had been issued, and the newspapers ran headlines like, 'Speedy Eviction of Squatters Sought'. But, he told Markson, there had been scares before, and they could still be living there ten years hence. They were not leaving with the idea of abandoning the place irrevocably, which was why they offered him the shack during their absence. The life was wonderfully healthy but Vancouver was culturally dead as a dodo and 'the abomination of desolation is already sitting in the holy place and at night the glare of new oil refineries compose a veritable City of Dis.' But Margerie had evidently worn him down. (Significantly, in the earlier version of *October Ferry*, Jacqueline Llewelyn loves Eridanus; by the 1953 version she hates it.) Living there constantly was too hard on her, he admitted, and he himself was feeling less than capable of surviving there alone.

> It is the suspicious element of the possible suicidal in all these constant small accidents that have plagued me which frightens me. And though I once prided myself on being a sometimes subtle if not good carpenter etc. I have become so clumsy and impractical I am almost ashamed

> to have anyone watch me do anything save swim and I'm scared . . . of the unnecessary risks I've got into the habit of taking even doing that, which is nearly my greatest joy. We also have taken to hitting the bottle, especially me, somewhat too hard – if not with consular vehemence or consistency – and though this can often be a joy too, there are few things worse than a bad hangover on a glorious day.

He had never been able to think of drinking as a vice, he admitted, but planned to go on the wagon shortly, at least until they came to New York. 'True, a hangover is an evil thing. But then a drink cures the evil and the specious reasoning begins again.' This intense self-awareness was part of a general gear-change. Since injuring his head, he had abandoned work on his novel, but had managed, with Jimmy Craige's help, to repair the pier and the platform. He had also enjoyed the pleasant respite of a glorious spring, swimming every day and getting sunburnt.[12]

Now he was off the Random House payroll and financially independent again, he could openly abandon *The Voyage that Never Ends*, and this he did in a letter to Erskine on 22 May. First, he said, since he was now working on his own again, he preferred to keep the status of his work a secret. He would not be sending any more bits and short pieces because he could not afford any more discouragement and the peculiar way in which he worked meant he could not predict its outcome. He had no idea whether or not he would be cutting two hundred pages from *October Ferry*'s five hundred and would not know until the final version was typed. The grand design was all but dead. It looked to him, he told Erskine, as if he would have three books ready for him by the final deadline, perhaps more, but all 'a little outside the main scheme'. He no longer wished to make promises which he could not keep or which Random House felt were not being kept well enough. He was unable to continue working in that way, but had to let things age and gather dust. However, he hoped that he could be thought to have stopped the deadline clock at 11.59 p.m. on 31 October 1953, or, if Erskine preferred, on 31 January 1954. He asked for confirmation of this as it was worrying him to death.[13]

He was annoyed at having to pay tax in two countries, and told Erskine that apart from the threat of eviction and Margerie's ill health, if he did not leave Canada soon he would be landed with a tax bill of $1,000. And Margerie was also looking for a change. With the pressure of Malcolm's deadline gone, she set out to pick up her own literary career. She had decided that calling herself Margerie Lowry was no longer advantageous, so she told Marie Moore she was back to being Margerie Bonner.

Their friends Harvey Burt and Dorothy Templeton were now as close to them as anyone, and they spent a great deal of time together in the summer. The two men shared the same sense of humour and had similar views on politics and literature. Burt recalled that the neon sign advertising the Shell Oil refinery across the Inlet lost its S, so the sign glowing in the darkness at night read HELL. It was too perfect, for was not Eridanus situated on the River Po which was also the Styx across which the sinner was ferried to damnation? One night on the beach, Lowry astonished Burt by propositioning him, and he told him to go to hell. He was still not averse, it seems, if it caused outrage, to flirting with homosexuality.

In a letter to George Robertson at the beginning of June, he wrote that until July he was 'immolated within a huge cheese of prose . . . '[14] *October Ferry* was still possessing him, but now he was writing it, or perhaps just staring at it, for himself at his own pace rather than for Random House and an arbitrary deadline. At the end of the month Erskine wrote to say that his metaphor of having 'stopped the clock' on his contract seemed an apt one. In mid-July Markson heard that the Lowrys would be arriving at New York's La Guardia Airport from Los Angeles at 9 p.m. on 25 August, hoping to sail for Genoa early in September; Erskine was also told to expect to hear from them on their arrival.

Lowry did very little work for a month until mid-July, except to read *Ushant*. Aiken's obsession with his childhood home in Savannah, Georgia, and Jeake's House in Rye, which almost exactly replicated its layout, had struck a deep chord with him. Aiken's pain at leaving Jeake's, he told Markson, was one with which he could identify as he faced having to leave The Wicket Gate. Consciousness itself had never seemed to him to be much of an aid or goal; 'Man forget yourself', he wrote, unconvincingly had too often been his motto. But now, for the first time, he felt that Aiken might have been right. 'All aboard for the good ship Solipsism, boys, in short, and don't forget your sea boots.'[15] On finishing *Ushant*, he told Aiken that reading the book had been a self-revelatory experience which had saved him psychologically from the abyss. It had also saved *October Ferry*, which might otherwise have been routed or even abandoned. But as with Markson, he said nothing about his near-rejection by Random House. He was honoured not hurt by *Ushant*, he said, and would have written at length earlier about it, but for certain 'auxiliary circumstances' – specifying only his broken leg, Margerie's dog-bite and the threat of eviction. His problem was that the noose of eviction was drawing tight around them – the oil refinery encroached more and more, its oil slicks polluted the Inlet and at night its flaring oil-towers lit up the sky and HELL announced itself across the water. And yet, on the site of their old shack, on the ground which had been burned ten years before, dogwood was bursting into blossom.

His problem was 'how both to abandon [the house] without treason and remain without going cuckoo but at the same time go . . . while yet leaving the door open to come back, and supposing there not to be a door, how to keep one in the heart . . .' The situation had been aggravated by his trying to write about it whilst actually living through it. To have observed and recorded the approaching horror was 'like making a tape recording of one's own execution.' He had been lost in the dark until the beneficial beams of *Ushant* had appeared to guide him, and he had been able to act decisively. For all that the decision had been taken to 'retreat in good order', this was to be a saga of 'withdrawal and return', and the house would be left in good hands awaiting their home-coming. Aiken's own complex and passionate relation to houses had saved him by taking on his own suffering about leaving home. Without that he would have been heading towards the abyss and his work would have been abandoned. Now he felt excited about the future.[16] *Ushant* had, it seems, sent him back to *October Ferry* with a new verve, suggesting that with an inspiring and critical presence such as Aiken's, he might have been saved from wallowing aimlessly through the slough of literary despond in which Erskine had left him.

As his letter to Aiken implied, Lowry was loth to leave Eridanus – his attachment was psychologically deep and he feared the parting, remembering no doubt what had happened when he left in 1944, 1945 and 1947. But eviction loomed and tripper-ships passing along the Inlet were broadcasting commentaries to the passengers saying 'This eyesore has to go.' Moreover there was the new and pressing problem of being taxed twice over, and, most importantly, there was Margerie's health.

Dorothy Templeton felt that she made more of this than was warranted, to make Malcolm feel guilty about remaining in Dollarton. She remembers saying to her doctor, also Margerie's, how worried she was that she might have caught Margerie's 'strep' throat, and his responding that there was nothing at all wrong with her friend. Margerie, she believed, had long planned to get Malcolm abroad and had told her that after Sicily she would take him to England and then, since they could now afford it without help, to Switzerland to see Jung. And despite her extravagant expressions of love and admiration for Malcolm in his presence, behind his back she would say, 'The bastard! He's impossible!'[17] But there was little love lost between the two women. If Dorothy was right, then the fiction of the idyll, at which they had worked so hard for so long, had begun to wear thin for one of them, no longer sure whether or not the genius was capable of fulfilling itself. When Margerie told Harvey that Malcolm was finished, he was horrified, and simply refused to believe it. Nevertheless, he feared for Lowry's future.

After celebrating their birthdays on the beach for the last time – Margerie forty-nine on 18 July and Malcolm forty-five on the 28th – they renewed their passports and applied for Italian visas. There was a birthday party too for Dorothy on the 21st, so much celebratory drinking went on over a period of ten days. Harvey agreed to care for the shack and ensure Malcolm's books and manuscripts were not vandalized by marauding adolescents or trippers. There were last-minute hitches. Their sailing date was postponed till 10 September, and they wrote to Markson telling him to expect them in New York on Wednesday 1st.[18] A week later, Lowry wrote to Erskine saying there had been a further delay; they would be sailing on 12 October aboard the SS *Giacomo*, together with a cargo of 'inflammable substances', and would now be in New York on the 3rd. He also announced that, 'I have largely revised Gabriola but that is another story. In fact, it is another story.'[19]

Just before he left he wrote a farewell letter to Downie Kirk, saying 'I have good news . . . though I am going temporarily, largely on account of Margie's health – the real estate evaluator figured we would all be here 15 years at least, so don't give up the ship.'[20] He had heard at the last moment that eviction was unlikely for some years, but Margerie had insisted there be no turning back, that she must leave for her health's sake, and that their life on the beach was no way for the wife of a celebrated writer to live. There was also the little matter of tax to avoid.

His farewell meeting with the Neilsons seems to have been an emotional one. They had seen him at his lowest and worst, but never ceased to love this tortured and gifted eccentric. The saddest farewell, however, must have been saying goodbye to the shack which they had built together, and the pier which meant so much to Lowry. Their trunks were sent care of Markson in New York, but Lowry kept with him the manuscript of *October Ferry*, and also his battered ukulele, with one string broken. For a couple of days before leaving they stayed at Vancouver's Hotel Georgia, where Lowry had first stayed in Canada in 1939, and from which he had sent Margerie such passionate love letters persuading her to stick by him. On Monday 30 August, the morning of their departure for Los Angeles, Harvey and Dorothy, and the faithful Jimmy Craige, took them to the airport. They went through the gate and Craige followed them up the ramp leading to the aircraft. Burt remembered their parting.

> He turned and clasped old Jim, who was a frail little man, who was only about five feet and weighed about a hundred pounds. [He] smothered him, and it was as though he were seeking the kind of assurance a child needs when it's being sent away from his parents. That image struck me then, and it stayed with me for a long time. I often think of [it] . . . He was going away forever in a sense, now I can see that. That's what it represented. He may not have been thinking that, but certainly his gestures were saying that.[21]

Craige told Burt afterwards that Lowry's last words to him on the ramp were, 'I'm afraid, I don't think that we'll ever come back here. I'm afraid to leave. I feel that we'll never come back.'[22] His friends were sure that he was coerced into leaving, and believed that by now he was no longer in charge of his own life, and, fearful of being deserted, simply did as he was told. Margerie certainly had no wish to return. Like the caged bird Yvonne frees in the *Volcano*, she was about to fly off to some kind of new freedom, and a literary success she had failed to gain in the backwoods. Lowry, however, like the Consul, was heading towards his Farolito.

When she saw him in LA, Priscilla thought him much changed. He had become bloated from drink and his mind, she thought, was worse in every way. She insisted again that he did not stay at her house, and perhaps because they did not feel very welcome, they left early and had to cable Markson to expect them in New York on the morning of the 2nd.[23] When they arrived they found that their luggage was not on the plane; the manuscript of *October Ferry* had gone missing, and Lowry was beside himself. For the next three days, bunked up at Markson's small West 113th Street apartment, near Columbia University, Malcolm was in a state of high anxiety until the luggage finally turned up. He had now reverted to his old drunken, disordered self: sly and foxy and mischievously delinquent in the pursuit of more liquor. He arrived drunk and was to depart drunk, so that David Markson was able to say afterwards that he had never known Malcolm Lowry sober.

He often had the shakes and occasionally hallucinated, assuring Markson that there was an owl perched outside his window. Nevertheless, he could still be entertaining, and when he met one of Markson's neighbours, Scipio Sprague, who loved the *Volcano* and was dazzled to meet him, he was at his dramatic best. In one afternoon's drinking session he told the story of Davenport visiting him at the hospital in Vernon where the nuns had fed him red wine. 'It started at least eight times,' recalled Markson, 'But after digressions about the China Sea, and Mexican jails, and the reading habits of James Joyce, and certain Manx fishing customs, it spiralled finally into absolute incoherence.' When Markson asked him what the hell he was talking about, his eyes lit up, 'Well, it's difficult. But you have to listen. It's . . . *contrapuntal*!' he said, and then added, 'And there *was* an owl!'[24]

He was anxious to get in touch with old friends, and scrawled a telegram to Aiken inviting him to meet up in New York. Markson, however, had found him to be in a generally deplorable state. His trousers, held up with an old tie, kept falling down, he was unable to shave himself, and unable to keep a steady hand to eat breakfast unless he had first had two or three ounces of gin in his orange juice. On several occasions he drank until he collapsed, once across Markson's phonograph, almost destroying it and nearly skewering himself on the raised spindle. He managed an evening with Erskine, where amity was restored between them (though Lowry still felt deeply hurt about his 'rejection'). Then, towards the end of his stay, he spent an evening with Jimmy Stern, from whom he borrowed Italo Svevo's *The Confessions of Zeno*, of which he commented, after describing its plot for two hours without having read it, 'And I am going to learn from it, a method of treating consciousness.'[25] Stern wrote to Aiken a few weeks later, 'I am afraid I fear for the old boy, no matter what the price of Sicilian wines. The real trouble lies in that he is a slave to M. – at least that's my opinion.'[26]

Scipio Sprague's fiancée, Kitty, saw mad genius in Lowry's piercing blue eyes, and found Margerie's behaviour distinctly odd. She spent most of her time trying to keep him sober, and dramatizing her role as the 'keeper' of the great genius.[27] Markson was disturbed that Malcolm ate so little and that Margerie, like a mother with a young child, spoon-fed him at the table. He was also concerned that at night, when Lowry was often at the point of alcoholic collapse, she fed him handfuls of pills – 'she used to literally jam the pills down his throat, nights, once he was half-way under.'[28] When he first saw her doing this he asked what they were. They were vitamins, she said, to help him survive the next morning's hangover. There were several extraordinary scenes in which she yelled at him hysterically and then flounced from the room in a huff. After one of these histrionic displays, Lowry said, 'I cannot live with that woman!' Then added, giggling, 'Of course – I naturally cannot live without her either.'[29]

Sometimes he did manage to escape from his 'keeper'. Markson had introduced him to a married woman friend, 'an old Bohemian broad',[30] Ruth, in the nearby West End bar, and Lowry had said that he would like to meet her again. Later he went back to the bar alone and the woman took him home intending to introduce him to her husband, a heavy drinker and also a great fan of the *Volcano*. Sometime that evening the husband returned, and finding his wife chatting to a tipsy stranger, threw him out. Lowry somehow managed to find his way back to Markson's apartment and spent the rest of the night sitting on the stairs outside the door. The husband accosted Markson next day, having discovered who he had ejected from his apartment. 'Now Jeeeses,' he said, 'how the Christ was I to know he was *that* Malcolm Lowry? I would of thrown Ruth out and talked to him instead.'[31]

As a break from New York, the Lowrys went to spend a night up along the Hudson River at Snedens Landing, with Joan Black and her husband Viscount Peter Churchill. Churchill, a cousin of the Blenheim Palace Churchills, was, like Lowry, the family black sheep. A friend of Nancy Cunard, he had lived in Paris in the 1930s, had formed the Medical Aid Committee, serving with it in Spain during the Civil War, and had spent the last war as an NCO in the US Air Force. He and Lowry became instant friends. Another visitor to the Churchills that evening was the critic Malcolm Cowley. In a letter to Mary Aiken shortly afterwards, he described what happened:

> It wasn't a very successful meeting with Malcolm L, my almost namesake, because he had been drinking too long and deep and was living withdrawn in a private universe, out of which came friendly but portentous mumbles that didn't register on my hearing aid. He looked unshaven, like a small bristly animal. It turned out that he didn't want to leave British Columbia or spend the winter in Sicily and was drinking as a protest (which doesn't mean that he doesn't drink at other times for other motives) – this time he was saying in effect,

> 'See, it's the suicide of my talent and it's all your fault, Marjorie.' When a man is killing himself one always asks, 'Who is he committing suicide against?' Whom, I mean. Joan Churchill gave him hell and he took it meekly. There was a sweetness about him and I wish I had met him at a more communicative moment . . . [32]

The visit to the Churchills ended in farce. Hurricane Edna was expected to hit the area any time and Lowry became obsessed by it. On the morning of their departure, while the Churchills were still in bed, Margerie burst into their bedroom to announce dramatically that Malcolm had vanished. A search party was organized, but Churchill noticed a bottle of gin missing and saw that the branches of the large tree outside the window were unaccountably swaying. There, among the leaves, he saw the pyjama-clad Lowry clinging on frantically and shouting 'Hang on! Here comes Edna. Don't let go!' The hurricane had actually not yet arrived, so Churchill steadied the branches and casually asked Lowry if he could lend him a razor blade. He promptly forgot Edna, climbed inside and meekly found a blade for his host.[33]

Since Churchill was interested in writing, Lowry promised to introduce him to Matson. It was arranged that they should return to Markson's to smarten up and then meet at the Waldorf, much favoured by the New York English set, and that Markson should join them. But the Churchills took so long getting ready that by the time they dropped the Lowrys back at the apartment, Malcolm decided it was too late to change and went as he was. They arrived late with Markson, and because of Lowry's unwashed appearance and blue denims, the doorman refused him entrance, until the immaculately dressed Churchill appeared and said they were his guests. 'Yes my Lord,' replied the doorman obsequiously, and they were promptly admitted. Lowry, delighted that the officious doorman had been squashed in this grand manner, broke out into gales of gleeful laughter.

Aiken, knowing that he would not get up to see him in Cape Cod, agreed to come to New York. Frank Taylor had arranged a party on 11 September, the day before they left, and Erskine, Stern and James Agee were also invited with their wives. Markson was working at his editorial job that afternoon, and Margerie had to go out, leaving Malcolm alone in the apartment for a few hours. Margerie was determined to get him to the party sober, so all the liquor was concealed and he was left with a six-pack of beer. When Markson returned, there was a faint aroma in the air and a silly grin on Lowry's face. 'I have something funny to tell you,' he said. But Markson already knew. In the bathroom he had found and consumed Markson's full bottle of Mennen's Skin Bracer, a shaving lotion fifty per cent alcohol. Nevertheless, they got him ready for the party. Markson shaved him, strangely reliving the scene in the *Volcano* where Hugh shaves the Consul before they go to the bullfight, and he was lent a jacket and tie and made to look respectable.

At Aiken's 'coldwater' apartment on East 33rd Street en route to the party, there was a fumbling shy reunion over the poet's favourite tipple, martini, each man unsure of how to greet the other. When Aiken enquired about work in progress, Lowry launched into a rambling account of the plot of *October Ferry*, and then concluded, 'Well, nothing happens. Nothing should, in a novel.' To which Aiken replied 'No. No *incidents*.'[34] Lowry, it seems, was now fully converted to Aiken's commitment to exploring human consciousness to the exclusion of almost everything else. He was obviously distressed at leaving Dollarton, saying, 'I have to slide through this time of crisis on my unconscious,'[35] and was then gripped by an attack of the shakes which he talked about openly in an apparently detached fashion. In a letter to Ed Burra six weeks later, Aiken wrote that it was impossible to talk to him.

> Just a non-stop mystic monologue full of groping pauses and wordless intensities. Marjie [*sic*] was ordered by the medicos to quit Vancouver, as being too tough a climate for her, and Malc is revenging himself by as it were drinking the Great Genius to Death. You see how it works? a fine drama, with Random House putting up the dibs.[36]

It was a typically stifling New York summer's night, and at Taylor's party he was soon in a sweat, as was the ailing James Agee.[37] Lowry withdrew almost at once into a corner and wrapped himself in a remote silence, while Margerie, back in the social scene she craved, was enjoying Agee's account of his writing career up to the screenplay of *The African Queen*, and chatting away about their *Tender is the Night* script, which Agee had read and admired so much.

After about an hour of silence, Lowry cupped his hands to his mouth and, apparently oblivious to the others, began to imitate jazz sounds, 'trumpeting' old Dixieland numbers to himself, like Beiderbecke's 'Singin' the Blues', 'I'm Comin', Virgina' and 'In a Mist'. After half an hour of this, Aiken, put out by Lowry's rudeness, decided to leave.

As he left he simply said to him, 'Goodnight, Disgrace.' Now out of his trance, Lowry hurried after him, insisting that he would see him home. Markson followed and reached the street in time to see Aiken hail a cab. As he tried to get into it, Lowry attempted to follow, and had to be fended off. They wrestled in the street for a time, and when Markson came up and pulled Lowry back, Aiken fell on to the floor of the taxi in an undignified heap. The door was slammed and the cab drove off.[38] In the empty street it had begun to rain and Lowry stood, suddenly very sober, and began to cry. 'He is an old man,' he said. 'And now I shall never see him again.'[39] They had wrestled at their first meeting – just twenty-five years earlier; it may seem appropriate if not symbolic that they should wrestle also at their last.

A few weeks later, Aiken wrote to Mary:

> Malc did seem reproachful towards Marjie [*sic*] for (even if on medical advice) having to leave BC, as if it were a real fault that she couldn't take it. All very sad . . . Malc had been too long indulged by ALL his friends as a sort of self-indulgent geyser of genius whose mystic spoutings were worth the boredom and the patience. I suppose he'll now go off and kill himself, and leave on Marjie [*sic*] the blame for his latter failures[40]

If there is an element of self-reproach in this it might be thought well deserved. This was the man who had set out to ensnare the twenty-year-old Lowry in a spider's web, to absorb him into his own consciousness regardless of the psychological consequences. He had encouraged him over Jan until he became jealous, and attempted to undermine their marriage in 1937; he had then cruelly represented him in *Ushant* as a wretched if inspired plagiarist and cuckold. It is true he offered help when he was in trouble during the early 1940s, but if there was a threatening monster lurking not far below the skin of Malcolm Lowry, Conrad Aiken must take responsibility for consciously, for his own lurid experimental purposes, having been its Frankenstein.

Markson shaved him one last time, and Lowry reiterated again his advice to the young writer: 'Whatever you do, wherever you go, MAKE NOTES!' Erskine joined them and they all took a cab to the Brooklyn pier from which the SS *Giacomo* was due to sail. Crossing the Brooklyn Bridge he talked of Hart Crane and the 'drama' of the New York skyline, and urged Markson to read Stern's short stories, Agee's *Let Us Now Praise Famous Men* and Aiken's *Great Circle* – 'Though I did not write that. The only one I wrote in another life was *Blue Voyage*.' And all the time he kept repeating in a pseudo-Southern accent a line he said was from Faulkner: 'Ah can stand anything. Ain't nothin' wrong with me that a good bour-bon won't cure.'[41]

At the dockside, Lowry said, 'I must see the skipper. If he's not a company man, this will be a happy ship.' They must tip the steward at once, he added. 'Italian ships have holds *full* of Chianti.' Erskine and Markson helped them aboard with their luggage, then, back on deck, Lowry began to act the old sailor, talking to the crew as if he was one of them. Noticing the looks they exchanged, Erskine scented trouble ahead for him if he carried on in that way. The sailing had been postponed for some hours and Lowry was soon drinking heavily. Erskine left and Markson stayed to see them off. Lowry's last words to him before they sailed were: 'I'm a pretty bad man, but you should really come to Sicily with us. We love you, you know, but not so that you have to shove a cork up your arse, old man.'[42]

The voyage was a disaster – 'an inferno of a voyage', he told Markson, '– though miraculously calm on one plane . . . and I forgot to say a steward named Dante, who at grave risk to his life gave one a skin-bracer and coffee at breakfast.'[43] What he did not report was that for most of the trip he was drunk, and after misbehaving at the Captain's table was threatened with the brig. He disembarked at Genoa in a deep depression and after two days went to Milan, where they contacted Eric Linder, his European agent, and Giorgio Monicelli, his Italian translator. At first he was too intoxicated and confused to be of much help to Monicelli, and when he finally sobered up for one morning's work, he suddenly collapsed and began vomiting black blood. Taken hurriedly to hospital with suspected liver damage, it was a week before he managed one of his miraculous recoveries, astonishing the doctors by his powers of recuperation. He sent Markson a postcard bearing the simple message, 'Bang!'[44]

On 17 October, they flew to Catania and then on to Syracuse in south-eastern Sicily. He sent a card to Downie Kirk, with another cryptic comment on his reluctant exile: 'Serve him damn well right for being responsible for all those forest fires.'[45] And to Markson: 'Only against death shall he cry in vain . . . And against etc etc hath he devised escapes.'[46] To this Margerie added the chirpy postscript, 'Dave, it's a gorgeous place & how you would love it – come & see us soon!' One night he devised an escape from Margerie, sneaking from the hotel for a bar crawl. Late that night the police called her. He had been arrested in a delirious rage and was in gaol. When she collected him, she fed him a handful of vitamin pills as Markson had seen her do in New York, to lessen the following day's hangover, and put him to bed.

After ten days they moved to Taormina, duplicating another step in Lawrence's exiled wanderings. They took a room at a small *pensione*, the Villa Eden ('Yes,' wrote Margerie, 'it has a Paradise Garden.'),[47] which seemed ideal, high on the cliffs overlooking the sea and in sight of the smoke and flames of Mount Etna. It was not Dollarton, but seemed a pleasant enough approximation, with strange overtones of Mexico. The villa was at 52 Via San Pancrazio and their room number was seven – 'the numerology will not escape you,' Lowry wrote Markson on the Day of the Dead, 2 November. The street was exactly the same as the Calle Nicaragua in Cuernavaca, he said. 'Am situated . . . here at last, immediately above the cemetery, to which a procession of people are taking chrysanthemums – Christian-anthems – if not quite like that old Typhoeus, adjacent.' They bathed every day in the old city of Naxos, and he swam up and down, pondering a story called 'Tremor in Taormina'. If he had been drunk or ill for most of the time since leaving Canada, the effect on Margerie was miraculous. 'Margie', he said, 'is getting better by leaps and bounds.'[48]

Matson forwarded a letter from Frank Taylor at MGM asking them to sign a release for their *Tender is the Night* screenplay. David O. Selznick had now purchased the film rights and was planning a movie. Now they could be open about it, and Lowry replied that if Selznick went ahead they deserved a crack at the script, adding proudly that although they had made mistakes, 'We solved nearly every difficulty of transposing a long sprawling novel into the different medium of the film, and few people can possibly know so much about that book by now as we do.'[49]

Across the Atlantic there were strange echoes of the past, when 'Strange Comfort' was reprinted in a Mentor Books *World Literature* anthology. A clearly embittered Burton Rascoe wrote, apparently to Edward Weeks, editor of *Atlantic*, resurrecting events of twenty years before, complaining angrily that Lowry had been hailed as one of the 'great modern authors of world literature'. He had told the story before, he said, but never named the plagiarist. Now, faced with Lowry's literary acclaim, he both named him and denounced him to Weeks.[50] Lowry was never to know about this outburst, but the strength of feeling behind the letter indicates just why he had felt so shattered all those years ago.

CHAPTER XXV

EUROPEAN DISASTERS 1954–1956

He that is mad, and sent into England . . . he shall recover his wits there; or, if he do not, it's no great matter there.
SHAKESPEARE, *Hamlet*, Act V, Scene 1

For the first two months in Sicily he seems to have maintained a fragile stability, swimming regularly and writing the occasional coherent letter. But whenever he tried to work on *October Ferry* it plunged him into a dark depression about Dollarton and raised again the many ghosts the book was attempting to lay. He wrote longingly to Kirk about the beach and struggled with several drafts of a letter to Monicelli, but never posted one.

Either Eden eventually palled or they thought a change of scenery might spark him into action. In any event, on 13 December they moved into the nearby Villa Margherita, which they hired for a month, together with a whole family of servants. Manuscripts were unpacked from trunks and the typewriter set up, and Lowry went swimming in full view of the Isles of Sirens and the Cyclops. The Villa Margherita was a little more convenient for the daily plunge, but hardly the place for a solitary writer pining for the silent forests of British Columbia. However, any thought of returning to Canada was squelched when Margerie again began to complain of sore throats. If they were going anywhere next, she insisted they go to England where medical treatment was free. He was caught in a trap, and quarrels were inevitable. He tried rising before dawn to write in the quiet of early morning, but to no effect. His initial burst of creativity did not last.

As he told Monicelli in one of his unfinished letters, they had shifted from one heavenly place to another, 'though all has so far been anything but heavenly with us, largely due to my own ghastly incapacity to look my own grief in the face.' He was having trouble with his eyesight, scarcely being able to see by electric light. He tried to write, but it was so bad he tore it up. He had difficulty relating to the Sicilians, their hard lives and antipathy to public drunkenness, and it must have brought back miserable memories of being openly mocked in Spain and Mexico. He wrote that he loathed Sicily as much as he loved Italy:

> It is the worst & most hypocritical place in the world. And, I think, the most hopeless. They know neither how to live or to die; & endless are the hypocrite lectures I receive about drinking their bloody wine even at the moment I am being overcharged for it & cheated everywhere. I put a malediction – as did Lawrence – upon the whole place.[1]

When finally he did get a letter off to Monicelli, it was a catalogue of complaints and self-torturings, for which he apologized in another letter as a 'damnfoolish compilation of self-pity'. His situation was perilous both psychologically and physically, and he was becoming his 'deranged abnormal fat self again under the influence of vast quantities of Gorgonzola cheese and mineral water . . .' But in Taormina there were abysses at every corner; what had been a paradise to him not long before was now a new kind of hell. He found the country barren and unappealing. The weather was 'bloody awful', the sea virtually unswimmable, Margerie had another sore throat, there was snow in Calabria, and they were being served by gorillas and Neanderthals. Most Sicilians, he said, were 'not human beings at all, but vultures preying on the tourists', and yet he found 'a stern . . . beauty' in their culture. It was difficult to imagine that Pirandello first drew breath there. But, he added wryly, Margerie of course thought it romantic. He searched out D. H. Lawrence's house, but, 'I . . . disrespected him for having taken it, I'm afraid – even though I cried.'[2]

The Villa Margherita, it was decided, was too small and too far from the beach, so in February they took a lease on a villa at Mazzaro, the beach below Taormina. The Villa Mazzullo was bigger with a larger family attached to it. Nevertheless problems soon became evident. They were close to the coast road along which buses and cars and lorries and scooters roared, hooted and popped at all hours, and close to the railway line which also regularly invaded the silence. People in the streets screamed at each other, donkeys brayed and cocks crowed all night. The house was full of the housemaid's children, and the noise outside compounded by the noise inside began to drive Lowry to despair. He tried wearing earplugs, but found it impossible to work; his continuing eye trouble, added to the sirocco, made life still more uncomfortable.

He continued to swim every day, but gave up trying to write. He found it impossible to read and took to drinking wine all day long. Margerie, however, remained cheerful, writing to Markson, 'We have a nice house, finally, a good cook, & a spare bed & we wish you were here.'[3] But by then they both knew that coming to Sicily had been a mistake.

Gradually Lowry sank into a state of permanent drunkenness and inactivity. If he was drinking the genius to death to revenge himself on Margerie, by March it had begun to have its effect. She began speaking openly about going to England where she could get free medical treatment and he could see a psychiatrist. He was suffering badly from the DT's and ultimately became so low and frightened that he said, 'Catch me at a lucid interval and I will talk it over.'[4] Later she told Markson, 'He was increasingly losing any contact with reality, and finally the strain was quite literally killing me. We faced it together . . . & one night he gave me his word he would go,'[5] a hard decision for Lowry, who had never wanted to return to England. They decided to take a freighter from Palermo to London after their lease expired on 15 June.

In April she wrote to Erskine: 'Malc has been trying to write to you for two weeks, but the letter became more and more involved . . . and in trying to say everything, poor soul, he ended saying nothing comprehensible, so I'm trying to figure out what he really meant to say, and say it for him.' They had realized that Sicily was not for them, and had decided to leave for England at the beginning of July. The noise where they were living had driven them both crazy and neither was doing much writing. In any case, Malcolm had to work at his own pace and when he tried to get back to his novel it filled him with anguish. Now they were hoping that once settled in England he could finish it off quite quickly. Meanwhile, he was still in demand in France. Maurice Nadeau wanted to translate and publish 'Strange Comfort' which he had read in *New World Writing*, and Margerie believed that, because of his reputation in Europe, *October Ferry* would ultimately not only be a great novel but would be given a great reception.

In the middle of May she wrote to tell the Sterns, now living in Dorset, that they expected to leave on 1 July and be in England some two weeks later.[6] At the same time, they had heard from Dorothy Templeton, who was in Europe and had asked if she could join them in Taormina. Margerie was delighted, eager for the company. She met Dorothy off the boat, and en route to the villa told her that she would be treated as a paying guest, which surprised her since they were now, she thought, comfortably off. She found Malcolm in a wretched state, permanently drunk, writing nothing, eating nothing and hardly leaving the house. 'He says there are no trees here,' said Margerie, 'but look at all those olive trees.' For Lowry, however, real trees grew wild and proud in the primeval forest, not in cultivated rows. Margerie kept a hoard of liquor locked in one of their trunks, and his wine intake was rationed; she was also feeding him two nembutal tablets and a cognac at bedtime. This knocked him out until after twelve noon the following day. The whole scene, decided Dorothy, was grim. 'He wouldn't get up till noon, and he *couldn't* get up until he had a drink, and then we'd sit for two hours watching him try to get through a piece of bread and a piece of cheese. It was just . . . agony.'[7] By the time he left Sicily he had lost forty-two pounds through lack of food.[8]

The two women shared a room, with Malcolm next door. One night, when he was still awake and pleading for drink, Dorothy asked Margerie if she could try to get him to stop voluntarily. 'It's no use,' she said. But Dorothy claimed that after one drink she simply told him he could have no more, and he accepted it and went to sleep. Her impression was that his drinking was aimed solely at Margerie. And by this time, she noticed, he no longer went swimming, even though the beach was right outside the front door, and she decided that he was very angry that she had taken him to Sicily.

Relations between the two women were fragile. Secretly Margerie thought Dorothy overemotional and unreliable. Dorothy, in turn, regarded Margerie as a liar. After a week, they had a tremendous quarrel and Dorothy moved out. For one thing, despite being charged for upkeep, she found there was no decent food at the villa, and servants would not stay because Margerie yelled at them and accused them of stealing. Dorothy moved to a nearby *pensione*, but still saw the Lowrys every day. Despite the quarrel, the women often went out together and Lowry was left alone, but on one occasion, after he had visited the dentist, Dorothy found him at home. There he told her a gruesome story (probably one of his voodoo tales): 'He told a story about a girl eating a live bird . . . it was the most fantastic thing. He went all through how she was chewing it, and how the feathers were falling out. The description was absolutely ghastly, and I believed every word of it. But he'd just made it up.'[9] But she remained convinced when he said that Margerie hated and despised him, stayed with him only for his money, had control of their joint bank account and had forced him to make the will she had witnessed in Dollarton leaving everything to her. She had also threatened to leave him.

Dorothy wrote to Harvey, 'I am witnessing such a tragedy: two souls disintegrating.'[10] Margerie, she claimed, had told her back in Canada that she had plans to leave him and had a nest egg put by for that eventuality.[11] By now they were living in a self-enclosed world. On the one hand it was the fantasy world of El Leon and Miss Harteebeeste, on the other it was a world of mad violence and dark threats of desertion. Some might regard this as normal enough for a marriage of some fifteen years; others might see in it strange, claustrophobic, Strindbergian danks and darks.

Somewhat recovered, he wrote to Markson at the end of May, 'Sicily – or at any rate Taormina – is a first class disaster . . . I fear you would like it.' On the back of this letter, Margerie scrawled, 'Sicily has been hell. Malc doesn't like it. But he doesn't like anywhere except Dollarton.' They were leaving for England the second week in June, and hoped to find a country cottage not far from London. 'It seems both of us need some doctoring & – remember – no cost in England.'[12]

Just before they left Sicily, Dorothy received news from Jimmy Craige that a severe storm on the night of 22 June had washed Lowry's pier away. On hearing this Margerie swore Dorothy to silence, fearing that the news would push him over the brink. Their lease on the Villa Mazzullo expired and they spent a little over a week island-hopping – Vulcano, Lipari, Strómboli. By now he was more sober and towards the end of June they went to Palermo and after about ten days flew to England.

Arriving in London on 9 July 1955, Margerie was given a three-month visitor's visa. If she wanted to stay for any greater length of time she would have to register as an alien and report her whereabouts to the police. She began house-hunting immediately, searching for that secluded country cottage where Malcolm could finish *October Ferry* and get back on good terms with Random House. In the middle of July they were holed up in the Goodwin Hotel in Queensborough Terrace, one of those slightly sleazy hotels catering mostly for itinerants, close to Paddington railway station. On the 27th they moved to 77 Onslow Road, Richmond, to get a little further from the centre of town, and were in touch with Ralph Case, now a GP in west London, and Davenport, who had just lost his BBC job and was reviewing books for the *Observer*.

The England to which Lowry had returned after almost exactly twenty years was lacklustre and exhausted after the war. The political excitement which had enlivened pre-war cultural life was gone, and although there were stirrings of a new initiative in the arts, generally the scene was one of inertia and dreariness. Lowry's own condition was similarly very poor. He could not write letters, his hands shook so badly Margerie had to light his cigarettes, and he could not be left alone for long. On 19 August he did manage to scrawl a few words on a postcard to Markson who had kept writing to him: 'Dear old Dave: Thank you. Wait. Malcolm.' Margerie, meanwhile, got herself admitted to the London Hospital for an operation and expected to be in for a month because, she told Markson, she was very run down and needed building up before they could operate. While she was away Malcolm stayed at Davenport's flat in Chelsea. His eye trouble had cleared up – he needed glasses for reading – and there was talk of his seeing a psychiatrist at last, something he had not done voluntarily since being treated by Dr Mars in Haiti.

Davenport, still as rotund as a sumo wrestler, still drinking heavily and as pugilistic as ever, had been having a bad time, not only with his work. His wife Marjorie had been unwell with depression and on 28 July, Lowry's forty-fifth birthday, his first wife Clement had died of a cerebral haemorrhage. The Davenports were living with their two young sons, Hugo and Roger, at Rossetti House in Flood Street, and John, though pleased to see Lowry, was shocked by his condition. He had disliked Margerie since Vernon, considering her hysterical and self-obsessed, and decided she had come to England hoping to achieve literary celebrity on Malcolm's coat-tails, seeing him and Jimmy Stern as ways into the literary establishment.

Marjorie's sister, Evelyn, who was staying at Rossetti House at the time, remembered one evening, after a convivial dinner, the two men reading the whole of *Ultramarine* through together late into the night, long after the others had gone to bed. Next morning, at about 10 a.m., Lowry crept into the kitchen and asked in a shy whisper for a cup of tea, as if afraid to disturb anyone. Evelyn found his lack of pomposity endearing.[13] He was clearly on his best behaviour, and, without Margerie around, apparently lucid enough.

After two weeks in hospital she returned and took Malcolm off to Richmond to see about getting him psychoanalysed. Shortly afterwards Stern, up from the country, called at Rossetti House, and later wrote to Markson,

> [I] spent an hour with John Davenport – talking, needlessly to say, of Malc. – or rather, more of HER. She appears to have fallen very

> near the Edge . . . According to Davenport, 'the brain is as quick as ever, the memory still unbelievable.' But there's talk of psychoanalysis. This, I'd say, is HER. But you probably know far more about this than I do . . . Malc is far too fond of the flames. It's an annihilation, which of course is why he does it, or at least talks of it so much.[14]

Dorothy had arrived in London and taken a room in Knaresborough Place off the Cromwell Road. When she went to visit the Lowrys in Richmond she was surprised, as she approached the house, to see Margerie hanging from the window waving and yelling in a loud voice, 'We've been thrown out!'

Their drinking and fighting had been too disturbing for the other tenants. Dorothy had brought a present from Harvey, a perfect replica of their shack, complete with pier, lovingly constructed from matchsticks and set in a cardboard box painted blue for the sea. Malcolm was overjoyed, but Margerie was worried, thinking it might make him hanker after Dollarton. And he did, writing to Jimmy Craige, asking him to pass on his love to 'the gang . . . & the good Harvey'. He had never stopped thinking about them, he said.[15]

At Davenport's suggestion, and encouraged by Margerie, he called his old friend, George Northcroft, now a consultant neurosurgeon. Pleased to hear from him after so long, he invited the Lowrys to dinner at a fashionable restaurant in Gerrard Street near Leicester Square. Malcolm was obviously ill at ease in a restaurant, and Northcroft was struck by how disoriented and confused he was. He ate little except what Margerie fed to him, and the doctor thought he was so bad that he might not have long to live. Margerie asked if he could help and said that she too was ill, suffering from stomach pains. He thought the best he could do was to get Malcolm into a side-ward at the Brook Hospital in Woolwich where he had a consultancy, and simply let him rest and dry out. He could also arrange for Margerie to be admitted for tests for what might be a peptic ulcer.

First, however, he saw them both at his office in Harley Street. Margerie said that what Malcolm needed was psychiatric treatment for his alcoholism, but since Northcroft was a neurosurgeon she enquired whether Malcolm ought to have a lobotomy (in Britain called a leucotomy). Modified leucotomies were being carried out by one of Northcroft's colleagues at the Brook, but only for those with tension states who had failed to respond to drugs and ECT. He discussed it with her, but with no intention of agreeing to it, knowing it would be ruinous to Malcolm's creativity. Yet he got the distinct impression that she wanted him to be leucotomized to make him more amenable to live with. All he really needed, the doctor decided, was a rest and no liquor, but he did not say as much to Margerie who evidently thought he would be getting psychoanalysis, and probably the brain operation. She said later that Northcroft had been keen to do the leucotomy and when she mentioned it to Malcolm he had replied, 'I'll do it if you want. I know you can't stand me any longer as I am,' to which she had replied, 'Never.' However, when he wrote to Jimmy Craige on 11 September the matter seemed to have been settled. 'I go in hospital for a brain operation thing tomorrow,'[16] and next day Margerie wrote to him, 'Malc has gone into hospital today for a minor operation & a rest & I'm going on Wednesday for about the same.'[17] Before leaving she gave Harvey's model of the shack and pier to Dorothy to look after. She took it back to her bedsitter, and left it on the window ledge, but while she was out one day the landlady threw it out, thinking it was rubbish.

Put into a side-room in Northcroft's neurosurgical ward at the Brook, Lowry was given a few routine tests, but basically was placed on bed-rest. Margerie was put into a medical ward in the care of Dr Bruce Pearson (considered by Northcroft an outstanding medical doctor), given tests for possible gall-bladder infection and ulcer, and allowed to see Malcolm daily. Pearson found nothing wrong with her, and Northcroft decided her symptoms were faked so she could stay close to Malcolm and keep an eye on him. A few days after being admitted, she wrote to Markson:

> Malc has been becoming worse & worse the last few years. They say he's only a 'secondary alcoholic' which I could have told them & the trouble is actually his mind – which of course I've know for years . . . he will have psychiatric treatment from a Harley St man for some weeks – or months – but they feel in the end they *may* have to perform a small brain operation to relieve the tension & anxiety if it can't be done other ways. I shall have to give my consent & shall *not* do so unless I'm convinced. But he's written nothing for over a year . . . & was losing all contact with reality. He should have had treatment years ago, of course, but they feel very hopeful because of his still phenomenal memory . . . The brain operation is *not* a classic lobotomy but something new & much less drastic. George Northcroft, who will perform it, is a very old friend & agrees Malcolm's genius

> *must* be saved, for if he should try to write again & couldn't, things could even be worse.

As Malcolm did not want anyone to know about his condition she asked him not to tell a soul. (Northcroft in fact did not carry out leucotomies but she apparently thought that he did and might.) She was herself, she said, in the middle of a nervous breakdown.[18]

Just after posting this she received a letter from a horrified Markson, alarmed about Lowry's health and hospitalization. She replied instantly, a little worried that he was so shocked, telling him that she had lived in terror of this situation for years, knowing it would only be a matter of time before treatment was necessary. What concerned her most was to get Malcolm to agree, get the right therapist and be able to afford him. What had to be understood was that he had never been normal and should have had help twenty years before. Despite becoming dramatically worse over the past few years, he had somehow held his mind together by sheer willpower. 'He will of course never be normal – whatever that is – but they are sure they can help him greatly. But can it be done without destroying his genius? No one knows.' The thing that had finally persuaded him was his inability to write even a letter, his losing contact with reality and the strain it was putting on her. He was about to see a psychiatrist, and was 'frightened, resigned, determined, even cheerful sometimes'.[19]

Although the hospital was some way out of town, Dorothy and Davenport visited regularly, John Sommerfield came and so did Peter Churchill. After just a week there Lowry was asking for writing paper, determined to write to Markson himself, but he could not quite summon the will to start. However, after another week of alcohol-free rest, he had regained the weight lost in Sicily and was considered fit enough to get up. He was allowed to walk and exercise on the cricket pitch behind the hospital, where, he told Erskine, he spent most of his time shirtless in the dew.[20] Northcroft found him no longer disoriented and confused, but once again the cheerful and charming Malcolm he had known at Cambridge.

On one of his visits Davenport spoke to Northcroft, then relayed the latest news to Jimmy Stern, who passed it on to Markson.

> Margerie L thought she had something wrong with her gall bladder & wanted Malc to see a psychiatrist, so they both went in. Old Moby after a fortnight of tea-totalism [*sic*] is as fit as a double bass: the

> psychiatrist regards *Margerie* as the problem. X-rays prove that there's nothing whatsoever the matter with her innards – 'a perfect little gall bladder', the surgeon told me. She's suffering from nervous exhaustion due to gin & a prolonged menopause. Of course she's perfectly furious that things should have turned out like this. It's sad & at the same time funny to see her impotently breathing clouds of peraldehyde, while M happily plays snooker with the doctors and does physical jerks on the cricket pitch . . . [21]

After three weeks at the Brook, Lowry felt well enough to return to work on *October Ferry*, and by 7 October, thanks to Davenport, the manuscript was sitting on his bedside table. He was now determined to re-establish his position with Erskine. Sitting in bed he composed a lucid three-page letter renewing his commitment to the book and his writing programme. He said nothing about alcoholism or psychological problems, maintaining that old injuries had led doctors to think he might need a minor brain operation but X-rays showed no need for it. He would be having an operation for haemorrhoids, and he hoped that that was not where they thought he kept his brain. His problems and Margerie's illness (which he assured Erskine had nothing whatsoever to do with alcohol, though she was sicker than he was) had held up work over the past year, and now bad eyesight prevented him reading his own handwritten manuscript easily. After eighteen months of not working he needed to refamiliarize himself with his work and revise his working methods. Until recently, holding a pencil for more than five minutes had been impossible. He had also become discouraged, he said, at receiving no acknowledgement from America of his recent success in publishing stories like 'The Bravest Boat' and 'Strange Comfort' from his *Hear Us O Lord* collection, and of his continuing success in Europe. Above all, he asked Erskine to reconfirm that the clock had been stopped when it had and that he still had time to catch up with his work, uncertainty about this being the main source of his emotional tension. To this Margerie added that further news about their joint illnesses could be obtained from Markson. She then wrote to warn Markson that Malcolm wanted no one to know the truth and was anxious to avoid news of his condition going around New York. She now felt guilty at having written so openly in the first place, and was fearful that this might get back to him.[22] It was not the last time she asked Markson to keep the truth to himself.

By mid-October, after five weeks in hospital, Lowry seemed to have made a miraculous recovery. 'The magnificent old boy has done it again,' Margerie told Markson: the doctors had definitely decided against an operation, but had said that if that path *were* taken she would have to be fit enough to cope afterwards. 'Thank God,' she wrote, having realized by now the alarm the idea of a leucotomy had caused among his friends. His genius, phenomenal memory, wit and sense of humour were all intact, and he was in great form. 'You should hear his descriptions of the horrors of his ward . . . I had a long talk with George Northcroft last night & he says if we're not yet out of the woods there is at least light at the end of the tunnel.'[23] No doubt all of this was due for inclusion in *October Ferry*. (*She* was all right, she said, just exhausted and with a possible tumour on the pituitary gland.) What Markson did not know was that Davenport had also heard about the suggested leucotomy and had confronted Margerie, who swore that the suggestion had not come from her and that she had rejected it anyway.[24]

Having received this news update, Markson duly passed it on to Erskine, adding, 'I guess Malc is not supposed to know that we know anything about psychiatric treatment, or we should not mention it to him, or some such. She is vague but insistent on that point.'[25] Erskine promptly wrote to Lowry assuring him that the clock was indeed stopped, and Random House still hoped and expected something important from him.

Thinking the Lowrys needed a rest from each other, on 24 October Northcroft suggested to Margerie that she go for a holiday to Cornwall leaving him in charge of Malcolm. He would keep him in hospital for a time then, using half his monthly cheque, put him in a boarding house allowing him two pounds a week to spend. Alternatively, he would put him up himself or admit him to a sanatorium where he could be easily supervised. 'After all, Margerie,' he said, 'he has opened his heart to me as to no other. And . . . I feel he has a better side, and all we need to do is appeal to it. He won't break his word to me.'[26] She was furious at this and, having discovered that Malcolm had received no psychiatric treatment, was determined to leave the Brook and find alternative help. When Northcroft conveyed all this to Dr Pearson, he said, 'Be careful there, George. This is a *folie à deux*.' And Northcroft thought his colleague had hit the nail squarely on the head.

Meanwhile, Bob Pocock, the ex-policeman, now at the BBC, prompted by Davenport, had written suggesting a visit, and they arranged to meet on 4 November at a pub near to the hospital. Lowry turned up in hospital blues, looking for all the world like a wounded soldier. With him he brought a battered copy of the *Volcano*, which he insisted on showing to the mystified landlady, and talked mostly about the 1930s as if nothing had happened in between. He kept looking at Pocock and saying, 'You know, you've changed,' and Pocock kept reminding him that it was twenty years since they had met. But whenever he mentioned the war, he saw that Lowry seemed embarrassed and quickly changed the subject. At closing time he saw Pocock to the bus stop, still saying, 'You've changed, you know, you've changed.'[27] He returned to the hospital drunk. All of the doctor's good work seemed undone, and Northcroft blamed Pocock for completely upsetting the cure. The following day Lowry walked out and Margerie followed.[28]

According to Stern, the first thing Lowry did on leaving the Brook was head for the nearest bar, get helplessly drunk and almost get himself arrested.[29] As they had been thrown out of the Richmond flat, they moved into the Frobisher Hotel on Cromwell Road. Malcolm was now completely off the wagon and back to being his old alcoholic self. Ralph Case and his brother Robert were anxious to help, and because Margerie was so worried, Ralph sent them to Harley Street to Sir Paul Mallinson, senior consultant psychiatrist at the Atkinson Morley Hospital in Wimbledon, where they had a few beds for alcoholics. After seeing Lowry, Mallinson agreed to admit him, but warned there might be a delay of four or five weeks. He was delighted. 'Oh, good, that will give me time to enjoy myself before going in there,' he said.[30] Three days before being admitted, Davenport and the Sterns took Malcolm and Margerie to dine with Julian and Mary Trevelyan at their studio at Durham Wharf in Hammersmith. Trevelyan, recalling that evening, remembered Davenport arriving drunk, although seeming amazingly sober compared with Lowry, and warning him to lock away the hard liquor.

They all went to the local pub, the Black Lion, and there Lowry told several times the story of his shack burning. Afterwards, at the studio, he wandered into the kitchen where Mary was preparing the meal, and said, 'Do you mind if I have a swig of your cooking sherry?' then promptly drank the whole bottle.[31] Ultimately it was difficult getting him to leave to catch the last train; he kept insisting he was going to sleep on the studio roof-beams, and had to be frog-marched into the street. Somehow they got him to Hammersmith station, but he was so drunk he just lay down on the platform. Davenport later told Trevelyan, 'We just rolled him into the train.'[32]

On the morning of Monday 25 November, Davenport went with

him to Wimbledon to see him admitted to the Atkinson Morley. Before doing so they repaired to a nearby pub for a last drink together. When they met Margerie at the hospital, Malcolm was completely drunk. She remembered him being led away by an orderly after checking in, dancing a little jig, then waving and beaming as he disappeared round a corner. Dr Michael Raymond, Sir Paul Mallinson's Senior Registrar, who took responsibility for his daily treatment, simply recorded in his notes, 'The patient arrived very drunk and was with difficulty persuaded to go to bed in a side-room. He was sedated.'[33]

Margerie, interviewed by the doctor, told him, 'You are really dealing with a genius; the greatest writer since Proust,' adding that he had a trunkful of partly finished novels which publishers were extremely anxious to get hold of but he would not finish them because he was a perfectionist. 'He had a ghastly childhood . . . and was blind for four years and had great fears about being impotent. [However] we have been wonderful together sexually.' But now he was in a bad way, and since coming to England had been drinking three bottles of wine and two bottles of beer a day.

To begin with, after his admission, he refused to talk, saying he just wanted to sleep. He was put on parentrovite (a concentration of vitamin B often used with alcoholics) and a high-protein diet, and finally he did begin to communicate. He said he could not give a medical history because it would involve a breach of confidence; his memory in any case was unreliable and he was not sure he wanted to be cured. He was incoherent and secretive, and when questioned closely would shrug and turn away. The doctor decided he showed no symptoms of schizophrenia, and when asked about his state of mind he said he was 'in a hell of a mood'. On 29 November, the doctor noted, 'Asked about hallucinations he said he heard very distinct voices mumbling from time to time as if in a dream. He denied hallucinations.' (Having planned the elaborated version of *The Voyage that Never Ends* on a claimed hallucination, he was being evasive to say the least.)

The doctor found his answers witty and lucid. He was, of course, well aware of what he was doing. He had met psychiatrists before – in Bellevue, at La Crescenta, in Haiti, Paris and Rome, and enjoyed pitting his wits against them. They, after all, were endeavouring to wean him away from the very alcohol that was a necessary crutch to his persona. He *was* the Consul, as he liked to admit, and still clung to the belief that alcohol was a source of inspiration in the way he had learned as a boy from Rabelais. He *was* the drunken sailor, the awkward little boy who identified with the drunken lawyer and the inebriated Bindon, and was now drinking the genius to death. Alcohol, too, was the drug that transformed, the deceitful medicament, the bottle that said 'Drink me!' The doctors were attempting to resocialize him, to unpick the complex psychic entanglements of a lifetime, to deprogramme him, not just the man but more importantly in Lowry's case, the writer. No wonder he turned his face to the wall and refused to co-operate.

With the prospect of Malcolm receiving proper psychiatric care, Margerie felt better, and moved into a place near Dorothy in Knaresborough Place, a miserable unheated little room with just a gas-ring for cooking, but convenient for Earls Court station and trains to Wimbledon. She sent Marie Moore news of Malcolm, but wrote gloomily that there were only two English magazines for serious stories, so little hope of publishing much there.[34] Through Davenport she again met Caitlin Thomas, still mourning angrily for Dylan, furious with Malcolm Brinnin's book, *Dylan Thomas in America*, and writing her own autobiographical cry of anguish, *Leftover Life to Kill*. One evening, Margerie, Dorothy and Caitlin went out together, but, according to Dorothy, Margerie so irritated Caitlin that she stopped their cab, threw her out, and drove off with Dorothy.[35]

It took until the end of his first week in hospital for Lowry to be well enough to start talking. He told Dr Raymond he was suffering mostly from fears – 'fear of everyone – fear of myself and of my wife, a general failure of my nerves'. He also complained of alcoholism of which he did not want to be cured. However, he gave the doctor his medical history, from corneal ulceration as a child to his broken leg of three years earlier. He talked about nearly going blind as a child, and not being allowed to play games or read at school for three years. He said he had gone to university only grudgingly and told of the incident which had scarred him ever afterwards – Fitte's suicide – and how, while drunk he had encouraged his friend to kill himself saying, 'It would be a good idea. You would probably find it a good deal better there than here.'[36] He did not, however, mention helping Fitte to seal the room and leaving him to his fate. The failure of *Ultramarine*, he said, had been a major disaster for him because he had hoped to earn enough money to be independent of his father. He talked about France and Mexico, the burning of the shack and the coincidence of the *Volcano*'s acceptance by two publishers on the same day in letters delivered by the postman who was a character in the book. He told of having to leave Mexico because of an expired visa, the threat of eviction, and

Margerie's inability to stand the life in Canada any longer, about being ill in Milan and permanently drunk in Sicily.

He dwelt on his sexual fears at length, talking about his childhood phobia of going blind from masturbation, his fear of contracting syphilis from sex, and of how he had started having sex with prostitutes even as a schoolboy. Finally, he said, he had been 'beautifully seduced' on Dartmoor by a married woman. He talked about his marriage to Jan and her pregnancy and abortion, claiming that the abortion had happened without his knowledge or consent – she being afraid of pregnancy, and he disliking using contraception. 'I was thoroughly immature,' he said, 'and developed a profound inferiority complex.' Of Margerie he said he had given her a good deal of help with her novels but all three had been failures. After his own success he had wanted to give up writing, because, 'Half of what I want to say is unbearable; the rest is inexplicable.' As for his sexual preferences he denied ever having a homosexual experience. Drinking had always been a sexual substitute, he said, and he began drinking in his teens to compensate for lack of sexual skill. Although he had suffered attacks of the shakes and nightmares, he denied ever having hallucinated. He claimed no religion, saying he had once believed in spiritualism but had abandoned it. (Nevertheless he talked about the importance of the spirit. It did not matter much if you damaged the body or the mind, he said, but to damage the spirit was sinful.)

Notwithstanding the spiritual risk from lying, he maintained that his father had died of cirrhosis of the liver and had been an alcoholic (Arthur Lowry was teetotal and died of cancer of the bowel). Dr Raymond noted, 'Patient said that he saw very little of him and now thinks he was a good man – gloomy, prone to worry, a fine swimmer and very much a Puritan. As a child, however, he thought his father was brutal.' He made much of his having sent Stuart packing for marrying a Catholic. 'It became a blasphemy to say any good word for Father.' As for his mother, 'If one did something nice for her it was thought to be disloyal to my eldest brother' – suggesting that he *was* more deeply affected by what happened to Stuart than might have been supposed in his attitude towards his parents. He said he was very anxious to appear stronger than he was. 'I can be quite happy alone, but can enjoy being with other people. I want to love people. I am appallingly self-conscious. I am given to both self-aggrandizement and self-belittlement, according to the circumstances.'[37]

The doctor thought he might suffer from a form of dipsomania connected with a romanticization of drinking, like Dylan Thomas, and thought that a change of attitude was required as much as anything. When he told him about his pioneering a modified form of aversion therapy – a combination of Pavlovian conditioning and attitude change – Lowry's response was that it would never work ('I'll bet you couldn't'). Nevertheless he seemed interested in what was said and hinted that he might be prepared to undergo the treatment. 'If you have the time to waste, so have I,' he said.[38]

George Northcroft phoned a week after Lowry's admission to warn Raymond that Margerie did not seem to him to have Malcolm's interests at heart. She appeared jealous of his success, had made him entirely dependent upon her and had been keen to have him leucotomized, which would certainly have ruined him as a writer. Confronted with this by Raymond, Margerie strongly denied the story, claiming that the leucotomy had been Northcroft's idea but that she had said all other therapies should be tried first. He had also suggested a separation which would have been intolerable, and anyway she thought he was hostile to her and jealous of their happy marriage. She later asked Dorothy to write to Dr Raymond supporting her, and she did so, saying that although she thought Margerie a liar, she believed she had done everything possible to get Malcolm well. Davenport also confirmed this, but added that there was little doubt that she was jealous of Malcolm, and socially impossible – a truly hysterical person who had but one topic of conversation, the Lowrys, and who took offence if one got bored and did not want to hear. Most people disliked her, he said, but she was worth tolerating because Lowry was worth saving. Whatever he made of all this, the doctor noted how, strangely, his patient had become institutionalized, not from living inside an institution, but from inside his own marriage. He could do nothing on his own, even dress himself or tie his own shoelaces. When Margerie visited him on 8 December, he told her that if he was moved out of his side-room into the general ward he would walk out of the hospital. She said that if he did she would leave him, and they had a long argument. When the doctor saw him later he was in tears.

Given methedrine – a form of truth drug – he said he felt on the verge of saying something useful, but the drug wore off; he hoped he would have it again. Four days later, he was given a larger dose (it took three doses to be effective) and finally he began to talk, warning that what he had to say would be painful and would cause the doctor to despise him. Firstly he spoke about his unhappy schooldays and being ridiculed on bath-night because of his under-sized penis. This, he said, had subsequently made him impotent and later in life he had taken to boasting, trying to make it appear that he had been a Don Juan while still at school, while at sea, and while at university.

At sea he had read Grieg's *The Ship Sails On*, and its picture of a crew riddled with syphilis had probably led to him becoming a syphilophobe later on. He so identified with Grieg's hero, Benjamin Hall, that his own book, *Ultramarine*, was in some passages a pastiche or plagiarism of Grieg, and he had then had to rewrite it to delete the offending passages. When the manuscript was stolen while with Chatto & Windus, he had first gone on a binge, then discovered a copy of the original which Martin Case had salvaged, and he had sent this straight off to the publishers. He implied that because of this the plagiarism and pastiche had thereby got into print, and since then he had been fearful that his borrowings from Grieg would be discovered. He said he had visited Grieg, confessed all this to him, and that the great man had been amused. As the doctor noted, 'He's never been able to bring himself to publish a novel and only published *Under the Volcano* under duress. It is probable, he thinks, that his reluctance to publish and become successful is due to the fact that, because of his shady first novel, it is better for him to remain obscure.'

Truth drug or no truth drug, Lowry said nothing about the Rascoe affair, nor about the disaster with Random House. On that day, 12 December, under methedrine, Lowry spoke nonstop for over five hours, and when the proceedings were terminated he complained that it was a bit like spiritual *coitus interruptus*. When he telephoned Margerie, as he did every day, she was surprised by how talkative he was. The day after this great outpouring he was back where he started – indecisive, incoherent and depressed. Because of this he was given the first of several courses of electroconvulsive therapy (ECT). When Margerie saw him that afternoon he was befuddled, forgetful and frightened; she, in turn, was shattered by his appearance, but Dr Raymond said it was not an unusual reaction to such treatment.

She wrote to Markson reminding him to send 'old monster Moby' a Christmas card, and followed that with a longer letter, urging him not to spread around what she was about to tell him. The Brook had been a disaster because he had not had psychiatric treatment; now he was getting it he was fighting it 'with all his savage will'. But when she saw him after his first two ECTs she found him bright and cheerful and was much reassured. He was of course a voluntary patient; she would never have him committed, but if he walked out she did not know what to do. It was as well the treatment was free because they had spent four months' income in the month before his admission.[39] Despite her attempts to keep his illness quiet, before the end of the year his old tormentor Ed Burra had informed Aiken that 'old Moby Malc' was in a home for alcoholics on the National Health.[40]

He was still having ECT over Christmas, including one dose on Christmas Eve and one on Boxing Day. However, this did not stop him borrowing two or three pounds from another patient and slipping out for a drink. According to Margerie he was missing for forty-eight hours and they sent a policeman to guard her, thinking he might be coming to do her violence. Finally he was picked up and returned, roaring drunk, to the hospital.[41] When she visited him late on Christmas Day he badgered her to give him money to repay his loan, but she refused and he shouted and abused her and loudly demanded drink.

After that he was told he would not be allowed out over the New Year period and would have no drink unless it was a part of aversion therapy treatment. He promptly asked for aversion therapy, and by 2 January the treatment was in progress. He was placed in a dark, windowless room with only a small red light and fed on brandy. At the same time he was fed, at intervals, apomorphine and occasionally ematine to make him nauseous. When Margerie asked about the light he replied, 'It adds to the mounting horror.' However, despite the nausea, he continued to gulp down everything he was offered. He was very uncooperative and aggressive at first, and not until he had been treated for over a week did the treatment began to have effect. At one stage he told Margerie, 'I was so thirsty I tried to drink my own piss.' She spoke to Dr Raymond and said that if his behaviour did not improve when he left hospital she would probably leave him. When the doctor put it to her that part of the trouble was her inability to settle, she said she was perfectly prepared to settle in England, and was hoping to find a cottage by the sea which she could make ready for him.

After ten days he asked to come off aversion therapy. When the doctor saw him he was pacing the room looking very worried. The very thought of neat spirits now made him vomit, he said, though he thought he might not feel so bad about a gin and lime. He now saw he had to be cured of his alcoholism, otherwise he was heading for the abyss: no doubt Margerie's threat to leave him had had an effect. In the past he had been flattered by alcohol and not taken it seriously, and had only started treatment to please Margerie, but now he really wanted to be cured. It was noted, however, that despite being so thirsty that he had tried drinking his own urine, when given milk he had used it to wash his hands and clean his nails. Now he was allowed food and non-alcoholic drinks, as much as he wanted.

Just after finishing the aversion therapy he was locked up for causing a disturbance when denied permission to see a film being shown in the general ward. The next day he was demanding paper, saying he had an insatiable desire to write, even if only about the way he was being treated. The respite was only brief and he was again subjected to aversion therapy, this time for just six days, and on 24 January Dr Raymond noted that he had had two bottles of beer in his room for a week without touching them. This annoyed Lowry, who complained to Margerie that while he liked Dr Raymond and could imagine him as a friend, he was insulted by his tricks and stratagems for testing his mental condition.[42] In any case, those claiming credit for his cure were misled – he had done it himself by an effort of will. That he *had* improved there was no doubt, and he settled down to a great burst of work on *October Ferry*, which Margerie had brought along.

Things were looking up and Margerie was feeling more optimistic. *Lunar Caustic* was due to appear in France, and she wrote buoyantly to Marie Moore saying that she hoped to have more good news for her by the springtime.[43] To Markson she wrote, 'The old monster has of course confounded everybody & made everything 10 times worse for himself, & everybody else than *any*one they've ever known . . .' He would never be 'normal', she wrote, for about the third time, 'My God! how could he be, & he Malcolm'. He could not simply be told to adjust and give up pipe dreams of being a great writer – he *was* a great writer. It was not every day, they had told her, that they had to deal with a genius, but at least they had taken this into account when treating him.[44]

The physical effects of aversion therapy were evident to her when she first visited him after the treatment was finished. He looked skeletal, his clothes hung on him and his face was deeply lined. She was shocked. When she asked him how he felt he replied, 'Like Lazarus.'[45] Dr Raymond thought that although Margerie was a hysteric, she would cope quite well with him after his discharge. He talked to her at length about their plans. They agreed that for the foreseeable future, Malcolm's best chance of survival lay in living under special restrictions – no travelling, no cities, no distractions, no drinking companions, frequent check-ups – but the most potent therapy for him was the peace and quiet in which to write. He had, she learned, amazed the doctors by surviving so much aversion therapy – most people collapsed after five days, he had stuck it for ten. However, although he was more collected, more aware, clear-minded and definite than he had been for ten years, he would need to see the doctor every two weeks, and could have further relapses, even dangerous and violent ones. But the house by the sea would be the answer. She wrote giving Markson an update on all this, stressing no more travel and the need for him to stay closely in touch with Dr Raymond.[46] She now had a very powerful argument against ever returning to Canada and life in the wretched shack again.

The right place to live was all important. Dr Raymond had heard from a patient of a furnished cottage to let in the Sussex village of Ripe, not far from where he himself lived at Burgess Hill, and suggested she look at it. She told him that Malcolm still suffered from free-floating anxieties and that unless these were cleared up by talking through his childhood, life with him would be impossible for her. She could not stand his egocentricity as she once could. However, by 25 January she was telling Markson about the dream cottage she had found, the one in Ripe that the doctor had told her about, a charming little eighteenth-century house called the White Cottage.

> This miraculous cottage is 3 miles from any station but 1½ hrs from Victoria Station in London. It has living room, dining room (which will be Malc's work room,) huge country kitchen, dairy, on first floor 2 bedrooms, *bath* on second floor, & attic bedroom & storeroom on 3rd floor. Front rooms look across meadow, with sheep & thatched roofed farm, brook, & up to the Great South Downs. We have a walled garden with flowers, & a kitchen garden where I can grow lettuce, herbs, etc . . . 2 of the houses in our town are in the Domesday Book but you won't find the town on any map, it's too small.[47]

It would be most convenient for travelling up to London for treatment every fortnight. Malcolm saw it as a good omen, and he loved the name Ripe.[48]

Besides writing, he was exercising daily, joining with other patients playing ping-pong – and looking forward to leaving. But he was annoyed that anyone should suggest that alcohol was a permanent weakness for him. Though he did not deny that the weakness was chronic, he declared that 'There is nothing more calculated to provoke the imp of the perverse than the insistence on weakness with a person who has just proved himself strong.' He was, however, delighted to hear Margerie's description of the cottage, and wrote to announce himself a changed man with a totally altered attitude to things and to 'the hell dance' he had led her. 'I shall try to make amends & am optimistic that you shall have real good & happy ripe & ripe & fun & the ducks will be themselves & be happy again.'[49] Before leaving hospital he asked to see his case notes so that he could write the experience from his point of view – and no doubt include it in *October Ferry*. In any event, he worked on it solidly for sixteen days, and on 3 February announced to Dr Raymond that he had completely revised it.

Despite an arctic winter, Margerie began moving things down to Sussex – those trunkfuls of manuscripts as well as their luggage – and informing friends of their new address. Now with a prospect of a more permanent home, she registered as an alien with the local police at Hailsham close to Ripe. Lowry began to write Miss Harteebeeste letters again. It looked as though the *folie à deux* was still intact and about to be transplanted permanently from Dollarton to Ripe. On 7 February he was discharged from the Atkinson Morley, and sent off with a supply of pills, a list of outpatient appointments with Dr Raymond, and the stern injunction not to drink. Only one thing worried him slightly: Margerie had told him that just at the end of the lane leading to the White Cottage, there was a pub.

The move to Ripe held promise of a new-found paradise. The village was delightful and remote, the cottage idyllic and picturesque (built in 1740 and with original oak beams). All their London friends, she told Marie Moore, were green with envy. They had told them that no such place existed since the war. Well, they had found that place and intended to remain there for some time.[50] Their landlady, an elderly widow, Edwina ('Winnie') Mason, lived next door – a pious, particular, somewhat snobbish woman who took an instant liking to the gentlemanly Lowry and his outgoing American wife. She sensed a spiritual quality in her new lodger with the sometimes distant look, as though he were searching for something beyond this earthly realm. The rent was a modest fifty shillings a week, well within their means, and they had a woman to clean and cook for them, although Mrs Mason also provided meals from time to time. The maid, said Margerie later, was so good she could clean Malcolm's desk without even disturbing him. They could walk through deserted lanes for miles, or visit nearby Deanland Wood and indulge their passion for bird-watching. Margerie bought a copy of *A Field Guide to British Birds*, and for their first month in Ripe they took trips to the coast, to Seaford and Eastbourne, and spent whole days spotting seabirds. For Lowry, too, the place had its literary associations – no absence of ghosts here. 'Hudson lived hereabouts,' he told Markson. 'Henry James' ghost prowls not far. So does that of almost every other writer you can think of, for that matter . . . '[51] They were on the telephone and a mere hour from the heart of London.

Lowry was busy catching up with letter-writing and his work in progress, as he told Markson at the end of February. He was now even well enough to offer his young friend some encouragement of his own and, still hankering after some kind of collaboration, suggested he come to England and they form 'a mutual aid society'. He needed no help with his new regime, however. 'I drink Cydrax (Cyder's non-alcoholic little sister) and behind a Melvillean boskage ponder the usage of the introverted coma.'[52] He asked Markson to send him copies of the *Partisan Review* and *New World Writing* carrying 'The Bravest Boat' and 'Strange Comfort'.[53] He needed to see himself in print again, to confirm his significance as a writer, but meantime he was working on *Hear Us O Lord*, and Margerie wrote urgently to Marie Moore for copies of 'In the Black Hills' and 'Elephant and Colosseum' which were missing from the trunk. In France, the February issue of *Esprit* carried the first of three parts of 'Le caustique lunaire', a worthy welcome back for 'Lazarus' to the land of the living, except that it would be months before he saw a copy. Margerie was also hoping to break into the literary scene, and they contemplated dispatching a copy of *The Last Twist of the Knife*, complete with last chapter, to T. S. Eliot at Faber and Faber, and Lowry even drafted a note to him recommending it as a 'masterpiece'.

Once he had settled down and was basking in the peace and country pleasures of Ripe, he wrote a long chatty letter to Davenport, who had surprised him by phoning to see how he was. He had also come back home in another way, and was tuning into a new literary scene. Listening to the radio, he had heard his old Cambridge friend Hugh Sykes Davies talking about one of his favourite poets, John Clare. There was more than one pretext to write to Davenport reporting on life in the new cottage and that he seemed to have found a second Eridanus – almost. 'It is small, an 18th century poet's paradise – or a 15th century one for that matter; all it lacks is yourself.'[54] But he still thought nostalgically of the beach, and when his friend Craige fell ill, he wrote to him that although they liked Ripe a great deal, he should not think that they had abandoned Dollarton; indeed they thought of it constantly, as they thought of him and the good times they were missing. However, for reasons of health it seemed better to stay put for the moment, though the beach would forever be home to them.[55] Margerie added, 'We are 8 miles from the sea, which is *awful*, but . . . the whole coast here is one huge resort & we don't like it. It's rather nice, friendly countryside with farms roundabout & the town of Ripe has about 8 houses altogether so we are quiet & peaceful. But oh dear our mountains! our forest! our *sea*! We shall come home, never doubt it, & have a fine time singing Loch Lomond.'[56] Margerie in fact had no desire to return to Dollarton. But what else could she say on the birthday of an elderly man suffering from cancer? However, Lowry also told Davenport that they were well and happy at Ripe and had no plans to move.[57]

At the end of March they had their first real visitors to the White Cottage, Peter and Joan Churchill, who brought a draft of Peter's autobiography for Malcolm to look at. They talked about a theme they had in common: the exile's return – Churchill after years in America and Lowry after years in Canada. When he had read it, and after making various suggestions about style, he urged Churchill to write a novel based on his exile. He could talk about two books, he said, and even imply a sequel, not a bad thing when dealing with publishers – a revealing piece of advice, confirming that the vast *Voyage that Never Ends* was probably as much a ploy to get a publisher to pay him a salary as something he truly expected to complete. The fascinating thing about doing a novel, he told Churchill, was that in establishing the universality of a protagonist you could project one or all sides of your 'many-sided self' and make it quite distinct from your 'auto-biographical self'. And the theme of the return of the wanderer to his own country was what Henry James had regarded as essentially the most dramatic of all.

Curious to see her translation of *Lunar Caustic*, he asked Clarisse to send a copy of *Esprit* and tell him how it had been received. 'We live in an ancient cottage in an ancient village, where there is not even a village idiot, unless you count myself,' he told her.[58] And there were certainly those in Ripe who did think that the new tenant at the White Cottage was a little soft in the head – it had something to do with his painful silences, standing still in the lanes staring ahead, and the strange fixed grin on his flushed face. He was well aware of doing all this – he had done it in Dollarton.

When Markson had his first success, placing a story with the *Saturday Evening Post*, they celebrated as if it had been their own. Telling him that he would now be in demand, Lowry urged him to retain his own 'native downbeat, personal three-point landing' style, and resist being 'typed' by editors. It was up to the novelist to establish self-editorship in order to resist such constraints, he wrote, but he might in so doing establish a touchstone which may both constrain and liberate others. 'Sometimes the originator himself gets caught in a "type" he's helped to invent.'[59] No doubt Lowry felt that the *Volcano* had 'typed' him and that was why he had difficulty satisfying editors with what he was now writing.

There was a glorious spring to enjoy and countryside to explore. Lowry was able to view life in a rustic timewarp with a cool ironic eye: 'The wild scarlet windflower of Greece is blooming in the garden and the cemetery is a riot of henbane. The stinking goosefoot is out, the mobile frying fish shop is advancing from the southwest, and there are two swallows nesting in the woodshed.' Soon they would have a cat and the landlady had lent him *The Psychic Life of Jesus*. Life on the whole seemed pretty good.[60]

A few days later he wrote Markson 'a note between paragraphs', telling him he would find the village enchanting. While Margerie planted hollyhocks and sweet peas in the garden, he weeded sentences full of contorted lousewort which he kept neatly in rows for later use. Although they missed the beauty and drama and old times on the beach, and without abandoning their shack in the forest completely, they had a good feeling about their temporary home in Ripe, were having fun and living very cheaply by American standards.[61] He was slowly putting down roots, though the sense of home being in Dollarton was still there.

Towards the end of the month, however, the idyll was suddenly under threat. When Clarisse announced that she might visit them, Lowry suggested she postpone her visit for a couple of months, announcing that Margerie had been ill, and there had even been the possibility of their moving from Ripe.[62] Two weeks earlier he had assured Markson that Margerie's health was the best she had enjoyed for years. While he had stuck religiously to Cydrax, however, Margerie had never stopped drinking. He later told Dr Raymond that she was drinking to excess and was drunk almost every evening, and he had said to her, 'This is more than Alcoholics Anonymous, this is Alcoholics Synonymous.'[63] Her illness therefore was probably drink-related, and talk of moving may have come from her feeling too isolated in the village.

Their regular trips to London to Dr Raymond's outpatient clinic in Knightsbridge were a good excuse to stay up in town to see a play, a ballet or a film. Once they went to the Criterion Theatre to see Samuel

Beckett's *Waiting for Godot*, which later, after hearing it again on the radio, Lowry called, 'one of the most inspired pieces of bloody-mindedness since the Crucifixion'.[64] They also visited Eric Estorick, his old New York acquaintance, now married and living in St John's Wood. But even such short expeditions to the big city ultimately had a disturbing effect on Lowry.

On 31 May, at St George's, Margerie told Dr Raymond, 'He is quite different. He thinks of other people more. His mind is clearer than I have ever known it.' Before returning home that day they visited the Tower and for some reason, while reflectively 'treading Raleigh's walk', Lowry began to think about the shack in Dollarton. Later, strolling moodily beside the Thames, he suddenly headed for a pub. Once he began drinking there was no stopping him, and although she managed to get him back to Ripe, hoping he would sober up, he promptly dived into the Lamb, the pub at the end of their lane, and ordered a bottle of gin. There was a loud argument over this, in which Malcolm got violent and threatened to do Margerie an injury. When the publican intervened he turned on him, too, and they were both ejected and told never to come back. Lowry ran off, stumbling around the countryside, cursing everyone – the landlord, Margerie, and the doctor who had predicted that this would happen if he drank alcohol again.[65]

Next day he tried calling Davenport, who had promised to visit them but never had, only to find he was in Rome. (In fact, working on his Norman Douglas biography, Davenport was at the Hotel Inghilterra where he met and began an affair with Mary McCarthy. On his return he lay low and was 'unavailable' because McCarthy followed him to England and he was trying to avoid her.) Davenport's absence depressed him, as did a letter from Harvey Burt announcing that he was coming to England to join Dorothy, and asking about finding someone to look after the shack.

Lowry managed to survive this lapse in sobriety alone, but was clearly disappointed with himself for having given in to an impulse. Just over a week later, Margerie reported him hard at work,[66] and he was well enough to reply to Burt, saying what he thought should happen to the shack in his absence, and revealing that the thought of returning was still there. It was important, he said, that whoever lived there should love it, too, and the more of their things that were left there, the less desolate it would appear.

He still knew nothing about the loss of the pier, which clearly held a deep psychological significance for him: 'To me, too, childish though it may seem, there is the pier, which we built, which I cannot imagine myself living without, even if it isn't there or myself am dead.' There was much love about the place, he added, which other lovers would enjoy. As to the manuscripts left behind, 'Leave 'em lay where de Lawd hath flung them.'[67] His prayer was that The Wicket Gate and Eridanus remain untouched. But he must have known that the future of both was limited, and that William Blackstone would have nowhere to go once the Puritans had conquered the whole land.

CHAPTER XXVI

GOING DOWN FIGHTING
1956–1957

> It seemed to me at that moment that the only thing that could come out of it was my own death, either by murder or suicide, or by some other unique distortion in the general pattern . . .
>
> MALCOLM LOWRY, *La Mordida*

> Writers, like children, have diseases peculiar to writers alone, the terrors of hysterical identification, for example, the uncanny dying through the death of another character, and so forth, frightening things which may indeed end in death for the author himself without another word.
>
> MALCOLM LOWRY, (letter to Harry Ford, 5 November 1949)

The flow of visitors to the White Cottage was modest, mainly because of its isolation. But Ralph Case visited a few times and felt that Margerie and Malcolm were more at ease with one another than they had been previously in London. The Churchills also dropped by, soliciting Malcolm's opinion of Peter's book, and talking of taking a cottage nearby. Ed Burra sent Aiken news of Lowry being in Ripe, reporting a cynical friend saying, 'They all end up in English villages, don't they?' In mid-June, Churchill came to stay for a few days and he and Margerie sat happily knocking back the gin and orange and telling Malcolm, 'You are so much better now, so much more considerate. How wise you are to leave this stuff alone.' The hypocrisy of this was too much for him, and coming on top of Davenport's absence and worry over the shack, his resistance finally broke and he gave in once more to his 'imp of the perverse', and was soon hitting the bottle again.

Alcohol had the same effect it had had two weeks earlier, and before long he was alternately in a stupor or violently raving. After two days of this, Margerie called their GP, Dr Troupe, from the nearby village of Alfriston. When he arrived he found Lowry incoherent, wild-looking and delirious. He refused to go to hospital, but the doctor signed an order compelling him to go. He was sedated, an ambulance was called and he was taken to the mental observation ward at Brighton Hospital. Margerie visited him three times that week, but then on the morning of 30 June they called her to say that he was causing such a rumpus, complaining about being kept there against his will, they no longer wanted him. She went to fetch him, but he then agreed to voluntary treatment and shortly after he was being driven back to Wimbledon to the Atkinson Morley. To her, remembering what he had previously gone through there, it was a heroic decision.

When Dr Raymond interviewed her after Malcolm's admission, she said she was now at the end of her tether, and that he had twice tried to strangle her and once attempted suicide. She added that he was intensely paranoid, always imagining people were plotting against him or following him in the street, especially policemen. He was helplessly dependent on her, unable even to cross the road alone, open his own mail or handle money. On top of that she was extremely afraid of him.[1]

The doctor was struck by the fact that on admission he was coherent, clear and concise, saying that he had been working hard and abstaining from drink, but was worried about his potency and lack of sex-drive. Margerie, though, had been drinking excessively while commending him for his sobriety, and on occasions had torn up his manuscripts and then stitched them up again.[2] She was happy at Ripe and got on well with the villagers, but he hated it. Because she tended the garden so carefully it seemed a betrayal of their house in Dollarton which he was worried about with Harvey Burt no longer there. He thought Davenport had let him down by not visiting them and not inviting them to Chelsea on their trips to town. He also said he felt suicidal. As for Margerie, 'She always wanted a child and I suppose that's what I've become.' When frustrated, she flew into hysterical rages, but he could not live without her. He denied feeling any more paranoid than was healthy in this world, but said he had to live the lives of his characters and that in some ways he experimented with himself and Margerie.[3] He was still inhabiting a fictional world, interacting with his own inventions.

Aversion therapy began immediately and lasted a week; the 'darkened room' treatment was more intense this time, but shorter. Afterwards he told the doctor that if he were denied alcohol completely then suicide would be inevitable. He said his attitude to alcohol had certainly changed and he now saw it as a menace rather than a joke, but said there must be a middle way of moderation for him. If there was not, his life would simply not be worth living. The important thing, the doctor decided, was to build up his self-confidence, make him more self-reliant and able to exist independently of Margerie. He decided to allow him to go freely in and out of the hospital, feeling that the risk of him getting excessively drunk was one worth taking.

Two weeks after aversion therapy ended, Lowry was allowed out of the hospital alone occasionally, twice even visiting a local pub for a couple of beers. He also underwent medical tests, and one of these was a barium enema. The resulting X-ray threw light on his lifelong chronic constipation. He described it gleefully to Margerie as 'an organic defect not to say phenomenon; hereditary . . . in fact [a] crashing deformity of the gut,' and quoted the radiologist with relish. It had been 'like pouring barium into a huge empty hall.' Dr Raymond called it 'megacolon with transposition of the gut' – his lower gut was grossly enlarged and out of place. Technically it was Hirschprung's Disease, a condition dating most likely from childhood and resulting in great difficulty in passing a motion. A partial colectomy was discussed (the removal of part of the lower gut), but it was deemed too hazardous. However, Lowry was delighted, especially when the doctor agreed that it could have contributed to his alcoholism. The 'great empty hall', he told Margerie, was greedy to be filled with anything alcoholic. It was a far more agreeable explanation of his past behaviour than wilful self-destruction, dipsomania, or simple lack of willpower. And he did not mind surgery to remove the 'hall', even if it meant some loss of mobility. But it certainly explained the mess his digestive system was in, he thought, and probably explained his father's death, too.[4]

He told Margerie he would try to meet her on her birthday, 18 July, at Victoria railway station, but, in the event, she spent her fifty-first birthday with him at the hospital. It was their first meeting for three weeks, and she brought along his manuscripts so that he might have them to hand when well enough to work again. He told her the doctors had put him through the worst aversion therapies they could devise and it had not worked. So he had asked them to do something even worse, saying they would have to dig much deeper to find out what was wrong with him.

Next day she wrote to Markson, saying that he had his psychiatrist 'on the run' and on one occasion the doctor had said, 'Let me get away from your Satanic tongue –'. She remained very open with Markson: 'Malc has, of course, among many others, a "free-floating anxiety neurosis", which they're trying to help. He said to me, "I don't suppose I'll ever get over it, but if it gets better, could you endure my derangements at half-buzz?"'[5] She felt very alone, she said, not surprisingly perhaps, because when Malcolm did write to her, he penned rather childish letters from El Leon to Miss Harteebeeste, complete with drawings.

Her solitude was not to last, however. Harvey Burt had arrived in England on 20 July, and visited the cottage with Dorothy – Margerie was pleased to have the company. She asked him to not to mention the loss of the pier to Malcolm, fearing it would only pitch him back into confusion. Because the visitors wanted somewhere to be alone, Margerie suggested they stay at the cottage while she spent some time in the local Hellingly Mental Hospital, resting and having more tests. They had to pretend they were married so as not to upset the pious Mrs Mason, but were delighted to stay. Margerie seems not to have told Malcolm about this, but did visit him on the evening of 21 July and told him harshly that if he was not cured this time, she would have him committed to a mental institution and would herself return to California – something she had also mentioned to Dorothy. Ironically, he had just written to say that the doctors were again 'astounded and confounded' by him, but pleased because there was a psychological change, and he was now able to dress and undress himself, had even organized a clock golf tournament at the hospital, and was generally getting himself fit for the big world outside.[6] In that world outside, Colonel Nasser, the Egyptian dictator, had just nationalized the Suez Canal, and a period of political upheaval lay ahead.

The threat of Margerie's leaving him appeared to upset Lowry deeply, and over the next few days he had to be collected more than once from the Crooked Billet pub on Wimbledon Common, where he was causing drunken disturbances. Back at the hospital he also caused trouble among the other patients, one of whom he had encouraged to go drinking with him. Finally on 27 July he was told that if he continued to regress like this there was little point in him remaining. The following day, no doubt fearful of the consequences of being thrown out uncured, he asked for a further course of aversion therapy, and the kindly Dr Raymond agreed. This might be his last chance to beat his addiction and gain control over his tortured mental life. The therapy started immediately and lasted for ten days. During that period, at his own request, he was kept incommunicado, and as a result of Margerie's threat and his decision to have more treatment he spent his forty-seventh birthday in a darkened room drinking alcohol and being violently sick.

The doctors found him co-operative and in good spirits about the treatment, regarding it as something of a joke, but after six days he appeared to be responding and showing at last some aversion to the large amount of alcohol which he was allowed. Apart from just one rest mid-course, the treatment continued until the evening of 7 August, and the following morning, when Margerie rang, she offered to take him back to Ripe at the end of the week, when she was, in any case, coming to London to renew her US passport.

Because of the disturbances he had caused and because he had encouraged another patient to go drinking with him, the Chief Consultant and Director of the Unit told Lowry that he would not be admitted to the Atkinson Morley again. However, Dr Raymond said that he could continue with him as an outpatient at St George's Hospital. Margerie later claimed that he had been discharged as incurable, but Dr Raymond testified that this was untrue.[7] The doctor had decided that Lowry was a manic-depressive, tending more towards the depressive, and could probably also be described as an alcoholic psychopath, who, when drunk, acted entirely on impulse.

When Margerie came to collect him, just before leaving, she announced dramatically to Dr Raymond that she had Simmonds Disease and would probably die shortly. She said she was to have tests at the Middlesex Hospital and wanted to know whether she should tell Malcolm. He advised her not to tell him for a week and promised to keep in touch through the outpatient clinic at St George's. Lowry left the hospital with what he called 'a grossgrandfather beard'.

It was a glorious summer, and the garden at the White Cottage was in full bloom when the 'new' Lowry arrived back home. Margerie felt she had to stay close to him and reverted to the old life of doing everything for him, and both his sleeping and waking hours were now carefully controlled by drugs. Harvey and Dorothy came to visit for the day and Harvey presented him with a model boat he had built. After dinner they went for a walk in the garden and Harvey asked Lowry about *October Ferry*, but he seemed depressed about it, saying it was not nearly so powerful as The *Volcano*. Then Lowry asked, 'Tell me, how is the pier?' Despite Margerie's dire warning, Burt decided that Lowry was adult enough to take the news. 'Well, in fact, it was washed away in the spring,' he said. Probably he had gauged better than Margerie

Malcolm's determination to present a more mature persona to the world. After all, he had learned to be more independent while in hospital. Now, to the news of the pier, he simply replied, 'I knew it.' Later he wrote thanking Burt for 'the bravest boat' and lamenting the passing of what had become to him an icon.

> I cannot believe our poor pier has been swept away: that pier, that gave so much happiness to many and us, WAS US in a sense; we risked our lives building it, especially on the further reaches . . . where there was a 35-foot perpendicular drop on to the granite . . . nobody could understand how it survived so long, not even engineers, and it was nicknamed "The Crazy Wonder" on the beach. Ramshackle from certain angles though it was, and the hand-rails puerile (but oh the washing hung out on the line there, like great white stationary birds beating their wings against the gale). Margie and I built it together with practically no tools and I am broken hearted it has gone.[8]

In more Shakespearian mood he wrote to Markson, 'Alas, our fool is dead, after 16 years.'[9]

Slowly he got back to work, and Margerie travelled back and forth to London for tests, and was, presumably, found not to have Simmonds Disease or to be on the verge of death. However, by the end of September, probably in reaction to what she had been through, she did show signs of a breakdown – shaking, crying uncontrollably and finding it impossible to sleep. When tests showed that there was nothing wrong with her physically, she was admitted on 18 October to St Luke's Woodside Hospital, in Muswell Hill, north London, for psychiatric treatment. It was arranged for Malcolm to sleep at the Rectory and be looked after by Mrs Spooner, the housekeeper, though he also spent time at the cottage, sometimes working there and keeping his eye on the garden, and feeding Merlin the cat. At the same time, he plunged into yet another revision of *October Ferry* which reflected his recent experiences and new-found stability, but he still found time to write to Margerie every day.

To begin with he sent her his usual 'El Leon' letters, full of winsome nonsense. But in October the mood changed suddenly and he told her, 'In passing it has struck [me] we might both write each other more real letters . . . Considering [our] profession it's just struck me as wonderful that we avail ourselves so little of writing as a means of serious communication, especially when otherwise incommunicable.'[10] This new and 'adult' mood was just what Dr Raymond had been hoping to achieve, and from the letters which followed, it seemed he had succeeded. There were detailed descriptions of life at the Rectory and accounts of Mrs Spooner's huge and fattening meals, the latest village gossip, and some expression of pleasure at living in Ripe. 'All in all a better place from both our points of view could not have been found.' (Since he had told both Dr Raymond and Harvey Burt that he hated Ripe, he had either changed his mind or simply told people what they wanted to hear. And of course his relationship with Margerie was one of fathomless Strindbergian depths.) There were descriptions of almost every flower in the garden and what it was doing – from the roses and nasturtiums to the dahlias and Michaelmas daisies, 'a dramatic . . . altogether beautiful flowering with quite a Dollartonian stillness & peace (despite the fact it's blowing like hell)'.

Perhaps because it was thought there might be some danger in his travelling to Knightsbridge alone, on Sunday 21 October, Dr Raymond came over from Burgess Hill to visit him at the Rectory. He found his patient busily working and consuming glass after glass of Cydrax. He claimed that it helped enormously with his constipation, somehow washing out that vast megacolon, and said that was why he would probably never give up beer drinking. As he wrote to Margerie the following day,

> Doc. Raymond arrived yesterday at the Vicarage for awfternoon tea, looking a mixture between Oscar Wilde & the Uncle in War & Peace, & bearing, in a hand like a malt-shovel, a half-dozen sodium amytals to tide me over nights & he's sending the rest later, & substituting grand things like yours for the pink objects on my days of benzydrene abstinence, the pink things latterly upset me slightly: in this way there's no temptation to overdose (or for that matter underdose) – too much of one makes you a headache, the other simply sick.[11]

The fact that he was conscious of the dangers of overdosing reflected a positive and optimistic outlook, now turning its attention towards work. He had proudly shown his visitor a trunkful of manuscripts and the doctor stressed the importance of getting back to work on them. In fact, as he said, he *was* working hard, when the cat would let him. The doctor had every right to feel that his treatment had been so far eminently successful.

Lowry rang the hospital for news about Margerie every day, and became worried when they said her main problem was worrying about him. He wrote trying to put her mind at rest; he was doing fine, leading a 'positively Jane Austen-like' existence, enjoying the solitude and finding it a God-sent opportunity to work.[12] Nor should she worry about him forgetting to take his medicine; if he forgot, Mrs Spooner always reminded him. The medicine, he thought, was doing him a lot of good, though he was looking forward to doing without it. He also worried in his usual paranoid way that his letters were being read by hospital staff. Alone, too, he seemed even more rooted to their country retreat. Mrs Mason was 'a good egg' and he was devoted to her, he said. 'And I'm growing quite fond of the cottage & mostly so of your garden.' He confirmed his growing independence by going alone on the bus to Lewes and back. He spent most of his time there shopping – a postal order for Dr Raymond, a pipe, a tobacco pouch, a bar of Lifebuoy soap. He changed his library books at Boots and bought a couple of Penguin Classics. Showing optimism about his work, he also bought a packet of large brown envelopes – 'a Talisman', he said. Finally, he bought a cup of coffee – 'price 7*d.* (Tip 4*d.*)' – before catching the three o'clock bus back to Ripe. He returned in triumph to the Rectory with a great sense of achievement.[13]

The Rectory – a large comfortable house with a lot of land and marvellous views – was for sale, he told Margerie, suggesting they tell the Churchills about it. But he was fed up with friends who, despite promising, never visited them. He was 'browned off on all friendships or even acquaintances' until they had sorted out their lives properly, which was the main problem they faced together. And world news concerned him too. 'I'm writing in the rectory against a radio blaring about disturbances in Poland,'[14] adding, with some satisfaction, as he recalled his own prediction of the ultimate collapse of East European communism, 'sounds damn good news too, not going to say I told you so, but I did nevertheless'.

Margerie was being treated by deep narcosis, so once she was into her sleep there were no letters and not much news to be had of her by telephone. Strangely enough, he wrote, he missed her even more now she had gone into her 'Great Schnooze', and would probably ring up about her just as often. Perhaps it was this acute feeling of missing her that led him to revert to a nonsense letter from El Leon to Miss Harteebeeste. On Halloween he became nostalgic about making jack-o'-lanterns on the beach at Dollarton. And, with house agents showing people over the Rectory ('I begin to feel like Firs in the Cherry Orchard, for some reason'), suggested that they themselves might consider buying it.

By November it was so cold in the cottage, he told Margerie, that he was writing wearing gloves. He still talked about staying in Ripe, despite the appalling climate, and even suggested they buy the White

Cottage and her garden to which even he had now grown to feel loyal. This sudden love affair with Ripe might have been just to cheer Margerie; or it may have reflected a genuine feeling of contentment from living alone and being fussed over by women who cooked him huge meals, cleaned the house, and generally took care of him. His reservations were not just the climate but the fact that he felt there was nothing in Sussex which one could 'wind one's heart quite all the way round'. Nevertheless, 'I'm very fond of our ghost-whistling engine-room drawingroom-little-white cottage though which reminds me of a flying saucer, with garden, does about 18 kn[ots].'[15]

On 2 November he reported,

> I am in FULL BUZZ at work: with six piles on the rectory table comprising the end of a chapter, six piles on the White Cottage table . . . comprising the beginning of the same chapter, and six piles on my arse to denote my belief in Sinclair Lewis' dictum that inspiration is the art of the application of the seat of the trousers to the seat of the chair.[16]

He was eating well, enjoying working again, and was quite able to organize himself – tending the garden and arranging for his clothes to be laundered. After another trip into Lewes, he wrote in triumph about going into a pub for cigarettes and sheltering there for twenty minutes from the rain without once being tempted to buy a drink. He was obviously in good form – he loved the cottage, could get to Lewes and back with only small incidents to worry him, resist the lure of the pub, and report all this with good humour even though Margerie was not replying to him. This was a different Lowry from the one who, apparently unable to live without her, got drunk in 1949 and broke his back falling off his pier. On 4 November, Dr Raymond visited again, and he was well able to entertain him, as he told Margerie:

> Raymond arrived Sunday & found me working in the kitchen like a demon: I gave him a cup of tea so strong it gave him the shake, & he sang the song the psychoanalyst sings in the Cocktail Party for me, only a bawdy version of it: since you don't know the song I don't think that conveys much.[17]

He was taking ever more interest in world affairs. The Hungarian uprising riveted his attention in early November, and recalling the extreme reactionary nature of pre-war Hungary from Jan's researches, he wondered whether it had been quite as the press made out or whether anti-Semites and ex-Nazis financed by the Americans were behind it. 'And yet there seems to be truth in the spontaneity of the uprising too, not to mention . . . a real hope of a better thing.' But any American intervention, he thought, would be a disaster. However, when it came to troops being sent to retake the Suez Canal from Nasser, imperialist attitudes not evident since his youth surfaced again. 'I myself, though still with a heart slightly to the leftward sometimes, am all in favour both of Israel's and our own action.'[18]

Dr Raymond's words were well heeded. 'I have got to WORK, as per your advice,' he told him, '& I mean WORK & no backtalk about it.' But he realized that that meant maintaining his stability in some form or other, which depended on getting the right kind and amount of drugs.

> I am much beholden to you for causing me to be sent a fortnight's supply of Sodium Amytal: i.e. 28. Having started 9 days ago I now have 10 left: I shall therefore be out of them by this Thursday. I have enough benzedrine at the moment – 3 a day & twice a week the pink things instead. I have, however, abandoned taking 1 pink object per day after the last benzedrine: in short I take no sedatives during the day, which works fine, so long as I'm alone, at least.

He did not think there was any longer a danger in his visiting Dr Raymond at St George's alone, but he did not want to commit himself until he saw exactly when he could see Margerie in hospital, especially now that he was working hard. He asked for more instructions about pills he should take.[19]

Margerie was in the middle of 'her Rip Van Winkle snooze', he told Markson on 5 November, and 'while she is away I am living on an absolutely incontrovertible wagon in a rectory haunted by a phantom billiard ball that bounces down the stairs at midnight and seeing no one (apart from the billiard ball of course).' Despite Hungary and Suez and riotous crowds burning Anthony Eden in effigy on the Sussex Downs, he still maintained his Micawberish optimism – 'all manner of things will be well soon here – at least with us.'[20]

The old dream of working in movies was revived when Matson wrote that a producer had taken a six-month option on the *Volcano*, naming José Quintero as director. Lowry was delighted with Quintero, who had had a great success in the New York theatre latterly with *Long Day's Journey into Night*; wherein O'Neill 'has four drunks, one dope-fiend &

one miser to cope with & which besides last 4½ hrs' so he could be trusted to come up with something special.[21] Meantime, he was again deep into his novel. 'I have got a real egg-like horror a-brewing in Gabriola,' he told Margerie, and worried what to do with a $35 cheque received as royalties on the *Volcano*. He had not wanted to go to the bank in Lewes, so asked at the post office if he could send it by post. 'Hadn't your wife better have it?' he was asked. 'Christ,' he wrote, 'whatever impression of me have you given at that place, oh deary deary me.' Then just to make it clear that he was no longer so dependent and incapable, he added, 'El Leon has managed on the whole quite well solo . . . '[22] And considering that it was *THAT* month and *THAT* anniversary was approaching, he was doing *very* well.

By 8 November, Margerie was awake enough to read Malcolm's accumulated letters and to reply to them. She had slept through the Russian invasion of Hungary, Eisenhower's re-election and the seizing of the Suez Canal by Britain and its allies. He in turn responded, beginning in the style of El Leon to Harteebeeste, but soon switching to that of his new mature self. For once he felt that his position over Suez would coincide with her conservative views. He approved of what Eden had done and thought that she would approve, too. 'TEN DAYS THAT SHOOK THE WORLD indeed.' With unconscious irony he added, 'I must say that between you and me about the only thing we can really have reason to feel optimistic about is – er – you & me.'[23]

Two days later, Margerie telephoned to say she would soon be discharged, and he wrote yet another love-letter-cum-newsletter, telling her about the film option, and how he felt he had let her down by not insisting on controlling what happened to her in hospital. He emphasized how busy he was and how difficult it was for him to come all the way to Muswell Hill to collect her, seemingly fearful of his flow of work being interrupted, and suggested that they meet instead at Victoria Station.[24]

But then he had a real crisis to handle. A letter came from Margerie's mother, and another arrived simultaneously from Bert and Priscilla announcing that she was dead. She had died aged ninety-one having just returned from voting for Eisenhower. Lowry opened both letters, but read about her death before reading her own last letter. It was yet another of those eerie coincidences which happened to him. Luckily for him when Margerie's doctor heard, he decided to return from holiday to give her the bad news himself.

Malcolm set about preparing for her homecoming, arranging for a health visitor and doctor to drop by on her return, and assuring her that all would be clean and ready. He also said that this time he was pleased that Eisenhower was re-elected and was sorry that the Suez war had failed, believing that Eden should have gone on to the end. But he was obviously nervous about the homecoming, and apologized for a confused letter. 'I just lit my nose & threw away my cigarette.'[25]

On 16 November Margerie returned to Ripe. On her arrival, Malcolm took her upstairs and carefully helped her undress. She had lost so much weight – she was down to seventy pounds – that when he saw her he cried. As a homecoming present he had bought her a suntan lamp to help her get through a grey overcast English winter. But in fact she was soon back on form, expressing delight about the film option on the *Volcano* in a letter to Marie Moore, and indicating that she would hope and expect to work on the movie while Malcolm was busy with his novel.[26]

In early December, Alfred Knopf wrote, asking permission to reprint the *Volcano* as a Vintage Book, and Lowry wrote to Markson that life was grand and he was working like sin on *October Ferry* with which he was now completely in love. 'But I am managing to eat it a little more than it eats me so far.'[27] Two days later he told Erskine that, as far as work was concerned, he had never been better. 'In fact I have to go back to work now, mine being the bow & me to bend it (as opposed to the elbow)'.[28] This sudden new burst of energy on *October Ferry* was all-consuming, and he had little mind for anything save work. He rose at 7.15 a.m., he told Dr Raymond, attended to the chores, then got down to work which was 'as intensive as it could be'. He had lost weight and seemed about to enjoy a sexual rebirth. Apart from entering for the Olympic Games he could do little more to demonstrate his all-round improvement, and he thanked the doctor very much for his help. Also, he said, the book was greatly changed for the better and while it was ten times more difficult to write, it seemed easier. 'In short I much doubt, whatever trials the future may have in store, I shall ever view that future again, or for very long even if I did, from the same abysmal standpoint; which coming from me is saying a good deal.'[29]

He wrote telling Downie Kirk that he was working like mad on *October Ferry* and all because he [Kirk] had liked it. It was better than the *Volcano*, 'a veritable symphony of longing for the beach'. They hoped to return, God willing, thought of him often and were frequently homesick.[30] His industrious equilibrium, however, was still dependent on drugs, and just before Christmas he asked Dr Raymond for a new prescription. He had cut down on benzedrine and relied mostly on sodium amytal to sleep at night, but wanted the doctor's approval.[31] He had also cut down on tranquillizers, but was anxious not to experiment further without Raymond's approval.[32]

They decided to move to London for a couple of weeks over Christmas. Before leaving, Lowry was called by Peter Churchill, then recovering from a heart attack, and Jimmy Stern who was visiting him. As Stern told Markson.

> We phoned, & there they both were, sounding as though they were 20 years old & had never heard the word *lc*h*l! He claimed in stentorian tones that he was 'writing like hell', and she – well, I really can't remember what she said, but I don't think she even uttered a complaint . . . I did not remind him that I had written him at least twice in the last 9 months . . .[33]

In fact Davenport as well as Stern had written several times in the past year but Lowry had chosen not to answer, partly because he was, as he said, 'browned off' with his friends, and partly because of illness and work. But he was clearly delighted to hear from them.

In London for the festive season, they attended the Christmas Day service at Westminster Abbey, then went to cinemas, dined out at good restaurants – Lowry particularly enjoyed Chinese ones – saw all the plays they had time to see, and visited the Royal Academy. On Boxing Day they went to the New Theatre to see the stage version of Dylan Thomas's *Under Milk Wood* (Thomas's title being quite likely in part a satirical twist on his friend's infernal *Under the Volcano*). Margerie hated the set so much she kept her eyes closed during the performance. As for Malcolm, 'I thought it curiously remote and tinny on the stage, like something going on in a music-box, and also in parts excessively sentimental, whimsical and generally pseudo Dickensian, but a bloody unusually splendid piece of work for all that.'[34]

In the New Year he resumed work on *October Ferry*, and was so engrossed in his writing that he put off seeing Dr Raymond until the end of January.

> I feel I should go on biting on the nail without intermission for another 3 weeks or so, having given myself that week off and just got down to a routine again, and an extremely tough one it is, though I can't say I'm not enjoying it, having acquired that beautiful & life-giving

> & indeed necessary paranoia in regard to Gabriola without which I suspect works of this kind would rarely be completed . . .[35]

He was too busy now to go into Lewes for shopping; that was left to Margerie. The book had begun to reflect his present situation. In one fragment, a little sketch describing Eridanus deserted after eviction, he seemed to be weaving together recent psychiatric experiences and life at Ripe, likening the village to 'a psychiatric ward at noon, waiting for the doctors to pass through, with two tall nurses at anchor,' or 'one emptied of its patients doubtless taking electric shock treatment, while one or two others moaned as though purposely . . . doubtless wanting to take the alcoholic aversion treatment'. It was as though Ripe's quaint claustrophobia enabled him to see Dollarton heightened to the state of a psychiatric illusion. And having come to love Ripe in his own way despite yearnings for Dollarton, he could look at the events which inspired the novel from a distance and with a different focus, as he had in rewriting the *Volcano* in Canada. That can only have given his creativity a new surge of energy. To Markson he wrote,

> I am these days almost continuously in the grip of that thing used to be call: inspiration, hombre . . . The trouble is, the lightning usually strikes at a tangent [and] it's sometimes wearing work dashing round picking up your charred smithereens or even bright illuminations and piecing them together, especially when they often seem to mean buggerall or as Dylan would say Llareggub . . .[36]

He wrote to Downie Kirk about his inspired work on the novel, and Kirk replied hoping that he was giving it the attention to detail which had so distinguished the *Volcano*, adding that since he had left, 'There has been a literary slump around here.'[37]

It is a measure of how recovered he was that he could, on 22 February, write a monumental thirteen-page witty, scholarly and inspiring letter to Markson who, now an editor with Lion Books, had written proposing a reprint of the *Volcano*. Lowry replied that Knopf's offer had gone through and a contract for a reprint was due at any time (though he was annoyed that Harcourt Brace had demanded fifty per cent of royalties for releasing it). He detailed cuts he wanted to see made in the book, even though Knopf had required none (an interesting reversal of the Cape situation of 1946), and reported sadly that the film option on the book had come to nought.

He offered Markson the plot for a novel which he thought he was well placed to write – 'one of the happiest ideas for a novel since Miss Lonelyhearts and Nathanael West were apprentice seamen,' he called it, and offered 'in a serious spirit of Pushkinship to your creative Gogolatry'. As ever with Lowry, the drama came down to a struggle between Thanatos and Eros, the Dark Dopplegänger and the Bright Doppelgänger, and, in even more predictably Lowryesque fashion, it became a novel about the writer writing it:

> it occurred to me that by starting a novel with such a short story, then proceeding to the motives of the author in writing it and the frustrations and despairs involved, you would have achieved a kind of *absolute* of construction, with the possibility of extending the frontiers of the novel.[38]

It sounded like a commentary on the making of *October Ferry*. He argued that the pluralistic morality of the artist often comes into conflict with the rigid morality of Art, and in a veiled warning to Markson to learn from his experiences, confessed that it was 'from the confusion of the two worlds, of the domains of art and life, that my own troubles have mostly arisen, not to say that of many other writers'.[39] All the writer's bloody-mindedness could go into his art 'but Life itself should strive towards a Happy Ending since however much this may seem to outrage us aesthetically, this is what we are meant for, even should the earth itself be cast into the uttermost dustcart.'[40] This long letter read at times like a writerly last will and testament bestowing his accumulated wisdom upon his young friend.

In March the contract from Knopf was signed and returned, though the book would not appear for another eleven months. But this boost to his confidence was timely, followed shortly by a most enthusiastic and flattering letter about the *Volcano* from the American writer George Sumner Albee who had just read it for the first time. He had easily out-written Faulkner and Hemingway, said Sumner, and it was Lowry who ought to have the Nobel Prize. It was the kind of encouragement on which he thrived, and he replied at length by hand, reflecting ironically that, by contrast with the US, in England where he had come to rest, the book had been poorly received and he was virtually unknown, though Canada had been no better.

In his new mood of optimism he asked Davenport to help find outlets in England for his and Margerie's work. Davenport suggested taking things out of the hands of Innes Rose, who had grown apathetic, and he would see what he could do with 'Strange Comfort' and Margerie's mysteries. But if he was having little success in England, he was in demand elsewhere. In April he heard from Ralph Gustafson, the Canadian poet, wanting to include two of his poems, 'Lupus in Fabula' and 'The Glaucous Winged Gull' in the *Penguin Book of Canadian Verse* which he was editing. This prompted a reply which ranged across poetry, his relationship to Canada, and his strong nostalgia for the beach. He did not know, he said, whether he counted as a Canadian, never having taken Canadian citizenship. However, he had long wanted to contribute something to Canadian literature, and had lived so long at Dollarton, in a shack on the beach which he loved more than his life and where he wrote his best work. He had left because of his wife's health, but hoped to return soon. Perhaps he was trying to please Gustafson in expressing his love for Dollarton as he did to his other Canadian friends, but there is passionate conviction in what he wrote. He thought of little else but poetry when he was not thinking about his shack at Dollarton, he wrote, and as a result, he was composing 'a huge and sad novel about Burrard Inlet . . . that I sometimes feel could have been better stated in about ten short poems – or even lines – instead.' Undoubtedly, writing *October Ferry* served to keep his mind preoccupied with his much-missed Eridanus. As to his poetry, he told Gustafson, he did not think very much of his poetic ability and asked him for advice about his work, though he thought that having had some youthful success as a jazz composer he must have a talent for verse of some sort.[41]

This increasing transatlantic interest in his work can only have served to further draw his attention westwards. On top of that, the death of Joseph McCarthy on 2 May and the awarding of the Pulitzer Prize to O'Neill a few days later must have made North America a somewhat more appealing place to him than it had been for many years. However, American writers were still being persecuted for their beliefs and at the end of May Arthur Miller was found guilty of contempt of the House of Representatives UnAmerican Activities Committee. Sometime that spring Lowry began a letter to a newspaper, but it soon grew into an essay, called 'Halt, I Protest!',[42] on the freedom of the press and the privacy of the individual, into which he put all his strong views about the evils of McCarthyism and the dangers of siding with one form of totalitarianism against another.

He and Margerie had decided to spend their summer holiday in the Lake District. They joined the Royal Society for the Protection of Birds in order to visit the bird sanctuaries on the Farne Islands before making for Wordsworth country. They were going there, he said, not because of Wordsworth but because if they half-shut their eyes they could imagine they were back on Burrard Inlet.[43] Perhaps Margerie thought it might temper his longing for Dollarton to enjoy a kind of substitute homecoming.

She had told him that she did not wish to read the *Volcano* again until they could work on it for a movie script. But he went out of his way to dedicate a copy of the Reynal & Hitchcock edition to her with the words, 'For Margerie with devotion from Malcolm – XCIXCLVII – Spring!' He also wrote and then crossed out 'viz à mon colombe sans pareil de ton sigisté.' (Namely: to my dove without parallel from your cicisbeo). And that spring, there was a beautiful comet visible in England which they stared at through binoculars for hours: every night Malcolm insisted on looking at it.

On 12 May, Joan Churchill died suddenly of hepatitis, and they were both deeply shocked. Unaccountably, they failed to attend the funeral, which upset Churchill, though possibly Margerie kept Malcolm away for fear that a funeral might precipitate another plunge into depression. Two weeks later, on 27 May, they left Ripe for their holiday up north, well armed with bird-watching guide and notebooks.

It was a sign of Lowry's alertness that his notebook for the trip was so detailed and comprehensive, with occasional passages of reflection, such as

> Importance for a writer, once having learned something, to repossess the position of his own former ignorance: the impressions life makes on the uninstructed consciousness, viz. upon one's ignorance, may have a poetic truth in the presentation they will lose as one acquires more knowledge, because the knowledge is likely to be corrupted by misinformation (amid the knowledge), whereas the ignorance is naturally pure, may indeed be near to a sort of absolute (in my case).[44]

But out among people again he referred to 'the agony of necessary discourse . . . breakdown of all communication'. Nor was he impressed by other bird-watchers on the trip to Farne Island, noting 'Inhumanity . . . [and] compulsive neurosis of fidgety bird-watchers vaulting fences, frightening the birds to death.' On their second day on the island, Lowry insisted they separate themselves from the others and go around on their own.

By 2 June, after taking four trains and two buses, they were in Grasmere and the notes were more detailed – an epitaph on a seat overlooking

Rydal Water, Wordsworth's name carved on a bench, a conversation overheard with the skipper of an old-fashioned lake boat, the intrusive trippers, a murder report in a local paper, a tiny hearse outside a funeral parlour, the sweet sinister smells around a large gabled house doubling as a hotel and crematorium, graveclothes dancing on a washing line, walks between Watersedge and Grasmere. He made a point each day of swimming in the icy lake, trying to somehow recapture life at Dollarton. They rowed across the lake, picnicked on an island, took midnight walks and listened to waterfalls, and rambled to Ambleside and Hawkshead ('just like Tlaxcala in Mexico') where he sat in Wordsworth's chair. Over the month of their stay, there were more days of walking through sun and showers, always taking notes, to pay homage at Wordsworth's grave and to visit Grasmere village, with half an eye open for a place to live. On 15 June, he sent a postcard to Markson with a panoramic view of Grasmere and the message:

> Dollarton? That's what we thought but it's Grasmere where Wordsworth designed the chimney pots and you may see de Quincey's room (smoking prohibited) in de Quincey's house to which, on payment of 1/6 you may be admitted on all days save Sundays as Wordsworth's cottage, which it was for 5 years . . .[45]

But, despite his alertness and apparent good humour, something dark was brewing. On the journey home on 22 June, Lowry's all but last note on the final page of his notebook in large block capital letters read 'OUT OF ORDER' – perhaps a sign of things to come. Margerie wrote later that he had never been so well and happy and mature as over the past months but on their return she had a black feeling of something hanging over their heads.

Certainly the trip seems to have unsettled him and they returned to an uncertain future. In particular he was worried by the failure of the people left to guard their Dollarton shack to reply to letters, and he must have been only too aware that 22 June was the second anniversary of the destruction of the pier. Margerie wrote urgently to Harvey and Dorothy, somewhere in Germany, asking for the latest news of what was happening at the beach.[46] Lowry in a letter to Burt misquoted from memory some apt lines from Wordsworth's 'The Prelude':

> Ye lonely cottages wherein we dwelt
> A ministration of your own was ours
> Can I forget you, being as you were

So beautiful among the pleasant fields
In which you stood? Or can I forget
The plain countenance with which
You dealt out your plain comforts.[47]

He did no more work on *October Ferry*, but clearly, with worry over the shack heightened and the strong yearning for Dollarton which the Grasmere trip had aroused, he became more and more agitated. Nor were there any of his friends around for him to talk things over with. Davenport was still hiding from Mary McCarthy, and Peter Churchill was away in France.

He is reported to have started drinking steadily again after returning from Grasmere, and there were quarrels. Quite likely these were about the drinking, but also about returning to Dollarton. Margerie had threatened that if he regressed into alcoholic delirium again she would have him committed and leave him. He still pined for Canada and she was determined never again to live the primitive life on the beach. But now he was less dependent on her; he had proved that he could exist without her, and she knew that if ever they divorced she would lose any inheritance she stood to get from him, including any control over the manuscripts which she had been so much a part of producing. A score of currents and cross-currents must have been swirling between them, for within the *folie à deux* El Leon and Miss Harteebeeste could only love one another – there was no language there for them to quarrel with or to handle hatred. Inside this maelstrom of dark, unsleeping passions, old terrors must have been stirred, and other spectres roused from their slumbers.

On the evening of Wednesday 26 June they went to The Yew Tree pub in Chalvington, which they had occasionally visited since being banned from the Lamb. Malcolm had, according to Margerie, got very drunk the night before, so going back to the pub was risky. However, throughout his months on the wagon she had continued drinking steadily and sometimes heavily. During the day, Lowry had worked on 'Halt! I Protest!' which in good Lowry style had grown into a lengthy piece of prose. He also wrote to Peter Churchill, whose home was now in Brighton. The plan that evening was to return to the cottage for a meal and to listen to a London Symphony Orchestra concert conducted by Leopold Stokowski on the BBC Home Service.

According to the landlord of The Yew Tree, Charlie Baker, Lowry was a quiet and friendly customer who usually sat silently drinking only beer before going quietly home. That evening he and Margerie sat apart from other drinkers, apparently having quarrelled, and before long she had begun to cry. Lowry then came to the bar and bought a bottle of gin – hoping it would cheer her up, he told the landlord – and saying that she was upset about their home in Canada, which they had now not seen for three years. But she was crying inconsolably and became even more hysterically angry about the bottle of gin. Lowry, disturbed and embarrassed, hurried her out of the pub, and Baker and his wife followed them to the door, watching as Margerie strode angrily down the lane towards Ripe, with Lowry swaying along in her wake still clutching the bottle of gin.

If they hoped to listen to the radio concert they would have to have left before 7.45 p.m. What happened that evening can only be pieced together from what Margerie later told Markson and others. The radio was in the bedroom, and it seems they drank gin and orange together as they listened to the concert. When it ended, just after 10 p.m., Margerie went down to the kitchen to prepare and bring up a meal. Back in the bedroom, she said, she found Malcolm had all but consumed the rest of the gin and had turned morose and wild. As they ate, he turned up the volume of the radio and when she turned it down, remembering that Mrs Mason's invalid sister slept in the adjoining room next door, he simply turned it up even more. They quarrelled, Margerie grabbed the almost-empty gin bottle and smashed it against the bedroom wall. Malcolm then snatched up the broken bottle and lunged at her. She said she had never seen him like this before; he was raving. 'I feared he'd hurt me badly & feel so awful the next day, I knew from 18 years experience the only thing was to get away till he calmed down,' she wrote to Markson later.[48] She fled from the room, she said, and ran down the stairs with Malcolm in drunken pursuit wielding the broken bottle-neck, and took refuge next door. The time, she told Markson, was 10.30 p.m. and her hope was that he would finish his dinner and sleep it off. Mrs Mason had made coffee and she stayed there for the rest of the evening, going outside occasionally to check whether the bedroom light was still on. She checked last at 1 a.m. and, seeing it still alight, assumed Malcolm was working and returned to spend the rest of the night at Mrs Mason's.

In the morning at nine o'clock, according to Mrs Mason, she went back to get Malcolm a cup of tea, saying that she had decided now to go to Liverpool to obtain powers of attorney over him. Within a few minutes she came running back, saying, 'Oh, Winnie, he's gone.' When

Mrs Mason asked, 'Where? To Liverpool?' she replied, 'No. He's gone. He's dead.' The two women ran back to the house and there he was lying at the foot of the bed with the gin bottle, a plate, and orange squash bottle all smashed to smithereens, and bits of food scattered around the room. He was indeed dead. Margerie's bottle containing twenty sodium amytal sleeping pills was missing from the bedside table. It was later found hidden in a drawer among Margerie's gloves in the other upstairs bedroom – empty.[49]

The doctor refused to sign the death certificate, and the police were called. Margerie and Mrs Mason were questioned, and Lowry's body removed. Because of the circumstances of his death there had to be an inquest. By eleven o'clock that morning Margerie had cabled Markson and Priscilla. 'Malcolm suddenly dead. Margerie.' Markson phoned Harvey Breit of the *New York Times*, who had met Lowry at the time of the *Volcano*'s publication. He in turn cabled his friend Stern in England. Stern heard the news on the night of Friday the 28th, and next morning telephoned Margerie, who, he said later, 'did not make too much sense'. On the day of Malcolm's death she had phoned Ralph Case and Davenport. Case went straight down to Ripe and found her lying on the bed weeping mostly, but also drinking gin to console herself. For some reason known only to herself, she did not inform the Lowry family. That was left to Davenport, who arrived on the Saturday afternoon. Of the three brothers, Wilfrid was too ill and Russell too busy and disinclined to attend. A cable was sent to Stuart, then on holiday in Chartres, and he dropped everything to try to get back in time for the funeral.

From the beginning, Lowry's friends were uncomfortable not only about the apparent circumstances of the death but also about the garbled and contradictory versions of events which Margerie had begun to recount. There was an 'official' version which she gave over the phone to Stern: Malcolm had died from a sudden heart attack in the early hours of Thursday morning. However, to others she hinted at suicide. She told Ralph Case's wife Adrienne that she wanted above all to ensure that Malcolm was buried in the churchyard, and said it was imperative therefore that the inquest did not bring in a verdict of suicide; she thought it would be bad for his reputation because the world's press would certainly turn up and make a sordid scandal out of it. She blamed herself, she said, for not going back to the cottage that evening; perhaps she could have saved him. And, that is exactly what Lowry's friends were beginning to think. And when she told them that Malcolm had died by his own hand they refused to believe it. (Mrs Mason was so confused that she told one story at the inquest and two different versions three years later to radio and television reporters.)

After Davenport arrived on the Saturday afternoon, he phoned Stern to say that the inquest was set for 1 July at Eastbourne and the funeral for two days later at Ripe. On 30 June, Harvey and Dorothy, now married, arrived from Metz, where Harvey had been teaching. Staying at the White Cottage, they found Margerie distraught and refusing to eat. She told them she was sure Malcolm had done this for her, implying suicide, but they remained sceptical. When Dorothy went down to the kitchen one night to get a glass of milk, she found Margerie wolfing down a chicken, and concluded that her refusal to eat was an act and she was not so much distraught about Malcolm as terrified about the inquest and about the possible intrusion of the world's press. As it happened, none of the world's press showed up; in fact the world's press was overwhelmingly ignorant of Lowry's death.

The *Brighton Argus*, however, thought it worth sending a reporter to cover the inquest of an unknown writer called Clarence Lowry, and on 2 July it ran a report under the headline 'She Broke Gin Bottle – Found Husband Dead':

> One evening last week Mrs Marjorie Lowry, of Ripe [White] Cottage, Ripe, tried to stop her 47-year-old writer-husband, Clarence, from starting on the gin. She smashed the bottle on the floor. And he hit her. Afraid, Mrs Lowry fled next door, and did not go back to the cottage until nine o'clock the next morning. When she did she found her husband dead. This was the story told at the Eastbourne Inquest, when the Coroner, Dr A. C. Sommerville, recorded a verdict of death by misadventure. Mrs Lowry said her husband had been treated in hospital for alcoholism, but was discharged last year as incurable. 'When he hit me,' she said, 'he was under the influence and in a bad temper.' PC William Ford said he found Mr Lowry on the floor beside his bed. Near him was a smashed gin bottle and a smashed orange squash bottle. *A bottle of 20 sodium amytal sleeping tablets belonging to his wife was missing*. This was found later, empty.
>
> 'In the house,' said PC Ford, 'I found a number of bottles containing tablets prescribed for Mrs Lowry.'
>
> Medical evidence showed that Mr Lowry died from acute barbiturate poisoning associated with a state of chronic alcoholism.

Had he been present, Dr Raymond would have contradicted Margerie's claim that Lowry had been discharged as incurable; indeed, in his opinion he was as good as cured. But he would not have been surprised at the many bottles of tablets prescribed for Margerie, knowing her tendency to hypochondria. The verdict, however, seemed to satisfy most people, especially the pious Mrs Mason, who was delighted when the local Vicar, Revd Frederick Talbot Baines, called to say that Malcolm could be buried in consecrated ground.

His death certificate reads:

> Twenty-seventh June 1957. Found Dead White Cottage. Cause of Death:
>
> 1a. Inhalation of stomach contents, 1b. Barbiturate poisoning. 2. Excessive Consumption of Alcohol. Swallowing a no. of barbiturate tablets whilst under the influence of alcohol. Misadventure P.M. Cert. received from A. C. Sommerville, Coroner for East Sussex (Lewes Dist.) Inquest held 1st July, 1957.

The Sterns arrived the day before the funeral and Margerie confided the suicide story to Jimmy. But after discussing it with Harvey Burt, Stern said, 'He could not have done it.' Later Burt gave an account of the inquest, which he attended, saying why he thought suicide was unlikely.

> The autopsy revealed that all of Malc's organs were in perfect condition; that his stomach contained alcohol and barbiturates; that there was food in his stomach; and that he had died by inhaling vomit – he had literally been drowned in his own vomit, as babies are apt to do unless precautions are taken to keep them on their stomachs.[50]

He could not have committed suicide, he said, because he was well, witty and cogent, at last standing on his own feet, and writing at full stretch. If he had been as drunk as Margerie claimed, he would have been incapable of the fine muscle control required to unscrew a pill bottle, and why was the empty bottle found only later hidden under clothes in a drawer in another bedroom? It was neither the alcohol nor the pills which killed him but the inhaling of vomit. It was, concluded Burt, 'a foul accident'.

Margerie was distraught, blaming herself for Malcolm's death, phoning around desperate to contact Peter Churchill. She did not know that Churchill had been staying with the Sterns and was studiously avoiding her, because, it was suggested, she was pursuing him rather too eagerly.

The Burts were convinced she was keen to make up to Churchill now that Malcolm was dead, and that she had written to him following Joan's death saying that Malcolm was finished and they should go off together.[51] But he did not answer her calls and did not appear at the funeral. Shortly thereafter he disappeared to France to stay with Julienne LaPierre in Vernon, and Julienne was more than capable of keeping persistent callers at bay.

The funeral was held at 3 p.m. on Wednesday 3 July at the Ripe Parish Church. After much confusion and misinformation from the police, Stuart Lowry arrived at 2.15 p.m. The vicar and then Margerie, he reported to his brothers, looked quite frightened when they saw him. The Vicar may have wondered whether he was someone from 'the world press' that she had been going on about – it was her insistence to the police that unwanted reporters would try to attend which had led them to misdirect Stuart. Nevertheless the sympathetic Stuart felt sorry for her and held her hand throughout the ceremony, leaving the rest of the mourners – Davenport, Jimmy and Tania Stern, Harvey and Dorothy Burt, Mrs Mason and a few villagers – wondering who on earth he was (Jimmy Stern thought he was a hired mourner). The service, Margerie wrote later, was 'macabre, grotesque & very High Church & he [Malcolm] would have loved it.'[52] Buried somewhat obscurely in a walled-off corner of the churchyard near to the gate, his headstone bears the simple inscription: 'Malcolm Lowry 1909–1957'. The weather had been fine until that day. During the funeral a thunderstorm broke and it rained solidly for weeks afterwards.

Margerie was admitted to the Hellingly Mental Hospital in Hailsham the day after the funeral. She asked the Burts to stay and sort out Malcolm's notes and manuscripts, some lying around the house, others in a big trunk. They were there for ten days until she returned. She later told them that after they had gone she had found a suicide note which Malcolm had hidden. But they, having searched the house thoroughly for manuscripts, letters and notes, had found nothing and thought she had made this up because it suited her to play the martyr – she who had sacrificed so much for the genius and to whom he felt so indebted that he had taken his life to prove his love. Her line was that he had committed suicide but that she had managed to persuade a sympathetic coroner to hand down a verdict of 'Misadventure' to save his reputation and her suffering at the hands of the press.

While in the hospital and afterwards, she wrote letters to Markson also suggesting suicide, and saying that she had told only Priscilla and

Davenport. She pleaded: 'Please write & say you forgive me. He has I know & anyhow he didn't mean it – he was sure I'd get there in time. But I didn't.'[53] She wrote in another, underlining the sentence,

> *If I'd gone back at 1 am he'd be alive now.* . . . I don't know why he did it. Despair? Bravado? (Margie will find me and get a Dr in time) Sense of failure at having done what he swore he'd never do again? No one will ever know what he felt those last hours. Not even me.[54]

But she also urged silence.

> What I wrote about Malc was for you alone. Only Jimmy Stern & John Davenport here & my sister in America know the truth & none of them know it all or know really. The official version is that he died suddenly in his sleep, which is all too true. But I would be racked & burnt at the stake rather than have some distorted scandalous mess get into circulation. So you must not talk about it. However difficult it is for you don't talk.

She had had difficulty over this at the inquest, she said, but had managed to keep it quiet.[55] But by telling one version to a small group while hinting at another, and offering an 'official' version to others, she ensured that distortions did get into circulation. Nor could she prevent Lowry's friends from talking about it to other friends.

In New York, Harvey Breit heard the conclusion of the story from Stern and wrote an obituary for the *New York Times* which was syndicated across North America. The tone of Breit's article implied that for an artist as self-destructive as Lowry, a verdict of 'Misadventure' could only be construed in one way.

> Even Mr Lowry's closest friends could not know the nightmares of his soul and the demons of his vision. There was only the perhaps too glib sense one had that Mr Lowry had no regard for the instincts of preservation and the unmistakable one that he was freewheeling along the road to self-destruction.[56]

When Margerie finally saw this she was furious and accused Markson of talking to Breit, complaining it was no fun to be thought the widow of a suicide. The fact that her first husband had been an alcoholic who killed himself may explain this reaction, and the feeling that she would be blamed for driving him to suicide.

On leaving hospital she asked Dr Raymond to visit her and take her on as a patient, and when he declined told him, too, that she had found a suicide note from Malcolm, but had destroyed it. The doctor did not believe her – Malcolm had so often told him that he thought suicide was an offence against the spirit. He thought that she told him this because she resented him having done so much to get Malcolm back on his own feet. She told a different story to Eric Estorick; Malcolm had died in his sleep and nothing more. And writing to Clarisse Francillon she said nothing about leaving the house that night but claimed she had slept in the next bedroom so as not to disturb him, a story Mrs Mason also told a few years later, despite having testified at the inquest that Margerie had stayed at her house all night.

She told only a selected few that Malcolm had killed himself, also enjoining them to utter secrecy for the sake of his reputation and to save herself from scandalous press stories. Because she confused matters so and told so many different versions, others were left to speculate darkly on what might have happened. Stuart wrote a long letter to Russell in which he had to apologize for sounding 'sinister' about what had occurred, but said categorically that he did not believe Malcolm had committed suicide. Some thought that at best Margerie should have taken more care of a man who when drunk might easily do himself a mischief. And indeed, he might have taken the pills in a fit of bravado while drunkenly 'acting out' a dramatic role for himself. 'And so I die!' But Dorothy Burt could not forget that when they first arrived in Ripe, Margerie, hysterical about having been questioned by the police, had sobbed, 'They think I murdered him!' Markson could never forget Margerie feeding him handfuls of vitamin pills when he was drunk, saying how this helped him cope with a hangover next day, leaving open the possibility that on the night of the 26th Lowry had swallowed what he thought were vitamin pills – after all, there were so many bottles of tablets lying around the cottage. It also leaves open the question of whether they were accidentally self-administered or whether they were administered by someone else. Suicide was Margerie's version, which no one believed, and she did hint that she had not told all, even to Lowry's close friends, but she was to take that dark secret with her to her grave.

Whatever suspicions may remain, and whatever the truth of the matter, there is another curious feature of Lowry's death which has never been noticed or discussed. Bearing in mind his obsession with dates and their significance, and his carefully ensuring that significant things happened on significant dates, we might consider the date on which

Lowry died. If it was an accident and nothing more suspicious, then it was at the least a very strange coincidence; if he committed suicide then he chose the day well. For it was on 27 June four years earlier that he had broken his leg at Dollarton, and the day that, two years before, Jimmy Craige had written to Dorothy to say that the pier had been washed away. More significantly, perhaps, 27 June was the date in his story 'The Bravest Boat' when the young Sigurd Storlesen set his model ship adrift in the Pacific Ocean bearing a message for whomsoever one day might find it. But more strangely still, 27 June was the birthday of Paul Fitte.

Perhaps the furies which had pursued him so constantly since the night of 15 November 1929 had finally caught up with him.

POSTFACE

The 'foul accident' of Lowry's death brought a strange and significant literary life to a close – a life lived half hidden in the shadows by dint of Lowry's determination to withdraw from society, to act differently from others, to live remotely, and, when in company, to retreat into his own alcoholically inspired world of familiars and daemons and the haunting past of his childhood and dissolute youth. With men he could share the simple friendship of the outdoors or a manly bonhomie lubricated by alcohol, though certain men – like some of his brilliant contemporaries at Cambridge – intimidated him, and he sheered away from those with literary pretensions.

With women he had more acute problems, caught between a powerful sexual lust and an overwhelming fear of contracting venereal disease. His ideal woman, according to Jan Gabrial, was a mother who was a good lay, but probably not one with too strong a mind of her own. In the end, Jan was too independent, and unwilling to be absorbed by the myth of intoxicated genius. Margerie, on the other hand, was ready to sacrifice herself to a belief in Malcolm's brilliance. But this only drew them in to a fairytale world of their own invention in which he could write nothing but masterpieces and she could produce only first-rate fiction in his shadow. Deeper inside this fantasy world lie his fictional women – two-dimensional and compliant. The two versions of womanhood merge as his marriage comes under strain in Mexico – a barely disguised Margerie appears in *La Mordida* as an exasperated woman, rapidly approaching the point of abandoning him. Nevertheless, the string of fictional women Lowry sketched using Margerie as a model – Yvonne Firmin, Primrose Wilderness, Jacqueline Llewelyn – lack the grit and substance of the first version of Yvonne, as featured in early drafts of the *Volcano* – a character, of course, based on Jan. The Margerie-inspired females are neatly summed up in Lowry's observation that the past life of Primrose Wilderness was best symbolized by Disney.

Despite often being uneasy in the presence of females, two of his favourite saints were women – Isabel la Católica, the saint of dangerous and desperate causes, and the Virgin of Soledad, the saint of lonely mariners. And yet, despite being educated as a Methodist and flirting with Spiritualism, he was not at all religious in any orthodox way. His sense of life's mystery was satisfied by a strong and enduring belief in supernatural powers which determine our fates, and he saw coincidences and other strange events as the manifestation of such powers. These forces were threatening to him and needed placating, and in the form of his familiars they could be enrolled as the cast of ghostly voices in his multi-vocal fiction, giving it at times a peculiarly religious quality, or the tone of Greek tragedy. His sense of religious awe also inspired his passionate feeling for nature, which drew him to Blake and through Blake to Swedenborg, but he would pray in any church, drunk or sober.

To the extent that he clung to his youthful socialist beliefs they were neither focused enough nor sufficiently ideologically grounded to attach him firmly to any political party, and he abandoned any faith he might have had in a revolutionary utopia with the 'betrayal' of the Hitler-Stalin pact. He never rid himself entirely of certain old colonialist attitudes, and faced with punitive post-war British tax rates, and under Margerie's influence, he shifted towards the centre of the political spectrum. And, although as an artist he detested McCarthyism, he tried to stand aloof from Cold War politics. Today he would probably have been most engaged, if at all, by Green issues, and the need to save the planet from the destructive onrush of material science.

Because the crisis in his first marriage coincided with the European crisis of 1939, in exploring his own suffering with such savage honesty through the Consul in *Under the Volcano*, he was able to reach beyond himself to achieve a great and enduring work of universal significance. His love-affair with American and European literature, and the spell which Hollywood and the cinema cast over him, provided him with a wider vision than most British novelists of his time, and in his first piece of American fiction, *The Last Address* (*Lunar Caustic*), he was already reaching towards the *Volcano*.

As a writer his tragedy was that he was unable to follow that masterpiece. This was in part due to an inability to concentrate his efforts on any single work – he was too easily diverted by private terrors, accidents, and grandiose projects. Also, despite its bizarre nature and internal strife, his relatively stable second marriage robbed him of the kinds of crises which underlay the earlier great work. The tormenting horror of a haunting past and its transformation through art – the personal crisis at the heart of *Dark as the Grave Wherein My Friend is Laid*

– lacks an obvious wider political significance, and *October Ferry to Gabriola*, exploring the same obsessive theme, was set in a country which had no ghosts for him. Back in Britain he might have made something of this final, Canadian novel, as he had when writing in Canada about Mexico to produce the *Volcano*. After all, he had once again been expelled from the Garden of Eden, and this experience provided the kind of myth he needed to produce his best work. Indeed, there are those who believe that *October Ferry* could have emerged as his finest work. That, I believe, is doubtful, but his early death leaves the question forever unresolved.

A book with more promise perhaps, which would have shown Lowry at his most Kafkaesque, *La Mordida*, was abandoned too early to be publishable. However, as Aiken noted, Lowry's novels mostly lack the depth of characterization and motivation to sit easily in that category, and a novel like *Dark as the Grave* (even in its posthumously published stitched-up version), can be seen as little more than a highly subjective travelogue, though it contains fascinating reflections on the process of creating fiction in general, and the *Volcano* in particular. His short stories, especially 'The Forest Path to the Spring', 'Strange Comfort Afforded by the Profession' and 'Elephant and Colosseum', are subtle and abiding works, finely conceived. However, there is in Lowry a tendency to recycle ideas, many of them present even in his earliest stories – the tortured childhood, the nameless but terrible sin committed in youth, the pain of remorse, the call of the sea and of nature, the destructive obsession with alcohol, the exiled writer reflecting on the sources of his creativity, the stalking furies, and the inevitable dialogue between ego and alter. Because writing was to him a form of therapy, his fictional landscape mirrors his own internal landscape, one readily recognized by those familiar with his fiction and verse.

Less of an achievement is the work he did as a poet, in the narrow sense. His poetry comes off only occasionally, and, although he often said he saw himself primarily as a poet, he lacked technical sophistication – often a promising verse is spoiled by a thoroughly clumsy line, as if in the midst of composition he grew bored and his inspiration failed him. Nevertheless, he did forge a distinctive style so that a Lowry poem has a recognizable voice of its own.

There is, however, one other form of writing, apart from fiction, in which Lowry does stand out but for which he is perhaps least recognized – letter writing. As is evident from his boyhood letters to Carol Brown, from an early age he was a compulsive, eccentric, but superbly gifted correspondent with a marvellous sense of the absurd. Some of his letters, like the long one to Jonathan Cape justifying every word in *Under the Volcano*, rank among the finest of the century, and are accomplished essays in their own right. A new selection of Lowry's letters would bring this aspect of his immense talent as a writer to the attention of a wider audience.

Almost certainly Lowry is the least-known British literary genius of the twentieth century. He bore a talent to rival Joyce's, and, like Joyce, he has played a seminal role in the growth of many younger novelists: Lowry's work stands at the fulcrum of twentieth-century English literature. But few writers can ever have absorbed so many influences as Lowry and come so close to plagiarizing so often, and yet he managed to produce work often superior to that from which he borrowed. Undoubtedly his output would have been greater had he lived a less confused, accident-prone and alcoholic life, but then he might not have produced works of the stature of the *Volcano* or *Lunar Caustic*. His life is littered with lost or abandoned good intentions, lost or abandoned manuscripts, lost or abandoned literary dreams and ambitions. Nonetheless, his influence on other writers has been considerable. Among those who have admitted a debt to him are the British writers Anthony Burgess, Robert Nye, Allan Massie, and J. G. Farrell, the Americans Thomas Pynchon, William Gass and Allen Ginsberg, and South Americans Guillermo Cabrera Infante and Gabriel García Márquez. And it is difficult to believe that Graham Greene had not read *Under the Volcano* before writing *The Honorary Consul*.

Despite his many sins and delinquencies, Lowry was not an evil man, in the way that Aiken probably was, but rather a good man fatally flawed. Among friends and acquaintances he is rarely recalled with bitterness, and despite the overriding sense of doom which clings to the man and to his works, in the latter there are many moments of great humour and there is forever the impetus towards the Better Thing, a hope of salvation for sinful Mankind. ('Whosoever unceasingly strives upward . . . him can we save.') He absorbed an aesthetic of self-destruction from Aiken and was inspired by others, like Rimbaud and Melville, who believed in the necessity of descending to hell and returning in order to testify in great art. Even so, Wodehouse is never at too great a remove to put in a wry, self-deflating comment. But he did return from the hell and the gutter, often enough and for long enough periods, to create one, and possibly more, masterpieces wherein anyone who has ever caught up with Lowry in the toils of human confusion can find a kind of grace and a kind of release. That is enough for one man.

At his death Lowry's estate was worth £47,000 – ironic when one thinks of the years of poverty and want in Canada. However, much of this money (£32,000) was held in trust and Margerie inherited only the income, and it would be some months before she received the £14,000 balance minus death duties. The value of his royalties is listed as £358, plus £35 12*s.* 6*d.* from France, and none of his novels were in print in his own language.

A series of accidents, illnesses, and diversions had interrupted his work, so that, although he had written tirelessly over the previous ten years, nothing substantial had been brought to a satisfying conclusion. The final diversion which undermined and then destroyed his grand conception, *The Voyage that Never Ends* (in so far as it was ever a serious or practical design), was *October Ferry to Gabriola.* If ever a novel murdered its author – 'Joyced on his own petard', as Lowry would have it – then *October Ferry* killed off the author of *The Voyage.* But whether *The Voyage* belonged to a real or a fantasy world remains a matter for speculation. As he himself wrote, 'in all concerning his work a writer assumes the most extraordinary pretensions . . .'[1]

Despite his own reluctance to see into print what he had written, Lowry had not been dead long before Margerie was thinking of publishing it. In his will he had named no literary executor, but Margerie, when she spoke to Stuart Lowry at the funeral, said it was John Davenport. A few months later, however, she declared that she and she alone now had that responsibility. She had visited Davenport after leaving hospital but, she said, received no words of comfort from him (nor, for that matter, she added, from Peter Churchill). Davenport, however, had his own problems, his wife having just committed suicide, and he found Margerie impossible anyway. She wanted him to read through Malcolm's poems and stories, and Davenport was probably insufficiently malleable for her liking, so she decided to take on the work herself – and consult with others, like Aiken, as she chose.

She felt very much alone in England after Malcolm's death; people who had tolerated her because they loved him no longer visited or invited her to visit. Her only attraction for the people she admired was the man to whom she had been married. Now he was dead the only hope of retaining their attention was as his literary executor and editor of his work. And that was the path she chose.

Barely three weeks after Malcolm was buried, back at the White Cottage where Harvey and Dorothy Burt had sorted out his manuscripts and notes, Margerie wrote to Markson, 'I shall salvage what I can of his work, poems, 2 novellas, some short stories, letters, journal, but I'll publish *nothing* that isn't worthy of him and *nothing* about us.'[2] On 10 August, she wrote to Aiken, 'Now I have to cope with his work, a trunk full [sic], largely unfinished, and I shall never publish anything unworthy of him or try to fill in the gaps or *write* anything for him, but those things I can merely edit for him, as I always did and he relied, I'm proud to say, on my judgement there, those things I can publish, and I feel I should . . . The literary executor is myself and no one else.' She was considering making a selection of poems, and Davenport told her that Stephen Spender might publish some in *Encounter*, and Cape were considering a book of them.

The first thing she got to work on was 'Elephant and Colosseum'. Davenport had told her that the Italian magazine *Botteghe Oscura* wanted a Lowry story, so she set about cutting it in the hope of selling it to them to pay for a Sicilian holiday. She sent the MS, cut by thirty pages, to Markson, asking him if he thought the joins showed, then asking him to send it to Marie Moore at Matson's. Some time after that, in Taormina, she got to work on 'Through the Panama' and 'Present Estate of Pompeii', hoping first to sell them separately to magazines and then to offer them, plus the remainder, to Erskine as a collection, *Hear Us O Lord*.

Some of Lowry's friends – Davenport, Erskine, Ralph Case, Jimmy Stern – expressed fears that Margerie would now go hell for leather to bring out work which he himself considered unready for publication. But, having failed as a writer herself, she was about to fulfil herself as the editor of Malcolm's work – a job, she argued, that she had always done when he was alive. Indeed he would not submit anything without her approval. By 1961 she had already had three of Lowry's best short stories published in prominent literary magazines, and in that year *Hear Us O Lord From Heaven Thy Dwelling Place* was also published in America (British publication followed in 1962).

When Ernst Klett and Clarisse Francillon asked about *Ultramarine*, mention of which made Lowry very nervous and defensive, she said that he had changed his mind about it just before he died and decided it was quite an original work after all, although he had intended it to be, in his sequence of novels – his 'Yoknapatawpha of the soul' – a novel which Sigbjørn Wilderness wrote in Canada. Yet only on 22 February had he told his friend Markson, who enquired about it for Lion Books, 'Thank you for thinking of Ultramarine but it has to be rewritten first.'[3] In 1962 Margerie allowed the original version of *Ultramarine* (with only minor alterations indicated by Lowry in notes to the original edition, and with the dedication to Tom Forman and Elizabeth Cheyne removed) to be published.

But when she sent Lowry's poems to Aiken, he told her they were no good. This reaction is strange since he told Lowry in 1940, after he had looked at *The Lighthouse Invites the Storm*, that they grew on him and he sent them to Robert Linscott to consider for publication. But to Margerie such judgements were unacceptable and she came to contend that Malcolm was incapable of writing badly, despite the fact that she had edited and corrected and rewritten passages of his work during his lifetime and afterwards. However, over the next twenty years she managed to get over a hundred and fifty of Lowry's poems published, many with the help of Earle Birney.

Also with Birney, she edited *Lunar Caustic* (published in 1963), piecing it together from a variety of manuscript versions, not necessarily in the way that Lowry would have approved, though it still stands as one of his most powerful pieces of writing. When Birney, having published a selection of Lowry's poems in 1962, was asked by Margerie to edit a larger selection, the project finally foundered on her insistence that all his known poems go into the book, even when it was pointed out to her that that whole included copies of other poets' work and heavy plagiarisms.[4] Margerie, in her turn, claimed that Birney was tinkering with Lowry's verse.

She edited his *Selected Letters* in 1965 with Harvey Breit, the writer she had so hated for implying in his *New York Times* obituary of Lowry that he had committed suicide. The letters are poorly edited and a number of them are wrongly dated. In 1968 she collaborated with Douglas Day, Lowry's first biographer, to produce from notes and drafts a complete version of *Dark as the Grave Wherein My Friend is Laid*, which also stands as a coherent work because Lowry was far enough along with the writing, though here again it is doubtful that he would have sent it to a publisher himself in quite that form.

Perhaps the most controversial is Margerie's version of *October Ferry to Gabriola*, which she edited alone and had published in 1970 – for here was the book Lowry was working on when he died – it was the book which had disrupted his literary plans and taken over as a kind of long confession or self-analysis, and it shifted about as his own mental anguish ploughed its storm-driven course through his final years. The book was poorly received and roused academic critics to argue that the manuscripts were best left as they were rather than patched together in so uncertain a fashion.[5] In one last throw, in 1975, Margerie published in America a selection of short stories and reminiscences of Lowry entitled *Malcolm Lowry – Psalms and Songs*, but it was in many ways an odd and unsatisfactory collection.[6]

Interestingly enough, despite the mammoth correspondence with Albert Erskine, and the contract of 1952, neither before nor after his death did Random House publish anything by Lowry. In America, Lippincott eventually took over the copyright of *Under the Volcano* from Harcourt Brace, and they published also *Hear Us O Lord From Heaven Thy Dwelling Place* (in 1961) and *The Selected Letters of Malcolm Lowry* (in 1965). The New American Library published *Dark as the Grave* (in 1968) and the World Publishing Company published *October Ferry* in 1970. In England, Cape published almost everything. But even they did not publish *Malcolm Lowry – Psalms and Songs*. (Latterly, most of Lowry's fiction has been republished by Picador in their Modern Classics paperback series.)

The history of plans and proposals to film *Under the Volcano* is a sorry and complex one,[7] and Wieland Schulz-Keil, a producer who finally purchased the film rights in 1982, counted sixty-six screenplays of the novel including a treatment by Margerie. In 1984, thirty-seven years after the book was first published, a film was finally made, directed by John Huston, with Albert Finney as the Consul. The Lowrys' own attempt at film-making, their screenplay of *Tender is the Night*, was partly published in 1990, mostly excluding original material from the Fitzgerald novel. It has not yet been filmed.

Jan Lowry remarried in 1944 and had a very successful career in real estate in the San Fernando Valley area west of Los Angeles. In 1993 she was working on a book about her life with Lowry.

On 29 September 1988, Margerie Lowry died in Los Angeles aged eighty-three, after several years of paralysis following a stroke. She was buried in the churchyard at Ripe.

NOTES

The following abbreviations have been used for frequently cited titles; the editions cited are those to which page references refer:

CP	*The Collected Poetry of Malcolm Lowry* (ed. Kathleen Scherf), (Vancouver, UBC Press, 1991)
DAG	*Dark as the Grave Wherein My Friend is Laid* (London, Penguin, 1969)
HUOL	*Hear Us O Lord From Heaven Thy Dwelling Place* (London, Penguin, 1979)
MLR	*Malcolm Lowry Remembered* (London, Ariel Books 1985)
OFG	*October Ferry to Gabriola* (London, Penguin, 1979)
PAS	*Malcolm Lowry: Psalms and Songs* (New York, New American Library, 1975)
SL	*Selected Letters of Malcolm Lowry* (London, Penguin, 1985)
SPML	*Selected Poems of Malcolm Lowry* (ed. Earle Birney), (San Francisco, City Lights, 1962)
U	*Ultramarine* (London, Penguin, 1974)
UTV	*Under the Volcano* (London, Penguin, 1963) Page numbers in brackets refer to (London, Penguin, 1985 edition).

The vast majority of Lowry's letters and unpublished manuscripts are quoted with permission of The Special Collections of the University of British Columbia in Vancouver, where the bulk of Lowry's papers are kept.

[Tex] indicates that the item is published with the permission of The Harry Ransom Research Center, University of Texas, at Austin – plus all letters of Lowry to Gerald Noxon.
[V] indicates that the item is published with the permission of The Special Collections Department of the University of Virginia.
[P] indicates that the item is published with the permission of the Manuscripts Division of the Department of Rare Books and Special Collections, Princeton University.
[T] indicates that the item is published with the permission of the Special Collections Department of the McFarlin Library, the University of Tulsa.
[H] indicates that the item is published with the permission of the Huntington Library.

CHAPTER I

1. From handwritten additions to the MS of 'Enter One in Sumptuous Armour'.
2. *The Leys Fortnightly*, 26 February 1926.
3. Malcolm sometimes claimed his ancestry went back to Robert the Bruce. This story was widely swallowed, but the truth is that Stuart, in order to impress an officer in a distinguished regiment in World War One decided that he needed a family crest and contrived one. Years later a mail order company hustling for business suggested a Lowry Scottish connection which it would research at a price. The offer was not taken up, but the Bruce connection became a family joke, one which Malcolm was happy in turn to play on gullible friends. (Russell Lowry).
4. 'Forest Path to the Spring', *HUOL*: 226.
5. *U*: 110–111.
6. *DAG*: 25.
7. John Boden's Death Certificate.
8. No doubt such medals were often handed out by the shrewd Sandow organization for improved performances. But the silver medal from the Liverpool Shipwreck and Humane Society was well deserved.
9. 'Through the Panama', *HUOL*: 72.
10. Arthur Lowry to Malcolm Lowry, 25 November 1942.
11. Lowry to Derek Pethick: 28 September 1950.
12. Arthur Lowry to Evelyn Lowry, 8 December 1911.
13. Miss Bell, 'A Letter from "Bey" ', *MLR*: 15–16.
14. See, e.g. the account of childhood abuse he passed on to Clarisse Francillon ('Malcolm, Mon ami,' *Les Lettres Nouvelle* (July/August, 1960): 8–19), and William McConnell ('Recollections of Malcolm Lowry', *Canadian Literature* (Autumn, 1960): 24–31).
15. I owe a great deal to Russell Lowry for the information about the home background of Malcolm and himself.

CHAPTER II

1. 'Elephant and Colosseum', *HUOL*: 125.
2. *U*: 68.
3. *Lunar Caustic*: *HUOL*: 298.
4. Russell Lowry's manuscript on his family.
5. Handwritten notes to MS of 'Enter One in Sumptuous Armour'.
6. 'Through the Panama', *HUOL*: 68.
7. *U*: 96.
8. Lowry to Downie Kirk, 2 March 1950.
9. Notes to MS of 'Enter One in Sumptuous Armour'.
10. *U*: 171.
11. Russell Lowry.
12. *ibid.*

13. Notes to MS of 'Enter One in Sumptuous Armour'.
14. Ralph Izzard to GB: interview, 20 November 1987.
15. Hywel Jones to GB: 31 May 1984.
16. 'Enter One in Sumptuous Armour', *PAS*.
17. Wilfrid Lowry to parents, 18 May 1912.
18. Ralph Izzard to GB: interview 30 November 1987.
19. Russell Lowry's manuscript on his family.
20. Notes to 'Enter One in Sumptuous Armour'. The lumber room at Inglewood is referred to as a means of punishment throughout the notes to this story, although Russell states there was no such room.
21. Notes to 'Enter One in Sumptuous Armour'.
22. *ibid.*
23. Clarisse Francillon and Clarissa Lorenz were both treated to sad tales of his childhood blindness. See Clarisse Francillon, 'Malcolm, mon ami,' *Les Lettres Nouvelles*, No. 7 (October 1960): 200, and Clarissa Lorenz, *Lorelei Two* (University of Georgia Press, 1983).
24. Lowry to parents, February 1922.
25. Lowry told Dr Raymond, his psychiatrist in 1955 just how much of an obsession it was with him.
26. *UTV*: 25. (65)
27. Richard Holmes, *Walter Greenaway, Spy* (Blackwood, London, 1917).
28. *ibid.*
29. *UTV*: 92. (132)
30. Hywel Jones to GB: 31 May 1984.
31. Ralph Izzard to GB: interview, 30 November 1987.
32. K. N. Hargreaves, memoir of Lowry at Caldicott School.

CHAPTER III

1. Notes to 'Enter One in Sumptuous Armour'.
2. *ibid.*
3. *ibid.*
4. *UTV*: 26. (66)
5. Notes to 'Enter One in Sumptuous Armour'.
6. The term before Lowry arrived at The Leys was Vladimir Nabokov's final term at Trinity, where he graduated in French and Russian.
7. 'Through the Panama', *HUOL*: 69.
8. 'The Forest Path to the Spring', *HUOL*: 280.
9. Lowry told his second wife, Margerie, that he was jeered at at The Leys for his interest in nature study. However, there were occasional talks by visiting lecturers on topics such as bird-watching.
10. Thomas Boden Hardy to GB: interview 30 April 1989.
11. S. C. Gillard, memoir of Lowry at The Leys.
12. Notes to 'Enter One in Sumptuous Armour'.
13. *ibid.*
14. John Stirland (Leys master) interviewed by Robert Duncan for National Film Board of Canada documentary film, *Volcano*, 1976.
15. M. F. Howard, 16 October 1961.
16. 'The Light that Failed Not', *The Leys Fortnightly*, 13 March 1925.
17. Notes to 'Enter One in Sumptuous Armour'.
18. W. J. Locke, *The Morals of Marcus Ordeyne*: 303.
19. The 'Sard' in Sard Harker was short for 'Sardonic', just as 'Lobs' was short for 'Lobster'. If one was to become an adventuring sailor perhaps one was required to have a mysterious-sounding nickname.
20. 'Enter One in Sumptuous Armour', *PAS*.

21. 'Through the Panama', *HUOL*: 80.
22. Notes to 'Enter One in Sumptuous Armour'.
23. Thomas Boden Hardy to GB: interview 30 April 1989.
24. *ibid.*
25. 'Travelling Light', *The Leys Fortnightly*, 18 June 1925.
26. Lowry to Carol Brown, May 1926. (T)
27. Thomas Boden Hardy to GB: interview, 30 April 1989.
28. 'Der Tag', *The Leys Fortnightly*, 1 April 1925.
29. Notes to 'Enter One in Sumptuous Armour'.
30. *ibid.*
31. *ibid.*
32. *ibid.*
33. 'The Blue Bonnet', *The Leys Fortnightly*, 9 October 1925.
34. 'A Rainy Night', *The Leys Fortnightly*, 23 October 1925.
35. *U*: 184.
36. Ralph Izzard to Neville Braybrooke, 10 May 1989.
37. Lowry to Carol Brown, May 1926. (T)
38. 'Satan in a Barrel', *The Leys Fortnightly*, 12 February 1926.
39. Ralph Izzard to Neville Braybrooke, 10 May 1989.
40. Hockey Reports, *The Leys Fortnightly*, 12 February 1926.
41. *ibid.*
42. *ibid.*
43. *The Leys Fortnightly*, 26 February 1926.
44. *ibid.*
45. Hockey Reports, *The Leys Fortnightly*, 26 March 1926.
46. *ibid.*
47. Lowry to Carol Brown, May 1926. (T)
48. Ralph Izzard to GB: interview, 30 November 1987.
49. *UTV*: 268. (308)
50. Hockey Report, *The Leys Fortnightly*, 7 May 1926.
51. *The Leys Fortnightly*, 14 October 1926.
52. Notes to 'Enter One in Sumptuous Armour'.
53. Dr Michael Raymond.
54. 'Autopsy', *CP*: 158–159.

CHAPTER IV

1. Lowry to Carol Brown, April 1926. (T)
2. Lowry to Carol Brown, 29 April–2 May 1926. (T)
3. *ibid.*
4. Lowry to George Sumner Albee, March 17 1957, *SL*: 399.
5. Lowry to Carol Brown, May 1926. (T)
6. *ibid.*
7. *ibid.*
8. *ibid.*
9. Thomas Boden Hardy to GB: interview, 30 April 1989.
10. Lowry to Carol Brown, May 1926. (T)
11. Lowry to Carol Brown, June 1926. (T)
12. *DAG*: 224.
13. Thomas McMorran to Carol Brown, 5 July 1926.
14. 'The Repulsive Tragedy of the Incredulous Englishman', *The Leys Fortnightly*, 4 June 1926.
15. Alan Baddeley, the then editor of the *Fortnightly*, cannot recall him ever attending meetings. (Baddeley to GB, 12 December 1985.)
16. Lowry to parents, 21 October 1926.
17. *ibid.*
18. Ronnie Hill, *MLR*: 23.
19. *ibid*: 26.
20. *UTV*: 159–60. (199–200)
21. 'The Rain Fell Heavily', *The Leys Fortnightly*, 26 November 1926.
22. 'Through the Panama', *HUOL*: 85.
23. 'Macbeth', *The Leys Fortnightly*, 29 October 1926.

24. *The Leys Fortnightly*, 16 December 1926.
25. *The Leys Fortnightly*, 12 November 1926.
26. *The Leys Fortnightly*, 6 December 1926.
27. *The Leys Fortnightly*, 14 December 1926.
28. *UTV*: 178–9. (218–9)
29. Thomas McMorran to Carol Brown, 7 February 1927.
30. *The Leys Fortnightly*, 18 February 1927.
31. *The Leys Fortnightly*, 18 March 1927.
32. McMorran's sister, reported by M. C. Bradbrook in *Proceedings of the London Conference on Malcolm Lowry 1984*: 12.
33. Herman Melville, *Moby Dick* (Penguin): 208.
34. *UTV*: 162. (202)
35. Stuart Lowry interviewed by George Woodcock for George Robertson's 1961 CBC Television programme, *Remembrance of Lowry*.
36. Lowry to David Markson, 25 August 1951.
37. 'Marching Down The Highway to China', *Collected Poetry of Malcolm Lowry*: 357.

CHAPTER V

1. 'Rich Boy as Deck Hand', *Liverpool Echo*, 14 May 1927.
2. *UTV*: 163. (203)
3. *U*: 20–21.
4. *UTV*: 166. (206)
5. *UTV*: 163. (203)
6. 'The Forest Path to the Spring', *HUOL*: 242.
7. *U*: 22.
8. *SPML*: 21; *CP*: 168.
9. Lowry to Conrad Aiken, 16 July 1954.
10. *SPML*: 21; *CP*: 168.
11. Joseph Ward, *MLR*: 34.
12. A. D. Kellett-Carding to GB, 16 August 1989.
13. *UTV*: 167. (207)
14. Joseph Ward, *MLR*: 34.
15. John Sommerfield remembered Lowry telling him that the man in the next bunk on the *Pyrrhus* had 'a bad dose of the clap'.
16. *U* draft: 39.
17. Tessa (Evans) to Lowry 1927. (H)
18. 'China', *PAS*.
19. Joseph Ward, *MLR*: 33–4.
20. *U*: 90–91.
21. Russell Lowry, Notes on Malcolm's Sex Life: 3.
22. Lowry to David Markson, 25 August 1951 (draft).
23. 'Seeing the World with a Ukelele', *Liverpool Echo*, 30 September 1927, reprinted in *MLR*.
24. Tessa (Evans) to Lowry, 1927. (H)
25. *U*: 21.
26. Notes to 'Enter One in Sumptuous Armour'.
27. Russell Lowry, *MLR*: 37.
28. 'The Glory of the Sea', *The Leys Fortnightly*, 15 December 1927.
29. Ronnie Hill in Conrad Knickerbocker, 'Swinging the Paradise Street Blues', *Paris Review*, 38 (Summer 1966): 22.
30. E. E. Kellett, *Suggestions, Literary Essays*, (Kegan Paul, London, 1927)
31. Conrad Aiken, *Blue Voyage*, (Scribner's, New York, 1927): 60.
32. Lowry to Seymour Lawrence, 28 November 1951, *SL*: 279.
33. Lowry to David Markson, 25 August 1951.
34. *ibid.*
35. Conrad Aiken, *Blue Voyage*: 18.
36. *ibid.*: 16.
37. *ibid.*: 186–9.
38. Lowry to Conrad Aiken, 10 June 1940.
39. Lowry to Conrad Aiken, 14 September 1952.
40. Conrad Aiken, *Blue Voyage*: 27.
41. Russell Lowry, *MLR*: 36.

42. Edward Butscher, *Conrad Aiken: Poet of White Horse Vale* (University of Georgia Press, 1988): 130.
43. Geoffrey Chaucer, *The Maunciple's Tale.*
44. Stuart Lowry to George Woodcock for CBC *Remembrance of Lowry.* Intense anguish over the generation lost in the war and a sense of guilt at missing it tormented many of Lowry's contemporaries and led to a sense of being dislocated from society. R. C. Sherriff's play *Journey's End*, produced the following year and shortly after Graves's *Goodbye to All That* and Remarque's *All Quiet on the Western Front*, swung public sentiment away from glorification of war to a belief in its utter futility. (See Valentine Cunningham, *British Writers of the Thirties.*)
45. Lowry to Conrad Aiken, 13 March 1929, *SL*: 6.
46. *The Leys Fortnightly*, 1 June 1928.
47. Lowry to Ten Holder: 23 April 1951.
48. Lowry to Ten Holder, 1951, *SL*: 240.
49. *SL*: 239.
50. He had seen several German plays at the Cambridge Festival Theatre and read about them and their authors in the theatre programmes.
51. John Best to GB: interview, 12 December 1990.
52. Lowry to Conrad Aiken, February 1929, *SL*: 3.
53. Conrad Aiken, *Selected Poems* (Scribner's, New York, 1929): 145.
54. Lowry to Conrad Aiken, February 1929, *SL*: 4.
55. S. C. Gillard.
56. Conrad Aiken, *Selected Poems*: 96.
57. Lowry to Conrad Aiken, 13 March 1929, *SL*: 7.
58. Conrad Aiken to John and Jane Aiken, 8 April 1929. [H]
59. Conrad Aiken to John Aiken, 25 June 1929.
60. *HUOL*: 72.
61. Clarissa Lorenz, *Lorelei Two*: 73.
62. Conrad Aiken to John and Jane Aiken, 22 July 1929. (Lowry said later that the first place he landed in North America was St John, in New Brunswick, Canada: Lowry to Earle Birney: 20 October 1947.) [H]
63. Conrad Aiken in 1961 CBC TV documentary, *Remembrance of Malcolm Lowry.*
64. Clarissa Lorenz, *Lorelei Two*, University of Georgia Press, 1983: 72.
65. Conrad Aiken, *Ushant* (W. H. Allen, London, 1963): 292.
66. Conrad Aiken to Robert Firuski, 8 August 1929. [H]
67. Clarissa Lorenz, *Lorelei Two*: 73.
68. Conrad Aiken to Robert Firuski, 8 August 1929. [H]
69. Conrad Aiken interviewed by George Robertson, 1961.
70. Gerald Noxon.
71. Conrad Aiken, *Blue Voyage*: 146.
72. Conrad Aiken, *Ushant*: 294.
73. *ibid*: 27–8.
74. *ibid*: 294–5.
75. *ibid:* 294.
76. Edward Butscher, *Conrad Aiken: Poet of White Horse Vale*: 109.
77. *Ushant*: 32.
78. Lowry claimed he found an ex-libris edition of the book in England in a secondhand bookshop before sailing on *Pyrrhus*, but the book was not published in England. More likely he found it in Boston.
79. Conrad Aiken *Selected Letters of Conrad Aiken* (ed. Joseph Killorin), (Yale University Press, 1978): 154.
80. Conrad Aiken, *Ushant*: 291.
81. Conrad Aiken to Robert Linscott, 29 May 1926.

82. Lowry to Seymour Lawrence, 28 November 1951.
83. 'Goya the Obscure', the *Venture*, 6 (June 1930).
84. Lowry to Dolly Lewis, September 1929.
85. Nordahl Grieg: *The Ship Sails On*, (Knopf, New York, 1927): 2.
86. *ibid.*: 95.
87. *ibid.*: 96.
88. *DAG* (MS): 342.
89. Lowry to Gerald Noxon, 21 September 1940.

CHAPTER VI

1. *UTV*: 180. (220)
2. St Catharine's was a hearty, games-playing College, but Lowry barely mixed with other students, considering them too young for him.
3. Lowry to his parents, 7 November 1929.
4. 'Through the Panama', *HUOL*: 74.
5. Maurice Hickin to GB, 3 March 1989.
6. T. R. Henn in 'Portrait of Malcolm Lowry', BBC Radio Third Programme, 16 September 1967.
7. T. R. Henn in E. E. Rich (ed.), *St Catharine's College, Cambridge*: Essays to Commemorate the Quincentenary of the Foundation of the College.
8. T. R. Henn to B. Stewart-Stubbs, 20 March 1961.
9. Earle Birney to B. Stewart-Stubbs, 8 April 1961.
10. Kenneth Wright's portrait of Malcolm Lowry.
11. T. R. Henn to B. Stewart-Stubbs, 20 March 1961.
12. Kathleen Raine, *The Land Unknown* (Hamish Hamilton, London, 1975).
13. Lowry to Charles Stansfeld-Jones, May–June 1944.
14. Jan Gabrial to GB, 3 March 1989.
15. Julian Trevelyan, *Indigo Days* (MacGibbon & Kee, London, 1957): 17.
16. *UTV*: 180. (220)
17. Dr Sydney Smith to GB: interview, 20 February 1988.
18. *Cambridge Daily News*, 16 November 1929.
19. Clarissa Lorenz, *Lorelei Two*: 125.
20. *DAG* (MS): 356.
21. *DAG* (draft): 357.
22. *OFG*: 71.
23. 'Through the Panama', *HUOL*: 27.
24. Robert Lazarus to GB: interview, 11 January 1989
25. Emile Marmorstein quoted in Kilgallin, *Lowry*, (Press Porcepi, Erin, Ontario, 1973): 23.
26. Edward Butscher, *Conrad Aiken: The Poet of White Horse Pass*: 274–6.
27. John Davenport, *MLR*: 46.
28. Julian Trevelyan, *Indigo Days*: 17.
29. Alistair Cooke to GB, 17 July 1988, confirms that Davenport was a habitual name-dropper.
30. Probably an error of memory as Traven does not appear to have been translated into English until 1934. (See Karl S. Guthke, *B. Traven: The Life Behind the Legend*, Lawrence Hill Books, New York, 1991: 467.) It is just possible, but unlikely, that he had brought some German editions of Traven books back with him from Bonn in 1927.
31. John Davenport, *MLR*: 46–7.
32. Valentine Cunningham, *British Writers of the Thirties*, (OUP, London, 1988): chapter 5.
33. Gerald Noxon to GB: interview, 15 October 1988.
34. Reported by Dr Ralph Case in conversation.
35. Martin Case in Knickerbocker, 'Swinging the Paradise Street Blues: Malcolm Lowry in England', The *Paris Review* Vol. 10 No. 38 (Summer 1966).
36. Charlotte Haldane, *Truth Will Out*

(Weidenfeld & Nicolson, London, 1949): 29–30.

37. Charlotte Haldane, *I Bring Not Peace* (Chatto & Windus, London, 1932): 36–7.
38. Robert Lazarus to GB: interview, 11 January 1989.
39. John Davenport in Conrad Knickerbocker, *op. cit.*
40. Kathleen Raine to GB in conversation, 3 December 1988.
41. *St Catharine's College Magazine*, December 1929.
42. John Davenport to Conrad Aiken, 18 April 1947.
43. John Davenport, *MLR*: 47.
44. Lowry to David Markson, 25 August 1951 (Draft).
45. 'Port Swettenham', *Experiment* 5 (February 1930): 22.
46. Hugh Sykes Davies, 'He Was Different From The Rest of Us', *MLR*: 44.
47. George Northcroft to GB: interview, 2 June 1989.
48. Kenneth Wright's portrait of Malcolm Lowry.
49. *ibid.*
50. George Northcroft to GB: interview, 2 June 1989.
51. Lowry to Giorgio Monicelli, December 1954.
52. William Empson in Kilgallin, *Lowry*: 19.
53. *Granta*, 10 May 1930.
54. F. R. Leavis, *The Cambridge Review*, 16 May 1930.
55. The *Times Literary Supplement*, 29 May 1930: 462.
56. Gerald Noxon, 'Malcolm Lowry 1930' (*Prairie Schooner*, Winter 1963–4). Reprinted in *MLR*: 51–52.
57. 'Goya the Obscure'.
58. Roy Pascal in the *Cambridge Review*, 13 June 1930: 509.
59. Russell Lowry in Anne Smith (ed.), *The Art of Malcolm Lowry* (Visions Press, London, 1978): 11–12.

CHAPTER VII

1. Possibly the letter to Lowry from 'Arthur' in Cap Ferat where he is undergoing a cure for gonorrhoea and also intent on picking up sailors.
2. Douglas Day, *Malcolm Lowry: A Biography* (OUP, 1973): 120.
3. Jane Aiken to GB, January 1989.
4. John Aiken, 'Malcolm Lowry: Some Reminiscences', *Encounter*, 49 (September/October 1987): 38–9.
5. Conrad Aiken to Walter Piston, 25 April 1931, *Selected Letters of Conrad Aiken*: 174.
6. *ibid*: 93.
7. John Davenport, Preface to *Ultramarine*, reprinted in *MLR*: 48.
8. Gerald Noxon, 'Malcolm Lowry: 1930', *Prairie Schooner* (Winter 1963–4).
9. Clarissa Lorenz, *Lorelei Two*: 84–5.
10. *ibid*: 87.
11. *ibid*: 87–8.
12. Julian Trevelyan, *Indigo Days*: 16.
13. Jacob Bronowski in Tony Kilgallin, *Lowry*: 24.
14. Lowry to Conrad Aiken, October 1930.
15. John Davenport in Conrad Knickerbocker, 'Swinging the Paradise Street Blues' in the *Paris Review*, Vol. 10, No. 38 (Summer 1966): 23.
16. Dr Sydney Smith to GB: interview, 20 February 1988.
17. Margerie Bonner Lowry to Conrad Knickerbocker.
18. Lowry to Conrad Aiken, Autumn 1930.
19. John Aiken to GB: interview, 10 January 1989.
20. Martin Case in Conrad Knickerbocker, 'Swinging the Paradise Street Blues' in the *Paris Review*, Vol. 10, No. 38 (Summer 1966): 27.
21. Ralph Case to GB: interview, 12 August 1984.

22. Lowry to Conrad Aiken, New Year 1931.
23. 'Those Cokes to Newcastle Blues', *Festival Theatre Programme*, 14 February 1931: 8–9.
24. Lowry to Conrad Aiken, 4–11 March 1931.
25. Conrad Aiken, *Ushant*: 226.
26. Clarissa Lorenz, *Lorelei Two*: 111.
27. *ibid*: 111.
28. *ibid*: 103.
29. Lowry to Conrad Aiken, 17/24 April 1931.
30. 'Punctum Indifferens', the point of indifference, as Coleridge points out in his *Aids to Reflection*, is the point which bisects its own extension. Lowry used this together with Grieg's title to set the present in relation to past and future – we exist only in the present because the present embodies both the past and the future – and in the world of coincidences and correspondences we see evidence of this mystical triangularity. The idea is also embodied in *Under the Volcano*. (See William New, *Malcolm Lowry*, McClelland & Stewart, Toronto, 1971: n23).
31. 'Punctum Indifferens Skibet Gaar Videre', *Experiment*, No. 7 (Spring 1931): 65.
32. Quoted in Lowry to Aiken 17/24 April 1931.
33. The *Times Literary Supplement*, 4 June 1931.
34. Lowry to Conrad Aiken, *SL*: 10 (where this letter appears wrongly dated as Summer 1932 instead of Summer 1931.)
35. Houston Peterson, *The Melody of Chaos* (Longmans, New York, 1931) was a full-length study of Aiken's work which had just appeared.
36. Lowry to Conrad Aiken (probably June 1931), *SL*: 8 (where it is wrongly dated).
37. *ibid*: 8.
38. *ibid*: 8.
39. Lowry to David Markson, 25 August 1951, *SL*: 255.
40. Lowry to Conrad Aiken, *ibid*: 8.
41. Edmund Wilson, *Axel's Castle*, 1931: 215.
42. *ibid*: 212.
43. Conrad Aiken to Alfred Claghorn Potter, 27 June 1931.
44. Draft of *DAG* (MS): 343.
45. Lowry to David Markson, August 25 1951, *SL*: 261.
46. Draft of *DAG*: 669.
47. Lowry later used this as the first line of a poem. (See 'Cain Shall Not Slay Abel Today on Our Good Ground' in *The Book of Canadian Poetry*, ed. A. J. M. Smith, (W. J. Gage & Co., Toronto, 1948: 372–3) and as 'A Poem of God's Mercy' in *SPML*: 17–8.
48. From Grieg's play *Barabbas* produced at the National Theatre in Oslo four years earlier, in 1927.
49. Draft of *DAG*: 351.
50. In *DAG* Lowry says it was a book on Elizabethan dramatists, probably also alluding to Brooke's work.
51. Conrad Aiken, *Ushant*: 222.
52. Rupert Brooke, *John Webster and the Elizabethan Drama* (Sidgwick & Jackson, London, 1916).
53. T. S. Eliot, 'Whispers of Immortality', *Collected Poems 1909–1935* (Faber, London, 1936): 53.
54. *Hamlet* in fact ante-dates *The Malcontent* not post-dates it.
55. Lowry is here quoting John Webster's *The White Devil*, Act V, Scene vi, quoted by Eliot *Collected Poems 1909–1935*: 83.
56. Lowry to Conrad Aiken, summer 1931; Lowry to Jan Gabrial, June 1933.
57. Lowry to David Markson, 25 August 1951.
58. *SPML*: 77. *CP*: 66–7.
59. Nordahl Grieg, *Die unge Død*,

(Gyldendal Forlag, Oslo, 1932). See also Edvard Hoem, *Til Ungdommen: Nordahl Grieg Liv* (*To Youth: Nordahl Grieg's Life*), (Gyldendal Norsk Forlag, Oslo, 1989.)

60. Lowry: *DAG*.
61. Lowry to David Markson, *SL*: 263.
62. Lowry to Albert Erskine, 5 June 1951, *SL*: 242.
63. Maurice Hickin to GB, 3 March 1989.
64. Lowry to David Markson, 25 August 1951.
65. The *Gownsman*, 30 May 1931.
66. Published in Britain by Jonathan Cape in 1932 under the title, *The Best Stories of 1931*. Jan Gabrial pointed out to me that the title 'Seductio Ad Absurdum' was the title of a story by Emily Hahn, an American writer who published a collection of stories, including this one, in America in 1927, the year that Malcolm first visited Aiken in Cambridge, Mass.
67. Arthur Lowry to Evelyn Lowry, November 1931.
68. Draft of *DAG*: 669.
69. Russell Lowry to GB.
70. Brian O'Kelly to M. C. Bradbrook, 20 January 1975.
71. Kathleen Raine to Malcolm Lowry (probably sometime in 1932). (H)
72. Reported by Arthur Calder-Marshall at London Conference on Malcolm Lowry, 1984. Published in the *Proceedings* of the Conference.
73. Lowry to Grieg, spring 1938, *SL*: 15–16.
74. Howarth, *Cambridge Between Two Wars* (Collins, London, 1978): 187.
75. Conrad Aiken letter to the *Times Literary Supplement*, 16 February 1967.
76. *Granta*, 9 June 1932: 504.
77. Dr George Rylands, in conversation, 20 November 1993.
78. *UTV*: 180. (220)
79. *ibid*: 180. (220)

CHAPTER VIII

1. Conrad Aiken, *Great Circle*, (Wishart, London) 1933: 260.
2. Max Perkins to Conrad Aiken, 30 January 1933.
3. Clarissa Lorenz, *Lorelei Two*: 111.
4. Russell Lowry to GB: interview, 25 February 1989.
5. Lowry to Aiken, probably summer 1932.
6. 'China' in *PAS*: 54.
7. 'Tramps' MS: 7.
8. 'Enter One in Sumptuous Armour', *PAS*: 228–49.
9. Ralph Case to GB: 12 August 1984.
10. *ibid.*
11. Martin Case to Conrad Knickerbocker, 'Swinging the Paradise Street Blues' in the *Paris Review*, Vol. 10, No. 38 (summer 1966): 31.
12. John Davenport to George Woodcock for CBC TV film, 1961.
13. John Davenport, *MLR*: 66–67.
14. George Northcroft to GB: interview, 2 June 1989.
15. John Sommerfield, *MLR*: 69.
16. *ibid*: 72–3.
17. *UTV*: 105. (145)
18. James Hepburn, *MLR*: 60–1.
19. Anna Wickham to Lowry, (sometime in 1932 or 1933). (H)
20. Oliver Warner – Report on *U*, 30 September 1932.
21. Ian Parson, *Times Literary Supplement*, 13 April 1967, *MLR*: 81.
22. *Best Stories of 1931*, edited by Edward O'Brien, Jonathan Cape, London, 1932.
23. Ian Parsons, *TLS*, 13 April 1967, *MLR*: 82.

24. Russell Lowry, *MLR*: 64–65.
25. Arthur Calder-Marshall, *Proceedings of the London Conference on Malcolm Lowry 1984*: 26.
26. *U*: 133.
27. James Hepburn, *MLR*: 61.
28. Drafted on verso of letter from Arthur Lowry dated 14 February 1933.
29. Reported by Arthur Calder-Marshall, *Proceedings of the London Conference on Malcolm Lowry 1984*: 28.
30. Conrad Aiken to Alfred Claghorn Potter, 29 March 1933.
31. Clarissa Lorenz, *Lorelei Two*: 149.
32. *ibid*: 151.
33. *ibid*: 152.
34. *ibid*: 153.
35. *ibid*: 153.
36. *ibid*: 155.
37. *ibid*: 156.
38. *ibid*: 157.
39. T. E. B. Howarth, *Cambridge Between Two Wars*: 156.
40. Conrad Aiken, *Ushant*: 297.
41. Jan Gabrial's journal. Jan says that what Lowry later remembered her saying, i.e. 'I'm not going to have an affair with you, Mr Lowry', is a more accurate account of what she said to him.
42. *Ushant*: 157.
43. *Ushant*: 158.
44. *Ushant*: 352.
45. Jan Gabrial's journal.
46. *ibid.*
47. Conrad Aiken to Lowry, 17 December 1939.
48. Clarissa Lorenz, *Lorelei Two*: 158.
49. Lowry to Jan Gabrial, May 1933.
50. *ibid.*
51. Clarissa Lorenz, *Lorelei Two*: 159.
52. Conrad Aiken, *Ushant*: 30.
53. Jan Gabrial to GB in conversation, 23 November 1988.

CHAPTER IX

1. E. Kenneth Wright's portrait of Malcolm Lowry, 1933.
2. Conrad Aiken to Kempton P. A. Taylor, 6 December 1933, *Selected Letters Conrad Aiken*: 200.
3. Lowry to Jan Gabrial: May 1933.
4. Jan Gabrial to GB in conversation, 12 April 1988.
5. Lowry to Jan Gabrial, June 1933.
6. Draft of *DAG*: 692.
7. Lowry to Jan Gabrial, June 1933.
8. Draft of *DAG*: 692.
9. Robert Pocock to Bob Duncan for National Film Board of Canada: 25 March 1975.
10. Draft of *DAG*: 693.
11. The Liverpool *Post and Mercury*, 29 June 1933.
12. The *Bookman*, (July 1933) Vol. 84, No. 502: 211.
13. The *Times Literary Supplement*, 13 July 1934.
14. The *London Mercury*, 28 August 1933: 363.
15. Richard Aldington to Lowry, 25 July 1933.
16. Paul Ferris, *Dylan Thomas* (Penguin, 1978): 166.
17. Robert Pocock to Bob Duncan for NFBC: 25 March 1975.
18. Hugh Sykes Davies: 68.
19. David Markson to GB: interview, 19 October 1988.
20. Jan Gabrial, *MLR*: 94.
21. *UTV*: 185. (225)
22. *UTV*: 185. (225)
23. Mrs E. Vanderheim to Jan Gabrial, 1933. (Reported by Jan Gabrial).
24. 'On Board the West Hardaway', *Story*, October 1933: 13.
25. Jan Gabrial, *MLR*: 95.
26. Jan Gabrial to GB: interview, April 12 1988.
27. John Sommerfield, *The Last Weekend*: 95, reprinted in Douglas Day, *Malcolm Lowry: A Biography*: 154.
28. *ibid*: 127.

29. *ibid*: 125.
30. *ibid*: 134.
31. Jan Gabrial to GB: 12 April 1988.
32. Anaïs Nin, *Journals*, Vol. 2 (Peter Owen, London, 1967): 117.
33. Anna Wickham to Natalie Barney, 1 December 1934.
34. Jan Gabrial to GB in conversation, 12 April 1988.
35. P. D. Ouspensky, *A New Model of the Universe* (Arkana, London, 1984): 240–41.
36. Richard Ellmann, *James Joyce* (OUP, 1982): 668.
37. 'Hotel Room in Chartres', *Story*, V, 26 (September 1934): 53.
38. *ibid*: 58.
39. Lowry to Jan Gabrial, April 1934.
40. 'In Le Havre', *Life and Letters*, X, 55 (July 1934): 464.
41. *ibid*: 466.
42. James Stern, 'Malcolm Lowry: A First Impression', *Encounter*, XXIX September 1967: 58–68.
43. *UTV*: 205. (245)
44. Screenplay for *Tender is the Night*: Paul Tiessen and Miguel Mota, *The Cinema of Malcolm Lowry* (UBC Press, Vancouver, 1990): 79.
45. Lowry to David Markson, 22 February 1957.
46. Jean Cocteau, *La Machine Infernale* (Editions Bernard Grasset, Paris, 1934).
47. Julian Green to GB, 30 August 1989.
48. Reported by Jan Gabrial in conversation, August 1989.
49. *UTV*: 18. (58)
50. Lowry, Haitian Notebook (conversation in French with Philippe Thoby-Marcelin.)
51. Lowry to Sylvia Beach, May–June 1934. (P)
52. 'Metal' – (Later 'June 30 1934' in *PAS*.)
53. Lowry later implied that the advance was never paid back for the uncompleted story cycle.
54. Lowry to Conrad Aiken, 9 May 1941.
55. Lowry to Margerie Bonner, September 1939.
56. 'Bulls of the Resurrection' in *PAS*.
57. Lowry to Jan Gabrial, July 1934.

CHAPTER X

1. 'Through the Panama', *HUOL*: 74.
2. Jan Gabrial to GB: interview, 6 November 1988.
3. *Lunar Caustic*, *HUOL*: 340–1.
4. Dolly Lewis to GB: interview, 14 January 1988.
5. Lowry to Whit Burnett, 31 August 1934.
6. Jan Gabrial, *MLR*: 99.
7. *ibid*: 101.
8. *ibid*: 101.
9. Jan Gabrial to GB.
10. Lowry to Mrs John Stuart Bonner, 16 April 1940, *SL*: 26.
11. Jan Gabrial to GB.
12. *DAG*: 63.
13. Lowry to Burton Rascoe, 19 May 1940.
14. Burton Rascoe to Edward Weeks, 22 November 1954.
15. Lowry to Markson (Draft), 25 August 1951.
16. *HUOL*: 74–5.
17. Waldo Frank, 1958 Preface to Hart Crane's, *Complete Poems* (reprinted by Bloodaxe Books, Newcastle, 1984): 21.
18. Hart Crane, *ibid*: 101.
19. *UTV*: 267. (207)
20. Eric Estorick in *MLR*: 103.
21. Arthur Lowry to Lowry, 6 April 1935.
22. Jan Gabrial, *MLR*: 100–101.
23. 'Portrait of a Conquistador'.
24. Lowry to David Markson, 20 May 1954.
25. Lowry to Robert Giroux: 11 January 1952.

26. She recalled later that at the time he was drinking brandy and strychnine, a primitive cure for alcoholism.
27. Lowry to Clemens Ten Holder, 21 March 1951.
28. Lowry to Derek Pethick, 6 March 1950, *SL*: 197.
29. 'Delirium on the East River'.
30. Hilda Doolittle (H. D.) to Conrad Aiken, November 1934, reported in *Selected Letters of Conrad Aiken*: 197.
31. Conrad Aiken to Ed Burra, 22 August 1936, *Selected Letters of Conrad Aiken*: 208.
32. *ibid*: 208.
33. Lowry to Seymour Lawrence, 28 November 1951, *SL*: 277–8.
34. Lowry to Innes Rose, summer 1936. (H)
35. Whit Burnett to Harold Matson, 14 January 1942.
36. Arthur Calder Marshall, *Proceedings of London Conference on Malcolm Lowry 1984*: 35.
37. John Davenport to Conrad Aiken: reported by Aiken, *Selected Letters of Conrad Aiken*: 211.
38. Jan Gabrial to GB: in conversation, 1 January 1988.
39. *HUOL*: 31.

CHAPTER XI

1. *La Mordida* (MS): 21.
2. Lowry quotes from his passport in the MS of *Dark as the Grave*.
3. *UTV*: 48. (88)
4. *UTV*: 61. (101)
5. *La Mordida* (MS): 30.
6. *ibid*: 48–9.
7. Jan Gabrial to GB: interview, 6 November 1988.
8. *UTV*: 34. (74) See also C. Ackerley & L. Clipper, *A Companion to Under the Volcano* (UBC Press, Vancouver, 1984): 192.
9. *UTV*: 34. (74)
10. *UTV*: 204. (244)
11. *UTV*: 134. (174)
12. During the time they were at 62 Calle Humboldt they were to have three gardeners. One told Jan he would knock her down if she were a man, a second knifed his mistress and the third robbed them. Jan Gabrial to GB, January 1988.
13. *DAG*: 111.
14. Jan Gabrial to GB, April 1988.
15. *DAG* (MS): 330.
16. *DAG*: 115.
17. *DAG*: 133.
18. Lowry to John Davenport, 31 August 1937.
19. What he probably did not know at this time was that Sommerfield, in Spain fighting with the International Brigade, had been reported 'killed in action' on 26 November. It proved to be a false report, however.
20. Mexican Notebook.
21. Evelyn Lowry to Lowry, 9 November 1936.
22. *DAG* (MS): 332.
23. *DAG*: 332–33.
24. *DAG*: 334.
25. *DAG*: 165.
26. *DAG*: 72.
27. Jan Gabrial to GB.
28. Conrad Aiken, *Ushant*: 348.
29. Jan Gabrial to GB: interview, 6 November 1988.
30. Conrad Aiken to Harry Murray, 27 May 1937, *Selected Letters of Conrad Aiken*: 216.
31. Conrad Aiken, *Ushant*: 348.
32. *Ushant*: 351.
33. Jan Gabrial to GB: interview, 6 November 1988.
34. *ibid*.
35. Conrad Aiken, *Ushant*: 349–50.
36. Jan Gabrial to GB: interview, 6 November 1988.
37. Conrad Aiken to Harry Murray, 12 June 1937, *Selected Letters of Conrad Aiken*: 217.
38. *ibid*: 217.

39. 'Prelude to Mammon', in *CP*: 108–8. This poem was not included by Lowry in his collection *The Lighthouse Invites the Storm*, but it was composed along with those which he did.
40. Lowry to Jan Gabrial Lowry, June 1937.
41. Conrad Aiken to Robert Taylor, 23 June 1937, *Selected Letters of Conrad Aiken*: 218.
42. Conrad Aiken to Henry Murray, 12 June 1937, *Selected Letters of Conrad Aiken*: 218.
43. Conrad Aiken, *Ushant*: 355.
44. *Ushant*: 356.
45. *Ushant*: 354–5.
46. Lowry to Jan Gabrial Lowry, June 1937.
47. *UTV*: 347. (387)
48. John Davenport to Lowry, 12 April 1947.
49. Jan Gabrial to GB: interview: 6 November 1988.
50. Lowry to John Davenport, 31 August 1937.
51. Lowry to Margerie Bonner, September 1939.
52. Indeed, he had just published in *Fact* (No. 4, July 1937) what some saw as the definitive call-to-arms to writers to mobilize in the cause of revolution. (Valentine Cunningham, *British Writers of the Thirties*: 327.)
53. Arthur Calder-Marshall, *MLR*: 111.
54. *DAG* (MS): 336–40.
55. Ara Calder-Marshall, 'Portrait of Malcolm Lowry' (BBC Third Programme, 16 September 1967). See also *The Listener*, 12 October 1967: 461–63.
56. Arthur Calder-Marshall, *MLR*: 76.

CHAPTER XII

1. Mensch is called Hölscher in *DAG*.
2. *DAG*: 104.
3. *DAG* (MS): 161.
4. *DAG* (MS) 163.
5. *DAG*: 91.
6. *DAG*: 109.
7. *DAG*: 232.
8. *DAG* (MS): 331.
9. *UTV*: 365. (405)
10. *UTV*: 366–7. (406–7)
11. *UTV*: 346–7. (386–7)
12. *UTV*: 367. (407)
13. 'Portrait of a Conquistador'.
14. *UTV*: 41. (81)
15. Lowry to Juan Fernando Márquez, January 1938.
16. *DAG* (MS): 282.
17. Lowry to James Stern, 7 May 1940, *SL*: 29.
18. Lowry to John Davenport, January 1938, *SL*: 11 [where it is wrongly dated].
19. Lowry to Conrad Aiken, January 1938: *SL*: 15 [where it is wrongly dated].
20. *DAG*: 142.
21. *DAG*: 210.
22. *DAG*: 163.
23. *DAG*: 70.
24. *DAG*: 247.
25. *UTV*: 12. (52)
26. *DAG*: 240.
27. Lowry to Albert Erskine, 22 June 1946.
28. *UTV*: 132. (172)
29. The true meaning is 'Do you like this garden that is yours? See to it that your children do not destroy it!' – Hugh's reading, *UTV*: 235.
30. 'In the Oaxaca Jail', *SPML*: 28, *CP*: 59–60.
31. Lowry to Clarisse Francillon, 1 March 1950, *SL*: 192.
32. *DAG*: 77.
33. Jan Gabrial to GB: interview, 6 November 1988.
34. Jan Gabrial Lowry to British Consul, Mexico City, 3 February 1938.
35. *DAG*: 251.
36. *DAG*: 101.
37. *DAG*: 220.
38. *DAG*: 223.

39. *DAG*: 221.
40. *DAG*: 101.
41. *DAG*: 226.
42. Ann Watkins to Lowry, 31 January 1938.
43. Jan Gabrial Lowry to British Consul, Mexico City, 15 February 1938.
44. The climate turned against foreigners, especially the English, and Graham Greene reports them sometimes being spat at in the streets and readily deported under the notorious Article 33.
45. Jan Gabrial to GB: interview, 6 November 1988.
46. Basham & Ringe to Ayrton & Alderson-Smith (Arthur Lowry's lawyers), 8 April 1938.
47. *La Mordida*: 41.
48. *CP*: 73–4.
49. The poem quoted, which appears in *UTV*: 331 (371), is a slightly more polished version of the one on the original menu.
50. Basham & Ringe to Ayrton & Alderson-Smith, 18 June 1938.
51. Reported by Jan Gabrial to GB.
52. Carol Phillips to GB: interview, 11 November 1988.
53. Jesse Dalton (for Basham & Ringe) to Ayrton & Alderson-Smith, 30 August 1938.
54. *DAG* (MS): 158.

CHAPTER XIII

1. Benjamin Parks to Ayrton & Alderson-Smith, 11 August 1938.
2. Jan Gabrial to GB: 6 November 1988.
3. Jan Gabrial in *MLR*: 124.
4. Lowry to Arthur Lowry, first letter from Los Angeles, August 1938.
5. Benjamin Parks to Ayrton & Alderson-Smith, 18 November 1938.
6. Lowry to Margerie Bonner, September 1939.
7. *UTV*: 105. (145)
8. Joe London to GB: 26 June 1989.
9. James Osborne to GB: interview, 25 June 1989.
10. Benjamin Parks to Alderson-Smith, 5 April 1939.
11. Evelyn Lowry to Lowry, 28 February 1939.
12. Benjamin Parks to Alderson-Smith, 19 April 1939.
13. *ibid.*
14. Carol Phillips to her mother, May 1939.
15. Lowry to Carol Phillips, May 1939.
16. Carol Phillips to her mother, May 1939.
17. Carol Phillips to her mother, May 1939.
18. Carol Phillips to her mother, 17 May 1939.
19. Arthur Lowry to Lowry, 5 May 1939.
20. Alderson-Smith to Benjamin Parks, 5 May 1939.
21. Margerie Bonner Lowry to Conrad Knickerbocker.
22. Priscilla Woolfan to GB: interview, 28 October 1988.
23. *ibid.*
24. 'Delirium in Vera Cruz', *SPML*: 32, *CP*: 62 & 127.

CHAPTER XIV

1. Lowry to Margerie Bonner, 30 July 1939.
2. Benjamin Parks to Ayrton & Alderson-Smith, 16 August 1939.
3. *ibid.*
4. Lowry to Carol Phillips, (probably 11 August), 1939.
5. Benjamin Parks to Ayrton & Alderson-Smith, (Cable), 8 September 1939.
6. Lowry to Margerie Bonner, (probably 9 September) 1939.
7. Lowry to Margerie Bonner, ('sometime in September') 1939.

8. Lowry to Conrad Aiken, early November 1939. (Edited version in *SL*: 18–25.
9. Maurice Carey, 'Life with Malcolm Lowry' (MS at University of British Columbia).
10. Maurice Carey to Arthur Lowry, 19 October 1939.
11. Lowry to Mrs John Stuart Bonner, 19 October 1939.
12. Reginald Makepeace Lott to Benjamin Parks, 23 October 1939.
13. Lowry to Conrad Aiken, reported in *Selected Letters of Conrad Aiken*: 233.
14. Conrad Aiken to Lowry, 29 October 1939: *Selected Letters of Conrad Aiken*: 235.
15. Edward Butscher, *Conrad Aiken: Poet of White Horse Vale*: 274–5.
16. A. B. Carey to Benjamin Parks, 26 October 1939.
17. Thomas Rafferty to Benjamin Parks, 7 November 1939.
18. A. B. Carey to Benjamin Parks, 7 November 1939.
19. Lowry to Benjamin Parks, 8 November 1939.
20. Lowry to Carol Phillips, November 1939.
21. Lowry to Conrad Aiken, (early November) 1939 (edited version in *SL*: 20).
22. *SL*: 25–6. Lowry said that *The Last Address* became *Swinging the Maelstrom* in 1939, 40, 41 – 'which even then had the alternative title Lunar Caustic.' (Lowry to Robert Giroux, 21 January 1952.)
23. Conrad Aiken to Ed Burra, 26 November 1939. [H]
24. 'Hollywood at War', the *Vancouver Daily Province*, 12 December 1939; 'The Real Mr Chips', *Vancouver Daily Province*, 13 December 1939.
25. Conrad Aiken to Lowry, 15 December 1939, *Selected Letters of Conrad Aiken*: 239. [H]
26. Lowry to Conrad Aiken, mid-December 1939.
27. Conrad Aiken to Lowry, 17 December 1939, *Selected Letters of Conrad Aiken*: 240.
28. Lowry to Conrad Aiken, 24 December 1939.
29. Conrad Aiken to Lowry, 27 December 1939. [H]
30. Lowry to Conrad Aiken, (around 12 January) 1940.
31. Conrad Aiken to Lowry, 19 January 1940, *Selected Letters of Conrad Aiken*: 242.
32. Lowry to Conrad Aiken, 27 January 1940.
33. *ibid.*
34. Margerie Bonner to Mary Aiken, 29 January 1940.
35. Conrad Aiken to Lowry, 1 February 1940, *Selected Letters of Conrad Aiken*: 243.
36. Lowry to Conrad Aiken, 7 February 1940.
37. Conrad Aiken to Lowry, 21 February 1940, *Selected Letters of Conrad Aiken*: 243. [H]
38. Lowry to Conrad Aiken, 23 February 1940.
39. Margerie Bonner Lowry to Conrad & Mary Aiken, 23 February 1940.
40. Lowry to Conrad & Mary Aiken, (about 24 February) 1940.
41. Conrad Aiken to Arthur Lowry, (Cable) 27 February 1940.
42. Lowry to Benjamin Parks, 27 February 1940.
43. Conrad Aiken to Lowry, 7 March 1940. [H]
44. Lowry to Arthur Lowry, March 1940.
45. *ibid.*
46. Conrad Aiken to Lowry, 1 April 1940. [H]
47. Arthur Lowry to Lowry, 5 April 1940.
48. Lowry to Conrad Aiken, 9 April 1940.

49. Conrad Aiken to Lowry, 28 April 1940. [H]
50. James Stern to Lowry, 1 May 1940.
51. Lowry to Conrad Aiken, 24 April 1940.
52. Lowry to James Stern, 7 May 1940, *SL*: 28. (Tex)
53. *SL*: 31.
54. Thomas Rafferty to Benjamin Parks, 14 May 1940.
55. Lowry to Conrad Aiken, 10 June 1940.
56. Lowry to Conrad Aiken, 15 May 1940.
57. Lowry to Juan Fernando Márquez, Spring 1940.
58. Jan Gabrial to GB: interview, 6 November 1988.
59. Lowry to Conrad Aiken, 10 June 1940.
60. Conrad Aiken to Lowry, 17 June 1940. [H]
61. Lowry to Whit Burnett, 22 June 1940. [P]
62. Lowry to Conrad Aiken, 19 July 1940.
63. Lowry to Harold Matson, 27 July 1940, *SL*: 32.

CHAPTER XV

1. Lowry to Gerald Noxon, 26 August 1940, Paul Tiessen (ed.), *The Letters of Malcolm Lowry and Gerald Noxon* (UBC Press, Vancouver, 1988): 27–8.
2. Lowry to Conrad Aiken, 6 September 1940.
3. *Atlantic Monthly*, August 1940: 221–223.
4. Lowry to Conrad Aiken, 6 September 1940.
5. Lowry to Gerald Noxon, 21 September 1940, *The Letters of Malcolm Lowry and Gerald Noxon*: 31.
6. *UTV*: 21. (61)
7. Margerie Bonner Lowry interview with Conrad Knickerbocker.
8. *ibid.*
9. Lowry to Gerald Noxon, 21 September 1940, *The Letters of Malcolm Lowry and Gerald Noxon*: 31.
10. Margerie Lowry interview with Conrad Knickerbocker.
11. Martha Foley to Harold Matson, 27 August 1940. [P]
12. Lowry to Harold Matson, 12 October 1940.
13. Reader's report for Story Press. [P]
14. *CP*: 59.
15. *CP*: 174.
16. Quoted by Robert Linscott to Lowry, 19 November 1940.
17. Lowry to Conrad Aiken, 22 November 1940. Also *SPML*: 74, and *CP*: 117–8.
18. *Field Book of the Skies*, by William Tyler Olcott and Edward W. Putnam, (Putnam's Sons, New York, 1936).
19. Lowry to Conrad Aiken, 11 December 1940. Also *SPML*: 62.
20. Conrad Aiken to Lowry, 15 December 1940.
21. Margerie Lowry notes.
22. Lowry to Conrad Aiken, 3 January 1941.
23. Lowry to Harold Matson, 4 March 1941.
24. Lowry to Conrad Aiken, 9 May 1941.
25. Eridanus Notebook.
26. Gerald Noxon quoted in *The Letters of Malcolm Lowry and Gerald Noxon*: 38.
27. *ibid.* 38.
28. Lowry to Gerald Noxon, Summer 1941, *ibid*: 40.
29. Robert Linscott to Lowry: 11 July 1941.
30. *Atlantic Monthly*, 4 October 1941: 501, *CP*: 186.
31. Lowry to Harold Matson, 4 August 1941.
32. Lowry to Conrad Aiken, 13 August 1941.

33. Klaus Mann to Lowry, (undated but probably October) 1941.
34. Edward Weeks, 22 October 1941.
35. Margerie Bonner & Malcolm Lowry to Harold Matson, 6 January 1942, *SL*: 37 (where it is wrongly dated).
36. Whit Burnett to Harold Matson, 14 January 1942.
37. Lowry to Harold Matson, 30 January 1942.
38. Arthur Lowry to Lowry, 22 April 1942.
39. Lowry to Arthur Lowry, 26 May 1942.
40. Lowry to Harold Matson, 25 June 1942.
41. *The Letters of Malcolm Lowry and Gerald Noxon*: 39.
42. Malcolm (& Margerie) Lowry to Gerald (& Betty) Noxon, 28 July 1942, *ibid*: 42.
43. *ibid*: 42.
44. Lowry to Priscilla Woolfan & Mrs John Stuart Bonner, 7 August 1942.
45. Arthur Lowry to Lowry, 25 November 1942.
46. *UTV*: 350 (390). Lowry could well have taken this much-quoted sentence in part from Klaus Mann's *The Turning Point*, which appeared that year, 1942, and which includes the passage, 'The spaces of the microcosm resound with the groan of orgasms and agonies as battlefields do with the cries of the wounded and victors.' (Serpent's Tail, London, 1987): 80 Lowry was also briefly in touch with Mann at the time.
47. Lowry to David Markson, 20 June 1951.
48. *UTV*: 42. (82)
49. *UTV*: 149. (189)
50. Lowry to Gerald Noxon, 15 June 1943, *The Letters of Malcolm Lowry and Gerald Noxon*: 42–46.
51. *SPML*: 53, *CP*: 136.
52. Lowry to Gerald Noxon, 15 June 1943, *The Letters of Malcolm Lowry and Gerald Noxon*: 56.
53. Lowry to Gerald Noxon, 7 September 1943, *ibid*: 57.
54. Lowry to Clemens Ten Holder, 21 March 1951.
55. S. Schuster, *The Legacy of the Beast*, (W. H. Allen, London, 1988): 207.
56. Lowry to Clemens Ten Holder, 21 March 1951.
57. S. Schuster, *op. cit*: 207.
58. Lowry to Clemens Ten Holder, 21 March 1951.
59. *UTV*: 178. (218)
60. Lowry to Gerald Noxon, 14 November 1943, *The Letters of Malcolm Lowry and Gerald Noxon*: 62.
61. Lowry's favourite phrase from Max Brod's postscript to the book expressed his sense of being at the mercy of hostile hidden forces.
62. Lowry in Margerie Lowry to Gerald Noxon, 15 February 1944, *The Letters of Malcolm Lowry and Gerald Noxon*: 73.
63. Lowry to Gerald Noxon, 24 April 1944, *ibid*: 82.
64. Lowry to Albert Erskine, 6 July 1946.

CHAPTER XVI

1. Sheryl Salloum, *Malcolm Lowry: Vancouver Days*, (Harbour Publishing Company Ltd., British Columbia, 1987): 22.
2. Lowry to Albert Erskine, 22 June 1946, *SL*: 113.
3. Eridanus Notebook.
4. Lowry to Gerald Noxon, Cable, June 1944, *The Letters of Malcolm Lowry and Gerald Noxon*: 92.
5. Gerald Noxon, in Paul Tiessen, 'In Connection with Malcolm Lowry', and 'On Malcolm Lowry', the *Malcolm Lowry Review*, 1987: 11–25.

6. Lowry to Conrad Aiken, fall 1945, *SL*: 48.
7. *UTV*: 283. (323)
8. Lowry to Margerie Lowry, July 1944.
9. *ibid.*
10. Gerald Noxon to GB: interview, 15 October 1988.
11. Lowry to Margerie Lowry, July 1944.
12. *DAG*: 168–9.
13. Margerie Lowry to Harold Matson, 2 September 1944.
14. Gerald Noxon in Paul Tiessen, *On Malcolm Lowry*, 1987: 18.
15. Gerald Noxon to GB: interview, 15 October 1988.
16. Lowry to Max Perkins, 15 September 1946.
17. Margerie Lowry interview with Conrad Knickerbocker.
18. Conrad Aiken to Lowry, 22 August 1944.
19. *ibid.*
20. Lowry to Noxons, September 1944, *The Letters of Malcolm Lowry and Gerald Noxon*: 93.
21. Lowry to Conrad Aiken, Fall 1945.
22. Lowry to Clemens Ten Holder, 23 March 1951.
23. Margerie Lowry interview with Conrad Knickerbocker.
24. Lowry to Conrad Aiken, Xmas 1944.
25. Margerie Lowry to Betty Noxon, 7 February 1945, *The Letters of Malcolm Lowry and Gerald Noxon*: 94.
26. Gerald Noxon to Conrad Aiken, 2 March 1945.
27. *ibid.*
28. *ibid.*
29. Margerie Lowry to Betty Noxon, 3 April 1945, Tiessen, *The Letters of Malcolm Lowry and Gerald Noxon*: 107.
30. Eridanus Notebook Diary, 18 April 1945.
31. Margerie Lowry to Betty Noxon, 3 April 1945.
32. Conrad Aiken to Ed Burra, April 1945.
33. Eridanus Notebook Diary, 12 April 1945.
34. *ibid*: 18 April 1945.
35. *ibid*: 18 April 1945.
36. *ibid*: 15 April 1945.
37. *ibid*: 18 April 1945.
38. *ibid*: 22 April 1945.
39. Lowry to Harold Matson, 1 July 1945.
40. Harold Matson to Lowry, 31 July 1945.
41. Margerie Lowry to Harold Matson, 10 August 1945.
42. Lowry to Jonathan Cape (draft). This letter seems to have been modified later by Lowry after seeing Cap Pearce's comment about the book lacking focus. He appears to have added the paragraph which Cape quotes back at Lowry in his letter of 29 Nov. (That letter also indicates that Lowry sent it to him in August – presumably after receiving Matson's letter of 31 July quoting Pearce's comments.) Most likely this draft was written on or about 23 July 1945.
43. Eridanus Notebook Diary, 14 September 1945.
44. Lowry to Aiken, 24 October 1945.
45. Conrad Aiken to Lowry, 14 September 1945. [II]
46. Lowry to Conrad Aiken, 24 October 1945.
47. Jonathan Cape to Lowry, 15 October 1945.
48. Lowry to Jonathan Cape, 2 January 1946, *SL*: 87.
49. Lowry to Conrad Aiken, 24 October 1945.

CHAPTER XVII

1. *DAG*: 21.
2. *DAG*: 20.
3. *DAG*: 42.

4. *UTV*: 47. (87)
5. Lowry to Ronald Button, 15 June 1946, *SL*: 92.
6. *DAG*: 64.
7. *DAG*: 31.
8. *DAG*: 94.
9. *DAG*: 99.
10. *DAG*: 112.
11. Cuernavaca Notebook.
12. *DAG* (MS): 572.
13. *DAG*: 414.
14. *DAG*: 419.
15. *DAG*: 183.
16. Jonathan Cape to Lowry, 29 November 1945.
17. William Plomer's Report on *UTV* for Cape.
18. *DAG*: 191.
19. Lowry to Jonathan Cape, 2 January 1946, *SL*: 87.
20. *DAG*: 193.
21. *DAG* (MS) 278.
22. Lowry to Jonathan Cape, 2 January 1946, *SL*: 61–2.
23. *ibid*: 64.
24. *ibid*: 65.
25. *ibid*: 65–6.
26. *ibid*: 66.
27. *ibid*: 66.
28. *ibid*: 66.
29. *ibid*: 67.
30. *ibid*: 88.
31. Preface to the French edition of *UTV*, also in G. Bowker, *Malcolm Lowry: Under the Volcano*, (Macmillan (Casebook) London, 1987): 30.
32. *UTV*: 11.
33. *DAG* (MS): chapter 9.
34. *DAG*: 223.
35. *DAG*: 230.
36. *DAG*: 257.
37. *La Mordida* (Final Margerie Lowry typescript): 4.
38. *ibid*: 10.
39. *ibid*: 25.
40. *La Mordida* (Penultimate Margerie Lowry typescript): 83.
41. *ibid*: 89.
42. *La Mordida* (Final Margerie Lowry typescript): 33.
43. *La Mordida* (Penultimate Margerie Lowry typescript): 155.
44. *La Mordida* (Final Margerie Lowry typescript): 148.
45. 'Song', *CP*: 128.
46. Margerie Lowry to Gerald Noxon, April 1946, *The Letters of Malcolm Lowry and Gerald Noxon*: 123.
47. Margerie's *La Mordida* Notebook.
48. Lowry to Bert Woolfan, 19 April 1946, *SL*: 89.
49. *La Mordida* (Final Margerie Lowry typescript): 229.
50. Lowry to Ronald Button, 15 June 1946, *SL*: 110.

CHAPTER XVIII

1. Lowry to Harold Matson, 8 May 1946.
2. Priscilla Woolfan interviewed by Conrad Knickerbocker.
3. Margerie Lowry interviewed by Conrad Knickerbocker.
4. Priscilla Woolfan to GB: interview, July 1989.
5. Lowry to Ronald Button, 15 June 1946, *SL*: 91–112.
6. Eridanus Notebook. Lowry to Clemens Ten Holder, 21 March 1951.
7. *La Mordida*. (Draft)
8. Lowry to Mrs John Stuart Bonner & the Woolfans, 7 June 1946, *SL*: 90.
9. Lowry to Jonathan Cape, 28 May 1946.
10. Lowry to Mrs John Stuart Bonner & the Woolfans, 7 June 1946, *SL*: 90.
11. Harold Matson to Lowry, 6 June 1946.
12. Lowry to Albert Erskine, 30 June 1946, *SL*: 115.
13. Lowry to Albert Erskine, 22 June 1946, *SL*: 114.
14. Lowry to Harold Matson, 28 June 1946.
15. *ibid*.

16. Lowry to Albert Erskine, 16 July 1946.
17. Lowry to Gerald Noxon, 29 July 1946, *The Letters of Malcolm Lowry and Gerald Noxon*: 126.
18. Albert Erskine to Lowry, 8 July 1946.
19. *ibid.*
20. Eridanus Notebook.
21. Lowry to Harold Matson, 29 July 1946.
22. Lowry to Harold Matson, 14 August 1946.
23. Lowry to Gerald Noxon, 29 July 1946. *The Letters of Malcolm Lowry and Gerald Noxon*: 126.
24. Lowry to Conrad Aiken, 5 August 1946.
25. John Davenport to Lowry, 13 April 1947.
26. Lowry to John Davenport – notebook draft of reply to Davenport letter.
27. Lowry to Max Perkins, 15 September 1946, *SL*: 118.
28. Max Perkins to Lowry, (Cable) 19 September 1946, *ibid*: 426.
29. Charles Scribner to Margerie Lowry, 9 October 1946, *ibid*: 428–9.
30. Albert Erskine to Lowry, 28 August, sent on 20 September 1946.
31. Lowry to Erskine, 26 January 1954, *SL*: 362.
32. Lowry to Erskine, (probably) 30 October 1946.
33. Lowry to Jonathan Cape, 30 October 1946, *SL*: 130–31.
34. Margerie Lowry, Notebook.
35. Lowry to John Davenport, 6 December 1946.
36. Lowry to Albert Erskine, 17 December 1946.
37. Lowry to Albert Erskine, December 1946, *SL*: 133.
38. James Stern to Lowry, 20 December 1946.
39. 'Haitian Dream' in *La Mordida* (penultimate Margerie Lowry typescript): 181.
40. Conrad Aiken to John Davenport, 29 December 1946. [H]
41. Haitian Notebook and in *La Mordida* (pentultimate Margerie Lowry typescript): 206.
42. *La Mordida*: 163.
43. *ibid*: 164.
44. Preface to *Under the Volcano*, dated 31 December 1946, on board the SS *Donald S. Wright.*
45. *La Mordida*: 169.
46. *ibid*: 214.
47. *ibid*: 214–5.
48. Jonathan Cape to Lowry, 18 December 1946.
49. *La Mordida*: 216.
50. Kathleen Ann Porter to Albert Erskine, 4 January 1947. (M)
51. James Stern to Lowry, 6 January 1947.
52. Edgar D. Brooks quoted in Douglas Day, *Malcolm Lowry: A Biography*: 374.
53. Lowry to Jonathan Cape, 10 January 1947.
54. Margerie Lowry's Haitian Notebook.
55. *ibid.*
56. *La Mordida*: 175.
57. Lowry to Albert Erskine, 18 January 1947.
58. Margerie Lowry interview with Conrad Knickerbocker.
59. Albert Erskine to Lowry, 22 January 1947.
60. Alfred Kazin to Albert Erskine, 6 January 1947.
61. Albert Erskine to Lowry, 22 January 1947.
62. Margerie Lowry to James Stern, 5 February 1947. (Tex)
63. Lowry to Albert Erskine, 11 February 1947, *SL*: 140.
64. Lowry to Gerald Noxon, 11 February 1947, *The Letters of Malcolm Lowry and Gerald Noxon*: 135.
65. James Stern to Margerie Lowry, 8 February 1947. (Tex)

66. James Agee to Albert Erskine, 11 February 1947.
67. Malcolm Cowley to Albert Erskine, 9 January 1947.
68. Conrad Aiken to Mary Aiken, 29 June 1947.
69. Lowry to James Stern, 16 February 1947. (Tex)
70. Lowry to Philippe Thoby-Marcelin, 18 February 1947.

CHAPTER XIX

1. Lowry to David Markson, 20 May 1954.
2. *MLR*: 188.
3. Lowry to Philippe Thoby-Marcelin, 7 April 1947.
4. Margerie Lowry to Noxons, 20 February 1947.
5. Albert Erskine to GB, 6 December 1989.
6. Margerie Lowry notes.
7. John Woodburn, the *Saturday Review*, 22 February 1947: 9–10.
8. Harvey Breit, 'In and Out of Books', *New York Times*, 14 July 1957.
9. Lowry to Clemens Ten Holder, 26 April 1952.
10. *MLR*: 147.
11. Lowry to John Davenport, (probably 21 February) 1947.
12. Lowry to Harold Matson: 2 October 1951.
13. Leslie Black to GB: interview, 5 December 1988.
14. James Stern in *MLR*: 147.
15. Margerie Lowry notes.
16. Dawn Powell to Lowry, 1 July 1947.
17. Jonathan Cape. See Michael S. Howard, *Jonathan Cape, Publisher*, (Cape, London, 1971): 212.
18. Conrad Aiken to Lowry, 23 February 1947, *Selected Letters of Conrad Aiken*, 277–279.
19. Gerald Noxon to GB: interview, 15 October 1988.
20. Maurice Carey, 'Life with Malcolm Lowry' (MS at University of British Columbia).
21. *ibid.*
22. Conrad Aiken to John Davenport, 11 April 1947. [H]
23. Harold Matson to Lowry, 25 March 1947.
24. Conrad Aiken to John Davenport, 20 March 1947. [H]
25. Lowry to Chester Kerr, 26 March 1947.
26. 'After Publication of Under the Volcano', *SPML*: 78; *CP*: 214.
27. Bestseller List, *New York Times*, 6 April 1947.
28. Bennet Cerf, *Saturday Review of Literature*, 5 April 1947.
29. Gerald Noxon to Lowry (Cable), 10 April 1947, *The Letters of Malcolm Lowry and Gerald Noxon*: 140.
30. Gerald Noxon to Lowry, mid-April 1947, *ibid*: 141.
31. Elizabeth Hardwick, 'Fiction Chronicle', the *Partisan Review*, March–April 1947: 199.
32. Edward Weeks, 'Mexico and Moscow', the *Atlantic Monthly*, May 1947: 144–46.
33. The *Toronto Globe and Mail*, 22 March 1947.
34. Eridanus Notebook.
35. John Davenport to Lowry, 12 April 1947.
36. Lowry to John Davenport, early May 1947.
37. Eridanus Notebook.
38. Lowry to John Davenport, May 1947.
39. Conrad Aiken to John Davenport, 17 April 1947.
40. John Davenport to Conrad Aiken, 18 April 1947.
41. Conrad Aiken to John Davenport, 20 April 1947.
42. Lowry to Frank Taylor, 20 April 1947, *SL*: 141.
43. Albert Erskine to Lowry, 26 April 1947.
44. Rubina Stansfeld-Jones to Charles Stansfeld-Jones, 1 May 1947.

45. John Davenport to Lowry, 1 May 1947.
46. James Hepburn to GB: in conversation, 18 June 1991.
47. Lowry to Jacques Barzun, 6 May 1947, *SL*: 146.
48. Jacques Barzun, *Harper's Magazine*, May 1947: 487.
49. Lowry to Jacques Barzun, 6 May 1947, *SL*: 148.
50. Jacques Barzun to Lowry, 10 May 1947.
51. Lowry to Harold Matson, 12 May 1947.
52. Lowry to Conrad Aiken, 4 October 1947.
53. Margerie Lowry to James Stern, 16 June 1947. (Tex)
54. Lowry to Conrad Aiken, 24 June 1947.
55. Conrad Aiken to Mary Aiken, 29 June 1947. [H]
56. Dawn Powell to Lowry, 1 July 1947.
57. *Toronto Globe & Mail*, 16 July 1947.
58. Margerie Lowry to Albert Erskine, 23 July 1947.
59. Some of this material was also incorporated into *OFG*.
60. Sheryl Salloum, Malcolm Lowry: *Vancouver Days*: 30.
61. Lowry to Albert Erskine, 13 August 1947, *SL*: 151.
62. Panama Notebook, 12 November 1947.
63. 'Through the Panama' (Draft): 53.
64. Lowry to Mona Harrop, 1 September 1947.
65. Margerie & Malcolm Lowry to Harold Matson, 11 September 1947.
66. Earle Birney to Lowry, 18 September 1947.
67. 'Sestina in a Cantina', *SPML*: 41, *CP*: 123.
68. The *Times Literary Supplement*, 20 September 1947: 477.
69. The *Observer*, 21 September 1947.
70. The *Illustrated London News*, 27 September 1947.
71. The *Spectator*, 10 October 1947.
72. The *Listener*, 30 October 1947.
73. The *New Statesman & Nation*, 6 December 1947.
74. Malcolm Bradbury, 'Malcolm Lowry as Modernist', in *Possiblities: Essays on the State of the Novel*, London 1973): 181–91, Anthony Burgess, 'Europe's Day of the Dead', *Spectator* (20 January 1967): 74.
75. Ed Burra to Conrad Aiken, November–December 1947.
76. Lowry to Conrad Aiken, 4 October 1947.
77. Lowry to Earle Birney, 20 October 1947.
78. Margerie Lowry to Dorothy Livesay, 23 October 1947.
79. Lowry to Alan Crawley, 26 October 1947.
80. Earle Birney to Lowry, 24 October 1947.
81. Lowry to Albert Erskine, 29 October 1947, *SL*: 157.
82. Margerie Lowry to Harold Matson, 2 November 1947.
83. Lowry to Albert Erskine, 2 November 1947.
84. Margerie Lowry to James Stern, 4 November 1947. (Tex)
85. Lowry to Robert Linscott, 5 November 1947.

CHAPTER XX

1. Lowry, Panama Notebook.
2. *ibid.*
3. Lowry to John Davenport, 10 November 1947, *SL*: 158.
4. Lowry, Panama Notebook, 11 November 1947.
5. Priscilla Woolfan interview for Conrad Knickerbocker.
6. The same name as mythical ferryman who carries souls of the dead across the River Styx.
7. 'Through the Panama', *HUOL*: 38.

8. Margerie Lowry, Panama Notebook, 17 November 1947.
9. *ibid.*, 18 November 1947.
10. *HUOL*: 37.
11. 'Through the Panama', *HUOL*: 66.
12. Lowry, Panama Notebook.
13. 'Through the Panama', *HUOL*: 73.
14. 'Through the Panama' (Draft): 60.
15. Margerie Lowry, Panama Notebook, 5 December 1947.
16. Lowry, Panama Notebook.
17. Leslie Black to GB: Interview, 5 December 1988.
18. Margerie Lowry notes.
19. Russell Lowry to GB.
20. Lowry to Albert Erskine, 18 April 1948, *SL*: 164. (V)
21. Margerie Lowry notes.
22. Margerie Lowry, Notebook.
23. Margerie Lowry, Notebook: 7 June 1948.
24. Lowry to Clarisse Francillon, February 1949, *SL*: 169.
25. 'Elephant and Colosseum' Notes.
26. 'Strange Comfort Afforded by the Profession', *HUOL*: 103.
27. Lowry to Albert Erskine, July 1948, *SL*: 164.
28. Margerie Lowry, Notebook.
29. *ibid.*
30. *ibid.*
31. Albert Erskine to GB: interview, 13 August 1989.
32. Clarisse Francillon, 'Malcolm Lowry, mon ami': 200.
33. Margerie Lowry to Albert Erskine, 23 July 1948. (V)
34. Lowry to Albert Erskine, 23 July 1948. (V)
35. Allanah Harper to GB: interview, 15 June 1989.
36. William Le Page Finley, letter to Anne Chisholm quoted in her biography, *Nancy Cunard* (Penguin, 1981): 371–2.
37. Lowry to Albert Erskine, 9 August 1948, *SL*: 165.
38. Lowry to James Craige, 20 October 1948.
39. Earle Birney to Lowry, 9 November 1948.
40. Margerie Lowry to Harold Matson, 15 November 1948.
41. Russell Lowry to GB.
42. Clarisse Francillon, 'Malcolm Lowry, mon ami'; and A. J. Frédérique, 'Malcolm Lowry, Au-dessous du volcan', *Liens*, 33, (February 1950): 1 & 12.
43. Julian Trevelyan to GB: interview, 11 September 1984.
44. Norman Matson, *MLR*: 151. Originally in *PAS*. Lowry later incorporated 'the herring' into his screenplay for F. Scott Fitzgerald's *Tender is the Night*, where it is transformed into 'a carp'.
45. Lowry to Harold Matson, 23 February 1949, *SL*: 171.

CHAPTER XXI

1. George VI was suffering from varicose veins.
2. Arthur Calder-Marshall, *MLR*: 156.
3. Lowry to Clarisse Francillon, 16 February 1949, *SL*: 167.
4. *ibid*: 167.
5. *ibid*: 168.
6. *ibid*: 168–9.
7. Dr C. G. McNeill, *MLR*: 158–60.
8. Douglas Day, *Malcolm Lowry: A Biography*: 413.
9. Lowry to Jonathan Cape, 12 February 1949.
10. Some confirmation of this predicted influence on younger writers came later in the year when a letter arrived from a then unknown young writer, Allen Ginsberg.
11. Albert Erskine to Lowry, 16 February 1949.
12. Evelyn Lowry to Lowry, 24 February 1949.
13. Lowry to Evelyn Lowry, March 1949.

14. Albert Erskine to Lowry, 28 February 1949.
15. Lowry to Albert Erskine, 5 March 1949, *SL*: 173.
16. *ibid.*
17. Frank Taylor to Lowry, 28 February 1949.
18. Jonathan Cape to Lowry, 11 April 1949.
19. Lowry to Albert Erskine, May 1949, *SL*: 179.
20. Albert Erskine to Lowry, 25 May 1949.
21. S. Salloum, *Malcolm Lowry: Vancouver Days*: 73.
22. Earle Birney, *MLR*: 161–2.
23. Lowry to Frank Taylor (Draft 1), July 1949.
24. Dr Victor Drache to GB: interview, 7 July 1989.
25. Dr Victor Drache to Bert Woolfan, 6 August 1949.
26. Dr Victor Drache to GB: interview, 7 July 1989.
27. Lowry to Frank Taylor, *op. cit.*
28. Lowry to Frank Taylor (Draft 2), July 1949.
29. Lowry to Frank Taylor (Draft 1), July 1949.
30. Frank Taylor to Lowry, 20 July 1949.
31. Lowry to Frank Taylor (Final draft) August 1949, quoted by Paul Tiessen, *Notes on a Screenplay for F. Scott Fitzgerald's 'Tender is the Night'*: xi.
32. Margerie Lowry to Harold Matson, 10 October 1949.
33. Lowry to Frank Taylor, September 1949.
34. Frank Taylor, quoted in Tiessen, *Notes on a Screenplay for F. Scott Fitzgerald's 'Tender is the Night'*: xiii.
35. Miguel Mota & Paul Tiessen, *The Cinema of Malcolm Lowry*: 15ff.
36. Mentioned in Margerie Lowry to Harold Matson, 17 January 1950.
37. *ibid.*
38. Lowry to Conrad Aiken, December 1949.
39. *ibid.*
40. Margerie Lowry to Harold Matson, 17 January 1950.
41. Lowry to Harold Matson, 17 January 1950.
42. Lowry to Harold Matson, 4 February 1950.
43. Margerie & Malcolm Lowry to Harold Matson, 13 February 1950.
44. Lowry to Philippe Thoby-Marcelin, 24 February 1950.
45. Lowry to Clarisse Francillon, 1 March 1950, *SL*: 193.
46. Rubina Stansfeld-Jones reported in Kilgallin, *Lowry*: 52.
47. Lowry to Clarisse Francillon, 1 March, 1950, *SL*: 192
48. Lowry to Harold Matson, 28 February 1950.
49. Lowry to Clarisse Francillon, *SL*.
50. Lowry to Downie Kirk, 2 March 1950, *SL*: 195–6.
51. Paul Ferris (ed), *The Collected Letters of Dylan Thomas*, (Dent, London, 1985): 756.
52. Margerie Lowry notes.
53. George Robertson in Sheryl Salloum, *Malcolm Lowry: Vancouver Days*: 76–7.
54. Malcolm & Margerie Lowry to Frank Taylor, 12 April 1950, *SL*: 205.
55. Frank Taylor to Lowry, 25 April 1950.
56. Clarisse Francillon to Lowry, 14 May 1950.
57. Frank Taylor to Lowry, 24 May 1950.
58. 'Garden of Etla', *United Nations World*, IV, No 6, New York, June 1950: 45–7.
59. Lowry to Stuart Lowry, 15 June 1950.
60. Christopher Isherwood to Lowry, 12 June 1950.
61. Lowry to Albert Erskine, 21 June 1950.

62. Innes Rose to Lowry, 27 June 1950.
63. Lowry to Stuart Lowry, 15 June 1950.
64. Ortega y Gasset, *History As A System: Towards a Theory of History*, (Norton, New York, 1962): 108.
65. Lowry to Downie Kirk, 23 June 1950, *SL*: 210–11.
66. *ibid*: 213.
67. Lowry to Gode, 4 July 1950.
68. Lowry to Harold Matson, 17 July 1950.
69. *ibid.*
70. *ibid.*
71. Lowry to Gode, 4 July 1950.
72. Lowry to Evan Morton, 30 August 1950.
73. Lowry to Evan Morton, 20 September 1950.
74. Lowry to Harold Matson, 21 September 1950.
75. Lowry to Conrad Aiken, 28 September 1950.
76. Lowry to Harold Matson, 23 October 1950.
77. Lowry to Harold Matson, 14 November 1950, *SL*: 215–16.
78. *ibid*: 216.
79. Lowry to Stuart Lowry, October 1950, *SL*: 224.
80. Evelyn Lowry's birth certificate has defied all searches, so no official confirmation of her birthday is to hand. Her death certificate gives her date of death as 7 December 1950.
81. Lowry to Downie Kirk, 13 December 1950.

CHAPTER XXII

1. Lowry to Downie Kirk, January 1951.
2. Lowry to Albert Erskine, 13 February 1951. (V)
3. Lowry to Clemens Ten Holder, 5 February 1951.
4. Lowry to Downie Kirk, February 1951.
5. Lowry to Albert Erskine, 13 February 1951. (V)
6. *ibid.*
7. Lowry to Albert Erskine, 23 February 1951.
8. Lowry to Harold Matson, 20 March 1951.
9. Lowry to Albert Erskine, 20 March 1951.
10. Margerie Lowry interview with Conrad Knickerbocker.
11. Frank Taylor to Lowry, 3 April 1951.
12. James Agee to Lowry, 18 April 1951.
13. Earle Birney from *Rough Passage*, BBC Television documentary, 1967.
14. David Markson to Lowry, 3 June 1951.
15. Lowry to David Markson, 16 June 1951.
16. Lowry to David Markson, 20 June 1951.
17. *ibid.*
18. Lowry to Albert Erskine, 5 June 1951, *SL*: 243.
19. *ibid*: 243.
20. *ibid*: 244.
21. Margerie Lowry notes.
22. Lowry to Albert Erskine, 5 June 1951, *SL*: 246.
23. Lowry to David Markson, 13 August 1951.
24. Lowry to Albert Erskine, 2 October 1951.
25. Samuel Taylor Coleridge, 'The Rime of the Ancient Mariner'.
26. Fletcher Markle to Lowry, 6 August 1961.
27. Draft of Lowry to David Markson, 25 August 1951.
28. Lowry to Harold Matson, 2 October 1951, *SL*: 267.
29. ibid.
30. Margerie Lowry to Harold Matson, 2 October 1951.
31. Margerie Lowry to Albert Erskine, 2 October 1951.

32. Ernst Klett to Lowry, 19 September 1951.
33. Hildegaard Ten Holder to Lowry, 22 September 1951.
34. Lowry to Harold Matson, 2 October 1951.
35. Margerie Lowry to Harold Matson, 29 October 1951.
36. Lowry to Ernst Klett, 31 October 1951.
37. Lowry to Clemens Ten Holder, 31 October 1951.
38. Lowry to David Markson, November 1 1951, *SL*: 269–76.
39. Terence Kilmartin, Introduction to Marcel Proust, *By Way of Sainte-Beuve* (Hogarth Press, London, 1984): 1.
40. Lowry to Harold Matson, 23 November 1951.
41. Lowry to Albert Erskine, 23 November 1951. (V)
42. Lowry to Robert Giroux, 11 January 1952.
43. Lowry to Stuart Lowry, 28 November 1951, *SL*: 270.
44. Clemens Ten Holder to Lowry, 30 November 1951.
45. Lowry to Harold Matson, 8 December 1951.
46. Robert Giroux to Harold Matson, 11 December 1951.
47. Harold Matson to Lowry, 13 December 1951.
48. Lowry to Albert Erskine, 19 December 1951.
49. *ibid.*
50. Lowry to Harold Matson, 20 December 1951.
51. Albert Erskine, to Lowry, 21 December 1951.
52. Lowry to David Markson, 26 April 1952 (unsent draft).
53. Harold Matson to Lowry, 14 January 1952.
54. Lowry to David Markson, 15 January 1952.
55. In no letter prior to this does he use the title *Swinging the Maelstrom*.
56. Lowry to David Markson, 26 April 1952.
57. Lowry to David Markson, 23 January 1952.
58. Margerie Lowry to Harold Matson, 9 February 1952.
59. Lowry to Albert Erskine, 21 March 1952. (V)
60. Harold Matson to Lowry, 6 March 1952.
61. Margerie Lowry to Albert Erskine, 11 March 1952. (V)
62. Lowry to Albert Erskine, 14–18 March 1952. (V)
63. *ibid.*
64. *ibid.*
65. *ibid.*
66. Robert Giroux to Lowry, 19 March 1952.
67. Lowry to Albert Erskine, 20 March 1952.
68. Lowry to Albert Erskine, 21 March 1952. (V)
69. Lowry to Albert Erskine, 21–23 March 1952.
70. Lowry to Robert Giroux, 21 March 1952 (Unsent).
71. Lowry to Albert Erskine, 9 April 1952.
72. Albert Erskine to Lowry, 21 March 1952.
73. Albert Erskine to Robert Haas, 25 March 1952. (V)
74. Lowry to Albert Erskine, 25 March 1952. (V)
75. Lowry to Albert Erskine, 9 April 1952. (V)
76. Albert Erskine to Lowry, 31 March 1952.

CHAPTER XXIII

1. Lowry to Erskine, (probably) 9 April 1952, *SL*: 306.
2. Lowry to Conrad Aiken, 2 April 1952.
3. Lowry to Albert Erskine, 5 April 1952.

4. Lowry to Harold Matson, 7 April 1952.
5. Lowry to Albert Erskine, 7 April 1952.
6. Harold Matson to Lowry, 14 April 1952.
7. Hildegaard & Clemens Ten Holder to Lowry, 13 April 1952.
8. Lowry to Albert Erskine, April 1952, *SL* (dated April): 309. Lowry headed the letter 'Ash Wednesday (with reservations)', probably a private joke.
9. Lowry to David Markson, 26 April 1952 (Unsent draft).
10. Lowry to Harold Matson, 26 April 1952.
11. Lowry to Gerald Noxon, spring 1952, *The Letters of Malcolm Lowry and Gerald Noxon*: 158.
12. 'Present Estate of Pompeii', *HUOL*: 177.
13. Lowry to Albert Erskine, 3–10 May 1952. *SL*: 315–322.
14. Lowry to Harold Matson, 14 June 1952.
15. Lowry to Albert Erskine, 17 May 1952.
16. Lowry to Albert Erskine, 14 June 1952. By making his hero in 'Forest Path' a jazz musician, the Primrose character begins to look rather like Sheila London, Joe's wife. The wife in *OFG* also bears some resemblance to her, being adopted and of Scottish ancestry. This could well have been Lowry's private joke, to base the character Margerie thought was her on someone else. Joe London to GPB, 17 October 1991.
17. Margerie Lowry to Marie Moore, 12 July 1952.
18. Lowry to Harold Matson, 14 June 1952.
19. Lowry to Harold Matson, 24 July 1952.
20. David Markson, 'Rough Passage', BBC Television documentary, 1967.
21. *ibid.*
22. *ibid.*
23. David Markson to GPB: interview, 19 October 1988.
24. Lowry to Albert Erskine, 5 August 1952. (V)
25. Lowry to Albert Erskine, 12 August 1952, *SL*: 322.
26. Lowry to Norman Newton, August 1952.
27. Albert Erskine to J. B. Marshall, 8 September 1952. (V)
28. Lowry to Clarisse Francillon, (undated, but probably early Autumn) 1952.
29. Lowry to Albert Erskine, 9 September 1952.
30. Lowry to Conrad Aiken, 14 September 1952.
31. Lowry to David Markson, 3 October 1952.
32. Lowry to Ernst Klett, 28 October 1952.
33. Lowry to Albert Erskine, (around 12 October) 1952.
34. *ibid.*
35. Lowry to William McConnell, October 1953.
36. Lowry to Irmgard Rexroth Kern, November 1952.
37. Albert Erskine to Lowry, 19 November 1952.
38. Lowry to Albert Erskine, April 1953, *SL*: 335 (Wrongly dated 'Early Summer 1953. This 'Pantagruel' letter was not sent.)
39. Lowry to Marie Moore, 10 December 1952.
40. Margerie & Malcolm Lowry to the Neilsons, 30 December 1952.
41. Lowry to Harold Matson, 8 January 1953, *SL*: 327.
42. *ibid*: 328.
43. Lowry to Albert Erskine, 22 February 1953.
44. Gloria Olney in Sheryl Salloum, *Malcolm Lowry: Vancouver Days*: 84.

45. Norman Newton, *ibid*: 84.
46. *ibid*: 88.
47. Lowry to Albert Erskine, April 1953. (V)
48. Lowry to David Markson, 17 February 1953.
49. Lowry to Albert Erskine, 11 April 1953.
50. Malcolm & Margerie Lowry to Albert Erskine, April 1953.
51. Lowry to Albert Erskine, (probably April 1953), *SL*. 333–40.
52. Lowry to Albert Erskine 22 April 1953. (The posted version).
53. Lowry to Albert Erskine, 10 July 1953, *SL*: 342.
54. Lowry to Downie Kirk, 10 August 1953.
55. Margerie Lowry to Albert Erskine, 15 August 1953.
56. Lowry to David Markson, 21 September 1953.
57. Douglas Day, *Malcolm Lowry: A Biography*: 16.
58. Lowry to Albert Erskine, 14 October 1953.
59. *ibid*.
60. Lowry to Albert Erskine, (Halloween) 31 October 1953, *SL*: 344–5. (V)
61. *ibid*: 345.
62. Albert Erskine to Lowry, 18 December 1953.
63. Lowry to Harold Matson, 25 January 1954.
64. Lowry to Albert Erskine, 27 December 1953. (V)
65. Albert Erskine interviewed for National Film Board of Canada documentary, *Volcano*, 1976.
66. Robert Haas to Albert Erskine (undated). (V)
67. Lowry to Albert Erskine, 4 January 1954.
68. Lowry to Albert Erskine, 6 January 1954. (V)
69. Lowry to Einar Neilson, (January) 1954.

CHAPTER XXIV

1. Lowry to Harold Matson, 25 January 1954, *SL*: 358.
2. Lowry to Albert Erskine, 26 January 1954, *SL*: 361–364.
3. Albert Erskine to Lowry, 29 January 1954.
4. Margerie Lowry to Albert Erskine, 1 February 1954. (V)
5. Albert Erskine to Lowry, 4 February 1954.
6. Lowry to David Markson, 5 February 1954, *SL*: 366.
7. *ibid*: 365.
8. Margerie Lowry notes.
9. Lowry to David Markson, 10 May 1954, *SL*: 368.
10. *ibid*: 369.
11. 'The Bravest Boat', *Partisan Review*, Vol. XXI No. 3 (May–June 1954): 275.
12. Lowry to David Markson, 20 May 1954.
13. Lowry to Albert Erskine, 22 May 1954, *SL*: 372.
14. Lowry to George Robertson, (probably 1 June) 1954.
15. Lowry to David Markson, 10 July 1954, *SL*: 373.
16. Lowry to Conrad Aiken, 16 July 1954.
17. Dorothy Burt to GB: interview, 8 July 1989.
18. Margerie Lowry to David Markson, 14 August 1954.
19. Lowry to Albert Erskine, 23 August 1954.
20. Lowry to Downie Kirk, 29–30 August 1954.
21. Harvey Burt to GB: interview, August 1982.
22. Harvey Burt interviewed for George Robertson's 1961 CBC TV documentary.
23. Margerie Lowry to David Markson, 31 August 1954.
24. David Markson, *MLR*: 172.
25. *ibid*: 180.

26. James Stern to Conrad Aiken, 12 December 1954.
27. Kitty Sprague to GB, 11 April 1989.
28. David Markson to Douglas Day, 29 June 1967.
29. David Markson to James Stern, 8 May 1964.
30. David Markson to (Mr) Raining (Conrad Knickbocker), 21 February 1966.
31. *ibid.*
32. Malcolm Cowley to Mary Aiken, 16 September 1954.
33. Peter Churchill, *All My Sins Remembered*, (Heinemann, London 1964): 199.
34. David Markson, *MLR*: 175.
35. *ibid*: 176.
36. Conrad Aiken to Ed Burra, 24 November 1954.
37. James Agee died some eight months later.
38. David Markson, *MLR*: 176–7.
39. *ibid*: 177.
40. Conrad Aiken to Mary Aiken, (probably September) 1954. [H]
41. David Markson, *MLR*: 181.
42. *ibid*: 182.
43. Lowry to David Markson, 22 September 1954.
44. Lowry to David Markson, 17 October 1954, *SL*: 374.
45. Lowry to Downie Kirk, 23 October 1954.
46. Lowry to David Markson, 23 October 1954.
47. Margerie Lowry to Marie Moore, 3 November 1954.
48. Lowry to David Markson, 2 November 1954.
49. *Tender is the Night* was made finally in 1961, though not by MGM. Henry King directed with Jennifer Jones (Selznick's wife) as Nicole, and Jason Robards Jr as Dick Diver. The script was by Ian Moffat.)
50. Burton Rascoe to Edward Weeks, 22 November 1954.

CHAPTER XXV

1. Lowry to Giorgio Monicelli (unsent draft), December 1954.
2. Lowry to Giorgio Monicelli, December 1954, *SL*: 375.
3. Margerie Lowry to David Markson, (probably February) 1955.
4. Margerie Lowry interviewed by Dr Michael Raymond, November 1955.
5. Margerie Lowry tc David Markson, 19 September 1955.
6. Margerie Lowry to the Sterns, 18 May 1955.
7. Dorothy Burt to GB, *MLR*: 206.
8. Lowry to Albert Erskine, 7 October 1955.
9. Dorothy Burt to GB, *MLR*: 206.
10. Douglas Day, *Malcolm Lowry: A Biography*: 206.
11. Dorothy Burt to GB: interview, 19 April 1985.
12. Malcolm & Margerie Lowry to David Markson, Spring 1955.
13. Evelyn Morrison to GB, 8 October 1988.
14. James Stern to David Markson, 9 September 1955.
15. Lowry to Jimmy Craige, 11 September 1955, *SL*: 382. (There dated 12 September).
16. *ibid.*
17. Margerie Lowry to Jimmy Craige, 12 September 1955.
18. Margerie Lowry to David Markson, 18 September 1955.
19. Margerie Lowry to David Markson, 20 September 1955.
20. Lowry to Albert Erskine, 7 October 1955.
21. James Stern to David Markson, 29 September 1955.
22. Margerie Lowry to David Markson, 7 October 1955.
23. Margerie Lowry to David Markson, 16 October 1955.
24. Dr Michael Raymond.

25. David Markson to Albert Erskine, 20 October 1955.
26. Quoted by Dorothy Templeton in a letter to Harvey Burt, 26 October 1955.
27. Robert Pocock interviewed for National Film Board of Canada 1976 TV documentary, *Volcano*, 1977.
28. Note: Lowry told Dr Raymond on 29 November 1955 that he left the Brook on 5 November 1955.
29. James Stern to David Markson, 21 December 1955.
30. Ralph Case in *MLR*: 202.
31. Julian Trevelyan to GB: interview, 11 September 1984.
32. *ibid.*
33. Dr Michael Raymond.
34. Margerie Lowry to Marie Moore, 3 December 1955.
35. Dorothy Burt to GB: interview, 19 April 1985.
36. Dr Michael Raymond.
37. *ibid.*
38. Dr Michael Raymond to GB, 21 February 1989.
39. Margerie Lowry to David Markson, 17 December 1955.
40. Ed Burra to Conrad Aiken, 28 December 1955.
41. Margerie Lowry to David Markson, 30 December 1955.
42. Lowry to Margerie Lowry, 20 January 1956.
43. Margerie Lowry to Marie Moore, 14 January 1956.
44. Margerie Lowry to David Markson, 14 January 1956.
45. Margerie Lowry to David Markson, 25 January 1956.
46. Margerie Lowry to David Markson, 14 January 1956.
47. Margerie Lowry to David Markson, 25 January 1956.
48. Lowry to Margerie Lowry, 20 January 1956.
49. *ibid.*
50. Margerie Lowry to Marie Moore, 17 March 1956.
51. Lowry to David Markson, 21 February 1956, *SL*: 383.
52. *ibid.*
53. *ibid.*
54. Lowry to John Davenport, 22 March 1956.
55. Lowry to Jimmy Craige, 25/26 March 1956, *SL*: 384. (There dated April.)
56. Margerie Lowry to Jimmy Craige, 25/26 March 1956.
57. Lowry to John Davenport, 22 March 1956.
58. Lowry to Clarisse Francillon, 21 April 1956, *SL*: 385.
59. Lowry to David Markson, May 1956.
60. Lowry to John Davenport, 9 May 1956.
61. Lowry to David Markson, 12 May 1956.
62. Lowry to Clarisse Francillon, 27 May 1956.
63. Dr Michael Raymond.
64. Lowry to David Markson, 22 February 1957.
65. Dr Michael Raymond.
66. Margerie Lowry to Marie Moore, 8 June 1956.
67. Lowry to Harvey Burt, 9 June 1956.

CHAPTER XXVI

1. Elsewhere it is said that she told Sir Paul Mallinson that her sex life with Malcolm had been non-existent for the past two years, although she later denied having said that. Day, *Malcolm Lowry: A Biography*: 36.
2. Day suggests this demonstrated the extent to which she had come to take powers of editorship over Lowry's material – powers she would be free to exercise after his death – and which she did exercise

freely after his death. Day, *ibid*: 36–37.

3. Dr Michael Raymond.
4. Dr Raymond also thought it might explain why he could drink so much and suffer so little apparent organic damage – the large gut simply absorbing the alcohol.
5. Margerie Lowry to David Markson, 19 July 1956.
6. Lowry to Margerie Lowry, 20 July 1956.
7. Dr Michael Raymond to GB: Dr Raymond denied Margerie's suggestion that Malcolm was discharged as incurable from the Atkinson Morley.
8. Lowry to Harvey Burt, August 1956, *SL*: 388.
9. Lowry to David Markson, 3 September 1956.
10. Lowry to Margerie Lowry, 20 October 1956.
11. Lowry to Margerie Lowry, 22 October 1956.
12. *ibid.*
13. Lowry to Dr Michael Raymond, 23 October 1956. Also to Margerie, 22 October 1956.
14. Polish demonstrators were demanding that the Russians withdraw from Poland.
15. Lowry to Margerie Lowry, 1 November 1956.
16. Lowry to Margerie Lowry, 5 November 1956.
17. Lowry to Margerie Lowry, 6 November 1956.
18. Lowry to Dr Michael Raymond, 4 November 1956.
19. *ibid.*
20. Lowry to David Markson, 5 November 1956.
21. Lowry to Dr Michael Raymond, 18 December 1956.
22. Lowry to Margerie Lowry, 7 November 1956.
23. Lowry to Margerie Lowry, 9/10 November 1956.
24. Lowry to Margerie Lowry, 10/11 November 1956.
25. Lowry to Margerie Lowry, 15 November 1956.
26. Margerie Lowry to Marie Moore, 28 November 1956.
27. Margerie & Malcolm Lowry to David Markson, 11 December 1956, *SL*: 394.
28. Lowry to Albert Erskine, 13 December 1956. (V)
29. Lowry to Dr Michael Raymond, 18 December 1956.
30. Lowry to Downie Kirk 19 December 1956.
31. Note: He referred to all anti-depressants as benzedrine, known usually as amphetamines in the UK.
32. Lowry to Dr Michael Raymond, 18 December 1956.
33. James Stern to David Markson, 24 December 1956.
34. Lowry to David Markson, 22 February 1957.
35. Lowry to Dr Michael Raymond, 7 January 1957.
36. Lowry to David Markson, 22 February 1956.
37. Downie Kirk to Lowry, 1 February 1957.
38. Lowry to David Markson, 22 February 1957.
39. *ibid.*
40. *ibid.*
41. Lowry to Ralph Gustafson, 29 April 1957, *SL*: 409.
42. 'Halt I Protest!' – the manuscript of which is lost.
43. Lowry to Ralph Gustafson, 29 April 1957, *SL*: 410.
44. Notebook, Summer 1957.
45. Lowry to David Markson, 15 June 1957, *SL*: 413.
46. Margerie Lowry to Harvey Burt & Dorothy Templeton, June 1957.
47. *Wordsworth* (OUP), 1986: 388.
48. Margerie Lowry to David Markson, 23 July 1957.

49. *ibid.*
50. Harvey Burt to Einar & Muriel Neilson, 25 October 1957.
51. She wrote much the same to Markson: 'I've known for years & last summer his psychiatrist told me it was hopeless & too late to help him.' Margerie Lowry to David Markson, 23 July 1957.
52. Margerie Lowry to David Markson, 13 July 1957.
53. *ibid*
54. Margerie Lowry to David Markson, 23 July 1957.
55. Margerie Lowry to David Markson, 14 July 1957.
56. Harvey Breit, 'In And Out Of Books', *New York Times*, 14 July 1957.

POSTFACE

1. Preface to *Under the Volcano*, 31 December 1946.
2. Margerie Lowry to David Markson, 23 July 1957.
3. Lowry to David Markson, 22 February 1957.
4. Earle Birney to GB: in conversation, August 1982.
5. Matthew Corrigan, 'Malcolm Lowry, New York Publishing and the "New Illiteracy" ', *Encounter*, 35 (July, 1970): 82–93.
6. *PAS*.
7. See J. Howard Woolmer, *Malcolm Lowry: A Bibliography*, (Woolmer/Brothers Ltd., Revere, Pennsylvania) 158. Also see Wieland Schulz-Kiel in *The Proceedings of the London Conference on Malcolm Lowry, 1984*: 45–61.

SELECT BIBLIOGRAPHY

LOWRY'S PUBLISHED WORK

'Port Swettenham', *Experiment*, 3 (February 1930), pp. 22–6

'Goya the Obscure', the *Venture*, 6 (June 1930), pp. 270–8

'Punctum Indifferens Skibet Gaar Videre', *Experiment*, 7 (Spring 1931), pp. 62–75

Ultramarine, Jonathan Cape (London 1933); rev. ed. Lippincott (Philadelphia 1962); Jonathan Cape (London 1963); Penguin (London 1974)

'On Board the West Hardaway', *Story*, III, 15 (October 1933) pp. 12–22

'In Le Havre', *Life & Letters* (July 1934), pp. 462–6

'Hotel Room in Chartres', *Story*, V, 26 (September 1934) pp. 53–8

Under the Volcano, Reynal & Hitchcock (New York 1947); Jonathan Cape (London 1947); Vintage (New York 1958); Penguin (London 1962); Penguin (London 1962); Lippincott (Philadelphia 1965); Signet (New York 1965)

'Economic Conference 1934', *Arena*, 2 (Autumn 1949) pp. 49–57

'Garden of Eden', *United Nations World*, New York IV, 6 (June 1950): pp. 45–7

Hear Us O Lord From Heaven They Dwelling Place, Lippincott (Philadelphia 1961); Jonathan Cape (London 1962); Penguin (London 1969)

Letters Between Malcolm Lowry and Jonathan Cape about 'Under the Volcano', Jonathan Cape (London 1962)

Selected Poems of Malcolm Lowry (ed. Earle Birney), City Lights (San Francisco 1962)

Lunar Caustic (ed. Earle Birney and Margerie Lowry), *Paris Review*, 29 (Winter/Spring 1963): pp. 15–72; Jonathan Cape (London 1968)

'Bulls of the Resurrection', *Prism International*, 5 (Summer 19965) pp. 5–11.

The Selected Letters of Malcolm Lowry (ed. Harvey Breit and Margerie Lowry), Lippincott (Philadelphia 1965); Jonathan Cape (London 1967)

Dark as the Grave Wherein My Friend is Laid, New American Library (New York 1968); Jonathan Cape (London 1969); Penguin (London 1972)

October Ferry to Gabriola, World (New York 1970); Jonathan Cape (London 1971); Penguin (London 1979)

'Ghostkeeper', *American Review*, 17 (May 1973) pp. 1–34
Malcolm Lowry: Psalms and Songs (ed. Margerie Lowry), New American Library (New York 1975)
Scherf, Kathleen (ed.), *The Collected Poetry of Malcolm Lowry*, UBC Press (Vancouver 1992)
The letters of Conrad Aiken and Malcolm Lowry 1929–54 (ed. Cynthia Sugars), ECW Press (Toronto 1992).
The 1940 Under the Volcano, edited by Paul Tiessen and Miguel Mota, with introduction by Frederick Asals, MLR Editions (Waterloo, Ontario 1993).

BOOKS AND ARTICLES ON LOWRY

Ackerley, C. & Clipper, L., *A Companion to 'Under the Volcano'* UBC Press (Vancouver 1984)
Binns, Ronald, *Malcolm Lowry*, Methuen (London and New York 1984)
Bowker, G. P., (ed.), *Malcolm Lowry Remembered*, Ariel Books (London 1985)
Bowker, G. P., (ed.), Casebook on *Under the Volcano*, Macmillan (London 1987)
Bradbrook, M. C., *Malcolm Lowry: His Art and Early Life*, Cambridge University Press (London 1974)
Costa, Richard Hauer, *Malcolm Lowry*, Twayne (New York 1972)
Cross, Richard K., *Malcolm Lowry: A Preface to his Fiction*, University of Chicago Press (1980); Athlone Press (London 1980)
Day, Douglas, *Malcolm Lowry: A Biography*, Oxford University Press (New York 1973; London 1974)
Francillon, Clarisse, 'Malcolm mon ami', *Les Lettres Nouvelles* (July/August, 1960) pp. 8–19
Grace, Sherrill, *The Voyage that Never Ends*: Malcolm Lowry's Fiction, UBC Press (Vancouver 1982)
Knickerbocker, Conrad, 'Swinging the Paradise Street Blues: Malcolm Lowry in England', *The Paris Review*, Vol 10, No 38 (Summer 1966) pp. 13–38
Lorenz, Clarissa, 'Call it Misadventure', *Atlantic Monthly* (June 1970)
Lorenz, Clarissa, *Lorelei Two*, University of Georgia Press (Atlanta 1983)
Markson, David, *Malcolm Lowry's Volcano: Myth, Symbol, Meaning*, Times Books (New York 1978)
Mota, Miguel & Tiessen, Paul, *The Cinema of Malcolm Lowry*: A scholarly edition of Lowry's 'Tender is the Night', UBC Press (Vancouver 1990)
Salloum, Sheryl, *Malcolm Lowry: Vancouver Days*, Harbour Publishing Company Ltd., (Vancouver 1987)

Smith, Anne (ed.), *The Art of Malcolm Lowry*, Barnes & Noble (New York 1978); Vision Press (London 1978)

Stern, James, 'Malcolm Lowry: A First Impression', *Encounter* XXIX (September 1967) pp. 58–68

Tiessen, Paul, (ed.), *The Letters of Malcolm Lowry and Gerald Noxon*, UBC Press (Vancouver 1988)

Vice, Sue, (ed.), *Malcolm Lowry: Eighty Years On*, Macmillan (London 1989)

Wood, Barry (ed.), *Malcolm Lowry: The Writer and His Critics*, Tecumseh Press (Ottawa 1980)

Woodcock, George (ed.), *Malcolm Lowry: The Man and His Work*, UBC Press (Vancouver 1971)

Woolmer, J. Howard, *Malcolm Lowry: A Bibliography*, Woolmer/Brotherson (Revere, Penn. 1983)

The Malcolm Lowry Review is published by the Department of English, Wilfrid Laurier University, Waterloo, Ontario, Canada. A British Lowry appreciation society (Friends of Malcolm Lowry) is at 28, Stainsdale Green, Whitwick, Leicestershire.

The major collection of Lowry manuscripts is held at the University of British Columbia in Vancouver. Some of the manuscripts, main texts, notebooks and letters are available on microfilm at the Senate House of the University of London.

INDEX